Constitutional Law

BLACK LETTER OUTLINES

Constitutional Law

by Jerome A. Barron

Harold H. Greene Professor of Law Emeritus
George Washington University Law School

C. Thomas Dienes

Lyle T. Alverson Professor of Law Emeritus
George Washington University Law School

NINTH EDITION

WEST®

Mat #41292056

COPYRIGHT © 1991, 1995 WEST PUBLISHING CO.
© West, a Thomson business, 1999, 2003, 2005
© 2010 Thomson Reuters
© 2013 LEG, Inc., d/b/a West Academic Publishing
    610 Opperman Drive
    St. Paul, MN 55123
    1–800–313–9378

West, West Academic Publishing, and West Academic are trademarks of West Publishing Corporation, used under license.

Printed in the United States of America

ISBN: 978–0–314–28193–7

Preface

This "Black Letter" is designed to help a law student recognize and understand the basic principles and issues of law covered in a law school course. It can be used both as a study aid when preparing for classes and as a review of the subject matter when studying for an examination.

Each "Black Letter" is written by experienced law school teachers who are recognized national authorities on the subject covered.

The law is succinctly stated by the authors of this "Black Letter." In addition, the exceptions to the rules are stated in the text. The rules and exceptions have purposely been condensed to facilitate quick and easy recollection. For an in-depth study of a point of law, citations to major student texts are given.

If the subject covered by this text is a code or code-related course, the code section or rule is set forth and discussed wherever applicable.

FORMAT

The format of this "Black Letter" is specially designed for review. (1) **Text.** First, it is recommended that the entire text be studied and, if deemed necessary, supplemented by the student texts cited. (2) **Capsule Summary.** The Capsule Summary is an abbreviated review of the subject matter which can be used both before and after studying the main body of the text. The headings in the Capsule Summary follow the main text of the "Black Letter." (3) **Table of Contents.** The Table of Contents is in outline form to help you organize the details of the subject and the Summary of Contents gives you a final overview of the materials. (4)

Practice Examination. The Practice Examination in Appendix B gives you the opportunity to test yourself with the type of questions asked on an exam and compare your answer with a model answer.

In addition, a number of other features are included to help you understand the subject matter and prepare for examinations:

Perspective: In this feature, the authors discuss their approach to the topic, the approach used in preparing the materials, and any tips on studying for and writing examinations.

Analysis: This feature, at the beginning of each section, is designed to give a quick summary of a particular section to help you recall the subject matter and to help you determine which areas need the most extensive review.

Examples: This feature is designed to illustrate, through fact situations, the law just stated. This, we believe, should help you analytically approach a question on the examination.

Glossary: This feature is designed to refamiliarize you with the meaning of a particular legal term. We believe that the recognition of words of art used in an examination helps you to better analyze the question. In addition, when writing an examination you should know the precise definition of a word of art you intend to use.

We believe that the materials in this "Black Letter" will facilitate your study of a law school course and assure success in writing examinations not only for the course but for the bar examination. We wish you success.

THE PUBLISHER

Summary of Contents

APPENDICES

Table of Contents

PART TWO: INDIVIDUAL RIGHTS AND LIBERTIES: CONSTITUTIONAL LIMITATIONS ON GOVERNMENTAL POWER

Capsule Summary of Constitutional Law

■ PART ONE: THE ALLOCATION OF GOVERNMENTAL POWER: NATIONAL AND STATE

I. JUDICIAL REVIEW

Jurisdiction is the power to hear a case. In addition to jurisdictional rules, there are prudential principles limiting the occasions when a federal court will decide a case on the merits. If jurisdiction is present and these prudential limits are overcome, courts can exercise the power of judicial review.

A. Establishing Judicial Review

1. Judicial Review Defined

Judicial review is the doctrine that the courts have the power to invalidate governmental action which is repugnant to the Constitution.

2. Review of Federal Action

While there is no explicit textual authority for federal court review of the acts of the President and the Congress, this power has been inferred from a number of sources, including the Art. III grant of judicial power to the Supreme Court and inferior federal courts and the principle that it is the judicial power to say what the law, *i.e.*, the Constitution, is.

3. Review of State Action

a. The Supremacy Clause of Art. VI establishes federal judicial power over the acts of state officials.

b. Art. VI requires state courts to make decisions in conformity with the U.S. Constitution. These "cases arising under the Constitution" are reviewable by the Supreme Court under Art. III.

B. Source of Judicial Power: Article III Jurisdiction

The "judicial power" is vested by Art. III in the Supreme Court and inferior federal courts created by Congress.

1. Federal "Judicial Power" Defined

a. Unless a case falls within one of the "cases or controversies" identified in Art. III, § 2, an Art. III federal court (as distinguished from an Art. I court) must dismiss the case for want of subject matter jurisdiction.

b. Congress exercises broad powers over the existence and jurisdiction of lower national courts, within the limits provided by Art. III.

2. Supreme Court Jurisdiction

a. Original Jurisdiction

Supreme Court original jurisdiction is defined by Art. III. It cannot be enlarged or diminished by Congress.

b. Appellate Jurisdiction—Congressional Power

The Supreme Court's appellate jurisdiction is vested by Art. III subject to congressional exceptions. This congressional power may be subject to limitations arising from separation of powers principles and constitutional rights and liberties.

c. Discretionary Review

Supreme Court review of lower court decisions is almost entirely a matter of discretion.

C. Constitutional and Policy Limitations on Judicial Review

Even where an issue concerns the subject matter set forth in Art. III, it may not *necessarily* be heard on the merits. For example, Art. III requires that a "case or controversy" must be present for an Art. III court to have jurisdiction. Further, there are prudential limitations borne of judicial self-restraint limiting the use of judicial review. The jurisdictional requirements and policy restraints are frequently referred to as justiciability.

1. Constitutional Limitations

a. Eleventh Amendment

The Eleventh Amendment, as interpreted, provides that the judicial power does not extend to suits against a state or its agencies by citizens of another state or of a foreign country or by its own citizens. However, there are exceptions:

(1) local governmental units are not covered;

(2) states may waive sovereign immunity if clearly done;

(3) acting under the Fourteenth Amendment, § 5, Congress can grant remedies against state action that violates the Fourteenth Amendment, § 1, if it makes its intent to abrogate state immunity unmistakably clear. The Court has become increasingly restrictive in its interpretation of Congress' enforcement powers under the Fourteenth Amendment, § 5. Congress may not abrogate Eleventh Amendment immunity using its Commerce Powers;

(4) unconstitutional acts of state officials are not state acts and may be enjoined by federal courts. But, if a suit involves a retroactive monetary charge against the state or violation of state law, the Eleventh Amendment is a bar. Prospective relief and ancillary relief are permitted.

b. Case or Controversy

A case must be in an adversary form and a context that is capable of judicial resolution and its resolution must not violate separation of powers principles, or an Art. III federal court lacks jurisdiction. Art. III federal courts cannot furnish advisory opinions.

2. Policy Limitations (Judicial Self–Restraint)

a. Rules for Constitutional Review. The *Ashwander* rules are used to avoid unnecessary constitutional decisions.

b. Presumption of Constitutionality.

c. Judicial Restraint to Avoid Unnecessary Use of Judicial Review. The Court follows a policy of "strict necessity" before deciding constitutional questions.

d. Congressional legislation can override prudential (i.e., non-jurisdictional) limitations.

D. Specific Doctrines Limiting Judicial Review

There are specific doctrines, based on the case or controversy requirement and judicial self-restraint, through which Art. III federal courts determine *who* may litigate a constitutional question, *when* the constitutional question may be litigated, and *what* constitutional questions may be litigated.

1. The Standing Limitation—*Who* Can Litigate?

a. Constitutional Standing

(1) Art. III requires that a plaintiff seeking to litigate a federal constitutional question demonstrate a personal stake in the outcome by establishing (1) injury in fact; (2) fairly traceable to the defendant's act being challenged; and, (3) redressable by the requested remedy. This assures the requisite adversity and reflects separation of powers concerns.

(a) *"Injury in Fact."* Any significant factual injury, economic, aesthetic, etc., will suffice. The injury must be "concrete and particularized and actual or imminent, not conjectural or hypothetical."

(b) *"Fairly Traceable."* Plaintiffs must establish causation by showing that the injury is "fairly traceable" to the defendant's action being challenged.

(c) *Redressability.* They must also demonstrate a "substantial likelihood" that the injury is "redressable" if the court grants the requested relief. The focus is on the relation of the injury and the remedy.

(2) Taxpayer and Citizen Standing

    (a) *Federal Taxpayers.* A federal taxpayer must allege (1) that the enactment being challenged is an exercise of the taxing and spending power, and (2) that the challenged enactment offends a specific limitation on the taxing and spending power.

    (b) *State and Municipal Taxpayers.* State taxpayers have no standing under Art. III to challenge state tax or spending decisions simply by virtue as their standing as taxpayers. But a municipal taxpayer does have standing to challenge municipal spending because the injury is more direct.

    (c) *Citizen Standing.* At least in the absence of congressional legislation authorizing the suit, under Art. III standing a citizen lacks a sufficient personal interest to raise the constitutional claim.

    (d) *State Standing.* A State does not have standing to sue the federal government as parens patriae on behalf of its citizens. A State may sue the federal government on its own behalf to protect its own interests.

(3) Statutory Standing

Congress can, by statute, create legal interests, the denial of which constitute injury in fact. However, Congress cannot ignore the Art. III standing requirements of injury in fact, and causation, *i.e.,* fairly traceable and redressability. Congress can remove prudential obstacles to standing.

b. Prudential Standing

(1) *Third Party Standing.* A litigant usually lacks standing to raise the rights of others, but there are exceptions.

    (a) The jus tertii rule is a rule of judicial self-restraint which can be overcome when the balance of interests warrants hearing the claim.

(2) *Associational Standing.* An association can raise the rights of its members if the members have Art. III standing to sue in their

own right, the suit is germane to the organization's interests and there is no need for individual participation.

2. The Timing Limitation—*When* Can Constitutional Litigation Be Brought

a. Mootness

Art. III requires dismissal of a case when, because of changes, the court's determination of the legal issue cannot have any practical effect in achieving the desired result. But there are exceptions to the doctrine:

(1) voluntary cessation of the allegedly illegal conduct;

(2) unsettled collateral consequences;

(3) there is a reasonable likelihood that the constitutional issue is "capable of repetition, yet evading review."

b. Ripeness, Prematurity and Abstractness

(1) The Art. III requirement of ripeness requires that there be *present* injury or an *imminent threat* of injury. In determining if a case is ripe, consider the effect of delay on plaintiffs, the effect of judicial intervention on administrative actors, and whether courts would benefit from the delay.

(2) Even if jurisdiction is technically present, judicial self-restraint may dictate dismissal of issues as premature and abstract.

c. Discretionary Abstention

(1) Vagueness

If a state statute is capable of a narrow saving construction, federal courts should exercise restraint and abstain from decisions on constitutional issues.

(2) Pending State Proceedings

Absent a showing of bad faith harassment, a federal court should abstain in a suit seeking declaratory or injunctive relief if state criminal or analogous civil proceedings are pending.

3. The Subject Matter Limitation—*What* Can Be Litigated

a. The Political Question Doctrine

Political questions, which are non-justiciable, have their origin in classic, functional, and prudential considerations.

  (1) Constitutional commitment to another branch;

  (2) lack of judicial resources and capabilities for deciding the case;

  (3) prudential or policy considerations relating to the proper use of judicial power.

b. Adequate and Independent State Grounds

Where adequate and independent substantive or procedural state grounds for a lower court decision clearly exist, the Supreme Court will decline to exercise jurisdiction.

II. NATIONAL LEGISLATIVE POWERS

Congress has only such powers as are granted by the Constitution. Under the Tenth Amendment, powers not granted to the national government are retained by the states and the people. The crucial inquiry is whether there is a constitutional source of power for congressional legislation.

A. The Scope of the National Legislative Power

1. Express Powers

Art. I, § 8, expressly grants specific powers to Congress.

2. Implied Powers

Under the Necessary and Proper Clause of Art. I, § 8, Congress can enact laws which are reasonably designed to achieve its delegated powers.

3. Inherent Powers

Congress has no inherent domestic legislative powers. This does not preclude the existence of inherent foreign affairs powers.

4. Delegation of Powers

Congress can delegate legislative authority so long as it prescribes some standards to guide use of the granted powers.

5. The Tenth Amendment

Powers that were previously exercised by the states which are not delegated are reserved to the states or to the people. There has been persistent controversy over whether the Tenth Amendment is a substantive limitation on Congress' ability to legislate as to private parties and the states.

6. The Supremacy Clause

Art. IV, cl. 2 establishes that national laws that are constitutional override contrary state laws.

B. Commerce Power

1. Definition

Congress has power to regulate "commerce among the states" which has come to mean interstate commerce. However, the commerce power provides the basis for congressional regulation even of local intrastate activities. Commerce is limited to economic activity and a majority of the justices have indicated that economic inactivity cannot be regulated by the federal government, even if this inactivity has an effect on interstate commerce. *National Federation of Independent Business v. Sebelius* (2012).

2. Achieving Social Welfare Objectives—A National Police Power

Congress' power to regulate the channels and instrumentalities of interstate commerce and persons and things in interstate commerce is plenary, permitting it to prescribe rules for the protection of commerce. Courts will not probe Congress' purpose in regulating interstate commerce.

    a.   While there is no national police power, Congress can achieve social welfare objectives through regulating interstate commerce. If Congress exercises its delegated powers, it may regulate matters traditionally regulated by the states.

b. *Tenth Amendment.* When Congress regulates *private* action, the Tenth Amendment is not a significant limitation on Congress' regulatory power.

3. Stream of Commerce

Local activities can be regulated if they are part of the "stream" of interstate commerce.

4. Instrumentalities of Commerce

Congress' plenary power to regulate and protect interstate commerce extends even to local activities that threaten the instrumentalities of interstate commerce and persons and things in interstate commerce.

5. The Affectation Doctrine

a. Substantial Effects

(1) Under the Necessary and Proper Clause, Congress can regulate local activities if it can rationally conclude that such activity has a substantial effect on interstate commerce. The courts generally defer to the congressional judgment.

(2) In assessing the effect, Congress may consider the *cumulative or aggregate impact* of all regulated activities.

(3) "Congress can regulate purely intrastate activity that is not itself 'commercial,' in that it is not produced for sale, if it concludes that failure to regulate that class of activity would undercut the regulation of the interstate market in that commodity." *Gonzales* v. *Raich* (2005).

(4) However, a majority of the justices have indicated that Congress may not regulate individuals not previously involved in commerce even if their failure to become active adversely affects interstate commerce. *National Federation of Independent Business v. Sebelius* (2012).

b. New Restrictions

There are limits. Consider if the matter regulated is commercial, if there is a jurisdictional nexus to interstate commerce, if there is congressional fact finding, and if the causal relation between the regulated act is remote or attenuated, including whether the regulation intrudes on areas of traditional state concern.

C. The Taxing Power

Congress has the fiscal power of raising monies through taxes. However, this is not a regulatory power and "penalties" may not be imposed in the guise of taxes.

1. Courts today tend to accept any tax as a fiscal measure if, on its face, it is a revenue producing measure.

2. Disclosure requirements will not make a tax into a penalty but such provisions raise problems of self-incrimination.

D. The Spending Power

Congress can spend, but cannot regulate, for the general welfare.

1. General Welfare

The Spending Clause of Art. I, § 8, cl. 1, is an independent fiscal power to spend for general welfare objectives. It is not limited to the regulatory powers of Art. I, § 8. Congress determines the scope of the general welfare.

2. Reasonable Conditions

Congress may impose any reasonable conditions for participation in federal spending programs even if this induces states to conform to federal standards. The courts defer to Congress' judgment of reasonableness. Such conditions must be explicitly stated so that states can make informed choices.

3. Constitutional Limitations

The Tenth Amendment is not likely to be a barrier to congressional spending so long as the states remain free to reject the federal grant and its conditions. While Congress may create incentives for states to act, if the conditions are so coercive as to compel State conduct, the law is unconstitutional.

4. Spending as a Contract: Explicit Conditions

Conditions on federal grants must be clear and unambiguous to be enforced.

E. Intergovernmental Immunities

The national government has greater immunity from state regulation and taxation and greater power to tax and regulate state functions (Art. VI Supremacy Clause).

1. State Taxation and Regulation

States cannot directly tax or regulate the federal government or federal instrumentalities. They cannot discriminate against the federal government or those who deal with the federal government.

2. Federal Taxation and Regulation

a. Federal Taxation of States

Non-discriminatory federal taxes, which reasonably reflect the benefits provided the state, are constitutional.

b. Federal Regulation of States

(1) *State Sovereignty Limitation.* Principles of state sovereignty, reflected in the Tenth Amendment, limit Congress' Commerce Clause power to regulate state activities.

(2) In *National League of Cities*, subsequently overruled, the national interest in including the states under the regulation was balanced against the intrusion on state sovereignty. Three conditions were used in determining if state sovereignty was violated:

(a) "States as states" (Direct regulation of state or its agencies);

(b) "Traditional state functions";

(c) Impairment of state ability "to structure integral operations in areas of traditional functions".

(3) Today, if Congress enacts a law generally applicable to private parties and the states, there is only a minimal state sovereignty

limitation. The Tenth Amendment and principles of state sovereignty, embodied in our constitutional structure, impose only minimal limits on congressional power, assuming that the national political process is functioning.

   (a) Federal courts should not determine what are "traditional" or "integral" functions of state government.

   (b) It is the structure of the federal government itself that protects federalism.

   (4) But if congressional regulations impose special burdens on states, state sovereignty and the Tenth Amendment impose limitations. Congress cannot constitutionally command states to regulate or to enforce a federal regulatory program, since this would undermine political accountability and dual sovereignty. In such cases, there is no judicial balancing of national and state interests. But Congress can require states to regulate or face preemption by a federal program.

III. STATE POWER IN AMERICAN FEDERALISM

States have inherent police power to legislate for the public health, morals, and well-being of its citizens. But this power is limited by the constitutional division of powers. The people of the entire nation, through the Tenth Amendment, reserved to the states only such powers as they had prior to ratification.

A. State Power to Regulate Commerce

1. Establishing the Foundations

Where a subject requires national regulation or where the particular state regulation would excessively burden interstate commerce, the state may not regulate absent congressional authorization.

a. The Nature of the Power

The commerce power is, at least partially, a concurrent power.

b. The Nature of the Subject—*Cooley* Doctrine

When subjects of commerce regulation are national in nature, *i.e.*, require a uniform system or plan of regulation, they are not amenable to state regulation. *Cooley v. Board of Wardens* (1851).

2. The Modern Focus: The Dormant Commerce Clause

The Dormant Commerce Clause, as interpreted by the courts, limits state power to enact regulations affecting interstate commerce. States may not discriminate against interstate commerce absent substantial justification. Nor may states place unreasonable burdens on interstate commerce.

a. Rationale

(1) Common Market Philosophy. No trade barriers.

(2) Lack of political protection for out-of-state interests.

b. Discrimination

If a state regulation is labeled "discriminatory" against interstate commerce, it is likely to be held unconstitutional. Economic protectionism violates the Dormant Commerce Clause. But laws which benefit public entities over private entities, yet which treat all private companies the same, do not discriminate against interstate commerce.

(1) Intentional Discrimination

A state law which purposefully discriminates against interstate commerce, e.g., by hoarding scarce resources against import or export to other states, is virtually per se invalid.

(2) Discriminatory Means and Effects

Even if a state law serves a legitimate police power objective, the law must regulate evenhandedly. Differential treatment favoring in-state against out-of-state interests constitutes discrimination. A local regulation may be discriminatory even if it curtails commerce by other state subdivisions as well as out-of-state interests. A law using discriminatory means or having a discriminatory impact must serve a legitimate local purpose that cannot be served as well by nondiscriminatory means. Watch for the following:

(a) Extraterritorial operation of state laws;

(b) Facial or factual imposition of unequal burdens or benefits;

(c) But differential impact or effects may be due to market structure rather than discriminatory laws.

c. **Undue Burdens—Ad Hoc Balancing**

In determining if a nondiscriminatory state regulation of interstate commerce is valid, the courts balance the local interests in maintaining the law against the burden on interstate commerce. Some members of the Court reject undue burdens balancing, limiting the Dormant Commerce Clause to a ban on discrimination.

(1) Important state interests in trade, conservation, and environment weigh heavily in the balance but cannot be achieved by means which excessively impede the free flow of interstate commerce.

(2) State highway laws enjoy a heavy presumption of validity but, even here, states cannot unreasonably burden our national Common Market system.

d. **State as Market Participant**

When the state acts, not as a regulator, but as a participant in the marketplace, the Dormant Commerce Clause doctrine doesn't apply. Even state discrimination in favor of its own citizens is permissible. Subsidies may involve such nonregulatory market participation. The more state actions affect parties not in privity with the state, the more likely the state will be held to be a regulator.

3. **Protecting Personal Mobility**

a. **Commerce Clause**

The Commerce Clause protects the free movement of persons from state to state.

b. **Interstate Privileges and Immunities**

Art. IV, § 2, prohibits unreasonable discrimination against out-of-state citizens in regard to fundamental interests basic to the livelihood of the Nation. There must be a substantial reason for the discrimination and the discrimination must bear a close relation to that reason. To justify discrimination in rights fundamental to national unity, it must be shown that out of state citizens are a peculiar source of the evil. Further, there must not be any less burdensome alternatives. The clause provides an alternative to the Dormant Commerce Clause for attacking state discrimination against out-of-state citizens and may be used when the State is acting as a market participant.

4. When Congress Speaks

a. Preemption

(1) If a state law conflicts with a valid federal law so that it is impossible to comply with both or if it impedes achievement of the federal legislative objective, the state law is invalid under the Art. VI Supremacy Clause.

(2) Congress may expressly preempt state law.

(3) If there is no conflict or express preemption, the courts must still determine if Congress intended to occupy the field and exclude the state regulation. Courts consider: (a) need for uniformity; (b) legislative history; (c) the pervasiveness of the federal regulation; (d) historic roles of national and local interest in regulating in the area (presumption of no preemption in areas of traditional state authority); (e) potential for future conflict; (f) availability of a federal agency to maintain continued control.

b. Legitimizing State Burdens on Commerce

In exercising its plenary powers, Congress may authorize the state to regulate even where the state law would otherwise violate the negative implications of the Dormant Commerce Clause. But Congress must expressly and unambiguously manifest such an intent.

5. The Compact Clause

Art. I, § 10, cl. 3, requires congressional consent to any agreement between states if it increases the political power of the states so as to potentially interfere with federal supremacy.

B. State Power to Tax Commerce

1. General Principles

a. Interstate commerce can be forced to pay taxes which reasonably reflect the benefits derived from the taxing state.

b. States *may not discriminate* against interstate commerce.

c.   *Due process* requires that the taxpayer have some minimal contacts with the taxing state.

d.   The *Commerce Clause* requires that a state tax be apportioned to reflect the extent of the taxable status the taxpayer has in the taxing situs to avoid *multiple burdens*.

2.   Modern Applications

Identify the local incidents being taxed and inquire into the actual economic effect of the tax. The tax is valid if:

(1)   the activity taxed is sufficiently connected to the taxing state;

(2)   the tax is fairly apportioned;

(3)   the tax does not discriminate against interstate commerce;

(4)   the tax fairly reflects the benefits received.

IV.   CONGRESS AND EXECUTIVE POWER

When executive and congressional powers conflict, formalist and functional approaches are used. In determining if separation of powers has been violated, consider whether one Branch is invading the constitutional prerogatives of another Branch or is usurping powers properly shared.

A.   The Domestic Arena

1.   Executive Law–Making

a.   Limited Domestic Law–Making Powers

Absent an emergency, the President has no inherent domestic law-making power. His powers as Chief Executive and his power to take care that the laws are faithfully executed may create some emergency powers subject to congressional review. Congressional acquiescence, custom and usage, may augment Executive powers.

b.   Veto Power

A presidential refusal to sign an act into law can be overridden by a two-thirds vote of both houses. But the Line Item Veto Act violates the Presentment Clause of Art. I, § 7. Instead of the law-making procedure outlined in Art. I, § 7, the Act allows the President to cancel or repeal particular spending provisions thus changing the signed law. This is inconsistent with the constitutionally prescribed Veto Power.

2. Executive Impoundment

It has not yet been decided whether a President's withholding or delay in expending appropriations is a constitutional exercise of the Executive power to faithfully execute the laws or an unconstitutional interference in Congress's law-making power.

3. Delegation and Control of Legislative Power

a. Congress can delegate power to the Executive if it formulates reasonable standards—an "intelligible principle"—to guide discretion. The courts defer to Congress in determining reasonableness.

b. *The Legislative Veto.* Retention of power by Congress to review and veto executive exercise of delegated power is legislative action which violates the Presentment and Bicameralism provisions of Art. I, § 7.

4. The Appointment and Removal Power

a. Art. II, § 2, cl. 2, vests the power to appoint federal officials, subject to the Senate's advice and consent, in the President. Congress may vest appointment of inferior officers in the President, courts of law, or heads of departments, but not in the Congress itself.

(1) Congress may not vest the appointment power in persons other than those specified in Art. II, § 2, cl. 2.

(2) Whether an official is a principal or an inferior officer depends on a functional analysis of her independence, power, jurisdiction, and tenure.

b. The President has the power to remove quasi-judicial or quasi-legislative officials subject to the standards established by Congress. The President has greater freedom to remove purely executive officials but it is not absolute. Consider whether Congress' removal restrictions impede the President's ability to perform his constitutional duty.

c. Congress may not vest executive functions in officials subject to congressional removal by means other than impeachment.

5. Separation of Powers Generally

Consider generally whether the challenged actions excessively intrude on the constitutional functions of another Branch or consolidate powers that should properly be dispersed.

B. The Foreign Arena

1. Foreign Affairs

Foreign affairs powers are shared powers between the President and Congress. States and courts play a limited role.

2. Treaties and Executive Agreements

a. *Treaties* are made by the President with the advice and consent of two-thirds of the Senators present. They prevail over state law but are subject to constitutional limitations. But a treaty is not binding domestic law unless Congress enacts implementing legislation or the treaty is self-executing. The President cannot unilaterally make treaties binding domestically.

b. *Executive Agreements*, not requiring Senate concurrence, are legal even though they are not mentioned in the Constitution and prevail over contrary state law.

c. Congressional legislation, which would not otherwise survive constitutional review, may be a legitimate means of implementing a treaty.

3. The War Power

While Art. I gives the Congress alone power to declare war, the President's Art. II power as Commander-in-Chief affords him power in making war. But he cannot order the indefinite detention of American citizens arrested on American territory without due process of law. Even aliens detained at Guantanamo are entitled to habeas corpus to test their status as enemy combatants. It is unconstitutional for Congress to authorize use of procedures which fail to provide the protections of habeas corpus to detainees, without suspending the writ.

C. Privileges and Immunities

1. Executive Privilege

The Court has recognized the existence of an executive privilege for internal confidential communications based on the separation of powers principle and Art. II. A claim of privilege is presumptively valid and the judiciary determines whether a sufficient need has been shown by the party seeking disclosure.

2. Impeachment

A President may be impeached by the House and tried by the Senate for "Treason, Bribery, or other high crimes and misdemeanors."

3. Presidential Immunity

The President is absolutely immune from civil liability for actions within the "outside perimeters" of his official responsibility. But the President does not have a general constitutional immunity for unofficial acts allegedly committed prior to assuming office. Presidential aides have a qualified immunity.

4. Congressional Immunity

Members of Congress and their aides enjoy absolute immunity under Art. I, § 6, for "legislative acts."

■ PART TWO: INDIVIDUAL RIGHTS AND LIBERTIES: CONSTITUTIONAL LIMITATIONS ON GOVERNMENT POWER

V.   HISTORICAL PERSPECTIVES

A.   The Original Constitution

1.   Natural Rights

The idea that there are extra-constitutional legally enforceable "natural rights" limiting governmental power has not been accepted by the Court.

2.   Express Rights

The original Constitution contains few express rights limiting governmental power.

B.   Bill of Rights

The first ten amendments were enacted only to limit the newly created federal government. They do not apply directly against the states. The Due Process Clause is used to apply the guarantees of the Bill of Rights to the states.

C.   The Civil War Amendments

1.   Thirteenth Amendment

This amendment abolishes slavery and involuntary servitude. Unlike other amendments, it applies to private action.

2.   Fourteenth Amendment

Persons born or naturalized in this country are citizens of the United States and of the state of their residence. No citizen of the United States can be denied the privileges and immunities of United States citizenship. No state shall deprive citizens of life, liberty, or property without due process of law or deny any person in the jurisdiction equal protection under the laws.

3. Fifteenth Amendment

Denial of the franchise because of race or previous condition of servitude by the state or federal government is prohibited.

D. Privileges or Immunities of National Citizenship

The Fourteenth Amendment Privileges or Immunities Clause does not make the Bill of Rights applicable to the states. The Clause has been narrowly interpreted to protect only those rights relating to a *U.S. citizen's relationship to the national government, e.g.,* to vote in federal elections. While it is seldom used today, it has recently been used to prevent discrimination against newly arrived residents based on their exercise of the right of interstate travel.

E. The Second Amendment

The Second Amendment confers an individual right to possess and carry weapons in cases of confrontation. The right is not unlimited but the Court has not determined the scope of permissible government regulation or the appropriate standards of judicial review. The Second Amendment right has been incorporated as a limit on states. *McDonald v. City of Chicago* (2010).

VI. DUE PROCESS OF LAW

While there are a few guarantees of liberty and property in the original Constitution, a central source of personal rights has been the Due Process Clause of the Fifth and Fourteenth Amendments. Fourteenth Amendment due process includes: (1) incorporated fundamental rights; (2) substantive rights limiting what government can do; (3) procedural limits on how government acts.

A. Ex Post Facto Laws

Neither the federal (Art. I, § 9) nor the state (Art. I, § 10) government may enact retrospective criminal laws significantly disadvantaging an offender. Civil laws are not covered by the Clauses.

B. Bills of Attainder

Neither Congress (Art. I, § 9) nor a state legislature (Art. I, § 10) may punish an individual without the benefit of judicial trial.

C. Impairment of Obligation of Contract

Art. I, § 10 limits state legislative ability to impair substantive contract obligations and the Fifth Amendment Due Process Clause prevents congressional impairment of substantive contract rights. It is occasionally used to limit government power, but infrequently.

1. Private Contracts

A state law substantially impairing pre-existing contractual relationships violates this guarantee unless the state establishes that the law is a reasonable means for achieving a significant and legitimate public purpose.

2. Public Contracts

A state may contract away its fiscal powers and may impair its contracts only if it is reasonable and necessary to serve important state interests.

D. The Takings Clause

1. Taking Property

"Private property" is generally defined by looking to rules and understandings stemming from an independent source such as state law.

2. Constitutional Text

The Fifth Amendment provides that private property is not to be taken by the federal government without just compensation. The Fourteenth Amendment Due Process Clause has been held to impose a similar obligation on the states.

3. What Is a "Taking?"

a. Regulatory Takings

The concept of taking goes beyond the formal condemnation of property to invalidate any regulation which is functionally equivalent to condemnation.

b. Reasonable Regulation

In determining if a regulation is a taking, factors to be considered include: economic impact of the regulation, effect on investment expectations, and the character of the government action. But the effectiveness of the regulation in furthering government interests is not relevant.

c.   Categorical (Per Se) Takings

If the government physically invades the property on a permanent basis or denies all economically beneficial or productive use of the land, there is a taking. A moratorium on property development, even for years, is not a categorical taking.

d.   Conditional Takings

In determining whether government imposition of a condition as a price of land development is a taking, two questions are asked:

(1)   whether there is an "essential nexus" between the legitimate state interest and the condition, and

(2)   whether the government has made sufficient individualized findings establishing that the exaction has a rough proportionality to the impact of the proposed development.

4.   Public Use

The taking must be for a public purpose, including economic development. Courts defer to the legislature.

E.   Due Process: The Incorporation Process

1.   Selective Incorporation

Only those provisions of the Bill of Rights which are "essential to the concept of ordered liberty" or "fundamental in the American scheme of justice" are made applicable to the states through the Due Process Clause. Rights thus far not incorporated as "fundamental rights" include the Third Amendment, Seventh Amendment right to jury trial in some civil cases, grand jury indictment, excessive bail, 12–person juries and a unanimous verdict for conviction.

2.   Full Incorporation

The incorporated fundamental right applies against the states in the same manner as the Bill of Rights provision applies against the federal government.

F.   Traditional Substantive Due Process

1.   The Rise and Fall of Economic Substantive Due Process

Under "Lochnerism," the courts invalidated federal and state laws as arbitrary and unreasonable interferences with the right of contract protected by the due process guarantees of liberty and property. Today, this active judicial review of socio-economic legislation has been replaced by judicial deference.

2. Modern Substantive Due Process: Non-fundamental Rights

In reviewing federal (Fifth Amendment) and state (Fourteenth Amendment) laws, the courts usually defer to the legislative judgment. If there is any *rational* basis that the legislature might have had for concluding that a law would further permissible legislative objectives, it does not violate due process. This deferential standard is used in reviewing most social and economic legislation.

a. Burden of Proof

The law is presumed constitutional and the burden of proof (which is essentially insurmountable) is on the challenging party.

b. Legitimate Objective

Any permissible government objective will suffice.

c. Rational Means

In assessing the rationality of the law in achieving the government's objective, the courts will not second-guess legislative fact finding or question the wisdom of the law.

d. Fundamental Rights Exception

Due Process challenges based on fundamental personal rights invoke a more searching judicial scrutiny.

G. Substantive Due Process Revisited: The Right of Privacy and Other Unenumerated Rights

1. Fundamental Rights

When laws burden the exercise of "fundamental rights" protected by the Due Process guarantee, the courts apply stricter scrutiny. The government bears the burden of showing that the law is narrowly tailored to further an overriding government interest. Often the review is "strict," requiring a showing that the means are "necessary" to a "compelling government interest."

2. Express, Implied, and Unenumerated Rights

A more stringent standard of review is used for all express rights, those rights implied from the express rights or the constitutional structure, and other unenumerated fundamental rights recognized by the courts. When the Court holds that a law burdens a significant or special liberty right, the Court uses strict scrutiny or employs a "particularly careful scrutiny."

3. Contraception and Abortion

a. The Privacy Right

There is no express right of privacy in the Constitution, but in early cases involving contraception and abortion, the Court held there is a constitutional right of privacy which limits the power of the government to regulate sexual activities involving marriage and family life.

b. The *Roe v. Wade* Revolution and Reaction

In *Roe v. Wade* (1973), the Court extended the fundamental right of privacy to protect a woman's decision to terminate a pregnancy. The Court found the privacy right in the Fourteenth Amendment guarantee of personal liberty and applied a "trimester test" to determine whether strict scrutiny was met.

c. *Casey*: The Essentials of *Roe*

(1) In *Planned Parenthood of S.E. Pennsylvania v. Casey* (1992), the Court verbally reaffirmed the "essential holding" of *Roe* including:

(a) the right of a woman to choose to have an abortion before viability without undue interference from the state;

(b) the state's power to restrict abortion after viability as long as there is an exception for the mother's life and health;

(c) the state's legitimate interests in protecting the health of the woman and the life of the fetus.

(2) The plurality in *Casey* did not discuss a right of privacy or fundamental rights, nor did it adopt strict scrutiny. Rather the

"undue burdens" test was used. A law is invalid "if its purpose or effect is to place a substantial obstacle in the path of a woman seeking an abortion before the fetus attains viability."

d. Abortion After *Casey*

A federal law banning partial birth abortion was upheld against a facial challenge despite the absence of any provision exempting mothers whose health was at risk. The Act did not impose an undue burden because there was medical uncertainty as to whether the prohibition on partial birth abortion created significant health risks and because other procedures were available. The prohibition is subject to as-applied challenges.

e. Rights of Minors

The minor woman's right of privacy also protects her contraception and abortion decisions. However, the greater state interest in minors and their usual lesser capacity permit a greater amount of state regulation. Parents cannot be given an absolute veto over the minor's decisions but requiring parental consent or notification, if a judicial by-pass is provided, has been upheld.

f. Abortion Funding

There is no right to abortion funding. Neither the right of privacy nor equal protection requires the state to make the abortion right effective even if maternal funding is provided.

4. Sodomy Laws

A state law criminalizing homosexual sodomy violates due process liberty. Liberty protects intimate decisional choices involving consensual adult sexual conduct in the privacy of the home. The state has no legitimate interest sufficient to justify the intrusion into the personal and private life of the individual.

5. Rights to Marriage and Family Life

The institutions of marriage and family, which are deeply rooted in our nation's history and traditions, are fundamental rights subject to the stricter form of judicial review. The Court has protected the right to marry, parents' right to the care, custody and control of their children and the right of close relatives to live together free from excessive government regulation. Particular associations and relationships may be held not to constitute a constitutionally-protected family or marriage.

6. Right of Travel

a. Interstate Movement

While the source of the right of interstate travel is unclear, it is a fundamental personal right subject to more stringent judicial protection.

b. Foreign Travel

The right to travel abroad guaranteed by Fifth Amendment due process is subject to reasonable regulation by the national government.

7. The Right to Care and Protection

Government has no affirmative constitutional duty, absent special circumstances, to provide care and protection for individuals. A limited duty may arise if government assumes custody of an individual.

8. The Right to Refuse Treatment

A person has a liberty interest in avoiding unwanted medical treatment. The government's interest may justify the regulatory burden on liberty, *e.g.*, the state's interest in preserving life justifies imposing a heightened evidentiary standard before life support is terminated.

9. The Right to Die

There is no fundamental right to commit suicide nor any fundamental right to assisted suicide. Such interests are neither traditionally protected nor implicit in the concept of ordered liberty as to be deemed fundamental. Criminal prohibition of such practices is rationally related to legitimate state interests such as preserving life, protecting the depressed and vulnerable groups, and avoiding euthanasia.

10. Rights in Restricted Environments

Stricter standards of due process review usually do not apply in special contexts such as the military, prisons, schools, and mental institutions. Balancing of the competing interests tends to reflect greater judicial deference.

H. Procedural Due Process

Whenever the government deprives a person of a significant life, liberty, or property interest, it must afford due process. Whether the interest is a right or a privilege, if it is a due process interest and is presently enjoyed, it is protected.

The question of what process is due is a matter of federal constitutional law for the courts. It is not determined by state law. In determining what procedures are required to assure due process, courts balance the competing interests, usually considering three factors:

(1) the severity of the harm to the litigant if the procedures are not provided;

(2) the risk of error if the procedures are not afforded; and,

(3) the administrative difficulty and other costs of providing the requested procedures.

1. What Is Property?

Property is limited to interests recognized by government, *e.g.*, entitlements.

2. What Is Liberty?

Liberty is not limited to freedom from confinement. It includes marriage, raising a family, etc. But reputation, without more, does not constitute a sufficient liberty interest.

3. What Is a "Deprivation"

Negligent injury by government officials to life, liberty or property interests does not constitute a deprivation.

4. Due Process Contexts

a. Welfare Benefits

Welfare benefits, once received, constitute a property entitlement. Courts balance the state interest in conserving resources against the recipient's interest in uninterrupted benefits.

b. Use and Possession of Property

Wages or a purchaser's interest in goods received under a contingent sales contract constitute property. Normally, notice and hearing are required prior to depriving the property interest.

c. Public Employment Rights

The mere subjective expectancy of continued employment or employment terminable at will are not property interests. There must be a state-created entitlement. A state-created cause of action is a property entitlement. The state may so condition an employment interest that it does not constitute property. But the court determines what procedures are due once a property interest exists—"No bitter with the sweet."

d. Institutional Due Process

While officials in public institutions do exercise broad discretion, liberty interests resulting from compulsory attendance at a school or involuntary confinement in a hospital require due process to be satisfied. Parole revocation or revocation of pre-parole conditional release involve liberty interests. The appropriate procedures are determined by balancing the liberty interest against institutional considerations.

e. Parental Rights

The important liberty interests of natural parents in the care, custody, and management of their children require significant procedural protection.

f. Student Rights

Due process does protect the liberty and property interests of a student. But the courts are reluctant to intrude on academic decision-making and the discretion afforded school authorities.

g. Access to Courts

Due process does not require that indigents be given free access to the courts in civil cases absent state monopoly of processes affecting fundamental due process interests. But once a state affords a right of access or significantly burdens fundamental rights, imposition of filing fees may violate due process (and equal protection). Procedures available in civil proceedings are determined by the balancing test, although there is a presumption against a right to appointed counsel in civil proceedings.

h. Fair Trial/Judicial Bias

While matters of judicial bias are normally dealt with through local rules and statutes, the Due Process Clause imposes some basic restrictions on when a judge must recuse himself from a case. If the judge has a direct, personal, substantial pecuniary interest in the outcome, recusal is constitutionally required. If an objective appraisal indicates that there is a serious risk of actual bias, the Due Process Clause requires that the judge recuse himself in the interest of a fair trial in a fair tribunal.

5. Conclusive Presumptions

When critical due process interests are lost through government action, due process generally requires that the individual be afforded an opportunity to prove that the facts presumed are not true in the particular case. But if the case involves a non-contractual claim to public benefits, it is possible that no liberty or property interest is involved.

VII. EQUAL PROTECTION

A. General Standards

The Fourteenth Amendment Equal Protection Clause and the Fifth Amendment Due Process Clause (which is read to guarantee equal protection) prohibit the state and federal government respectively from using unreasonable classifications. Reasonableness is dependent on: (1) the basis of the classification; (2) the character of the interests burdened by the classification; and (3) the government objectives supporting the classification. The courts generally use three principal standards of review: (1) the traditional rational basis test; (2) an intermediate standard requiring that the classification be substantially related to an important government interest; and (3) strict scrutiny requiring that the classification be necessary to a compelling state interest.

B. Traditional Equal Protection

1. The Rational Basis Test

In most cases, a classification will be upheld if it is rationally related to any permissible government objective. The fact that a classification is under- or over-inclusive will not result in its unconstitutionality.

a. Burden of Proof

The law is presumed valid and the burden of proof of its invalidity is on the challenger. The burden is usually insurmountable.

b. Permissible Government Objective

If the classification is rationally related to a permissible government objective, even if it is not the actual objective, it will be upheld.

c. Rational Means

If any facts can be ascertained that will sustain the classification, the existence of such fact finding by the legislature will be assumed. Only arbitrary classification is proscribed.

2. Rationality With Bite

In some cases, the Court has engaged in a more demanding balancing of the competing interests in determining the reasonableness of the challenged classification. This may reflect judicial concern with possible prejudice or animus against the disfavored class.

C. Heightened Review Equal Protection

1. Suspect Classifications

When a law purposely employs a suspect classification, the classification is subject to strict scrutiny. The ordinary presumption of validity no longer applies and the burden is on the government to demonstrate that the classification is necessary to a compelling government interest.

2. Criteria of Suspectness

Factors which have been considered in labeling a classification suspect include: the historical purpose of the Equal Protection Clause; the history of discrimination against the class; the stigmatizing effect of discrimination; classification based upon a status which the person cannot control; discrimination against a politically insular minority.

3. Purpose, Not Effect

Before strict scrutiny is used, the challenger must prove that the discrimination was purposeful, either overtly or covertly. While discriminatory impact or effect may be evidence of discriminatory purpose, it is usually not sufficient in itself to prove discriminatory purpose. Even if discriminatory purpose is shown, government can avoid strict scrutiny if it can prove that it would have taken the same action even apart from the discriminatory purpose.

4. Legislation and Administration

Legislation or administrative action which is purposely discriminatory is subject to strict scrutiny. A law or policy may be overtly or covertly discriminatory in purpose. Even if a law or policy is neutral, it may be administrated or enforced in an intentionally discriminatory fashion (unconstitutional "as applied").

5. The Rationale and Limits of Suspectness

a. Race and National Origin

Racial, ethnic and national origin classifications are suspect, subject to strict scrutiny review.

(1) Segregation in Education

(a) *De Jure Segregation.* Intentional racial segregation in public schools is inherently unequal and violates equal protection.

(b) *De Facto Segregation.* Government has no affirmative constitutional duty to remedy segregation it has not created.

(c) *Duty to Desegregate.* A *de jure* segregated school system is under an affirmative constitutional duty to desegregate. Action having a discriminatory *effect* impeding desegregation is prohibited.

(d) *Desegregation Remedies.* In remedying *de jure* segregation, equal protection does not require racial balancing, although racial composition may be used in measuring desegregation. District courts have broad equity powers, including the use of busing. Remedies must reflect the nature of the constitutional violation.

(e) *Interdistrict Segregation.* Segregation between school districts in a state does not violate equal protection unless it is caused by the government.

(f) *Resegregation.* A school district desegregates if it complies in good faith with the desegregation decree and eliminates vestiges of past discrimination to the extent practicable. There is no duty to remedy subsequent unintentional resegregation.

(2) Affirmative Action

    (a) Federal, state and local affirmative action programs are reviewed under the strict scrutiny test.

    (b) In applying strict scrutiny, a narrowly-drawn race-based program designed to remedy specific, identified racial discrimination is likely to be upheld.

    (c) An institution of higher education has a compelling interest in the diversity of its student body, which can include racial and ethnic diversity. A race conscious admissions program must be narrowly tailored; the process must be individualized, not mechanical. Quotas or racial balancing are unlikely to be upheld. Race may be a "plus" factor; it must not be determinative of the admissions decision. Narrow tailoring does not require exhaustion of every possible race-neutral alternative. Time limits to race conscious policies are relevant.

    (d) Race-based student placement programs by elementary and secondary schools were held to be unconstitutional because they were not narrowly-tailored. The Court did not decide whether the schools' interest in the benefits of racial diversity would be a compelling interest.

    (e) Congressional districting, where race is the predominant factor, is subject to strict scrutiny. Race is the predominant factor when the state subordinates traditional race-neutral districting considerations to race.

b. Alienage—The "Sometimes Suspect" Classification

(1) Strict Scrutiny

When a state classifies on the basis of alienage, strict scrutiny normally applies.

(2) Political Function Exception

Only rationality is required when the state sets voter qualifications or defines the qualifications for appointment to important government positions involving governance of the political community, *e.g.*, state police, teachers, probation officers.

(3) Preemption

State classifications involving aliens are preempted if they interfere with national policies regarding immigration and naturalization.

(4) Federal Discrimination

Action by the national government does not violate the Fifth Amendment if it is a reasonable means of implementing its immigration and naturalization powers.

c. **"Almost Suspect" Classifications—Gender and Illegitimacy**

When reviewing gender and illegitimacy classifications, courts generally use an intermediate standard of review. The classification must be substantially related to an important government interest.

(1) Gender Classification

(a) Sex Discrimination

In gender discrimination cases, the Court has referred to intermediate review as requiring "exceedingly persuasive justification." This may include consideration of alternatives available to government, making the review closer to strict scrutiny. Use of classifications that intentionally discriminate against women based on stereotypes seldom survive intermediate review. If the classification reflects real differences between the sexes, it is more likely to be upheld.

(b) Discriminatory Purpose

While a discriminatory impact on women is evidence of impermissible intent, it is only a discriminatory government purpose that will trigger use of the intermediate standard of review.

(c) Non-sex Classifications

Not all classifications that disadvantage only women will be treated as discriminatory sex classifications.

(d) Affirmative Action

Classifications providing benefits only to women which are actually designed to remedy past discrimination are likely to be upheld using intermediate review if they are narrowly tailored to achieve an actual remedial objective.

(e) Mothers and Fathers

A law which discriminates against fathers, in favor of mothers, where the parents are similarly situated, is subject to intermediate review and generally violates equal protection. But there may be real difference between mothers and fathers that justify the discrimination.

(2) Illegitimacy Classifications

An intermediate standard of review is also used for classifications burdening illegitimates—the classification must be substantially related to an important government interest. The more that it appears that a law is based on prejudice against illegitimates, the more likely it is that the law will be held unconstitutional.

d. Other Classifying Traits

Other classifying traits, *e.g.,* those which operate to disadvantage the poor, the aged, the mentally retarded or gays and lesbians (sexual persuasion) without more, are reviewed under the traditional rational basis test. But if the law suggests prejudice or animus, it may be reviewed using "rationality with bite."

6. Fundamental Rights

When a classification significantly burdens the exercise of fundamental personal rights, the government usually must prove that the classification is necessary to a compelling governmental interest.

a. In cases where the law does not deter, penalize, or otherwise *significantly* burden the constitutional right, the Court applies the traditional rational basis test.

b. Increasingly, the Court has moved to a variable standard of review. The more significant the burden on fundamental rights, the greater the degree of scrutiny used.

c. Examples of fundamental rights include:

(1) First Amendment Rights—When government classifications significantly burden the exercise of fundamental First Amendment rights such as freedom of speech or religion, the classification is closely scrutinized.

(2) The Right of Interstate Travel—When the government imposes a classification which deters, penalizes or otherwise significantly burdens the fundamental right to travel, the strict scrutiny standard of judicial review applies. In some cases, the Court has held that the law could not satisfy even rationality review. Recently, the Court has used the Privileges and Immunities Clause of the Fourteenth Amendment to prevent discrimination against newly arrived citizens of the state.

(3) The Right of Privacy and Marriage—Only if a fundamental right is significantly burdened will heightened scrutiny apply.

7. Fundamental Interests

The Court also has used a stricter standard of review to prevent discrimination in access to certain fundamental interests that are not technically constitutional rights but are protected by the Equal Protection Clause when discrimination is involved. This use of stricter review has been applied to the following interests:

a. Voting

(1) When the government discrimination significantly burdens the *exercise of the franchise,* in general or special purpose elections, strict scrutiny is applied.

  (a) *Special Purpose Districts.* A district may be so special purpose and its effects on citizens so disproportionate that strict scrutiny will not be applied.

  (b) *Durational Residency Requirements.* While reasonable residency requirements are constitutional, durational residency requirements burden the vote and the right of interstate travel.

(2) *Diluting the Franchise.* Dilution of the effectiveness of a vote of a particular class will often be reviewed under a more stringent standard of review than rationality.

  (a) *Access to the Ballot.* The requirements must be fair and not virtually exclusionary of independents and minority parties.

(b) *Reapportionment.* The one-person-one-vote principle is applied to congressional districting as a command of Art. I, § 2, and to both houses of a bicameral state legislature as a mandate of equal protection.

(c) *Multi-member Districts.* Multi-member districting violates equal protection and the Fifteenth Amendment if it is a purposeful device to exclude racial minorities from effective political participation.

(d) *Political Gerrymanders.* While equal protection challenges to political gerrymanders are presently justicable, the Court is sharply divided as to whether judicially manageable standards are possible. Political gerrymanders that are proven to be intentionally discriminatory and which have actual discriminatory effects on an identifiable political group violate equal protection.

(e) *Vote Processes.* In *Bush v. Gore* (2000), the Court held that equal protection may be violated by arbitrary and disparate treatment in the processes by which votes are counted but this may be limited to the unique circumstances involved in *Bush v. Gore.*

b. **Access to Justice**

Differences in wealth should not determine the ability of a person to secure criminal justice. Similarly, some civil cases involve matters of such fundamental concern, e.g., termination of parental rights, that equal protection requires equal access.

c. **Education**

While education is an important social and individual interest, the rational basis test is generally used for reviewing classifications burdening the interest in education. But when education is totally denied to a discrete underclass of children, the Court has required government to prove substantial justification.

8. **Other Interests**

Classifications burdening other social and economic interests, such as welfare, housing and medical care, are reviewed under the traditional rational basis test.

VIII.   FREEDOM OF EXPRESSION

A.   The Basic Doctrine

While the First Amendment is addressed only to Congress, its guarantees, express and implied, have been incorporated in due process liberty and have been applied to the states. When these fundamental rights are burdened, the courts employ heightened judicial scrutiny.

1.   First Amendment Rationale

a.   Marketplace of Ideas

Government must not prevent the free exchange of ideas in the marketplace. Free competition is the best test of an idea's worth.

b.   Citizen Participant

Free expression is necessary so that citizens can perform their democratic obligation of discussing public officials and public policy.

c.   Individual Liberty

Freedom of expression promotes individual autonomy and furthers self-determination.

2.   First Amendment Methodology

The Court employs a variety of methodologies designed to reconcile freedom of speech with other legitimate public interests.

a.   Categories of Speech

At times the Court has held that certain categories of speech are not entitled to First Amendment protection, requiring only rationality in lawmaking. These categories of speech can be regulated because of their constitutionally proscribable content. The Court has held that such categories are subject to First Amendment review when the law discriminates on the basis of content within the category of proscribable speech.

b.   Strict Scrutiny

On other occasions, the Court uses a test which imposes a heavy burden of justification on the government when it seeks to regulate speech content, making the law presumptively invalid. Strict scrutiny requires government to prove that the law is necessary to a compelling interest.

c.   Balancing

If the law indirectly or incidentally burdens freedom of speech, the Court is more likely to engage in some less stringent form of balancing to determine if the law is reasonable, weighing the interests of the government in regulating the activity against the burden on free speech interests. The degree of judicial scrutiny varies widely.

3.   **Content–Based v. Content–Neutral Regulation**

a.   Content–Based Regulation

When government undertakes to regulate expression because of the content of the speech, the law is presumptively invalid. Laws are content-based if they discriminate on the basis of viewpoint or if they categorize speech based on its subject matter. The courts apply the most exacting scrutiny to such laws and the government must either show that the law falls into a category of proscribable speech or that it is narrowly drawn to serve a compelling state interest.

b.   Content–Neutral Regulation

Government regulations that are unrelated to the content of speech are subject to a lesser degree of judicial scrutiny, even though speech may be incidentally burdened. If a law is justified without reference to the content of the speech, it may be held to be content-neutral.

(1)   The courts generally apply a less demanding form of balancing analysis to content-neutral time, place and manner regulations. Generally the law must be narrowly tailored to serve a significant government interest and leave open ample alternative channels of communication.

(2)   The *O'Brien* standard, which is essentially the same as the above balancing standard, is often used. The law must further an important government interest unrelated to the suppression of speech and the incidental restriction of speech must be no greater than essential to further that

interest. This requires only that the law directly and effectively further the interest.

4. The Doctrine of Prior Restraint: Forms of Control

Prior restraints involve government regulations of freedom of expression which operate prior to the time that the expression enters the market-place of ideas. This form of regulation is highly suspect, both substantively and procedurally, and there is a heavy presumption against the law's constitutionality; the Court imposes a demanding standard of justification in reviewing prior restraints. But if an injunction only incidentally affects expression and is content-neutral, the prior restraint doctrine does not apply. The court will ask "whether the challenged provisions of the injunction burden no more speech than necessary to serve a significant government interest."

5. First Amendment Vagueness and Overbreadth

Laws may be facially invalid or invalid as applied in a particular case. The former generally results in invalidation of the law itself.

a. Vagueness

A law is facially invalid under freedom of expression and due process if it is not drawn with sufficient clarity and definiteness to inform persons of ordinary intelligence what actions are proscribed.

b. Overbreadth

A law may be void on its face if it is overbroad, in that the law indiscriminately reaches both constitutionally protected and unprotected activity. Substantial overbreadth is required. A litigant may challenge the constitutionality of an overbroad statue even if her activities could be reached under a properly drawn statue.

B. Freedom of Association and Belief

The First Amendment guarantees a right of expressive association for First Amendment objectives, not a general right of social association. The validity of government burdens on the implied rights of association and belief is usually determined by a balancing test. A law is reasonable if the government interest outweighs the individual's right to associate and hold particular political, economic, or social beliefs. Increasingly the Court has employed more stringent forms of interest balancing, including strict scrutiny.

1. **Restraints on Membership and Associational Action**

   a. Membership in an organization cannot be penalized or punished unless the law is limited to active membership, which requires:

      (1) membership knowing of the group's illegal objectives (scienter);

      (2) specific intent to further those illegal objectives.

   b. The right includes the freedom to engage in legitimate group activity to further associational objectives but does not impose any constitutional duty on government to promote the group.

2. **Group Registration and Disclosure Requirements**

   These requirements only indirectly restrain free association. The Court will balance the extent of the interference with the right to associate against the interests of government in the regulation. Deference to legislative judgement has often been given when subversive or extremist groups are involved.

3. **Restraints on Government Employment and Benefits**

   Civil penalties for group membership and activities must satisfy First Amendment standards; the right-privilege distinction has been rejected. Government may not condition the receipt of government benefits on the surrender of First Amendment rights (*i.e.*, Unconstitutional Conditions). When reviewing restraints on expression by government employees, the courts employ a balancing test, weighing the interest of the government as employer against the burden on First Amendment rights.

   a. Loyalty Programs

      Programs designed to review the loyalty of government employees must be narrowly drawn to serve the government interest in security.

   b. Loyalty Oaths

      While narrowly drawn oaths are constitutional, broader oaths probing associational activities must be clear (vagueness) and narrowly drawn to include scienter and specific intent (overbreadth).

   c. Individual Membership Disclosure: Bar Admission Requirements

      (1) Failure to cooperate with a bar commission's inquiry, when the questions are narrowly drawn and have a substantial relevance

to determining an applicant's fitness and competence to practice law, is a grounds for denying bar admission.

(2) Broad-ranging inquiries into associational memberships which are not limited by scienter and specific intent requirements violate freedom of expression.

d. Political Patronage

Government may not discharge public employees or deny benefits to independent contractors for refusing to support a political party or its candidates, unless political affiliation is a reasonably appropriate requirement for the job or benefit in question. Government cannot unconstitutionally condition the exercise of fundamental rights.

4. Legislative Investigations and Forced Disclosure

a. Investigatory Power

The government can investigate in order to legislate pursuant to the necessary and proper clause, as long as the grant of authority is specific and explicit.

b. First Amendment Limitations

The Court often balances the government interests against the individual interests. More recently, the Court has held that when an investigation intrudes on First Amendment rights, the government must show a substantial relation between the information being sought and a subject of overriding and compelling government interest.

c. Disclosure Requirements and Self–Incrimination

Employees cannot be required to forgo their right against self-incrimination as a condition of employment. But if an employee is given immunity from prosecution, he may not refuse to answer questions specifically, directly and narrowly relating to the performance of his official duties.

5. Group Litigation

Group litigation, a form of expressive and associational conduct, can be regulated only for substantial reasons and only by specific regulations.

6. Support for Organizations

Regulations restricting support for lawful activities of organizations are constitutional if they are reasonable in imposing only a limited burden on associational rights and where the support endangers significant national security interests.

C. Freedom From Compelled Expression

The First Amendment protects the freedom to speak freely and the right to refrain from speaking. The constitutional right to associate and believe implies a correlative right to be free of compelled association and beliefs. If freedom to engage in expressive activity is significantly burdened by requiring support, compulsory fees or dues, or forced association, strict scrutiny applies.

1. Compelled Speech

"[F]reedom of speech prohibits the government from telling people what they must say." However, conduct can be regulated even if speech is incidentally burdened.

2. Compelled Association

If an organization engages in "expressive activity," being forced to accept certain persons as members may be inconsistent with that expression and can involve a significant burden on the right not to associate. However, mere forced interaction may not constitute association, which is focused largely on whether a group is forced to accept someone as a member.

3. Compulsory Fees and Dues

Being compelled to provide financial support for messages and programs that one opposes implicates the First Amendment right not to speak or associate. But reasonable fees and charges reflecting comparable benefits are generally constitutional.

4. Compelled Market Assessments

The freedom from compelled expression includes the right to refuse support for advertising with which one disagrees. However, the extent of the compulsion and the identify of the speaker bear on whether the First Amendment is violated.

D. The Electoral Process

Speech involving the electoral process is at the core of the First Amendment. The rigor of judicial review of electoral regulation depends on the extent to which the challenged provision burdens freedom of speech, association, and belief.

1. Political Speech and Association

Direct restrictions on what is said during an election campaign, including the electoral speeches of judges, are tested under strict scrutiny. The restriction must be necessary to achieve a compelling government interest or be a form of unprotected expression. But if there is only a "reasonable, non-discriminatory" restriction, the state's important regulatory interests are generally sufficient to justify reasonable, nondiscriminatory restrictions.

2. Regulating Political Parties

A heavy burden of justification is imposed when states seek to legislate extraterritorially by regulating national political parties. Limiting access to party primaries only to members of the party imposes a severe burden on association and is generally unconstitutional. But some limitations on access to primaries impose only a minimal burden on association and are reasonable and constitutional.

3. Limitations on Contributions and Expenditures

a. Campaign Spending

(1) Noncorporate Spending

Restrictions on *expenditures* by individuals and groups violate freedom of speech. Reasonable limitations on *contributions* by individuals and groups are permissible since such laws further the interest in avoiding the actuality or appearance of corruption.

(2) Political Party Spending

Expenditures by political parties that are independent of the candidate's control may not be limited. But expenditures that are coordinated with a candidate are deemed "contributions" subject to limitation. Regulation of soft money is a limitation on contributions. The regulation need only be "closely drawn to serve an important interest."

(3) Corporate Spending

Government prohibition of a corporation's independent expenditures for political speech is an unconstitutional restriction on a corporation's First Amendment freedom of speech. Such a prohibition cannot be justified under strict scrutiny review. *Citizens United v. Federal Election Commission* (2010).

b. Ballot Referenda

Limitations on contributions in ballot referenda disputes are generally invalid.

c. Disclaimer and Disclosure Requirements

Disclaimer and disclosure requirements are subject to "exacting scrutiny," which requires a "substantial relation between the requirements" and a "sufficiently important governmental interest." They are upheld if they are narrowly drawn to inform the public about sources of election-related spending.

E. Speech in the Local Forum

When government regulates speech protected by the First Amendment because of harms associated with the speaker's message, the law is presumptively invalid and must pass strict scrutiny. If the regulation is unrelated to content, a balancing test is used.

1. Controlling Speech Content

a. The Clear and Present Danger Test

Advocacy of illegal conduct, without more, is constitutionally protected. Only "where such advocacy is directed to inciting or producing imminent lawless action and is likely to incite or produce such action may the speech be suppressed because of its content." *Brandenburg v. Ohio* (1969).

(1) The Early Formulation

The original test focused on the danger of illegal conduct under the circumstances at the time of the speech. An alternative test, offered by Judge Learned Hand, focused on the language of incitement used by the speaker.

(2) The Doctrine Distorted

In *Dennis v. United States* (1951), the Court looked at the gravity of the evil discounted by its improbability in order to determine whether the First Amendment was violated.

(3) Advocacy vs. Incitement

Later, the Court retreated and declared that only advocacy of unlawful action was prohibited, not advocacy of abstract doctrine.

(4) The Modern Test: Incitement and Danger

The modern formulation of the clear and present danger test focuses on both the nature of the speech and the danger it presents. First, only incitement of unlawful conduct, not advocacy of abstract doctrine, can be punished. Second, only incitement to "imminent lawless action" which is "likely to incite or produce such actions," may be reached. *Brandenburg v. Ohio* (1969).

(5) Advocacy Supporting Lawful Activity

But the government may be able to proscribe advocacy even of lawful activity if it reasonably determines that a limited regulation is needed to protect critical national security interests. *Holder v. Humanitarian Law Project* (2010).

b. The Fighting Words Doctrine

Government can impose content-based regulation when the speech constitutes fighting words—"which by their very utterance inflict injury or tend to incite an immediate breach of the peace." *Chaplinsky v. New Hampshire* (1942). Government has the power to punish the use of fighting words under carefully drawn statutes not susceptible of application to protected expression.

(1) Rationale

The fighting words doctrine is based upon the theory that these verbal assaults are of such slight social value as a step to truth as to merit little or no First Amendment protection.

(2) Overbreadth and Vagueness

Rather than defining what are fighting words, courts have often held that the relevant statute is not limited to fighting words and therefore is overbroad or so unclear as to be unconstitutionally vague.

(3) "Protected" Fighting Words

Even if a law regulates fighting words, if it discriminates on the basis of subject matter or viewpoint to create subcategories of fighting words, government must demonstrate that the discrimination is necessary to a compelling government interest. However, when the content discrimination does not create the possibility that government is seeking to drive certain ideas from the marketplace, strict scrutiny does not apply.

c. Hostile Audiences

If the source of the impending violence is a crowd of listeners hostile to the speaker's lawful message, the police must proceed against the crowd and protect the speaker.

d. Offensive and Abusive Language

Government has no power to punish the use of words that are merely offensive, abusive, profane or vulgar.

e. True Threats

Statements where the speaker means to communicate a serious expression of an intent to commit an act of unlawful violence to a particular individual or group is a category of speech subject to regulation consistent with the First Amendment.

f. Equal Protection as a First Amendment Doctrine

Discrimination against certain speakers in the public forum usually involves content-based distinctions. Such content-based controls are subject to strict scrutiny.

g. Hate Speech

Some states, localities and public colleges have enacted laws or codes prohibiting expression that incites hatred of, or which is insulting or derogatory towards, traditionally vulnerable groups. *R.A.V. v. City of St. Paul* (1992) raises serious doubts about the constitutionality of such laws. Laws which punish racially motivated harmful conduct or which simply enhance the penalty for crimes when inspired by racial bias have been held to be constitutional.

2. Regulating Public Property

There is a right of access and a right of equal access to the public forum. But not all government controlled property is part of the public forum. And speech in the public forum is subject to reasonable regulation.

If government regulates speech in the public forum, content-based regulation must fall into a category of proscribable speech or be justified using strict scrutiny. Content-neutral regulation of speech in the public forum is constitutional if the law is narrowly-tailored to serve an important governmental interest and leaves open alternative channels for communication of information.

If government regulates speech in a nonpublic forum, the regulation must be viewpoint-neutral and reasonable. "Reasonableness" usually means "rational;" courts tend to defer to the regulators.

a. The Nature of the Forum

A categorical approach to determining the nature of the forum draws a strict line between government's proprietary and regulatory functions. It gives the government almost unlimited authority to restrict speech on its property. The minority approach focuses on the objective, physical characteristics of the property and the actual public access and uses which have been permitted to determine if speech is compatible with the ordinary use of the forum.

(1) Traditional Public Forum

A traditional public forum is public property that has been used primarily for the free exchange of ideas and which has historically been associated with expressive activity. Government cannot bar all speech activity from a traditional public forum.

(2) Designated Public Forum

When the practice or policy of government is to open a nontraditional forum for public speech, it is a designated public forum.

(3) Limited and Nonpublic Forums

Public property which is not by tradition or designation a forum for public communication is a nonpublic forum. Selective access for a class of speakers who must individually obtain permission to enter creates only a limited forum.

(4) Privately–Owned Property

Only when privately owned property has taken on all the attributes of public property can it become part of the public forum. Speech on private property can be restricted by reasonable means, such as trespass statutes.

b. The Demand for Reasonable Regulation

(1) The *O'Brien* Standards

The Court often employs the *O'Brien* standards, which are essentially the same as the standards used for content-neutral regulation of the public forum, in reviewing public forum regulation.

(2) Determining Reasonableness

When government regulates speech in the public forum, it must be done without reference to the content of the speech. The regulation must be narrowly drawn to further a substantial government interest but need not be the least restrictive or least intrusive means of achieving the interest. It is sufficient if the regulation is a direct and effective means of achieving the government's important interests. The *O'Brien* test is the same test as that used for content-neutral regulation of the public forum.

(a) Speech Plus

The Court frequently has suggested that when expression takes the form of speech plus conduct, it is not entitled to the same degree of protection as pure speech.

(b) Sound Amplification

Communication in the public forum can be subjected to content—neutral regulation in the interest of privacy and tranquility.

(3) Protecting the Homeowner

Canvassing, handbilling and solicitation of homeowners are constitutionally protected but may be subjected to clear, narrowly-drawn, non-discriminatory regulation protecting the privacy of homeowners, *e.g.*, targeted picketing, or to avoid fraud.

(4) Licensing, Prior Restraint and the Duty to Obey

Prior restraints on access to the public forum, *e.g.*, permit systems, licensing, injunctions, are constitutional if they are clear, narrowly-drawn, content-neutral, time, place and manner regulations.

(a) Facial Validity—Vagueness and Overbreadth

Laws vesting discretion in administrators must be drawn with precision, specificity, and clarity. They must not vest excessive discretion in administrators.

(b) The Duty to Obey

If a statute is not a prior restraint, its constitutionality may be tested in an enforcement action. If a licensing law is valid on its face, it must be obeyed, and its application must be judicially determined. However, if a licensing law is transparently invalid, it may be ignored and its invalidity established at the time of prosecution.

(c) Procedural Standards

A content-neutral permit system must contain adequate standards to guide administrative discretion and render the permit official's actions subject to judicial review.

F. Symbolic Speech (Expressive Conduct)

When conduct is alleged to embody the idea itself, the Court employs a two-part inquiry: (1) Is the conduct communicative? (2) If so, is the speech protected under First Amendment law?

1. Is the Conduct Communicative?

The nature, factual context, and environment are examined to determine if the actor has an intent to communicate and whether the viewing audience would understand the communication.

2. Is the Speech Protected?

a. Government regulation of expressive conduct is permissible if:

(1) it furthers an important or substantial government interest;

(2) the governmental interest is unrelated to the suppression of the idea; and,

(3) the incidental restriction on alleged First Amendment freedom is no greater than is essential to furtherance of that interest. It is sufficient if the means are direct and effective.

b. If the regulation is based on the content of the symbolic speech, *e.g.,* flag burning, the most exacting scrutiny applies.

G. Commercial Speech

1. Regulation of commercial speech, *e.g.,* lawyer advertising, is constitutional if it satisfies a four-part test:

(1) the speech is actually or inherently misleading or related to unlawful activity since such speech is not protected by the First Amendment.

(2) the asserted government interest must be substantial (paternalistic regulation of truthful commercial speech is seldom sufficient).

(3) the government regulation must directly advance the governmental interest asserted. It must be shown that the potential harms are real and that the regulation will alleviate them in a material way.

(4) the regulation must not be more extensive than is necessary to serve that interest. It is sufficient if there is a "reasonable fit," but the Court has become increasingly demanding, requiring the use of available alternatives.

2. Note that the overbreadth doctrine does not apply to commercial speech. Its greater hardiness and objectivity make a chilling effect on protected speech from overbroad regulations less likely.

3. Lawyer advertising of routine legal services is constitutionally protected commercial speech. While total bans on lawyer advertising are uncon-

stitutional, more limited regulations, *e.g.*, a ban on in-person solicitation for economic gain or a 30–day ban following an accident on direct mail solicitation of victims and relatives, have been upheld.

4. Regulation of advertising harmful activity (*e.g.*, smoking, gambling, alcohol) is subject to the *Central Hudson* test. While early cases suggested a deferential approach, later cases apply a "closer look" at paternalistic regulation of truthful commercial speech.

H. Freedom of the Press

The Press Clause is read with the Speech Clause as a single guarantee. The press enjoys no privileges or immunities beyond those afforded the ordinary citizen. While the media is subject to generally applicable laws, discrimination which threatens to suppress particular ideas is prohibited.

1. Defamation

a. Public Officials and Public Figures

Public officials and public figures may be awarded damages for publication of a defamatory falsehood only if they prove by clear and convincing evidence that the publication was made with actual malice, *i.e.*, subjective knowledge of its falsity or reckless disregard of its truth or falsity.

(1) In all matters of public interest, the plaintiff also bears the burden of proving falsity.

(2) A public figure may be an all-purpose public figure (*i.e.*, general fame or notoriety) or a limited purpose (vortex) public figure (*i.e.*, voluntary involvement in a public controversy).

b. Private Figures

(1) So long as a state does not impose strict liability, it may define for itself the appropriate standard of liability for a publisher or broadcaster in defamation actions by a private figure.

(2) Presumed and punitive damages cannot be recovered, absent a showing of actual malice, unless the subject of the defamation is a matter purely of private concern.

(3) The private figure plaintiff also bears the burden of proving falsity, at least where the statements involve matters of public concern.

c. Opinion

There is no constitutional privilege for opinion, although there cannot be liability if the publication cannot reasonably be interpreted as stating a defamatory fact.

2. Privacy

a. False Light Privacy

At least at present, a privacy action against the media cannot be maintained solely on the basis that the report was false—actual malice must be shown.

b. Disclosure of Private Facts

State laws providing civil damages for truthful publication of private facts are not necessarily unconstitutional. But accurate reporting of matters of public record is protected. And, if a newspaper lawfully obtains truthful information about matters of public significance, government may not constitutionally punish publication of the information absent a need to further a state interest of the highest order.

c. Disclosure of Illegally Obtained Information

Where the press plays no part in the illegal activity and the information is lawfully obtained, the disclosure of truthful information of public concern is constitutionally protected absent a need of the highest order.

3. Intentional Infliction of Mental Distress

Public officials and public figures must show that the defendant published with actual malice.

4. Newsgathering

Newsgathering is protected by the First Amendment. The protection available generally reflects a balancing of interests.

a. **Journalist's Privilege**

The First Amendment affords journalists no privilege, qualified or absolute, to refuse to give evidence to a grand jury at least so long as it is conducted as a good faith law enforcement effort. The Supreme Court has not decided whether a qualified First Amendment-based journalist's privilege is available in the context of other proceedings. Lower courts have recognized a First Amendment-based reporter's privilege in a variety of proceedings. The First Amendment does not prohibit civil damages awarded for breach of a journalist's promise of confidentiality.

b. **Access to Public Information and Institutions**

(1) Prisons

(a) Censorship of prisoners' outgoing mail is permitted only when the censorship is no greater than necessary to further a substantial public interest. Incoming and internal mail may be regulated if the law reasonably furthers legitimate penological objectives.

(b) A non-discriminatory, reasonable regulation limiting press interviews with prisoners is constitutional.

(2) Judicial Proceedings

(a) In determining if there is a right of public access, the courts consider whether the proceedings have traditionally been open and whether access would aid the functioning of the process.

(b) If there is a presumption of openness, closure must be based on specific findings that denial of access is essential to preserve higher values and that the closure order is narrowly-tailored to serve those interests.

c. **Newsroom Searches and Seizures**

The press, like the public, may be subjected to reasonable searches but warrant requirements are to be applied with searching exactitude.

d. **Cameras in the Courtroom**

Due process is not violated by broadcast media coverage of trials, absent a showing of prejudice to the defendant depriving him of a fair trial.

e. Copyright

The First Amendment does not protect the publishing of as yet unpublished copyrighted expression of a public figure from copyright liability.

f. Silencing Trial Participants

A rule prohibiting lawyers from making extrajudicial statements "if the lawyer knows or reasonably should know that it will have a substantial likelihood of materially prejudicing an adjudicative proceeding" is constitutional. *Gentile v. State Bar of Nevada* (1991).

g. Media Ride Alongs

Law enforcement officers violate the Fourth Amendment by allowing the media to accompany them into private homes in executing an arrest warrant.

5. Regulation of the Electronic Media

a. Regulating Broadcasting

Full First Amendment protection does not extend to broadcasting. Scarcity and the pervasiveness and influence of broadcasting allow greater content-based regulation and even government licensing. Compare telephone communications where a prohibition on indecent speech was held unconstitutional using strict scrutiny.

b. Regulating Cable Television

While the Court has not clearly held that cable is subject to the same standards as the print media, it has rejected application of the deferential broadcast standards, closely scrutinizing cable regulations.

c. Regulating the Internet

The Court has said that precedent provides no basis for qualifying the level of First Amendment scrutiny that should be applied to regulation of speech on the Internet. It is not a scarce resource and is not as invasive as broadcasting (it requires affirmative action to receive the communication and there are ways to avoid exposure). Overbroad regulation of indecent speech to minors was held unconstitutional.

6. Public Access to the Media

The First Amendment protects the public's right to receive suitable access to ideas and experiences.

a. Public Access to the Electronic Media

Government can require broadcasters to discuss public issues and provide balanced coverage or provide for a limited reasonable statutory right of access to broadcast time. But the First Amendment does not afford a constitutional right of public access to broadcasting.

b. Public Access to the Print Media

Since the First Amendment protects journalistic integrity and the editorial process, the print media cannot be compelled to publish that which they do not choose to publish.

I. Obscenity

1. No First Amendment Protection

Lewdness, indecency, offensiveness, and profanity are not excluded from First Amendment protection, but obscenity, which lacks social importance, is generally entitled to *no* protection under the First Amendment. But content-based discrimination within the category of obscene speech may be subject to strict scrutiny.

2. Defining Obscenity

Each element of a three-part test must be satisfied in order to define material as obscene:

(1) whether the average person, applying contemporary community standards, would find that the work taken as a whole appeals to the prurient interest;

(2) whether the work depicts or describes, in a patently offensive way, sexual conduct specifically defined by the applicable state law; and,

(3) whether the work, taken as a whole, lacks serious literary, artistic, political, or scientific value. *Miller v. California* (1973).

3. Applying the Standards

a. No National Community Standard

(1) In determining pruriency and patent offensiveness, the jury may apply "contemporary community standards." Community standards may be used in regulating the internet.

(2) Sensitive persons, but not children, are part of the community.

(3) No expert testimony is constitutionally required.

(4) Jury determinations are subject to appellate review to assure constitutional requirements are met.

b. Defining the Relevant Audience

(1) The Average Person

Obscenity is to be judged by the effect of the material on a person of average susceptibility.

(2) Variable Obscenity: Minors and Deviants

But if the material is directed at a particular audience, obscenity may be judged by its probable effects on that audience.

c. The Demand for Specificity

(1) *Vagueness.* If the three-part test is satisfied, a vagueness challenge to a law will fail.

(2) *Overbreadth.* The conduct to be proscribed must be specifically defined by applicable state law, but this specificity may be satisfied by judicial construction of state law in conformity to the *Miller* obscenity standards. Only the overbroad provisions of the statute are to be invalidated.

(3) *Pandering.* In determining whether the material is obscene, the circumstances of the presentation and dissemination of the material may be considered.

(4) *Serious Value.* "Serious" value (which is not judged by local community standards) can save material from being labeled obscene.

4. Privacy and Obscenity

The mere possession of obscene material cannot constitutionally be made a crime but possession of child pornography can be criminalized.

5. Civil Control of Obscenity and Indecency

a. Zoning laws, usually treated as time, place and manner regulations, must be reasonably designed to achieve a substantial government interest and leave open reasonable alternative channels of communication.

b. Civil controls of obscene material, *e.g.*, nuisance laws, must satisfy the three-part *Miller* test; indecent expression is protected. But if a regulation is directed to unlawful activity and does not significantly burden protected expression, only rationality is required.

6. Broadcasting and Indecency

FCC regulation of indecent, although not obscene, material in broadcasting is constitutional. However, regulation of indecent speech in other media contexts has been reviewed using more demanding standards and has often been held unconstitutional.

7. Child Pornography

Sexually indecent live productions or reproductions of sexually indecent live productions involving minors is not protected speech. Knowing distribution of such material may be criminally punished. But "virtual obscenity," not involving the actual use of minors in production of the materials, may not be proscribed unless obscenity standards are satisfied. However, the pandering or transaction of materials that the owner believes, or attempts to make others believe, contain real children can be made criminal.

8. Administrative Censorship

a. Procedural Fairness

Prior restraints on publication, alleged to be obscene, are burdened procedurally. Content-based censorship must satisfy the following requirements:

(1) burden on censor;

(2) prompt judicial proceeding;

(3) censor must secure judicial approval.

b. **Search and Seizure**

While seizure of a single copy of an allegedly obscene work, pursuant to a warrant for use as evidence is permissible even without a prior adversary determination of obscenity, large scale seizure for purposes of suppression must be preceded by a determination of obscenity.

J. Special Contexts

In certain "restricted environments," like the military, government employment, schools and prisons, and subsidized speech, First Amendment protection of expression is diminished.

1. Government Employees and Independent Public Contractors

a. First, when government employee speech or the speech of contractors involves matters of private interest rather than public concern, the courts exercise deference and apply a rationality test. This limitation applies to both the Speech and Petition Clauses.

b. Second, in determining if a restraint on speech on matters of public concern by government employees and contractors is constitutional, the courts normally balance the interests of the employee as citizen against the government's interest as employer. The courts look at the facts as the employer reasonably found them to be after investigation. However, when public employees make statements pursuant to their official duties, the employees are not speaking as citizens for First Amendment purposes, and the Constitution does not insulate their communications from employer discipline.

c. The employee or contractor must prove that the protected activity was a cause of the adverse government action.

2. The Academic Forum

a. Library Censorship

The First Amendment does impose limits on library book removal in an effort to limit student access to offensive ideas.

b.   Student Speech

(1)   Schools can bar speech or expressive action which intrudes on the work of the schools and their educational mission or which violates the rights of other students. Schools can also restrict student speech that reasonably can be understood as promoting illegal activity, at least in the context of illegal drug use.

(2)   Schools are public forums only if school officials have by policy or practice opened those facilities for general public use or for use by some segment of the public.

(3)   Schools can regulate "school sponsored" student speech that occurs in "curricular" activities if there is some pedagogical reason for the regulation.

c.   Academic Freedom

The First Amendment embraces a concept of academic freedom but it does not protect against all incidental burdens.

3.   **Subsidized Speech**

When government acts as a speaker or funds a selected private group to express its message, it need not fund alternative viewpoints. When government provides grants to selected speakers, *e.g.*, in creating a limited public form, it cannot discriminate on the basis of viewpoint. The Unconstitutional Conditions Doctrine applies.

IX.   FREEDOM OF RELIGION

The First Amendment guarantees of free exercise of religion and freedom from religious establishment are applicable to the states as part of Fourteenth Amendment due process liberty. The basic command is government neutrality.

A.   The Meaning of the Establishment Clause

The Establishment Clause is not limited to a command of equal treatment of religions. While the Court has increasingly asked whether the challenged law *endorses* religion, the three-part *Lemon* test is usually used to determine if the Establishment Clause is violated. *Lemon v. Kurtzman* (1971):

(1)   the government action must have a secular legislative purpose;

(2) the primary effect of the government action must neither advance nor inhibit religion (this often involves consideration of whether there is an endorsement or coercion of religion);

(3) the government must not foster an excessive entanglement with religion.

1. Religion in the Schools

a. Released Time

While released time for religious education is a constitutional accommodation of religion, on-premises religious instruction has the primary effect of advancing religion.

b. Prayers, Bible Reading, and Devotional Exercises

Required prayers, including moments of silent prayer, even when non-denominational and where objectors are excused, have the purpose and primary effect of aiding religion.

c. Teaching Religious Values

While a state has broad discretion over its curriculum and may foster the teaching of basic values and tradition, a state-sponsored program violates the Establishment Clause if it is primarily religious in character or has the purpose of advancing religion.

d. Equal Access

Discrimination among groups in the use of the public forum based on the fact that they are engaged in religious expression can be justified only by a compelling government interest. While compliance with the Establishment Clause can be a compelling interest, the *Lemon* test must be satisfied, e.g., there is an endorsement of religion. Laws promoting equal access to public schools by religious groups do not violate the Establishment Clause.

2. Financial Assistance to Religious Schools

a. Public Benefits

If the state provides public benefits to private school children only for the secular purpose of serving the public welfare, the incidental benefit to religion does not condemn the program.

b. Financial Aid for Schools

While financial aid usually is considered to be for a secular purpose, it may be found to have a primary effect that is sectarian, involving excessive government entanglement with religion. Specifically the Court today asks whether the program results in indoctrination, whether it defines recipients by reference to religion, and whether the aid creates excessive entanglement.

(1) Elementary–Secondary v. Higher Education

Since pupils in lower levels of education are likely to be more impressionable and political divisiveness is more common, aid to such schools is more likely to be held unconstitutional.

(2) Testing, Recordkeeping, and Other Services and Equipment

The dangers of religious indoctrination from a particular form of aid and the location where it occurs influence the constitutional validity of the program. But instruction by public employees on the premises of sectarian schools where safeguards were provided against indoctrination was upheld. A secular, neutral and nonideological program is constitutional.

(3) Tax Relief and Tuition Benefits

Aid directly to the religious institution rather than to citizens is more likely to be held unconstitutional but not all aid that directly benefits the educational activities of sectarian schools is unconstitutional. Financial support directed only to parents having children in private schools has the primary effect of aiding religion. A tuition benefits program (vouchers) which is neutral and which provides true free choice to parents on how tuition assistance benefits are to be directed is constitutional.

3. Other Establishment Contexts

a. Blue Laws

Thus far, Sunday closing laws have been upheld against Establishment Clause challenge on grounds that they serve the secular purpose of promoting a common day of rest.

b. Tax Exemptions

Tax exemptions for religious and other charitable institutions are constitutional given the historical experience with such benefits. But an exemption from sales and use taxes solely for religious activities has been held violative of the Establishment Clause.

c. Social Welfare Programs

If religious institutions are incidentally benefitted as participants in a generally applicable, secular governmental social welfare program, there is no Establishment Clause violation. However, if a significant portion of funds go directly to sectarian institutions, the Establishment Clause could be violated.

d. Legislative Prayer

History and tradition support the conclusion that opening prayer at the state legislature, led by government paid clergy, does not violate the Establishment Clause.

e. Public Displays

Public recognition of traditional holidays is permissible when the religious effect is only indirect, remote, and incidental. However, if the display endorses religious beliefs, the anti-establishment principle is violated.

f. Denominational Preference

When government provides benefits to only selected religions, it must demonstrate that the law is narrowly tailored to further a compelling public interest. The *Lemon* test must be satisfied.

g. Internal Church Disputes

While courts may not decide purely internal church disputes, they can decide legal questions when they involve only application of neutral principles of law.

h. Institutionalized Persons

A federal law intended to protect religious exercise by institutionalized persons was held to be a permissible accommodation of religion. It did not violate the Establishment Clause.

B. The Meaning of the Free Exercise Clause

If a law directly and significantly burdens the free exercise of religion by compulsion or coercion, government must demonstrate a compelling or overriding government interest. The availability of less burdensome alternatives will be considered. General First Amendment law will be applied.

A law that is generally applicable and religion-neutral, which imposes only incidental burdens on a particular religion, will not be judged by strict scrutiny. Incidental discriminatory impact on a religious practice or belief, even if it is significant, is subject only to rationality review since the First Amendment right is not implicated. *Employment Div. v. Smith* (1990).

1. Belief–Conduct

While religious belief is absolutely protected, religious conduct must be accommodated to valid government interests.

2. Centrality and Sincerity

While the courts cannot probe the truth or falsity of a religious belief, they can probe whether the belief is sincerely held. While courts have also probed the centrality of a belief or practice to a religion, there are indications that this approach may be eliminated from free exercise review.

3. General Indirect Burdens

Absent some significant burden on a claimant's free exercise of religion, strict scrutiny is not appropriate.

4. Blue Laws

Thus far, the Court has upheld Sunday closing laws against free exercise challenges by characterizing the burden as only an indirect economic hardship, outweighed by the public interest in a uniform day of rest.

5. Conditioning Public Welfare Benefits

The government cannot condition the receipt of public benefits on the surrender of constitutional rights, such as free exercise of religion. Loss of such benefits constitutes a significant burden on religion, requiring government to demonstrate a compelling interest which cannot be satisfied by less burdensome means. Benefits can be denied if this is only an incidental effect of applying a generally applicable and otherwise valid religion-neutral criminal law.

6. Compelled Action

Outside of the military context, when government requires an individual to engage in practices contrary to central tenets of his or her religion, only the showing of a compelling interest will justify such a direct (significant) burden on religion.

7. Noncoercive Laws

If the government regulation has the incidental effect of making it significantly more difficult to practice a religion, but does not compel or coerce action contrary to a religious belief, strict scrutiny does not apply. Government is not required to accommodate its internal practices to religious needs and desires.

8. Proscribed Religious Practices

Strict scrutiny is not used for a generally applicable, religion-neutral criminal law which has the incidental effect of prohibiting a religious practice. Application of the law is constitutional, even if the practice is central to a religion. Congressional legislation declaring that strict scrutiny does apply even to generally-applicable laws, if the free exercise of religion is significantly burdened, was held unconstitutional as applied to state laws because Congress lacked remedial power under the Fourteenth Amendment, § 5, to enact the law. *City of Boerne v. Flores* (1997). However, the congressionally-mandated strict scrutiny test was applied to actions of the federal government. The Government failed to demonstrate a compelling interest justifying prohibition of the groups communal use of *hoasca*, a banned hallucinogen. *Gonzales v. O Céntro Espirita Beneficente Uniao do Vegetal* (2006).

C. The Meaning of Religion

1. Defining Religion

While "religion" is not limited to theistic beliefs and practices, the Court has not yet defined the outer limits of religion.

2. Conscientious Objection—Parallel Beliefs

In conscientious objector cases, the Court has asked whether a given belief which is sincere and meaningful occupies a place in the life of its possessor parallel to that filled by the orthodox belief in God.

X. STATE ACTION

Most of the rights and liberties protected by the Constitution require a showing of "state action." It is government wrongdoing, not private misconduct, that is the focus of constitutional judicial review.

A. The State Action Requirement

1. The Civil War Amendments

While the Thirteenth Amendment prohibits the imposition of slavery or involuntary servitude regardless of its source, the Fourteenth and Fifteenth Amendments, at least in the absence of congressional legislation, require that governmental action be present in order to establish a violation.

2. The Present Standard—State Responsibility

It is only when government is so significantly involved in the challenged action that it can be said that government is actually responsible for it, that the state action threshold is satisfied. There must be a close nexus between government and the particular action being challenged. These requirements have become harder to satisfy.

B. Official Misconduct and Joint Action

1. Action Contrary to State Law

Laws and official action pursuant to law involve state action. Even if a state official acts contrary to state law, the state action requirement is satisfied since government has put the official in a position of power.

2. Public Administration

Official supervision, control, or management of a facility, even where the government is only indirectly entwined in the management, constitutes state action.

3. Joint Action

If a private individual engages in joint activity with government officials, state action is established.

C. Public Functions

If performance of a function is traditionally and exclusively a function of government, it will constitute state action, *e.g.,* white primaries, company towns.

D. Significant State Involvement

1. Symbiotic Relationships

In weighing the facts and circumstances to determine the significance of a public-private relationship, the existence of mutual benefits and supports (*i.e.,* symbiotic relationship) is critical. If the acts of the private actor may fairly be treated as the acts of the government itself, i.e., they are entwined, there is state action.

2. Government Regulation and Licensing

Even licensing and extensive government regulation of a private activity will not, without more, constitute state action.

3. Government Financial Support

Financial support of a private activity, unless it makes the government responsible for the challenged private action by encouraging, authorizing, or approving it, does not constitute state action.

E. Encouragement, Authorization, and Approval

1. Neutral Law Enforcement

Neutral state enforcement of state laws, without a showing of encouragement, authorization, or approval of the particular action being challenged, does not constitute state action.

2. Involuntary Discrimination

However, even a neutral enforcement of state laws cannot be used to force racial discrimination on unwilling parties.

3. Significant Encouragement

When the challenged private actions are overtly or covertly encouraged by government, state action is present.

4. Authorization and Approval

a. While acquiescence in conduct is not enough to establish state action, government compulsion or authorization of the particular act being challenged, whereby the state becomes responsible for it, is state action.

b. The Court has indicated that the challenger must show that the action being challenged is borne of a state policy, rule, right or privilege, and that the party charged with the action reasonably may be said to be acting for the state.

XI. CONGRESSIONAL LEGISLATION IN AID OF CIVIL RIGHTS AND LIBERTIES

A. In General: Federal Legislative Jurisdiction

1. Pursuant to the commerce and spending powers, Congress has power to legislate for social welfare purposes, including the protection of civil rights and liberties.

2. Congress can also legislate to protect "federal rights" against state or private interference.

3. The Civil War Amendments and a number of other amendments grant Congress power to enact legislation, which is reasonably appropriate, to enforce the rights secured by the amendments.

B. Enforcing the Thirteenth Amendment

1. Under the Thirteenth Amendment, § 2, Congress has power to enact legislation which is rationally related to eliminating all badges and incidents of slavery in the United States.

2. Pursuant to the power, Congress can legislate against even private conduct.

C. Enforcing the Fourteenth Amendment

The Fourteenth Amendment, § 5, authorizes Congress to enact legislation which is rationally related to protecting the privilege and immunities, due process and equal protection guarantees.

1. Scope of the Enforcement Power

a. The enforcement power is a remedial or corrective power, not a power to define the substantive rights.

b. There must be a congruence and proportionality between the injury to be prevented or remedied and the means Congress has used.

c. Congress may prohibit conduct which is not itself unconstitutional and even regulate conduct in areas reserved to the states.

2. Constitutional Limits on Enforcement Powers

Congress cannot violate other constitutional provisions in exercising its enforcement powers. The Tenth Amendment, however, does not limit Congress' powers under the Fourteenth Amendment, § 5. Congress can abrogate state sovereign immunity only if the law is congruent and proportional to the state's constitutional violation. Such a law is more likely to be upheld in situations where the state would be subject to more demanding standards of judicial review than rationality review.

3. Private Action

Under the Fourteenth Amendment, § 5, Congress is limited to remedying or preventing unconstitutional State action, not private misconduct.

D. Enforcing the Fifteenth Amendment

The Fifteenth Amendment, § 2, gives Congress power to enact legislation which rationally implements the Fifteenth Amendment's prohibition against racial discrimination in voting.

Perspective

■ THE STUDY OF CONSTITUTIONAL LAW

(1) The Document and Judicial Review

Constitutional law is concerned primarily with the exercise of judicial review. The focus is on the manner in which the courts generally, but the Supreme Court in particular, have interpreted the sometimes cryptic provisions of the United States Constitution. In your study, you should emphasize not only the principles, doctrines and rules developed in the cases but also the underlying policies and values. Further, you should consider the principles and policies rejected by the Court. The collegial character of the Supreme Court demands attention not only to the opinion of the Court but also to concurring and dissenting opinions which indicate alternatives and often suggest future currents and trends in constitutional decision-making. Remember, stare decisis, the rule of precedent, has less force in constitutional law than in other areas of your law studies. Constitutional law is an unsettled and rapidly evolving field. Its touchstone may be, variously, constitutional text, constitutional history, policy or recently-fashioned doctrine and practice.

(2) Approaches to Constitutional Interpretation

Two general approaches to constitutional interpretation and analysis should be noted. While these approaches are especially useful in the context of defining rights and liberties, they also inform the exercise of judicial review in the area of the allocation of powers.

a.   Interpretivism emphasizes reliance on the Constitution itself as the basic norm for decision in constitutional cases. The approach assumes various forms. Interpretivists may look to the "plain meaning" of the textual language (textualism), the original intent of the framers, the original historical understanding of the provision, the historical exegesis of the constitutional provision or the structure and relationships reflected in the document. A broad or narrow reading of the provisions may be adopted. But the focus of judicial review, the source of the principles and policies for decision, are all, according to the Interpretivists, to be derived from the Constitution.

b.   Non-interpretivism acknowledges the existence of an "unwritten constitution." Principles and policies used in judicial review are derived not only from the document but from external sources, such as historical experience, political realities, traditional social values, societal consensus or evolving concepts of justice and morality. The constitutional text and the historical origins of the provisions in question are, at best, only starting points for judicial review.

■ PRINCIPLES OF CONSTITUTIONAL LAW: COURSE OVERVIEW

The course in constitutional law is traditionally divided into two major parts. The first part is devoted to the allocation of powers at the national level (separation of powers) and between the national government and state governments (division of powers). The second part of the course focuses on the limitation of government power resulting from the guarantee of rights and liberties. The allocation of government powers is designed not only to assure that government can govern effectively but also to limit the exercise of government powers. In Madisonian democracy, which is reflected in the original Constitution, abuse of power is avoided primarily through the distribution and blending of power. The Bill of

Rights (the first ten amendments) was added *after* the Constitution was ratified.

The subject matter of constitutional law reflects the following basic principles of American constitutionalism that find expression throughout the course.

(1) Limited Government and Popular Sovereignty

The premise of American constitutionalism is that the national governmental power is derived from the people—government acts with the consent of the governed. The national government properly exercises such powers as "we the people" have delegated to it through the Constitution and subject to the limitations we have imposed. Thus, the political sector has a limited, essentially fiduciary, role to play in fulfilling the purposes for which government was created. This is a government of limited powers.

(2) Separation of Powers

Limited government is achieved in part through the separation of powers at the national level. Under the Articles of Confederation, the only national government unit was the Congress. But the Constitution created a separate national executive and judiciary as well as a Congress. The U.S. Constitution, Art. I, vests the legislative power in a bicameral Congress. Art. II vests the executive power in a President, and Art. III vests the judicial power in a Supreme Court and such inferior federal courts as Congress may create (*i.e.*, Art. III federal courts).

(3) Division of Powers

Governmental power is divided not only horizontally, but vertically—we are a nation of states. This is the division of powers. Federalism reflects a belief in the value of diversity and the need to prevent accumulation of power even while seeking the benefits of union. Under the Tenth Amendment, powers not delegated to the national government "are reserved to the states respectively, or to the people." The national government is limited to the exercise of powers delegated to it by the Constitution, either expressly or by reasonable implication. But if the national government constitutionally uses its delegated power, the U.S. Constitution, Art. VI (the Supremacy Clause), provides that the federal law, shall supersede inconsistent state law (preemption). The student should consider the extent to which the protection of the values of federalism is achieved through the constitutional division of powers or through the system of political representation in the Congress and the workings of our political system.

(4) Checks and Balances

The separation of powers and division of powers reflect the principle of checks and balances. Power is divided among institutions but the functions of government are blended. Congress legislates but the President can veto. The President makes treaties, but only with the advice and consent of the Senate. The federal courts can hold congressional or executive acts unconstitutional but the jurisdiction of the federal courts is largely subject to congressional control.

(5) Rights and Liberties

The principle of limited government is achieved not only by the distribution of governmental powers but also by the protection of rights and liberties. Some rights were recognized in the original Constitution, *e.g.,* Art. I, § 9, limits suspension of the writ of habeas corpus; Art. I, §§ 9 and 10 proscribe bills of attainder or ex post facto laws, neither Congress nor the states may impair the obligation of contract (Art. I, § 10 and Fifth Amendment due process). A Bill of Rights was the price for ratification. Most of the guarantees of the Bill of Rights have been applied to the states through the Due Process Clause of the Fourteenth Amendment (incorporation). Using the amending process of Art. V, another seventeen amendments have been added. Other rights have been implied from those that are granted and still others have been read into the Constitution. The First and Fourteenth Amendments will be especially important in your study of Constitutional Law.

■ GUIDE TO ANALYSIS: COMMON ISSUES

While the uncertainties of constitutional law adjudication and decision-making make any "all-purpose" guidelines questionable, there are certain basic issues that a student should consider in analyzing cases in this area.

(1) Court Jurisdiction and Reviewability

Before a constitutional case can be considered on the merits, the Court must decide whether it will review the constitutional issue. If the federal court lacks jurisdiction, it lacks power to determine the issue and the case will be dismissed, regardless of the merits of the constitutional claim. Even if jurisdiction is technically present, the court may, for a variety of functional and prudential reasons, exercise discretion and decline to decide a constitutional claim. These jurisdictional and prudential concerns are sometimes referred to as justiciability. Therefore, the student should first consider whether the court has jurisdiction and whether it might decline to review the constitutional claim. *NOTE:* Even if you decide that the court cannot or will not reach the merits of the case, do *not* end the analysis. You should always consider what would happen if the court does reach the merits. Your judgment on the questions of jurisdiction and reviewability could be wrong— protect yourself.

(2) Sources of Power

(a) National Law

If the court reaches the merits of the constitutional claim and the question involves the constitutionality of national law, ask yourself— does the government have the *power* to act? Since our government is one of enumerated powers, it must be ascertained whether there is a power, express or implied, delegated to the national government.

(b) State Law

If the court reaches the constitutional merits and the question involves the constitutionality of state or local action, it is *not* necessary (at least in the constitutional law course) to determine whether there is power to act. States and localities have inherent fiscal and police powers to legislate for the health, morals, and well-being of their citizens.

(3) Limitations on Power—National and State Law

Even if the national or state government has the power to act, this does not mean that its actions are constitutional. The student must consider whether the exercise of the power violates some constitutional limitation. Remember, there are two sources of limitations on governmental power: *First,* the separation and division of powers; *second,* rights and liberties guaranteed by the Constitution.

Always consider whether the manner in which the government actor has exercised its power excessively intrudes on the constitutional powers of another government actor, *e.g.,* the President takes action that constitutionally is the province of Congress, a state regulates in such a way as to unduly burden the free movement of interstate commerce.

Consider also whether the way in which the government has acted may unconstitutionally burden some right or liberty, *e.g.,* freedom of speech or religion, rights of association and belief, the right of privacy. Remember constitutional rights and liberties are not limited only to express guaranteed rights. Nor does the fact that a right is burdened mean that the government action is unconstitutional—burdens on rights can be justified.

■ APPROACH TO CONSTITUTIONAL LAW

Alexis deTocqueville wrote, more than a century ago, that in America every question ultimately becomes a constitutional question. With the expanded role of the Supreme Court, this is particularly true. More and more legal questions have a constitutional dimension. The course in constitutional law, like all courses in law school, is, to some extent, a course in a new vocabulary. Phrases that pepper the case law in the fields of free expression and equal protection will become second nature to you. You will find yourself talking easily about standards of review, about the differences among the rational basis standard of review, the intermediate standard of review, and the strict scrutiny standard of review. These are standards of review that have distinct meanings in constitutional law. In the free expression area, terms like content-based and content-neutral regulation, categories of speech, the public forum, the public law of libel, the distinction between political speech and commercial speech and obscenity and indecency, will become terms of art to you. That constitutional law will open up a new vocabulary to you is to be expected. What, perhaps, requires emphasis is that the course in constitutional law is for the law student also a course in humanities and a course in the social sciences. The basic values to which a society is dedicated and about which a society may be in conflict is the bedrock of a course in constitutional law.

■ DAY–TO–DAY STUDY

Because the course in constitutional law is so fundamental, the student's approach to study in constitutional law must be somewhat different than in other courses. In a course in torts or in contracts, the names of particular cases may not be especially important. Abiding principles may emerge in those fields of law. But the particular names of the plaintiffs and defendants who gave play to those principles usually are not particularly significant. This is not so in constitutional law.

After all, one of the greatest cases in constitutional law, *Marbury v. Madison,* does not involve just an ordinary person. Madison was Secretary of State of the United States and he later became President. To a very large extent, cases in constitutional law involve the way our society should be governed and the way our polity should be structured. Students sometimes ask their instructors in law school, are we responsible for the names of the cases? The classic response to this question by most law instructors is that what they are interested in is that students learn the basic legal method to approach particular problems and that the names of particular cases are irrelevant. But in constitutional law, case names like *Marbury v. Madison* (1803) or *United States v. Nixon* (1974) involve controversies and principles which are part of the liberal learning of any literate and educated lawyer. These cases are documents in American history and government to a degree not encountered in other courses. With respect to these most famous cases, the student should at least have an idea when he hears the name of cases like *Marbury v. Madison* or *United States v. Nixon* of the context in which those cases arose and of the principles for which they stand. In short, case names are more important in constitutional law than in other areas.

■ THE ROLE OF CASE LAW

If the case law is important in constitutional law, how should one approach those cases? The short answer to this question is—slowly. A case like *Marbury v. Madison* cannot be read quickly. Embedded in the magisterial prose of Chief Justice Marshall, one will find condensed the substance of controversies about the role of the Judiciary vis-a-vis the Executive and the Congress, which still absorb us as a people. A student in constitutional law will often say that it took her an hour or two to read ten pages. In the early period of a course in constitutional law, this should be considered standard rather than remarkable. It should take you an hour or an hour and a half to read the edited version of *Marbury v. Madison* that is found in most contemporary constitutional law casebooks. In the formative constitutional law cases, you are reading about fundamental and enduring controversies. These controversies raise deeper and more profound issues than obtain in the resolution of cases which involve automobile accidents or commercial disputes.

■ THE SIGNIFICANCE OF THE CONSTITUTIONAL TEXT

We have spoken about the role of case law and of how carefully it should be approached and studied in constitutional law courses. What about the constitutional text itself? There was a great constitutional law teacher at Harvard several generations ago named T. R. Powell. The story goes that Professor Powell used to tell his classes that they need not bother to read the Constitution because they would only find it distracting. This was Professor Powell's mischievous way of telling his students that the overlay of case law on the constitutional law text is truly significant and that the constitutional document is continually interpreted by each new generation of Americans through the doctrine of judicial review.

All this is true, but in our opinion, Professor Powell's witticism overstates the matter. You *should* read the constitutional text, particularly in those parts of the course which deal with the separation and division of powers. Reading the text of the Constitution will bring directly to your attention the difficulty and the magnitude of the task people like Chief Justice Marshall faced. Questions such as whether or not the Supreme Court could invalidate acts of Congress or whether the Supreme Court of the United States could review constitutional decisions of state courts are questions upon which there was very little prior law. In a sense, the prior law that had existed had been repudiated. The people who wrote the American Constitution had, to a considerable extent, rejected much of the body of English constitutional law when they declared their independence from the Crown. People like John Marshall wrote on a largely blank slate. There were few cases for them to construe. Their opinions were going to become the case law for tomorrow and they knew it. If you tackle the question of whether or not there is a basis for judicial review in the text of the American Constitution as an original proposition, you will be giving yourself the same task that John Marshall and his colleagues faced.

For this reason, many teachers of constitutional law—and we are among them—do not believe that it is wise for students new to the subject of constitutional law to attempt to bury themselves too quickly or too deeply in treatises or hornbooks. We think it is more profitable for the student to do what Marshall did—analyze the facts of a great case like *Marbury v. Madison,* read the constitutional text, try to identify the large principles which the framers had in mind, and then to reach a decision which seems to flow from the interstices of the document. If you take this approach, you will find that your task, at least initially, will take more time. But the conclusions you reach are likely to stay with you longer than if you merely parrot the summary of these great cases which you can easily find in some hornbook or treatise.

■ OUTSIDE READING

This is not to say that outside reading should be discouraged in a course in constitutional law. It is only to say that the timing of the appropriate moment for outside reading is crucial. One should not go too quickly to what others have thought about problems that you have been asked as students to confront for the first time. After you have spent a significant part of the course struggling with these ideas themselves, it may then be appropriate for you to seek some help on a particularly troubling point with the vast constitutional law literature.

For many years there was a dearth of constitutional law treatises particularly for students. This was partially because the Warren Court so rapidly changed our understanding of constitutional law. The law in this area, therefore, was thought to be too much in flux to warrant any easy summary. To a considerable extent, in the past few years this situation has altered. Recent books which can provide you a crisp and accurate summary of basic principles are the treatises, *Constitutional Law* (8th ed., 2010), by J.E. Nowak and R.D. Rotunda and *Constitutional Law: Principles and Policies* (4th ed., 2011) by Erwin Chemerinsky. Professor Tribe has written a two volume treatise, *American Constitutional Law* (Vol. I, 3d ed., 2000; Vol. II, 2d ed., 1988), which deals in a very sophisticated and thorough way with some of the more subtle and complex issues in contemporary constitutional law. Capsule summaries can prove useful. Illustrative are *Constitutional Law in a Nutshell* (8th ed., 2013), and *First Amendment in a Nutshell* (4th ed., 2008), by the authors of this Outline.

An outline such as this can also be helpful. But if it is going to be helpful, it should be approached with a clear understanding of what it can do and what it cannot do. What it can do is to put an organizational structure on a body of learning with which you are already significantly familiar. It can identify the highlights in that body of learning, and it can serve as a refresher for what you have, through your own study, both earned and learned. What this outline cannot do—and what no outline can do—is to serve as a substitute for the course itself. If you have not read the great cases in constitutional law, if you have not struggled with the text as Marshall did, for example, the principles and examples summarized here cannot mean as much to you as they will mean for those who have, to put it plainly, done their homework.

■ APPROACH TO THE EXAMINATION

(1) Studying for the Examination

How does one review for an examination in constitutional law? There are so many cases to read. Your class notes usually are quite extensive. Furthermore, your instructor may have mentioned or discussed a number of books and law review articles which bear on various aspects of the course. One good technique is to look at the table of contents of your casebook. The table of contents of the book will usually give you a detailed skeletal outline of the course. Since it lists the leading cases under the various topics, *e.g., Marbury v. Madison* under Judicial Review, *Roe v. Wade* under Substantive Due Process and the Right of Privacy, and *Massachusetts v. EPA* under Standing, the table of contents will itself serve to refresh your recollection. After you have looked at the Table of Contents, you probably will want to read your notes once through. Then you will want to read this outline because it provides a crisp review of the whole subject and it will put flesh and structure on the course. After having read your notes and the outline, certain aspects of the course may be less clear to you than others. For example, in the equal protection area, the constitutional significance of the distinction between discriminatory purpose and discriminatory effect may be unclear to you. In that case, you may want to reread a leading case in the field, such as *Washington v. Davis* (1976).

In studying for the examination, does it make a difference whether the examination is an open-book exam or a closed-book exam? It probably does not make a great deal of difference in terms of how you study for the examination. It is possible, however, that if you know you are going to take an open-book examination you should spend more time on analyzing concepts than devoting yourself to the brute memorization of facts. Does it make any difference whether the examination is entirely essay or semi-objective? On this point, it probably does make a difference. If the examination is semi-objective, you probably want to focus your study to a higher degree on detail; but principles and their application remain vital even in objective exams.

There is a technique for preparing for examinations which somehow law students resist which is the most effective guarantee for success that we can think of. This is to look at the past examinations of your instructor from previous years, if possible, and then to take those examinations for practice. You would not think of learning to drive a car by just reading the rules in the operator's manual. You would want to drive a car at some point before you are given your road test. Similarly, if you are going to take a test in constitutional law, does it not make sense that you actually practice by taking constitutional law examinations? We think it does. However, for this technique to work, you have to be honest. If the practice examination that you are taking is a closed-book examination, then you should not look at anything else when you are taking that particular examination. Also, you should follow the specific time allocations. In other words, you should make the simulated practice examination as close to the real thing as possible. At this point you may say, how do I know that what I am saying is right? You don't. But perhaps there are others in your class, who have demonstrated a gift for constitutional law, who can be of assistance. Or, at least, you can check your answer against the course material.

(2) Getting Started

All right, you are now at the examination. You have studied hard and you are ready to take the examination. What do you do first? The first thing you do—we are going to say that again—THE FIRST THING YOU DO IS READ THE EXAMINATION. This may seem like an easy thing to do—it isn't. Some of your classmates will be writing away as soon as they get their bluebooks passed to them. You may be tempted, because they are writing, to start writing too. Resist this temptation. Read the question first, read it carefully, and read the question in terms of the answer you are specifically requested to provide. For example, the first question might be a question that seems to involve interstate commerce. Some students will attempt immediately to convey to the instructor everything they know about the Commerce Clause. They will, therefore, recite the case law from *Gibbons v. Ogden* (1824) to

National Federation of Independent Business v. Sebelius (2012) (Affordable Care Act). Now such a chronological history of the Commerce Clause could make an impressive answer if anybody had asked you for it. But usually the constitutional law instructor will be asking you to apply specific principles to specific facts. The question will usually be directed to some such specific matter. If the question is, should the court order an injunction, you should begin with "yes" or "no" and then give your supporting reasons. Obviously, "yes" or "no" is not enough of an answer but at least you are, by answering the question, doing two things: you are flagging your view of the situation to the instructor and you are organizing your answer around a particular conclusion. On the other hand, some instructors will not even ask you to reach a conclusion. They are interested only in your analysis of the issues. In either case, keep your answer relevant to the particular issues raised by the facts.

(3) Analysis

How do you analyze the question itself? You should try to keep five things in mind when you are answering the examination questions. This is your Analysis Check List. (We are assuming as the norm for this check list the typical law school essay examination. The technique will be the same whether the format is short answer or long answer essay although if it is short answer essay, your answers must be particularly concise and terse.):

(1)   The first thing you should do is to try to identify the issues.

(2)   You should identify the principle or principles which apply to the resolution of those issues.

(3)   You should try to provide a supporting rationale as to why the particular principle or principles might be applicable to this set of facts.

(4)   You should be sure that you apply the principle to the facts in question.

(5)   You should include the principle or principles which may compete for application to the resolution of the particular facts presented. This demonstrates that, although you have chosen a particular principle to resolve the facts, you are aware that strong arguments exist for the applicability of a competing principle.

The technique of including in your answer competing principles even though you do not think they are the most appropriate principles is an excellent one.

First, you may be wrong in your assessment of what is the best principle available to govern the facts. If you have included the competing principle, the instructor will be aware that you saw this clash of principles. Usually, the instructor will not mind that the principle you selected is not the one he thought the best available if you at least present the one he thought the best available as an alternative. After all, we all have read enough five to four decisions of the Supreme Court to know, as Justice Frankfurter said, that constitutional issues are non-Euclidean problems.

There is an easy guide to the successful taking of constitutional law examinations. It is, like all good counsel, magnificent in its simplicity. First, READ THE QUESTION; SECOND, ANSWER THE QUESTION. In other words, answer the question you have been asked, not the question you would like to have been asked. The authors of this outline have been reading answers to constitutional law questions for many years. A phenomenon we have frequently encountered is that students answer the question they expected to be asked or that they would like to have been asked. That this is so is only human nature. We prefer to write about what we know more than what we do not know. The instructor, however, will be more impressed if you take a stab at what he asked than if you provide a great deal of information for which he did not ask.

Here is another technique for successful examination taking. What do you do if a particular question or sub-question draws a complete blank from you? Do you leave it blank? Here is our advice. Unless the instructor tells you that he will deduct for wrong answers, it usually is worth your while to attempt some kind of answer. Even the most liberal instructor cannot give a sympathetic construction to nothing. So try to write something.

(4) Time Constraints

You have to be mindful of the time problem in taking an examination. Many instructors will assign a specific number of minutes to a particular question. This allocation of time by the instructor has to be taken with great seriousness by the student. If the instructor says that a particular question is worth thirty minutes, then it is worth no more than that. Some students decide to put an hour into a thirty minute question. Their idea is that by fully exploiting a question where they happen to be comfortable, they will do so well it will outweigh the question which, by definition, they will not be able to answer as well since they have exceeded the time allocation. This is a mistake. Following the time allocations in an examination is a form of showing your mastery of the course. If the instructor gives you a series of questions and says that you should answer each sub-question in one or two sentences: DO THAT. The instructor is well aware that many times you would be able to answer the same sub-question in a hundred sentences. She knows that. What she is trying to do, however, is to give a comprehensive examination raising a large number of questions to test your overall knowledge of constitutional law. She cannot do that if you insist on saying more than she has asked for. The end result of doing that will be that toward the last third or half of the examination you will be way out of time. The solution for this problem is not to write TIME at the end of the bluebook because this is only a way of telling the instructor you did not follow instructions.

We have taken a great deal of space to emphasize the importance of respecting the time allocation of the instructor. We would like to make a couple of other observations with respect to time allocation. First, if you draw a blank on a question, although you certainly should plan to say something on the question, do not tarry over such a question. Go on to the next one and come back to it. The blank you drew may be only a temporary one. Furthermore, leave a couple of minutes in your time allocation for reading what you have written at the end of the examination. Did you by mistake leave out the answer to part of a question? Did you by mistake forget to turn the examination over and miss two questions on the other side? One way to find this out is to turn the examination paper over. These errors may seem obvious but experienced instructors will tell you that they happen with surprising frequency.

A question students often have is this: If I am going to be taking an open-book examination in constitutional law, is there any particular technique I should bear in mind while taking an examination? Some students develop elaborate colored tab indexes so they can reach a relevant point in their materials instantly. Is this kind of thing worth it? In our opinion, this kind of thing usually is not worth the time. The examination is not usually intended to be a research experience. Most instructors designate their examinations as open-book examinations in order to help their students relax so that they will not freeze if they forget a particular point or case. Usually, time is such a pressing problem during a constitutional law examination that the best thing one can do is to have such a mastery of the subject that you don't need to refer to your books and notes at all. If you do refer to them, you should do so rarely. If you are referring to the materials all the time, this could be a signal to you that you are going to run into a time problem. If you are allowed to use study-aids, such as this Outline, you may find time to at least refer to the Summary Outline. If you can bring only your own material into the exam, prepare an outline, or at least a checklist, to jog your memory.

The last thing you should do as part of the examination taking process is to forget the examination after you have written it. Do not engage in post-mortems with your classmates. They will invariably have put something on the examination that you did not. What they put in may have been right, but it also may have been wrong. The best thing to do after you complete the constitutional law examination is to go to a movie—unless you have another exam!

PART ONE

The Allocation of Governmental Power: National and State

■ *ANALYSIS*

I

Judicial Review

■ ANALYSIS

A course on American constitutional law deals primarily with the exercise of the power of judicial review. But before a court can review government action on its constitutional merits, the court must have jurisdiction, *i.e.*, power to hear the case. Even when a court has technical jurisdiction to decide a case, there are various policies and principles whereby final decision can be avoided, at least temporarily. This chapter deals with the jurisdiction of the federal courts, including the power of judicial review, and the constitutional, congressional and self-imposed limitations on the exercise of that judicial power.

A. Establishing Judicial Review

1. "Judicial Review" Defined

Judicial review is the doctrine that the courts have the power to invalidate governmental action which is repugnant to the Constitution. "It is emphatically the province and duty of the judicial department to say what the law is." Marbury v. Madison (1803).

2. Review of Federal Action

State and federal courts have the power to review and invalidate the acts of Congress and of the Executive which are contrary to the Constitution. Although the power of judicial review over the Congress has been long established, this power has now been explicitly extended to executive action as well.

a. Reviewing Acts of Congress—*Marbury v. Madison*

1) In *Marbury v. Madison* (1803), the Supreme Court held § 13 of the Judiciary Act of 1789 unconstitutional. The Act was read by Justice Marshall, perhaps erroneously, to enlarge the Supreme Court's original jurisdiction beyond the limits defined in Art. III of the Constitution. Since the Constitution prescribes the powers delegated by the people to the national government, a congressional act contrary to the Constitution is invalid. The Constitution is supreme over ordinary federal or state law under the Supremacy Clause of Art. VI.

2) There is no explicit textual authority for judicial review in the Constitution. But Art. III does extend the judicial power to all cases arising under the Constitution. Marshall reasons that it is the judicial duty to say what the law is. When the constitutionality of a

congressional act is drawn into question, the Court must give effect either to the Act or to the Constitution. Only federal laws "made in pursuance" of the Constitution are the Supreme Law of the Land under Art. VI.

3) The critical issue is whether Marshall is correct that the judicial judgment on constitutionality is controlling. The Court could have held that the judgment of Congress, the popularly elected branch of government, binds the courts on the meaning of the Constitution. Many countries, even some with written Constitutions, do not accept judicial review. The student should consider whether constitutional interpretation is analogous to judicial functions such as statutory interpretation or common law decision-making or is qualitatively different. The student should also consider the capabilities of the branches of government for interpreting the Constitution.

4) The holding in *Marbury v. Madison* might have been limited to acts of Congress dealing with federal court jurisdiction or to cases where judicial action is necessary to give effect to congressional legislation. Instead, it has come to stand for the broad proposition "that the federal judiciary is supreme in the exposition of the law of the Constitution, and that principle has ever since been * * * a permanent and indispensable feature of our constitutional system." *Cooper v. Aaron* (1958).

b. **Reviewing Executive Action**

The doctrine of judicial review also applies to Executive action. Courts may call executive officers to answer for their actions and review those actions as to their constitutionality.

1) In *Marbury*, the Court reasoned that where the Executive possesses legal or constitutional discretion, judicial review would be precluded. But it is the nature of executive action and not the office of the person that determines the appropriateness of judicial review. A mandamus order, therefore, could issue to an executive officer requiring the performance of ministerial (non-discretionary) duties.

2) While the President takes an oath to uphold the Constitution, his decisions regarding constitutionality are not decisive. The federal judiciary is supreme in the interpretation of the Constitution.

Example: The federal courts have the power to review claims of the Executive to withhold tape recordings and documents relating to conversations among staff subpoenaed by the Special Prosecutor for use in a pending criminal prosecution. "Notwithstanding the deference each branch must accord the others, the 'judicial power of the United States' vested in the federal courts by Art. III, § 1 of the Constitution can no more be shared with the Executive Branch than the Chief Executive, for example, can share with the Judiciary the veto power." *United States v. Nixon* (1974).

3. Review of State Action

The Supremacy Clause of Art. VI establishes that the Constitution of the United States binds state officials, "anything in the Constitution or laws of any state to the contrary notwithstanding." Thus, the federal courts can review the constitutionality of state statutes and the actions of state officials involving matters of federal law.

When the state courts decide federal constitutional questions, the Supreme Court has appellate jurisdiction under Art. III, § 2, over such decisions. A principal policy justification for extending Supreme Court appellate jurisdiction to the federal constitutional decisions of state courts is the need for uniformity in federal constitutional interpretation.

Examples: (1) Section 25 of the Judiciary Act of 1789 conferring appellate jurisdiction on the Supreme Court over the decisions of a state court is constitutional for the reasons stated above. *Martin v. Hunter's Lessee* (1816).

(2) The governor and legislature of a state act unconstitutionally in attempting to interpose state sovereignty as a justification for refusing to obey the Supreme Court's decision declaring state mandated school segregation unconstitutional. *Cooper v. Aaron* (1958).

B.   Source of Judicial Power: Article III Jurisdiction

The "judicial power," consisting of defined "cases and controversies," including cases involving constitutional questions, is vested by the U.S. Constitution, Art. III, in the Supreme Court and such inferior courts as Congress may establish. The U.S. Supreme Court, the U.S. Courts of Appeal, and the U.S. District Courts are created pursuant to this authority. The judicial power has been interpreted to include the power to review and invalidate as unconstitutional both federal and state action.

1. Federal "Judicial Power" Defined

Art. III, § 2, defines the subject matter jurisdiction of the Art. III federal courts. Unless a case falls within one of the "cases and controversies" identified in Art. III, § 2, an Art. III federal court must dismiss the case for want of jurisdiction. Article III courts cannot assume jurisdiction but must decide the jurisdictional question as an antecedent question prior to reaching the merits. "The statutory and (especially) constitutional elements of jurisdiction are an essential ingredient of separation and equilibration of powers. . . ." *Steel Co. v. Citizens for a Better Environment* (1998). *While Art. III is the source of federal judicial power, its implementation is largely dependent on congressional legislation.*

a. Art. III and Art. I Courts

1) The Supreme Court of the United States is the only federal court specifically required by the Constitution. Whether other federal courts were needed was left to Congress to determine. In the Judiciary Act of 1789, Congress created federal trial courts (district courts) and intermediate courts of appeal. Independence of Art. III judges is assured by protecting "their offices during good behavior" and prohibiting their salaries from being "diminished."

2) Art. III federal courts must be distinguished from "legislative" or Art. I courts created by Congress pursuant to its various powers under Art. I, *e.g.*, the military justice system, courts of the District of Columbia. Art. I legislative courts are not limited to the jurisdiction specified in Art. III and Art. I judges do not enjoy the tenure and salary protections provided by Art. III.

b. Subject Matter Jurisdiction

Art. III federal courts are courts of limited jurisdiction. They may hear and decide only those "cases and controversies" identified in Art. III, § 2. The more important categories of Art. III jurisdiction for you to remember are cases arising under the Constitution, laws and treaties of the United States, *i.e.*, federal question jurisdiction, and cases involving citizens of different states (diversity jurisdiction). If litigation does not fall under the designated categories, an Art. III federal court lacks subject matter jurisdiction and must dismiss the case.

c. Congressional Control

While the source of the federal judicial power is Art. III, the extent to which it is exercised is generally determined by Congress. See Ch. I, B,

2, b. This is especially true for the inferior federal courts whose very existence was left to the pleasure of Congress. But Congress cannot authorize the Art. III federal courts to take jurisdiction or perform functions beyond the limits of Art. III. *Marbury v. Madison* (1803). Nor can Congress "prescribe a rule for the decision of a cause in a particular way." *United States v. Klein* (1872).

> *Example:*   In 1991 the Supreme Court ruled that actions brought under the Securities Exchange Act of 1934 had to be brought within one year of discovery of the facts giving rise to the violation and within three years of the violation. Later when Congress changed the statute of limitations under the 1934 Act and reopened cases that had been dismissed under the Court's 1991 ruling, the Court held that the law violated the separation of powers. Retroactively requiring an Art. III court to reopen final decisions is in violation of *Marbury v. Madison. Plaut v. Spendthrift Farm, Inc.* (1995).

2. Supreme Court Jurisdiction

The "judicial power" vested by Art. III in the Supreme Court may be exercised in two ways: original or appellate jurisdiction.

a. Original Jurisdiction

Congress has passed legislation implementing the grant in Art. III to the Supreme Court of original jurisdiction in all cases affecting ambassadors, other public ministers and consuls, and those in which a state shall be a party. By assigning original jurisdiction, it is meant that such cases may commence in the Supreme Court. Congress cannot grant original jurisdiction to the Court beyond those cases specified in Art. III.

b. Appellate Jurisdiction—Congressional Power to Confer and Withdraw

Art. III, § 2, provides that in all other cases to which the federal judicial power extends, the Supreme Court shall have appellate jurisdiction. But this power is given "with such Exceptions, and under such Regulations as the Congress shall make." Congress must authorize the Court's appellate jurisdiction, and Congress may withdraw subjects from the Court's appellate jurisdiction. Congressional failure to authorize jurisdiction is considered an implied exception. How extensive such withdrawal can be is a matter of dispute.

1) Essential Functions: Internal Restraints

While Art. III, § 2, may be a grant of power to Congress to withdraw subjects from the Supreme Court's appellate jurisdiction, congressional powers are subject to constitutional limitations. It has been argued by some commentators that a statute preventing the Court from performing its essential role under Art. III of preserving the uniformity and supremacy of federal law would violate the principle of separation of powers.

2) Rights and Liberties: External Restraints

Apart from possible Art. III limitations, congressional statutes withdrawing Supreme Court review might also invade rights and liberties guaranteed in the Constitution, *e.g.*, Fifth Amendment due process. Even withdrawal of a particular remedy might, in some cases, prevent judicial protection of a constitutional right, *e.g.*, busing to implement a school desegregation order, and thus could be argued to violate that right.

> *Example:* A congressional statute withdrawing Supreme Court appellate jurisdiction to issue writs of habeas corpus was held constitutional, even though the case was already pending. But note that other methods for Supreme Court review still were available. The congressional statute did not foreclose all Supreme Court review of the constitutional issue but only precluded one particular remedy. Nevertheless, the Court did use sweeping language in describing congressional power over Art. III appellate jurisdiction. *Ex parte McCardle* (1869).

c. Discretionary Review

1) Certiorari

With a few minor exceptions, Supreme Court review of lower court decisions is discretionary. The losing party below petitions the Court for a writ of certiorari. Certiorari is granted when four justices vote to review the decision (the Rule of Four). A denial of certiorari is not a decision on the merits.

2) Basis for Review

a) Supreme Court rules indicate that certiorari will be granted only for special and important reasons and suggest the character of the considerations that govern the decision whether or not to grant certiorari. But these rules are not meant to be exhaustive.

b)   Court Conflict—Certiorari is often granted when federal courts of appeal are in conflict or there is a conflict between the highest courts of different states or between a state high court and a federal court of appeals.

c)   Novel Federal Questions—The exercise of certiorari often reflects the novelty of the federal question presented or the fact that an important federal question may have been incorrectly decided.

C.   Constitutional and Policy Limitations on Judicial Review

Even if a case appears to be within the technical jurisdiction of a federal court under Art. III, there is no assurance that the Art. III court will reach a decision on the merits. There are a number of doctrines, based either on the Constitution or on the policy of judicial self-restraint, whereby the federal courts may avoid a decision on the merits. Together these textually-required doctrines and judicially fashioned policies reflect a concern with justiciability—the proper use of the judicial review power. For example, the Court asks whether constitutional rights and duties can be judicially defined and appropriate relief fashioned.

1.   Constitutional Limitations

a.   Eleventh Amendment

The Eleventh Amendment provides that the judicial power granted in Art. III does not extend to suits against a state by citizens of another state or of a foreign country. Through judicial interpretation, the Eleventh Amendment has been extended to provide a bar to suits against a state by its own citizens. Hans v. Louisiana (1890). The Eleventh Amendment does not prevent the Supreme Court from reviewing cases arising in state courts which involve questions of federal law, even though the suit could not have been heard originally in federal court. The preservation of uniformity of federal law requires Supreme Court review of such decisions under the Constitution. *McKesson Corp. v. Division of Alcoholic Bev. and Tobacco, Fla.* (1990).

1)   State Immunity

The Eleventh Amendment grant of sovereign immunity is limited to the states and their agencies. It does not bar suits against cities, counties, local school boards or other local agencies. *Lake Country Estates, Inc. v. Tahoe Regional Planning Agency* (1979).

2) Waiver

A state may intentionally waive its Eleventh Amendment immunity if it does so expressly by statute or waiver is otherwise clearly implied. But state waiver cannot be inferred simply from participation in a program funded by the federal government. *Atascadero State Hospital v. Scanlon* (1985). "The Court will give effect to a State's waiver of Eleventh Amendment immunity 'only where stated by the most express language or by such overwhelming implication from the text as [will] leave no room for any other reasonable construction.' " *Port Authority Trans–Hudson Corp. v. Feeney* (1990).

3) Congressional Limitations

The Eleventh Amendment bar to suits against a state is limited by the power of Congress to authorize such remedies pursuant to its Fourteenth Amendment, § 5 legislative powers. *Fitzpatrick v. Bitzer* (1976). See Ch. XI, C, 2, b, on the scope of Congress' enforcement power. But congressional intent to remove the Eleventh Amendment bar and authorize a remedy against a state must be made "unmistakably clear in the language of the statute." *Atascadero.* Further, the power of Congress to subject states to suit in Art. III federal courts in spite of the *constitutional* bar of the Eleventh Amendment may be limited to statutes based on the Fourteenth Amendment, § 5. *Seminole Tribe of Florida v. Florida* (1996), held 5–4 that a statute authorizing certain suits against states in federal court based on Congress' Commerce Clause power over Indian tribes violates the Eleventh Amendment.

4) Unconstitutional Official Acts

A suit for injunctive relief against a state officer acting unconstitutionally or contrary to a statute is not a suit against the state and the Eleventh Amendment is therefore not a bar. Ex parte Young (1908). For example, the Eleventh Amendment did not bar a suit against named state officials for allegedly unconstitutional acts which resulted in the death of students at Kent State. *Scheuer v. Rhodes* (1974). The fact that a state is required to expend monies in order to comply with a court decree does not infringe the Eleventh Amendment prohibition. *Milliken v. Bradley* (1977). But the Eleventh Amendment does bar a suit against state officials where the official action violates only state law—federal court review is not necessary to assure supremacy of federal law. *Pennhurst State School & Hospital v. Halderman* (1984).

Exception: Where a suit directed against a public official results in a *retroactive* charge on the general revenues of the state and cannot be distinguished from an award of damages against the state, the Eleventh Amendment bars the award. *Edelman v. Jordan* (1974) (award of retroactive welfare benefits held to violate Eleventh Amendment). But the award of attorney's fees or other forms of ancillary relief requiring expenditure of state money does not violate the Eleventh Amendment even if paid by the state. *Hutto v. Finney* (1978).

b. Case and Controversy

The federal judicial power granted in Art. III is limited to certain defined "cases and controversies." This requires that a case be in an adversary form and context that is capable of judicial resolution and that its resolution would not violate separation of powers principles. If this requirement is not met, the federal courts lack jurisdiction and, therefore, power to act.

1) No Advisory Opinions

The federal courts may not furnish opinions on constitutional matters in a "friendly" nonadversary proceeding even at the request of a coordinate branch of government.

Example: The Supreme Court held that Congress could not authorize a certain class of Indians to bring suit against the United States to test the constitutionality of federal legislation limiting the property rights granted by earlier federal legislation to the same Indians. The Supreme Court held that what Congress sought was an impermissible advisory opinion because the interest of the defendant United States was not adverse to the Indians. Therefore, there was no case and controversy. *Muskrat v. United States* (1911).

2) Declaratory Judgments

Federal courts are often requested to decide what legal consequences will apply to the conduct of litigants, rather than provide damages or injunctive relief. Such declaratory judgments are not advisory opinions if they are sufficiently concrete to provide a true controversy that the court can decide.

2. Policy Limitations (Judicial Self Restraint)

a. Rules for Constitutional Review

Constitutional issues affecting legislation will not be determined: (1) in advance of the necessity of deciding them; or (2) if there are alternative grounds of disposition; or (3) if a construction of a statute is fairly possible by which the constitutional question may be avoided; or (4) in broader terms than are required by the precise facts to which the ruling is to be applied. *Ashwander v. TVA* (1936).

b. Presumption of Constitutionality

Some of the policies recited above are exemplified in the long-standing canon of constitutional construction, sometimes honored more in the breach than in the observance, that legislation challenged on constitutional grounds should be accorded a presumption of constitutionality by the reviewing court.

c. Judicial Restraint

The federal courts, where possible, have conventionally avoided judicial review, given: (1) the delicacy of the function; (2) the potential consequences; (3) the finality of the court's judgment; (4) the principle of separation of powers; and (5) the inherent limitations of the judicial process. The federal courts follow a policy of "strict necessity" in using the judicial review power.

d. Congressional Role

While Congress cannot directly remove an Art. III jurisdictional obstacle to judicial review, the above prudential limitations can be overcome by congressional legislation.

D. Specific Doctrines Limiting Judicial Review

There are a number of specific doctrines, based on the case and controversy requirement and policy considerations, through which the federal courts avoid a decision on the merits. They relate to WHO may litigate a constitutional question, WHEN a constitutional issue may be litigated, and WHAT constitutional questions may be litigated.

1. The Standing Limitation—Who Can Litigate?

a. Constitutional Standing

1) General Standards

   Art. III case and controversy requires that the party seeking to litigate a constitutional question, originally or on appeal, demonstrate "such a personal stake in the outcome of a controversy as to assure that concrete adverseness which sharpens the presentation of issues upon which the Court so largely depends for illumination of difficult constitutional questions." Baker v. Carr (1962). *A litigant has such a "personal stake" if he alleges (1) an "injury in fact" (2) "fairly traceable" to the defendant's action being challenged; and, (3) "redressable" by the judicial relief requested. The injury must be caused by the defendant's wrong.* The focus is on the party who is litigating, not on the issue being litigated. The student should note that the determination whether the asserted injury is sufficient and whether the requisite causal relationship exists often involve a highly subjective, value-laden judgment.

a) "Injury in Fact"

Standing does not usually turn on the legal claim but on the existence of factual injury. It may be economic, aesthetic, environmental injury, or even an intangible injury such as the ability to live in an integrated community. *The Court has stated that injury in fact requires "an invasion of a legally-protected interest which is (a) concrete and particularized and (b) actual or imminent, not conjectural or hypothetical."* Lujan v. Defenders of Wildlife (1992). While an interest may be widely shared, the plaintiff must still demonstrate a personal interest. Plaintiffs must satisfy the standing requirements *for each claim.* See *Los Angeles v. Lyons* (1983) (plaintiffs who suffered injuries from a police chokehold had standing to maintain a damage claim but not a claim for injunctive relief against future use of the chokehold policy since plaintiff failed to show actual or imminent injury) Compare *Gratz v. Bollinger* (2003) (plaintiff challenging University of Michigan affirmative action policy, who claims he was denied equal treatment because of the University's admissions policy and alleges that he is ready to apply for a transfer to the University, has standing to seek prospective relief).

Examples: (1) Harm to aesthetic, conservational and recreational values will suffice for injury in fact. However, the Sierra Club lacked standing to challenge a planned recreational development approved by federal authorities since it failed to show that any of its members would be personally harmed by the development. *Sierra Club v. Morton* (1972). On remand, the club included allegations of personal harm to members and was able to litigate the claim.

(2) An unwed mother seeking child support payments from the father of the child lacked standing to maintain an action to require state officials to enforce a child neglect law. First, there was no injury in fact since "a private citizen lacks a judicially cognizable interest in the prosecution or nonprosecution of another." Second, causation was lacking since there was "no showing that her failure to secure support payments results from the nonenforcement, as to her child's father, of [the statute]." *Linda R.S. v. Richard D.* (1973).

(3) Environmental groups lack standing to challenge a regulation by the Department of the Interior requiring agencies providing funds to projects affecting endangered species to consult with the Department only if the projects are domestic or on the high seas. Although a desire to use or observe an animal species is a judicially cognizable injury in fact, the groups failed to show that one or more of their members were personally affected in a concrete manner. A statement of a vague intent to visit the habitat of the species without concrete plans or dates, is not an actual or imminent, concrete injury. Claims of a nexus between the habitats and the professional interest of members, *e.g.*, zoologists, are "abstract and speculative." *Lujan v. Defenders of Wildlife* (1992).

(4) White voters residing in a majority-minority district, created by the Georgia legislature with "race as the predominant factor in [its] drawing . . . ," in order to increase the voting strength of African–Americans, have standing. *Miller v. Johnson* (1995). But white voters not living in such a legislative district lack standing to challenge the

creation of that district. Only resident voters suffer the requisite "individualized harm" necessary for Art. III standing. Voters in districts specifically created to increase the voting strength of the racial group are said to suffer "representational harm" because elected officials in those districts are more likely to represent the members of that racial group and not the district as a whole. A voter not living in such a district does not suffer "representational harm," absent specific evidence of a particular injury and asserts only a generalized grievance against governmental conduct which he or she does not approve. *United States v. Hays* (1995). See *Shaw v. Hunt* (1996), reaffirming *United States v. Hays*.

(5) Members of Congress who voted against the Line Item Veto Act do not have sufficient personal concrete injury to confer Art. III standing. The Members of Congress suing had not been singled out for "specially unfavorable treatment as opposed to other Members of their respective bodies." They had not been deprived of something to which they were personally entitled—such as their seats. See *Powell v. McCormack* (1969).

The Court held that the holding of *Coleman v. Miller* (1939) was limited: "legislators whose votes would have been sufficient to defeat (or enact) a specific legislative act have standing to sue if that legislative action goes into effect (or does not go into effect), on the ground that their votes have been completely nullified." Since the Members of Congress "have not alleged that they voted for a specific bill, that there were sufficient votes to pass the bill, and that the bill was nonetheless deemed defeated," there was no legislative standing under *Coleman v. Miller*. "[T]heir votes were given full effect. They simply lost that vote." *Raines v. Byrd* (1997).

(6) The Court appears to have eased the stringent injury in fact requirements of *Lujan*. Plaintiffs were held to have Article III standing based on their showing that they had a *reasonable* (not merely subjective) concern that the defendants discharge of pollutants into waterways would directly affect their recreational, aesthetic and economic interests. Even though there was no proof that the defendant had polluted the waterways, the plaintiffs geographic proximity and their ongoing desire to use the waterways made their interests more concrete and less speculative than the plaintiffs in *Lujan*. "The relevant showing is not injury to the environment but injury to the plaintiff." *Friends of the Earth, Inc. v. Laidlaw Environmental Services, Inc.* (2000).

(7) The "Millionaire's Amendment" to a federal campaign financing law allowed a candidate to receive contributions at three times the normal limit if his opponent contributed more than $350,000 in personal funds to his own campaign. Davis, a candidate who announced his intention to expend more than $350,000, was held to have standing to challenge the Amendment, even though when he filed suit he had not yet reached the cap, and when he finally did, his opponent would not have taken advantage of the discriminatory system. The Court concluded that, even though the threat faced by Davis was still "prospective" at the time the suit was commenced, his injury was still "real, immediate, and direct." He had declared his candidacy and his intent to spend more than $350,000 of personal funds in the general election campaign whose onset was rapidly approaching, and there was no indication that his opponent would forgo his opportunity to receive extra contributions under the statute. *Davis v. FEC* (2008). See Ch. VIII, D, 3, a, for a discussion of the case.

(8) The Court held 5–4 that an environmental group ("Earth Island") did not have standing to challenge a regulation of the U.S. Forest Service which exempted small-fire rehabilitation and timber-salvage projects from the notice, comment and appeals process the Forest Service used for more significant land-management decisions. In his opinion for the Court, Justice Scalia stated that the organization did not have standing because none of its individual members could prove a personal and concrete injury from a live dispute over a concrete application of the challenged regulation. See I, D, 1, b, 1) on Third Party Standing. While Earth Island did allege that one member was sufficiently personally affected by a salvage project (Burnt Ridge), the member had previously settled his claims. Earth Island also claimed that one of its members planned to visit unnamed national forests in the future, but the Court held that this did not involve a specific project affected by the challenged regulation and concrete plans sufficient to show actual or imminent injury. Earth Island also claimed standing for members because they suffered procedural injury in that they could not file comments on some Forest Service actions. "But deprivation of a procedural right without some concrete interest that is affected by the deprivation—a procedural right *in vacuo*—is insufficient to create Article III standing. Only a 'person who has been accorded a procedural right to protect *his concrete interests* can assert that right without meeting all the normal standards for redressability and immediacy.' " While statutory standing can result in a more relaxed standard for *redressability*, "the requirement of injury in fact is a hard floor of Article III jurisdiction that cannot be removed by statute." Justice Kennedy concurred in the judgment, noting that Congress had not provided redress for a concrete injury that would create a new basis for standing.

Justice Breyer, joined by Justices Stevens, Souter and Ginsburg, dissenting, argued that there was a "realistic likelihood" that other members of the environmental organizations would suffer harm from future salvaging projects subject to the challenged regulations—and that members had already been subject to the claimed injury. This claim was sufficient to satisfy the injury in fact requirement for organizational standing, even though the plaintiff cannot specify precise time, dates and places. The Court, however, rejected this "statistical probability" approach—the requirement of naming at least one member who is harmed or would suffer imminent harm is required. *Summers v. Earth Island Institute* (2009).

(9) An amendment to the Foreign Intelligence Surveillance Act (FISA) allows the government to acquire foreign intelligence information by surveillance of individuals who are not "United States persons" and are located outside the United States. A group of human rights groups and related organizations who were United States persons as defined by FISA brought suit seeking declaratory and injunctive relief. They claimed the amendment was unconstitutional as it affects their sensitive communications with individuals who are likely targets of FISA. The Second Circuit found the groups had Article III standing given the reasonable likelihood of future intercepts as well as present injuries stemming from costs to avoid future harmful government conduct. The Supreme Court reversed, 5–4.

Justice Alito, writing for the majority, found the injury was too speculative for Article III purposes under the established doctrine requiring "certainly impending" injury. It is "speculative whether the Government will imminently target communications to which respondents are parties" and it is too unclear under this standard whether the

Government will ever actually seek and get approval to monitor the groups' communications, and whether those communications will ever be successfully monitored. Additionally, current "costly and burdensome" measures taken by the respondents to avoid surveillance also fails to provide standing because the "harm respondents seek to avoid is not certainly impending." Respondents already have an incentive to take these measures due to pre-amendment Government surveillance and therefore cannot be fairly traced back to the amendment itself. "[R]espondents cannot manufacture standing by choosing to make expenditures based on hypothetical future harm that is not certain." This applies even if it insulates the amendment from judicial review.

The dissent, per Justice Breyer, focused on the removal of certain investigatory restrictions on the Government that were created by the new amendment and "common sense inferences" on how it increased the reasonable likelihood or probability that the Government will intercept some of the communications between the respondents and targets of FISA. "The Government does not deny that it has both the motive and the capacity to listen to communications of the kind described by the plaintiffs." The dissent argues that requiring that harm be "absolutely certain" is too limited. *Clapper v. Amnesty International USA* (2013).

b) Causation—"Fairly Traceable"

The Art. III case and controversy requirement also requires that a plaintiff establish an "actionable causal relationship" between the government action and the asserted injury. *Warth v. Seldin* (1975). *Plaintiffs must demonstrate that the injury is "fairly traceable" to the action being challenged.* Recent judicial application of the causation requirement has stressed separation of powers concerns, *i.e.*, the danger of judicial interference with executive policy choices. *Allen v. Wright* (1984).

Examples: (1) Black and low income litigants lack standing to challenge exclusionary zoning in the absence of any showing that a developer who would build housing suitable to their needs is prevented from doing so because of the zoning ordinance. Nor was there a developer who could identify a specific project then being impeded by the restrictive zoning. *Warth v. Seldin* (1975).

But a black litigant who seeks housing near his employment and shows that the zoning ordinance is barring a developer from building low-income housing suitable to his needs, has standing. The developer, who had expended funds and had a desire to build the low-income housing, also has Art. III standing. *Village of Arlington Heights v. Metropolitan Housing Development* (1977).

(2) Indigents and organizations composed of indigents lack standing to challenge a federal revenue ruling allowing favorable tax treatment to non-profit hospitals even though those hospitals provide only limited services to indigents. While the plaintiff may suffer from denial of services by the hospital, this is insufficient injury to maintain the present action since the hospital is not the defendant. It is pure speculation that the hospital's denial of services to indigents is attributable to the government's grant of tax exempt status. *Simon v. Eastern Kentucky Welfare Rights Organization* (1976).

(3) An allegation that the IRS failed in its legal duty to deny tax-exempt status to racially discriminatory private schools is a sufficient claim of injury to minority public school children in a suit by parents where such failure diminishes the ability of their children to be educated in a racially integrated school. (A claim of stigmatic injury to racial minorities was held to be too general to confer standing.) Furthermore, the plaintiffs failed to prove that the alleged injury is fairly traceable

to the IRS action. It is uncertain how many racially discriminatory schools received tax exemptions. And, it is speculative whether withdrawal of tax exemption from any particular school would lead that school to change its policies. Separation of powers principles bar suits simply designed to challenge the policies government agencies adopt to carry out their legal obligations. *Allen v. Wright* (1984).

(4) A construction contractors association has standing, on behalf of its members, to challenge a city ordinance which set aside money spent on city contracts for minority businesses. Although none of its members demonstrated that, but for the ordinance, they would have successfully bid for any of the contracts, members were "able and ready" to bid on the contracts and alleged that "a discriminatory policy prevents [them] from doing so on an equal basis." When a challenged government barrier makes it more difficult for members of one group to obtain a benefit than members of another group, it is not necessary for plaintiff to allege that the benefit would be obtained but for the government barrier. "The 'injury in fact' in an equal protection case of this variety is the denial of equal treatment resulting from the imposition of the barrier, not the ultimate inability to obtain the benefit." *Northeastern Florida Chapter of the Associated General Contractors of America v. Jacksonville* (1993).

c) Redressability

Article III requires that a plaintiff demonstrate that it is likely, as opposed to merely speculative, that the injury will be "redressed" by the remedy being sought. The redressability requirement is often treated as an aspect of causation.

Examples: (1) An environmental protection organization, alleging that the defendant manufacturer had violated the Emergency Planning and Community

Right-to-Know Act of 1986 (EPCRA) by failing to make timely filings of toxic and hazardous-chemical inventory forms and toxic-chemical release forms lacked standing. Even assuming that the plaintiff suffered a concrete injury in being deprived of information required under EPCRA, "the complaint fails the third test of standing, redressability."

None of the remedies sought by plaintiff would provide relief for late reporting or eliminate any effects of that late reporting on plaintiffs. Since there was no controversy that the defendant had filed late reports, a declaratory judgment would be worthless. Civil penalties were payable to the United States Treasury and therefore could not remedy plaintiff's injury. Prospective injunctive relief, e.g., receipt and inspection of future reports, cannot be remedial for past violations and plaintiff had not alleged a continuing or an imminently threatened future violation. *Steel Co. v. Citizens for a Better Environment* (1998).

(2) Plaintiffs seeking civil penalties for excessive discharge of pollutants into waterways in the quality of which they have a legally protectable interest satisfied the redressability requirement of Art. III. Where the defendant's violation is continuing at the time of the complaint, civil penalties payable to the government can encourage defendants to discontinue current violations and deter them from committing future ones. Plaintiffs also had standing to seek injunctive relief. *Friends of the Earth v. Laidlaw* (2000).

2) Taxpayer and Citizen Standing

a) Federal Taxpayers

(1) *In general, the interest of a federal taxpayer in the expenditure of federal monies is too fluctuating, remote, and imprecise to provide a basis for invoking federal jurisdiction to challenge such*

an expenditure. A showing that a federal enactment violates the federal taxing and spending powers delegated to Congress by Art. I, § 8 is insufficient in itself to furnish a basis for taxpayer standing in a federal court. *Frothingham v. Mellon* (1923) (federal taxpayer lacks standing to challenge federal law providing grants to states as violative of the Fifth Amendment Due Process Clause).

Exception: Federal taxpayer status may be a basis for Art. III standing if the taxpayer can satisfy a two-part test: (1) the taxpayer must be challenging an exercise of Congress' Art. I, § 8 taxing and spending power; and, (2) the enactment must be alleged to offend a specific constitutional limitation on the taxing and spending power. *Flast v. Cohen* (1968). In *Flast*, the taxpayer challenged a federal spending law as violative of the Establishment Clause of the First Amendment which limits government spending in support of religion. While *Flast* has not been overruled, it has been confined to its facts. It is unlikely today, in light of the citizen standing cases cited below, any other constitutional claim will satisfy the *Flast* test.

Examples: (1) Claiming standing as federal taxpayers under the *Flast* exception to the general rule of no federal taxpayer standing, the Freedom from Religion Foundation, Inc. challenged the expenditure of funds under President George W. Bush's Faith–Based and Community Initiative Program as violative of the Establishment Clause. The Court held 5–4 that the Foundation lacked standing under *Flast*. Justice Alito, writing for a plurality (he was joined by the Chief Justice and Justice Kennedy), concluded that, while the Foundation's Establishment Clause claim satisfied *Flast's* requirement of a specific constitutional limitation on the taxing and spending power, the taxpayers failed to satisfy the first prong of *Flast*. The agencies administering the Faith–Based program are funded through general Executive Branch appropriations without any express congressional authorization; plaintiffs were not asking the Court "to invalidate any congressional enactment or legislatively created program."

Justice Kennedy, concurring, stressed separation of powers concerns. He also endorsed *Flast*, whereas Justice Scalia, joined by Justice Thomas, concurring, would have the Court overrule *Flast*. Justice Scalia argued that standing based on psychic injury, even as limited by *Flast*, is inconsistent with constitutional limitations on the judicial power.

Justice Souter, joined by Justices Stevens, Ginsburg and Breyer, dissenting, argued that there was no meaningful difference in a taxpayer's stake in the outcome of challenges to congressional spending laws or Executive spending of congressionally-appropriated funds. *Hein v. Freedom from Religion Foundation, Inc.* (2007).

(2) Arizona taxpayers challenged an Arizona law authorizing tax credits for contributions to organizations providing scholarships to students attending private schools, many of which are religious, claiming the law violated the Establishment Clause. The Court held, 5–4, per Justice Kennedy, that the plaintiffs lacked standing under *Flast*. Justice Kennedy emphasized the distinction between government expenditures and tax credits. With tax credits there are no government funds that are given to a sectarian entity. Further, when Arizona taxpayers make a contribution, they spend their own money, not state money. The Court also held that plaintiffs failed to satisfy the requirements of causation and redressability.

Justice Kagan, writing for the dissent, argued that the distinction between tax credits and cash grants from the state treasury "finds no support in case law," and just as little in reason. Taxpayers experience the same injury for standing purposes. Tax credits come "out of what a taxpayer would otherwise be legally obligated to pay the State—hence out of public resources," and therefore cause the same injury for standing purposes. The Court's opinion, Justice Kagan argued, allows states to finance religious activity free of legal challenge; the state can structure the funding as a tax credit and "[n]o taxpayer will have standing to object." *Arizona Christian School Tuition Organization v. Winn* (2011).

b)   **State and Municipal Taxpayers**

Similar to federal taxpayers, "[s]tate taxpayers have no standing under Article III to challenge state tax or spending decisions simply by virtue of their status as taxpayers." *DaimlerChrysler v. Cuno* (2006). Municipal taxpayers may have standing to challenge illegal spending by the *municipality* because the injury is more direct. *Frothingham v. Mellon* (1923). However, a municipal taxpayer does not have standing to challenge *state* spending programs absent particularized injury. *DaimlerChrysler v. Cuno.*

Example: Residents of the city of Toledo and the state of Ohio challenged state tax breaks that would encourage the expansion of DaimlerChrysler in Toledo as violative of the Commerce Clause. The Court unanimously held that plaintiffs did not have standing to challenge the state tax breaks. Chief Justice Robert's opinion for the Court, echoing *Frothingham v. Mellon*, reasoned that, like federal taxpayers, state taxpayers do not suffer any cognizable injury simply as state taxpayers because the harm suffered by each individual taxpayer is minuscule. "A federal and state taxpayer's 'interest in the moneys of the Treasury is shared by millions of others; is comparatively minute and indeterminable; and the effect upon future taxation, of any payment out of the funds, so remote, fluctuating and uncertain, that no basis is afforded for an appeal to the preventive powers of a court of equity.' *Frothingham*. Plaintiffs' challenge based on loss of state funding for other projects due to the tax breaks does not present a particularized or imminent harm, but is merely the airing of a general grievance designed to direct state policy."

Nor did the plaintiffs have standing as *municipal* taxpayers to challenge the state tax credits. The fact that the revenues from the state tax would normally be distributed to individual municipalities did not support standing in this case. Any effect the taxpayers suit might have on the municipality was based on conjecture. *DaimlerChrysler v. Cuno* (2006).

c) Citizen Standing

At least in the absence of congressional legislation authorizing the suit, a citizen lacks a sufficient personal interest to challenge government acts as unconstitutional. Her interest is viewed as an "abstract injury" and a "generalized grievance" held in common with citizens generally. While individual justices have argued that the bar to citizen standing is a prudential rule of judicial self-restraint, the Court has generally treated it as an Art. III impediment.

Examples: (1) A citizen lacks standing to challenge the constitutionality of a federal statute authorizing the director of the CIA to certify expenditures as a violation of the constitutional requirement of a regular accounting of the use of public funds. *United States v. Richardson* (1974).

(2) A citizen has only a generalized interest, insufficient to maintain standing, in challenging the holding of reservist status by a congressman in violation of the Incompatibility Clause which prohibits members of Congress from holding other office. *Schlesinger v. Reservists Comm. to Stop the War* (1974).

(3) A citizen and taxpayer lacks standing to challenge an HEW grant of surplus land under a federal statute to a religious institution as a violation of the Establishment Clause. Since the challenge was to an HEW action rather than a federal statute and since the government grant was based on the property power rather than the Taxing and Spending Clause, the challengers did not have standing under *Flast* as taxpayers. Nor does a citizen qua citizen have standing to challenge government action merely to correct constitutional wrongs. An Establishment Clause claim does not eliminate the Art. III requirement of personal injury. *Valley Forge Christian College v. Americans United For Separation of Church and State* (1982).

(4) Colorado citizens challenged a Colorado Supreme Court ruling enjoining the state legislature from implementing a new redistricting plan after a state court redistricting plan had been put into effect following a prior legislative stalemate. The Colorado Supreme Court had interpreted Art. V of the Colorado Constitution to allow redistricting only once per census. However, plaintiffs argued that the Colorado Supreme Court's rejection of the state legislative plan violated their rights under the Elections Clause of the U.S. Constitution, which leaves the manner of holding congressional elections in the hands of state legislatures. The United States Supreme Court remanded the case with instructions to dismiss for lack of standing because the citizen plaintiffs did not suffer a personal injury as a result of the Colorado Supreme Court's ruling. "The only injury plaintiffs allege is that the law—specifically the Elections Clause—has not been followed. This injury is precisely the kind of undifferentiated, generalized grievance about the conduct of government that we have refused to countenance in the past." *Lance v. Coffman* (2007).

d) State Standing

A State does not have standing to sue the federal government as parens patriae on behalf of its citizens. *Massachusetts v. Mellon* (1923). But a State may sue the federal government on its own behalf to protect its own quasi-sovereign interests. *Massachusetts v. EPA* (2007).

Example: The Court held 5–4 that Massachusetts and other private and governmental petitioners had standing to challenge the EPA's failure to regulate the emission of carbon dioxide and other greenhouse gases as required by the Clean Air Act. The Court, in an opinion by Justice Stevens, relied on the fact that Congress had authorized a procedural right to bring challenges under the Act and the fact that Massachusetts had a special interest as a State in preserving its territorial integrity from the harms of global warming.

While plaintiffs must still personally suffer the particularized injury identified by Congress, "a litigant to whom Congress has 'accorded a procedural right to protect his concrete interest,'—here, the right to challenge agency action unlawfully withheld—'can assert that right without meeting all the normal standards for redressability and immediacy.' " This lower standard of redressability allowed the plaintiffs to seek an injunction against the EPA even though there was only "some possibility" that regulating would solve the alleged problems created by global warming.

Justice Stevens also emphasized the fact that Massachusetts is a sovereign state with special interest in protecting its territory. "There is a critical difference between allowing a State 'to protect her citizens from the operation of federal statutes' (which is what *Mellon* prohibits) and allowing a State to assert its rights under federal law (which it has standing to do)." While Massachusetts was "entitled to special solicitude in [the Court's] standing analysis," the Court also claimed that Massachusetts could have satisfied "the most demanding standards of the adversarial process." EPA's failure to regulate presented a risk of harm to the state that was "actual" and "imminent." Massachusetts had already experienced an injury in fact due to a rise in sea levels swallowing its coastal lands and there is potential for increased future damage from global warming. The EPA did not dispute the causal connection between greenhouse gas emissions and global warming; EPA's failure to regulate at least "contributes" to Massachusetts's injury. There is a "substantial likelihood" that a judicial remedy will prompt EPA to take steps to reduce Massachusetts' risk of harm. Even if EPA regulation cannot redress the harm from global warming, EPA regulation of auto emissions can be an important first step in slowing or reducing global warming.

Chief Justice Roberts, writing for the dissenting justices, rejected the Court's assertion of relaxed standing requirements for a State challenge under either Art. III or the Clean Air Act. And the plaintiffs could not establish standing on traditional Art. III terms. Massachusetts lacked "particularized" injury; the loss of coastal land was based on conjecture because there was inadequate actual evidence of loss and the threat of future loss was not "certainly impending." Causation is speculative; the loss of Massachusetts coastal lands cannot be traced back to the results of global warming resulting from inaction on the part of the EPA. Redressability was even more problematic. Even if the EPA were to regulate, it is not "likely" that such regulation would prevent the effects of global warming because the EPA could not prevent other countries from releasing greenhouse gases. *Massachusetts v. EPA* (2007).

3) Statutory Standing

Congress can, by statute, create legal interests, the denial of which satisfies the injury in fact requirement, "even where the plaintiff would have suffered no judicially cognizable injury in the absence of the statute." *Warth v. Seldin* (1975). For example, Congress can authorize "aggrieved persons" to bring actions to enforce a federal statute. Congress can also "articulate chains of causation that will give rise to a case or controversy where none existed before." *Lujan v. Defenders of Wildlife* (1992) (Kennedy, J., concurring). However, Congress cannot ignore the Art. III minima of injury in fact and causation.

Examples: (1) A village has standing to sue real estate brokers alleged to have engaged in "steering" prospective home buyers to different areas according to their race in violation of federal civil rights laws. The consequences of changing the village from an integrated to a segregated neighborhood are sufficiently concrete to give the village standing. Residents of the 12–13 block neighborhood to which blacks were alleged to have been steered also have standing, pursuant to the statute, because the transformation of their neighborhood from integrated to segregated, denied them the social and professional benefits of living in an integrated community protected by the federal civil rights law. The residents' desire to live in an integrated neighborhood was sufficient to satisfy Art. III requirements. Congress had authorized suit by parties suffering indirect injury from such racial steering. *Gladstone Realtors v. Village of Bellwood* (1979).

(2) The Court held 5–4 that a provision of the Endangered Species Act authorizing "any person" to bring an action to enforce the statute was insufficient to satisfy Art. III standing requirements. The environmental organizations bringing the action alleged only an abstract, generalized grievance against executive policy in implementing the Act. The lower court holding that the Act creates a procedural right to consultation in all persons which satisfies Art. III was rejected. A citizen "claiming only harm to his and every citizens'

interest in proper application of the Constitution and laws, and seeking relief that no more directly and tangibly benefits him than it does the public at large—does not state an Article III case or controversy." Prior cases of statutory standing involved Congress' elevating to the status of legally cognizable injuries concrete, *de facto* injuries.

Justice Kennedy, joined by Justice Souter, concurring, recognized that while Congress has the power to define injuries and chains of causation giving rise to a case or controversy, it must at "the very least identify the injury it seeks to vindicate and relate the injury to the class of persons entitled to bring suit." *Lujan v. Defenders of Wildlife* (1992).

(3) Acting under the Endangered Species Act (ESA), the Bureau of Reclamation determined that a proposed federal project might adversely affect two endangered fish species and requested a "Biological Opinion" from the Fish and Wildlife Service. The Service found that the project would jeopardize the species and suggested as a reasonable alternative that minimum water levels be maintained at certain reservoirs. The Reclamation Bureau indicated that it would run the project in compliance with the Biological Opinion. Irrigation districts and ranchers, fearing they would get less water, sued under the citizens suit provisions of the ESA.

The Court held that the plaintiffs had alleged sufficient injury in fact and causation to satisfy Article III. Since they alleged that the amount of available water would be reduced, "it is easy to presume specific facts under which [plaintiffs] will be injured." Causation is present since the Bureau is acting under the coercive effect of the Service's Biological Opinion. Through the ESA citizen-suit provisions authorizing "any person" to bring an action, Congress expanded the zone of interests to the full extent permitted by Article III, and removed any prudential standing obstacle to this action. *Bennett v. Spear* (1997).

(4) An ordinary voter has standing to challenge the refusal of the Federal Election Commission (FEC) to designate the American Israel Public Affairs Committee (AIPAC) as a "political committee," which would have subjected AIPAC to statutory record keeping and disclosure requirements. The Federal Election Commission Act (FECA) grants standing to "[a]ny person who believes a violation of this Act * * * has occurred." Since the voters' interest in obtaining information is within the zone of interests FECA seeks to protect, prudential standing is satisfied. The voters' injury in fact is the inability to obtain information under FECA to help them evaluate candidates for office and the role of AIPAC. Even though the injury is widely-shared, it is sufficiently concrete and particular to satisfy Art. III. Congress acted within its constitutional power in authorizing vindication of this informational interest in federal courts. The causation requirements of Art. III are also satisfied since persons adversely affected generally have standing to complain that the agency made its decision on an improper legal ground. *Federal Election Commission v. Akins* (1998).

(5) See *Friends of the Earth v. Laidlaw* (2000), at D, 1, a, 1), a), holding that plaintiffs, suing under an Act giving a cause of action to any person having an interest which is or may be adversely affected by discharge of excessive pollutants into waterways in violation of the Act, have standing based on their reasonable concern that the waterways might become polluted.

b. Prudential Standing

1) Third Party Standing—Raising the Rights of Others

a) *A litigant usually lacks standing to raise the rights of third parties not before the court.* The rule is based on the desire to avoid unnecessary litigation of constitutional rights, on the possibility that the third party might choose not to assert the constitutional claim, and on the belief that the third party is the best proponent of her own rights.

Examples: (1) Litigants lack standing as city taxpayers to raise the rights of low-income persons excluded by suburban restrictive zoning practices even though their city taxes are increased by the need to provide increased low income housing. There was no showing that either the rights of third persons would be adversely affected by denying standing or that there existed a special relationship between the litigants and those they sought to represent. *Warth v. Seldin* (1975).

(2) A father who had been deprived by state law of the right to sue as next friend on behalf of his child lacks prudential standing to challenge a school policy requiring daily recitation of the Pledge of Allegiance. Plaintiff, an atheist, claimed that the words "under God" in the Pledge of Allegiance impermissibly endorse religion in violation of the Establishment Clause. The mother, who had legal custody and authority over the child under state law, intervened, urging dismissal. The Ninth Circuit held that the father had Art. III standing to assert his state law right as a parent to expose his child to his values regarding religion. On the merits, the Ninth Circuit held that the words of the Pledge violate the Constitution.

In reversing, the Supreme Court balanced "the heavy obligation to exercise jurisdiction against the deeply rooted commitment not to pass on questions of constitutionality unless adjudication of the constitutional issues is necessary." The Court began by stressing the consistent practice of federal courts of declining to intervene in the realm of domestic relations. In this case, the state had recognized that the mother has final authority to make decisions for the child. The plaintiff father's rights derive entirely from his relationship to his daughter, but he lacks the right to litigate as her next friend. The interests of the father and the child are not parallel, but are potentially in conflict. Nothing done by the mother or the school impairs the father's parental right to instruct his child in his religious views. The father has no right to dictate what they say to the child respecting religion.

Chief Justice Rehnquist, joined by Justices O'Connor and Thomas, concurred in the reversal, but dissented on prudential standing. The dissent argued that the daughter is not the plaintiff's source of standing; "instead it is their relationship that provides his standing." Newdow sought to protect his parental rights, not his child's rights. On the merits, the dissent would hold that "under God" in the Pledge does not violate the Establishment Clause. *Elk Grove Unified School District v. Newdow* (2004).

b) *The third party standing doctrine is a rule of judicial self-restraint, not an Art. III requirement. Therefore, the values supporting the rule can be outweighed by competing considerations in a particular case. Further, Congress can grant a cause of action to persons who would otherwise be barred by prudential standing rules so long as Art. III requirements are satisfied.*

Examples: (1) Physicians may raise the rights of their patients to an abortion given: (a) the intimacy of the relationship of the physician to the patient; and (b) the relative inability of the patient to assert her own rights since she may be chilled from litigating by the desire to avoid publicity and by the imminent technical mootness. *Singleton v. Wulff* (1976).

(2) If a litigant has a substantial interest which depends on establishing the rights of the third person, the Third Party rule will not be applied. Thus, a beer vendor has standing to challenge a

state law barring sales to males under 18 but not minor females as a violation of equal protection, (*Craig v. Boren* (1976)), and a physician defending against a criminal charge for providing contraceptives has standing to raise the privacy rights of his patients. *Griswold v. Connecticut* (1965).

(3) A white criminal defendant has standing to raise equal protection and due process claims challenging racial discrimination against blacks in the grand jury selection process. In litigating the equal protection claim, the defendant satisfies all of the conditions required for third party standing. Discrimination in the grand jury selection process causes an injury-in-fact since it casts doubt on the fairness and integrity of the criminal proceeding. The accused has a definite interest in asserting the rights of excluded grand jurors, since a successful claim could lead to his conviction being overturned. Finally, excluded grand jurors face significant obstacles in asserting their own equal protection rights. *Campbell v. Louisiana* (1998).

2) Associational Standing

An association has standing to assert the claims of its members even if it has suffered no personal injury from the challenged activity. It must satisfy the following three requirements: (1) the members would otherwise have standing to sue in their own right; (2) the interest the association seeks to protect is germane to its organizational purpose; (3) neither the claim asserted nor the requested remedy would require participation by the individual members in the lawsuit. *Hunt v. Washington State Apple Adv. Comm'n* (1977). See *Summers v. Earth Island Institute* (2009) (group of environmental organizations lack standing to challenge agency regulations because they failed to name any member who suffered injury from a live dispute over a concrete application of those regulations).

2. The Timing Limitation—When Can Constitutional Litigation Be Brought?

a. Mootness

When a federal court's determination of a legal issue submitted by the parties is no longer necessary to compel the result originally sought because of changes after the suit was brought, the case is said to be moot and federal courts are without power to decide such an issue. The constitutional underpinning of the doctrine derives from the Art. III requirement that there be a case or controversy.

Examples: (1) An action brought by a rejected non-minority applicant to a state university law school who asserts that the Equal Protection Clause of the Fourteenth Amendment is violated because minority applicants with lesser credentials are admitted is rendered moot when he is registered for his last year of study at the school and will complete his studies regardless of the Court's decision. *DeFunis v. Odegaard* (1974).

(2) An action brought by members of Congress, challenging the President's "pocket veto" of a bill limiting further grants of military aid to El Salvador, was rendered moot since the bill expired by its own terms before the matter was reviewed by the Court. *Burke v. Barnes* (1987).

Exceptions: (1) Voluntary Cessation. The voluntary cessation of allegedly illegal conduct will not render a case moot where there is a reasonable expectation that the wrong will be repeated. The party asserting mootness bears a heavy burden of persuading the court that it is "absolutely certain" that the challenged action cannot reasonably be expected to recur. *Friends of the Earth, Inc. v. Laidlaw Environmental Services, Inc.* (2000).

(2) Collateral Consequences. A case will not be rendered moot if there remain unsettled important collateral consequences which may still have an adverse impact on the litigant, *e.g.*, a challenge to a criminal conviction following completion of the prison sentence.

(3) Repetitious Issues. *A constitutional issue will not be rendered moot when it is "capable of repetition, yet evading*

review." If the suit is maintained as a class action, mootness is avoided if it is "capable of repetition, yet evading review" for any members of the class. There must be a "reasonable likelihood" that the wrong complained of will recur.

Examples: (1) The fact that a woman who was pregnant when the case was instituted is no longer pregnant will not prevent her and members of her class from challenging the constitutionality of state abortion laws before the Supreme Court. Pregnancy will almost always end prior to appeal but is capable of repetition. *Roe v. Wade* (1973).

(2) A suit by an emotionally disturbed student under the Education of the Handicapped Act seeking injunctive relief against school officials who suspended him for violent and disruptive behavior related to his handicap was not moot although he was no longer enrolled in school. Absent evidence that the student has overcome his disabilities, there is a "reasonable expectation" that he would again be deprived of his rights because of classroom misconduct. A similar suit by a student who was no longer entitled to the benefits of the statute because of his age was held to be moot. *Honig v. Doe* (1988).

(3) A suit challenging the City of Jacksonville's affirmative action program is not rendered moot by the city changing its program. Under the previous Minority Business Enterprise ordinance, 10% of city contracts were set aside for the benefit of seven different minority groups. Under the new MBE program, "participation goals" of 5% to 16% are established for the benefit of women and blacks. The "voluntary cessation" of the challenged program does not deprive the federal court of its power. The new law presents essentially the same disadvantage in obtaining city contracts for the members of plaintiff Associated General Contractors as did the prior law. There is also the danger that the defendant could revert to the previous program after dismissal of the lawsuit. *Northeastern Florida Chapter of the Associated General Contractors of America v. Jacksonville* (1993).

(4) A prisoner's petition for a writ of habeas corpus challenging parole revocation procedures is rendered moot by the expiration of his sentence. The prisoner's claim is not within the "collateral consequences" exception to mootness. The possible future harm to the prisoner from parole revocation is significantly less than from a criminal conviction. The possibility that the revocation might be used to deny parole in the future or that it might be used against him in sentencing proceedings, is too speculative to overcome mootness. The prisoner's claim is also not within the "capable of repetition, yet evading review" exception. Although the claim may have been rendered moot as a result of delaying action by legal authorities, the courts still cannot rule on it. If a case has no demonstrable continuing legal effect, for any reason, an Art. III federal court has no power to decide it. *Spencer v. Kemna* (1998).

(5) The Court held that a suit brought by Davis, a self-financed candidate, challenging the "Millionaire's Amendment," which would allow his opponent to raise three times the normal limit because his self-financing exceeded $350,000, was not moot even though the election had passed since the issue was one "capable of repetition, yet evading review." First, the action "would not reasonably be resolved before the election concluded;" it would evade review. Second, the FEC conceded that the claim would be capable of repetition if Davis ran again, and Davis had subsequently indicated his intent to do so. *Davis v. FEC* (2008). See Ch. VIII, D, 3, a, for a discussion of the case.

b. Ripeness, Prematurity and Abstractness

A prerequisite to the adjudication of constitutional issues is the presentation for decision of concrete legal issues, presented in actual cases, not abstractions. For a case to be ripe, there must be present injury, or an imminent threat of injury. In determining if a case is ripe for review, the courts consider three issues: (1) whether delayed review would cause hardship to plaintiffs; (2) whether judicial intervention would improperly interfere with administrative action; and (3) whether the courts would benefit from further factual development of the issues presented. Further, a federal court will not decide a case where the controversy is at too premature a stage to permit proper judicial resolution.

1) Ripeness is generally considered to be a mandate of the Art. III case and controversy requirement. However, it blends almost imperceptibly into a prudential rule of judicial self-restraint based on the timing of the constitutional litigation.

2) Even when jurisdiction is technically present, a federal court will sometimes dismiss the issue as premature and abstract. Such a disposition reflects prudential concerns that the power of judicial review be used only when necessary to decide a case which "tenders the underlying constitutional issues in clean-cut and concrete form." *Socialist Labor Party v. Gilligan* (1972).

3) In determining whether a constitutional case has sufficiently matured to permit judicial resolution, consider whether there are any significant events yet to occur which will sharpen the dispute, whether the issues are sharply defined or remain speculative and uncertain and whether there is a realistic expectation that a threatened government action, *e.g.*, enforcement of a statute, will occur.

Examples: (1) Government employees who plan to engage in activities that might infringe on the Hatch Act prohibition against political activities fail to present an Art. III case and controversy. It is uncertain what political actions they would engage in and how the Civil Service Commission would react. *United Public Workers v. Mitchell* (1947).

(2) A ban on the use of contraceptives which is not being enforced is not justiciable. *Poe v. Ullman* (1961).

(3) The Texas Educational Code authorizes various sanctions for school districts that fail to meet state-mandated achievement standards, including the use of a master or a management team. When Texas submitted these code provisions for preclearance under § 5 of the Voting Rights Act, the United States determined that implementation of the above sanctions, "under foreseeable circumstances" could violate the Act which would require preclearance. Texas' suit for a declaratory judgment that the sanctions were not subject to preclearance was held by the Court not to be ripe since it was "speculative" whether the legal issue

on preclearance would ever need solving. The issues Texas raised were not presently fit for judicial consideration since a district would first have to fall below achievement levels and then the State would have to choose the questionable sanctions. There was no substantial hardship to Texas in waiting since it would not be required to do anything until the contingencies occurred. Even then it would suffer only an inconvenient delay or the need to legally defend its actions. Texas' claimed immediate hardship of a "threat to federalism" was an abstraction no graver than the "threat to personal freedom" from any agency regulation. *Texas v. United States* (1998).

(4) A challenge to a federal land and resource management plan, on grounds that it permits too much logging and clearcutting, is not ripe for judicial review where the plan itself merely sets guidelines and does not authorize any cutting of trees. Withholding review would not cause significant hardship to either party. There are no legal consequences to the challengers and they may challenge the plan and timber harvesting when logging is actually proposed. In addition, judicial review could hinder the government's ability to revise the plan before it went into effect. Finally, it would be difficult for courts to review the plan until specific proposals for logging were made. *Ohio Forestry Association v. Sierra Club* (1998).

(5) The Court held that a challenge by an association of concessioners to an administrative regulation rendering the Contract Disputes Act inapplicable to concession contracts is not ripe for review. Focusing on the lack of sufficient hardship to plaintiffs, the Court determined that the regulation did not have the "force of law" but was more like a policy directive. The regulation did not affect the challengers' "primary conduct," but left them free to conduct their business as they saw fit. The Court concluded that "further factual development would significantly advance [the Court's] ability to deal with the legal issues present-

ed." *Nat'l Park Hospitality Ass'n v. Dept. of the Interior* (2003).

c. Discretionary Abstention

1) Vagueness

   If a state statute is capable of a narrow saving construction, federal courts should abstain from decision even though important constitutional questions may be involved. This policy is based on the desire to avoid needless friction with state courts (comity) and unnecessary resolution of constitutional decisions. If the statute is unambiguous and not capable of a savings construction, abstention is inappropriate. Railroad Commission of Texas v. Pullman Co. *(1941).*

   > *Example:* Abstention is inappropriate in a case involving a First Amendment challenge to an ordinance making it unlawful to intentionally interrupt a police officer in the performance of his duties. The case involved a facial challenge to a law that was not ambiguous and was not fairly subject to a construction that would overcome the overbreadth claim. There was no core of constitutionally unprotected expression to which the law might be limited. *Houston v. Hill* (1987).

2) Pending State Proceedings

   Absent a showing of bad faith harassment, a federal court should abstain in a suit seeking declaratory and/or injunctive relief if a state criminal prosecution is pending even though the statute is alleged to be a vague and overbroad invasion of First Amendment rights. Younger v. Harris (1971).

   a) The principle of *Younger v. Harris* has been extended to civil proceedings analogous to state criminal proceedings, *e.g.,* enjoining operation of a state public nuisance statute used to close a pornographic movie house. *Huffman v. Pursue, Ltd.* (1975).

   b) No Pending Proceeding. Where there is no pending state court proceeding, a federal court need not abstain from granting either declaratory or injunctive relief where a statute is alleged to be a vague and overbroad invasion of First Amendment rights even though there is no showing of bad faith harassment. *Steffel v. Thompson* (1974) (declaratory relief); *Wooley v. Maynard* (1977) (injunctive relief).

3. The Subject Matter Limitation—What Can Be Litigated?

a. The Political Question Doctrine

Political questions, which does not mean cases dealing with political subjects, are non-justiciable. In defining what questions are political, the Court in Baker v. Carr *(1962) provided criteria, reflecting classic, functional, and prudential considerations. The Court has generally limited the doctrine to cases involving the federal court's role vis-a-vis co-equal branches rather than cases involving state power but it has been suggested as applicable to constitutional cases generally.*

1) Classic Doctrine

If the issue has been committed by the Constitution to the discretion of another government decision maker, federal courts will treat it as a political question. But whether the issue is constitutionally committed to a particular branch is itself a judicial question. Only the manner in which discretion is exercised is inappropriate for federal review.

2) Functional Considerations

A question may be labeled "political" because the Court determines that the judicial branch lacks the resources and capabilities for resolving it. For example, "a lack of judicially discoverable and manageable standards for resolving [the question]," *e.g.,* foreign affairs issues, may render the question political.

3) Prudential Considerations

Constitutional issues may also be labeled political because of prudential or policy considerations relating to the proper use of the judicial power. For example, *Baker v. Carr* (1962), noted the following considerations are relevant: "the impossibility of deciding without an initial policy determination of a kind clearly for nonjudicial discretion; or, the impossibility of a court's undertaking independent resolution without expressing lack of the respect due coordinate branches of government; or, an unusual need for unquestioning adherence to a political decision already made; or the potentiality of embarrassment from multifarious pronouncements by various departments on one question."

Examples: (1) The question whether state legislative apportionment satisfies equal protection is not a political question since it does not involve separation of powers concerns and equal protection standards for decisions are available. *Baker v. Carr* (1962). Similarly, the issue of partisan or political gerrymandering is justiciable. Judicially discernible and manageable standards for decision could be formulated as they were in the reapportionment context. *Davis v. Bandemer* (1986). See *Vieth v. Jubelirer* (2004).

(2) The question of whether the House of Representatives' refusal to seat Adam Clayton Powell was constitutional was held justiciable. The Supreme Court determined that Art. I, § 5, making each House "the Judge of the * * * Qualifications of its own members," is limited to the qualifications specified in the Constitution, *i.e.*, age, citizenship, and state residence. *Powell v. McCormack* (1969).

(3) Questions concerning the duration for state ratification of a constitutional amendment and whether a state can withdraw a prior ratification are left to Congress by Art. V. These questions are non-justiciable. *Coleman v. Miller* (1939).

(4) A plurality of the Court would treat the question of a President's power to unilaterally terminate a treaty as a political question since no constitutional provision directly controls the issue, the political branches have adequate resources to decide the issue, and the issue involves foreign affairs. *Goldwater v. Carter* (1979).

(5) A challenge to Senate rules allowing a Senate committee to hear evidence against an impeached federal judge and then allowing the committee to report the evidence to the full Senate involves a non-justiciable political question. Article I, § 3, cl. 6 states: "The Senate shall have the sole Power to try all Impeachments." "Sole" indicates the power "is reposed in the Senate and nowhere else." The grant of power is subject only to the specific requirements of Art. I, § 3, and other textual limitations in the Constitution. "Try" was not intended by the Framers to be an identifiable textual limitation on the broad discretion

vested in the Senate. Further, there are no judicially manageable standards for determining what is a trial. *Nixon v. United States* (1993).

(6) The issue of whether a person born in Jerusalem can elect to have their place of birth listed as Israel as authorized by a section of the Foreign Relations Authorization Act is *not* a political question. Menachem Zivotofsky's mother requested that his birthplace be recorded as Jerusalem, Israel as authorized by statute. The Secretary of State refused the request citing State Department policy that prohibits recording Israel as the place of birth for those born in Jerusalem. Zivotofsky's parents filed a complaint. The lower federal courts dismissed concluding that the political question doctrine barred judicial review since resolving the issue would necessarily involve deciding the political status of Jerusalem, an issue left to the Executive. The Court, per Chief Justice Roberts, held that the issue was not the political status of Jerusalem but rather, the constitutionality of the statute. This was not a political question but "demands careful examination of the textual, structural, and historical evidence put forward by the parties regarding the nature of the statute and of the passport and recognition powers. This is what courts do." *Zivotofsky v. Clinton* (2012).

b. Adequate and Independent State Grounds

1) Substantive Rules

Where a decision of a state court includes a "plain statement"—"clearly and expressly"—that it rests on adequate and independent state grounds, the Supreme Court will not take jurisdiction even though the state court may also have erroneously decided a federal constitutional question. But federal jurisdiction over state court decisions exists when the state's "decision fairly appears to rest primarily on federal law, or to be interwoven with the federal law, and when the adequacy and independence of any possible state ground is not clear from the face of the opinion." Michigan v. Long (1983).

2) Procedural Rules

A litigant's failure to adhere to fair and reasonable state procedural rules can also result in Supreme Court dismissal of an appeal from a state court. Such failure would provide an adequate and independent state ground for the decision. But the state procedural rule must advance substantial state interests and must not unnecessarily impair decision of the federal constitutional question.

Example: The Court invoked the principle of "comity," or proper respect for state functions, to bar a suit in federal court which raised a constitutional challenge against a state civil judgment. Since the movant had not sought the requested relief in the state court, the Court assumed that state procedures could have afforded an adequate remedy. The moving party did not sustain its burden of forwarding unambiguous authority to the contrary. Although the question presented in federal court had never been addressed by the relevant state courts, there was no evidence that the state courts lacked the authority or inclination to address it. *Pennzoil Co. v. Texaco, Inc.* (1987).

E. Review Questions

1. **T or F** There is explicit textual authority for the doctrine of judicial review.

2. **T or F** The doctrine of judicial review only applies to legislation as the facts of *Marbury v. Madison* (1803) illustrate.

3. **T or F** State courts have the power to invalidate acts of Congress or Presidential acts on the grounds of their inconsistency with the federal Constitution.

4. **T or F** The Supreme Court of the United States does not have appellate jurisdiction over cases coming from the state courts because the only reference in Art. III to Supreme Court appellate jurisdiction is directed to such inferior federal courts as Congress may create.

5. **T or F** When a federal constitutional issue is presented along with nonconstitutional issues, the federal constitutional issue should be decided in order to remove uncertainty.

6. **T or F** As a textual matter, Congress can abolish federal courts, other than the Supreme Court.

7. **T or F** The Eleventh Amendment does not bar federal courts from enforcing federal constitutional obligations against state officials.

8. **T or F** Congress can authorize suits against states in federal court pursuant to its plenary commerce power.

9. **T or F** In order to have standing to litigate a federal constitutional question in an Art. III federal court, the litigant must demonstrate (1) injury in fact; (2) that the injury is fairly traceable to the defendant's conduct and (3) the injury is redressible by the remedy requested.

10. **T or F** A federal citizen has standing to challenge violations by federal officials of constitutionally imposed duties.

11. **T or F** Art. III prevents the plaintiff from litigating the legal rights of a party not before the court.

12. **T or F** When Congress, by statute, authorizes a citizen to maintain an action in federal court, the requirements of Art. III are satisfied.

13. **T or F** A pregnant woman brings an action challenging the constitutionality of an anti-abortion law. When the case is heard by a federal court she is no longer pregnant. Her claim must be dismissed as moot.

14. **T or F** If a state criminal prosecution is pending, a federal court generally should abstain from granting declaratory or injunctive relief with regard to the controversy even though a First Amendment claim is involved.

15. **T or F** A question is "political" and, therefore, non-justiciable because the problems the question presents are not appropriate for judicial resolution.

16. **T or F** The Court has held that a constitutional challenge to the impeachment of a federal judge is always a non-justiciable political question.

17. Which of the following is an Art. III requirement?

   a. The presumption of constitutionality.

   b. Third party standing rule.

   c. Ban on advisory opinions.

   d. Avoidance of prematurity and abstract questions.

18. Which of the following is *not* an exception to the Eleventh Amendment limitation on federal court jurisdiction?

    a. State waiver of immunity.

    b. Retroactive charges on state revenues.

    c. Suits against state officials acting unconstitutionally which seek injunctive relief.

    d. Ancillary monetary relief.

    e. Prospective relief which involves expenditures of state funds.

19. Suburbia, which adjoins the city of Metro, maintains a racially exclusionary zoning ordinance. Which of the following parties would be most likely to have the requisite standing to challenge Suburbia's law?

    a. Metro taxpayers.

    b. A builder who has been denied a permit to build a racially integrated housing project in Suburbia.

    c. Black persons living in Metro.

    d. An association of homebuilders.

20. In which of the following scenarios has the plaintiff satisfied the "injury in fact" requirement?

    a. Citizens of Colorado who are challenging the enforcement of a judicially-created redistricting plan as violating the Elections Clause of the U.S. Constitution, which leaves the mode of electing Congressmen to each State's legislature.

    b. An environmental group that is challenging a regulation of the US Forest Service which limited the ability to comment on proposed land-management actions. The members of the environmental group plan one day to study unnamed National Forests, but do not have any definite plans.

    c. State taxpayers are challenging a State decision to grant tax breaks to an automobile manufacturer in violation of the Commerce Clause.

    d. A State that is challenging the EPA's inadequate regulation of carbon dioxide emissions, where Congress has authorized a procedural right to bring suit under the Clean Air Act, and where global warming was causing the State to suffer from rising sea levels.

21. A state decides to grant an automobile manufacturer tax breaks as an incentive to expand its operations within the state. The tax revenues lost by the tax breaks are normally distributed to individual municipalities within the state. Which group of plaintiffs would have standing to challenge the tax breaks as violating the Commerce Clause in an action brought in federal Court?

    a. Federal taxpayers

    b. State taxpayers

    c. Municipal Taxpayers

    d. All of the above

    e. None of the above

22. A federal court, pursuant to the 1972 amendments to Title VII of the Civil Rights Act of 1964, has awarded back pay and attorneys' fees against the state to present and retired male state employees where the latter had suffered from state discrimination against them because of their sex. Congress had enacted this legislation pursuant to legislative authority granted it under Section 5 of the Fourteenth Amendment. The state has argued that the award is unconstitutional on the ground that it offends the Eleventh Amendment. Is it?

23. The state of Purity maintains a law prohibiting any person from sterilizing females. Doctor Kildare, a licensed physician in Purity, brings suit in federal district court seeking to enjoin the Purity Sterilization Law, alleging that the Sterilization Law violates the right of privacy of his female patients who wish to be sterilized. The state of Purity has moved to dismiss Doctor Kildare's suit for want of jurisdiction and, in the alternative, that Doctor Kildare cannot raise the rights of his patients. Discuss the validity of the state's claims.

II

National Legislative Powers

■ ANALYSIS

American government is limited government. The national government has only such powers as are granted to it by the people through the constitutional text, either expressly or impliedly. Powers not delegated are retained by the states and the people (Tenth Amendment). A broad view of the constitutional basis for federal legislative power originated with Marshall in the early nineteenth century, then a more or less contracted view of federal congressional power emerged, to be followed in turn by Supreme Court decisions which since the New Deal have once again taken a very expansive view of congressional power based on a generous interpretation of the implied powers granted to Congress in the Constitution. More recently, a more restrictive interpretation of Congress' power (at least under the Commerce Clause and the Fourteenth Amendment, § 5) has emerged.

In analyzing the constitutionality of federal statutes, always ask two questions: (1) Is there a constitutional source of power and, if so, (2) is there a constitutional limitation on the exercise of the power? Remember, limitations on the exercise of government power include both constitutional rights and liberties and the constitutional distribution of powers (*i.e.,* separation and division of powers).

A.   The Scope of the National Legislative Power

1.   Express Powers

Art. I, § 8 expressly grants a variety of powers to Congress including the powers to regulate commerce with foreign nations and among the several states and to lay and collect taxes to pay the debts and provide for the defense and general welfare of the United States. There are also other express congressional powers granted in the Constitution. For the enforcement clauses of the Thirteenth, Fourteenth and Fifteenth Amendments authorizing Congress to enforce the guarantees of those Amendments by appropriate legislation, see Ch. XI. And as indicated in Ch. I, Congress has various express powers in relation to the federal courts under Article III.

2.   Implied Powers

a.   "Necessary and Proper" Clause

Art. I, § 8 also provides that Congress shall have power "To make all Laws which shall be necessary and proper for carrying into Execution the foregoing Powers, and all other Powers vested by this Constitution in the Government of the United States, or in any Department or Officer thereof."

b.   Interpretation of "Necessary and Proper"

The terms "necessary and proper" have been interpreted to mean that if the end for which Congress legislates is legitimate, within the scope of the Constitution, then *"all means which are appropriate, which are plainly adapted to that end, which are not prohibited, but consist with the letter and spirit of the Constitution are constitutional."* McCulloch v. Maryland *(1819). Congress may use "reasonable" means for achieving its delegated powers.* The Court has generally adopted a deferential approach allowing Congress to use any legislative means rationally related to its granted powers.

Examples: (1) In an action to collect state taxes against a federal corporation, the Bank of the United States, the question was raised as to whether Congress had the power to incorporate the bank. The Court noted that among the enumerated powers of government the word "bank" or "incorporation" is not found. Nevertheless, the Constitution did not enumerate all the means by which the powers it confers may be executed. Congress has implied power to create such a corporation if it is appropriate to the beneficial exercise of an enumerated power, *e.g.,* incorporation of a national bank by Congress is a useful instrument for pursuing the fiscal powers of Congress. *McCulloch v. Maryland* (1819).

(2) A federal statute authorizing civil commitment of mentally ill and sexually dangerous federal prisoners beyond the date of their scheduled release was held 7–2 to be a constitutional exercise of Congress' power under the Necessary and Proper Clause. The Court, per Justice Breyer, reasoned that the Clause is satisfied if the "statute constitutes a means that is rationally related to the implementation of a constitutionally enumerated power." Citing *McCulloch*, the Court said Congress has "large discretion" in its choice of means. The civil commitment statue is reasonably related to Congress' power to act as a reasonable federal custodian; it is justified by the same enumerated power that justifies the creation of a federal criminal statute and provision of imprisonment of the convicted individual. Nor were the links between the statute and the enumerated Article I power too attenuated. The argument that the Necessary and Proper Clause permits no more than a single step between the enumerated power and an Act of Congress was rejected. The civil commitment authority "is a reasonably adapted and narrowly tailored

means of pursuing the Government's legitimate interest as a federal custodian in the responsible administration of its prison system." *United States v. Comstock* (2010).

3. Inherent Powers

Consistent with the principle that this is a limited government, i.e., *a government of enumerated powers, Congress has no inherent domestic legislative powers.* Kansas v. Colorado *(1907).* This does not necessarily preclude inherent foreign affairs powers. The Court has suggested that the national government has inherent powers of external sovereignty which do not depend on the Constitution. *United States v. Curtiss–Wright Export Corp.* (1936).

4. Delegation of Powers

Congress is free to delegate legislative authority provided it has exercised the essentials of the legislative function by determining the basic legislative policy and by formulating standards to guide subsequent conduct. The courts today are very liberal regarding what will suffice as adequate standards, *e.g.,* "just and reasonable," "fair and equitable."

5. The Tenth Amendment

The Tenth Amendment provides that, "[t]he powers not delegated to the United States by the Constitution, nor prohibited by it to the States, are reserved to the States respectively, or to the people." Only powers that the States had prior to ratification in 1789 are deemed to be "reserved." *U.S. Term Limits v. Thornton* (1995). The power delegated to the United States by the Constitution includes those specifically enumerated powers listed in Article I along with the implementation authority granted by the Necessary and Proper Clause. *United States v. Comstock* (2010). While the Tenth Amendment is not a substantive limitation on Congress' power to regulate private activities, *United States v. Darby* (1941), state sovereignty and the Tenth Amendment significantly limit Congress' power to regulate states. *Printz v. United States* (1997). See Ch. II, E, 2, b.

6. The Supremacy Clause

Art. VI, cl. 2, provides: "This Constitution, and the Laws of the United States which shall be made in Pursuance thereof; and all Treaties made, or which shall be made under the Authority of the United States, shall be the Supreme Law of the Land; and the Judges in every State shall be bound thereby, any thing in the Constitution or Laws of any State to the Contrary not withstanding." Under this critical clause, a constitutional exercise of the national legislative power can operate to override contrary state law. See Ch. III, A, 4.

B. Commerce Power

1. Definition

In *Gibbons v. Ogden* (1824), Justice Marshall initially defined "commerce" as "commercial intercourse," including navigation. He then broadly defined "commerce among the States" as "commerce which concerns more states than one," including those activities "which affect the states generally." But Justice Marshall noted that the federal commerce power did not extend to "the exclusively internal commerce of a state."

a. Territorial Movement

In subsequent years, the courts required a showing of movement of goods across state lines, *i.e.*, "interstate commerce." Production, mining, etc., were held antecedent to, and not part of, interstate commerce as such.

b. A Broader Commerce Power

However, as indicated below, the territorial limitation on the Clause is not indicative of the scope of Congress' commerce power, which today has been interpreted to encompass a wide range of activity.

c. The Regulatory Power

In *Gibbons*, Justice Marshall said that the power to regulate is the power to prescribe the rule by which commerce is to be governed. He described the power as plenary as to its objects; it is "complete in itself, may be exercised to its utmost extent, and acknowledges no limitations, other than are prescribed in the Constitution," subject only to political constraints.

2. Achieving Social Welfare Through the Commerce Power—A National Police Power?

Congress can regulate the use of the channels of interstate commerce and can protect instrumentalities of, and persons and things in, interstate commerce. While Congress is not given express authorization to legislate for police power purposes, i.e., to legislate on a national basis concerning the morals, health, well-being of the people, its power to "regulate" interstate commerce is plenary, is complete in itself, and is subject only to constitutional limitations. It follows that Congress can legislate to protect interstate commerce and prevent it from being misused. The courts will not probe the motive or purpose of Congress' regulation of interstate commerce. Congress, therefore, can achieve social welfare objectives by using its broad commerce powers.

a. Prohibiting Commerce

In *Champion v. Ames* (*the Lottery Case*) (1903), the Court held that the regulatory power of Congress over commerce included the power to prohibit the interstate shipment of lottery tickets. Congress could act for the purpose of preventing interstate commerce from being used to further a moral evil; it could decide that such commerce should not be "polluted."

b. Pretext Principle

But in *McCulloch*, Justice Marshall had indicated that if Congress uses its delegated powers as a pretext for regulating activities properly in the domain of the states, the Court would hold the law unconstitutional. In *Hammer v. Dagenhart* (1918), the Court held that federal regulation prohibiting the interstate transit of goods produced by child labor was an unconstitutional intrusion on state police powers and violative of the Tenth Amendment.

c. Protective Principle—The Modern View

Today, it is accepted that Congress can legislate for social welfare objectives using its commerce power. It can close the channels of interstate commerce to traffic and regulate locally to protect interstate commerce from pollution and misuse. *The Tenth Amendment, insofar as federal regulation of private activity is concerned, is a truism—anything not delegated is reserved to the states.* But if Congress exercises its delegated powers, express or implied, the Tenth Amendment is not a limitation on Congress' power to regulate private activity. Note that the Tenth Amendment is important in determining the scope of Congress' commerce power to regulate state activity. See Ch. II, E.

Examples: (1) Congressional wage and hour legislation prohibiting the interstate transit of goods produced under substandard conditions and regulating the wages and hours of employees is constitutional. *Hammer v. Dagenhart* is overruled. Since Congress can close the channels of interstate commerce, it also can regulate locally to effectuate the prohibition. Congress can also legislate to prevent unfair competition which would adversely affect interstate competition. *United States v. Darby* (1941).

(2) Congress may prohibit racial discrimination in places of public accommodation serving interstate travellers since

Congress could rationally conclude that such discrimination in service impedes interstate travel by Negroes. The fact that national police power purposes, *i.e.*, terminating racial discrimination, are accomplished by such legislation does not make the legislation an improper use of the commerce power. *Heart of Atlanta Motel, Inc. v. United States* (1964).

(3) Congress has power under the Commerce Clause to authorize states to preserve the confidentiality of reports filed in securing federal highway grants that indicate dangerous sections of the highways by prohibiting their discovery in legal proceedings. The legislation was "aimed at improving safety in the channels of commerce and increasing protection for the instrumentalities of interstate commerce." Congress could "reasonably believe" that protecting such materials would improve collection of the information, improve decision-making and "ultimately [provide] greater safety on our nation's roads." *Pierce County v. Guillen* (2003).

3. Stream of Commerce

Local activities can be regulated by Congress if they are part of the "stream" or "current" of interstate commerce. In defining interstate commerce, the Court rejected a technical inquiry into the non-interstate character of some of the incidents of the activity, focusing instead on the overall movement of which they are a part.

Example: Congress has the power to regulate the activities of local dealers in the Chicago Stockyards since the stockyards are but a throat through which the current of commerce flows from West to East. *Stafford v. Wallace* (1922).

4. Instrumentalities of Commerce

Congress has power "to regulate and protect the instrumentalities of interstate commerce, or persons or things in interstate commerce, even though the threat may come only from intrastate activities." *United States v. Lopez* (1995).

Example: The ICC can constitutionally regulate local rates of a railroad engaged in interstate commerce to prevent price discrimination against interstate commerce. The commerce power extends to all matters having "such a close and substantial relation to interstate traffic" that the regulation is appropriate to the protection of interstate commerce. *Houston, E. & W. Texas Ry. v. United States (The Shreveport Rate Cases)* (1914).

5. The Affectation Doctrine

Congress has power to regulate local activities to the extent such regulation is necessary and proper to fostering and protecting interstate commerce. The fact that the federal law has the purpose or effect of displacing state police power will not make the federal law invalid. But the fact that the federal law regulates in traditional core areas of state concern may bear on the validity of the law.

a. Regulating Local Activities

In the early years, the Court drew a sharp distinction between local activities subject only to state regulation such as manufacturing, mining and agricultural production and the "commerce" subject to congressional regulation. Such local activities were antecedent to interstate commerce. The sharp dichotomy between matters which under the Tenth Amendment were left to the states and the subjects of federal regulatory power has been termed "dual federalism." See, e.g., *United States v. E. C. Knight Co.* (1895) (Congress lacked constitutional commerce power to regulate a monopoly in the manufacture of sugar. "Commerce succeeds to manufacture, and is not a part of it.")

b. Direct–Indirect Test

Prior to the New Deal, Congress could regulate local activities having a "direct" effect on interstate commerce but not local activities having only an "indirect" or "incidental" effect on interstate commerce. This standard excluded consideration of the magnitude of the effect of local activities on interstate commerce, limiting the inquiry to the manner in which the effect was brought about.

Example: Congressional legislation regulating the hours and wages of workers in the coal mines was held unconstitutional. The Act was a regulation of production, not commerce. While strikes in coal mining might severely disrupt the flow of interstate coal and damage the national economy, the wages and hours were only an indirect, incidental cause of the effects on interstate commerce. *Carter v. Carter Coal Co.* (1936).

c. The Modern Affectation Doctrine

1) Substantial Effects

    Congress may regulate even local activity if it can rationally conclude that such activity has a substantial adverse effect on interstate commerce, regardless of whether the effect is "direct" or "indirect." The Courts defer to the congressional judgment. Again, the fact that the law has the purpose or effect of displacing state police power regulation does not make the federal law invalid.

2) Cumulative Effects

    In determining the adequacy of the effect, Congress may consider the cumulative effect of all the activities regulated even though the contribution of a particular activity may be trivial.

    Examples: (1) A farmer who grows wheat for home consumption may individually have only a trivial effect on the supply or demand for interstate wheat. However, such an effect is sufficient to include him under a federal regulation governing wheat production where Congress could reasonably determine that his production or consumption of wheat, when taken together with that of others similarly situated, has a substantial effect on the price paid for interstate wheat. *Wickard v. Filburn* (1942).

    (2) The provisions of the 1964 Civil Rights Act prohibiting racial discrimination by establishments providing lodging to transients in interstate commerce are constitutional. Record evidence established that local racial discrimination in services imposed a qualitative and quantitative burden on interstate travel of Black Americans. Congress can use reasonable means in regulating the use of the channels of interstate commerce, including regulation of local activities "which might have a substantial and harmful effect upon that commerce." The fact that Congress was legislating against a moral and social wrong does not invalidate the law. *Heart of Atlanta Motel v. United States* (1964).

    (3) Congress may prohibit racial discrimination in restaurants serving food which has traveled through

interstate commerce since Congress could rationally conclude that such discrimination causes less interstate goods to be sold, that it impedes interstate travel by Negroes and causes business to suffer generally. Even a small restaurant whose purchases of interstate goods is insignificant in itself may be regulated since the cumulative effect with others similarly situated is substantial. *Katzenbach v. McClung* (1964).

(4) A congressional statute prohibiting the use of extortionate credit transactions is within the power of Congress to regulate interstate commerce. A class of activities may be properly regulated by Congress in spite of its police power purpose without proof that the particular intrastate activity against which a sanction is laid has an effect on interstate commerce. Congress could reasonably conclude that local loansharking supports interstate crime; the courts will not consider the separate effect of the individual case. *Perez v. United States* (1971).

d. Restricting the Commerce Power

But the Court has indicated that there are limits to the congressional use of the Commerce Power. *There must be a rational basis for concluding that the regulated activity substantially affects interstate commerce. Among the factors discussed by the Court, the following appear especially relevant. First, the absence of any jurisdictional nexus between the regulated act and interstate commerce makes it more difficult to identify the requisite effect. Second, it is important to determine whether the regulated activity is economic or non-economic. While the Court has not adopted a categorical rule against aggregating the effect of non-economic intrastate activity in determining if the effect is substantial, the Court indicated that aggregation is appropriate "only where [the] activity is economic in nature." It is also likely that the causal relationship of alleged effects of non-economic activity on interstate commerce will be more closely scrutinized. Third, the absence of congressional findings of fact indicating a substantial effect makes it more difficult to evaluate Congress' judgment, although such findings are not required. Fourth, the effect must be "substantial." The causal relation of the regulated act on interstate commerce must not be attenuated or remote. The fact that the federal law regulates in areas such as criminal law, education or family law where states have historically been sovereign may bear on the reasonableness of a federal law.* United States v. Lopez *(1995);* United States v. Morrison (2000).

Examples: (1) For the first time since the New Deal, the commerce power was held inadequate to sustain a federal law. The Court held 5–4 that the Gun–Free School Zones Act, prohibiting knowing possession of firearms in a school zone, is unconstitutional. The Act did not have a jurisdictional nexus requiring that the firearms or the defendant have some connection with interstate commerce. The Court placed a new emphasis on the need for *commercial* regulation and a *substantial* effect. The possession of a gun in a local school zone is not an *economic* act that might, through repetition, substantially affect interstate commerce.

Congress had made no findings on the effect of school violence on interstate commerce. While findings are not required, their absence makes it more difficult to conclude that such a substantial effect exists. The Government argued that the use of guns in schools affects the national economy because of the substantial cost of violent crime, that violence impedes travel to unsafe places and that a less productive citizenry is produced by a handicapped educational process. The Court responded that accepting such an attenuated relationship would allow federal regulation of any activity, even in areas such as education, local law enforcement and family law where the states have historically been sovereign.

Justice Kennedy, joined by Justice O'Connor, concurring, argued that the Act is unconstitutional, given its significant interference with state sovereignty, "[a]bsent a stronger connection or identification with commercial concerns that are central to the Commerce Clause."

Justice Breyer, joined by Justices Stevens, Souter and Ginsburg, dissenting, stressed that the relevant standard of review was whether Congress could have "a rational basis" for concluding that the regulated act has a "significant" effect on interstate commerce. The absence of findings only deprives the statute of some extra leeway beyond the usual deference required. Congress could rationally conclude that gun-related violence near the schools, through its effect on education, has a significant effect on economic activity. Violence around the schools "is a commercial, as well as a human, problem." The effect of federal law on state regulation does not affect the validity of the federal law. *United States v. Lopez* (1995).

(2) The Court held 5–4 that a section of the Violence Against Women Act providing a federal civil remedy for victims of gender-motivated violence is unconstitutional. There was no jurisdictional element limiting the reach of the statute. Gender-motivated crimes of violence are not economic activity. While Congress had made extensive findings to support its conclusion that gender-motivated violence substantially effects interstate commerce such findings are not determinative on the courts. The Court rejected the government's reasoning that relied on a causal chain from the occurrence of a violent crime "to every attenuated effect upon interstate commerce." The regulation of intrastate crime that is not directed at interstate commerce is the province of the states. "The Constitution requires a distinction between what is truly national and what is truly local."

The dissent stressed the extensive congressional record documenting the effects of violence against women on interstate commerce and the need for judicial deference to congressional findings of a substantial adverse effect. The dissent suggested that the Court was substituting "a new criterion of review" for that used in the post-New Deal cases. The dissent also rejected "the formalistic economic/noneconomic distinction," which it claimed had been rejected in *Wickard v. Filburn* and argued that the use of traditional state concerns as a limitation on Congress' plenary commerce power had been disapproved in *Darby*. *United States v. Morrison* (2000).

e. Affectation After *Lopez* and *Morrison*

1) If Congress uses its commerce power to regulate local intrastate activity that is "economic" or "commercial," the courts are likely to adopt the deferential approach to the Affectation Doctrine used from the New Deal to *Lopez* and Morrison. [See Ch. II, B, 5, c].

Example: A debt restructuring agreement executed in Alabama by Alabama residents is "a contract evidencing a transaction involving commerce" under the Federal Arbitration Act (FAA). "Involving commerce" means "affecting commerce." Congress' power " 'may be exercised in individual cases without showing any specific effect upon interstate commerce' if in the aggregate the economic activity in question would represent a general practice . . . subject to federal control." There was a "sufficient nexus with interstate commerce" to make the local debt restructuring agreement enforceable under the FAA. First, the local builder Alafabco engaged in interstate business using loans documented in the agreements. Second, the restructured debt was secured by Alafabco's assets, including goods assembled from out-of-state parts and raw materials. Third, the economic transactions involved commercial lending, which has a broad impact on the national economy and which Congress has power to regulate under the Commerce Clause. *Citizens Bank v. Alafabco, Inc.* (2003).

2) "*Wickard* [*v. Filburn,* Ch. II, B, 5, c,] thus establishes that Congress can regulate purely intrastate activity that is not in itself 'commercial,' in that it is not produced for sale, if it concludes that the failure to regulate that class of activity would undercut the regulation of the interstate market in that commodity." *Gonzales v. Raich* (2005).

Example: The federal Controlled Substances Act (CSA) provisions which prohibit the cultivation and use of marijuana produced and consumed locally, even when in compliance with California law authorizing the use of marijuana for medicinal purposes, are a constitutional exercise of Congress' commerce power. Precedent "establishes Congress' power to regulate purely local activities that are part of an economic 'class of activities' that have a substantial effect on interstate commerce." The Court stressed the particular relevance of *Wickard v. Filburn.* "Like the farmer in *Wickard,* respondents are cultivating, for home consumption, a fungible commodity for which there is an established, albeit illegal, interstate market." Just as in *Wickard,* "Congress had a rational basis for concluding that leaving home-consumed marijuana outside federal control would similarly affect price and market conditions." It is likely that the high demand in the interstate market will draw local marijuana into the interstate market. The Court cited the enforcement difficulties in distinguishing marijuana grown locally from that produced elsewhere and concerns that "legal" marijuana could be diverted into illegal channels, for concluding "that Congress had a rational basis for believing that failure to regulate the intrastate manufacture and possession of marijuana would leave a gaping hole in the CSA."

Unlike *Lopez* and *Morrison* where the challenge was directed at a particular statute or provision which "fell outside Congress' commerce power in its entirety," in the present case the challenge seeks to excise a particular application "of a concededly valid statutory scheme (ie., the CSA)." Further, unlike *Lopez* and *Morrison*, "the activities regulated by the CSA are quintessentially economic" because it is "a statute that regulates the production, distribution and consumption of commodities for which there is an established, and lucrative, interstate market." Medicinal marijuana was part of the larger "class of activities" covered by the CSA. While the possession and consumption of medicinal marijuana was in accordance with California state law, the federal regulation was valid under the Supremacy Clause.

Justice Scalia, concurring, distinguished between the regulation of intrastate *economic* activities that substantially affect interstate commerce and the regulation of *noneconomic* intrastate activities that may be necessary and proper to effectuate a more general regulation of interstate commerce. Scalia writes that "Congress may regulate even non-economic local activity if that regulation is a necessary part of a more general regulation of interstate commerce" and "the relevant question is simply whether the means chosen are 'reasonably adapted' to the attainment of a legitimate end under the commerce power."

Justice O'Connor, joined by Chief Justice Rehnquist and Justice Thomas dissenting, again warned of the federal encroachment on state sovereignty and stressed the importance of the role of states as laboratories. The dissent argues that the Court's reliance on the fact that marijuana use is part of a larger interstate regulatory scheme provides Congress with a "perverse incentive to legislate broadly pursuant to the Commerce Clause— nestling questionable assertions of its authority into comprehensive regulatory schemes—rather than with precision." It makes *Lopez* "nothing more than a drafting guide." O'Connor adds that the Court's definition of economic activity is far too broad and "threatens to sweep all productive human activity into federal regulatory reach." Unlike the Court, the dissent argues this case is indistinguishable from *Lopez* and *Morrison* because of the tenuous link between the noneconomic acts of production and use of medicinal marijuana and interstate commerce.

3) Regulating Inactivity

However, the Court arguably limited Wickard *by placing a restriction on Congress' Commerce Clause power to regulate "intrastate activities." Five justices would hold that Congress does not have the power under the Commerce Clause to require individuals to engage in commerce on the basis that their abstaining from entering into the marketplace affects interstate commerce. The precedential value of these opinions is unclear.*

Example: The Patient Protection and Affordable Health Care Act (ACA) contains a provision, known as the "individual mandate" that requires any nonexempt individual who is not already covered by government or employer health insurance to purchase a "minimum essential" plan in the private market. If an individual fails to purchase a plan in a statutory time period, he is required to pay a "shared responsibility payment"—a "penalty" assessed with his federal taxes. The Court held that the individual mandate is a constitutional exercise of the taxing power. See Ch. II, C, 5.

Chief Justice Roberts announced the judgment of the Court. In one part of his opinion not joined by any of the other justices, he concluded that the individual mandate was not a constitutional exercise of the commerce power. The Chief Justice reasoned that the individual mandate "does not regulate existing commercial activity," but instead "compels individuals to become active in commerce by purchasing a product, on the grounds that their failure to do so affects interstate commerce." Compelling "individuals to become active in commerce by purchasing a product, on the grounds their failure to do so affects interstate commerce" would make "countless decisions an individual could potentially make within the scope of federal regulation." It "would fundamentally change the relationship between citizens and the federal government." Even *Wickard*, considered the "most far reaching example of the commerce clause" dealt with economic activity, i.e., the farmer was actively growing wheat. If the government's reasoning were applied to *Wickard*, it would allow Congress to impermissibly "command those not buying wheat to do so" on the grounds that "the aggregated decisions of some consumers not to purchase wheat have a substantial effect on the price of wheat, just as decisions not to purchase health insurance have on the price of insurance."

Additionally, the government's argument that the near certainty that an individual will at some point enter the health care marketplace does not provide a justification to compel the purchase of health care. While Congress can use the future effect of economic activity on commerce to justify a regulation, it cannot anticipate that activity itself in order to regulate individuals not currently engaged in it. The fact remains that "most of those regulated by the individual mandate are not currently engaged in any commercial activity involving health care." Differentiating the case from *Gonzales v. Raich*, where the Court upheld "comprehensive legislation to regulate the interstate market in marijuana," the Chief Justice argued that *Raich* "did not involve the exercise of any 'great substantive and independent power,' of the sort at issue here." Instead, "it concerned only the constitutionality of 'individual applications of a concededly valid statutory scheme.' "

Justice Kennedy, joined by Justices Scalia, Thomas, and Alito wrote separately. Without concurring in Chief Justice Roberts' opinion, they agreed that the individual mandate does not fall within Congress' Commerce Clause power. The Commerce Clause "is not carte blanche for doing whatever will help achieve the ends Congress seeks by the regulation of commerce." Although purchasing insurance is commerce, "one does not regulate commerce that does not exist by compelling its existence." Fundamentally, people targeted by the mandate "do not purchase" any items in the marketplace, and therefore cannot be defined as participants simply because there is a possibility they will become participants in the future. "If every person comes within the Commerce Clause power of Congress to regulate by the simple means that he will one day engage in commerce, the idea of a limited government power is at an end." The Justices distinguished this case from *Gonzales v. Raich* by arguing that in *Raich*, "growing and possession prohibitions were the only practicable way of enabling the prohibition of interstate traffic in marijuana to be effectively enforced;" whereas here, there are many other ways outside of the individual mandate by which the Act's goals could be achieved. Furthermore, the individual mandate, unlike *Raich* involved "the expansion of federal power into a broad new area."

Justice Ginsburg, joined by Justices Sotomayor, Kagan, and Breyer, dissented from Chief Justice Roberts opinion with respect to the Commerce Clause, finding instead that "the uninsured, as a class, substantially effect interstate commerce," and thus the ACA is an appropriate exercise of Congress' Commerce Clause power. Emphasizing that "Congress' authority under the Commerce Clause is dependent upon 'practical' considerations," Justice Ginsburg argued that, not only did Congress have "a rational basis for concluding that the uninsured, as a class, substantially affect interstate commerce," based on the "billions of dollars of healthcare products and services" the uninsured consume every year, but also that Congress "acted reasonably in requiring uninsured individuals, whether sick or healthy, either to obtain insurance or pay the specified penalty." The failure of the uninsured to pay for their health care costs "drives up market prices, foists costs on other consumers and reduces market efficiency and stability." Given the far reaching effect that refusing to purchase insurance has on interstate commerce, "the decision to forgo insurance is hardly inconsequential or equivalent to 'doing nothing'; it is, instead, an economic decision Congress has the authority to address under the Commerce Clause." The rationale used by the majority that the individual mandate regulates "economic inactivity" is not a reason to strike down the ACA, because Congress "delineates the boundaries of the market the Legislature seeks to regulate." Nothing in the Constitution limits Congress to "regulating those actively engaged in commercial transactions." Justice Ginsburg criticized Chief Justice Roberts' argument by emphasizing that "[e]veryone will, at some point, consume health-care products and services." Accordingly, the Court's prior precedent in this area "acknowledge Congress' authority, under the Commerce Clause, to direct the conduct of an individual today . . . because of a prophesized future transaction." *National Federation of Independent Business v. Sebelius* (2012).

f. Narrowing Construction

In order to avoid the constitutional problem indicated in *Lopez* and *Morrison*, the court may give a federal statute a narrow reading.

Examples: (1) The Court declined to read the federal arson statute, covering any building "used in interstate or foreign commerce or in any activity affecting interstate or foreign commerce," to reach an owner-occupied private residence. Congress had not clearly conveyed an intent to make such a significant change in the federal-state balance in the prosecution of crimes. The narrow reading was supported by "the interpretive rule that constitutionally doubtful constructions should be avoided where possible." *Jones v. United States* (2000).

(2) The Court held that a federal agency interpretation of the Clean Water Act conferring federal authority over an abandoned sand and gravel pit containing water that served as a habitat for wild birds exceeded the power conferred by Congress. "[W]here an otherwise acceptable construction of a statute would raise serious constitutional problems, the Court will construe the statute to avoid such problems unless such construction is plainly contrary to the intent of Congress." *Solid Waste Agency of Northern Cook County v. Army Corps of Engineers* (2001).

C. The Taxing Power

*Art. I, § 8 provides that "Congress shall have power to lay and collect taxes, duties, imposts, and excises, to pay the debts and provide for the common defense and general welfare of the United States * * *." While this textual authority gives Congress the power to raise revenue, it is a fiscal power and not an independent source of regulatory power. Congress can, of course, impose a tax if it is a necessary and proper means of achieving a granted regulatory power. And, taxes do not lose their character as taxes because of an incidental regulatory motive or effect. However, a taxing measure which betrays on its face penalizing features loses its character as a tax and becomes a regulatory penalty not authorized under the fiscal taxing power.*

1. Objective Constitutionality

This doctrine, sometimes called the doctrine of judicial obtuseness, permits the Court to uphold taxing measures by focusing only on the portions of the legislation which disclose a taxing purpose while ignoring other manifest regulatory features.

Example: The Court upheld a $0.10 per lb. tax on colored oleo but taxing white oleo at a rate of only $0.0025 per lb. The motive of the statute was clearly to give the dairy industry's butter a competitive advantage over colored oleo. However, by just looking at the four corners of the statute, the Court, using the doctrine of objective constitutionality, upheld the statute. *McCray v. United States* (1904).

2. The Penalty Doctrine

A taxing measure with the characteristics of regulation and punishment must be judged as a penalty, and not a tax. Note that the law may still be constitutional as a means of achieving one or more of the regulatory powers, *e.g.,* under the Commerce Clause. The constitutional problem arises only where Congress does not have power to regulate the activity that is taxed.

While the Court today is less willing to probe the congressional purpose, it will look for facial features extraneous to any tax need. It will consider: (1) the amount of the tax; (2) the consequences of a failure to pay; (3) scienter requirements; (4) the identity of the administering authority; and (5) the detail of the scheme or administration.

Example: The Federal Child Labor Tax imposing a heavy tax on employers using child labor was held an invalid penalty rather than a tax. Among other regulatory features was the provision that the employer would be liable only if he knew that a child was under the proscribed age limits. The Court held that scienters are associated with penalties and not with taxes. *Bailey v. Drexel Furniture Co.* (1922).

3. Modern Trend

The modern judicial trend is to accept any tax as a valid taxing measure if it purports to be and is, on its face, a revenue-producing measure.

Examples: (1) A tax on persons engaged in the business of gambling, having a regulatory effect but producing revenue, even though negligible in amount, was held to be a valid tax. Filing and disclosure provisions were held to be reasonable regulatory features incidental to effectuation of the tax. *United States v. Kahriger* (1953).

(2) The individual mandate provision of the Affordable Care Act of 2010 (ACA), requiring individuals to purchase insurance or pay a "shared responsibility payment," was held constitutional by the Court (5–4) as an exercise of Congress' taxing power. (See Ch. II, B, 5 on the rejection of the commerce power justification). Chief Justice Roberts, joined in part by Justices Ginsburg, Sotomayor, Breyer, and Kagan, concluded that while the individual mandate was labeled in the statute as a "penalty" and was defended by the Government primarily as a

regulation requiring individuals to purchase insurance, it could be read as a tax. The Chief Justice began by citing the basis for adopting the alternative interpretation. "If a statute has two possible meanings, one of which violates the Constitution, courts should adopt the meaning that does not do so." While the statute could be read as ordering individuals to buy insurance, it was "fairly possible" to read it "as imposing a tax on those who do not buy that product." The exaction "looks like a tax in many respects." It is paid to the Treasury when taxpayers file their tax returns. It doesn't apply to individuals who do not pay taxes because of low income. For taxpayers, the taxable amount reflects tax factors such as taxable income, number of dependents, and joint filing status. The payment requirements are in the Internal Revenue Code and are enforced by the IRS. And it has "the essential feature of any tax: it produces at least some revenue for the Government. *United States v. Kahriger.*"

The fact that Congress labeled the exaction as a penalty is not determinative. Rather the Court had adopted a "functional approach" in constitutional interpretation. "[F]or most Americans the amount due will be for less than the price of insurance," making it a "reasonable financial decision" for an individual to choose to pay the tax and not buy insurance. Additionally, "the individual mandate contains no scienter requirement" and provides no criminal sanction or penalty for the refusal to buy health insurance. While the ACA attempts to influence individuals to buy insurance, this does not mean that it cannot be a valid exercise of the taxing power. The ACA does not make the failure to buy insurance unlawful. It is estimated that some four million people would choose to pay the "penalty" rather than buy health insurance; Congress did not make them "outlaws." The imposition of a tax "leaves an individual with a lawful choice to do or not to do a certain act, so long as he is willing to pay a tax levied on that choice."

Justices Scalia, Kennedy, Thomas, and Alito, dissenting, argued that the penalty imposed by the individual mandate is not a constitutional tax. Arguing that the actual issue "is not whether Congress had the power to frame the minimum-coverage provision as a tax, but whether it did so," the dissent said, "there is simply no way, 'without doing violence to the fair meaning of the words used,' to escape what Congress enacted." The difference between a tax and a penalty is that "a tax is an enforced contribution to provide for the support of government," while a penalty, "is an exaction imposed by statute as punishment for an unlawful act." This case is the latter. Not only did Congress refer to the mandate as a penalty eighteen times in the Act, but the Act requires "every 'applicable individual shall . . . ensure that the individual . . . is covered under minimum essential coverage' " or pay a penalty for "violation of the law." Additionally, even though the "penalty is assessed and collected by the IRS, [it]is administered both by that agency and the Department of Health and Human Services." The Department of Health and Human Services is also responsible for defining "the substantive scope of the penalty." Additionally, it is not dispositive that the ACA "penalty" contains no scienter requirement; "[p]enalties for absolute-liability offenses are commonplace." Finally, "the mandate and penalty are located in Title I of the Act, its operative core, rather than where a tax would be found—in Title IX." For these reasons, "to say that the Individual Mandate merely imposes a tax is not to interpret the statute but to rewrite it." The individual mandate is in effect just what Congress labeled it, a penalty. *National Federal of Independent Business v. Sebelius* (2012).

4. Self–Incrimination

a. While disclosure requirements may not make a tax into a penalty, such provisions may violate the privilege against self-incrimination.

b. Where the information required would be a significant link in the chain of evidence tending to establish guilt, presenting a "real and appreciable" and not merely an "imaginary and unsubstantial" danger of self-incrimination, the Fifth Amendment is violated and the taxpayer need not provide the information. *Marchetti v. United States* (1968).

D. The Spending Power

Congress is expressly empowered to spend for the general welfare. While this does not permit Congress to regulate for the general welfare, it does authorize expenditures for any general welfare purpose. The Spending Power is a fiscal, not a regulatory power. Nevertheless, Congress can attach reasonable conditions to its grant of money. The Court has set forth four restrictions on Congress' spending power: (1) the spending must be for a general welfare purpose; (2) any condition must be unambiguous; (3) conditions must be related "to the federal interest in particular national projects or programs;" and (4) it must not infringe on any other constitutional provision. South Dakota v. Dole (1987).

1. General Welfare

a. Under the Necessary and Proper Clause, Congress can spend for the purpose of achieving any of its delegated regulatory powers.

b. But the Spending Clause is an independent source of fiscal power authorizing Congress to spend for general welfare objectives. General Welfare is not limited to the specific objectives specified in the Art. I, § 8 regulatory powers but includes all matters of national concern. Today, the Court defers substantially to Congress in determining the scope of the general welfare.

2. Reasonable Conditions

In implementing this spending power, Congress may impose any reasonable conditions upon the states as a prerequisite for participation in federal spending programs. While a condition that is totally unrelated to any federal interest in the program might be illegitimate, this limitation has little practical significance today given the judicial deference accorded congressional spending measures.

3. Constitutional Limitations

"Constitutional provisions may provide an independent bar to the conditional grant of funds." *South Dakota v. Dole* (1987).

a. The Tenth Amendment has historically been a barrier to a plenary exercise of the congressional spending power. *See United States v. Butler* (1936) (federal law providing grants to farmers paid for by a tax on processors, for the purpose of raising farm prices, held to be unconstitutional infringement on state power). Today, the Tenth Amendment is generally viewed as only as a truism since grantees remain free to reject the federal grant and its attached conditions. While there is inducement to participate, this is not the equivalent of coercion.

b. *However, the Court has noted that the financial inducement offered by Congress might, under particular circumstances, be so coercive as to pass that point at which "pressure turns into compulsion." South Dakota v. Dole (1987).* Until 2012, this limitation was more theoretical than real. See Ch. II, D, 2, c.

   Examples: (1) The Court upheld a tax on employers under the Social Security Act to be used for payment of unemployment compensation to employees against a claim that the legislation violated the Tenth Amendment on the ground that Congress may spend money to avoid the severe national consequences of unemployment. *Chas. C. Steward Machine Co. v. Davis* (1937).

(2) An act of Congress which authorized the withholding of a percentage of federal highway construction funds from states where the drinking age was under 21 is a valid exercise of the spending power; the Twenty-first Amendment granting the states control over importation and sale of liquor and the structure of the liquor distribution system is not, as South Dakota contended, an independent constitutional bar to the conditional grant of federal funds. Although in some situations financial inducements might be so coercive as to constitute compulsion, all South Dakota would lose if it did not comply was 5 percent of the funds otherwise obtainable under the highway grant program. The coercive argument was "more rhetoric than fact." Even if Congress lacked the power to impose a national minimum drinking age directly, the federal statute's relatively mild encouragement to the states to enact a higher minimum drinking age than they would otherwise choose was a valid use of the spending power. *South Dakota v. Dole* (1987).

(3) Congressional legislation authorizes states to impose a surcharge on radioactive wastes generated in other states. The Secretary of Energy then collects a portion of the surcharge which is placed in an escrow account which is used to provide grants to states meeting federal deadlines in establishing their own waste disposal sites. The grant of funds to states meeting the "reasonable condition" of developing waste facilities is a constitutional exercise of Congress' spending powers. The fact that the funds are placed in an account separate from the federal treasury and that the states themselves determine whether they will impose the surcharge or collect a share of the escrowed funds, does not change this result. The spending power does not "mandate a particular form of accounting;" Congress determines the structure of federal spending. *New York v. United States* (1992).

(4) A federal statute making it a crime to offer bribes to city or state officials working for entities receiving at least $10,000 in federal funds is not facially unconstitutional even though the statute does not require proof of a connection between the federal funds and the bribe. A jurisdictional hook is not required. Under the Spending Clause, Congress can appropriate money and, under the Necessary and Proper Clause, it has authority to assure that taxpayer dollars are spent to promote the general welfare. The criminal provision is a rational, narrowly-drawn means of safeguarding the integrity of federal monies. *Sabri v. United States* (2004).

c. *In 2012, for the first time, the Court held a federal law violated the Spending Clause. The condition was found to be so coercive that pressure had turned into compulsion. While Congress can create incentives for States to act, Congress cannot force the States to implement a federal regulation. Congress may not withhold previously authorized federal funds for a program, producing a massive effect on a state budget, if a State refuses to adopt a new federal program.* National Federation of Independent Business v. Sebelius (2012).

Example: The Court held 7–2 that a section of the Medicaid expansion in the Affordable Care Act of 2010 was unconstitutional as a coercive use of the congressional spending power. The Medicaid expansion required States to expand their Medicaid programs by 2014 to cover all individuals under the age of 65 with incomes below 133 percent of the poverty line and established a new health benefits' package, which States must provide to Medicaid recipients. However, it also granted authority to the Secretary of Health and Human Services to penalize states and withhold all Medicaid funding, not just funding for the expansion, if a state did not comply with the new Medicaid provisions. The Court found this "financial inducement is much more than 'relatively mild encouragement'—it is a gun to the head." The Chief Justice, writing for the Court, stated: "The threatened loss of over 10 percent of a State's overall budget . . . is economic dragooning that leaves the States with no real option but to acquiesce in the Medicaid expansion." The expansion was not simply a modification of the existing program that the states had agreed to; it was an element in a new plan of universal health coverage.

While the Court held 7–2 that Congress could not withhold existing Medicaid funds for failing to comply with the expansion, the Court held 5–4 that the provision could be severed and the rest of the Medicaid expansion upheld—as Congress had provided in the ACA. Thus, existing funds may be withheld for not complying with the existing Medicaid program and funds provided under the expansion may be withheld if a State does not comply with the expansion's requirements—it is the taking of existing funds for not complying with the new requirements that is unconstitutional. States remain free to accept the new Medicaid funding subject to the ACA conditions.

A joint opinion by Justices Scalia, Thomas, Kennedy, and Alito concurred in striking down the Medicaid expansion, finding it exceeded the federal Spending Power by coercing the states to accept new policy. "Coercing States to accept conditions risks the destruction of the 'unique role of States in our system.'" If such coercion was allowed, Congress could "dictate policy in areas traditionally governed primarily at the state or local level." But they would have invalidated all of the ACA expansion. The Court should not "solve a constitutional problem by rewriting the Medicaid Expansion so as to allow states that reject it to retain their preexisting Medicaid funds."

Justice Ginsburg and Sotomayor, dissenting, saw the expansion of Medicaid as an amendment of existing law, so that any conditions the federal government attaches to the expansion are legitimately attached to the entire program. The Court has previously always deferred to the federal government's conditional funding to the states, and the conditions here are reasonably related to the "general welfare." There is no limit on how Congress can amend its own legislation, and Medicaid has previously been modified or amended dozens of times; no constitutional issues were raised for the withholding of all Medicaid funds if a State did not comply with the amended law. The rule in this case is difficult for Congress to follow in the future because it is unclear what makes the expansion provisions a new program and not an amended program such that withholding funding is coercion on the States. *National Federation of Independent Business v. Sebelius* (2012)

4. Spending as a Contract: Explicit Conditions

Conditions imposed in federal grants are akin to contractual provisions and must be clear and unambiguous to be enforced. The conditions must be clearly delineated so that the states can make informed choices as to whether or not they will accept the grant subject to the condition. Language not sufficiently clear is to be considered only as a policy statement and not as a binding commitment on the part of the state.

Examples: (1) The words in the federal Developmentally Disabled Bill of Rights Act calling for "appropriate treatment" in "the setting that is least restrictive of personal liberty" was held to be only part of congressional findings of fact and policy statements and not to create a statutory right to treatment conditioning grants to the state made under the Act. *Pennhurst State School and Hosp. v. Halderman* (1981).

(2) The Family Educational Rights and Privacy Act, which conditions federal grants to state agencies and educational institutions upon compliance with requirements concerning the privacy of student records, did not create individual, enforceable rights. Congress must clearly intend to create such rights. "[W]here the text and structure of a statute provide no indication that Congress intends to create new individual rights, there is no basis for a private suit, whether under § 1983 or under an implied right of action." *Gonzaga University v. Doe* (2002).

E. Intergovernmental Immunities

Intergovernmental immunities deals with two problems: (1) the power of the state or local government to tax or regulate federal activities; and (2) the power of the federal government to tax or regulate the states. When dealing with questions in this area, remember that the Supremacy Clause (Art. VI) runs in one direction. It makes the Constitution "and the Laws of the United States" made pursuant to it the Supreme Law of the Land. This suggests that the national government has greater immunity from state taxation and regulation and greater power to tax and regulate state functions.

1. State Taxation and Regulation

a. The state cannot directly tax or regulate the federal government or a federal instrumentality. A state tax, for example, is unconstitutional if the legal burden of the tax falls on the federal government. The power to tax is the power to destroy. *McCulloch v. Maryland* (1819) (state tax on notes issued by the Bank of the United States held unconstitutional).

b. Nor can a state discriminate against the federal government or those who deal with the federal government absent proof that there are significant differences between the classes that justify the inconsistent treatment.

> *Example:* An operating subsidiary of a national bank is "subject to [federal Office of the Comptroller of the Currency] superintendence, and not to the licensing, reporting and visitorial regimes of the several States in which the subsidiary operates." While federally chartered banks are subject to generally applicable state laws, the Court reaffirmed *McCulloch* in protecting national banks from excessively burdensome and duplicative state regulations. State regulation which would significantly impair or impede activity (e.g., mortgage lending) of a national bank's operating subsidiary is similarly barred by federal supremacy. The Tenth Amendment expressly does not reserve any power delegated by the Constitution to Congress. Therefore, it is not an obstacle to congressional regulation of subsidiaries of national banks which is authorized under the Necessary and Proper Clause. *Watters v. Wachovia Bank, N.A.* (2007).

2. Federal Taxation and Regulation

a. Federal Taxation of States

If a federal tax imposed on state activities is non-discriminatory, *i.e.*, not applicable only to the state, is based on a fair return for federal benefits and the cost is not excessive in light of the benefits provided the state, the federal tax will be upheld. *Massachusetts v. United States* (1978) (federal tax on all civil aircraft using federal facilities, applied to state police aircraft, held constitutional).

b. Federal Regulation of States

The principle of state sovereignty reflected in the Tenth Amendment imposes some limitation on the power of Congress to regulate the State itself. However, the scope of the Tenth Amendment-state sovereignty limitation on Congress' regulatory power is unclear.

1) In *National League of Cities v. Usery* (1976), the Court held 5–4 that Congress' power to regulate the states under the commerce power was limited by principles of state sovereignty. Subsequent cases held that, under the Tenth Amendment, a federal law must satisfy each of three requirements.

"First, there must be a showing that the challenged statute regulates 'States as States.' Second, the federal regulation must address matters that are indisputably 'attributes of state sovereignty.' And third, it must be apparent that the States' compliance with the federal law would directly impair their ability 'to structure integral operations in areas of traditional functions.' " *Hodel v. Virginia Surface Mining & Reclamation Ass'n* (1981).

Example: An amendment to the Fair Labor Standards Act applying minimum wage and maximum hour provisions to public employees of States and their political subdivisions violates state sovereignty. The federal law operates "to directly displace the states' freedom to structure integral operations in areas of traditional governmental functions." States must be able to structure employer-employee relations in providing traditional governmental services as an attribute of state sovereignty. The federal law interferes with the considered policy choices of state officials on how traditional public services are to be provided. *National League of Cities v. Usery* (1976).

2) In *Garcia v. San Antonio Metropolitan Transit Authority* (1985), the Court 5–4 overruled *National League of Cities*. Judicial determination of which state government functions are "traditional" or "integral" was said to be unworkable and inconsistent with principles of federalism. It is the political process, not judicial determination of what state activities must be immune from federal regulation, that protects federalist values. The judicial role is limited to compensating for possible failings in the national political process.

Example: Application of the overtime provisions of the Federal Fair Labor Standards Act to the operations of the San Antonio Metropolitan Transit Authority does not violate state sovereignty and the Tenth Amendment. There is nothing in the application of the Act to the transit authority "that is destructive of state sovereignty or violative of any constitutional provision." While Congress has placed a financial burden on states and localities, the political process has also provided financial assistance. *Garcia v. San Antonio Metropolitan Transit Authority* (1985).

a) In cases following *National League,* the courts had been unable to fashion objective criteria for identifying the essential functions of the states in our federal system.

b) *Garcia* emphasizes that it is not the function of an unelected federal judiciary to define the nature and content of the limitations that our federal structure imposes on the commerce power. It is the structure of the federal government, *e.g.,* the role of the states in the selection of the Executive and the Congress, that defines these limits.

c) The *Garcia* Court did indicate that state sovereignty does impose some process limitations on congressional regulation of the states. But such restraints, which the *Garcia* Court does not define, appear to be minimal, designed only to provide a safeguard if the political process fails, *e.g.,* a congressional effort to dictate where a state locates its capitol. *Coyle v. Smith* (1911).

d) The *Garcia* dissent argues that it is the judicial role under *Marbury* to enforce the Tenth Amendment, that federal usurpation of the traditional functions of the states undermines their role as a counterpoise to federal power and that the political process is an inadequate safeguard for federalism. The dissent contends that the courts should balance the respective interests of the states and the federal government.

3) *In* New York v. United States *(1992), the Court held that Congress cannot constitutionally force states to regulate.* To allow Congress to coerce states to regulate, rather than directly regulating itself, undermines "political accountability." *Garcia* was distinguished as involving congressional legislation that subjects "a State to the same legislation applicable to private parties."

Example: A federal law providing that a State failing to provide for disposal of radioactive waste generated in the state by a set date shall take title to the waste is unconstitutional. Congress could not constitutionally order the states to take title to the wastes and this law fares no better. "A choice between two unconstitutional coercive regulatory techniques is no choice at all. Either way, 'the Act commandeers the legislative processes of the States by directly compelling them to enact and enforce a federal regulatory program.' "

However, a provision of the federal law authorizing states having disposal sites to increase costs or deny access to waste generated in states not meeting federal deadlines is constitutional. Congress can offer states the choice of regulating an activity in a way consistent with federal standards or having the state law pre-empted by federal regulation. This is encouragement, not coercion. There is no burden on the State as a sovereign arising from its failure to regulate. *New York v. United States* (1992).

4) *In* Printz v. United States *(1997), the Court held 5–4 that the Federal Government may not "command the States' officers, or those of their political subdivisions, to administer or enforce a federal regulatory program."* But note that state courts cannot refuse to apply federal law given the Supremacy Clause. *Testa v. Katt* (1947).

Example: The provision of the Brady Act, commanding state and local law enforcement officers to conduct background checks on prospective handgun purchasers, was held unconstitutional 5–4. Absent controlling constitutional text, the Court based its conclusion on historical understanding and practice, the structure of the Constitution, and on the jurisprudence of the Court.

In the area of history and practice, the Court noted that except for a few very recent exceptions, "there is not only an absence of executive-commandeering statutes in the early Congresses, but there is an absence of them in our later history, as well."

Turning to the structure of the Constitution, the Court found among its "essential postulates" a system of "dual sovereignty." In our system of federalism, the states retained "a residuary and inviolable sovereignty." The Congress has the power to regulate individuals, not States. State governments represent and are accountable to their citizens. Allowing the Federal Government to impress into its service the officers of individual states, at no cost to itself, is inconsistent with the structure of federalism. Further, the Act transfers the power to execute laws from the President to the States in violation of the principle of separation of powers. Finally, when federal law violates state sovereignty, it is not a reasonable means under the Necessary and Proper Clause for carrying into execution the granted powers—it is not an exercise of a *delegated* power and the Tenth Amendment applies.

Turning to its prior jurisprudence, the Court relied on decisions that have "made clear that the Federal government may not compel that States to implement, by legislation or executive action, federal regulatory programs." *New York v. United States* (1992) could not be limited to "making law," rather than "enforcing" it as in the Brady Act since such a distinction is unworkable. Further, it is not compatible with state independence and autonomy that its officers be "dragooned" into administering federal law. As in *New York*, the Brady Act violates the principle of accountability since it forces state governments to shoulder the burdens of a federal regulatory problem, allowing Congress to take credit for any success, while insulating itself from any of the monetary or political costs.

The "important purposes" served by the Act and the "minimal and temporary burden" placed on state officers, urged by the dissent, are not valid considerations in evaluating the constitutionality of the law. "[W]here, as here, it is the whole object of the law to direct the functioning of the state executive, and hence to compromise the structural framework of dual sovereignty, such a balancing analysis is inappropriate." *Printz v. United States* (1997).

5) Tenth Amendment-state sovereignty concerns can also influence the interpretation of congressional legislation.

Examples: (1) The Age Discrimination in Employment Act was held not to apply to provisions of the Missouri Constitution requiring state judges to retire at age 70. Congressional intent to interfere with the state's decision requires a "plain statement" to that effect. *Gregory v. Ashcroft* (1991).

(2) A private residence could not be construed to be "currently involved in interstate commerce" in applying the federal arson statute. A broad interpretation of the arson law would make almost every building in the country susceptible to coverage which was not likely the intent of Congress and would raise severe constitutional issues. *Jones v. United States* (2000).

6) But Congress can require the States to legislate or face federal preemption. And Congress can regulate State activities, so long as it does not commandeer the States regulatory or enforcement processes.

Example: A federal statute restricting the release of personal information about licensed drivers without the driver's consent is a valid exercise of Congress' power to regulate the interstate traffic in personal information even though it imposes obligations on the States. The law does not seek to control or influence the manner in which States regulate private parties. It regulates the States as the owners of databases. *Reno v. Condon* (2000).

F. Review Questions

1. **T or F** Congress has inherent power to legislate in matters where the states separately are incapable of acting.

2. **T or F** Congress can use its granted powers, *e.g.* the commerce power, in order to achieve social welfare objectives.

3. **T or F** Congress can regulate local activities which have a substantial adverse effect on interstate commerce even if the law displaces state police powers.

4. **T or F**   Under the Affectation Doctrine, Congress can use its commerce power to regulate any local activity.

5. **T or F**   If a law purports, on its face, to be a revenue producing measure, it is a valid taxing measure.

6. **T or F**   Congress can regulate to further the general welfare.

7. **T or F**   Congress can impose reasonable conditions as a precondition to receiving federal grants.

8. **T or F**   A federal law, even if otherwise valid under the commerce power, is unconstitutional if it regulates the state itself.

9. **T or F**   Congress can use reasonable means for implementing its granted powers, even if this involves regulation of matters traditionally subject to state regulation.

10. **T or F**   Since Congress can preempt state legislation, it can also direct the states to regulate a particular subject.

11. **T or F**   States can waive Tenth Amendment-state sovereignty limitations on congressional power, thus authorizing congressional regulation that might otherwise be unconstitutional.

12. **T or F**   Congress can require State officials to enforce federal law based on the commerce power if the national interest is sufficiently important and the enforcement burden on state officials is relatively minimal.

13. Congress imposes a $.10 tax on every gallon of gas sold, the revenues to be used to make federal grants to states for energy conservation programs. States' programs which are funded must meet federally-imposed standards. Which of the following is most accurate?

    a.   The tax is an unconstitutional penalty since it is intended to discourage use of gasoline.

    b.   The law is a valid regulation for the general welfare.

    c.   These exercises of the tax and spending powers are both constitutional.

    d.   The federal law violates the Tenth Amendment since it coerces the states to conform to federal standards.

14. Assume that the lifeguards who work at the municipal beach of Magnolia Beach, State of West Jefferson, were paid the federal minimum wage, but were not paid the federal overtime rate of time and a half by Magnolia Beach. In the summer, the lifeguards there worked eight hours a day, seven days a week. The federal government contends that the Fair Labor Standards Act requires that the federal overtime rate should be paid to the lifeguards. The largest part of the municipal payroll for the tiny resort town of Magnolia Beach consists of its lifeguard salaries. If overtime has to be paid, the city contends that it might have to dissolve itself and ask for annexation by its neighbor Jackson City. If the government seeks to enforce the FLSA against the town of Magnolia Beach, does the town have a constitutional defense or must the town bankrupt itself?

III

State Power in American Federalism

■ ANALYSIS

While the national government can exercise only such powers as are expressly or impliedly delegated in the Constitution, states have inherent police power to act for the health, morals, and well-being of their citizens. When dealing with the constitutionality of state laws, therefore, the student should focus on constitutional limitations on state power. Such limitations may take the form of constitutional rights and liberties or limitations arising from the constitutional allocation of powers. The focus of this Chapter is on federalist values reflected in the Division of Powers principle.

Federalist values are reflected in the Tenth Amendment which reserves all non-delegated powers to the "States respectively, or to the people." The text of the Tenth Amendment leaves open two possible interpretations of the nature of Federalism. The majority interpretation defines Federalism in favor of the national government, arguing that a State has only such reserved powers which it had before ratification and that the source of National power is the people of the entire Nation. The minority view would enlarge State power, interpreting the Tenth Amendment to limit the national government only to powers delegated by the people of each state. All powers not delegated remain with the people of the individual States who either delegate them to the State or retain them. Where the Constitution is silent, it raises no bar to action by the States or the people of the States.

Example: In a 5–4 decision, the Court held unconstitutional a "Term Limitation Amendment" to the Arkansas state constitution limiting ballot access for congressional candidates who had already served a specified number of terms. First, the Court held that the constitutional text, history and structure impliedly divested the States of power to add to or alter the qualifications for members of Congress. Art. I, §§ 2 and 3 specify qualifications, precluding all others. While States were authorized to control the qualifications of *electors*, the Framers fixed the qualifications of *members* of Congress in the Constitution, limiting State power to effect the character of the National Legislature. Structurally, the Constitution reflects the democratic principle that the sovereign people of the United States are free to choose their own representatives.

The dissent argued that the Constitution sets only the minimum qualifications of members, leaving to the people of the States the power to determine the qualifications of their representatives. Alternatively, the dissent argued that if the Constitution does not preclude state action setting term limits, under the Tenth Amendment the States are free to act. *The people* of *each State* decided what powers to delegate to the National Government, reserving all nondelegated powers to the State or to the people of the State.

But the Court held that, even if the Constitution did not impliedly divest the States of power to impose term limits, such a power was not delegated to them by the Constitution and it is not a power reserved by the Tenth Amendment. The Tenth Amendment reserves only such powers as the States possessed prior to ratification. There was no election of representatives to Congress before ratification, therefore regulation of the qualifications of members of Congress was not reserved. In creating the Constitution, popular sovereignty was divided. *The people of the United States, acting in a new collective capacity,* created a national Congress which is responsible to the people of the United States. *U.S. Term Limits, Inc. v. Thornton* (1995).

A. State Power to Regulate Commerce

1. Establishing the Foundations

Some constitutional powers are exclusively national, *e.g.,* the power to declare war or to legislate for the District of Columbia. Other powers are shared by both the states and the federal government. If the power is concurrent, in some instances, where Congress has not acted to exclude the states, the states may regulate even though Congress, if it chose, could also legislate in the same area. In other instances, however, where Congress could act, the particular state regulation is proscribed by the constitutional grant of power to Congress.

The rationalizing principle is that where a subject of the state regulation is by its nature national or where the state regulation would place an excessive burden on national concerns, the states may not regulate in the absence of congressional authorization.

a. The Nature of the Power—Exclusive or Concurrent

1) The Commerce Power Is, at Least Partially, a Shared Power
The text of the Commerce Clause addresses only Congress' regulatory power; the text does not mention state power to regulate. The existence of a plenary power over interstate commerce in Congress is not necessarily inconsistent with the existence of state regulatory power over that commerce. *Cooley v. Board of Wardens* (1851).

2) Primacy of Federal Regulation

When a state regulation conflicts with a federal law in a shared area or impedes the achievement of the federal objectives, the federal regulation must prevail by force of the Supremacy Clause (Art. VI) which states: "This Constitution, and the Laws of the United States which shall be made in Pursuance thereof * * * shall be the supreme Law of the Land * * *."

b. **The Nature of the Subject—The Cooley Doctrine**

In the determination of whether a state regulation of interstate commerce is permissible, the Cooley *doctrine focuses on the subject of the regulation. When subjects of commerce regulation are national in nature, i.e., require a uniform system or plan of regulation, they are not amenable to state regulation.* Cooley v. Board of Wardens *(1851) (holding that, in the absence of applicable federal legislation, a state may regulate local pilotage for navigation).*

The *Cooley* doctrine is criticized for focusing excessively on the subject of the state regulation rather than the nature of the regulation, *i.e.*, its effect on interstate commerce. Nevertheless, it continues to be used occasionally as a test of the state power to regulate interstate commerce.

2. **The Modern Focus: The Dormant Commerce Clause**

The text of the Commerce Clause does not address state regulatory power. *Nevertheless, it has been held that, even when Congress is silent, the Dormant Commerce Clause itself, as interpreted by the courts, imposes some limitation on the ability of states to regulate when the state regulation affects interstate commerce.* In determining whether a state regulation is barred by the negative implications of the Dormant Commerce Clause, the course of decisional law has moved away from nominalistic tests of direct and indirect interference with commerce to a new inquiry.

Today, the student should ask two questions derived from *Pike v. Bruce Church* (1970): *(1) does the state regulation impermissibly discriminate against interstate commerce; or, (2) are the incidental burdens imposed on interstate commerce "clearly excessive in relation to the putative local benefits."* If the answer to either question is "yes," the state law is unconstitutional. It should be noted that there are a number of justices on the Court who would limit the negative implications of the Dormant Commerce Clause to state regulations that are discriminatory.

a. Rationale

1) Common Market Philosophy

The central purpose of the Commerce Clause was the avoidance of state custom barriers and other economic barriers which spawn trade rivalries and retaliation. The Constitution "was framed upon the theory that the peoples of the several states must sink or swim together, and that in the long run prosperity and salvation are in union and not division." *Baldwin v. G.A.F. Seelig, Inc.* (1935).

2) A Political Rationale

When a law is framed so that its negative impact is directed solely at out-of-state interests, "legislative action is not likely to be subjected to those political restraints which are normally exerted on legislation where it affects adversely some interests within the state." *South Carolina Highway Dept. v. Barnwell Bros.* (1938).

b. Direct and Indirect Effects

An early effort to reconcile national and local interests in regulating commerce focused on whether the state regulation imposed a "direct" or an "indirect" burden on interstate commerce. The test provided little indication of how burdens were to be classified as direct or indirect and the distinction has been abandoned.

c. The Modern Standards

1) Discrimination

a) Intentional Discrimination

A state law which has no purpose other than favouring local interests against out of state competition is unconstitutional. Simple economic protectionism is "virtually per se" invalid.

Example: A state law prohibiting the sale of milk bought out-of-state at a price lower than the price set by law for the sale of milk in the state is unconstitutional. "[W]hen the avowed purpose of the [state law], as well as its necessary tendency, is to suppress or mitigate the consequences of competition between the states," it violates the Commerce Clause. *Baldwin v. G.A.F. Seelig, Inc.* (1935).

b) **Discriminatory Means and Effects**

Even if a state regulation is intended to serve a legitimate police power interest rather than simple economic protectionism, the law must regulate even-handedly. "The statute must serve a legitimate local purpose and the purpose must be one that cannot be served as well by available nondiscriminatory means." Maine v. Taylor (1986).

(1) If a state law operates extraterritorially to control activities occurring outside the state's borders, it may be labeled discriminatory and be subjected to more stringent judicial review.

> ***Examples:*** (1) A New York law requiring liquor distillers selling to wholesalers in New York to sell at a price that is no higher than the lowest prices that it charges wholesalers in other states violates the Commerce Clause. While a state may seek lower prices for its consumers, it may not insist that producers or consumers in other states surrender competitive advantages. The New York law impermissibly regulates extraterritorially. *Brown–Forman Distillers Corp. v. New York State Liquor Auth.* (1986).
>
> (2) A state law requiring out-of-state shippers of beer to affirm that their monthly posted prices for beer sold in the state are no higher than prices for their product in bordering states, including any price inducements, violates the Commerce Clause. The statute has the practical effect of "controlling commercial activities" occurring wholly outside the state. The law also serves as a disincentive for companies doing business in the state from engaging in interstate commerce. *Healy v. The Beer Institute, Inc.* (1989).
>
> (3) A Maine prescription drug plan that sought to provide discounted prescription drugs to state residents did not violate the Commerce Clause. Under the plan, the state would

negotiate with drug manufacturers for rebates to lower the price of prescription drugs,
but any manufacturer who did not enter into
a rebate agreement would be subject to a
"prior authorization procedure" that allegedly would result in decreased revenue and
market share for those manufacturers. An
association of out-of-state drug manufacturers argued "that the rebate requirement constitutes impermissible extraterritorial regulation." But "unlike price control or price affirmation
statutes" at issue in *Healy v. Beer Institute, Inc.*,
this prescription drug plan did not "regulate
the price of any out-of-state transaction" either facially or in effect, did not force "manufacturers [to] sell their drugs to a wholesaler
for a certain price," and did not "t[ie] the
price of [Maine's] in-state products to out-of-
state prices." *Pharmaceutical Research & Mfrs.
of Am. v. Walsh* (2003).

(2) If a state law facially imposes burdens on out-of-state
interests that are not imposed on in-state interests, it is
likely to be labeled as discriminatory and be subjected to
more searching judicial review.

> ***Examples:*** (1) A state law which prohibits the importa-
> tion of wastes from out-of-state for dumping
> in local landfills while allowing local traffic
> and dumping of wastes is unconstitutional.
> "[T]he evil of protectionism can reside in
> legislative means as well as legislative ends."
> While the law serves legitimate interests of
> the state, there is no reason to discriminate
> against interstate commerce. *City of Philadel-
> phia v. New Jersey* (1978).
>
> (2) A state statute forbidding the transporta-
> tion out-of-state for sale of free-swimming
> minnows taken from waters within the state,
> but not restricting local sales, was held to

violate the Commerce Clause. While conservation of natural resources is a legitimate state purpose, states may not seek to achieve this goal by choosing discriminatory means where non-discriminatory means are available. *Hughes v. Oklahoma* (1979).

(3) Nebraska's permit system limiting out-of-state export of ground waters to states granting reciprocity for sale of its waters in Nebraska is unconstitutional. The law did not satisfy the "strictest scrutiny" applicable to facially discriminatory laws. While Nebraska has an "unquestionably legitimate and highly important" conservation and health interest in ground waters, the state failed to show that the reciprocity requirement was narrowly tailored to this end. Even if the water could be used most beneficially in another state, the reciprocity requirement could bar the sale. *Sporhase v. Nebraska* (1982).

(4) A Maine criminal statute banning the importation of live baitfish from out-of-state is constitutional. The district court finding that the law served the state's important interest in protecting the integrity of its natural resources and that alternative means would not adequately serve that interest was not "clearly erroneous." The law was not deemed economic protectionism. *Maine v. Taylor* (1986).

(5) An Ohio law awarding a tax credit against the Ohio fuel sales tax for each gallon of ethanol sold as a component of gasohol, but only if the ethanol is produced in Ohio or in a state that grants similar tax advantages to Ohio ethanol, violates the Commerce Clause. The law imposes a facial disadvantage on out-of-state sellers. Reciprocity provisions would

not justify such disparity of treatment but would enhance the discrimination by seeking more favorable treatment for Ohio-produced ethanol. The state's health and commerce justifications were merely speculative and would not justify "this plain discrimination against products of out-of-state manufacture." *New Energy Co. of Indiana v. Limbach* (1988).

(6) A Michigan Act providing that solid waste generated in another county, state, or country cannot be accepted for disposal unless authorized in the receiving county's 20 year waste disposal plan is unconstitutional. The fact that other Michigan counties were subject to restriction did not negate the discrimination against interstate commerce. Michigan failed to meet its burden of proving that its legitimate health and safety concerns could not be adequately served by nondiscriminatory alternatives. *Fort Gratiot Sanctuary Landfill, Inc. v. Michigan Department of Natural Resources* (1992).

(7) A non-profit church camp for children, most of whom were not Maine residents, brought suit under the Dormant Commerce Clause challenging a Maine property tax that provided tax exemptions for charitable institutions incorporated in the state and that operated principally for the benefit of state residents. In a 5 to 4 decision, the Court invalidated the statute holding that it was facially discriminatory. "The Maine law expressly distinguishes between entities that serve a principally interstate clientele and those that primarily serve an intrastate market, singling out camps that serve mostly in-staters for beneficial tax treatment, and penalizing those camps that do a principally

interstate business." The not-for-profit nature of the camp did not affect the Commerce Clause analysis.

The majority also found unpersuasive Maine's claims that the exemption was like a "legitimate discriminatory subsidy of those charities that focused on local concerns," or that the state was merely acting as a "market participant," purchasing charitable services. Rather, the majority concluded, "that even the smallest discrimination invites significant inroads on national solidarity." *Camps Newfound/Owatonna, Inc. v. Town of Harrison* (1997).

(8) Michigan and New York laws permitting in-state wineries to sell directly to residents while prohibiting, or significantly burdening, direct sales by out-of-state wineries constitute explicit discrimination against interstate commerce and violate the Dormant Commerce Clause. The "object and design" of the laws was to give in-state wineries a competitive advantage. While federal statutes and § 2 of the 21st Amendment grant the states broad power to regulate liquor, this power "does not allow States to ban, or severely limit, the direct shipment of out-of-state wine while simultaneously authorizing direct shipment by in-state producers." The discrimination against interstate commerce "is neither authorized nor permitted by the Twenty-first Amendment." See Ch. III, A, 4, b.

"State laws that discriminate against interstate commerce face 'a virtually *per se* rule of invalidity.' " Here, the states were not able to make the "clearest showing" that the laws "advance a legitimate local purpose that cannot be adequately served by reasonable nondiscriminatory means." Although the States claimed that the laws were necessary to prevent underage drinking and to facilitate tax collection, the Court found that there was no "concrete evidence that direct shipping of wine is likely to increase alcohol consumption by minors," that "the States can take less restrictive steps to minimize the risk that minors will order wine by mail," and that "the States have not shown that tax evasion from out-of-state wineries poses such a unique threat that it justifies their discriminatory regimes." The Court noted that it had upheld state regulations that discriminate against interstate commerce only after finding, based on concrete record evidence, that a state's nondiscriminatory alternatives will prove unworkable. The states did not meet their burden. *Granholm v. Heald* (2005).

(3) Even if a state law is evenhanded in purpose and is facially neutral between out-of-state and in-state interests, *i.e.*, it is not discriminatory in means, it may impact more severely on interstate commerce than on local commerce and be labeled discriminatory. However, if the different effect is due to the way in which the market is structured rather than the operation of the state law, the Court might not label it discriminatory. *Exxon v. Governor of Maryland* (1978) (state law prohibiting oil producers or refiners from operating retail service stations held nondiscriminatory even though almost all oil producers and refiners were out-of-state concerns; there was no competitive discriminatory effect).

Examples: (1) A North Carolina state law requiring all closed containers of apples sold in the state to bear no grade other than the U.S. grade operates to discriminate against the Washington state apple industry. The law raises the costs of doing business in North Carolina thereby depriving Washington apple dealers of an economic competitive advantage over local sellers. Washington's apple industry is deprived also of its competitive marketing advantage resulting from displaying the superior Washington state grades. Even when considered as a law to prevent consumer deception, the law fails since marketing is permitted with no grades at all, sales in closed containers would apply only to wholesalers and brokers who are knowledgeable, and Washington state grades are in fact superior to U.S. grades. Finally, there are non-discriminatory alternatives to an outright ban such as requiring U.S. grades when other grades are used or banning state grades which are not equal to U.S. grades. *Hunt v. Washington State Apple Advertising Comm'n* (1977).

(2) A Clarkstown, New York flow control ordinance requiring that all solid waste be processed at a designated transfer station before leaving the city was held to have an unconstitutional discriminatory effect on interstate commerce in the processing and disposing of wastes. First, the requirement drove up the costs of handling waste coming from outside the town. Second, for in-town wastes, the ordinances prevented everyone other than the favored local facility from competing for the processing business—"the ordinance thus deprives out-of-state businesses of access to a local market." The local interest in generating revenue to pay for the local disposal facility could not justify discrimination. Further, less discriminatory alternatives were available. *C & A Carbone, Inc. v. Clarkstown* (1994).

(3) A Massachusetts pricing order imposed a tax on all fluid milk sold by dealers to Massachusetts retailers. The proceeds from

the tax were distributed as subsidies to Massachusetts dairy farmers. The "avowed purpose" and "undisputed effect" of the pricing order was to enable higher cost Massachusetts dairy farmers to compete with lower cost dairy farmers in other states. The order operated as an unconstitutional tariff which "neutraliz[ed] the advantage possessed by lower cost out-of-state producers." While the tax applied to all milk sold, its effect on local producers was offset by the subsidy. The fact that Massachusetts consumers also were burdened by the pricing order did not deny its discriminatory effect. While the state dairy industry was facing an economic emergency, this did not justify economic protectionism. *West Lynn Creamery v. Healy* (1994).

(4) Relying on *West Lynn Creamery v. Healy*, an association of out-of-state drug manufacturers argued that a state plan to provide discounted prescription drugs to state residents discriminated against interstate commerce because the prescription drug fund "would be created entirely from rebates paid by out-of-state manufacturers and would be used to subsidize sales by local pharmacists to local consumers." The Court rejected this argument, holding that the drug plan would "not impose a disparate burden on any competitors. A manufacturer could not avoid its rebate obligation by opening production facilities in Maine and would receive no benefit from the rebates even if it did so; the payments to the local pharmacists provide no special benefit to competitors of rebate-paying manufacturers." *Pharm. Research & Mfrs. Of Am. v. Walsh* (2003).

(4) County flow control ordinances which benefit public entities over private entities, but which treat all private com-

panies the same, do not discriminate against interstate commerce for purposes of the Dormant Commerce Clause. *United Haulers Association, Inc. v. Oneida–Herkimer Solid Waste Management Authority* (2007).

Examples: (1) Oneida and Herkimer Counties enacted flow control ordinances which required that all solid waste produced in the counties would be processed at the Oneida–Herkimer Solid Waste Management Authority, a public benefit company, created by New York state. The Authority charged "tipping fees," exceeding those on the open market, which allowed the Authority to dispose of wastes and perform other functions, e.g., recycling, hazardous waste disposal. An association of private haulers and six private haulers alleged that the ordinances violated the Dormant Commerce Clause because they discriminated against interstate commerce by preventing private haulers from disposing of waste at cheaper out-of-state facilities.

The Court held 6–3 that the flow-control ordinance did not violate the Dormant Commerce Clause. Chief Justice Roberts, writing for the Court, distinguished *Carbone v. Clarkstown*, *supra*. That case involved a private facility and therefore the Court had not addressed the public-private distinction. The flow control ordinances challenged here benefitted a clearly publicly owned and operated facility which treated all private in-state and out-of-state hauling companies the same. Such flow control ordinances do not discriminate against interstate commerce for purposes of the Dormant Commerce Clause. The Chief Justice reasoned that laws favoring public businesses are less likely to be a product of economic protectionism; such laws are likely to be directed towards a number of legitimate goals.

Treating public and private entities the same "would lead to unprecedented and unbounded interference by the courts with state and local governments." Further, waste disposal is a traditional local function and courts should be particularly hesitant to interfere with such core local functions. Finally, the costs fell on the very voters who supported the laws.

Chief Justice Roberts, now writing for a plurality, went on to argue that the ordinance did not unduly burden interstate commerce under the *Pike* test. Even if the ordinance imposed an incidental burden on interstate commerce, the arguable burden would not exceed the public benefits from the laws. Flow control ordinances provide a way to finance an integrated package of waste-disposal services.

Justice Scalia, concurring in part, did not join the plurality's undue burden analysis—"the so-called 'negative' Commerce Clause is an unjustified judicial invention, not to be expanded beyond its existing domain." Under *stare decisis*, discriminatory laws violate the negative Commerce Clause. But, as the Court holds, it is not discriminatory to treat public and private entities differently since they are not similarly situated. Justice Thomas concurred only in the judgment, rejecting the "negative" Commerce Clause as lacking a basis in the Constitution and as unworkable.

Justice Alito, joined by Justices Kennedy and Stevens, dissenting, argued that *Carbone* was determinative. The ordinances in *Carbone* and in the present case were essentially identical and "[t]he public-private distinction drawn by the Court is both illusory and without precedent." The facility in *Carbone* was not really "private;" the only real difference was that title to the facility had not yet formally passed to the municipality in *Carbone*. In any case, the Court has never treated discrimination differently simply because the entity was a public business. While the Court has recognized a defense to discrimination in the Market–Participant Doctrine (see Ch. III, A, 2, d) that was inapplicable here. While Government was acting as a market participant, Government was also regulating the market.

Justice Alito challenged the Court's rationale for exempting discrimination in favor of public entities. Economic protectionism is still threatened by the government discrimination since the laws benefit local residents employed at the facility as well as local suppliers and their local workers. *United Haulers Association v. Oneida–Herkimer Solid Waste Management Authority (2007)*.

(2) The Court relied on *United Haulers* in holding 7–2 that a Kentucky tax scheme which taxes the interest on out-of-state bonds, but does not tax the interest on in-state and local bonds does not violate the Dormant Commerce Clause. Justice Souter, for the Court, reasoned that Kentucky's tax exemption, like the law in *United Haulers*, is more likely motivated by legitimate health, safety and welfare objectives rather than simple economic protectionism. Courts must be hesitant to interfere where the government engages in a traditional government function; issuing debt securities for public projects is a "quintessentially public function" with a venerable history. Such tax schemes are employed by 41 states and it is a tax scheme affirmatively supported by all of them. Since "Kentucky's tax exemption favors a traditional govern-

mental function without any differential treatment favoring local entities over substantially similar out-of-state interests," under *United Haulers* it is not "discriminatory against interstate commerce" for purposes of the Dormant Commerce Clause.

In a part of his opinion joined only by Justices Stevens and Breyer, Justice Souter claimed that the outcome was also supported by the Market Participant Doctrine. Using an expansive view of the Doctrine, Souter argued that when government acts in the dual roles of market participant and regulator, its latter role does not necessarily invalidate its actions if the regulations are aimed at creating a market in which the government is a favored participant, rather than a market which simply favors in-state private actors. Kentucky's tax scheme did not create a commercial advantage for local actors in the market but for the state and local governments. Justice Souter described a number of ways in which the differential tax scheme was "critical to the operation of an identifiable segment of the municipal financial market as it currently functions."

After holding that the tax scheme was not discriminatory under the Dormant Commerce Clause, the Court held that it would not engage in a *Pike* balancing test. "What is most significant about these cost-benefit questions is not even the difficulty of answering them or the inevitable uncertainty of the predictions that might be made in trying to come up with answers, but the unsuitability of the judicial process and judicial forums for making whatever predictions and reaching whatever answers are possible at all."

Justice Stevens concurred arguing that policies which encouraged residents to lend money to the State did not constitute a "burden" within the context of the Dormant Commerce Clause. Kentucky was not engaging in trade or business, it was merely borrowing money needed for public improvements. Justice Roberts concurred in part on the basis of *United Haulers*. Justice Scalia, concurring in part, agreed that Kentucky's tax scheme was not discriminatory and that the negative Commerce Clause was therefore satisfied. However, he found the plurality's Market Participant analysis unnecessary and he would abandon the *Pike* analysis. Justice Thomas concurred in the judgement. He would abandon the negative Commerce Clause doctrine altogether and leave the prevention of burdens on interstate commerce to Congress.

Justice Kennedy, joined by Justice Alito, dissented, arguing that the Kentucky law is discriminatory and protectionist; it is inconsistent with the national, free market objective of the Commerce Clause regardless of state's police power objectives. Here, taxing out-of-state but not in-state bonds was a clear form of discrimination that was absent from the government activity at issue in *United Haulers*. *Department of Revenue of Kentucky v. Davis* (2008).

2)   Undue Burdens—Ad Hoc Balancing
Even if a state law is held to be nondiscriminatory, it may still violate the Dormant Commerce Clause if it imposes an undue burden on interstate commerce. In determining if a non-discriminatory state regulation of interstate commerce imposes an undue burden on interstate commerce, the Court balances the local interests in maintaining the regulation against the burden on the free movement of interstate commerce. This balancing inquires into: (1) the nature and function of the regulation; (2) the character of the business involved; and (3) the actual effect on the

flow of commerce. As a result of this inquiry, a court may conclude that a state law that burdens interstate commerce may be sustained because the regulation pertains to matters peculiarly local and does not unduly infringe the national interest in maintaining freedom of commerce across state lines.

A number of justices argue that such judicial balancing of interests is improper. They argue that, if the law is nondiscriminatory, the rationale of the Dormant Commerce Clause no longer applies; that courts lack the capacity for such interest balancing; that such balancing makes the courts a superlegislature; that federalism counsels judicial restraint; and that Congress can legislate to relieve any excessive burdens on interstate commerce. This approach would limit the Dormant Commerce Clause to cases of discrimination.

a) Important State Interests
    Certain state interests receive greater weight in the balancing test, *e.g.*, health, safety, prevention of fraud, conservation of resources, regulation of highways.

b) Trade, Conservation, Environment
    A state may regulate incoming and outgoing commerce in goods pursuant to its interests in protecting the health, safety, and well-being of its citizens, including the economic well-being of citizens. But the states cannot hoard their resources or adopt laws that are essentially protectionist. It cannot use means which, while rationally designed to achieve permissible police power objectives, excessively burden the free flow of interstate commerce.

    Examples: (1) An Arizona statute requiring a grower of cantaloupes to package its produce in the state at an added cost of $200,000 was held unconstitutional. The state interest in having the produce identified with the producing state was viewed as minimal and less substantial than the cost burdens on the grower. *Pike v. Bruce Church, Inc.* (1970).

    (2) A state ban on plastic nonreturnable milk containers was held not to violate the Commerce

Clause. The statute did not discriminate between interstate and intrastate commerce, but rather prohibited all milk retailers from selling their products in plastic containers. The incidental burden imposed on interstate commerce, *i.e.*, the statute was more burdensome on the out-of-state plastics industry than the Minnesota pulp wood industry, was not excessive in light of the local benefits achieved. The state demonstrated substantial interests in promoting conservation of energy and other natural resources and easing solid waste disposal problems. Most out-of-state dairies package their products in more than one type of container and it was only minimally inconvenient to conform to the particular packaging requirements of Minnesota. *Minnesota v. Clover Leaf Creamery Co.* (1981).

(3) The Illinois Business Takeover Act, imposing restrictions on corporate takeovers (not limited to Illinois corporations), beyond those imposed by federal law, is unconstitutional. Applying a balancing test, the Court held the state law excessively burdened interstate commerce. The ability to block nationwide tender offers substantially burdened interstate commerce and "directly" regulated commerce outside the state. The state interests were deemed speculative. *Edgar v. MITE Corp.* (1982).

(4) An Indiana statute providing that, when an entity or person acquires controlling stock of an Indiana corporation having a substantial number of Indiana shareholders, the acquiring party obtains no voting rights unless the shareholders agree to give voting rights, does not violate the Commerce Clause. The law is not discriminatory since it applies to all tender offers whether or not the offeror is an Indiana resident. Since the law applies only to Indiana corporations, there is no danger of businesses being subjected to inconsis-

tent state regulation. The law does not impose an undue burden on interstate commerce since the statute is limited to Indiana corporations and is designed to protect the shareholders of such corporations, including Indiana residents, from takeovers and to prevent the corporate form from being used as a shield for unfair business dealing. *CTS Corp. v. Dynamics Corp. of America* (1987).

(5) The Michigan Motor Carrier Act, which imposes a $100 annual fee on vehicles that engage in intrastate commercial operations does not violate the Dormant Commerce Clause. Petitioners claimed that the fee was discriminatory and burdensome on interstate commerce because trucks that carry both intrastate and interstate loads engage in less intrastate business but Michigan taxes all trucks at the same rate. The Court held that the petitioners challenging the fee "failed to show that Michigan's fee, which does not seek to tax a share of interstate transactions, which focuses upon local activity, and which is assessed evenhandedly, either burdens or discriminates against interstate commerce, or violates the Commerce Clause in any other relevant way."

Because the fee only applied to intrastate transactions, the Court found that the fee "does not facially discriminate against interstate or out-of-state activities or enterprises. The statute applies evenhandedly to all carriers that make domestic journeys. It does not reflect an effort to tax activity that takes place, in whole or in part, outside the State. Nothing in [the Court's] case law suggests that such a neutral, locally focused fee or tax is inconsistent with the dormant Commerce Clause."

Further, there was "little, if any, evidence that the $100 fee imposes any significant practical burden upon interstate trade." The facts in the record revealed little to "show that the flat assessment unfairly discriminates against interstate truckers." The purpose of the law is to defray the costs of "regulating vehicular size and weight," "administering insurance requirements," and "applying safety standards." Most such costs vary per-truck or per-carrier, indicating that a per-truck assessment is fair. While the petitioners claimed that a per-mile fee would provide a better alternative, they failed to "provide the details of their preferred alternative administrative system or point to record evidence showing its practicality."

Nor did the fee fail the "internal consistency" test, which asks, "What would happen if all States did the same?" "If all States did the same, an interstate truck would have to pay fees totaling several hundred dollars, or even several thousand dollars," "[b]ut it would only have to do so because it engages in *local* business in all those States." (emphasis in original). *American Trucking Associations, Inc. v. Michigan Public Service Commission* (2005).

c) Transportation

A state may regulate traffic passing through the state in order to achieve permissible police power objectives. *State highway laws enjoy a heavier presumption of validity given the historic and local interest in highway management. But the states may not regulate where the national interest requires uniformity of regulation, nor otherwise excessively burden the movement of interstate commerce. State laws granting exceptions in favor of local interests are more closely scrutinized.* State adoption of a regulation more burdensome than that used by surrounding states also increases the likelihood of its being held unconstitutional.

Example: An Iowa statute generally prohibiting the use of 65–foot double-trailer trucks within its borders was held to impose an unconstitutional burden on interstate commerce. While the Court accords special deference to state legislative judgments regarding highway safety regulations, in the present case the state did not prove that its safety interests justified the significant burden on efficient and safe interstate transportation. Studies indicated that the 65–foot doubles are safe and that the Iowa law would severely impair trucking firms using interstate highways. The use of smaller trucks being driven through the state or larger trucks being driven longer distances to bypass Iowa increased the danger of traffic accidents. Various exemptions in the state statutory scheme benefitted only state residents while shifting to neighboring states many of the costs associated with the statutory requirement. *Kassel v. Consolidated Freightways Corp.* (1981).

d. State as Market Participant

1) *When the State acts, not as a regulator but as a participant in the marketplace, it is not subject to the ordinary constraints of the Commerce Clause. The Dormant Commerce Clause does not prohibit the state from discriminating in favor of its own citizens incident to engaging in market transactions.* It has been argued, similarly, that subsidies given to local economic interests, when funded from general revenues, do not involve the kind of regulatory burden covered by the Dormant Commerce Clause. It has been suggested that the market participation exception to the Dormant Commerce Clause principle may not extend to state discrimination in regard to natural resources which the state has not expended effort to develop, but the Court has not, thus far, adopted such an exception.

Examples: (1) A state law discriminating in the sale of cement marketed by the state (*i.e.*, preference for in-state residents) does not violate the Commerce Clause. The negative implications of the Dormant Commerce Clause do not apply when the state acts as a market participant rather than as a market regulator. The historical purposes of the Commerce Clause and respect for state sovereignty indicate that any restraint should come from Congress rather than from the courts. *Reeves v. Stake* (1980).

(2) An executive order of a mayor requiring all construction projects funded wholly with city funds or

with city and federal funds be performed by a work force at least half of which are bona fide residents of the city does not violate the Dormant Commerce Clause. Since the city acted as a market participant rather than as a regulator, the negative implications of the Commerce Clause do not apply. The impact of the law on out of state firms and residents is relevant only if the state is regulating the market. Everyone affected by the law can be said to be working for the city. Insofar as federal funds were used, federal statutes and regulations permitted the parochial favoritism in the order—Congress can exempt states from the negative implications of the Dormant Commerce Clause. *White v. Massachusetts Council of Const. Employers* (1983).

2) The more that state action impacts on persons who are not parties to the state contract, the more likely it is that the state action will be treated as a regulation.

   Example: A state statute requiring buyers of timber sold by the state to process that timber in the state violated the Commerce Clause. While the state participated in the marketplace in selling its timber, a four-justice plurality reasoned that the conditions of the statute on downstream processing constituted a regulation of the processing market. That regulation is subject to the Dormant Commerce Clause and is clearly unconstitutional. *South–Central Timber Dev., Inc. v. Wunnicke* (1984).

3) Note that even if a law survives Commerce Clause scrutiny, it may violate the Privileges and Immunities Clause of Art. IV, § 2, or the equal protection guarantee.

   Example: A Camden municipal ordinance requiring contractors and subcontractors working on public work projects to use their best efforts to employ no less than 40% Camden residents is subject to Art. IV, § 2, even if the Commerce Clause is satisfied. Art. IV, § 2's concern with interstate comity in matters of fundamental concern applies whether the state is acting as a regulator or a participant. The opportunity to seek employment with a private employer is of fundamental national concern to come within Art. IV, § 2. The case was remanded to determine if Art. IV, § 2, was violated. *United Bldg. & Constr. Trades Council v. Camden* (1984).

e. Protecting Personal Mobility Through the Dormant Commerce Clause

The Commerce Clause has been used to invalidate state restrictions on the free movement of persons into a state.

Example: A state statute making it a misdemeanor to bring an indigent person into the state was held an unconstitutional burden on interstate commerce. While the influx of indigent migrants might burden the state, the problem of indigence is a national burden which must be shared and no state can isolate itself. *Edwards v. California* (1941).

3. Interstate Privileges and Immunities

Art. IV, § 2, providing that "the Citizens of each State shall be entitled to all Privileges and Immunities of Citizens in the several States," has been interpreted as a prohibition against unreasonable discrimination against out-of-state citizens in regard to fundamental national interests. The Court employs the following test. First, is the activity in question "fundamental" in that it is sufficiently basic to the livelihood of the Nation as to be within the privileges and immunities protected by Art. IV, § 2? Second, is there a substantial reason for the discrimination? Third, does the discrimination bear a close relation to that reason, including consideration of the availability of less restrictive means?

a. The term "citizens" does not include aliens or corporations.

b. State A must treat the citizens of state B in the same way it treats its own citizens with the exception that some reasonable distinctions such as a slightly higher fishing license fee for out-of-state commercial fishermen to pay state administration and conservation costs may be justifiable.

c. A law that does not expressly discriminate on the basis of citizenship or residency may still violate Art. IV, § 2, if the "practical effect" of the law is discriminatory. But the Court has not decided whether Art. IV, § 2 prohibits any classification with the practical effect of discriminating against out-of-state residents or only "classifications that are but proxies for differential treatment against out-of-state residents." *Hillside Dairy, Inc. v. Lyons* (2003).

d. But Art. IV, § 2, does not apply to all forms of interstate discrimination. It applies only if fundamental national interests are burdened, *i.e.,* those which bear on the vitality of the Nation as a single entity.

Examples: (1) A state statute requiring preferential employment treatment of residents in oil-or-gas-related jobs was held to violate the Art. IV Privileges and Immunities Clause. Non-residents were not the peculiar source of the evil attacked, *i.e.,* high unemployment among residents. Even if non-residents were the peculiar source of the evil, the broad employment preference given *all* residents was too loosely related to the goal of aiding unemployed residents. The state's interest in the oil and gas was inadequate justification for the discrimination. *Hicklin v. Orbeck* (1978).

(2) A state's imposition of substantially higher elk-hunting license fees on non-residents than on residents was held not to violate the Art. IV Privileges and Immunities Clause. Elk hunting is not a fundamental interest, so it does not fall within the scope of the Art. IV Privileges and Immunities Clause. The distinction between residents and nonresidents is a rational means of preserving a finite natural resource. *Baldwin v. Fish & Game Comm'n of Montana* (1978).

(3) A state supreme court rule limiting bar admission to state residents violates Art. IV, § 2. The opportunity to practice law is a national "fundamental right" under the Clause given the role of lawyers in national commercial intercourse and the importance of out-of-state counsel in protecting federal rights. There was no evidence indicating nonresidents would be deficient in practice. State interests in assuring the ready availability of counsel could be satisfied by less restrictive means. *Supreme Court of New Hampshire v. Piper* (1985).

(4) A state Supreme Court rule requiring out-of-state lawyers to become permanent residents of the state in order to be admitted to the state bar violates the Art. IV, § 2, Privileges and Immunities Clause. In applying *Piper,* the Court held that it was not necessarily true that lawyers admitted in other states are less likely to respect the bar

and further its interests solely because they are nonresidents. *Supreme Court of Virginia v. Friedman* (1988).

(5) Virgin Islands' court rules requiring applicants for admission to the bar to live in the Virgin Islands for one year and to declare an intention to reside and practice law there following admission violate the Art. IV, § 2, Privileges and Immunities Clause. Applying *Piper,* the discrimination against nonresidents was not justified by any substantial state objective. Less restrictive means existed to address the problems relating to the unique nature of the legal practice in the Virgin Islands. For example, assuring the presence of counsel could be met by requiring nonresident lawyers to retain a local counsel. *Barnard v. Thorstenn* (1989).

(6) A New York tax law that allows residents to deduct alimony expenses from their taxable income while preventing nonresidents from making such deductions violates Art. IV, § 2. The right to conduct business in another state without discriminatory taxation is one of the fundamental rights protected by the Privileges and Immunities Clause. Even though alimony payments are personal rather than business expenses, the law would deny deductions even if the expense is related to New York. Since the state could not provide a substantial justification for its treatment of nonresidents, the law was held unconstitutional. *Lunding v. New York Tax Appeals Tribunal* (1998).

4. When Congress Speaks

a. Preemption

CONFLICT. Under the Supremacy Clause (Art. VI), if a state regulation of interstate commerce conflicts with a federal regulation, the state law is invalid. Conflict arises if it is impossible to comply with both federal and state law or if the state law impedes the achievement of the federal objectives.

EXPRESS PREEMPTION. In the exercise of its plenary commerce power, Congress may expressly prohibit a specific form of state regulation or may entirely preclude state regulation of the subject. Where the area is one that has traditionally been occupied by the states, the congressional intent to supersede state law must be clear and manifest.

OCCUPYING THE FIELD. In the absence of conflict or express exclusion of state regulation, the courts must determine if Congress intended to occupy exclusively a field of regulation. The courts consider: (a) the need for uniformity; (b) legislative history; (c) the pervasiveness of the federal regulatory scheme; (d) the historical dominance of national or local interest in the area; (e) the potential for conflict from dual administration; and (f) the use of a federal regulatory agency to maintain continued regulatory control of an area in determining whether Congress has preempted the field. Preemption, therefore, turns on the particular facts of each case.

Examples: (1) A state sedition law was preempted by federal sedition legislation based on the following considerations: (1) numerous federal statutes in the field were so pervasive as to compel the conclusion that Congress intended to leave no room to the states to supplement the federal legislative program; (2) the state law touched a field in which the federal interest was so dominant that enforcement of state legislation on the same subject was assumed to be precluded; and (3) the enforcement of the state sedition law presented a serious threat of conflict with the administration of the federal program. *Pennsylvania v. Nelson* (1956).

(2) A state regulation providing for the permanent cancellation of producers' entitlements to natural gas for excessive delay in extraction does not violate the Supremacy Clause. In the National Gas Act, Congress divided the field of natural gas regulation, allocating to states the regulation of the production and gathering of natural gas. This was precisely the field of state regulation at issue. The regulation does not conflict with federal law regulating interstate purchasers' cost structures since there was no showing that the state regulation impaired the federal objective of promoting production of low cost natural gas. *Northwest Central Pipeline Corp. v. State Corp. Comm'n of Kansas* (1989).

b. Legitimizing State Burdens on Commerce

In the exercise of its plenary powers, Congress may decide to permit state regulation of an area even though the state would be barred from such regulation by the Commerce Clause in the absence of such congressional authorization. But Congress must expressly manifest an unambiguous intent before a statute will be interpreted as permitting discriminatory state laws.

Examples: (1) A discriminatory state tax imposed on out-of-state but not domestic insurance companies is valid where Congress expressly authorized states regulation and taxation of interstate insurance. *Prudential Insurance Co. v. Benjamin* (1946).

(2) The Federal Agriculture Improvement and Reform Act of 1996 provides that "nothing in this Act or any other provision of law shall be construed to preempt, prohibit, or otherwise limit" California from regulating either "(1) the percentage of milk solids or solids not fat in fluid milk products sold at retail or marketed in the State of California; or (2) the labeling of such fluid milk products with regard to milk solids or solids not fat." Although the Act expressly allows California to regulate "the composition and labeling of fluid milk products," the provision does not extend to the state's pricing and pooling laws. Because the Act does not "clearly express an intent to insulate California's pricing and pooling laws from a Commerce Clause challenge," the lower court erred in dismissing such a challenge. *Hillside Dairy, Inc. v. Lyons* (2003).

(3) In a 5 to 4 decision striking down Michigan and New York laws that discriminated against out-of-state direct wine sales to consumers (see Ch. III, A, 2, c), the majority held that, although federal statutes and § 2 of the 21st Amendment "allow the States to maintain an effective and uniform system for controlling liquor" Congress did not give states "the authority to pass nonuniform laws in order to discriminate against out-of-state goods." The Court concluded: "[T]he Twenty-first Amendment does not supersede other provisions of the Constitution and, in particular, does not displace the rule that State may not give a discriminatory preference to their own producers."

The dissent, disagreeing with the Court's interpretation of federal statutes granting states broad power to regulate alcohol, argued that Congress "completely immuniz[ed] all state laws regulating liquor imports from negative Commerce Clause restraints." Although the dissenters believed the 21st Amendment did not need to be reached, they concluded that the 21st Amendment "made clear that States could regulate importation destined for in-state delivery free of negative Commerce Clause restraints." *Granholm v. Heald* (2005).

5. The Compact Clause

Art. I, § 10, cl. 3, requires that Congress consent to any agreement or compact by a state with another state or with a foreign country. This consent requirement is limited to agreements which increase the political power of the states in such a way as to potentially interfere with federal supremacy.

> *Examples:* (1) The Multistate Tax Compact does not give any member state powers beyond those a member state possesses when acting individually. Further, each state retains complete freedom to accept or reject rules of the governing commission and may withdraw from the compact at any time. There is no actual or potential interference with federal supremacy. *United States Steel Corp. v. Multistate Tax Commission* (1978).
>
> (2) State statutes authorizing regional bank holding companies to acquire in-state banks if the other state accords reciprocity does not create a compact. No mutual obligations are created and no regional authorities are established. Further, the laws do not enhance the political power of the states in the region or impact on our federal structure. *Northeast Bancorp, Inc. v. Board of Governors* (1985).

B.   State Power to Tax Commerce

State and local taxation of interstate commerce has increasingly become a subject for specialized courses. Therefore, no effort is made to survey this extensive and technical body of case law. Rather, the general principles governing the area and some of the modern applications of these principles will be provided.

The fact that a state tax burdens the free flow of interstate commerce does not necessarily mean it's unconstitutional. Interstate commerce can be made to pay its own way. In determining whether a state tax on interstate commerce is constitutional, the student should generally consider the following: (1) Is the tax discriminatory?; (2) Is the activity being taxed sufficiently related to the taxing state?; (3) Is the tax fairly related to the benefits provided the taxpayer?; and (4) Is the tax fairly apportioned in light of the local contracts and benefits received by the taxpayer? Complete Auto Transit, Inc. v. Brady *(1977). Remember, Congress has plenary commerce power to determine the permissible extent of state taxation.*

1. General Principles

a. Concurrent Power

Not all state taxation of interstate commerce is impermissible. Interstate commerce can be forced to pay its own way as long as the burden imposed by the taxing state is commensurate with the benefit the taxpayer receives from the taxing state.

b. Discrimination

A state may not discriminate against interstate commerce in imposing taxes. It cannot, for example, use one tax rate for local commerce and a higher rate for interstate commerce if there is no essential difference between the two classes. *Nippert v. City of Richmond* (1946).

Example: A Florida statute prohibiting out-of-state banks, bank holding companies and trust companies from owning or controlling businesses selling advisory services violates the Commerce Clause. Since only out-of-state banking interests were subject to the regulation, it was discriminatory. There was no showing that this disparate treatment was only an incidental product resulting from furthering legitimate local concerns. *Lewis v. BT Investment Managers, Inc.* (1980).

c. Due Process

In order for a state to levy a tax on an interstate concern, the taxpayer must have a taxable situs in the state. *Minimum Connection*—If a state seeks contribution from a person, the Fourteenth Amendment Due Process Clause requires some benefit to justify the burden, *i.e.,* some definable link, some minimum connection (jurisdictional contacts) between the taxpayer and the taxing state. The taxing formula used must be reasonable "in relation to the opportunities which [the state] has given, to protection which it has afforded, to benefits which it has conferred." *Wisconsin v. J. C. Penney Co.* (1940). But the Due Process Clause does not require a physical presence in the state. *Quill Corp. v. North Dakota* (1992).

d. Interstate Commerce

1) "Multiple Burdens"

Since a taxpayer frequently acquires more than one taxable situs, there is a danger of an excessive burden on interstate commerce if each state is allowed to impose an unapportioned tax. Interstate commerce would be placed at a competitive disadvantage to local competition.

2)   Apportionment

The taxing state must apportion its tax to reflect the extent of the taxable situs the taxpayer has acquired with the taxing state.

2.   Modern Applications

Even a state tax nominally imposed on the "privilege of doing business" which is applied to the taxpayer doing interstate business may be constitutional if it satisfies the *Complete Auto Transit, Inc. v. Brady* test. The Court's modern focus is increasingly on the actual economic effects of the state tax.

a.   Under *Complete Auto Transit*, a tax is valid under the Commerce Clause if the tax: (1) is applied to an activity having a "substantial nexus" with the taxing state; (2) is fairly apportioned; (3) does not discriminate against interstate commerce, and (4) is fairly related to the services provided by the taxing state.

Examples: (1) A state severance tax on each ton of coal mined in the state was held constitutional, using the four-part *Complete Auto Transit* test. Since the act of severance occurs in Montana and no other state could tax that local activity, the first two parts are satisfied. Since the tax is computed at the same rate regardless of the final destination of the coal, it was not discriminatory. Finally, because the tax is measured as a percentage of the coal mined, it reflects the taxpayer's activities within the state and thus is fairly related to the services provided by the state. *Commonwealth Edison Co. v. Montana* (1981).

(2) North Dakota imposes an unconstitutional burden on interstate commerce when it requires an out-of-state mail order house with neither outlets nor sales representative in the state to collect and pay a use tax on goods purchased for use in the state. The *Complete Auto* test is violated since such a vendor lacks the "substantial nexus" with the taxing state required by the Commerce Clause. The due process concern with fundamental fairness was satisfied by the significant activity of the mail order house in North

Dakota. The Commerce Clause, however, emphasizes the burdensome effects of the state regulation on the national economy. Congress is free to decide that there should not be a bright-line rule against forcing mail order houses, lacking contacts with the state, to collect and remit use taxes. *Quill Corporation v. North Dakota* (1992).

(3) Oklahoma's tax on the full sale price of bus tickets for interstate travel originating in the state was held to be constitutional under the *Complete Auto Transit* test. First, in accordance with the four-part test, the sale of the bus tickets in Oklahoma provided a "substantial nexus with the State."

Second, the tax was "fairly apportioned" since the tax was both internally and externally consistent. Internal consistency exists if an identical tax levied by every other state would not place interstate commerce at a competitive disadvantage. Here, even if every state were to impose an identical tax, no ticket sale would be subject to more than one State's tax, preserving internal consistency. External consistency is satisfied since the unique and discrete taxable event is the agreement, payment, and delivery of some of the service, all of which take place in Oklahoma. Since no other State can claim to be the site of the same combination of events, the State taxes only its fair share of the transaction. The third and fourth parts of the test are satisfied because the tax does not discriminate against out-of-state businesses and the tax is fairly related to the services provided by the taxing state, such as police and fire protection. *Oklahoma Tax Commission v. Jefferson Lines, Inc.* (1995).

b. States may not assess taxes on out-of-state businesses by methods which discriminate against interstate commerce. The Commerce Clause prohibits a state from imposing taxes placing a much heavier burden on out-of-state businesses that compete in an interstate market than it imposes on its own residents who also engage in interstate commerce. *See American Trucking Associations, Inc. v. Michigan Public Service Commission* (2005), Ch.III, A, 2, C, 2), b).

Example: North Carolina imposed an "intangibles tax" on the value of a corporation owned by state residents. The tax was inversely proportionate to the corporation's exposure to state income tax. Therefore, the more business a corporation did out-of-state, the less income tax they paid to North Carolina and the higher the "intangibles tax." The Court held that this tax facially discriminated against interstate commerce. The North Carolina tax failed all three requirements for a tax to be compensatory and not discriminatory. First, "[t]he tax must serve some purpose for which the State may otherwise impose a burden on interstate commerce." Second, "the tax on interstate commerce must approximate, but not exceed, the tax on intrastate commerce." Third, "the different taxes on in-staters and out-of-staters must fall on substantially equivalent events." *Fulton Corp. v. Faulkner* (1996).

C. Review Questions

1. **T or F**   The Tenth Amendment reserves to the States only such powers as they exercised prior to ratification of the Constitution.

2. **T or F**   The plenary power of Congress over interstate commerce precludes state regulation of such commerce.

3. **T or F**   In the absence of congressional legislation, states are free to regulate interstate commerce.

4. **T or F**   State regulation which purposefully favors local economic interests against out-of-state concerns is permissible under the Commerce Clause if it is reasonably related to a valid state interest.

5. **T or F**   When a state law is discriminatory in means or effect, a state must use any less burdensome alternatives available.

6. **T or F**   A law will not be labeled discriminatory so long as local economic interests or other political subdivisions of the State are burdened since this provides political checks.

7. **T or F**   A subsidy program for the benefit of local wheat farmers facing an economic emergency, funded by a nondiscriminatory tax on the sale of wheat in the state, is constitutional.

8. **T or F** A nondiscriminatory state law is necessarily valid under the Commerce Clause.

9. **T or F** Under the Dormant Commerce Clause, state regulation cannot prefer a public entity over out-of-state competitors.

10. **T or F** State highway laws are presumed to be valid in spite of the negative implications of the Dormant Commerce Clause but factual balancing may result in their invalidity.

11. **T or F** Under contemporary Commerce Clause decisions a state may discriminate in favor of its own citizens when it acts as a participant in the marketplace.

12. **T or F** State discrimination against out-of-state citizens does not violate the Art. IV, § 2, Privileges and Immunities Clause, unless fundamental national interests are involved.

13. **T or F** If a state cuts and sells timber from its own lands, it may choose to sell only to its own citizens without violating the Commerce Clause.

14. **T or F** State taxation of out-of-state business concerns is prohibited by the Commerce Clause.

15. **T or F** A state tax on the "privilege of doing business" in the state imposed on an out-of-state business is unconstitutional.

16. The state of Montana imposes a substantial severance tax on each ton of coal mined in the state regardless of the coal's destination. Which of the following is most accurate?

   a. The tax is unconstitutional because of the economic costs to out-of-state users.

   b. The tax discriminates against interstate commerce and is, therefore, unconstitutional.

   c. The tax is constitutional even though it imposes an excessive burden on out-of-state businesses.

   d. The tax is constitutional since the tax is on the local act of severance, is nondiscriminatory, and reflects the services provided by the state.

17. **T or F** When Congress regulates in a field, state regulation in the same field is preempted.

18. **T or F**   Congress cannot authorize the states to regulate in a manner that would violate the Dormant Commerce Clause.

19. Which of the following factors are considered in determining if a federal law is intended to preempt state law?

     a.   The pervasiveness of the federal law.

     b.   The need for uniformity.

     c.   The potential for administrative conflict.

     d.   The existence of a federal regulatory agency.

     e.   All of the above.

20. During the 1973 oil embargo, the state of West Lincoln conducted a study which showed that gasoline stations operated by producers or refiners received preferential treatment in terms of oil supplies during this scarcity. As a result, the West Lincoln legislature enacted a law which prohibits producers or refiners from operating retail service stations within West Lincoln. Furthermore, producers or refiners now are required in West Lincoln to extend all "voluntary allowances" uniformly to all stations that are supplied. Colossal Oil Company, one of the nation's largest producers and refiners, has brought suit in the federal district court in West Lincoln on the ground that the state law is unreasonable and will frustrate rather than enhance competition. Colossal Oil also argued that the West Lincoln scheme discriminated against out-of-state competitors in favor of in-state independent dealers, since the burden of the legislation fell on interstate companies which will have to divest themselves of their West Lincoln service stations. Is the West Lincoln legislation constitutional? Why or why not?

IV

Congress and Executive Power

■ *ANALYSIS*

Art. II, § 1 vests the Executive Power in the President of the United States. It has never been determined whether this Vestiture Clause is itself a separate source of power, only a reference to all Art. II powers, or a reference to the Framers' choice of a single rather than a plural Executive. In any case, the modern presidency has broad domestic and foreign affairs powers. The President is Head of State, Chief Executive, Chief Legislator, and Commander-in-Chief. But in examining the constitutional place of the Executive in our separation of powers system, keep in mind the wide gap between the President's paper powers and his real powers. A reading of the Constitution provides only a shadow of the modern presidency.

Most of the express executive powers are vague and lie in areas where power is shared with Congress. What happens when the executive and congressional actions come into conflict? In the past, the tide of power has tended to flow to the Executive. But Congress has been trying to stem the tide by enacting laws which at least ostensibly seek to promote Executive responsibility and accountability. *The question is whether such laws unconstitutionally invade the constitutional prerogative of the Executive or usurp powers properly shared by the other Branches.*

In answering this question, the Court at times adopts a *formalist* approach. This approach stresses a stricter emphasis on constitutional text, a strict separation of powers between the Branches, and a preference for bright-line rules. At other times, the Court adopts a more *functional* approach stressing the interrelation of the Branches and the need for checks and balances. Constitutional text tends to be downplayed and the focus is on the balancing of competing interests.

A. The Domestic Arena

1. Executive Law–Making

a. Limited Domestic Law–Making Powers

The President has no inherent domestic law-making powers, at least in the absence of extreme emergency. In emergencies, his power as Chief Executive under Art. II, § 1, and his power to "take care that the laws be faithfully executed" (Art. II, § 3), do appear to create some power to act subject to congressional authority.

Example: The seizure of the steel mills by President Truman to avert a crippling strike during the Korean War was held unconstitutional since Congress had previously legislated regarding the scope of executive power to curtail strikes. Art. I gives Congress the power to make law. A majority of the justices indicated that, in the absence of such a specific congressional legislation, the President would have independent power to act in an emergency. *Youngstown Sheet & Tube Co. v. Sawyer* (1952).

b. Veto Power

1) A bill passed by Congress and signed by the President is law. If the President refuses to sign, he returns it to Congress with a statement of objections. Congress may make the bill law by a two-thirds vote of both houses. Art. I, § 7.

2) The President has ten days to determine if he will veto a bill or it automatically becomes law unless Congress by its adjournment prevents its return. The President is thus able to "pocket veto" a bill by not acting on it prior to adjournment. While a brief recess is not an adjournment, *Wright v. United States* (1938), the nature of an adjournment permitting use of the pocket veto has not been judicially determined.

3) The Line Item Veto

   Congress has sought to achieve greater budgetary control while preserving executive accountability through the Line Item Veto Act. After signing a bill into law and making certain findings, the President can cancel certain spending provisions of the law. The cancelled provisions are then returned to Congress which can nullify the cancellations by enacting a disapproval bill which is subject to presidential veto. In a "formalist" opinion, the Supreme Court held that the Line Item Veto Act, as enacted, violated the Presentment Clause, Art. I, § 7.

   Example: The Line Item Veto Act violates the Presentment Clause of Art. I, § 7 which requires that the President either sign or veto a piece of legislation passed by Congress. The legal and practical effect of the presidential cancellation is to amend the signed law by repealing a portion of it. It alters the President's constitutional Veto Power. Given the extensive debates and compromises over the Art. I procedures, the silence of the Constitution on the President's power to amend or repeal portions of a statute is "equivalent to an express prohibition." Art. I sets forth a "single, finely wrought and exhaustively considered procedure" for making law. Unlike prior suspension authority whereby Congress authorizes executive discretion in spending, the Act gives the President unilateral power to change the law. Since the procedure created by the Line Item Veto Act is inconsistent with the Art. I procedure, the Act is unconstitutional. The Court did not consider whether the Act would violate the separation of powers. *Clinton v. City of New York* (1998).

2. Executive Impoundment

The President impounds when he withholds or delays the expenditure of congressionally appropriated funds. This may defeat a congressional program or policy.

a. Justification

It is argued that such impoundment is justified by statutorily-imposed budgetary constraints in the light of the constitutional mandate that the President should faithfully execute the laws and by the Vestiture Clause.

b. Critique

Conversely, it is claimed that such frustration of a congressional program or policy violates Congress' power to make the law and hence the separation of powers principle. Further, it arguably constitutes an executive veto in a manner not prescribed by the Constitution. The Supreme Court has not yet ruled on the constitutionality of impoundment. Congress has enacted legislation limiting the executive power to impound. The constitutionality of such a restraint on executive power has not been tested in the Supreme Court. The decision of the Court in *Chadha*, discussed below, raises serious doubt as to the validity of the provisions in federal legislation embodying a legislative veto of executive impoundments.

3. Delegation and Control of Legislative Power

a. Legislative Delegation

Much executive law-making results from conscious congressional delegation of legislative power. Such delegation is constitutional provided Congress exercises the essentials of the legislative function by determining policy and formulating reasonable standards to guide the exercise of executive discretion. *Congress must provide an "intelligible principle" guiding the exercise of the delegated power. The courts have generally exercised restraint and deferred to Congress in reviewing the adequacy of such standards.*

Examples: (1) Congressional legislation creating the United States Sentencing Commission in the Judicial Branch and delegating to it power to formulate Sentencing Guidelines binding on the courts does not violate separation of powers. The Act set forth the policies and principles governing Commission operations and provides specific directives to govern formulation of the Guidelines. There was, therefore, no violation of the nondelegation doctrine.

Delegation of some rulemaking authority to a Commission located in the Judicial Branch does not violate separation of powers if it does not intrude on the prerogatives of another Branch and is appropriate to the central mission of the Judiciary. Setting sentencing policy is a shared responsibility of the Branches and the Judiciary has always played a role.

The fact that Art. III judges serve on a Commission with nonadjudicatory functions does not violate separation of powers. Art. III judges may perform extrajudicial duties if such service does not "undermine the integrity of the Judicial Branch." Nor does the fact that the President appoints and removes members of the Commission for good cause pose a sufficient threat to judicial independence to violate separation of powers. *Mistretta v. United States* (1989).

(2) Provisions of the Clean Air Act delegating authority to the EPA to set national ambient air quality standards was held not to violate Art. I, § 1, vesting all legislative power in Congress. An agency cannot cure an unlawful delegation of legislative power by adopting a limiting construction of the statute. But the Clean Air Act requirement that "[f]or a discrete set of pollutants and based on published air quality criteria that reflect the latest scientific knowledge, [the] EPA must establish uniform national standards at a level that is requisite to protect public health from the adverse effects of the pollutant in the ambient air," pro-

vides an "intelligible principle" to which the EPA is to conform. Even in sweeping regulatory schemes, the Court has never demanded that statutes provide a determinate criterion of how much of the regulated harm is too much. The Court stressed the broad congressional discretion recognized in its nondelegation precedent. *Whitman v. American Trucking Associations* (2001).

b. The Legislative Veto

One method by which Congress has sought to achieve executive accountability in exercise of broad delegated power is the legislative veto. Congress delegates power to the Executive but reserves authority to review and veto executive action taken pursuant to the grant. In a "formalist" opinion, the Supreme Court held that such a veto is legislative action violative of the Art. I, § 7, separation of powers requirements of Bicameralism and Presentment.

Example: In the Immigration and Naturalization Act, Congress delegated authority to the Attorney General to suspend deportation of aliens. However, Congress reserved control over executive action by allowing either House to review and veto the suspension order. This legislative veto violates the Presentment Clause which requires legislation be presented to the President for approval or veto. The one House veto also violates Bicameralism (Art. I, §§ 1, 7), requiring that both houses enact a measure in order for it to become a law. The veto in this case was a "legislative act" in both purpose and effect in that it altered "legal rights, duties and relations of persons." Thus, the structural requirements of Art. I, designed to preserve checks and balances and maintain the separation of powers, must be followed. The veto provision is severable from the remainder of the Act and is unconstitutional. *Immigration and Naturalization Service v. Chadha* (1983).

4. The Appointment and Removal Power

a. The Appointment Power

Art. II, § 2, cl. 2, provides that the President "shall nominate, and by and with the advice and consent of the Senate, shall appoint Ambassadors, other public Ministers and Consuls, Judges of the Supreme Court, and all other Officers of the United States, whose appointments are not herein otherwise provided for, and which shall be established by law, but the Congress may by law vest the Appointment of such inferior Officers, as they think proper, in the President alone, in the Courts of Law, or in the Heads of Departments."

1) *Congress may not vest the Appointment Power in persons other than those specified in Art. II, § 2, cl. 2.*

>   ***Example:*** A majority of the voting members of the Federal Election Commission were appointed by the President pro tem of the Senate and the Speaker of the House. Neither the Speaker of the House, nor the President pro tem of the Senate comes within the terms "Courts of Law" or "Heads of Departments" as required by Art. II, § 2, cl. 2. The power given to Congress under the Twelfth Amendment to regulate parties in connection with presidential elections does not permit Congress to create a federal commission to regulate such elections in a manner violative of the Appointments Clause. Accordingly, except in the case of its investigatory and informative power, Congress, in permitting the Commission to exercise administrative and law enforcement powers, violated Art. II, § 2, cl. 2. *Buckley v. Valeo* (1976).

2) *Whether an officer is a principal or inferior officer depends on a functional analysis of the extent to which there is subordination or independence, the scope of the officer's jurisdiction and the extent of the functions performed.* If the officer is an inferior officer, interbranch appointments are permissible unless it impairs the ability of a Branch to perform its functions or is incongruous.

>   ***Example:*** Congressional legislation vesting the appointment of independent counsel to investigate and prosecute executive officials in a Special Division of the U.S. Court of Appeals does not violate the Appointments Clause. The independent counsel is an "inferior officer." She is subject to removal for good cause by the Attorney General and has a limited jurisdiction. She performs only limited duties of investigation and prosecution, and does not make general policy. The office is limited in tenure to the completion of the appointed task. *Morrison v. Olson* (1988).

b.   The Removal Power

1)   Executive Removal

Historically, the scope of the President's power to remove executive officials has turned on whether the official was deemed a "purely executive" official or an official who exercised "quasi-legislative" or "quasi-judicial" powers. In the former case, the President had exercised unfettered removal power. In the latter case, the removal power was subject to congressional restrictions. More recently, the Court has cast doubt on excessive use of these "rigid categories" to define the removal power. *While accepting the relevance of the categories, the Court emphasized a functional approach focusing on "whether the removal restrictions are of such a nature that they impede the President's ability to perform his constitutional duty."* Morrison v. Olson (1988).

Example: The provision of the Ethics in Government Act that the Attorney General can remove an independent counsel only for good cause is not of such a nature as to interfere impermissibly with the President's constitutional obligation to ensure the faithful execution of the laws. Law enforcement functions are executive functions. But the President's need to control the exercise of discretion of the independent counsel, an "inferior official" with limited jurisdiction, tenure and power, is not so central to the functioning of the Executive Branch as to require as a matter of constitutional law that counsel be terminable at will by the President. Counsel can still be removed for misconduct. Independence could be achieved only by limiting the removal power. Congress has not sought to usurp any added role in the removal of executive officials. *Morrison v. Olson* (1988).

2)   Congressional Removal

Congress may not constitutionally vest executive functions in officials who are subject to removal by Congress by means other than impeachment.

Example: Provisions of the Gramm–Rudman Act vesting in the Comptroller General authority to specify spending reductions binding on the President violate the separation of powers. The Act vests executive functions in the Comptroller since he has the ultimate authority to determine the budget cuts to be made; he interprets and implements the legislative mandate and this constitutes execution of the laws. The Comptroller is an agent of Congress since by earlier legislation he is removable for designated, but broadly-phrased, causes, *e.g.*, inefficiency, neglect of duty. This allows removal for transgressing of the legislative will. By retaining in its own agent control over the execution of the Gramm–Rudman Act, Congress violated separation of powers. *Bowsher v. Synar* (1986).

5. Separation of Powers Generally

Apart from the specific contexts discussed above, the Court will often examine the separation of powers question generally. *The Court examines the degree of intrusion on the constitutional functions of the other Branch and the extent to which the challenged actions consolidate powers that should properly be shared.*

Examples: (1) The Ethics in Government Act, providing for the appointment of independent counsel to investigate and prosecute high executive officials, taken as a whole, does not unduly interfere with the role of the Executive Branch. Nor is there any congressional usurpation of any Executive Branch functions. The Attorney General has sole and unreviewable power to request the appointment of the independent counsel. He retains several means for supervising and controlling the independent counsel's prosecutorial powers. He may remove the independent counsel for good cause. While the counsel is to some degree independent and freer from Executive supervision than most federal prosecutors, the Act provides the Executive Branch "sufficient control * * * to ensure that the President is able to perform his constitutionally assigned duties." *Morrison v. Olson* (1988).

(2) A congressional act authorizing transfer of National and Dulles airports to a new Authority created by a regional compact was held violative of separation of powers. In exchange for the transfer, decisions of the Authority's board of directors were subject to review by a Review Board consisting of nine members of Congress, which wielded a veto power over

policy decisions made by the directors. If the Review Board were said to be performing executive functions, the Act is unconstitutional because Congress cannot vest executive functions in a body subject to its control (*Bowsher*). If the Review Board functioned as a legislative body, its acts were still unconstitutional because Congress must follow the Bicameralism and Presentment requirements when performing legislative acts (*Chadha*). *Metropolitan Washington Airports Authority v. Citizens for the Abatement of Aircraft Noise* (1991).

B. The Foreign Arena

The respective roles of Congress and the Executive in the exercise of foreign affairs and the war powers remain unclear. The Court in *United States v. Curtiss–Wright Export Corp.* (1936) spoke of inherent foreign affairs powers vested in the national government and suggested an executive primacy in their exercise. The Constitution, however, provides a wide range of express and implied foreign affairs powers to each branch. Whatever the source of the national foreign powers, their distribution has yet to receive a consistent and clear judicial definition. A few items should be noted. Congress has broad discretion to vest foreign affairs powers in the Executive. Since foreign affairs and the war powers are exclusive, states have a very limited role to play. Finally, remember that the political question doctrine plays an especially important role in the foreign affairs arena, inviting judicial avoidance of constitutional questions.

1. Foreign Affairs

a. Presidential Powers

The President has power to receive Ambassadors and other public ministers (Art. II, § 3), to recognize or withdraw recognition of foreign governments, and to act on behalf of the United States in day-to-day dealings with foreign governments. This is augmented by his role as Commander-in-Chief.

b. Congressional Powers

Congress has express authority to regulate foreign commerce, to fashion a uniform rule of naturalization, to raise and maintain armies and to declare war as well as the vital power to tax and spend.

c. Shared Powers

The power to determine foreign policy is arguably a shared power, although the Executive has become dominant. The executive control of information and its ability for quick response gives it an advantage in this area. When the Executive acts with congressional authorization, its constitutional powers are maximized. When it acts contrary to congressional action, its powers are at their lowest. When Congress has not acted, the Executive acts in a "zone of twilight," where the distribution of power is uncertain. *Youngstown Sheet & Tube Co. v. Sawyer* (1952) (Jackson, J., concurring).

Example: In his Executive Order nullifying attachments on Iranian assets and transferring Iranian assets, the President acted within his statutory authority. Prior legislation reflects a congressional purpose to put control of foreign assets in the hands of the President for use in negotiating the resolution of a declared national emergency. With respect to his order suspending claims against Iran in U.S. courts, congressional acquiescence in past presidential action supports such authority. Past practice does not by itself create power but "long continued practice known to and acquiesced in by Congress raises a presumption that the action has been taken in pursuance to its consent." When the President acts on a vital issue of foreign affairs with congressional approval and authorization, his constitutional power is maximized. *Dames and Moore v. Regan* (1981).

2. Treaties and Executive Agreements

a. Treaties

The President has the power to make treaties but to become law, two-thirds of the senators present must concur.

b. Executive Agreements

Executive Agreements do not require Senate concurrence. While Congress is often consulted concerning such agreements, this is not required. While there is no express constitutional authority for such agreements, their legality is now established. *United States v. Belmont* (1937).

c. Supremacy

Art. VI provides that all treaties which are made "under the authority of the United States" are the supreme law of the land. They prevail, as do Executive Agreements, over inconsistent state law. Treaties and Executive Agreements are subject to constitutional limitations. *Reid v. Covert*

(1957). Treaties and Acts of Congress are on a par, *i.e.,* the last in time controls. *The Chinese Exclusion Case* (1889).

> *Example:* Executive agreements between the United States and several European countries concerning settlement and disclosure of insurance policies sold in Europe before World War II (dealing with Holocaust victims claims) preempted a California law requiring insurance companies doing business in the state to disclose the existence of such insurance policies. Even absent an express preemption provision, there was sufficient evidence of a "clear conflict" between the state law and federal executive policy "to require the state law to yield." *Am. Ins. Ass'n v. Garamendi* (2003).

d. Self–Executing Treaties

Congressional legislation, which would not be constitutional otherwise, is constitutional when it reasonably implements a treaty. Some treaties are self-executing and do not require congressional implementing legislation. A treaty which is NOT self-executing does not preempt state law. And a presidential order, absent implementing legislation, has no authority to establish binding rules of decision that preempt contrary state law. See *Medellin v. Texas* (2008).

> *Examples:* (1) Legislation implementing a treaty with Canada regulating the movement of migratory birds was held constitutional even though the Court had previously indicated that the Commerce Clause was not a source of power for the legislation. *Missouri v. Holland* (1920).
>
> (2) The International Court of Justice (ICJ) had held that, under the Vienna Convention, Mexican nationals who had not been informed of their right to contact their embassy when arrested have a right to have their state convictions reviewed even though they failed to raise the issue as required by state law. But the Supreme Court subsequently held that the Vienna Convention does not prevent the application of state procedural rules barring review. The President then issued a Memorandum indicating that the United States would "discharge its international obligations" and state courts must conform to the ICJ decision by granting habeas corpus review of the convictions.

In the present case, the Supreme Court holds that neither the ICJ decision nor the President's Memorandum constitute enforceable federal law preempting contrary state law limiting review. The international obligations do not become domestic law "unless Congress has either enacted implementing statutes or the treaty itself conveys an intention that it be 'self-executing' and is ratified on these terms." The relevant international agreements do not provide for implementation of ICJ judgments through direct enforcement in domestic courts.

While the President has broad power to enforce international obligations, he does not have power to convert a non-self-executing treaty into domestic law; that power belongs to Congress. Nor does the President have independent foreign affairs authority to settle international claims disputes sufficient to preempt state law. Under the principles provided in *Youngstown*, the President lacks power to create domestic law. *Medellin v. Texas* (2008).

3. The War Power

a. Shared Power

1) Congress has the power to declare war, to create and regulate the armed forces, and to provide for the general defense. From these express powers are implied broad powers to prepare for war (*e.g.*, to assure electricity, to register and draft for the military), to regulate during wartime (*e.g.*, economic controls, Japanese–American internment in World War II), and to remedy wartime disruptions (*e.g.*, veteran's benefits, rent controls).

2) The President is Commander-in-Chief but the scope of this power is not clear. An executive claim of national security does not justify an injunction against newspaper publication of classified material, at least in the absence of congressional authorization or direct, immediate, and irreparable damage to the Nation. *New York Times Co. v. United States* (1971).

b. Declaring and Making War
Since Congress has the constitutional power to declare war (Art. I, § 8), the President cannot formally initiate a "war." But, as Commander-in-Chief (Art.

II, § 2), the President has power to repel sudden attack, to make war, and to control the disposition of our armed forces. These powers may often be used in such a way that the country may be committed to hostilities.

1) War Powers Resolution

Congress has enacted a War Powers Resolution which seeks to limit executive power to engage the armed forces in hostilities. Sixty days after the President is required to report the use of the armed forces, such use shall terminate unless Congress affirmatively acts. Whether the War Powers Resolution is an unconstitutional delegation of Congress' power to declare war or excessively intrudes on the President's power as Commander-in-Chief, his duty to execute the laws and his status as Chief Executive, has not been judicially determined. The constitutionality of the legislative veto provision of the War Powers Resolution is in doubt as a result of *Chadha*.

c. The Militia Clauses

The Militia Clauses of Art. I, § 8, cls. 15 & 16, do not limit the war powers of Congress. Instead they are additional grants of power to Congress. The Clauses recognize the supremacy of federal power in the areas of military affairs.

d. Military Detentions

The Court has often applied Justice Jackson's concurring opinion in *Youngstown* in reviewing the use of executive war powers in prosecuting the war against terror. Even if Congress can authorize military detention of an American citizen captured on a foreign battlefield, due process requires that an alleged "enemy combatant" be given an opportunity to contest his classification as an enemy combatant through a writ of habeas corpus. *Hamdi v. Rumsfeld* (2004). Further, if the Executive undertakes to try a detainee using a military commission, it is obligated to comply with the Rule of Law that prevails in the jurisdiction, at least absent express expansion of Executive power by Congress. *Hamdan v. Rumsfeld* (2006). The constitutional limitations on suspension of habeas corpus apply to military detentions, even where the United States does not exercise sovereign authority (e.g., Guantanamo Bay), including the right of detainees to contest their status as "enemy combatants." If Congress denies the privilege of habeas corpus, even to aliens detained at Guantanamo, without providing an adequate substitute, this has the effect of an unconstitutional suspension of the writ. *Boumediene v. Bush* (2008).

Examples: (1) Hamdi, an American citizen, captured in Afghanistan, was held in indefinite military detention as an enemy-combatant, with no means of challenging his detention. While the Fourth Circuit ordered his habeas petition dismissed, the Supreme Court vacated the judgment and remanded. A plurality opinion by Justice O'Connor, joined by Chief Justice Rehnquist and Justices Kennedy and Breyer, held that "although Congress authorized the detention of combatants in the narrow circumstances alleged here, due process demands that a citizen held in the United States as an enemy combatant be given a meaningful opportunity to contest the factual basis for that detention before a neutral decision maker." The plurality concluded that the Authorization for the Use of Military Force (AUMF), passed by Congress after 9/11, authorized Hamdi's military detention. Therefore, it did not reach the question whether the President's powers under Article II would authorize military detention of citizens. The plurality reasoned that battlefield detention is so incident to war as to be part of the "necessary and appropriate force" that the AUMF authorized. But even if detention is legally authorized, a citizen-detainee is still entitled to bring a writ of habeas corpus in order to assert his due process right to contest his detention by presenting and rebutting evidence.

Justices Souter and Ginsburg, dissenting in part, disagreed with the plurality's holding that the AUMF authorized the detention and would have released Hamdi. But they concurred in the judgment ordering remand to allow Hamdi to contest his detention as an enemy combatant. Justices Scalia and Stevens, dissenting, argued that absent a suspension of habeas corpus, detainees had to be prosecuted or released. Justice Thomas, dissenting, argued that the detention was authorized by the Federal Government's war powers and that the courts lacked the expertise and capacity to challenge that decision. He would have dismissed the habeas challenge. *Hamdi v. Rumsfeld* (2004). On procedural due process in *Hamdi*, see Ch. IV, 4, h, 5.

(2) The military commission convened by the Executive to try Hamdan, a detainee at Guantanamo Bay, "lacks the

power to proceed because its structure and procedures violate both the UCMJ [Uniform Code of Military Justice] and the Geneva Convention." First, the Court held that the kind of military commission trying Hamdan had not been authorized by Congress through its Authorization for Use of Military Force (AUMF) law, the Code of Military Justice (CMJ) or the Detainee Treatment Act (DTA). At least absent specific congressional authorization expanding Executive power, under Justice Jackson's *Youngstown* concurrence, Justice Stevens for the Court ruled that "in undertaking to try Hamdan and subject him to criminal punishment, the Executive is bound to comply with the Rule of Law that prevails in this jurisdiction." In this case, the procedure that the Executive has decreed to govern Hamdan's trial by commission will violate the American common law of war, the UCMJ and the "rules and precepts of the law of nations," including the Geneva Convention. *Hamdan v. Rumsfeld* (2006).

(3) Aliens designated as enemy combatants and detained at Guantanamo Bay under the authority of the United States have the right to avail themselves of habeas corpus which cannot be withdrawn except in conformity with the Suspension Clause, Art. I, § 9, cl. 2. The Detainee Treatment Act of 2005 (DTA), provides procedures for review of detainees' rights which are not an adequate and effective substitute for habeas corpus. Therefore, section 7 of the Military Commission Act of 2006 (MCA), which denies federal courts jurisdiction to hear pending habeas corpus actions (including the petitioners' habeas corpus applications), operates as an unconstitutional suspension of the writ of habeas corpus.

The privilege of habeas corpus or an adequate substitute, as well as the limitations imposed by the Suspension Clause, apply to the Guantanamo detainees. First, the status of the alien detainees or enemy combatants is still a matter of dispute and they have not been afforded adequate procedural protection in determining their status. Second, while the United States does not claim sovereignty over Guantanamo, "it is within the constant jurisdiction of the United States." Third, while there are costs to holding the Suspension Clause applicable to military detention abroad, they are not dispositive.

The Court held that there were excessive constraints "on the detainee's ability to rebut the factual basis for the Government's assertion that he is an enemy combatant." An adequate substitute for habeas corpus must allow the detainees to challenge the President's authority to detain them indefinitely, to contest the factual findings of the Combatant Status Review Tribunals (CSRTs), to supplement the record on review with exculpatory evidence and to request an order of release. Because the procedures provided by Congress are not an adequate substitute for the writ of habeas corpus, the removal of habeas corpus jurisdiction of federal courts by MCA § 7 effects an unconstitutional suspension of the writ. *Boumediene v. Bush* (2008).

C. Privileges and Immunities

1. Executive Privilege

While nowhere expressly mentioned, the need for candor and objectivity in confidential communications has been held to give rise to a privilege against disclosure which is constitutionally based. It is based on the separation of powers principle and flows from the need to implement the powers enumerated in Art. II.

a. Limitations

However, this privilege, at least in the domestic sphere, is not absolute and may yield when the proven need for disclosure is sufficiently great. While a claim of privilege for confidential communication by the President is presumptively privileged, it is the duty of the judiciary to determine if sufficient need has been demonstrated by the party seeking disclosure.

b. Unsettled Areas

The treatment of claims of executive privilege for military, diplomatic or sensitive national security matters, or the claim of privilege against congressional demands for information, have not yet been determined by the Supreme Court.

Examples: (1) President Nixon's claim of privilege for tapes and other materials relating to Watergate from disclosure to a grand jury for use in a criminal proceeding was held subject to judicial review. The generalized interest in confidentiality did not prevail over the fundamental demands of the fair administration of criminal justice to prevent *in camera* judicial determination of what materials were relevant to the criminal proceedings and what should remain confidential. *United States v. Nixon* (1974).

(2) Vice-president Cheney is not required to assert executive privilege as a precondition to challenging discovery orders on separation of powers grounds. Sierra Club and Judicial Watch sued Cheney, claiming that a presidential energy policy group he chaired violated open meeting and disclosure laws. The Supreme Court held that the rejection of executive privilege in *United States v. Nixon* (1974) did not apply because this was a civil case; government-withholding information did not impair the "essential functions" of the judiciary; and the broad scope of the discovery orders placed a heavy burden on the Executive Branch, especially considering the involvement of the Vice–President. Cautioning against requiring the government to assert executive privilege, a result that sets "co-equal branches of the Government on a collision course," the Court held the lower courts must first consider other broad separation of powers claims made by the government. *Cheney v. U.S. Dist. Ct.* (2004).

2. Impeachment

a. Grounds

Art. II, § 4 provides that "[t]he President, Vice–President and all civil Officers of the United States, shall be removed from Office on Impeachment for, and Conviction of Treason, Bribery, or other high Crimes and Misdemeanors."

b. Procedure

The House of Representatives has the sole power to impeach (Art. I, § 2) and the Senate the sole power to try impeachments (Art. I, § 3). Conviction requires the concurrence of two-thirds of the members present. The Chief Justice presides when the President is tried.

c. Unsettled Questions

Whether "High Crimes and Misdemeanors" is limited to criminal offenses or includes some acts of political maladministration or failure to discharge the constitutional duties of the office has not been judicially determined. Moreover, while Andrew Johnson was impeached, he was not convicted by the Senate. As a result, the full meaning of the clause "High Crimes and Misdemeanors" has yet to be resolved.

3. Presidential Immunity

a. A civil damages suit cannot be maintained against the President for action taken while in office that is within the "outside perimeter" of his official responsibility. The President's unique role in the constitutional scheme demands that he be free to vigorously execute the duties of his office without the distraction of civil suits. Consequently, he is accorded absolute immunity from damages for all action taken under any of his broad areas of constitutional authority. Other measures, including congressional oversight, impeachment, and scrutiny by the press still exist to deter presidential misconduct. *Nixon v. Fitzgerald* (1982). However, the President does not enjoy immunity from civil suit for actions allegedly done prior to assuming office, which are not official acts. *Clinton v. Jones* (1997).

b. Presidential aides generally have only a qualified immunity—they are subject to liability only for violation of clearly established constitutional or statutory rights which would have been known by a reasonable person. *Harlow v. Fitzgerald* (1982). The Attorney General enjoys only a qualified immunity even when performing national security functions. *Mitchell v. Forsyth* (1985).

4. Congressional Immunity

a. Art. I, § 6, provides immunity for members of Congress "for any Speech or Debate in either House." Legislative aides enjoy immunity when performing acts for which a member would be immune.

b. Only "legislative acts," *i.e.,* matters which are "an integral part of the deliberative and communicating processes" by which Congress acts are protected. *Gravel v. United States* (1972).

> *Example:* Neither Senator Gravel nor his aide could be questioned or prosecuted for reading portions of the Pentagon Papers into

the public record at a subcommittee meeting. Immunity also extended to preparations for the meeting. However, arrangements between Senator Gravel and a private publisher to publish the Papers was not an immune legislative act. *Gravel v. United States* (1972).

D. Review Questions

1. **T or F** The President has inherent domestic law making power.

2. **T or F** Congress can choose to perform legislative acts through a special committee whose actions are not subject to presidential veto.

3. **T or F** There is a constitutionally based executive privilege against disclosure.

4. **T or F** The President is free to remove any public official he selects.

5. **T or F** Congressional delegation of executive functions to an official who is not fully subject to presidential supervision and control violates separation of powers.

6. **T or F** Foreign affairs powers are shared powers.

7. **T or F** Executive agreements, even when made without congressional consultation, prevail over state law.

8. **T or F** Under the Constitution, Congress has the exclusive power to declare war.

9. **T or F** The President can be made to answer in civil damages for his wrongful acts even if committed in an area of his constitutional authority.

10. **T or F** The President has inherent Art. II power to detain U.S. citizens as enemy combatants without providing due process.

11. **T or F** The Supreme Court has held that the President, acting under his war powers, can order the detention of American citizens who are determined to be "enemy combatants."

12. **T or F** Aliens, designated as enemy combatants and detained at Guantanomo Bay, can claim habeas corpus protection even though Congress has provided procedures for review of their status.

13. **T or F** The Supreme Court has held that an alien captured in a war zone and detained at Guantanamo Bay cannot be tried by a military commission.

14. Which of the following is most accurate?

    a. The Executive has power under his Art. II War Powers to order the detention of citizens as "enemy combatants."

    b. Citizens may be detained by the Executive as enemy combatants, when authorized by Congress.

    c. Citizens may not be detained as enemy combatants, even when authorized by Congress, unless the writ of habeas corpus has been lawfully suspended.

15. Which of the following is the most accurate?

    a. The President has absolute executive privilege from judicial subpoenas.

    b. The Court engages in ad hoc balancing in assessing a claim of executive privilege.

    c. A claim of executive privilege against a subpoena is presumptively valid.

    d. It is for Congress to finally resolve whether a claim of executive privilege should prevail.

16. Which of the following is most accurate?

    a. Members of Congress enjoy absolute immunity from criminal prosecution.

    b. Legislative aides do not share in legislative immunity.

    c. Only acts pursuant to the legislative process are immune.

    d. Art. I, § 6, does not provide any protection to members of Congress from criminal prosecution for bribery and fraud.

17. In the original legislation creating the Federal Election Commission, Congress provided that a majority of the voting members of the Commission should be appointed by the President pro tem of the Senate and the Speaker

of the House. The selection procedure mandated by this legislation was challenged on the ground that it was unconstitutional. Was it?

PART TWO

Individual Rights and Liberties: Constitutional Limitations on Governmental Power

■ *ANALYSIS*

V

Historical Perspectives

■ *ANALYSIS*

A. The Original Constitution

1. Natural Rights

Despite some contrary judicial opinion in the early years of the Republic, the claim that there are extra-constitutional "natural rights" limiting governmental power has generally not been accepted by the courts. If the federal government exercises one of its delegated powers or the states exercise their reserved powers, some express or implied constitutional, statutory, or common law limitation must be found if the government action is to be successfully challenged.

2. Express Rights

a. The original Constitution contained few express rights. Art. I, §§ 9 and 10 prohibit the use of Ex Post Facto laws and Bills of Attainder. Art. I, § 9 protects the Great Writ, Habeas Corpus, from suspension except in cases of rebellion or invasion, and Art. I, § 10, prevents states from enacting laws impairing the obligation of contract. Art. IV, § 2 protects the right of nonresidents entering a state from discrimination in regard to fundamental national rights. See Ch. III, A, 3. Religious tests may not be used as a qualification for office. Art. VI.

b. During the debates over ratification, Federalists argued that since this is a government of limited power, no specification of rights was necessary. Further, they argued that inclusion of some rights might be used to deny other rights not enumerated or provide a basis for the federal government claiming powers beyond those delegated. Efforts to include a Bill of Rights were defeated at the Constitutional Convention.

c. Anti–Federalists argued that our English heritage *e.g.*, Magna Carta, demonstrated the need for written limitations on government. During the ratification debate, promises were given that a Bill of Rights would be added to the Constitution.

B. Bill of Rights

One of the acts of the first Congress was to initiate the enactment of ten amendments to the Constitution, popularly called the Bill of Rights. These amendments were designed to protect the individual from various infringements on freedom which might emanate from the newly created federal government. The provisions of the Bill of Rights do not directly limit state action. *Barron v. The*

Mayor and City Council of Baltimore (1833). Most of the guarantees of the Bill of Rights apply to the states as part of the liberty protected by The Fourteenth Amendment Due Process Clause.

C. The Civil War Amendments

1. Subsequent Amendments

The Constitution has subsequently been enlarged to a total of twenty-seven amendments. The most important limitations on state governmental action are found in the Thirteenth, Fourteenth and Fifteenth Amendments adopted during the Reconstruction following the Civil War.

2. The Thirteenth Amendment

Ratified in 1865, The Thirteenth Amendment abolishes slavery and involuntary servitude. Unlike the other amendments, the Amendment applies even to private action. However, the rights secured by the Thirteenth Amendment, § 1, have been narrowly construed, limited essentially to formal bondage and forced labor.

3. The Fourteenth Amendment

a. Ratified in 1868, the Fourteenth Amendment, § 1, establishes that persons born or naturalized in this country are citizens of the United States and of the state of residence. This provision rejects *Scott v. Sanford* (1857) (*Dred Scott*) which had held that a Negro slave was not a citizen entitled to sue in federal court.

b. Section one of the Amendment guarantees that no state shall deny the privileges or immunities of *citizens* of the United States. It also provides that states shall not deprive any *person* of life, liberty, or property without due process of law or of equal protection of the laws.

4. The Fifteenth Amendment

Ratified in 1870, the Fifteenth Amendment, § 1, prohibits denial of the franchise because of race or previous condition of servitude. It applies to both the federal government and the states. It does not establish a general right to vote.

D. Privileges or Immunities of National Citizenship

1. The Slaughterhouse Cases

In the *Slaughterhouse Cases* (1873), the Supreme Court definitively held that the Privileges or Immunities Clause of the Fourteenth Amendment did not make the Bill of Rights applicable to the states.

a. Function of the Clause

It was held in the Slaughterhouse Cases *that the sole function of the Privileges or Immunities Clause of the Fourteenth Amendment was to protect the rights secured to individuals in their relationship to the federal government,* i.e., *in their capacity as federal citizens.* The fairly narrow list of rights of federal citizenship secured by the Privileges or Immunities Clause of the Fourteenth Amendment was declared to include the following rights: (a) to petition Congress; (b) to peaceably assemble; (c) to use the Writ of Habeas Corpus; (d) to use the navigable waters of the United States; (f) the right to interstate travel; (g) to claim the rights secured by the Thirteenth and Fifteenth Amendments; and (h) the right to vote in federal elections.

b. Rationale

The Court in the *Slaughterhouse Cases* reflected federalism values in rejecting the view that the Privileges or Immunities Clause was intended to make all the fundamental rights traditionally protected by state law into federal constitutional rights which could be protected in federal court.

2. Reviving the Clause

a.   This limited interpretation of the Privileges or Immunities Clause of the Fourteenth Amendment dashed the hopes of those who sought to use the Clause to protect fundamental rights whenever endangered as a result of state action or inaction. It was the Due Process Clause of the Fourteenth Amendment that was to be the vehicle for making the fundamental rights in the Bill of Rights into limitations on state action.

b.   The Court resurrected the Privileges or Immunities Clause to protect that aspect of the right to travel that guarantees to travelers who elect to become permanent residents of a state, the right to be treated like other citizens of that state. Discrimination against the newly arrived citizen based on the exercise of the right to travel, even if only an incidental burden, is a penalty, apparently subject to strict scrutiny. See Ch. VIII, C, 6, b, on the use of Equal Protection to challenge discrimination penalizing the right to travel.

Example: A California law providing that families that move into the state and seek welfare benefits during the first year of residence are limited to the amount of benefits payable by the State of the family's prior residence violates the Four-teenth Amendment Privileges or Immunities Clause. While the law might serve the State's legitimate fiscal objective by reducing welfare expenditures, the State may not discriminate among equally eligible needy citizens. *Saenz v. Roe* (1999).

c.　Whether *Saenz v. Roe* portends a general revival in the use of the Clause as a substantive source of protection for fundamental rights is unlikely. It is possible to argue that a State can still seek to assure that a newly arrived traveler is maintaining a bona fide residence before it provides state benefits.

E.　The Second Amendment

1.　Text

The Second Amendment provides: "A well regulated Militia, being necessary to the security of a free State, the right of the people to keep and bear Arms, shall not be infringed."

2.　A Personal Right

a.　*In* District of Columbia v. Heller (2008), *the Court held, 5–4, that the Second Amendment guarantees "the individual right to possess and carry weapons in cases of confrontation." The right of self-defense is a core Second Amendment right. The Court rejected the argument that the Amendment "protects only the right to possess and carry a firearm in connection with militia service."*

　　Example:　The District of Columbia banned the possession of usable handguns in the home. D.C. law, the most stringent in the country, made it a crime to carry an unregistered firearm, prohibited the registration of handguns and provided that no person may carry a handgun without a license. The law also required that registered, lawfully owned firearms, be kept unloaded and either disassembled or bound by a trigger lock or similar device. Handguns are the most preferred firearm in the nation "to keep and use for protection of one's home and family." The Court held that the law violated the Second Amendment. *District of Columbia v. Heller* (2008).

b.　*Methodology.* In interpreting the meaning of the Second Amendment, Justice Scalia, for the Court, joined by Chief Justice Roberts and Justices

Thomas, Alito, and Kennedy, uses an originalist approach which focuses on the *"Original Meaning"* of the Amendment. He focuses on the text and the understanding of the Amendment when enacted.

c. *Textual Analysis.* Justice Scalia begins with the Operative Clause of the Amendment rather than the Prefatory Clause. He reads "right of the people" to protect individual rights. The natural meaning of the phrase "to keep and bear Arms" and its meaning in the 18th Century was to carry arms for confrontation, and did not to refer to the militia. History confirmed that the Amendment codified a preexisting personal right. The Court found nothing in the Prefatory Clause inconsistent with interpreting the Amendment to protect an individual right to bear arms for self-defense.

d. *History.* Justice Scalia also examined the arms bearing provisions in state constitutions, the drafting history of the Second Amendment and post-ratification interpretation of the Amendment, finding that they all supported the Court's individual rights interpretation of the Second Amendment.

e. *Precedent.* No Supreme Court holding rejects the Court's individual rights interpretation. *United States v. Miller* (1939) is read narrowly, as standing "only for the proposition that the Second Amendment right, whatever its nature, extends only to certain weapons."

3. Scope of the Right

a. The Court accepts that the Second Amendment right is not unlimited—it is "not a right to keep and carry any weapon whatsoever in any manner whatsoever and for whatever purpose."

b. The Court says that nothing in its opinion casts doubt on long standing prohibitions on possession of firearms by felons and the mentally ill, laws forbidding carrying firearms into sensitive public places such as schools and government buildings or laws imposing conditions and qualifications on the commercial sale of arms.

c. Limitations on the type of weapons protected have been said to be limited to those "in common use at the time." *Miller.* While the modern militia may require the use of sophisticated arms, this does not determine the scope of the Second Amendment right.

d. Heller *does not address the standard of review the Court will use in reviewing gun control laws under the Second Amendment. The Court said the D.C. law was unconstitutional under any standard of scrutiny.*

4. The *Heller* Dissent

a. Justice Stevens, joined by Justices Souter, Ginsburg and Breyer, dissenting, accepted that the Second Amendment protects "a right that can be enforced by individuals," but rejected the claim that it protects "the right to possess and use guns for nonmilitary purposes like hunting and personal self-defense." For the dissent, "[t]he Second Amendment was adopted to protect the right of the people of each of the several States to maintain a well-regulated militia." The Steven's dissent also uses Originalism. But it focuses on original intent of the Framers and ratifiers and on precedent.

b. *Textual Analysis.* The preamble to the Second Amendment "identifies the preservation of the militia as the Amendment's purpose." The phrase "the people" in the Second Amendment reminds us that "it is the collective action of individuals having a duty to serve in the militia that the text directly protects and, perhaps more importantly, that the ultimate purpose of the Amendment was to protect the State's share of divided sovereignty created by the Constitution." The phrase "To keep and bear Arms" "describe a unitary right: to possess arms if needed for military purposes and to use them in conjunction with military activities."

c. *Framers' Intent.* The history of the Second Amendment reflects a concern about the potential threat to state sovereignty that a federal standing army would pose and a desire to protect the States' militias as a means of protecting against that danger and against the danger that Congress could disarm them. The Amendment was not motivated by a fear that Congress might regulate civilian use of weapons. "[T]here is no indication that the Framers of the Amendment intended to enshrine the common-law right of self-defense in the Constitution."

d. *Precedent.* "[T]he *Miller* Court unanimously concluded that the Second Amendment did not apply to the possession of a firearm that did not have 'some reasonable relationship to the preservation or efficiency of a well-regulated militia.' " Since *Miller*, hundreds of judges have relied on its militia-based view of the Second Amendment.

e. Justice Breyer, joined by all of the other dissenting justices, wrote a separate dissenting opinion. He agreed with Justice Stevens "that the Second Amendment protects militia-related, not self-defense-related interests." But he also argued that the Court failed to show that the District's gun control law "is unreasonable or inappropriate in Second Amendment terms." The DC law would be constitutional under the rational basis standard of review. Justice Breyer would adopt an "interest-balancing inquiry," given that the law "implicates competing constitutionally protected interests in complex ways." He argues that the DC handguns control law is "a proportionate, not a disproportionate, response to the compelling concern that led the District to adopt it."

5. ***Heller* Perspectives**

a. The Court and the Stevens dissent both accept Originalism in determining the meaning of the Second Amendment. Yet they focus on different evidence to support their view of Originalism and differ 5–4 on the proper interpretation of the Second Amendment.

b. *Heller* holds that the Second Amendment establishes a personal right to possess usable handguns for defense of the home. But it leaves critical questions concerning the scope of the Second Amendment right undecided. What is the status of government regulation of weapons other than handguns, of regulation of the possession of firearms outside of the home or of the myriad of other gun control laws? What standard of review should a court use in reviewing such laws?

6. **Incorporation**

Heller did not decide whether the Second Amendment right extends to the states through the Fourteenth Amendment. But in *McDonald v. City of Chicago* (2010), the Court, 5–4, held: "Applying the standard that is well established in our case law, we hold that the Second Amendment right is fully applicable to the States."

Example: Chicago and Oak Park, Illinois had laws banning possession of handguns. Justice Alito, writing for a plurality, declined to overrule the *Slaughter–House Cases* and hold that the Second Amendment right is among the privileges or immunities protected by the Fourteenth Amendment, citing the lack of consensus on what rights should be included among the protected privileges or immunities and the well-established use of the Due Process Clause to analyze what rights are protected against state infringement by the Fourteenth Amendment. Instead, the plurality used selective incorporation (see Ch. VI, E, 3). Writing for the Court, Justice Alito stated: "Self-defense is a basic right, recognized by many legal systems from ancient times to the present day, and in *Heller*, we held that individual self-defense is 'the central component' of the Second Amendment right. *Heller* makes it clear that this right is 'deeply rooted in this Nation's history and tradition,' *Glucksberg*." The Court supported the *Heller* analysis with historical evidence from Reconstruction. The Court remanded the question whether the Illinois ordinance violated the Second Amendment right to the lower courts.

Justice Thomas, concurring, did not accept the due process incorporation analysis; the Due Process Clause is only a guarantee of processes, not substantive rights. Instead, Justice Thomas looked to what ordinary citizens at the time of the ratification of the Fourteenth Amendment would have understood "privileges or immunities" to mean. He concluded that "the right to keep and bear arms is a privilege of American citizenship that applies to the States through the Fourteenth Amendment Privilege or Immunity Clause." He provided an extensive historical record to support his argument that the Second Amendment was essential to the preservation of liberty, part of "the minimum baseline of federal rights" protected by the Clause.

While the dissent believed *Heller* was incorrectly decided, they argued that, even if correct, the Second Amendment should not be incorporated. Justice Stevens, dissenting, focused on the substantive question whether the Constitution guaranteed a fundamental personal right enforceable against the states to possess handguns. He concluded that the states' laws did not violate values "implicit in the concept of ordered liberty." Justice Breyer, joined by Justices Ginsburg and Sotomayor, dissenting, argued that it had not been shown through "text, history, or underlying rationale" that the Second Amendment right is "fundamental to the American scheme of justice." The dissent rejected the Court's "history—constrained approach" in favor of a broad ranging inquiry into the place of the personal right to possess and bear arms for self-defense in our society. *McDonald v. City of Chicago* (2010).

F. Review Questions

1. **T or F**   The Bill of Rights applies only to the national government.

2. **T or F**   The Fourteenth Amendment Privileges or Immunities Clause protects essentially the same rights as the Due Process Clause.

3. **T or F**   The Constitution does not confer an individual right to own a firearm for private use.

4. **T or F**   The right to possess and bear arms protected by the Second Amendment is a privilege or immunity of federal citizenship protected by the Fourteenth Amendment against state abuse.

5.   Recently, the legislature of the state of West Lincoln enacted a statute stating that before a new entrant into the dry cleaning industry can be licensed, the State Board of Dry Cleaners must ascertain the "necessity" for the new entrant and find that the existing dry cleaning establishments in the state "are not adequate to meet the public needs." Kris Kleen wants to go into the dry cleaning business in the state of West Lincoln. He has consulted a lawyer. His lawyer thinks that the statute is constitutionally invalid on a number of grounds. He thinks that the statute is particularly vulnerable because he believes it violates the Privileges or Immunities Clause of the Fourteenth Amendment. Kris Kleen's lawyer has filed suit in the appropriate state court. He alleges that the right to choose one's calling is one of the privileges or immunities of United States citizenship protected by the Fourteenth Amendment. Is he right?

VI

Due Process of Law

■ *ANALYSIS*

Express protection for personal liberty in the original Constitution can be found in Art. I, §§ 9 and 10, prohibiting either the federal or state governments from enacting Ex Post Facto laws or Bills of Attainder. Economic liberty and property rights were protected by a provision prohibiting state impairment of contract obligations (the Contract Clause). This protection of economic rights was augmented by the Fifth Amendment which provided that property should not be taken for public use without just compensation (the Takings Clause). This "Takings" limitation on government regulation burdening economic interests is receiving renewed attention in recent years.

But it is the Due Process Clauses of the Fifth and Fourteenth Amendments that have traditionally been central to the protection of personal liberty and property rights. First, the Due Process Clause of the Fourteenth Amendment became the vehicle for *incorporation* of fundamental rights of the Bill of Rights as limitations on state action. Second, the Due Process Clauses have been interpreted by the Court to impose a *substantive* limitation on what government can do. Third, the Due Process Clauses provide *procedural* protection when government regulation burdens life, liberty or property.

A. Ex Post Facto Laws

1. Constitutional Text

Art. I, § 9, cl. 3 prohibits the federal government from passing ex post facto laws. Art. I, § 10, cl. 1 imposes a similar limitation on the states. This prohibition against retrospective punishment seeks to assure that legislative acts give fair warning of their effect, allowing individuals to rely on their meaning until changed. It also implements the basic legal principle in western civilization that a person should not be penalized without a pre-existing law. *Nulla poena sine lege.* While the constitutional clauses apply only to legislation, action by the courts or the executive which imposes retrospective punishment can be challenged under the Due Process Clauses.

2. Criminal Punishment

An ex post facto law is a statute which imposes punishment retrospectively to conduct which occurred prior to passage of the law. The classic example is a statute that makes conduct criminal which was not an offense when committed. But the *Ex Post Facto* Clauses also prohibit other legislation which retrospectively disadvantages an offender, *e.g.*, by aggravating a crime, or imposing a greater punishment, or by changing the rules of evidence or the defenses available, thereby making it easier to convict. *Calder v. Bull* (1798).

Examples: (1) A state statute repealing an earlier statute and reducing the amount of "gain" time for good conduct deducted from a convicted prisoner's sentence, is an unconstitutional ex post facto law as applied to the petitioner, whose crime was committed before the new statute's enactment. Since the petitioner lost gain time that had been available under the repealed statute, the effect of the repealer statute was to retrospectively impose a punishment more severe than that assigned when the defendant was convicted and thereby retrospectively disadvantaged him. *Weaver v. Graham* (1981).

(2) A state statute extending the statute of limitations for sex-related child abuse crimes was an ex post facto law as applied to the prosecution of an individual for offenses the prosecution of which was previously time-barred by the statute of limitations. The statute authorized prosecution of specified crimes for which the statute of limitations had already tolled where the victim reported an allegation of abuse to the police, there was independent evidence that "clearly and convincingly" corroborated the victim's allegation, and prosecution was begun within a year of the victim's report. Allowing a previously time-barred prosecution to proceed was equivalent to aggravating the underlying crime by authorizing punishment for conduct to which no liability previously could have attached. The law also changed the rules of evidence with respect to that prosecution because it allowed conviction based on a quantum of evidence whereas, before the law, no quantum of evidence was sufficient to convict. *Stogner v. California* (2003).

3. Civil Laws

Civil laws are not covered by the Ex Post Facto Clauses. Although the legislature may not escape the ban simply by labeling a statute as "civil"—it is the effect of the law, not its form, that is critical—the courts have often been deferential, allowing retrospective laws with onerous effects to pass as civil enactments. Professional disqualification, deportation, imposition of an increased sanction for a three time offender enacted after the defendant had committed the first two offenses (i.e., "three strikes and you're out") have been treated as civil or prospective and therefore not violative of the Ex Post Facto Clauses. Laws which simply alter procedural rules without disadvantaging a person do not violate the limitation. *In determining whether the effects of a law make it punitive, the court will consider factors such as, "whether, in its necessary operation, the regulatory scheme: has been regarded in our history and traditions as a punishment; imposes an affirmative disability or restraint, promotes the traditional aims of punishment; has a rational connection to a non-punitive purpose; or is excessive with respect to this purpose.*" Kennedy v. Mendoza–Martinez (1964).

Examples: (1) The deportation of aliens whose membership in the Communist Party ended before a law making such membership punishable by deportation does not violate the Ex Post Facto Clause. "Deportation, however severe its consequences, has been consistently classified as a civil rather than criminal procedure." *Harisiades v. Shaughnessy* (1952).

(2) A state Sexually Violent Predator Act providing that a person convicted of a sexually violent crime, upon release from prison, can be involuntarily civilly committed if he "suffers from a mental disorder which makes [him] likely to engage in the predatory acts of sexual violence," is not an ex post facto law. Such a proceeding is civil, not criminal. On its face, the statute is a civil commitment scheme designed to protect the public. It does not implicate either of the two primary objectives of punishment, retribution or deterrence. No finding of scienter is required. The potentially indefinite duration of confinement is linked to the mental abnormality. The absence of any legitimate "treatment" does not establish that the confinement is disguised punishment. *Kansas v. Hendricks* (1997).

(3) A state statute that imposed retroactive registration and community notification requirements on persons convicted of sex offenses against children did not violate the Ex Post Facto Clause because it was not so punitive in purpose or effect as to negate the legislature's intent to create a civil, non-punitive regulatory regime intended to protect the public from sex offenders. The statute, one of many "Megan's Laws" passed by states, required persons convicted of sex and kidnapping offenses against children to register prior to release, providing personal information. The information was posted to provide a convenient and cost-effective means for the public to access the information, most of which was already publicly available. Nor did the regime impose a restraint or disability on the offenders, because it did not require the state's approval to move or change jobs, and did not involve supervision, like probation.

Finally, even if the legislature had an incidental purpose to deter future crimes, the statute had a rational connection to a non-punitive purpose, which was to promote safety. *Smith v. Doe* (2003).

B. Bills of Attainder

1. Constitutional Text

Art. I, § 9 prohibits Congress from enacting Bills of Attainder and Art. I, § 10 contains a similar prohibition directed to the states. In a sense, a Bill of Attainder is a specific illustration in the Constitution of the separation of powers principle, *i.e.,* punishment is a judicial and not a legislative function.

2. Punishment Without Trial

Functionally, the Bill of Attainder clauses prohibit the legislature from punishing individuals without the benefit of judicial trial. The meaning of punishment in this context is not limited to imprisonment.

C. Impairment of Obligation of Contract

1. Constitutional Text

Art. I, § 10, provides that "no state shall * * * pass any * * * law impairing the obligation of contract." While there is no comparable clause applicable to the federal government, the Fifth Amendment Due Process Clause guarantees procedural fairness which would bar unreasonable impairment of substantive vested legal rights. Fifth Amendment due process review has been characterized by the Court as "less searching" than review under the Contract Clause.

2. Present Scope

By giving a broad construction to the concept of "contract," courts could invalidate state police power measures. During most of the twentieth century, the clause has been accorded only limited importance. While the Court has revived the Contract Clause on occasion, it is unlikely today that it will be used as a significant limitation on government power.

3. Judicial Construction

The guarantee applies only against legislative (not judicial) action impairing substantive legal rights (not procedures for enforcement of contracts). While both private and public contracts are protected, the state may reserve the power to subsequently revise its licenses and other contracts.

a. Private Contracts

In the case of private contracts, a challenger must initially establish that the law substantially impairs pre-existing contractual relationships. If this threshold is met, the government must demonstrate that the law imposes reasonable conditions appropriate to achieving a significant and legitimate public purpose. In most cases, the courts defer to the legislative judgment.

A severe impairment will be particularly vulnerable (1) if it is not designed to deal with a broad generalized economic or social problem, (2) if it is a permanent rather than a temporary impairment, (3) if the area regulated has never before been subject to regulation by the state, and (4) if the impairment in question has an extremely narrow focus. *Allied Structural Steel Company v. Spannaus* (1978) (state statute providing for vesting of employee pension rights if an employer closes a facility in the state or terminates a pension program held unconstitutional).

Example: A state law imposing price controls on interstate natural gas sales, and retroactively prohibiting application of private contract clauses allowing (1) price escalation if the government fixes prices at higher than the contract price, and (2) redetermination of prices, does not violate the Contract Clause.

First, the state act does not meet the threshold test since it does not operate as a substantial impairment of the contractual relationship. The heavily-regulated character of the natural gas industry and the inclusion of the contract clauses indicate that the parties knew that their contractual rights were subject to price regulation. Even assuming the Act substantially impaired the contractual relation, the Act was a reasonable means of achieving the significant and legitimate public purposes of protecting consumers from the escalation of prices caused by deregulation and preventing imbalances in intrastate and interstate markets. The Act's prohibitions are limited to the context posing the greatest dangers from price escalation. *Energy Reserves Group, Inc. v. Kansas Power & Light Co.* (1983).

b. Public Contracts

In the case of public contracts, (1) the state may reserve the power to subsequently revise its licenses and other contracts; (2) a state may not abandon its sovereign power to legislate for the public health, safety, and well-being by a contract and if it does so then any such contract is invalid; and (3) while the state may contract away its financial powers, it may impair such contracts if this is reasonable and necessary to serve important state interests.

Example: State statutes repealing a statutory covenant made by the two states limiting the ability of the Port Authority of New York and New Jersey to subsidize rail passenger transportation from revenues and reserves violates the Contract Clause. The repeal on the limitation eliminated an important security provision of bondholders and thus impaired the obligation of the state's contract. In this instance the repeal was not necessary to encourage users of private automobiles to shift to public transportation, and it was not reasonable in light of any changed circumstances since the contract was entered into. *United States Trust Co. of New York v. New Jersey* (1977).

D. The Takings Clause

1. Taking Property

The federal and state governments have power to take private property for public use (eminent domain). An exercise of the eminent domain satisfies the "public use" requirement if it is rationally related to a conceivable public purpose. *Hawaii Housing Authority v. Midkiff* (1983). The federal government must in addition show that a taking is authorized under its Art. I powers, *e.g.,* condemnation of land to build a post office under the postal power.

Example: Interest income generated by funds held in an Interest on Lawyers Trust Account (IOLTA) program used by Texas to provide legal services to the poor, is the "private property" of the owner of the principal. A well-established common law rule states that "interest follows principal." Therefore, the interest is the property of the owner of the principal even though its economic value may be minimal. In remanding, the Court expressed no view on whether public use of this interest income is a "taking" requiring "just compensation." *Phillips v. Washington Legal Foundation* (1998).

2. Constitutional Text

The Fifth Amendment provides that private property is not to be taken for public use without just compensation. A similar limitation is applicable to the states as part of Fourteenth Amendment due process. A principal purpose of the Takings Clause is "to bar Government from forcing some people alone to bear public burdens which, in all fairness and justice, should be borne by the public as a whole." *Armstrong v. United States* (1960).

3. What Is a "Taking"

a. Regulatory Takings

While formal condemnation of property for a public use is the classic example of a "taking" requiring compensation, the concept is broader. "[W]hile property may be regulated to a certain extent, if regulation goes too far it will be recognized as a taking." *Pennsylvania Coal Co. v. Mahon* (1922). But the mere fact that property values are diminished by government regulation does not create a compensable taking of property. The Court's attempt to identify regulatory actions that are equivalent to the classic taking of condemnation.

b. Reasonable Regulation

Generally, if government regulation reasonably advances legitimate public interests, and merely diminishes the value of the property, the regulation will not constitute a compensable taking. *In determining if government action is a compensable taking, courts will consider: (1) the economic impact of the regulation to the claimant; (2) the extent to which the regulation has interfered with distinct investment expectations; and, (3) the character of the governmental action.* See Penn Central Transportation Co. v. New York City (1978). *Regulations must meet the requirement of public use, but judicial examination of a regulation's effectiveness "has no proper place in [the Court's] takings jurisprudence."* Lingle v. Chevron (2005).

Examples: (1) A municipal zoning ordinance, enacted after plaintiff's purchase of land, which limits the uses of the land is not a "taking" without just compensation in violation of the Fifth and Fourteenth Amendments. The ordinance, as interpreted, did not bar all residential uses. The ordinance substantially advanced the public's interest in avoiding the ill effects of urbanization by controlling land development. Plaintiffs share in the benefits and burdens of the controls. The ordinance neither prevents economically viable uses of the land nor extinguishes fundamental attributes of ownership. There has been no denial of "justice and fairness." *Agins v. City of Tiburon* (1980).

(2) A Pennsylvania statute prohibiting mining of 50% of the coal beneath certain pre-existing public buildings, dwellings, and cemeteries in order to prevent damage to these structures does not constitute a state "taking" for which the owner is entitled to compensation. The owners of the mining rights are not denied all economically viable use of their property. The Court deferred to the legislature's finding that mining damage posed a significant threat to the common welfare. The prohibition was a legitimate exercise of state police power, narrowly tailored to its significant and legitimate purposes. *Keystone Bituminous Coal Association v. DeBenedictis* (1987).

(3) A person who purchases waterfront property with notice that the State had used its wetlands regulations to deny a number of development proposals for the property is not barred from challenging the State's regulation as an inverse condemnation constituting a taking requiring compensation. A transfer of property which occurs after enactment of a land use regulation does not absolve the state of its obligation to defend the reasonableness of its regulation. "Future generations, too, have a right to challenge unreasonable limitations on the use and value of land." Further, precluding such taking claims "would work a critical alteration to the nature of property, as the newly regulated landowner is stripped of the ability to transfer the interest which was possessed prior to regulation." In this case, however, the property still had significant economic value for use as a private residence—use of the regulation was not a deprivation of all economic value. The case was remanded to determine if the government action was a reasonable regulation or a compensable taking. *Palazzolo v. Rhode Island* (2001).

(4) A Hawaii statute capping the rent an oil company can charge the lessee-operator of a company-owned service station cannot be unconstitutional as an uncompensated taking without an analysis of the burden imposed on the claimant by the statute. The trial court's determination that the statute was a taking because it was ineffective in substantially advancing any legitimate public interest re-

vealed "nothing about the *magnitude or character of the burden*" the regulation imposed on private property. Therefore, the "substantially advances" formula examining the effectiveness of a statute is not a valid takings test. *Lingle v. Chevron* (2005).

c. Categorical (Per Se) Takings

If the government physically invades the property on a permanent basis, there is a compensable taking. No specific inquiry into the public interest is required. Similarly, a "confiscatory taking," where the regulation "denies all economically beneficial or productive use of land," is a compensable taking. Just compensation must be paid unless the state can show that the state law of property or nuisance had previously limited the ownership of the property. *Lucas v. South Carolina Coastal Council* (1992).

Examples: (1) A New York statute which requires owners of rental housing units to permit the installation of cable T.V. equipment on their property constitutes a state "taking" for which the owner is entitled to just compensation under the Fifth Amendment. Since the cable equipment is affixed to the building, there is a physical occupation which deprives the owner of his rights to possession, use, and disposition of his property. No balancing of interests is required. Requiring the property owner to install equipment such as smoke alarms, *which would be owned by the property owner* is distinguished. *Loretto v. Teleprompter Manhattan CATV Corp.* (1982).

(2) State regulations banning housing construction on a coastal island to preserve the state's beaches deprived a private property owner of all economically beneficial uses of property and thus could result in a confiscatory taking, requiring compensation regardless of the public interest. The regulation would not be a taking if the state can show its restrictions are innate in the owner's title by being part of the state's property or nuisance law. *Lucas v. South Carolina Coastal Council* (1992).

(3) A temporary moratorium on development of property imposed during the process of devising a comprehensive

land-use plan does not constitute a *per se* categorical taking of the property. Property owners of land in the area of Lake Tahoe challenged the 32 month moratorium which prohibited virtually all development as categorical takings under the decision in *Lucas*. But the Court held 6–3 that since the owner was not deprived of "*all* economically beneficial uses" of his land, the "essentially ad hoc, factual inquiries" of *Penn Central*, involving an examination of all the relevant circumstances, in the interests of "fairness and justice," should be used. *Tahoe–Sierra Preservation Council, Inc. v. Tahoe Regional Planning Agency* (2002).

(4) A Washington law requiring lawyers to place client funds incapable of earning interest into special accounts called IOLTAs (interest on lawyer's trust accounts), the interest on which had to be paid by the bank to the Legal Foundation of Washington for law-related charitable purposes, constituted a per se taking. But just compensation is measured by the property owner's loss, not the government's gain. Since the clients could not expect to have otherwise earned interest on their funds, just compensation in this case was zero. *Brown v. Legal Foundation of Washington* (2003).

d. Conditional Takings

1) Government imposition of conditions on a person seeking to use or develop property are limited by the Takings Clause. Under the *unconstitutional conditions doctrine*, "the government may not require a person to give up a constitutional right—here the right to receive just compensation when property is taken for a public use—in exchange for a discretionary benefit conferred by the government where the property sought has little or no relationship to the benefit." *Dolan v. City of Tigard* (1994).

2) In determining whether a condition is a reasonable regulation or a compensable taking, the Court asks two questions: First, whether there is an "essential nexus" between the "legitimate state interest" and the condition (Nollan). *Second, whether the government has made sufficient individualized findings establishing that the condition, in nature and extent, has a "rough proportionality" to the impact of the proposed development.* (Dolan).

Examples: (1) A state requirement that an ocean-front property owner grant a public easement across his property for beach users as a condition of securing a permit to rebuild a residence on the property is a compensable taking. Assuming that the state might have denied the permit if it reasonably determined that the proposed development would impair legitimate state interests, conditioning of the permit would be allowed only if it served the same governmental purpose as the ban. If it did serve that objective, it would be a reasonable regulation of land use rather than a compensable taking. *Nollan v. California Coastal Comm'n* (1987).

(2) A taking of property occurs where a city conditions approval of a business owner's application to expand her store and pave her parking lot upon dedication of land for a public greenway along a creek and a pedestrian bicycle pathway. There is the "essential nexus" between dedication of land for a greenway which will minimize flooding and the pathway dedication to reduce traffic congestion. However, the city's findings did not establish the requisite reasonable relationship, *i.e.,* "rough proportionality."

The city failed to establish that a *public* easement, as opposed to a *private* greenway was required for flood control. Nor did the city meet its burden of showing that the additional traffic congestion from the development necessitated the pathway easement. "No precise mathematical calculation is required, but the city must make some effort to quantify its findings in support of the dedication for the pedestrian/bicycle pathway beyond the conclusory statement that it could offset some of the traffic demand generated." *Dolan v. City of Tigard* (1994).

e. **Public Use**

The Takings Clause requires that takings be for a "public use." Government cannot take property solely for the purpose of conferring a private benefit on a particular private party. But public use does not require that the taken property be put to use for the general public. The Court has interpreted the requirement broadly to require only a public purpose and has followed a policy of deference to legislative judgment. *Berman v. Parker* (1954); *Hawaii Housing Authority v. Midkiff* (1984). If the takings is pursuant to a carefully considered development plan which serves a public purpose, it satisfies the public use requirement. *Kelo v. City of New London* (2005).

Example: The City of New London, Connecticut carefully formulated an integrated economic development plan it believed would provide new jobs, increase tax revenues and generally rejuvenate an economically distressed area. It then bought most of the property needed in the development area and used eminent domain to take the property of unwilling owners. The Court 5–4 held: "Given the comprehensive character of the plan, the thorough deliberation that preceded its adoption, and the limited scope of our review, it is appropriate for us * * * to resolve the challenge of individual owners, not on a piecemeal basis, but rather in light of the entire plan. Because the plan unquestionably serves a public purpose, the takings challenged here satisfy the public use requirement of the Fifth Amendment." The Court rejected the challengers proposed bright-line rule that economic development does not qualify as a public use. Nor would the Court require a "reasonable certainty" that the expected public benefits will actually accrue.

Justice Kennedy, concurring, using a rational basis standard of review, concluded that the takings in this case was not "intended to favor a particular private party, with only incidental or pretextual public benefits." Justice O'Connor, joined by Chief Justice Rehnquist and Justice Scalia, dissenting, argued that economic development takings are not constitutional. To reason "that the incidental public benefits resulting from subsequent ordinary use of private property render economic development takings 'for public use' is to wash out any distinction between private and public use of property" and effectively delete the public use requirement. It makes all private property vulnerable to being taken and transferred to other private owners, usually those with disproportionate power and influence in the political process. Justice Thomas, dissenting, urged that the Court's precedent be reconsidered. The Court should return to the original understanding, limiting the Takings Clause to authorize the taking of property "only if the public has a right to employ it, not if the public realizes any conceivable benefit from the taking." *Kelo v. City of New London* (2005).

E. Due Process: The Incorporation Process

The guarantees of the Bill of Rights do not directly limit the states. *Barron v. The Mayor and City Council of Baltimore* (1833). The present section deals with whether the Due Process Clause makes all or some of the Bill of Rights applicable to the states, whether the clause has an independent meaning, and whether Bill of Rights guarantees made applicable to the states apply to the same extent and in the same manner as they operate against the federal government.

1. Total Incorporation

The Court has rejected the argument that the Due Process Clause incorporates all of the Bill of Rights and makes them applicable against the states.

2. Flexible Due Process

In the 1940s and 1950s, a Court majority employed a flexible approach which viewed the Due Process Clause as having a meaning independent of the Bill of Rights. The Court determined whether a proceeding was so unfair as to offend fundamental standards of decency.

3. Selective Incorporation

The Court has held that some, but not all, of the provisions of the Bill of Rights are incorporated by the Due Process Clause and thus made applicable to the states. Note that the guarantees of the Due Process Clause are not limited to those rights in the Bill of Rights.

a. Standard of Incorporation

The standard of incorporation has been variously stated as whether the Bill of Rights guarantee is essential to "the concept of ordered liberty" or whether it is "fundamental to the American scheme of justice."

Example: In *McDonald v. City of Chicago* (2010), the Court held that the Second Amendment was a limit on the states through the Due Process Clause of the Fourteenth Amendment. A plurality of the Court applied the "well established" Due Process Clause standard of selective incorporation: "whether the right to keep and bear arms is fundamental to *our* scheme of ordered liberty, [*Duncan v. Louisiana* (1968)] or as we have said in a related context, whether this right is 'deeply rooted in this Nation's history and tradition.' *Washington v. Glucksberg* (1997)." Using the analysis in *Heller* that the Second Amendment is a fundamental right and that the right of self-defense has historically been recognized as a basic right and as a "central component" of the Second Amendment, the Court held that the Second Amendment right was incorporated.

b. Provisions Not Incorporated

Most of the provisions of the Bill of Rights have been incorporated. Those which today do not apply to state governments are the Seventh Amendment right to trial by jury in civil cases, the right to grand jury indictment, freedom from excessive bail, the requirements of a 12–person jury and of a unanimous verdict for conviction.

4. Full and Partial Incorporation

The Court has held that the incorporated right applies against the states to the same extent and in the same manner as the Bill of Rights provision applies against the federal government. Caveat: Later cases appear to have narrowed the scope of certain Bill of Rights guarantees to accommodate state procedures.

Example: The Sixth Amendment right to trial by jury is "fundamental to the American scheme of justice" and thus is incorporated in Fourteenth Amendment due process. *Duncan v. Louisiana* (1968). But the right to a 12–person jury is not a Sixth Amendment right and thus is not constitutionally required in federal or state criminal trials. *Williams v. Florida* (1970). A jury of five persons is not constitutionally permissible (*Ballew v. Georgia* (1978)) and a state conviction by a non-unanimous six-person jury for a non-petty offense violates due process. *Burch v. Louisiana* (1979). While the requirement of unanimity is not incorporated in Fourteenth Amendment due process, a split among the justices indicates it may still be a Sixth Amendment requirement. *Apodaca v. Oregon* (1972).

F. Traditional Substantive Due Process

During the last part of the nineteenth century, the Court began to strike down state social and economic legislation as unreasonably interfering with the liberty and property rights guaranteed by the Fourteenth Amendment Due Process Clause. Federal socio-economic legislation was similarly invalidated under the Fifth Amendment Due Process Clause.

Legislation which upset settled expectations based on the common law were almost presumptively unconstitutional. The exercise of judicial review in this area imported substantive economic concepts such as freedom of contract and the principles of free market economics into the process of due process interpretation, hence the description, substantive due process. Reaction against large-scale court invalidation of social and economic legislation gradually produced judicial restraint and a new deference to the legislative judgment in economic matters and finally today to almost total judicial abdication with respect to due process challenges to economic legislation.

1. The Rise and Fall of Economic Substantive Due Process

a. Rise of Economic Substantive Due Process

Prior to the New Deal, the courts used the Due Process Clauses of the Fifth and Fourteenth Amendments to invalidate a variety of federal and state social and economic laws as arbitrary and unreasonable interferences with the freedom to contract protected by the Due Process guarantees of liberty and property.

Example: In the heyday of economic substantive due process, the Supreme Court invalidated a state law setting maximum hours of employment for bakery employees on the ground that the statute unreasonably interfered with the right of contract between the employer and the employee. Freedom of contract was declared to be part of the liberty of the individual protected by the Fourteenth Amendment.

The Court probed the purpose of the law, questioning whether it was really a police power measure designed to serve the general public interest or an arbitrary interference with private labor relationships. Further, the Court closely scrutinized the reasonableness of the hours requirement as a means of promoting employees' health, holding the law to be an excessive burden on liberty of contract. In a famous prophetic dissent, Mr. Justice Holmes insisted that constitutional interpretation should be governed, not by the economic theories of the justices, but by whether the legislative judgment was reasonable. *Lochner v. New York* (1905).

b. Decline of Economic Substantive Due Process

In the 1930s, in the face of rising adverse public reaction to judicial invalidation of the New Deal, the doctrine of economic substantive due process began to ebb in importance and the doctrine followed a process of steady decline and erosion.

Example: The Court upheld state legislation setting milk prices against a due process challenge. While the Court spoke of the milk industry as a business "affected with a public interest," this meant only that the law was a reasonable exercise of the police power. Questions concerning the wisdom of the law are for the legislature, not the courts. The Court's evaluation of the reasonableness of the regulation reflected deference to the legislative judgment. *Nebbia v. New York* (1934).

2. Modern Substantive Due Process: Non–Fundamental Rights

RATIONAL BASIS. Today, social and economic regulatory and tax legislation which does not interfere with fundamental rights will not be closely scrutinized by the federal courts. If there is any rational basis that the legislature might have had for concluding that the legislation would further permissible legislative objectives, it will be sustained. The law must not be arbitrary or irrational. But the law is presumed to be constitutional and the burden of proving that the law is irrational is on the challenging party. This burden is essentially insurmountable and no economic legislation has been held unconstitutional by the Court, using this rationality test, since the New Deal.

GENERAL APPROACH. When examining a statute under the Due Process Clause, if there is no basis for invoking a stricter standard of review, the rationality test should be adopted. Use the following approach: (1) ascertain the objective of the law (a court will not probe for the true purpose of the law); (2) identify the means used by the state to achieve the objective; and (3) examine the rationality of the means for achieving the objective by reviewing the relevant facts. In your analysis, remember that the courts adopt a position of extreme deference to the legislative policy judgment when this standard is used.

a. In using the rationality test, the courts will not question the legislative objective. In the case of state laws, any permissible police power objective (public health, morals, and well-being) will suffice. If the law serves a valid purpose, the fact that the law incidentally serves other purposes will not make it unconstitutional.

b. While the law must be rationally related to the achievement of the objective, the courts will not second-guess the legislative fact-finding. If there are facts that would sustain the law, the courts will generally assume the legislation was based on those facts.

Examples: (1) The federal Price Anderson Act setting maximum limits on tort liability for nuclear power plant accidents is constitutional. The law is rationally designed to promote nuclear power development while providing a fair and adequate basis for recovery. Any dollar ceiling is necessarily an arbitrary determination. *Duke Power Co. v. Carolina Environmental Study Group* (1978).

(2) A state law requiring pharmacies to be operated or controlled by pharmacists does not violate due process despite the fact that the state supreme court had relied on an earlier substantive due process Supreme Court precedent to the contrary. *North Dakota State Board of Pharmacy v. Snyder's Drug Stores, Inc.* (1973).

c.   ***Punitive Damages.*** The Court usually applies "[a] strong presumption of validity in rejecting challenges to state rules governing the award of punitive damages." *TXO Production Corp. v. Alliance Resources Corp.* (1993) (upholding a punitive damage award 528 times actual damages given the magnitude of the potential harm). However, the "Court has found that the Constitution imposes certain limits, in respect both to procedures for awarding punitive damages and to amounts forbidden as 'grossly excessive,' " *Philip Morris USA v. Williams* (2007) (overturning Oregon jury's award of $79.5 million in punitive damages against Philip Morris because the damages were calculated to punish harm caused to others, as well as to the plaintiff).

In determining whether a punitive damages award is grossly disproportionate to actual damages, the Court will consider three factors: (1) the degree of reprehensibility of the defendant's conduct; (2) the disparity of the harm or potential harm suffered by the plaintiff and the punitive damages award; and (3) the difference between the punitive damages remedy and the civil penalties authorized or imposed in comparable cases. *BMW of North America, Inc. v. Gore* (1996) (overturning a $2 million punitive damages award based on BMW's policy of repairing and reselling damaged automobiles as new when the damage was less than 3% of the total cost and where actual damages to purchaser were calculated at $4000). In *State Farm Mutual Automobile Insurance Co. v. Campbell* (2003), the Court applied *BMW* to overturn as excessive a $145 million punitive damages award against State Farm Insurance, where compensatory damages were only $1 million. The Court noted that, "in practice, few awards exceeding a single-digit ratio between punitive and compensatory damages will satisfy due process." Additionally, a State may not prohibit judicial review of the reasonableness of jury awards of punitive damages. *Honda Motor Company v. Oberg* (1994).

Due process also governs the procedures for awarding punitive damages. Standards must be in place in order to assure that damage awards are not arbitrary and that defendants have "fair notice of the severity of the penalty that a State may impose." *BMW of North America*. For instance, a State may not "use a punitive damages award to punish a defendant for injury that it inflicts upon those who are, essentially, strangers to the litigation," because the defendants would not be able to fully defend themselves against a party who was not present and because allowing the injury of non-parties to be a factor "would add a near standardless dimension to the punitive damages equation." *Philip Morris USA*. While a jury may consider the harm caused to non-parties in determining the level of reprehensibility, it may not directly punish the defendant in its damage award for harm done to non-parties. Potential harm—but only to the plaintiff—can also be considered in the calculation of damages. *Philip Morris USA*.

G. Substantive Due Process Revisited: The Right of Privacy and Other Unenumerated Rights

1. Fundamental Rights

Just as procedural rights were incorporated into due process and made applicable to the states, various substantive limitations on government power became part of Fourteenth Amendment due process. State legislation was declared unconstitutional not because it was an arbitrary and unreasonable deprivation of liberty but because it violated the guarantee of free speech, or religious freedom, or privacy which are fundamental rights guaranteed by Due Process Clause.

"FUNDAMENTAL RIGHTS": STANDARD OF REVIEW. *When legislation intrudes on "fundamental rights" applicable to the states through the due process guarantee, courts do not apply the rational basis test. A more demanding standard of review is adopted. Often this takes the form of "strict scrutiny," i.e., the government must demonstrate that the legislation is narrowly tailored or necessary to further a compelling state interest.*

RATIONALITY TEST DISTINGUISHED. *This standard departs from the rationality test of due process in the sense that it requires a much more specific showing that the means are reasonable, a much more urgent showing of state interest must be made in order to validate the challenged legislation, and the burden of justification is on the government,* i.e., *the usual presumption of the law's validity does not apply. If such a law is not precisely drawn, it can be held to be unconstitutionally overbroad.*

2. Express, Implied and Unenumerated Rights

While a more stringent standard of review than the rationality standard is used for all *express* rights, *e.g.*, speech, religion, the Court has also applied the more demanding standard to rights that are not expressly enumerated in the Constitution. In some cases, the rights are implied from the express rights, *e.g.*, rights of association and belief implied from the First Amendment. In other instances, the judicial determination of whether a fundamental right is significantly burdened reflects considerations such as tradition, contemporary morals, precedent and analogy, logic and reason, or the consequences of the law for the individual.

In some cases, the Court declines to fashion a separate "fundamental right" but determines whether the government regulation substantially burdens a significant liberty interest guaranteed by the Due Process Clause. The Court may avoid use of "strict scrutiny" in these substantive due process cases. Instead, the Court adopts a "continuum" approach reflecting the reasoning "that certain interests require particularly careful scrutiny of the state needs asserted to justify their abridgement." *Poe v. Ullman* (1961) (Harlan, J., dissenting). The Court balances the government interest in regulating the conduct against the burden on protected liberty. While such substantive due process review does not reach the rigors of strict scrutiny, it generally does not reflect the deference of rationality review used for social and economic laws.

3. Contraception and Abortion

a. The Privacy Right

1) There is no express right of privacy in the Constitution. But in early cases involving contraception and abortion, the Court held that there is a constitutional right of privacy which limits the power of government to regulate intimate sexual activities. In *Griswold v. Connecticut* (1965), Justice Douglas, for the Court, reasoned that the privacy right could be implied from the

penumbras of the First, Third, Fourth, Fifth and Ninth Amendments. Concurring justices found the privacy right "implicit in the concept of ordered liberty" (Harlan) or emanating from the "traditions and collective consciences of our people" (Goldberg). Justice Goldberg used the Ninth Amendment as support for the existence of unenumerated rights. Members of the Court variously stressed the intimate relationship of husband and wife and the place of home and family in our society in recognizing an unenumerated fundamental right of privacy.

2) In *Griswold*, the Court rejected the traditional rational basis standard of review but was unclear on the appropriate standard. The law was held to "sweep unnecessarily broadly" on the privacy right. Concurring members of the Court employed "strict scrutiny" or "particularly careful scrutiny" given the fundamental right at stake.

> *Example:* A state criminal statute proscribing the use of contraceptives even by married persons or aiding and abetting the use of contraceptives is a violation of the right of privacy. It is an impermissible intrusion on the right of association protecting the marital relationship. Enforcement of the law threatens police intrusion into the marital bedroom. *Griswold v. Connecticut* (1965).

3) In *Griswold*, the Court protected a right of privacy extending to the use of contraceptives within the *marital relationship*. Marital privacy reflects traditional values associated with marriage and family life. In *Eisenstadt v. Baird* (1972) (statute prohibiting distribution of contraceptives to unmarried persons violates equal protection), the Court indicated that the right of privacy includes the right of an *individual* to be free from excessive governmental intrusion into decisions relating to procreation.

b. The *Roe v. Wade* Revolution and Reaction

1) In *Roe v. Wade* (1973), the Court extended the "fundamental right" of privacy to protect a woman's decision to terminate a pregnancy. The Court held that the right of privacy has its source in the Fourteenth Amendment's guarantee of personal liberty. Some lower courts had used the Ninth Amendment.

The harm to the woman and the unwanted child were cited as justifying extension of the privacy right to abortion.

2) When a fundamental right is burdened, the *Roe* Court said, the law must be necessary to a compelling state interest. In determining whether this standard was met, the Court applied a "trimester" test. The state's interest in protecting a mother's health becomes compelling after the end of the first trimester of pregnancy. Therefore, the state may regulate the abortion procedure after the first trimester to the extent reasonably required to protect maternal health. Prior to the end of the first trimester, the attending physician and the patient are free to jointly determine the woman's medical care, without significant state regulation. After viability, the state has a compelling interest in the potentiality of human life and state regulation is permissible even if it goes so far as to prohibit abortion. But the law must provide an exception when abortion is necessary to preserve the life or health of the mother.

Example: A Texas statute making it a crime to procure or perform an abortion except "for the purpose of saving the life of the mother" violates the right of privacy founded in the Fourteenth Amendment concept of personal liberty. The law makes no distinction between an abortion performed early or late in pregnancy and allows abortion only to save the mother's life. The law is not narrowly drawn to further a compelling state interest. *Roe v. Wade* (1973).

3) From 1973 to 1992, the Court sought to apply *Roe*. There was increasing criticism of *Roe* and of the trimester test among the justices, leading to an expectation that *Roe* might soon be overruled.

c. *Casey*: The Essentials of *Roe*

1) *In 1992,* in Planned Parenthood of Southeastern Pennsylvania v. Casey, *the Court 5–4, at least formally reaffirmed the "essential holding" of* Roe v. Wade. *This was said to have three parts. First is the recognition of "the right of the woman to choose to have an abortion before viability without undue interference from the State."*

Second, the Court confirms the state's power to prohibit abortion after fetal viability, so long as it provides an exception for the mother's life or health. Third, the Court recognizes the principle "that the State has legitimate interests from the outset of the pregnancy in protecting the health of the woman and the life of the fetus that may become a child." The reaffirmation of Roe *was said to be based on the strong liberty interests involved, concerns over institutional integrity if* Roe *were overruled and the rule of* stare decisis.

2) In evaluating the right of the woman to terminate a pregnancy, the Court stressed "reasoned judgment." *Precedent established that "the most intimate and personal choices a person may make in a lifetime, choices central to personal dignity and autonomy, are central to the liberty protected by the Fourteenth Amendment."* Abortion was said to involve a similar intimate and personal decision which the woman must be free to make without government interference. The Court employed precedent and analogy to establish that liberty includes the decision of a woman to terminate a pregnancy.

3) But the unusual joint opinion crafted by Justices Kennedy, Souter and O'Connor in *Casey* does not talk of a right of privacy or even of "fundamental rights." The Court in *Casey* does not adopt strict scrutiny and expressly rejects the trimester test as based on a misconception of the pregnant woman's interest and an underevaluation of the state's interest in potential life throughout pregnancy. Only Justice Blackmun, concurring, adhered to strict scrutiny and the trimester test of *Roe.*

4) A plurality of the Court adopts an "undue burdens" test. *"An undue burden exists and therefore a provision of law is invalid, if its purpose or effect is to place a substantial obstacle in the path of a woman seeking an abortion before the fetus attains viability." The law must be designed to inform the woman's choice, not hinder it.*

> ***Example:*** A statute that requires that a woman seeking an abortion give informed consent following a 24–hour waiting period after receiving information about alternatives to abortion with an exemption for medical emergencies is not an undue burden. A requirement that physicians give truthful, non-misleading information about the nature of the

procedure, health risks and gestational age of fetus is not an undue burden. "What is at stake is the woman's right to make the ultimate choice, not a right to be insulated from all others in doing so." Given the state's interest in potential life from conception, the state may require that information about the fetus and abortion alternatives be provided designed to persuade a woman to choose childbirth over abortion. These requirements ensure that the woman makes an informed choice.

In addition, a 24–hour waiting period requirement is not an undue burden in a facial challenge to the statute. The abortion decision will be more informed and deliberate if there is time for reflection. The joint opinion seems to permit challenge to a waiting period *as applied* in particular cases, *e.g.*, poor women who could not afford an overnight stay.

A provision requiring a married woman seeking an abortion to sign a statement indicating that she notified her husband of her decision to get an abortion is an undue burden and therefore is unconstitutional. The spousal notification requirements are likely to prevent a significant number of women from seeking an abortion because of the potential of spousal and child abuse by husbands.

Reporting requirements, such as the name of the physician, the facility, prior abortions, gestational age of fetus and marital status, which respect a patient's confidentiality and privacy, are constitutional. They are reasonably directed at the preservation of maternal health. A reporting provision that requires a reason for failing to provide notice to a husband, however, is an undue burden. *Planned Parenthood of Southeastern Pennsylvania v. Casey* (1992).

d. Abortion After *Casey*

1) In *Casey*, the plurality distinguished between laws imposing a substantial obstacle to a woman's free choice and laws that create structural mechanisms for a state to express its respect for prenatal life. *Roe* and *Casey* also required that, in regulating abortion, a state must provide an exception "where it is necessary in appropriate medical judgment, for the life or health of the mother." *Roe*. Both of these principles were critical in the partial birth abortion cases.

2) *Stenberg v. Carhart* (2000)

   a. The Court held 5–4 that a Nebraska partial birth abortion law was facially unconstitutional. Partial birth abortion (or D & X) was defined as partially delivering vaginally "a living unborn child before killing the unborn child and completing the delivery." The statute required the intentional delivery into the vagina of "a living unborn child or a substantial portion thereof" for the purpose of killing the unborn child. D & X is used primarily for late-term abortions.

   b. First, the state law lacked any exception for the health of the mother. The state failed to show that its ban on D & X "may not create significant health risks for women, because the record shows that significant medical authority supports the proposition that in some circumstances, D & X would be the safest procedure."

   c. Second, the statute "unduly burdened" the woman's abortion choice by using broad language which could be read to ban some abortions using the most commonly used method for performing protected previability abortions (D & E)—"All those who perform abortion procedures using that method must fear conviction and imprisonment."

   d. The dissent, which included Justice Kennedy who was a member of the *Casey* plurality, argued that the Act advanced critical state interests, denied no woman the right to chose a safe abortion and imposed no undue burden on the right. The Act furthered state interests in expressing concern for the life of the unborn, in preserving the integrity of the medical profession and expressing the state's moral condemnation of the procedure which some believe resembles infanticide. The Act deprived no woman of a safe abortion. Any possible marginal safety difference would not be a substantial obstacle to the abortion right. Rules of statutory construction established that the Act was limited to a ban on D & X; D & E would not fall within the ban.

3) *Facial and As–Applied Validity.* In *Stenberg* the Court held the law facially unconstitutional; the law was invalidated wholesale. But the Court has held that even if a statute would be unconstitutional in some of its applications, invalidating it in its entirety is not always necessary. It may be possible to provide narrower injunctive and declaratory relief.

> *Example:* New Hampshire had enacted a statute requiring parental notification before a minor could receive an abortion, and did not explicitly allow a physician to perform an abortion on a minor without notification in a medical emergency. Because there are cases where the minor mother needs an immediate abortion in order to preserve her health, the application of the statute in those select cases would be unconstitutional. Rather than striking down the whole statute, the Court remanded for the lower court to consider a declaratory judgment and injunctive relief prohibiting only the unconstitutional applications of the statute. *Ayotte v. Planned Parenthood of Northern New England* (2006).

4) ***Gonzales v. Carhart* (2007)**

a) The Court held 5–4, per Justice Kennedy, that the federal Partial Birth Abortion Ban Act of 2003, banning partial birth abortions (intact D & E) was not facially unconstitutional. The Act provided a limited exception to preserve the life of the mother but did not include any health exception. Instead Congress included legislative findings that "[a] moral, medical and ethical consensus exists that the practice of performing a partial birth abortion is a gruesome and inhumane procedure that is never medically necessary and should be prohibited."

b) Justice O'Connor, who had joined the Court's opinion in *Stenberg*, had resigned and was replaced by Justice Alito. Chief Justice Rehnquist had died and had been replaced by Chief Justice Roberts. Both of the new justices joined Justice Kennedy's opinion, as did Justices Scalia and Thomas.

c) *The Status of Casey*. Justice Kennedy noted that not all members of the majority support *Casey's* re-affirmation of *Roe's* essential principles. But the Court would "assume" those principles for its opinion. Justice Ginsburg, dissenting, argued that the Court "refuses to take *Casey* and *Stenberg* seriously."

d) *Vagueness*. The Act "sets forth 'relatively clear guidelines' as to prohibited conduct and provides 'objective criteria' to evaluate whether a doctor has performed a prohibited procedure." Its use of "anatomical landmarks" and mens rea requirement, "defines the line between potentially criminal conduct on the one hand and lawful abortion on the other."

e) *Overbreadth*. Unlike *Stenberg*, which prohibited intentionally delivering into the vagina a living unborn child "or a substantial portion thereof" before killing it, the federal Act requires the extraction of the entire fetus by providing anatomical landmarks to define the prohibited act. Further, the federal law has intent requirements which preclude liability for accidental intact D+E. The doctor must "deliberately and intentionally vaginally deliver a living fetus before performing the overt act." The "vast majority" of D+E procedures are safeguarded.

f) *Undue Burden*

(1) The Court held that the law did not facially impose a substantial obstacle to a woman seeking a previalidity abortion. *"Where it has a rational basis to act, and it does not impose an undue burden, the State may use its regulatory power to bar certain procedures and substitute*

others, all in furtherance of its legitimate interests in regulating the medical profession in order to promote respect for life, including the life of the unborn."

(2) *Purpose.* Congress acted rationally to express respect for the dignity of human life, to protect the integrity and ethics of the medical profession, and to protect women in making a "difficult and painful moral decision" which she may come to regret. The Court's focus on the claimed state interest in dealing with the emotional and moral difficulty for the woman and the claim that some undetermined number of women will regret their decision is a new and controversial argument in *Gonzales*. The state can claim an interest in protecting women and not only the unborn child.

(3) *Effect.* The Court held that the absence of an exception to protect a woman's health did not make the Act facially unconstitutional. *"The medical uncertainty over whether the Act's prohibition creates significant health risks provides a sufficient basis to conclude in this facial attack that the Act does not impose an undue burden."* While not placing dispositive weight on Congress' findings, some of which are factually incorrect, Congress' findings are reviewed under a deferential standard. The medical uncertainty over whether the barred procedure is ever necessary to preserve a woman's health does not make the Act facially unconstitutional *"given the availability of other abortion procedures that are considered safe alternatives."*

g) Note that *Gonzales* holds only that the federal Act is not *facially* unconstitutional—the Act would not be unconstitutional "in a large fraction of relevant cases." But the Act would be "open to a proper as-applied challenge in a discrete case."

h) Justice Ginsburg, dissenting, argued that in fact, the Court's decision was an effort "to chip away" at the woman's abortion right. Under *Stenberg*, a division in medical opinion means, at most, uncertainty, a factor which indicates the presence of risk to the woman's health, not its absence.

In fact, the record indicated that, "significant medical authority" accepted the proposition that "in certain circumstances and for certain women, intact D+E is safer than alternative procedures and necessary to protect women's health." Thus the Act subjected these women to added risk.

Further, the dissent argued that the Act does not further any legitimate governmental purpose. No fetus is saved since the Act bars only a *method* of abortion. Ultimately, the Court allows moral concerns to override fundamental rights. The concern over a woman's regret, an "antiabortion shibbolleth," for which there is concededly no evidence, is met, not by informing the woman's choice but by denying her that choice. Finally, the dissent criticizes the Court's handling of facial challenges. In determining if the law is unconstitutional "in a large fraction of relevant cases," the relevant class is not all women. "The absence of a health exception burdens all women for whom it is relevant—women who, in the judgment of their doctors, require an intact D+E because other procedures would place their health at risk."

e. Privacy Rights of Minors

The reproductive rights of the woman are constitutionally protected even if she is a minor. However, the Court, recognizing the greater state interest in protecting immature minors, has applied a less stringent standard of review in cases involving minors and allows a greater degree of state regulation. *Generally, parental notification and even parental consent can be required if provision is made whereby a judge can grant permission for the abortion where the minor has sufficient maturity or where parental involvement would not be in her best interests.*

Examples: (1) A parental notification statute which requires that a doctor notify both parents of a minor female seeking an abortion without provision for a judicial bypass, is unconstitutional. The requirement that both parents be notified serves no legitimate state interest and could have harmful effects on the pregnant minor. A provision in the law which provides that a judicial bypass procedure would be implemented if the dual parent notification section was enjoined by a court is constitutional, however, and saves the statute.

By allowing a minor to show that she possesses sufficient maturity to make an informed choice or that parental notification was not in her best interests, the bypass procedure addresses the very concerns which rendered the original statute unconstitutional. *Hodgson v. Minnesota* (1990).

(2) A statute that requires an unemancipated minor seeking an abortion to get the informed consent of one parent, but provides a judicial bypass if the minor does not wish to or cannot get parental consent, and which provides an exemption for medical emergencies, is not an undue burden and thus is constitutional. *Planned Parenthood of Southeastern Pennsylvania v. Casey* (1992).

f. Abortion Funding

But the abortion right is not significantly burdened if government fails to make the right effective by funding abortions even for those dependent on government for their medical assistance. There is no affirmative right to government aid.

Example: A state does not act unconstitutionally if it refuses to provide funding for indigent women who might otherwise be unable to secure an abortion. There is no constitutional obligation that government must affirmatively act to implement the abortion decision of the women. *Maher v. Roe* (1977). Nor does a federal statute denying public funding for certain medically-necessary abortions violate Due Process, Equal Protection or the Establishment Clause. While government may not place obstacles in the path of a woman's exercise of her freedom of choice, it need not remove those obstacles it did not create. *Harris v. McRae* (1980). States may prohibit public employees and public facilities from being used for facilitating abortions not necessary to save the life of the mother. States need not commit any resources to facilitating abortions. *Webster v. Reproductive Health Services* (1989).

4. Sodomy Laws

a. The *Bowers v. Hardwick* Precedent

1)   In *Bowers v. Hardwick* (1986), the Court held 5–4 that the Georgia gender-neutral sodomy law was constitutional as applied to

consensual adult homosexual activity in private. There is no fundamental liberty right to engage in such homosexual activity. Precedent recognizing a fundamental liberty right to family, marriage, and procreation was distinguished. Homosexual sodomy was not "implicit in the concept of ordered liberty" or "deeply rooted in this Nation's history and tradition," but instead, had been historically legally proscribed. Illegal conduct is not protected simply because it is performed in the home. The application of state law to homosexual sodomy is rationally related to furthering the majority's belief that homosexual sodomy is immoral.

2) A dissent written by Justice Blackmun, joined by Justices Brennan, Marshall and Stevens, reasoned that society's traditional proscription of homosexual sodomy should not control the outcome of the case. Precedent established that there is a fundamental right of privacy, which encompasses personal privacy and spatial privacy. Personal privacy stresses protection of decisional autonomy and intimate association. Spatial privacy affords special protection to home life. Homosexual sodomy in this case involved both forms of the fundamental liberty right of privacy.

3) Justice Stevens, dissenting, reasoned that a general ban on sodomy involves essential liberty to engage in private, non-reproductive, intimate social conduct, even between married heterosexual adults. Liberty is presumed to be the same for all citizens and the state failed to provide any essential, legitimate basis for treating homosexuals differently. The dissent of Justice Stevens would strongly influence the Court's analysis in *Lawrence v. Texas* (2003).

b. *Lawrence v. Texas* (2003)

1) In *Lawrence v. Texas* (2003), the Court, per Justice Kennedy, overruled *Bowers*, holding that a state law criminalizing homosexual sodomy violates due process liberty. The Court reviewed the substantive due process decisions after *Griswold* which protect decisional choices regarding intimate social activity, whether the parties are married or not. The issue is not, as *Bowers* claimed, whether there is a fundamental right to homo-

sexual sodomy, but whether the state can control intimate choices involving consensual adult sexual conduct in the privacy of the home.

2) The *Bowers* Court erred in claiming that the ban on homosexual sodomy has ancient roots. Nineteenth century sodomy laws were general and enforced only in limited factual contexts. It was not until the 1970's that homosexuals were targeted by sodomy laws.

3) *Modern laws and traditions show an* emerging awareness, *that liberty affords substantial protection to adult persons in deciding how to conduct their private lives in matters pertaining to sex.* The Court discussed the Model Penal Code, widespread non-enforcement of sodomy laws, and the increasing liberalization of laws regulating homosexual conduct in western countries and under international law.

4) The foundations of *Bowers v. Hardwick* have eroded. There has been no reliance on it; subsequent precedent has undermined it. Justice Kennedy emphasized *Planned Parenthood* v. *Casey*, where the Court had protected intimate decisions essential to happiness and *Romer v. Evans*, which brought the central holding of *Bowers* into question. While *Romer v. Evans* was decided using the Equal Protection Clause, "[e]quality of treatment and the due process right to demand respect for conduct protected by the substantive guarantee of liberty are linked in important respects."

5) *Bowers* was wrongly decided. The individual decisions of married and unmarried persons concerning the intimacies of their physical relationships, even if they do not involve procreation, implicate protected liberty. The fact that a majority of citizens traditionally view a practice as immoral is not a sufficient reason for upholding a law prohibiting the practice.

6) The Court holds: "The Texas statute furthers no legitimate state interest which can justify its intrusion into the personal and private life of the individual." The Court does not indicate what standard of review is being used. It might be considered strict scrutiny, a "particularly careful scrutiny" or a rationality test. Finally, the Court indicated it was not dealing with the issue of gay marriage.

7) Justice O'Connor, concurring, agreed that the Texas law was unconstitutional but would have decided the case on equal protection grounds, using a "more searching form of rational basis review." Therefore, she would not have overruled *Bowers*. The law involved discrimination based on homosexual status since it criminalized the conduct that defined the class. The prohibition reflected a decision to harm a politically unpopular group, an illegitimate state interest, and inhibited personal relationships which also supported using heightened judicial review. Moral disapproval of a group does not provide a rational basis for discrimination. Like the Court, she indicated that gay marriage was not at issue.

8) Justice Scalia, joined by Chief Justice Rehnquist and Justice Thomas, dissenting, criticized the Court for using "an unheard-of form of rational basis review that will have far reaching implications beyond this case." He argued that the Court ignored stare decisis. *Bowers* had upheld laws prohibiting homosexual sodomy and held that homosexual sodomy does not involve a fundamental right. There is a long-standing history in this country of laws prohibiting sodomy in general and emerging traditions do not make the practice "deeply rooted." Justice Scalia sharply criticized the Court's use of foreign law in interpreting the Constitution. The Texas law was rationally related to the legitimate state interest in furthering the belief of its citizens that certain forms of sexual behavior are immoral and unacceptable.

5. Rights to Marriage and Family Life

a. The institutions of marriage and family life are deeply rooted in our nation's history and traditions. Through them, basic moral and cultural values are passed down. They involve intimate, personal relationships. They are, therefore, fundamental rights guaranteed by the Due Process Liberty Clause. Similarly the Court has accepted that a parent has a fundamental right in the care, custody and control of children. See also Ch. VI, H, 4, e. A more stringent standard of review is appropriate when these rights are significantly burdened.

b. But not all relationships and associations are within the "marriage" and "family life" and "parental rights" that are protected by due process liberty. The claimed interest may be defined by the Court in such a way that it does not qualify for constitutional protection.

Examples: (1) A state statute prohibiting interracial marriage violates due process liberty and the Equal Protection Clause. Marriage is one of the "basic civil rights of man" and is fundamental "to our very existence and survival." The state failed to prove that the law is necessary to the achievement of an overriding government interest. *Loving v. Virginia* (1967). See *Zablocki v. Redhail* (1978), Ch. VII, C, 6, d.

(2) A legal ordinance limiting occupancy of dwelling units to a single family and defining family so narrowly as to prohibit a grandmother from living with her two grandsons violates due process. A plurality reasoned that familial rights are not limited merely to the nuclear family. Laws limiting personal choice in matters of marriage and family life are subject to careful judicial scrutiny. The ordinance has only a marginal relation to valid government interests in preventing overcrowding, minimizing traffic and parking congestion, and avoiding excessive financial burdens on the school system. *Moore v. City of East Cleveland* (1977).

(3) A local ordinance limiting dwellings to a single family, but defining family to mean not more than two unrelated persons, does not violate due process. The law excludes land uses such as boarding houses, fraternities, communes, etc. No fundamental right of privacy or association is involved. The law is rationally related to permissible police power objectives of controlling population density and preventing noise and congestion. *Belle Terre v. Boraas* (1974).

(4) A state statute establishing a conclusive presumption that a child born to a married woman cohabiting with her husband is a child of the marriage does not violate the substantive due process rights of the natural father or the child. In a plurality opinion, Justice Scalia argued that our society has not traditionally

awarded parental rights to a natural father when the child is born into an extant marital union. It is the relationships that develop within the unitary family that have traditionally been protected as due process liberty interests. However, it appeared that a majority of the justices did accept the possibility that a natural father might have a constitutionally protected liberty interest in his relationship with a child born into an extant marital union. *Michael H. & Victoria D. v. Gerald D.* (1989).

(5) The Washington Supreme Court held that a state statute providing that "any person" may petition the court for visitation rights, and authorizing the court to grant such visitation rights when it was in the best interests of the child, was facially unconstitutional. Grandparents using the statute had successfully obtained a court order which allowed greater visitation rights with their granddaughters than the mother was willing to provide. The U.S. Supreme Court affirmed the holding that the law was unconstitutional 6–3 but there was no majority opinion.

A four-justice plurality argued that the "breathtakingly broad statute," was unconstitutional *as applied* because it violated "the fundamental rights of parents to make decisions concerning the care, custody, and control of their children." The lower court had not given any special weight to the traditional presumption that a fit parent will act in the child's best interest. Only Justice Scalia clearly rejected the argument that a parent has a special liberty right in the care, custody and control of children. The plurality and two concurring justices expressly accepted such a fundamental right. *Troxel v. Granville* (2000).

6. The Right of Travel

a. Right of Interstate Movement

The Court has never clearly identified the source of the right of interstate movement. It has been variously ascribed to the Privileges or Immunities

Clause of the Fourteenth Amendment, Art. IV, § 2, or has been held to be an inherent national right. If the right is burdened, the more stringent standard of judicial review applies. Since most of the cases involving this right have been decided under the Equal Protection Clause, it will be discussed more fully below.

b. Right of Foreign Travel

The right of travel abroad is a guarantee flowing from the Due Process Liberty Clause of the Fifth Amendment. Because of the national interest in foreign affairs and the behavior of citizens abroad, reasonable regulations, e.g., area restrictions on passport use, will be upheld. Zemel v. Rusk (1965).

Example: The Secretary of State has the power to revoke a passport when the holder's activities are causing or likely to cause serious damage to national security or foreign policy. Such a revocation does not constitute a violation of procedural due process, the right to travel or the First Amendment right to criticize the government. The right to travel abroad is subordinate to national security and foreign policy considerations and subject to reasonable government regulation. *Haig v. Agee* (1981).

7. The Right to Care and Protection

As the abortion funding cases indicate, government generally has no affirmative constitutional duty to provide care and protection for individuals. However, in some limited cases, where the State exercises custody of an individual, the Due Process Clause imposes a duty on government to assume some responsibility for that person's care and well-being.

Examples: (1) Due process liberty protects the right of involuntarily committed mentally retarded persons to "minimally adequate or reasonable training to ensure safety and freedom from undue restraint." When this right is burdened, the courts must undertake a balancing of the liberty interests against the relevant state interests. The judgments of the medical profession are presumptively valid and violation can be based only on a showing of a "substantial departure from accepted professional judgment." *Youngberg v. Romeo* (1982).

(2) The state's failure to protect a child from physical abuse by his father does not deprive the child of any due process liberty

right. There is no affirmative right to government aid, even though the welfare department has investigated reports of child abuse, and after reports of continuing abuses, has taken various steps, short of removing the child, to try to protect him. No constitutional duty has been violated. *DeShaney v. Winnebago County Dept. of Social Servs.* (1989).

(3) The state does not violate Fourteenth Amendment substantive due process by unreasonably failing to protect a city sanitary worker who dies of asphyxia while working in a manhole, even if the city manifested a policy of deliberate indifference to the employee's safety. "The Due Process Clause does not impose an independent federal obligation upon municipalities to provide certain minimal levels of safety and security in the workplace and the city's failure to train or to warn its sanitation department employees was not arbitrary in a constitutional sense." *Collins v. City of Harker Heights* (1992).

(4) A police officer does not deprive a suspect of any due process liberty right by causing his death through indifference to human life in a high-speed chase. The allegations, although serious, do not rise to the level of a constitutional violation. In the context of a high-speed chase, given the need for quick decisions, "only a purpose to cause harm unrelated to the legitimate object of arrest will satisfy the element of arbitrary conduct shocking to the conscience, necessary for a due process violation." *Sacramento v. Lewis* (1998).

8. The Right to Refuse Treatment

A person possesses a significant liberty interest in avoiding unwanted medical treatment. But the state's regulatory interest may justify the burden on the protected liberty interest.

Examples: (1) Nancy Cruzan is in a persistent vegetative condition. Her parents want artificial feeding and hydration terminated but the hospital refuses. In such circumstances, a state may constitutionally require clear and convincing evidence of the patient's desire that life-sustaining treatment be withdrawn. The competent patient has a significant liberty interest in refusing unwanted medical treatment. The state's interest in the preservation of human life and its interest in safeguarding the personal element of the choice of life and death is sufficient to justify the imposition of heightened evidentiary standards. Such a standard protects against abuse, promotes more accurate fact-finding and reflects the importance of the decision. The state is not constitutionally required to repose judgment in such matters with anyone but the patient herself; it need not accept the substituted judgment of close family members. *Cruzan v. Director, Missouri Dept. of Health* (1990).

(2) Involuntary administration of antipsychotic drugs to a mentally ill criminal defendant in order to render him competent to stand trial for serious, but nonviolent, crimes does not violate due process, "if the treatment is medically appropriate, is substantially unlikely to have side effects that may undermine the fairness of the trial, and, taking account of less intrusive alternatives, is necessary significantly to further important government trial-related interests." *Sell v. United States* (2003).

9. The Right to Die

There is no fundamental right to commit suicide nor any right to assisted suicide. Such interests are not "deeply rooted in this Nation's history and tradition" and are not "implicit in the concept of ordered liberty" such that "neither liberty nor justice would exist if they were sacrificed." *Washington v. Glucksberg* (1997). A law regulating assisted suicide need only be rationally related to legitimate government interests.

Example: The Supreme Court reversed a court of appeals holding that a ban on causing or aiding a suicide violated due process as applied to physicians aiding terminally ill competent adults. The Court began with a "careful description" of the asserted fundamental liberty interest—"a right to commit suicide which includes a right to assistance in doing so." The Court then found "a consistent and almost universal tradition that has long rejected the asserted right, and continues explicitly to reject it today, even for terminally ill, mentally competent adults." The history of the legal rejection of assisted suicide establishes that it is not a fundamental liberty interest. The assisted suicide law is rationally related to legitimate state interests in preserving life, protecting those suffering from depression, protecting medical ethics, protecting vulnerable groups and avoiding euthanasia.

Four concurring justices described the interest in assisted suicide in broader terms of autonomy, dignity and avoidance of extreme pain. They concluded that the law was facially constitutional since there was no indication that terminal patients could not obtain palliative care to relieve extreme pain even if it causes death. Justice Souter, concurring, urged a balancing approach, focusing on the importance of the claimed interest, the severity of the burden and the strength of the State interest. A majority of the justices appeared to leave open the possibility of an as applied challenge if palliative care was denied. *Washington v. Glucksberg* (1997). See *Vacco v. Quill* (1997) (holding that a prohibition on assisted suicide does not violate equal protection).

10. Rights in Restricted Environments

In certain special contexts, such as the military, schools, government employment and the prisons, the stricter standards of judicial scrutiny do not apply. While persons in such contexts do not lose their constitutional rights, the courts tend to defer to decisionmakers in the other branches of government. See *Goldman v. Weinberger* (1986) (military); *Morse v. Frederick* (2007) (schools); *Garcetti v. Ceballos* (2006) (government employees). In prison cases, for example, restrictions on fundamental rights are valid if they are reasonably related to legitimate penological objectives.

Examples: (1) A state restriction upon correspondence between inmates survives constitutional review, but a regulation that severely limits the ability of inmates to marry does not. Recognizing a special need for judicial deference in cases involving prison regulation, the Court employed a diminished standard of review—"the regulation is valid if it is reasonably related to legitimate penological objectives." The restraint on correspondence was not content-based and "logically advanced" the legitimate government interest in promoting institutional security and safety. It was not an "exaggerated response" to concerns over prison security; there were no "obvious, easy alternatives" available. In contrast, the restriction on marriage was not logically connected to the state's proffered objective of preventing "love triangles" that threaten prison security or rehabilitation. Additionally, the almost complete ban on marriages was excessive in that it covered marriage with civilians and male inmates, whose marriages generally posed no security threat. *Turner v. Safley* (1987).

(2) A state policy authorizing involuntary treatment with drugs of an incarcerated felon who suffers from a "mental disorder" and who is "gravely disabled" or poses a "likelihood of serious harm to himself, others or their property," does not violate substantive due process. While the inmate has a significant liberty interest in avoiding the unwanted administration of drugs, the state policy recognizes both the prisoner's medical interests and the state interests. The policy is "reasonably related to legitimate penological interests of the State." Where the root cause of the threat to prison security is mental illness, the state interest encompasses provision of medical treatment. The impact of the due process right on guards, other inmates and prison resources generally also suggests the reasonableness of the policy. Finally, there were no "ready alternatives" to involuntary treatment. *Washington v. Harper* (1990).

H.   Procedural Due Process

The Fifth and Fourteenth Amendment Due Process Clauses guarantee procedural fairness. Whenever a state or federal practice is challenged as violative of due process, two questions must be asked.

INTEREST INVADED. *First, is there a deprivation of a significant life, liberty, or property interest so that the Due Process Clause applies? It does not matter whether the interest is characterized as a "right" or a "privilege." If it is a significant due process interest, procedural fairness is required. However, thus far the Court has only recognized due process as applying to benefits that are "presently enjoyed," i.e., due process is not applied to the application for benefits. A negligent injury to life, liberty or property is not a "deprivation."*

PROCEDURES REQUIRED. *Second, in the particular factual context, what procedures are required to assure fundamental fairness? The question of what procedures are required is a federal constitutional question to be decided by the courts; it is not determined by the state law. The Court has rejected the proposition that an individual takes "the bitter with the sweet."*

The minimum procedures demanded by due process are notice and a hearing. What is fair is determined by balancing the interests favoring summary determination against the harm to the person aggrieved. Courts in making this determination consider three factors: (1) the severity of the harm to the litigant if the requested procedures are not granted; (2) the risk of error if the procedures are not afforded; and (3) the administrative difficulty and cost of providing the added procedures. Mathews v. Eldridge (1976). *However, the*

Court has noted that *Mathews* is not "an all-embracing test for deciding due process claims." *Dusenbery v. United States* (2002) (using "a more straightforward test of reasonableness under the circumstances" in holding that notice of forfeiture sent by certified mail to the federal prison where the claimant was incarcerated satisfies procedural due process); see also *Hamdi v. Rumsfeld* (2004) (although a U.S. citizen captured on the battlefield fighting for Taliban and designated an "enemy combatant" could be held in military detention, he is entitled to due process under the *Mathews v. Eldridge* test to determine whether he is an enemy combatant, but a plurality would afford special deference to the government, taking into account separation of powers concerns and the military context). Ch. IV, H, 4, h.

1. What Is "Property"?

While property is not limited to interests in realty or personalty, the fact that an interest is important to an individual is inadequate to create "property" for due process purposes. Property has thus far been limited to interests recognized by government. For government benefits to constitute property, therefore, the person seeking due process must show some entitlement created by government.

Example: A woman who obtained a restraining order against her husband to protect herself and her children "did not, for purposes of the Due Process clause, have a property interest in police enforcement of the restraining order against her husband." Gonzales claimed that the property right was created by a Colorado statute which stated: "A police officer shall use every reasonable means to enforce a restraining order." However, the Court, per Justice Scalia, noted the "deep-rooted nature of law-enforcement discretion, even in the presence of seemingly mandatory legislative commands." Justice Scalia asserted that "a true mandate of police action would require some stronger indication from the Colorado Legislature" than the language of the statute. Colorado law did not necessarily give *"respondent* an entitlement of *enforcement* of the mandate." (emphasis in original). Even though the statute spoke of "protected person[s]" such as respondent, it did so in connection with matters other than a right to enforcement.

The Court went on to state that even if it had decided that Colorado had created a statutory entitlement, Gonzalez's interest in the enforcement of a restraining order would not constitute a property interest for purposes of the Due Process Clause. A property right in having a restraining order enforced would not "resemble any traditional conception of property." There were three barriers to the enforcement of a restraining order constituting a property right. First, "the right to have a restraining order enforced does not 'have some ascertainable monetary value.'" Second, "the alleged property interest here arises incidentally, not out of some new species of government benefit or service, but out of a function that government actor have always performed—to wit, arresting people who they have probable cause to believe have committed a criminal offense." Finally, an "indirect and incidental result of the Government's enforcement action does not amount to a deprivation of any interest in life, liberty or property," citing *O'Bannon v. Town Court Nursing Center* (1980). *Castle Rock, Colo. v. Gonzalez* (2005).

2. What Is "Liberty"?

Liberty is a broad concept not limited to conditions of confinement such as imprisonment. It includes interests such as marriage, raising a family, working in the common occupations of the community. It includes reputation but the Court has held that the imposition of stigma by government officials, without more, does not violate liberty.

Example: Distribution of a flyer by the police identifying a person as a shoplifter, even though the person had only been arrested, not convicted of the offense, does not violate due process liberty. The action of the state officials did not alter any status of the individual recognized and protected by law nor was he deprived of a tangible interest such as employment. Where there is no state created interest involved such as employment or schooling, even a charge of criminal conduct does not create a basis for an actionable due process violation although it may give rise to a claim for defamation. *Paul v. Davis* (1976).

3. What Is a "Deprivation"?

When an individual is injured by a negligent rather than a deliberate act, there is no "deprivation" requiring due process protection.

Examples: (1) A prison inmate who is injured as a result of slipping on a pillow negligently left on a stairwell by a prison guard cannot sue for damages for violation of procedural due process rights. There has been no "deprivation" of life, liberty or property to be remedied. *Daniels v. Williams* (1986).

(2) The negligent failure of prison officials to guard an inmate who informs the officials of threats made against him by another prisoner does not implicate the Due Process Clause. The lack of due care by government officials does not constitute the kind of abusive treatment that the Due Process Clause was designed to protect against. Since there is no "deprivation" of due process, no remedy is required. *Davidson v. Cannon* (1986).

4. Due Process Contexts

a. Welfare Rights

1) **The Statutory Entitlement Concept**

   A person who qualifies to receive welfare benefits has a statutory entitlement to receive benefits. Whether welfare is deemed a right or a privilege, this is a significant property interest and due process must be afforded when benefits are terminated.

2) **Balancing to Determine Fairness**

   In determining what process is due, the state interest in conserving fiscal and administrative resources is balanced against the importance to the welfare recipient of uninterrupted benefits.

   Examples: (1) Welfare benefits to a qualified AFDC recipient cannot be terminated prior to a hearing. Given the dependence of the recipient on the benefits for subsistence, the importance to the state that persons receive such subsistence and the absence of any emergency justifying summary procedures, due process requires timely notice indicating the basis for termination, and a hearing before an impartial examiner in which the recipient may appear personally, with or without counsel (counsel need not be provided by the state) to present evidence and confront and cross-examine adverse witnesses. *Goldberg v. Kelly* (1970).

   (2) Social security disability benefits may be terminated without a prior hearing. *Goldberg* is distinguished. The individual hardship is not as great since disability benefits are not based on need, there is less risk of error given the medical basis of the disability

determination, and the administrative difficulty and costs the additional procedural safeguards would entail would severely burden the government. *Mathews v. Eldridge* (1976).

b. The Right to Use and Possess Property: Constitutionalizing the Consumer Credit Relationship

1) Wages as a Property Interest

Wages constitute a specialized type of property interest protected by due process. Given the effect of even a temporary loss of such wages by garnishment, notice and a hearing must be afforded prior to statutorily-recognized garnishment. *Sniadach v. Family Finance Corp.* (1969).

2) Contingent Interests in Property

The purchaser of goods under a contingent sales contract has a significant property interest in the use and possession of such goods. The due process guarantee has thus been extended in some situations to relationships which have not yet matured into property rights. Due process must be afforded but in some cases summary adjudication may provide sufficient fairness.

Example: Procedural due process requires that before a state may authorize the summary seizure of goods or chattels in a person's possession under a writ of replevin, upon the mere *ex parte* application by a creditor to a court clerk, the state must provide an opportunity for hearing to the person in possession of the goods. The function of the hearing is to prevent unfair and mistaken deprivation of the "property" interest. *Fuentes v. Shevin* (1972).

c. Employment Rights of the Public Sector

1) Conditions of Employment

Whether a public employee has a due process property interest in continued employment, requiring at least notice and hearing, depends on the conditions of the employment. A person must have more than a subjective expectancy of continued employment. The expectation must be created by the state.

Examples: (1) A state university teacher on a one-year contract has not suffered a due process violation by the refusal of the university to renew his contract. To have a property interest in a benefit, a person must have a legitimate claim of entitlement. If non-renewal is based on factors involving good name, reputation, honor or integrity (a liberty interest) then a hearing would be necessary. *Board of Regents v. Roth* (1972).

(2) A state college teacher who has held his position for a number of years may be able to show a legitimate claim of entitlement to job tenure even in the absence of a formal tenure system. The college rules, regulations, and practices can create a de facto system of tenure, *i.e.*, an entitlement. Although a mere subjective "expectancy" is not protected by due process, the teacher is entitled to be given an opportunity to prove the legitimacy of a claim of entitlement. If such a property interest is proved, the teacher is entitled to hearing by the college where he could be informed of the grounds for his nonretention and challenge the sufficiency of the grounds. *Perry v. Sindermann* (1972).

2) Employment at Will—Conditional Property Interests

a) The termination of a policeman's employment without a hearing pursuant to a city ordinance providing for discharge for negligence, unfitness, and unsuitable conduct, was held not to violate due process. A public employee whose position is terminable at the will of the employer is not deprived of "liberty" when there is no public disclosure of the reasons for the discharge. Similarly, there is no "property" interest infringed when the ordinance involved is construed as "granting no right to continued employment" but merely conditions removal on satisfactorily complying with certain specified procedures. *Bishop v. Wood* (1976).

b) *But remember, the issues of whether a life, liberty or property interest is implicated and what procedures are required to satisfy due process are separate. While a state may so condition the employment interest that it does not constitute "property," the courts, not state law, define what processes are due once a property interest is found to exist. The public employee does not take "the bitter with the sweet."*

Example: In order to satisfy due process a statute governing discharge of public employees must provide at least for pre-termination notice and an opportunity to respond, coupled with adequate post-termination administrative procedures. A public employee has a property interest in continued employment; property cannot be defined by the procedures provided for its deprivation.

Nor does the fact that the statute defines applicable procedures determine the federal constitutional question of what procedures are due. Given the severity of depriving a person of a livelihood, the danger of factual error, the issues likely to surround the appropriateness of discharge, and the absence of any significant administrative burden on the state, due process requires at least pre-termination notice and "some kind of hearing" designed to assure that there are reasonable grounds for the discharge. A fuller administrative proceeding can follow termination. Since the employees involved alleged they had not been given an opportunity to respond prior to discharge, they stated a cause of action. *Cleveland Bd. of Educ. v. Loudermill* (1985).

d. Institutional Due Process

Procedural due process issues have frequently arisen in the context of the judicial review of the practices of public institutions such as prisons, schools, and mental hospitals. While officials in such institutions exercise broad discretion, the courts have demanded adherence to fair processes in admission and administration. For example, while confinement in a mental hospital may not constitute imprisonment, it does involve significant curtailment of a liberty interest requiring due process. *Addington v. Texas* (1979) (involuntary confinement requires at least "clear and convincing evidence").

Examples: (1) Transfer of an incarcerated prisoner to a mental hospital implicates a liberty interest protected by due process. A liberty interest is created by a statute specifying certain conditions for transfer and by commitment to the mental hospital. The stigma and subjection to mandatory behavior modification treatment also implicate significant liberty interests. The Court weighed the interest of the prisoner in not being arbitrarily stigmatized and subjected to involuntary treatment and the substantial risk of error against the state's interest in segregating and treating mentally ill prisoners. Due process requires written notice, a hearing at which evidence is heard, including a right of presentation, confrontation and cross-examination, an independent decisionmaker, a written statement by the fact-finder, effective and timely notice of rights, and qualified and independent assistance of legal counsel. *Vitek v. Jones* (1980).

(2) A child voluntarily committed by its parents to a mental institution has a constitutionally protectible liberty interest at stake given the confinement and stigma involved. In determining what procedures are due, the interests of the parents and the child are presumed to be the same since parents generally act in the child's best interests. State interests in effective use of its resources and avoidance of excessive procedures are also to be considered. The risk of error is sufficiently great to require some inquiry (an informal medical hearing would suffice) by a neutral fact-finder to assure admission requirements are satisfied, and thereafter to assure that there is a continuing need for confinement. *Parham v. J.R.* (1979).

(3) A state policy establishing a nonjudicial procedure for involuntary treatment with antipsychotic drugs of mentally ill felons does not violate procedural due process. Although the inmate has a substantial liberty interest in avoiding unwanted administration of drugs, the state procedures satisfy due process. The treatment decision is made by a psychiatrist and is reviewed by a board of medical professionals not involved in the case. There is

notice to the inmates and an opportunity to attend the hearing and cross-examine witnesses. *Washington v. Harper* (1990).

(4) The state was not required to provide released sex offenders with a hearing to determine their "current" dangerousness for the purposes of a statute requiring all released sex offenders to provide DNA samples, updated photographs, addresses, and phone numbers for ten years after release (life for violent sex offenders). The information was published on a website maintained by the state's Department of Public Safety, which was searchable by zip code. Because the statute applied to *all* released sex offenders (the website indicated that officials had made no determination regarding the registrant's current dangerousness), the Court reasoned that none of the offenders were entitled to a hearing on whether they were currently dangerous. The registry requirement was based "on the fact of previous conviction, not the fact of current dangerousness." *Connecticut Department of Public Safety v. Doe* (2003).

e. Parental Rights

The interest of natural parents in the care, custody, and management of their children involves a fundamental liberty interest. See Ch. VI,G, 5. In determining what process is due, this liberty interest of the parents is commanding and weighs heavily. *See M.L.B. v. S.L.J. (1996)* (holding that a state violates due process and equal protection when it conditions appeals from trial court decrees terminating parental rights on the affected parent's ability to pay record preparation fees). But the state interests may still outweigh the parental liberty interest.

Examples: (1) Due process requires use of the "clear and convincing" evidentiary standard before parental rights are terminated for unfitness. Use of the "fair preponderance" standard violates due process. There is a significant risk of error and the consequences of erroneous termination of parental rights generally outweigh the consequences of erroneous failure to terminate the parental relation. Accuracy in fact-finding also serves the state interest in the child's welfare by preserving the natural familial bonds while doubt remains. Since the clear and convincing standard is regularly used in other proceedings, there would be no excessive administrative burden on the state fact-finders. *Santosky v. Kramer* (1982).

(2) An indigent parent is not necessarily denied procedural due process guarantees where the state fails to appoint counsel in a parental-status termination proceeding. There is a general presumption that the due process safeguard of appointed counsel will only be required where there is a possible deprivation of personal liberty. To rebut this presumption, the private interests at stake, the risks of an erroneous decision, and the state's interest must be considered. While the balancing of these factors does favor the parent's interests in many cases, whether it is sufficient in a particular case to overcome the presumption against appointed counsel must be determined on a case-by-case basis. The record in the present case indicated that the absence of counsel had not denied fundamental fairness. *Lassiter v. Department of Social Services* (1981).

f. Student Rights

Courts have been reluctant to intrude into the sensitive area of school-student relationships and have generally recognized broad power in school authorities to act in *loco parentis.* But the Court has now indicated that due process does protect the liberty and property interests of a student.

Examples: (1) A state statute allowing school principals to suspend students for misconduct for up to ten days without a hearing violates due process. Because the state confers a system of free public education on its children, there is an "entitlement," *i.e.,* a property interest. Since the suspension could impose a stigma, the child's liberty interest is infringed. Balancing these interests against the state's interests in maintaining order and discipline, the Court held that due process requires that the student be furnished at least notice of the charges, an explanation of the evidence against him and an opportunity to reply. *Goss v. Lopez* (1975).

(2) Charlotte Horowitz failed to graduate from medical school because of poor performance in clinical courses and

her lack of concern for personal hygiene. She was notified of the reasons for the school's actions and afforded a hearing and appeal at which she could respond. She was not, however, accorded an opportunity to appear personally. Assuming that such a dismissal denies a property or liberty interest, the Court was unanimous that due process was satisfied by the procedures afforded. A number of justices indicated that due process standards are more easily satisfied when the procedures involve academic rather than disciplinary considerations. *Board of Curators v. Horowitz* (1978).

g. Access to Courts

1) Filing and Record Fees

While the Due Process Liberty Clause imposes significant demands to assure due process in criminal cases, with some exceptions, due process does not require that indigent plaintiffs be given free access to the courts in civil cases.

Examples: (1) A filing fee imposed on indigents seeking a divorce violates due process. Marriage occupies a fundamental position in our society and the state monopolizes the means of dissolving it. *Boddie v. Connecticut* (1971).

(2) A filing fee imposed on an indigent seeking a discharge in bankruptcy does not violate due process. The individual's interest in a bankruptcy is not as fundamental as marriage dissolution since the position of the individual who is denied is not materially altered. The government's role is qualitatively and quantitatively less than in *Boddie* since there are other methods for debt adjustment. *United States v. Kras* (1973).

(3) A state violates due process and equal protection when it dismisses an appeal from a trial court decree terminating a mother's parental rights because of her inability to pay record preparation fees. While the Constitution does not guarantee a right to appellate review, once a state affords that right, *Griffin v. Illinois*

(1956) establishes that there must be open and equal access to the courts. The present case falls within "a narrow category of civil cases in which the State must provide access to its judicial processes without regard to a party's ability to pay court fees." Reviewing State intrusions on family relationships, "the Court has examined closely and contextually the importance of the governmental interest in defense of the intrusion." Since the present case involves the State's authority to permanently sever the parent-child bond, it requires the "close consideration" required for associational rights "of basic importance to our society." When measured against the magnitude and permanence of the loss the mother faces and the importance of the transcript to her interests, the State's interest in offsetting the costs to its court systems is unimpressive. The State may not withhold from the parent a record of sufficient completeness to permit proper appellate consideration of her claim. *M.L.B. v. S.L.J.* (1996).

2) Effective Access

The procedures that are available in civil proceedings are generally determined by the three-part balancing test. However, there is a presumption against a right to appointed counsel in civil proceedings that requires a case-by-case determination whether counsel is needed under the circumstances.

Example: A state statute which provides that in paternity actions the cost of blood grouping tests is to be borne by the party requesting them violates due process when applied to deny such tests to indigent defendants. Applying the three-part test for determining what process is due to the facts in the present case, the Court held that the denial of free blood tests denied the putative father a meaningful opportunity to be heard. First, the father has a strong pecuniary interest in avoiding support obligations and a liberty interest threatened by possible sanctions for non-payment as well as an interest in the creation of a parent-child relationship which is shared with the child. Second, blood tests are a highly effective method for negating paternity and thus avoiding the risk of error. Third, the state has an interest in securing support for a child on public assistance and securing a just determination of paternity. While the state seeks to determine paternity as economically as possible, federal reimbursement is available and costs can be offset. *Little v. Streater* (1981).

h. Fair Trial/Judicial Bias

While matters of judicial bias are normally dealt with through local rules and statutes, the Due Process Clause does impose some requirements identifying when a judge must recuse himself from a case. Due Process incorporates the common law rule that a judge must recuse himself when he has "a direct, personal, substantial, pecuniary interest in a case." *Tumey v. Ohio* (1927). Further, Due Process requires recusal "when 'the probability of actual bias on the part of the judge or decisionmaker is too high to be constitutionally tolerable.'" *Withrow v. Larkin* (1975). Recusal is required where an objective appraisal of the circumstances indicate "that there is a serious risk of actual bias." *Caperton v. A.T. Massey Coal Company* (2009).

Example: Justice Brent Benjamin of the West Virginia Supreme Court of Appeals refused to recuse himself in a case where the defendant Massey had contributed over $3 million to Justice Benjamin's campaign which occurred while an appeal from a $50 million judgment adverse to the defendant was pending. Benjamin was elected to the bench by less than 50,000 votes. The state Court of Appeals then granted Massey's appeal and the judgement was reversed 3–2. The Supreme Court held 5–4 that, in these "rare" and "extraordinary" circumstances, the Due Process Clause was violated. Justice Kennedy, writing for the Court, reasoned that, in the present case, "there is a serious risk of actual bias—based on objective and reasonable perceptions—when a person with a personal stake in a particular case had a significant and disproportionate influence in placing the judge on the case by raising funds or directing the judge's election campaign when the case was pending or imminent." While Justice Benjamin had made an extensive search for actual bias, given Massey's "significant and disproportionate influence—coupled with the temporal relationship between the election and the pending case," an objective appraisal indicated that the probability of actual bias reached an unconstitutional level. Justice Kennedy stressed that it is only in the "extraordinary situation where the Constitution requires recusal."

Chief Justice Roberts, dissenting, joined by Justices Alito, Scalia, and Thomas, claimed that the Court's new uncertain rule would increase challenges to judicial neutrality and eventually erode the public's confidence in the judiciary. Chief Justice Roberts argued that cases other than those where there was a direct interest (i.e., financial interest in the outcome or criminal contempt), should be regulated by state rules rather than constitutional standards. *Caperton v. A.T. Massey Coal Co.* (2009).

i. Miscellaneous

While the above indicates recurring contexts in which procedural due process issues have arisen, the question of when due process applies and what procedures are required to assure fairness can arise in any context where the government significantly burdens important liberty or property interests.

Examples: (1) A routine 27–day delay in affording an administrative hearing to adjudicate a claim for a refund of a towing fee resulting from a disputed parking ticket did not violate procedural due process. The Court applied *Mathews v. Eldridge* (1976). First, because the plaintiff's interest was monetary, his interest was minimal because the loss could be easily compensated by an interest payment. Second, given the nature of an administrative hearing and the straightforward nature of the facts at issue, the delay was unlikely to spawn significant factual errors. Third, the government interest in administrative necessity was strong, given the number of similar claims and limited city resources. A predeprivation hearing was impossible if the city was to be able to enforce the parking rules. *Los Angeles v. David* (2003).

(2) An American citizen captured on the battlefield in Afghanistan, allegedly fighting for the Taliban, and held in military detention in Virginia, was entitled to due process

to challenge his status an "enemy combatant" in a habeas corpus proceeding. Writing for a plurality, Justice O'Connor applied *Mathews v. Eldridge* (1976). Hamdi has a fundamental right to be free of involuntary physical confinement and loss of liberty without due process of law. This must be weighed against "the weighty and sensitive governmental interests" involved in the military combat context. A majority of the Court agreed that this would include "notice of the factual basis for his classification, and a fair opportunity to rebut the Government's factual assertions before a neutral decision maker."

The plurality, however, indicated that the exigencies of the situation may demand that, beyond the core elements of due process, enemy combatant proceedings might be tailored "to alleviate their uncommon potential to burden the Executive at a time of ongoing military conflict." The plurality made clear that due process requirements would not apply to initial captures on the battlefield, but only to persons that the military continued to hold (possibly on U.S. soil). It also left open the possibility that these requirements could be met by a military tribunal, rather than an Art III court in a habeas proceeding. *Hamdi v. Rumsfeld* (2004).

(3) Before the government takes and sells a person's property for delinquent taxes, it must make reasonable efforts to inform him. Actual notice is not required. *Dusenberry v. United States* (2002). But when certified mail notice to the property owner went unclaimed and government had other reasonable alternatives for notifying him, due process was violated. What constitutes reasonable notice requires balancing the state and individual interests involved. The Court emphasized the extraordinary use of government power involved in taking and selling a person's house, the government's knowledge that the mailed notice was unclaimed and the alternatives available to the state, e.g., ordinary mailed notice or posting a notice on the door, in holding that due process had been violated. *Jones v. Flowers* (2006).

5. Conclusive Presumptions

DEFINITION. *Conclusive presumptions are created when laws conclusively presume that certain facts exist which categorize individuals into a class subjected to burdens not visited on others, even though the presumptions may be wrong in a certain case.*

LEGAL EFFECT. *The denial of an opportunity to challenge the presumption has generally been held to violate due process. When critical due process interests of the individual are lost by government action, he or she must normally be afforded an opportunity for a hearing to prove that the fact presumed is not true in his or her case.*

a.   A plurality of the Court argues that the conclusive presumptions doctrine does not rest upon procedural due process. Such cases, it is claimed, do not question the adequacy of the procedures, but the fit between the classification established by the law and the policy underlying the classification. *Michael H. & Victoria D. v. Gerald D.* (1989).

>   *Example:*   School board rules requiring every pregnant school teacher to take a maternity leave without pay a specified number of months (five and four months in the two statutes challenged) before the expected birth of her child violate due process. The presumption that all women teachers were physically unfit to continue employment beyond the designated date assumed a fact that was not true in individual cases. Since the critical interests in marriage and family life were at stake, the use of the conclusive presumption of unfitness violated due process. Individualized determinations were required to satisfy due process. The Court held also that the rules had no relationship to the school's interest in assuring continuity of instruction. *Cleveland Board of Education v. LaFleur* (1974).

>   *Exception:*   When the irrebuttable presumption involves a non-contractual claim to receive public funds, and claimants are permitted to present evidence that they meet objectively defined statutory requirements for eligibility, the presumption is constitutional if rationally based. No significant liberty or property interest is impaired.

>   *Example:*   A Social Security Act provision preventing wage earners, widows and step-children from recovering benefits if their relationships with the wage-earner began less than nine

months before the wage-earner's death is constitutional. Congress could rationally conclude that a presumption would preclude the use of sham marriages to obtain Social Security benefits and that it would avoid the expense and difficulty of individualized determinations. It was therefore permissible to bar a widow from recovery even though the wage-earner was in good health at the time of the marriage. *Weinberger v. Salfi* (1975).

I.   Review Questions

1.   **T or F**   A reasonable law will generally be constitutional even if it retroactively impairs private contract relationships.

2.   **T or F**   Once a state has contracted away its fiscal powers, it is thereafter barred from any changes in the contract.

3.   **T or F**   If a state law has the effect of reducing property values, the law constitutes a "taking" requiring "just compensation."

4.   **T or F**   A law which denies all economically beneficial use of property is a compensable taking regardless of the public interest in regulating.

5.   **T or F**   Government can condition development on dedication of property if the condition is rationally related to the public interest.

6.   **T or F**   In most cases, due process is satisfied if the law is rationally related to a permissible government objective.

7.   **T or F**   The Court has now held all of the guarantees of the Bill of Rights applicable to the states as part of the Fourteenth Amendment Due Process "Liberty" Clause.

8.   **T or F**   An incorporated right applies against the states but the scope of the Bill of Rights guarantee that is being incorporated may be re-defined by the Court.

9.   **T or F**   When a fundamental right is significantly burdened, the Court requires the government to justify the law under a stricter standard of review.

10.   **T or F**   A law prohibiting abortion prior to viability is unconstitutional.

11. **T or F** Regulation of abortions in the second trimester of pregnancy is constitutional only if the regulation is necessary to a compelling interest.

12. **T or F** A regulation on abortion procedures which does not include an exception when the mother's health is in danger is facially constitutional.

13. **T or F** Due process is not violated by a law which provides funding for maternity but denies funding for abortion.

14. **T or F** The Court has held that there is a fundamental right to die.

15. **T or F** The Court has held that the right of interstate movement is a fundamental right derived from the Due Process Clause of the Fourteenth Amendment.

16. **T or F** Whenever a state procedure is alleged to violate due process, the courts balance the interests of the person affected against the government interests in not affording the requested procedures.

17. **T or F** Reputation, when burdened by government, can qualify as a liberty interest.

18. **T or F** Although a state may define the nature of a property interest, state law is not determinative of what processes are required if a property interest is burdened.

19. **T or F** Conclusive presumptions always violate due process.

20. **T or F** Procedural due process applies only when life, liberty, or property rights are burdened.

21. **T or F** Due Process is not violated by a judge's failure to disqualify himself if he makes a good faith determination that he is not biased and he has no direct financial interest in the outcome.

22. **T or F** If a life, liberty or property interest is significantly burdened, the process that is due is usually determined by some form of balancing test.

23. Which of the following is *not* an element of the traditional rational basis test?

    a. Probe to discover the true legislative objective.

   b.   Ascertain if the means are rationally related to the objective.

   c.   Assume any state of facts that would sustain the law.

   d.   All of the above (a, b, and c) are elements of the traditional due process rationality test.

24. Which of the following sodomy laws would be most likely to survive a constitutional challenge?

   a.   A law prohibiting sodomy between adult persons of either sex.

   b.   A law prohibiting sodomy between adult persons of the same sex.

   c.   A law prohibiting sodomy between adult males.

   d.   None of the above laws would survive a due process challenge.

25. Which of the following abortion laws would be *least* likely to survive constitutional challenge?

   a.   A substitute consent law for minors requiring approval of parents for the abortion, with a judicial bypass provision.

   b.   A law requiring the presence of a second physician in post-viability abortions unless there is an emergency.

   c.   A law requiring abortions to be performed in a hospital.

   d.   A law requiring spousal consent.

26. Which of the following would most likely violate the Ex Post Facto Clause if enforced?

   a.   Sanctions imposed under a "Three Strikes and You're Out" type law enacted after the defendant had committed the first two crimes, but before he committed the third.

   b.   Sanctions imposed under a law providing for the deportation of resident aliens who are members of the Communist Party enacted after the aliens terminated their membership in the party.

   c.   Sanctions imposed under a law making conduct a crime where the law was enacted after the defendant had engaged in the conduct.

    d.   Sanctions imposed under a law disbarring attorneys for ethics violations enacted after an attorney had committed such a violation.

27. Which of the following is *least* likely to qualify as a sufficient interest for invoking the due process guarantee?

    a.   The interest of a purchaser in a contingent sales contract.

    b.   The interest of a state employee under an "at will" contract.

    c.   The interest in a state cause of action.

    d.   A student's interest in not being suspended from school.

28. A state law requires that pharmacies be operated by pharmacists in good standing or by a corporation or association predominantly controlled by pharmacists. The West Lincoln State Board of Pharmacy denied a permit to a drugstore chain because it did not comply with the stock ownership requirements of the statute. The rejected drugstore chain has contended that the state statute violates the Due Process Clause of the Fourteenth Amendment. Is the West Lincoln statute constitutional?

VII

Equal Protection

■ *ANALYSIS*

A. General Standards

1. Constitutional Text

The Fourteenth Amendment provides that no state shall deny to any person within its jurisdiction the equal protection of the laws. While there is no corresponding provision applicable to the federal government, unreasonable classifications by the federal government violate Fifth Amendment due process. *Bolling v. Sharpe* (1954).

2. Unreasonable Classification

Not all classification violates equal protection since law generally involves different treatment of persons. Only when a classification is unreasonable, arbitrary and invidious, does it violate equal protection.

3. Standards of Reasonableness

The reasonableness of a classification is dependent on: (1) the basis of the classification; (2) the nature of the interests impaired by the classification; and (3) the government interests supporting the classification.

During the Warren Court era, the Court developed a two-tier standard of judicial review. In reviewing socio-economic classification, the Court employs a traditional, deferential rational basis test. But when the law intentionally classifies on the basis of a suspect classification or significantly burdens fundamental rights, "strict scrutiny" is used, i.e., the classification must be necessary to a compelling government interest. During the Burger Court era, a third intermediate approach emerged, primarily in gender and illegitimacy cases, asking whether the classification is substantially related to an important government interest. Various justices have suggested that there is only one standard of review, with the degree of judicial scrutiny varying with the nature of the discrimination and the significance of the interests burdened by the classification.

B. Traditional Equal Protection

1. The Rational Basis Test

The Equal Protection Clause of the Fourteenth Amendment traditionally has been interpreted to grant the states a wide measure of discretion with respect to making classifications in enacting legislation. As long as the classification set forth in a statute has some rational basis, i.e., it is rationally related to a permissible government interest, the Equal Protection Clause is not violated because the particular measure results in some inequality.

This rational classification test operates as follows: (1) When a classification is challenged on the basis of the Equal Protection Clause, if any state of facts reasonably can be conceived that would sustain the law, the existence of that state of facts at the time the law was enacted will be presumed. (2) One who challenges a law on the basis of the Equal Protection Clause has the burden of showing that the classification has no rational relationship to a permissible governmental purpose and is essentially arbitrary. This burden of proof has proven essentially insurmountable.

Examples: (1) A city ordinance prohibited ads on the side of trucks but made an exception for those who owned their trucks and used their vehicles to advertise their own business. It was contended that the prohibition drew an arbitrary line between advertisements of products sold by the owner of the truck and other truck and general outdoor advertising. The Court held that the local authorities may reasonably have concluded that those who advertise their own wares on their trucks do not present the same traffic safety problems in view of the nature or extent of the advertising which they use. *REA v. New York* (1949).

(2) A ban on plastic nonreturnable milk containers while permitting the sale of milk in other nonreturnable containers, such as paperboard milk cartons, does not violate the equal protection guarantee. The state legislature could rationally have decided that its ban on plastic milk jugs might foster greater use of environmentally desirable alternative containers. Where the evidence on whether the classification would help to conserve energy and landfill space was at least debatable, the courts are not to substitute their judgment for that of the legislature. *Minnesota v. Clover Leaf Creamery Co.* (1981).

(3) New York laws making it a crime to aid another to commit or attempt suicide, but allowing patients to refuse even lifesaving medical treatment, do not violate equal protection. While the laws do not facially discriminate, it was argued that the laws allow some competent terminally ill people (*i.e.*, those on life support systems) to hasten death while other terminally ill people (*i.e.*, those seeking physician-assisted suicide) are denied that choice. But the Court held that the distinction between assisting suicide and terminating life support is rational; it comports with legal principles of causation and intent. The patient refusing treatment dies from the underlying illness; the

patient committing suicide intends and does die from the lethal medication. The doctor who withholds treatment intends to respect the patient's choice; the doctor who assists a suicide intends primarily that the patient be made dead. New York has legitimate objectives in recognizing this distinction including prohibiting killing and preserving life, preventing suicide, maintaining the physician's role as healer, protecting vulnerable people from indifference, prejudice and coercion, and avoiding euthanasia. *Vacco v. Quill* (1997).

(4) A state statute that imposes a higher tax rate on slot machines at race tracks than on slot machines on riverboats does not violate equal protection. Applying the deferential rationality standard of review, the Court reasoned that a law might predominantly serve one general objective, while containing subsidiary provisions that serve other desirable (perhaps even contrary) ends as well. The legislature could balance objectives, even while serving the general objectives seen as a whole. The state law authorizing racetracks to operate slot machines rationally serves to help racetracks economically to some degree, even while the imposition of the tax means that the law is less helpful than some would like. The tax rate differential serves the subsidiary objective of providing help to the riverboats, which are also facing financial hardships. *Fitzgerald v. Racing Ass'n of Central Iowa* (2003).

(5) Indianapolis had a law to apportion payment for a sewer project by creating an initial assessment, then apportioning the cost of the project among affected lots and allowing homeowners to pay in either a lump sum or in installments. When the city changed its payment plan to one that was cheaper for homeowners, it forgave any installments not yet paid, but the city did not provide any refund for homeowners who had paid a lump sum. The Court held, 6–3, per Justice Breyer, that equal protection was not violated. An economic distinction based on payment method is not a "suspect classification;" when "ordinary commercial transactions are at issue, rational basis review requires deference." The City's claimed justification of avoiding administrative costs of calculating refunds and the difficulties of "line-drawing" involved in multiple payment schemes are sufficient to provide a "rational basis for distinguishing be-

tween those lot owners who had already paid their share of project costs and those who had not." The dissent argued that when a tax scheme creates a 30–1 discrimination between "abutting lots," and when state law requires taxpayers be treated alike, "administrative costs" cannot justify disparate tax treatment. *Armour v. City of Indianapolis* (2012). See *Allegheny Pittsburg Coal Co. v. County Com'n* (1989) (Ch. VII, C, 2, a).

2. Rationality With Bite

a. In some cases, the Court has indicated a willingness to utilize a somewhat more stringent approach in traditional review. In these cases, the Court's analysis more closely approximates true ad hoc balancing to determine the reasonableness of the law.

Examples: (1) A Food Stamp Act provision which generally excludes from participation any household containing an individual who is unrelated to any other member of the household violates equal protection. The provision does not rationally further any legitimate state objective. For example, it is clearly unrelated to safeguarding public health and raising the nutrition levels of members of low-income households. *United States Dept. of Agriculture v. Moreno* (1973).

(2) An Alaskan law whereby income derived from the state's natural resources is distributed to Alaskan citizens based on the length of residence violates equal protection. The Court found it unnecessary to determine whether a more stringent standard of review should apply since the law failed to satisfy even the minimal rationality test. While Alaska may have an interest in encouraging residents to remain in the state, and in promoting prudent use of the state's resources, these ends are not rationally furthered by distinguishing among past residents. Rewarding citizens for past contributions is not a legitimate state purpose. *Zobel v. Williams* (1982).

(3) A state domestic preference tax imposing a substantially lower tax rate on domestic insurance companies than on out-of-state insurance companies vio-

lates the Equal Protection Clause. A state may not constitutionally favor its own residents by taxing foreign corporations at a higher rate solely because of their residence. Promotion of domestic businesses within the state by discriminating against foreign corporations that wish to compete is not a legitimate purpose under the Equal Protection Clause, nor is the encouragement of investment in state assets and governmental securities a legitimate purpose when furthered by discrimination. *Metropolitan Life v. Ward* (1985).

(4) A county policy which assesses real property on the basis of recent purchase price, but which makes only minor modifications to assessments of properties not recently sold, violates equal protection. The valuation scheme results in a gross disparity in the assessed value of comparable properties over a long period of time. While the government may reasonably seek to promote tax appraisal based on the true market value of property, the law must provide for some reasonable attainment of a rough equality of similarly situated property owners. While the state purported to treat all property uniformly in determining tax assessments, the county had engaged in "intentional systematic underevaluation" for ten years. *Allegheny Pittsburgh Coal Co. v. County Com'n.* (1989). *Allegheny* was distinguished in *Armour v. City of Indianapolis* (2012) (See Ch. VII, B, 1), as involving "a clear state law requirement clearly and dramatically violated" which precluded rationality justification.

(5) A property owner who claims that the city irrationally and arbitrarily imposed a more stringent easement on her when she sought to hook up to the municipal water supply than was imposed on other property owners states a claim for relief under the Equal Protection Clause. Olech could constitute a class of one since "the number of individuals in a class is immaterial for equal protection analysis." *Village of Willowbrook v. Olech* (2000).

b. Some of the cases purporting to use rationality review to invalidate discriminatory laws appear to reflect judicial concern that the challenged law reflects prejudice or animus towards a particular group rather than legitimate governmental interests.

Examples: (1) Mental retardation is not a "quasi-suspect" classification calling for a more exacting standard of judicial review. But application of a zoning ordinance to exclude a group home for the mentally retarded but not other similar uses is not rationally related to any legitimate government interest. Denial of a special use permit in this case appears to rest "on an irrational prejudice against the mentally retarded." *City of Cleburne v. Cleburne Living Center* (1985).

(2) An amendment to the Colorado state constitution preventing state and city legislatures from enacting antidiscrimination laws for the protection of homosexuals in housing, employment, education, public accommodations and health and welfare services, violates equal protection. A law that imposes "a broad and undifferentiated disability on a single group," which is "inexplicable by anything but animus towards the class it affects" fails even rationality review. A law making it more difficult for one class of citizens to seek legal protection is inconsistent with equal protection. *Romer v. Evans* (1996). See Ch. VII, C, 5, g for discussion of *Romer* as discrimination based on sexual persuasion.

C. Heightened Review Equal Protection

STRICT SCRUTINY. *When a law employs a "suspect classification" or significantly burdens the exercise of a "fundamental right," the Court strictly scrutinizes the relation of the classification to the government purpose. When the Court uses strict scrutiny, the burden is on the government to demonstrate that the classification is necessary to achieve a compelling state interest. There must not be a less burdensome alternative available for achieving the government objective. The ordinary presumption of constitutionality no longer pertains. It is extremely difficult for the government to satisfy this burden.*

1. Suspect Classifications

Strict judicial scrutiny may be used when the basis of the classification, *i.e.,* the basis on which governmental benefits are awarded or penalties imposed, significantly burdens a protected group.

2. Criteria of Suspectness

Some of the factors that have been considered in labeling a classification suspect include: (1) the historical purpose of the Equal Protection Clause; (2) a history of pervasive discrimination against the class; (3) the stigmatizing effect of the classification (commentators sometimes refer to "caste" legislation); (4) classification based on an immutable status or condition which a person can't control; and (5) discrimination against a "politically insular minority."

3. Purpose, Not Effect

Before strict scrutiny is used, the challenger must prove that the discrimination was purposeful, either overtly or covertly. While discriminatory impact or effect may be evidence of discriminatory purpose, it is usually not sufficient in itself to prove discriminatory purpose. If a decision is motivated in part by discriminatory purpose, the state may avoid strict scrutiny if it proves that it would have reached the same decision regardless of the discriminatory purpose.

Examples: (1) The fact that blacks are four times as likely as whites to fail a police qualifying test does not establish an equal protection violation. Discriminatory impact, standing alone, does not trigger strict constitutional review. Such a rule would have far-reaching effects, raising serious questions concerning the constitutional validity of a whole range of laws. Racially discriminatory purpose must be shown to justify strict scrutiny under the Equal Protection Clause. *Washington v. Davis* (1976).

(2) A zoning ordinance may not be challenged as racially exclusionary solely on the basis that it has a racially disproportionate impact. Racial discrimination need not be the sole basis for the law but it must be a "motivating factor." Racially discriminatory intent was not sufficiently evidenced by racially disproportionate impact, historical background, specific prior events, departures from usual procedures, or contemporaneous statements of the decision-makers involved. *Village of Arlington Heights v. Metropolitan Housing Development Corp.* (1977).

(3) Mobile's at-large election of city council members does not violate the rights of black voters under the Fourteenth and Fifteenth Amendments unless it is purposely discriminatory. There is no right for a political group to have its candidate selected, only a right not to have a purposeful denial or abridgement of the franchise. There was inadequate showing

that Mobile had "conceived or operated a purposeful device to further racial discrimination." *City of Mobile v. Bolden* (1980). Compare *Rogers v. Herman Lodge* (1982), where the Court upheld a lower court finding that the at-large voting scheme was maintained as a purposeful device to further racial discrimination. Looking at the totality of the evidence, the lower court had considered the historical discrimination in elections, the failure of any blacks to be elected to local government despite their majority status in the general population, the unresponsiveness of public bodies to the needs of black constituents and other factors.

(4) A state statute affording veterans an absolute lifetime preference for civil service positions does not violate equal protection even though it impacts severely on public employment opportunities of women. Volition or awareness of consequences is not discriminatory purpose. Many male non-veterans are also disadvantaged. Absent a showing that the preference was established for the purpose of discriminating against women, the classification need not meet the more stringent standard of review. It was not shown that the statute was enacted "because of" a desire to discriminate. The law serves legitimate and worthy purposes of assisting veterans to readjust to civilian life, of encouraging military enlistments and rewarding those who have served the country. *Personnel Adm. of Massachusetts v. Feeney* (1979).

(5) A study showing that there is a statistically greater risk that race will be considered by state decision makers weighing whether or not to impose the death penalty upon racial minorities does not establish purposeful discrimination under the Equal Protection Clause. In the absence of evidence specific to the challenger's case, statistical evidence such as this study establish discriminatory purpose only where the statistics establish a "stark" pattern of discrimination. Most important, the Court stressed that the decision of a constitutionally-selected jury upon whether or not to impose the death penalty is entitled to great deference. Finally, since discretion is essential to the criminal justice process, evidence of any type would have to be exceptionally clear in order to support the inference that this discretion has been abused. *McCleskey v. Kemp* (1987).

(6) In a trial for capital murder, the prosecution's use of peremptory challenges to exclude ten of eleven potential black jurors (where it had fourteen total peremptory challenges at its disposal) was sufficient evidence of a racially discriminatory purpose to constitute a substantial showing of the denial of a constitutional right (prima facie case). The defendant was entitled to review of the lower court's denial of habeas relief. While the prosecution had used peremptory challenges to exclude 91% of the available African–American jurors, only 13% of the non-black jurors were removed using peremptory strikes. In addition, the prosecutors had apparently subjected jurors to different lines of questioning during voir dire on the basis of race and had "shuffled" panels of prospective jurors, i.e., changed the order in which they were questioned in order to increase the chances that a non-African–American juror would be empanelled before an African–American one. There was also evidence of past and present policies of excluding African–American jurors by the Dallas District Attorney's office. Three of the race-neutral reasons the state proffered to justify striking African–American jurors applied equally to white jurors who had ended up serving on the jury, suggesting that the rationales were pretextual. The defendant had thus satisfied his burden of proof under *Batson v. Kentucky* (1986) (Ch. VII,C, 5). *Miller–El v. Cockrell* (2003).

4. Legislation and Administration

Legislation may be challenged as overtly or covertly discriminatory, i.e., discriminatory on its face or by extrinsic evidence showing a racially discriminatory purpose. In such cases, the statutory classification is suspect. Even if the law is neutral, it may be administered or enforced in a discriminatory fashion (unconstitutional as applied). If it is shown that the purpose of the administrators is to classify on a suspect basis the government must show that the classification is necessary in order to achieve a compelling state interest.

Examples: (1) A state anti-interracial marriage statute, discriminatory on its face, violates equal protection. Racial classifications are suspect and cannot be upheld when there is patently no legitimate overriding purpose—invidious racial discrimination is not a legitimate objective—which justifies the classification. *Loving v. Virginia* (1967).

(2) Two hundred Chinese who applied for laundry licenses

were denied, while all applications by persons who were not Chinese were granted. The Court held that even where legislation is racially neutral, if it is applied and administered by public authorities with an unequal hand so as to make unjust discriminations between persons in similar circumstances, a violation of equal protection has occurred. *Yick Wo v. Hopkins* (1886).

(3) Defendants claiming that the prosecutor had intentionally singled them out for prosecution because of their race, failed to make the threshold showing required for discovery since they failed to prove that the Government failed to prosecute similarly situated suspects of other races. Evidence that every one of the 24 crack cocaine cases closed by the Federal Public Defender's Office during 1991 involved blacks did not constitute "some evidence tending to show the essential elements" of a selective prosecution claim since it failed to identify individuals who were not black who were not prosecuted. Defendants were not entitled to discovery. *United States v. Armstrong* (1996).

5. The Rationale and Limits of Suspectness

a. Race and National Origin

The very purpose of the Fourteenth Amendment was to prevent legal discrimination against racial minorities. There is seldom any justification for a classification that discriminates against a racial minority. Race is a highly visible classifying trait, historically having a stigmatizing effect. It is an immutable condition. Black persons have been unable to protect their interests through ordinary political processes. Thus, race is a suspect classification. Purposeful racial discrimination imposes a heavy burden of justification on government, *i.e.*, strict scrutiny applies.

Examples: (1) An amendment to the city charter requiring voter referendum approval for any city council action involving racial discrimination in housing violated equal protection. The law imposed a heavier burden on legislation involving fair housing than on other legislation. Race classifications are "constitutionally suspect." The city could not meet its "far heavier burden of justification." *Hunter v. Erickson* (1969).

(2) A wartime conviction under a military order excluding Americans of Japanese ancestry from designated areas on

the west coast was held constitutional. While racial classifications are subject to the "most rigid scrutiny," the law was justified by wartime necessity and the alleged inability to adequately separate the loyal from the disloyal. *Korematsu v. United States* (1944).

(3) A state court's overt reliance on the potential harm to the child from community racial bias in determining whether a white natural mother cohabiting with a black male should retain custody violates equal protection. Private racial bias cannot be given legal effect. *Palmore v. Sidoti* (1984).

(4) A prosecutor cannot use his peremptory challenges to exclude certain jurors based solely on their race. The state denies a black defendant equal protection when it puts him on trial before a jury from which members of his race have been excluded. A defendant makes a prima facie case by showing purposeful discrimination in selection of a jury in his particular case. The burden then shifts to the state to come forward with a neutral explanation for challenging the black jurors. *Batson v. Kentucky* (1986).

(5) A white defendant has standing to challenge a prosecutor's race-based exclusion of black jurors since "a prosecutor's discriminatory use of peremptory challenges harms the excluded jurors and the community at large." Further, there is third-party standing since the white defendant is likely to fully litigate the equal protection claim and there is not likely to be an effective alternative way for the claim to be raised. *Powers v. Ohio* (1991). A white defendant has standing to raise an equal protection claim alleging racial discrimination against black persons in the selection of his grand jury and to raise his own due process claim. *Campbell v. Louisiana* (1998). Race-based peremptory challenges by a defense attorney also violate the Equal Protection Clause. *Georgia v. McCollum* (1991). And exclusion of potential jurors because of their race in civil litigation also violates the equal protection rights of potential black jurors. The Court found the requisite state action. *Edmonson v. Leesville Concrete Co.* (1991).

(6) A California Department of Corrections policy of racially segregating prisoners in double cells for up to sixty days after they enter a new facility is subject to strict scrutiny. Racial classifications are "immediately suspect," and strict scrutiny is as necessary here as in other contexts to "smoke out illegitimate uses of race." Furthermore, racial classifications not only stigmatize individuals but also "perpetuate[e] the notion that race matters most," which could "breed further hostility among prisoners and reinforce racial and ethnic divisions." The case was remanded for review using strict scrutiny. *Johnson v. California* (2005).

1) Segregation in Education

a) De Jure Segregation

Intentional racial segregation in public schools is inherently unequal and violates equal protection. Brown v. Board of Education *(1954). This principle was summarily extended to public facilities generally,* e.g., *beaches, golf courses, parks, without any showing of particularized harm resulting from the racial classification.*

b) De Facto Segregation

The Supreme Court has held that *de facto* segregation, *i.e.,* segregation which is not intentionally created by government action, does not violate equal protection.

c) Duty to Desegregate

A de jure *segregated school system has an affirmative duty to desegregate and achieve a unitary school system.* Green v. County School Bd. of New Kent County (1968). A school district determined to be *de jure* segregated may not take any action that has the *effect* of impeding desegregation. *Wright v. Council of City of Emporia* (1972).

Examples: (1) Lower court findings that a school board's past actions were animated by a segregative purpose and had a current segregative impact throughout the school system provided adequate basis for finding a violation of equal protection. Actions having a foreseeable and anticipated disparate racial impact are relevant evidence of a forbidden racial purpose. Proof of purposeful segregation in a substantial part of a system is prima facie proof that a dual school system exists. There was no showing that the school board had satisfied its affirmative duty to disestablish its dual school system. *Columbus Board of Educ. v. Penick* (1979).

(2) Maintenance of a dual school system in 1954, coupled with a failure to disestablish that dual system, provides prima facie proof that present segregation was caused, at least in part, by prior intentionally segregative acts. The affirmative duty not to take any actions that have the *effect* of increasing or perpetuating segregation in the *de jure* segregated system had been violated. The school board was under a "heavy burden" of showing that pupil assignment policies and school construction and abandonment did not perpetuate its dual system and served legitimate and important objectives. *Dayton Board of Educ. v. Brinkman* (1979) (*Dayton II*).

d) Desegregation: Balancing, Quotas and Busing

(1) In *Brown v. Board of Education* (1955) (*Brown II*), the Court ordered the defendant school districts to desegregate "with all deliberate speed." Lower federal courts were to retain jurisdiction, apply equitable principles and assure that school districts sought, in good faith, to desegregate as soon as possible. Resistance to desegregation eventually produced a Court holding demanding prompt conversion to a unitary school district. *Alexander v. Holmes County Board of Education* (1969). Today, lower federal courts exercise broad supervisory powers over school districts that have engaged in *de jure* segregation.

(2) *In remedying de jure segregation, equal protection does not require racial balancing but racial ratios may be used as measures of desegregation.* A federal court, in the exercise of its broad equity powers, may order busing in order to achieve desegregation. *Swann v. Charlotte–Mecklenburg Bd. of Educ.* (1971).

(3) While lower courts have broad discretion in fashioning remedies, there are limits. Generally, the nature of the remedy must reflect the nature of the constitutional violation.

Examples: (1) A district court order increasing local taxes to satisfy a school desegregation decree violates the principles of federal/state comity. However, a district court may order local governments to levy taxes greater than the limit set by state statute and may enjoin the operation of state laws where they interfere with implementing federal constitutional guarantees. In providing desegregation remedies, the power of the federal courts to enforce the Fourteenth Amendment against the states is in no way diminished by the Tenth Amendment's reservation of non-delegated powers to the states. *Missouri v. Jenkins* (1990). A federal court may not order salary increases and funding of remedial programs designed to increase "desegregation attractiveness" as a remedy for past discrimination. The goal of the district court must be not only to remedy the violation to the extent practicable but also to restore state and local control of a school system operating in compliance with the constitution. *Missouri v. Jenkins* (1995).

(2) A district court order imposing monetary sanctions upon individual Yonkers city council members for failure to vote to implement a housing desegregation order was held invalid as an abuse of discretion. The imposition of sanctions upon individual legislators subverts the normal legislative process by forcing them to act for their own interests instead of the city's. The district court's imposition of a daily fine for the duration of the

contempt *on the city* had a reasonable probability of success. *Spallone v. United States* (1990).

(4) *Anti–Busing Laws.* The Court has not yet formulated a clear position on the validity of laws designed to prohibit busing. If the anti-busing law restructures the government decision-making process for racial reasons or adopts different government processes for decisions involving race, it is likely to violate equal protection. *Washington v. Seattle School Dist.* (1982). Compare *Crawford v. Board of Educ.* (1982) (State amendment prohibiting state courts from ordering busing held constitutional. The law was racially neutral on its face and was not enacted for a racially discriminatory purpose).

e) Interdistrict Segregation

The mere showing of segregation between school districts does not establish an equal protection violation. "It must be shown that racially discriminatory acts of the state or local school districts, or of a single school district has been a substantial cause of interdistrict segregation." *Milliken v. Bradley* (1974).

f) Resegregation

(1) Once a formerly *de jure* segregated school district has desegregated, a court may not require constant revision of attendance zones to reflect a changing racial composition. *Pasadena City Board of Educ. v. Spangler* (1976). A school district once under a judicial decree to desegregate can implement a new busing plan which would result in one-race schools *if the school district had complied in good faith with the initial decree and "vestiges of past discrimination had been eliminated to the extent practicable." Board of Education of Oklahoma City v. Dowell* (1991).

(2) A district court can relinquish supervision and control of a school district in incremental stages, prior to achieving full compliance with the Constitution. The Court held that the district court's end purpose must be to remedy the constitutional violation and return control of the school system to local authorities. *Freeman v. Pitts* (1992).

2) Affirmative Action

a) Standard of Review

Equal Protection does not preclude the voluntary use of racial classifications where a proper factual showing is made. But race-based federal, state and local affirmative action programs are subject to strict scrutiny. The government must establish that the race-conscious program is necessary to a compelling state interest.

(1) A minority of justices have argued for intermediate review—that a classification must be substantially related to an important government interest—since the rationale of suspectness is not applicable to "benign" classifications. Emphasis was placed on the lack of "stigma"—affirmative action classifications do not presume one race is inferior and do not reflect prejudice or race hatred. Race consciousness was claimed to be a necessary tool in remedying past societal discrimination and in promoting equality. See, e.g., *Regents of the University of California v. Bakke* (1978) (Brennan, J., concurring in the judgment and dissenting).

(2) But in *City of Richmond v. J.A. Croson Co.* (1989), the Court held that strict scrutiny applied to state and local affirmative action programs. Equal protection creates a personal right to be treated with equal dignity and respect, not a group right. Further, strict scrutiny is needed for "smoking out" covert racism. It ensures that allegedly "benign" plans are not in fact based on racial prejudice or stereotype.

(3) There was precedent, now rejected, indicating that, given the deference accorded Congress under the Fourteenth Amendment, federal affirmative action programs need satisfy only intermediate scrutiny. This standard could be satisfied even if the federal action was not designed to remedy an identifiable legal wrong.

Examples: (1) The Court upheld a congressional statute requiring that 10% of federal funds granted for local public works projects must be used by the grantee to procure services or supplies from businesses owned and controlled by members of statutorily identified minority protection. While there was no agreement on the standard of review, the Court did "closely examine" the program. The program was a limited and tailored program, operating prospectively, designed to remedy prior discrimination in the construction industry. There was no showing that Congress' choice of particular minority groups to benefit from the remedy worked an invidious discrimination against other identifiable minorities making it under-inclusive. The burden on nonminorities was only "incidental." The program was not facially over-inclusive since it provided reasonable assurances that it would be limited to the remedial objectives of Congress and that improper applications would be promptly remedied administratively. *Fullilove v. Klutznick* (1980).

(2) Two FCC minority preference policies designed to promote diversity in radio and television programming do not violate equal protection. After a number of efforts to promote greater minority participation in broadcast ownership and management, the FCC adopted the two challenged policies. First, the FCC awards an "enhancement" to a license applicant with minority participation in ownership and management which is then weighed with other factors in comparing applications for new broadcast stations. Second, the FCC maintains a "distress sale" policy which allows a licensee whose qualifications are questioned to transfer the license to a qualified minority enterprise without having to undergo an FCC hearing.

Using intermediate review, the Court held 5–4 that the minority preference policies serve the important government interest of promoting program diversity. Such diversity is vital to the FCC mission of serving the public interest and serves First Amendment values. The programs were substantially related to this objective since the FCC and Congress found that a nexus exists between minority ownership and diversity. *Metro Broadcasting, Inc. v. F.C.C.* (1990).

(4) In *Adarand Constructors Co. v. Pena* (1995), the Court held 5–4 that all racial classifications, imposed by whatever federal, state or local governmental actor, must be analyzed by a reviewing court under strict scrutiny. A plurality indicated that strict scrutiny is not necessarily "strict in theory, fatal in fact." The Court overruled *Metro Broadcasting* to the extent that it prescribed a different standard of review for federal programs.

Example: A Department of Transportation ("DOT") program provides financial incentives to government contractors to hire subcontractors certified as small businesses controlled by "socially and economically disadvantaged" individuals. The legislation on which the DOT program is based, the Small Business Act, establishes a government-wide goal for participation of such concerns at "not less than 5 percent of the total value of all prime contract and subcontract awards for each fiscal year." The Act further establishes a rebuttable presumption that members of racial and ethnic minority groups are socially disadvantaged. Adarand Co. is a nonminority firm which submitted the low bid on a DOT subcontract. However, the prime contractor awarded the subcontract to a minority-owned firm that was presumed to be socially disadvantaged in order to receive the additional compensation from DOT. Adarand sued DOT.

The Court held 5–4 that strict scrutiny is the standard of constitutional review for federal affirmative action programs that use racial or ethnic classifications as the basis for decision making. Three general propositions govern affirmative action programs: *Skepticism*—the need for searching review for all race and ethnicity classifications in order to smoke out covert invidious discrimination. *Consistency*—since equal protection is a personal right, standards of review should not depend on the race of the person benefitted or burdened. A plurality indicated that this does not mean that the classification is necessarily unconstitutional. Consistency applies to the standards of review in race-based cases, not to the applications and outcomes. The plurality sought to "dispel the notion that strict scrutiny is strict in theory, but fatal in fact." *Congruence*—equal protection analysis under the Fifth and Fourteenth Amendments uses the same standard of review. *But this does not necessarily mean that strict scrutiny will apply in the same way; courts may give greater deference to federal programs.* The case was remanded to determine if strict scrutiny was satisfied. *Adarand v. Pena* (1995).

b) Applying Strict Scrutiny: Education

(1) *Remediation.* Although four concurring justices in *Bakke* would have upheld an affirmative action program designed to remedy past societal discrimination, the Court has generally rejected remedying societal discrimination as sufficient to justify a racial classification. *On the other hand, the Court will uphold a narrowly drawn race based program designed to remedy specific identified illegal racial discrimination.*

Examples: (1) A race-based layoff program in a collective bargaining agreement between a school board and a union was held not to be narrowly tailored to achieving a compelling government interest. Remedying societal discrimination, not traceable to the board's actions, is not a compelling justification. Remedying past or present discrimination by the state actor would suffice as a compelling interest for a narrowly tailored affirmative action program. But the layoff plan in question was not narrowly tailored given the burden on white workers and the availability of less intrusive means such as hiring goals. *Wygant v. Jackson Board of Education* (1986).

(2) A city ordinance requiring prime contractors awarded city construction contracts to subcontract at least 30% of the dollar amount of each contract to minority businesses violated equal protection. A plurality held that elimination of government's passive support for private racial discrimination would be a compelling interest. But the city ordinance was not based on sufficiently specific statistical findings that the city was actually remedying the effects of specific identified past illegal racial discrimination in the city's construction industry. Further, the city's plan was not narrowly drawn. Racially neutral alternatives must be considered. Racial quotas may not be used where case-by-case consideration is available. The city must consider the effects of its program on third parties and must limit the program in duration and scope. *City of Richmond v. J.A. Croson Co.* (1989).

(2) *Student Body Diversity*

(a) In *Bakke*, a majority of justices had indicated that a narrowly tailored race-conscious university admissions program designed to promote diversity in the student body could be constitutional. But only Justice Powell had used strict scrutiny in reaching this conclusion.

Example: Where a state university medical school voluntarily set aside a set number of places for minority students, a non-minority, otherwise qualified, applicant who had no opportunity to be considered for any of these places cannot be denied admission solely because of his race. However, five justices held that race or ethnicity could be a factor in the decision to admit an applicant. Justice Powell, who provided the crucial fifth vote, argued that the university had a compelling interest in promoting diversity in the student body given its educational mission. However, he concluded that race could only be one factor in the admissions decision and that the school's program was not narrowly-tailored to promote diversity. *Regents of the University of California v. Bakke* (1978).

(b) In *Grutter v. Bollinger* (2003), the Court held that a narrowly drawn race-conscious law school admissions policy designed to promote diversity in the student body, was constitutional. *Diversity in the student body, at least in the university educational context, can be a compelling government interest. But the affirmative action program must be narrowly tailored; it must be individualized, non-mechanistic, using race only as a "plus" factor in the admissions decision.*

Examples: (1) The University of Michigan Law School's admissions policy, designed to achieve, *inter alia,* racial and ethnic diversity in the student body, does not violate equal protection. The Court based its analysis on Justice Powell's concurring opinion in *Regents of the University of California v. Bakke* (1978). Applying strict scrutiny, the Court held that the Law School's interest in diversity of the student body was compelling, emphasizing deference to the "Law School's educational judgment that such diversity is essential to its educational mission." The Court emphasized the First Amendment interest in educational autonomy in selecting students (i.e., academic freedom), the educational benefits of diversity in the learning process, the importance of preparing students for business and the military and for citizenship and leadership roles.

The Court held that the Law School policy was narrowly tailored, focusing on the individualized, non-mechanical nature of the admissions process, in which race was taken into account, but not given determinative weight. While the Law School sought a "critical mass" of minority students to provide diversity, the program did not use quotas, place different racial groups on different admissions tracks, or award a set number of points to an applicant based on minority status. Rather, "[u]niversities could consider race or ethnicity more flexibly as a 'plus' factor in the context of individualized consideration of each and every applicant." Narrow tailoring does not require exhaustion of every possible race-neutral alternative. Turning to the absence of formal time limits in the Law School program, the Court noted that it would not recognize the validity of race conscious admissions policies indefinitely, noting that "[w]e expect that 25 years from now, the use of racial preferences will no longer be necessary to further the interest approved today."

Each of the four dissenters in *Grutter* wrote a separate opinion. Chief Justice

Rehnquist and Justice Kennedy argued that the program was not narrowly tailored but sought to achieve racial balancing. While the law school claimed it was seeking a critical mass for each minority group, it produced a disproportionate number of African–Americans compared with Hispanics and Native Americans. Further, the percentage of admitted minority applicants for each group closely tracked the percentage of the minority group's applicants in the applicant pool. Justices Scalia and Thomas challenged the Court's holding that racial diversity constitutes a compelling government interest. Justice Scalia's dissent argues that the benefits from diversity claimed by the Law School could be claimed by any public institution to justify race-conscious programs and warned of spawning litigation challenging the specifics of various affirmative action programs. Justice Thomas, dissenting, argued that the law School program served "aesthetic" interests but produced, at best, marginal educational benefits. The program was in fact aimed at maintaining an "elite law school" serving no pressing public need. In fact, the school had a race-neutral alternative to achieving diversity—abandon its exclusionary admissions program and admit applicants meeting minimum qualifications on a color blind basis, e.g., a lottery. *Grutter v. Bollinger* (2003).

(2) In a companion case, the University of Michigan's undergraduate admissions policy was held to violate equal protection because it was not narrowly tailored. Membership in a designated racial or ethnic minority (African–American,

Hispanic, or Native American) resulted in applicants being awarded 20 points, one-fifth of the amount needed to guarantee admission. While consideration was given to a variety of other factors, including high school GPA, activities, and standardized test scores, the 20–point bonus resulted in an offer of admission for "virtually every minimally qualified underrepresented minority applicant." The lack of individualized consideration and the rigid treatment given racial and ethnic status in the program did not satisfy narrow tailoring. The fact that more individualized and wholistic treatment might not be administratively feasible given the number of applicants "did not render constitutional an otherwise problematic system."

Justices Souter and Ginsburg, dissenting, argued that the University admissions process did not involve a quota comparable to that in *Bakke* which forecloses applicants from competing for certain seats. Race is only one factor in the admissions decision and it can be outweighed. There is no essential difference between "holistic" review and the system used by the University. Arguably, it is preferable that educational institutions are open about the weight assigned to various factors, rather than operating covertly. *Gratz v. Bollinger* (2003).

(c) In *Parents Involved in Community Schools v. Seattle School District No. 1* (2007), the Court held 5–4 that two local school districts that had voluntarily used race in assigning students violated equal protection because the plans were not narrowly drawn to further a compelling state interest. *The Court did not decide whether the educational and social benefits from racial diversity (ie., preventing racial isolation or promoting a racially integrated student body) in public elementary and secondary schools could be a compelling state interest.*

Example: The Seattle, Washington, school district had never been under a school desegregation order. Under the threat of litigation, Seattle had adopted an open-choice plan under which students were generally assigned to the school of their choice. If a school was oversubscribed, the district used tiebreakers, including whether the student was white or nonwhite and whether the school's racial makeup deviated from the district-wide overall racial composition. After one year at the assigned school students could transfer without regard to race. Jefferson County, Kentucky, school district had been subject to a court-ordered desegregation order but in 2000 the order had been dissolved based on a finding that the school district had achieved unitary status. In 2001, Jefferson County adopted a choice plan in which students could choose a school in a nearby geographic zone unless space was not available or if it would cause the percentage of "black" students to fall below 15% or rise above 50%. Transfer requests were also based on space and race.

The Court, per Chief Justice Roberts, began from the premise that whenever "the government distributes burdens or benefits on the basis of individual race classifications," the action is reviewed under strict scrutiny. In the school context, the Court had recognized compelling interests in "remedying the effects of past intentional discrimination" and in "diversity in higher education." The remediation interest was inapplicable to Seattle since the schools had never been "segregated by law, and were not subject to court-ordered desegregation decrees." Jefferson County school district "had achieved unitary status." The second compelling interest did not apply to the two plans since race was not "considered as part of a broader effort to achieve exposure to widely diverse people, cultures, ideas and viewpoints." Race was not simply one factor; when it came into play, it was decisive by itself. Race was used in the "non individualized, mechanical way," rejected in *Grutter–Gratz*. Further, the districts used only a limited notion of diversity—white/nonwhite in Seattle and black/other in Jefferson County—producing results that failed to consider the diverse racial/ethnic composition of students. Finally, the districts failed to consider race-neutral alternatives, evidenced by the minimal effect of the racial classification on school enrollment. The Chief Justice also noted that higher education in *Grutter* involved unique considerations bearing on diversity not shared by elementary and secondary education.

In a part of his opinion, joined only by Justices Alito, Scalia and Thomas, the Chief Justice rejected the districts' argument that the plans were justified by the educational and social benefits claimed to flow from racial diversity. But the plurality did not decide whether or not racial diversity could be a compelling interest. Rather, the plurality focused on the lack of narrow tailoring. In design and operation, the plans were directed to racial balancing, which is illegitimate. The plans were based on the racial demographics of the districts' students not the level of diversity needed to provide the alleged educational and socialization benefits. More generally, the plurality argued that *Brown v. Board* had rejected the use of race in assigning students. Finally, the plurality endorsed a Colorblind Constitution. "The way to stop discriminating on the basis of race is to stop discriminating on the basis of race." This principle was developed further by Justice Thomas in a concurring opinion.

Justice Kennedy concurred in part and concurred in the judgment. Since Justice Kennedy provided the crucial fifth vote, his separate opinion is especially important. He agreed with the Court that the Seattle and Jefferson County plans were not narrowly tailored. But he argued that the plurality had gone too far in rejecting race-conscious programs. "A compelling interest exists in avoiding racial isolation, an interest that a school district in its discretion and expertise may choose to pursue." School districts can devise race conscious measures such as strategic selection of sites for new schools, or drawing attendance zones reflecting neighborhood demographics. "If necessary, a more-nuanced individual evaluation of school needs and student characteristics that might include race as a component" could be used for student assignment. But the use of race must be informed by *Grutter*.

Justice Breyer, joined by Justices Stevens, Souter and Ginsburg, dissented. They argued for a contextual approach to review, differentiating inclusive and exclusive use of race, even in applying strict scrutiny. The challenged plans were narrowly tailored. Student choice was the predominant criterion; race was only one factor to be used as a tiebreaker. Use of race-based numerical *goals* to desegregate is permissible. Further, the dissent argued that racial diversity is a compelling interest. The quest to promote racial diversity seeks to remedy past school segregation (Justice Breyer criticizes the Court's application of an extreme de jure and defacto segregation standard). Also, such plans allow school boards to seek the educational benefits of integration and to further democratic values reflecting our pluralistic society. The dissent especially condemned the plurality's misuse of *Brown*. *Brown I* and *II* promised racially integrated education which would permit and, at times, require race-consciousness. *Parents Involved in Community Schools v. Seattle School District No. I* (2007).

c) Congressional Districting

A state may consider race as one of the factors influencing redistricting decisions. However, *when race is the predominant factor in formulating a redistricting plan, that plan is subject to strict scrutiny. Race is the predominant factor when the state subordinates traditional race-neutral districting considerations to race.* A state may not assume that a group of voters share a common interest simply because they are members of the same race. Such a race-based assignment of voters reflects racial stereotypes.

Examples: (1) An equal protection challenge by white constituents to state reapportionment legislation creating an extremely irregularly shaped majority black district, which could not rationally be understood as anything other than racially motivated districting, may state a claim even though the legislation was passed to comply with the federal Voting Rights Act. The Court in remanding held that when race is used to separate voters into districts it is subject to strict scrutiny and is invalid when it can only be rationally explained as a race-conscious gerrymander. *Shaw v. Reno* (1993) (*Shaw I*).

(2) A redistricting plan creating three majority black congressional districts is subject to strict scrutiny and violates equal protection, even though none of the districts in question was extremely bizarre in shape. A plaintiff can show that race was the predominant factor in redistricting decisions either by circumstantial evidence (i.e. bizarreness of shape), or by direct evidence of legislative intent. Race is the predominant factor in redistricting decisions when the state subordinates traditional race-neutral districting principles to racial considerations. There is a compelling government interest in eradicating the effects of past discrimination but this plan was designed simply to satisfy the Justice Department's preclearance demands. The Justice Department's requirement that states maximize majority-minority districts whenever possible is based on an incorrect reading of the Voting Rights Act. Such race-based districting is not reasonably necessary to satisfy the Act. *Miller v. Johnson* (1995).

(3) On remand from *Shaw v. Reno*, the Court ultimately holds that the irregularly shaped district violates equal protection principles. Although the state did take account of several race-neutral districting principles, race was still the predominant factor, and therefore strict scrutiny is applied. Since the creation of majority-minority districts was not motivated by past discrimination, eradicating the effects of past discrimination is not a compelling state interest in this case. Assuming that compliance with the Voting Rights Act

can be a compelling state interest independent of any interest in remedying past discrimination, the plan in question goes beyond the requirements of the Voting Rights Act, and is therefore not narrowly tailored. *Shaw v. Hunt* (1996) (*Shaw II*).

(4) A redistricting plan creating three majority-minority districts is held unconstitutional. Although the redistricting decisions were not "purely race-based," the Court applies the "predominant factor" test and holds that since traditional districting principles were subordinated to race, the plan is subject to strict scrutiny. (Two justices reiterate their belief that any government classification based on race is automatically subject to strict scrutiny.) Although the Court assumes without deciding that compliance with the Voting Rights Act can be compelling, it holds that the plan in question goes beyond the minimum requirements of the Voting Rights Act. The plan is therefore not narrowly tailored and fails under strict scrutiny. Nor is the plan justified as a remedy for past discrimination, requiring that there be specific, identified discrimination to be remedied and that there be a strong basis in evidence that the remedial action is necessary. The districting plan was not narrowly tailored to any identified discrimination. *Bush v. Vera* (1996).

(5) After the Court's ruling in *Miller v. Johnson*, the Georgia legislature was unable to agree upon a revised redistricting plan. As a result, a federal district court was forced to formulate its own plan. The district court's plan contained only one majority-minority district, which was two fewer than the original plan. The Supreme Court upheld the district court's plan because it violated neither the Constitution nor the Voting Rights Act. Although the plan did reduce the number of majority-minority districts, it reflects traditional districting principles such as respect for political boundaries

and maintaining communities of interest. *Abrams v. Johnson* (1997).

(6) In response to *Shaw II*, the legislature enacted a new districting plan. The Court reversed a district court grant of plaintiff's motion for summary judgment, holding that a genuine issue of material fact existed as to whether the legislature was racially motivated or, as the state claimed, politically motivated. *Hunt v. Cromartie* (1999). On remand, the district court again held that the districting was predominantly motivated by race. Again, the Supreme Court reversed, holding that the finding was clearly erroneous. While race correlated with political behavior, the plaintiff must show that the districting was done because of race *rather than* political and other nonracial factors. *Easley v. Cromartie* (2001).

b. Alienage—The "Sometimes Suspect" Classification

1) Compelling Justification
When a state classifies on the basis of alienage, strict scrutiny normally applies. Such a classification involves a discrete and insular minority requiring judicial solicitude.

Example: A state court rule restricting admission to the bar to United States citizens violates equal protection. The state failed to show that the classification was "necessary to the accomplishment of its purpose or the safeguarding of its interests." *Application of Griffiths* (1973).

2) Political Functions Exception
However, a state need only satisfy the rational relation test when it sets qualifications for voting or for appointment of officials to important government positions which involve the definition and self-government of a state.

Examples: (1) A state law limiting appointment to the state police to U.S. citizens was upheld under traditional equal protection standards. Generally, alienage classifications are suspect. However, a state need only satisfy the rational relation test when defining eligibility for positions held by "officers who participate directly in the formation, execution, or review of broad public policy." Because of the high degree of discretion afforded police, police officers fall within this exception as officers who execute broad public policy. *Foley v. Connelie* (1978).

(2) Elementary and secondary public school teachers play a vital role in preparing individuals to participate as citizens and in preserving basic societal value. A state law excluding from teaching all aliens who were unwilling to apply for United States citizenship satisfies traditional equal protection. The classification is rationally related to promoting civic virtues and understanding. *Ambach v. Norwick* (1979).

(3) A state requirement that notaries public be United States citizens was held unconstitutional under the Equal Protection Clause. Utilizing a two-part test, the Court first examined the specificity of the classification to determine if it was sufficiently tailored to serve legitimate ends. The Court did not resolve this issue, however, because the state requirement failed the second prong of the test—the classification did not apply to a position lying at the heart of representative government. Therefore, the notary position did not qualify for the political function exception. The state failed to show that the law furthers a compelling state interest by the least burdensome means available. *Bernal v. Fainter* (1984).

3) Preemption

Note that state classifications against aliens may interfere with the national power to legislate regarding matters of immigration and naturalization. Such laws would violate the Art. VI Supremacy Clause.

Examples: (1) A state university policy preventing "nonimmigrant" aliens from qualifying for tuition preference was held invalid under the Supremacy Clause. The policy imposed an ancillary burden on certain aliens not contemplated by the congressional laws admitting them. *Toll v. Moreno* (1982).

(2) In a 5–3 decision (Justice Kagan recused herself), the Court held three provisions of an Arizona immigration statute (S.B. 1070)—enacted to address the problem of illegal aliens in the state—were preempted under the Supremacy Clause. However, the Court, per Justice Kennedy, reversed a lower court injunction against a fourth provision, finding that it was not facially unconstitutional but leaving room for an "as applied" challenge after its implementation.

Section 3 of S.B. 1070, making failure to comply with federal alien-registration requirements a state misdemeanor, was preempted because it intruded on the field of alien registration where Congress has implemented a "single integrated and all-embracing system" that does not leave room for States to curtail or complement federal law. Section 5(C), making it a misdemeanor for an unauthorized alien to seek or engage in work in Arizona, was preempted because the text, structure, and history of the Immigration Reform and Control Act (IRCA) indicated that Congress decided that it would be inappropriate to impose criminal penalties on employees. Section 5 (C)'s method of enforcement was in conflict and an obstacle to the federal regulatory system. Section 6 of S.B. 1070 authorizing state and local officers to arrest a person without a warrant where the officer has probable cause to believe that person has committed any public offense that makes the person removable from the United States, was preempted because it authorized arrest beyond the limited and specific circumstances authorized by federal law. The provision "creates an obstacle to the full purposes and objectives of Congress."

Section 2(B) of the S.B. 1070 requires Arizona officers making a stop, detention, or arrest to verify the person's immigration status with the Federal Government "if reasonable suspicion exists that the person is an alien and is unlawfully present in the United States." Various limitations are provided. The United States had brought suit before the law had gone into effect and before it had been interpreted by state courts. Justice Kennedy reasoned that, under these circumstances, it would be inappropriate to assume that the provision would be implemented in a way that creates a conflict with federal law. He said: "The opinion does not foreclose other preemption and constitutional challenges to the law as interpreted and applied after it goes into effect." *Arizona v. United States* (2012).

4) Federal Discrimination

The broad power given to Congress over immigration and naturalization (Art. I, § 8, cl. 4) results in a more limited standard of judicial review being applied to federal laws discriminating against aliens which are challenged under the Fifth Amendment.

Example: A federal statute conditioning an alien's eligibility for participation in a federal medical insurance program on continuous residence in the United States for five years and admission for permanent residence does not deprive ineligible aliens of due process of law guaranteed by the Fifth Amendment. Those qualifying under the test may reasonably be presumed to have a greater affinity to the United States than those who do not and it is therefore rational. *Mathews v. Diaz* (1976).

INTERMEDIATE REVIEW: GENDER AND ILLEGITIMACY. *In recent years the Court has reviewed equal protection classifications in selected areas using an intermediate standard of review. The Court examines the classification to assure that it is* substantially *related to achieving an* important *government objective. This intermediate form of equal protection review has been applied to sex discrimination and illegitimacy classifications.*

c. **Gender Classifications**

1) Sex Discrimination

No Supreme Court majority has held that sex classifications are suspect. As a result, the "strict scrutiny" standard is not used.

However, discrimination against women does share common characteristics with race, *e.g.*, it has been historic and pervasive and gender is highly visible and immutable. Such discrimination often reflects archaic stereotypes rather than meaningful differences between the sexes.

a)   *The Court today applies an intermediate standard of review—purposeful gender classifications against women or men "must serve important governmental objectives and must be substantially related to achievement of those objectives."* Craig v. Boren *(1976).* In most intermediate review cases, the Court will use the actual government purpose and demand close correspondence of the classification to that end. Classifications are most likely to fail because the classification is not substantially related to the government interest.

Examples: (1) A state law denying a widower death benefits under workmen's compensation laws unless he proves dependence or physical or mental disability while granting death benefits to widows without such proof violates equal protection. Such a law discriminates against women workers who receive less protection for their spouses. And it discriminates against male widowers since they have a heavier burden than widows in order to recover. The classification was not substantially related to an important government interest. While providing for needy spouses is an important objective, the administrative convenience of presuming dependency will not support the discrimination. *Wengler v. Druggists Mutual Ins. Co.* (1980).

(2) A women-only admissions policy at a state nursing school violates equal protection. The classification, which the state claimed was compensatory, in fact served to reinforce a stereotype of nursing as a profession for women. Since women had not been discriminated against in nursing, there was no need for compensation. Compensation was not the *actual* purpose of the government. While promoting educational diversity might

serve as an important interest, the law was not substantially related to that end since the choice was given only to women, not to men. *Mississippi University for Women v. Hogan* (1982).

(3) The Equal Protection Clause forbids the use of peremptory strikes on the basis of gender, just as it forbids the use of those strikes on the basis of race. The intentional striking of a juror on the basis of gender was not proven to further the "litigant's effort to secure a fair and impartial jury." Virtually no proof was offered that gender is an accurate predictor of juror's attitudes. Intentionally striking jurors on the basis of gender simply furthers "archaic and overbroad" stereotypes about the relative abilities of men and women, causing harm to the "litigants, the community, and the individual jurors who are wrongfully excluded from participation in the judicial process." Parties can still use strikes to remove jurors whom they feel may be less acceptable than others on the panel, as long as gender is not the motivating factor. If gender discrimination is alleged, there must be "a prima facie showing of intentional discrimination before the party exercising the challenge is required to explain the basis for the strike." *J.E.B. v. Alabama* (1994).

b) *Recently, the Court has referred to the intermediate review standard as requiring "exceedingly persuasive justification." Some critics argue that the Court has made the standard more like strict scrutiny by imposing a less restrictive means test.*

Example: Virginia Military Institute (VMI), the only single-sex public institution of higher learning in Virginia, uses a unique "adversative method" of training to produce "citizen soldiers." The United States sued VMI and Virginia claiming a violation of equal protection. The lower court held that the VMI program violated equal protection and the case was remanded for fashioning a remedy. Virginia proposed creating a parallel program for women at Virginia Women's Institute for Leadership (VWIL) at Mary Baldwin College. A task force of educational experts fashioned a leadership program appropriate for "most women" but with marked differences from the VMI military model. The Fourth Circuit held that the program would provide "substantial comparability" and satisfied equal protection. The Supreme Court 7–1 affirmed the holding that Virginia violated equal protection but reversed the judgment approving the remedy.

The intentional gender-based program at VMI requires "exceedingly persuasive justification." While the Court purports to apply intermediate review, Justice Scalia, dissenting, argues that the Court, by demanding an "exceedingly persuasive justification" abandons intermediate review and uses de facto strict scrutiny by applying a less restrictive means test.

The Court argues that *diversity* of educational choice is not the actual state purpose. While diversity may serve the public good, the VMI program didn't serve that objective since there was no single sex program for women. The State interest in maintaining the adversative method of education does not provide exceedingly persuasive justification since the program's goals and methods are not inherently unsuitable for women. Justice Scalia argues that Virginia has an important interest in promoting effective education and that the single sex program at VMI satisfies intermediate review given the traditional acceptance of single sex education and the existence of private all-female colleges. The program is still *substantially related* even if some women who could participate were excluded since less restrictive means is not applicable to intermediate review.

The dual program at VMI and VWIL does not constitute an adequate remedy for the wrong since the VWIL program does not provide a comparable military program. VWIL is a pale shadow of VMI. The Court rejects the argument that the differences were justified by real gender differences; the programs reflect stereotypical thinking. While adjustments would be required, VMI could accommodate women who sought admission. *United States v. Virginia* (1996).

c) *In some cases, the Court has determined that the sexes are not similarly situated. A gender classification based on real differences rather than sexual stereotypes is more likely to be upheld.* Perhaps reflecting a determination that the use of gender in classifying in such cases is not suspect, the Court tends to apply a lesser standard of review. Emphasis is on mixed legislative motives and less on a particular actual purpose. The fit of the classification to the state interest need not be as precise and close as in most intermediate review cases.

Examples: (1) A state "statutory rape" law which makes men alone criminally liable for the act of sexual intercourse with a female minor does not violate the equal protection guarantee. This gender-based classification realistically reflects the fact that the sexes are not similarly situated in certain circumstances. The different treatment of males and females bears a "fair and substantial relationship" to the "important" governmental interest of preventing illegitimate teenage pregnancies, which was at least one of the purposes of the law. Because virtually all the significant harmful and identifiable consequences of teenage pregnancies fall on the female, a legislature acts reasonably when it elects to punish only the male who suffers few of the consequences of his conduct. *Michael M. v. Superior Court* (1981).

(2) A federal statute authorizing male-only draft registration does not violate the Fifth Amendment equal protection guarantee since such a gender classification realistically reflects the fact that the

sexes are not similarly situated in regard to the need to provide combat troops. In matters of national defense and military preparedness, great discretion must be given to Congress. Since women are not used for combat duty, the exemption of women from registration for the draft is "closely related" to Congress' "important governmental interest" in developing a pool of potential combat troops. *Rostker v. Goldberg* (1981). The Government now has authorized the use of women in combat roles.

2) **Discriminatory Purpose**

While discriminatory effect may be evidence of discriminatory purpose, it is not enough to trigger intermediate review. Only a governmental purpose to discriminate justifies departure from the traditional rationality standard.

Example: While veteran preference laws have the effect of disadvantaging women, this is not their purpose. Therefore, only rational basis analysis applies. The laws rationally compensate veterans for the disruptions of military service. *Personnel Adm'r of Massachusetts v. Feeney* (1979).

3) **Non-sex Classifications**

Remember that not all classifications which operate to the disadvantage of women or classes of women are necessarily sex classifications.

Example: A state public health program which exempts any work loss resulting from normal pregnancy from coverage is not a sex classification. The classification is not between men and women but between "pregnant women and non-pregnant persons." In the interests of economy, a state may reasonably exclude a particular physical condition. *Geduldig v. Aiello* (1974).

4) **Affirmative Action**

Classifications providing benefits to women (but not to men) to remedy disadvantages have been held constitutional if narrowly drawn to compensate for past wrongs. But the Court will probe to determine if the alleged benign purpose is the real purpose.

Examples: (1) A state law granting a property tax exemption to female widows but not male widowers is constitutional given a lone woman's greater financial difficulty. *Kahn v. Shevin* (1974).

(2) A federal statute requiring discharge of male officers passed over twice for promotion after nine years of service and of female officers after 13 years is constitutional. Congress could reasonably conclude that women line officers had less opportunity for promotion. *Schlesinger v. Ballard* (1975).

(3) An amendment to the Social Security Act permitting women to exclude more lower earning years in computing benefits than males is constitutional. The classifications worked directly to achieve the important government interest in reducing the disparity in the economic condition between men and women caused by a long history of discrimination. *Califano v. Webster* (1977).

(4) A state statute authorizing courts to award alimony to wives but not to husbands violates equal protection. Sex was not a reliable proxy for need in this case since individualized hearings on financial need already occur—actual dependency could be determined on a gender-neutral basis. The law was not carefully tailored to achieving any compensatory objective. *Orr v. Orr* (1979).

(5) A state-supported university's policy of denying admission to its nursing school to otherwise qualified males violates the Equal Protection Clause. This classification cannot be justified as compensating women for past discrimination, since women do not otherwise suffer a disadvantage in this area. The classification actually tends to perpetuate the traditional stereotype that nursing is a woman's job. *Mississippi University for Women v. Hogan* (1982).

5) Mothers and Fathers

A law which discriminates against fathers and in favor of mothers where the parents are similarly situated except for their gender violates equal protection under the intermediate standard of review.

Examples: (1) A state law permitting the mother, but not the father, of an illegitimate child to block the child's adoption by withholding consent, violates equal protection. The classification was based on the overbroad generalization that the maternal role is invariably more important for children, regardless of the child's stage of development. Nor did the law bear a substantial relation to the state's interest in securing homes for illegitimate children. *Caban v. Mohammed* (1979).

(2) A state law barring the father of an illegitimate child who has not legitimated the child from suing for the child's wrongful death does not violate equal protection. A plurality in the 5–4 decision used only the rational basis test on grounds that the parents are not similarly situated where only the father is in a position to legitimate the child. The statute was rationally related to the state interest in proving paternity and the avoidance of spurious claims against intestate estates. The concurring opinion and the dissent would use intermediate review. *Parham v. Hughes* (1979).

(3) A federal statute requiring that illegitimate children born outside the United States to fathers who are U.S. citizens obtain proof of paternity by age 18 in order to obtain U.S. citizenship, but not requiring such action if the mother is a U.S. citizen, does not violate equal protection. There is a significant difference between the relationship of mothers and fathers to the potential citizen at the time of birth. First, there is proof of biological parenthood from the mother's presence at birth but the father is not necessarily present at birth. Second, the citizen mother and the child have a demonstrated opportunity or potential to develop a relationship to each other (and, in turn, the United States) from the event of birth that does not exist for the citizen father. Congress could properly seek to assure a reasonable substitute for the citizen father and child. *Nguyen v. INS* (2001).

(4) The Supreme Court divided 4–4 (Justice Kagan recused herself) in deciding if a statute dealing with

United States citizenship requirements violated the Equal Protection Clause. The statute imposed a requirement that an illegitimate child reside in the United States for five years after the age of fourteen if born to a United States citizen father, but not to a United States mother, before the child could claim citizenship. Because the Court deadlocked, the 9th Circuit Court of Appeals decision—which held that the statute does not violate the Equal Protection Clause in light of *Nguyen v. INS*—was affirmed. *Flores–Villar v. United States* (2011).

d. Illegitimacy Classifications

Illegitimacy classifications have many of the characteristics of suspectness, *e.g.*, they are based on a status beyond the control of the child, there is a history of pervasive discrimination, illegitimates are a politically insular minority. The Court has been ambivalent in its treatment of classifications based on the legitimacy of the child. *Today, the Court uses an intermediate standard of review, i.e., the classification must be substantially related to an important government interest. The more that it appears that a law is based on prejudice against illegitimates, the more likely it is that the law will be held unconstitutional.*

Examples: (1) Under a state workmen's compensation law, unacknowledged dependent illegitimate children would recover benefits only if there were not enough surviving legitimate dependents to exhaust the maximum statutory benefits. The Court declared that Louisiana's denial of equal recovery rights to the dependent unacknowledged illegitimate children violated equal protection. The Court said the inferior treatment of dependent unacknowledged illegitimates bore no significant relationship to those recognized purposes of recovery underlying workmen's compensation statutes. *Weber v. Aetna Casualty & Surety Co.* (1972).

(2) A state law providing that illegitimate children can inherit by intestate succession only if a court of competent jurisdiction has, during the lifetime of the father, made a finding of paternity is constitutional. The burden placed on illegitimates substantially furthers the important state interest in assuming the just and orderly disposition of

property at death. The law aids in the difficult task of establishing paternity. *Lalli v. Lalli* (1978).

(3) A Texas statute providing that a paternity suit to identify the natural father for purposes of obtaining support must be brought before the child is one year old or the suit is barred violates equal protection. The state has a legitimate interest in preventing the prosecution of stale or fraudulent claims but the "unrealistically short time limitation" of one year is not "substantially related" to this interest. There is no real threat of loss or diminution of evidence or an increased vulnerability to fraudulent claims with the passing of one year. Nor does this period provide a time sufficiently long in duration to present a reasonable opportunity for those with an interest in such children to assert claims on their behalf. Five justices, concurring, noted that a longer period of limitations would probably also fail to justify the discrimination against illegitimates. *Mills v. Habluetzel* (1982). The Court later adopted this suggestion, holding a state's two-year limitation unconstitutional. *Pickett v. Brown* (1983).

(4) A six year statute of limitations does not necessarily provide a reasonable opportunity to assert a claim on behalf of an illegitimate child. Since the statute was not substantially related to the state's interest in avoiding litigation of stale or fraudulent claims, it violated equal protection. *Clark v. Jeter* (1988).

OTHER CLASSIFYING TRAITS. *Thus far, stricter standards of equal protection review has been limited to classifications drawn on the basis of race and national origin, alienage, gender, and illegitimacy.*

e. Wealth and Age

In the absence of infringement on some fundamental right or interest, a classification which operates to disadvantage the poor or which classifies on the basis of age, is not suspect. The Court will use the traditional rationality standard of review.

Examples: (1) A state constitutional provision requiring referenda before any government-sponsored low income housing could be built in a community was held not to violate equal protection. The provision was not racially-discriminatory on its face or in its impact. *James v. Valtierra* (1971).

(2) A state law requiring retirement of police officers on attaining the age of 50 does not violate equal protection. Discrimination against the aged has not been as historically pervasive or been used as a stereotype to the degree of race, and there is no "discrete and insular minority" of elderly persons needing judicial protection. The law rationally serves the public interest in the physical preparedness of its police. *Massachusetts Bd. of Retirement v. Murgia* (1976).

f. Mental Retardation

Generally a law which disadvantages the mentally retarded as a class is subject only to rationality review. However, in some circumstances the courts might use "rationality with bite." (See Ch. VII, B, 2)

Example: Mental retardation is not a "quasi-suspect" classification since it is a characteristic which government may legitimately consider in a wide range of its decisions. The question of how this class is to be treated under the law is more often a question for legislatures rather than courts. The class is not politically powerless and legislatures have been responsive to the needs of the mentally retarded. There are often real differences between the mentally retarded and others. It is difficult to find a principled means for distinguishing many other groups claiming prejudice based on an immutable trait if the mentally retarded were afforded special judicial protection. *City of Cleburne v. Cleburne Living Center* (1985). But note that the law in question was held unconstitutional using rationality review.

g. Sexual Orientation

1) In *Bowers v. Hardwick* (1986), the Court rejected any fundamental right of adults to engage in homosexual sodomy, even in private. But the Court noted that it was not deciding whether discrimination based on sexual orientation might violate equal protection. (*Bowers* was overruled by *Lawrence v. Texas*, Ch. VI, G, 4).

2) The Court still has not decided whether discrimination based on sexual persuasion is suspect or quasi-suspect, deserving of a heightened standard of judicial review. Advocates of heightened scrutiny cite the historic, pervasive discrimination against gays, that classifications based on sexual orientation often reflects prejudice and stereotypes, and the possible genetic basis of sexual orientation (immutability). But critics argue that gays were not intended to be special beneficiaries of the Fourteenth Amendment, that gays increasingly have the ability to protect their interests politically and that homosexual activity can be controlled. Almost all lower courts have applied rationality review to classifications based on sexual orientation.

3) *While the Court has not held whether classifications based on sexual persuasion are subject to heightened scrutiny, it has held that a law imposing a broad, undifferentiated disability against gays, which reflects animus towards the class, is irrational and violates equal protection.* Romer v. Evans (1996). (*Romer* is also discussed in Ch. VII, B, 2). This may indicate that a greater scrutiny will be given to laws imposing special burdens on gays as a class.

Example: An amendment to the Colorado state constitution preventing state and city legislatures from enacting anti-discrimination laws for the protection of homosexuals in employment, education, public accommodations, and health and welfare services is irrational and violates equal protection. The state interests in protecting the freedom of association and conservation of resources cannot justify such a broad status-based enactment. The law is so unrelated to any legitimate state interest as to suggest that it is born of animus—a desire to harm a politically unpopular group. Further, the law denies legal access to specific protection of the laws. "A law declaring that in general it shall be more difficult for one group of citizens than for all others to seek aid from the government is itself a denial of equal protection of the laws in its most literal sense." *Romer v. Evans* (1996).

6. Fundamental Rights and Interests

FUNDAMENTAL RIGHTS. *Strict scrutiny is also used because of the nature of the interests which are burdened by the classification. When a classification significantly burdens the exercise of a fundamental personal right, the government usually must prove that the classification is necessary to a compelling governmental interest. But note that the Court has occasionally used varying terminology in defining the standard of review, suggesting a movement away from the strict scrutiny formulation. Fundamental rights may be derived independently from provisions of the Constitution or may be dependent on the Equal Protection Clause itself, e.g., voting, access to justice.*

SIGNIFICANT BURDEN. *The fact that a classification has some effect on the exercise of a fundamental right does not necessarily mean that a more stringent standard of review than rationality will be applied. In some cases, where the law does not deter, penalize or otherwise significantly burden the exercise of the protected right, the Court has applied the traditional rational basis test.*

a. First Amendment Rights

When the government classification significantly burdens the exercise of a fundamental First Amendment right such as freedom of speech, freedom of belief and association, or the free exercise of religion, the Court will apply a stricter standard of review.

Example: A statute prohibiting the picketing of residences except where it involves a place of employment in a labor dispute was held to violate the First Amendment and the Equal Protection Clause. "When government regulation discriminates among speech-related activities in a public forum, the Equal Protection Clause mandates that the legislation be finely tailored to serve substantial state interests, and the justifications offered for any distinction it draws must be carefully scrutinized." Neither the state interests in maintaining the privacy of the home nor in controlling labor disputes justified this discrimination. *Carey v. Brown* (1980).

b. The Right to Travel

1) *While the Court has never clearly indicated its constitutional source, there is a fundamental constitutional right of interstate movement. When the government makes recent exercise of interstate travel a basis for denying benefits, the classification burdens the fundamental right to travel and the strict scrutiny standard of judicial review applies. But if the classification does not deter, penalize, or otherwise significantly burden the protected right, the Court will not apply strict scrutiny. In some cases, the Court has*

held that the law could not satisfy even rationality review and therefore has not considered whether a stricter standard should be used.

Examples: (1) A state law which denies welfare assistance to the residents of the state who have not resided within the jurisdiction for at least one year immediately preceding their application for assistance is invalid. Such a classification burdens the fundamental right of interstate movement, and, when judged by the stricter equal protection standard of whether it promotes a compelling state interest, clearly violates the Equal Protection Clause. *Shapiro v. Thompson* (1969).

(2) A one year state residency requirement for divorce was held valid against an equal protection attack because of the importance of the state interest in divorce and because of the different character of the alleged deprivation, *i.e.*, the petitioner was not foreclosed but merely delayed. *Sosna v. Iowa* (1975).

(3) In *Zobel v. Williams* (1982) the Court invalidated Alaska's scheme for distributing state income derived from its natural resources among its citizens on the basis of duration of residency on equal protection grounds using a rationality standard. A plurality, however, in a concurring opinion, urged that the law violated the right to travel, requiring "intensified equal protection scrutiny." Alaska's scheme was deemed "inconsistent with [our] Federal structure."

(4) A New York Civil Service law giving an employment preference solely to resident veterans who lived in the state at the time they entered military service violates the constitutionally protected right to travel *and* the Equal Protection Clause. A plurality reasoned that, since a penalty is put on the exercise of a fundamental right, the state must have a compelling justification. The benefits involved in this case are of substantial importance and the veteran is permanently deprived of them. Since New York could satisfy its interest by giving preference to *all* qualified veterans, there were "less drastic means" available. Two concur-

ring justices found the state law irrational and arbitrary. *Attorney General of New York v. Soto Lopez (1986).*

2) The Court has held that newly arrived citizens of a state have the right to the same privileges and immunities enjoyed by other citizens of the state. Discrimination in public benefits against bona fide residents based on their recent exercise of the right to travel violates the Privileges or Immunities Clause of the Fourteenth Amendment. *Saenz v. Roe (1999).* See Ch. V, D, 2.

c. The Right of Sexual Privacy

The decision whether or not to bear a child is a fundamental right. Government classifications significantly burdening exercise of the right are subject to stricter scrutiny in determining if equal protection is violated. Eisenstadt v. Baird *(1972). However, if the government does not penalize or otherwise significantly burden the fundamental right, the rationality test will be used.*

Example: State denial of abortion funding for welfare recipients, even while funding childcare services, does not violate equal protection. The government does not interfere with or place any obstacle in the path of the woman seeking an abortion but only encourages an alternative activity. Since no fundamental right is significantly burdened, only rationality is required. The law rationally furthers the state's strong and legitimate interest in encouraging normal childbirth. *Maher v. Roe* (1977). This principle applies even when therapeutic abortions are involved. *Harris v. McRae* (1980) (federal law); *Williams v. Zbaraz* (1980) (state law).

d. Right to Marry

Marriage is one of the "basic civil rights of man." It is deemed fundamental "to our very existence and survival." Loving v. Virginia *(1967). Government classifications which significantly interfere with this right are subject to a rigorous standard of review. But, if the classification does not significantly interfere with the exercise of the fundamental right, only the rational basis test is used.*

Examples: (1) A statute requiring persons having minor children not in their custody to whom they owe support payments to get court approval before they marry was held invalid under "new equal protection" standards. The statute significantly interfered with the fundamental right to marry. If the person lacks financial means, the statute bars remarriage. The classification was not "closely tailored" to effectuate "legitimate and substantial" state interests in counseling parents regarding support obligations or protecting the welfare of the children. *Zablocki v. Redhail* (1978).

(2) A Social Security Act provision under which benefits received by a disabled dependent child of a wage earner terminate when the child marries an individual not entitled to benefits under the Act does not violate equal protection. The classification is rationally related to the need of a recipient for continued benefits. Reasonable regulations that do not significantly interfere with the protected right to marry are constitutional. *Califano v. Jobst* (1977).

FUNDAMENTAL INTERESTS. *The Court has also used a stricter standard of equal protection review to prevent discrimination in regard to fundamental interests such as voting and access to criminal justice. Equality of access to these interests is protected by the Equal Protection Clause itself; the Court does not recognize an independent right. While the Court has not rejected this precedent, it has frequently rejected use of strict scrutiny based on the importance of other interests. Today, it is usually discrimination in the exercise of independent constitutional rights that triggers strict scrutiny under the Equal Protection Clause.*

e. Voting

The Court has thus far not recognized a right to vote in the Constitution. However, the Court has indicated that voting is a fundamental interest, preservative of other rights and closely related to First Amendment rights. When government classifications discriminate in the ability to vote or otherwise significantly burden access to the franchise, the government must prove the classification is necessary to promote a compelling governmental interest. This principle applies whether a general or special purpose election is involved.

1) Exercising the Franchise

a) Voting Qualifications

When government significantly burdens the franchise by imposing qualifications on voting beyond age, citizenship and residence in the jurisdiction, a stricter judicial scrutiny generally applies. Under this standard, "invidious discrimination," or discrimination that is unrelated to a voter's qualifications, is prohibited. *Harper v. Virginia State Bd. of Elections* (1996). However, "evenhanded restrictions that protect the integrity and reliability of the electoral process itself are not invidious." *Anderson v. Celebrezze* (1983). Reasonable, nondiscriminatory voting restrictions are judged by a lower scrutiny standard, e.g., a balancing test where the interests of the state in imposing the restriction are weighed against the burdens imposed on the electorate.

Examples: (1) Imposition of a state poll tax as a precondition for voting is unconstitutional. A state violates the Equal Protection Clause whenever it makes the affluence of the voter or payment of any fee an electoral standard. Voter qualifications have no relation to wealth or to paying the tax. *Harper v. Virginia State Board of Elections* (1966).

(2) A state law providing that residents who are otherwise eligible to vote in state and federal elections may vote in the school district election only if they (1) own (or lease) taxable real property within the district, or (2) are parents (or have custody of) children enrolled in the local public schools is unconstitutional. The classifications permit inclusion of many persons who have, at best, a remote and indirect interest in school affairs and, on the other hand, exclude many who have a distinct and direct interest in the school board decisions. The classifications are not necessary to assuring participation by an interested electorate. *Kramer v. Union Free School District* (1969).

(3) The Court, 6–3, rejected a facial challenge to an Indiana law requiring citizens voting in person to present a free government-issued photo identification. A majority of the justices agreed that a stricter review standard was not applicable. A plurality opinion by Justice Stevens, joined by Chief Justice Roberts and Justice Kennedy, argued that while the Indiana law might impose a special

burden on some voters, the State's legitimate interests in deterring and detecting voter fraud, including participating in a national effort to improve and modernize the election process, and protecting voter confidence were "sufficiently weighty to justify the limitation." The plurality stressed that petitioners had "a heavy burden of persuasion to maintain the facial challenge." Using the balancing test, the plurality explained that because the record suggests that the law imposes only a limited burden on a small percentage of voters, and that the state provides identification for free and allows eligible voters without identification to cast provisional votes, petitioners failed to show that the burden imposed by the statute was sufficiently broad and significant enough to require invalidation of the statute in all of its applications.

A concurring opinion by Justice Scalia, joined by Justices Thomas and Alito, stated that "a deferential 'important regulatory interests' standard" [*Burdick v. Takushi* (1992)], less demanding than the balancing standard used by the plurality, should be applied in this case because the regulation at issue was a "nonsevere, nondiscriminatory" constraint. Justice Scalia reasoned that the Court should look at the impact on voters as a whole—rather than the impact on different voters—in determining whether a burden is severe, because having a voter-by-voter evaluation would require too much judicial supervision of the state's constitutional power to determine voter qualifications. In this case, because the requirement that voters present identification was minimal for most voters and was applied equally to everyone, and because the state has legitimate interests, the regulation is constitutional.

Justice Souter, dissenting, joined by Justice Ginsburg, argued that even using the plurality's balancing test the regulation was unconstitutional. The travel and cost burdens on the poor and the elderly were much more severe than the plurality contended, and the numbers burdened, while not precisely established, were significant. The threat posed by potential voter fraud was less serious than the plurality maintained; there was no record evidence of in-person voter impersonation. Justice Breyer also dissented, disagreeing that the burden imposed was minimal; the Indiana law imposed a disproportionate burden on the poor, elderly and disabled. Further, other states used less burdensome photo ID laws. *Crawford v. Marion County Election Board* (2008).

b) **Special Purpose Districts**

However, if the district has such a special limited purpose that it is not truly a governmental body and if the districts affected have a disproportionate effect on certain segments of the populace, the franchise can reasonably be limited to the affected group. The Court will consider the nature of the district and the effect of the activities of the district on different classes in determining whether the franchise is significantly burdened. But even a limited purpose governmental body is subject to the equal protection requirement of reasonable classification.

> *Example:* A law permitting only landowners to vote in water storage district general elections and apportioning votes in those elections according to the assessed valuation of land is constitutional. The Court reasoned that the water storage district by virtue of its special limited purpose and of the disproportionate effect of its activities on landowners was an exception to the requirements of *Kramer. Salyer Land Co. v. Tulare Lake Basin Water Storage District* (1973).

c) **Durational Residency Requirements**

While residency requirements for voting do not violate equal protection, durational residency requirements significantly burden the exercise of the franchise and impair the fundamental personal right of travel.

Examples: (1) A one year state residency requirement as a precondition for voting is an unconstitutional denial of equal protection. The restriction is not necessary to achieve the state interests in avoiding fraud and assuring an interested electorate. *Dunn v. Blumstein* (1972).

(2) A 50–day duration residency requirement and a 50–day voter registration cut-off requirement for voting is a reasonable means of preventing fraud in the process of voter registration. *Marston v. Lewis* (1973).

d)   The Fifteenth Amendment

The Fifteenth Amendment prohibits the national government and the states from denying or abridging the right to vote on account of race, color or previous condition of servitude: "The design of the Amendment is to reaffirm the equality of races at the most basic level of the democratic process, the exercise of the voting franchise." *Rice v. Cayetano* (2000).

Example: Hawaiian state law limiting the franchise for election of a board of trustees to manage public trust lands to Hawaiians, defined as descendants of races who occupied the islands in 1778, violates the Fifteenth Amendment. "Under the Fifteenth Amendment voters are treated not as members of a distinct race but as members of the whole citizenry." *Rice v. Cayetano* (2000).

2)   Diluting the Franchise

The right to equal protection in voting can be significantly burdened not only by a denial of the franchise to a particular class of citizens through numerous voter qualifications, but also by a dilution of the effectiveness of the vote of particular classes. But the Constitution does not guarantee that your candidate will win or that you will be in a voting district with like-minded voters.

a)   Access to the Ballot

Attempts by the state to significantly limit access to the ballot by minority parties and independents will succeed only if the require-

ments imposed are fair and not virtually exclusionary. "The differences between requiring primary votes to qualify for a position on the general election ballot and requiring signatures on nominating petitions are not of constitutional dimension." Munro v. Socialist Workers Party *(1986)* (law requiring minor party candidate to receive 1% of primary vote to qualify for place on the general election ballot upheld).

Examples: (1) A state law provided that candidates of "major" parties could obtain ballot position by being nominated in a primary election. However, parties that polled less than 2% of the total gubernatorial vote in the preceding general election (or new parties) had to hold precinct, county and state nominating conventions and obtain signatures equalling at least 1% of persons voting in the last gubernatorial election. These and other distinctions for access to the ballot as between "majority" and "minority" parties were held not to violate equal protection since they were not unreasonably burdensome. *American Party of Texas v. White* (1974).

(2) A state law requiring a filing fee to obtain a place on primary election ballot or to be write-in candidate—in this case, 2% of the annual salary for the state office sought ($701.60)—violated equal protection when applied to indigents. In the absence of reasonable alternative means of ballot access, a state may not, consistent with constitutional standards, require from an indigent candidate filing fees he cannot pay. *Lubin v. Panish* (1974).

(3) A provision of the Texas state constitution that prevents state and local office holders from running for the state legislature before the term of their incumbency expires does not violate the Equal Protection Clause. In view of the minimal restriction on candidacy, and the fact that the candidacy is not itself a fundamental right, the

law need only bear a rational relation to a legitimate state interest. The law was sufficiently related to the goal of insuring that office holders do not abuse their position or neglect their duties because of their aspiration for higher office. *Clements v. Fashing* (1982).

b) Reapportionment

"ONE MAN–ONE VOTE" PRINCIPLE. Geographical boundaries of a governmental unit for voting may not be defined in such a way as to deny numerical equality among voters. *The basic command is one person-one vote—a voting district which has twice as many voters as another district is entitled to twice as many representatives.*

(1) Congressional Apportionment. *Art. I, § 2, requires that representatives be chosen "by the People of the Several States." This is a command that, as nearly as is practicable, each person's vote be equivalent to that of another.* Wesberry v. Sanders *(1964).*

   (a) *Limited Variance Permitted.* The Court has said that the constitutional provision permits only limited variances from numerical equality for which there is substantial justification. *Kirkpatrick v. Preisler* (1969). The Court in *Karcher v. Daggett* (1983) rejected a .7% maximum deviation between districts absent state showing "with some specificity that a particular objective required the specific deviation in the plan." But the Court, in a *per curiam* opinion, affirmed West Virginia's reapportionment plan which contained a .79% variance in population between its largest and smallest congressional districts. The State's objectives—not splitting political subdivisions, avoiding contests between incumbents, and minimizing population shifts—all qualified as "valid, neutral state redistricting policies" permitting the State to have limited variance in districts' populations. *Tennant v. Jefferson County Commission* (2012).

(2) State Legislative Apportionment. *The Equal Protection Clause of the Fourteenth Amendment requires the seats in both houses of*

a bicameral state legislature be apportioned on a population basis. A citizen has a right to equal representation and to have his vote weighted equally with those of other citizens. Reynolds v. Sims *(1964).*

    (a) *Greater State Variance Permitted.* Greater flexibility is constitutionally permissible with respect to state legislative apportionment than in congressional districting. A state must make a good faith effort to construct districts as nearly of equal population as is practicable but it may rationally consider traditional political subdivisions and make the necessary minimum deviations from numerical equality. *Mahan v. Howell* (1973) (permitting deviations of 16.4% from the ideal).

(3) Local Apportionment. *Whenever a local government decides to select its officials by popular election to perform governmental functions, and selects these officials from separate districts, equal protection requires that each district be established on a one man-one vote basis.* Hadley v. Junior College Dist. *(1970).*

    Exception: A district may be created for such a limited purpose that it is only marginally governmental, *i.e.,* it doesn't provide the variety of services normally associated with government. One man-one vote does not apply. *Salyer Land Co. v. Tulare Lake Basin Water Storage Dist.* (1973).

    Example: A system for electing the directors of a large water reclamation district which limits voting eligibility to landowners and which apportions voting power according to the amount of land the voter owns does not violate the equal protection guarantee even though it does not satisfy one man-one vote. The district was so specialized and narrow in purpose and its activities bore on the landowners so disproportionately as to distinguish the district from those public entities exercising more general governmental functions. While the district did regulate water supply and sell electricity to numerous consumers, this was not deemed a traditional element of governmental sovereignty. Since it was necessary to limit the franchise in order to get the district started, the voting scheme had a reasonable relation to the statutory objective of supplying water. *Ball v. James* (1981).

c) Multi-member Districts

(1) Representation by two or more legislators elected at large by voters of a district does not per se violate equal protection. Such representation does not inherently invidiously discriminate against racial or political minorities. *Whitcomb v. Chavis* (1971).

(2) *However, if a challenger proves that a particular multi-member district system purposely excludes racial minorities from effective political participation, it violates equal protection and the Fifteenth Amendment.* White v. Regester *(1973)*.

Examples: (1) Mobile's at-large election of city council members does not violate the rights of Black voters under the Fourteenth and Fifteenth Amendments unless it is purposely discriminatory. There is no right for a political group to have its candidates selected, only a right not to have a purposeful denial or abridgement of the franchise or purposeful discrimination affecting voting. There was inadequate showing that Mobile had "conceived or operated a purposeful device to further racial discrimination." *City of Mobile v. Bolden* (1980).

(2) An at-large voting scheme that is maintained as a purposeful device to further racial discrimination violates equal protection. The Court declined to overturn the district court's findings of racially discriminatory intent. These findings were properly based on evidence of historical discrimination in elections, the failure of any Blacks to be elected to local

government despite their majority status in the general population, the unresponsiveness of public bodies to the needs of Black constituents and other factors. *Rogers v. Herman Lodge* (1982).

d) **Political Gerrymandering**

Apportionment schemes whereby political districts are deliberately and arbitrarily distorted for partisan political purposes are justiciable (*Vieth v. Jubelirer* (2004)) and may violate equal protection. The challenger must prove both intentional discrimination against an identifiable group and an actual discriminatory effect on this group. Although the Court remains divided on the appropriate standards, it is established that the mere lack of proportional representation does not prove unconstitutional discrimination.

Examples: (1) Indiana's 1981 state apportionment scheme did not violate equal protection even though Democrats receiving 52% of the vote received only 43% of the seats. A plurality held that "unconstitutional discrimination occurs only when the electoral system is arranged in a manner that will consistently degrade a voter's or a group of voters' influence on the political process as a whole." While the lower court's finding of discriminatory intent was not clearly erroneous, the plurality concluded that the challengers had failed to establish a prima facie case of discriminatory vote dilution. In addition to discriminatory intent, there must be evidence of "continued frustration" of the majority will or of effective denial of a minority of voters of a fair chance to influence the political process. *Davis v. Bandemer* (1986).

(2) After a court-ordered redistricting plan for Texas had been put in place after the 2000 census, the Texas legislature, controlled by Republicans, voted to redistrict again in 2003. Operating under the new plan in 2004, Republicans won 21 congressional seats to the Democrats 11. The mid-

decennial redistricting was challenged on a host of statutory and constitutional grounds. Plaintiffs alleged that the redistricting was done for purely partisan advantage and had no legitimate public purpose and that it severely burdened the Democratic Party based on political beliefs and political affiliation. The Supreme Court did not revisit the question of the justiciability of the equal protection challenge to a political gerrymander. Because of its holding that part of the 2003 redistricting violated the Voting Rights Act, the Court did not address the claim that the Texas political gerrymander violated the Constitution.

As in *Veith*, the Court lacked a majority for any substantive standard for determining when a political gerrymander is unconstitutional. Only Justice Stevens, joined by Justice Breyer would have held the Texas gerrymander—which was done "all for purely partisan purposes"— unconstitutional. Justice Kennedy delivered the Court's judgment and, in an opinion joined by Justices Souter and Ginsburg, rejected the claim that a mid-decennial legislative decision to replace a court ordered plan with one of its own or the fact of mid-decade redistricting alone was "inherently suspect" or was "presumptively" unconstitutional even when "solely motivated by partisan objectives." A successful test must "show a burden, as measured by a reliable standard, on the complainants' representational rights." *League of United Latin American Citizens v. Perry* (2006).

e)　Inequality in Vote Processes

Equal protection involves more than the allocation of the franchise. "Equal protection applies as well to the manner of its exercise. Having once granted the right to vote on equal terms, the State may not, by later arbitrary and disparate treatment, value one person's vote over that of another." *Bush v. Gore* (2000).

Example: Florida recount procedures used in the 2000 presidential election were held not to satisfy "the minimum requirements for non-arbitrary treatment of voters necessary to secure the fundamental right [to vote] and violated the equal protection guarantee." While the recount was designed to determine the "intent of the voters," Florida lacked specific standards to ensure equal application. Formulation of uniform rules to determine voter intent based on recurring circumstances is practicable and necessary. The Court limited its consideration to the circumstances, "for the problem of equal protection in election processes generally presents many complexities."

Three dissenting justices argued that the Court had never before found a constitutional violation based on the substantive standard by which a state determines that a vote has been legally cast. They warned that numerous differences in voting procedures might violate equal protection if subject to similar judicial review. *Bush v. Gore* (2000).

f. Access to Justice

Access to the courts for a criminal defendant is of fundamental importance. Wealth differences should not determine the kind of criminal justice a person receives, at least when the initiative for the criminal proceeding comes from the government. Similarly, in some civil cases, such as termination of parental status for unfitness, equal justice requires that litigants not be denied access because of their inability to pay core costs. Cases involving equal access to justice are often decided on due process grounds.

Examples: (1) A state law which makes the only appeal which an accused criminal has of right under state law dependent on whether the accused can afford to hire counsel violates the Equal Protection Clause as such. *Douglas v. California* (1963). The Due Process and Equal Protection Clauses require the appointment of counsel for defendants, convicted on their pleas, who seek access to first-tier review in the state court of appeals. *Halbert v. Michigan* (2005).

Moreover, the defendant is entitled to effective assistance of counsel. *Evitts v. Lucey* (1985).

(2) When an indigent criminal defendant, charged with a capital offense, makes a preliminary showing that his sanity at the time of the offense is likely to be a significant factor at trial, due process requires that he have access to the psychiatric assistance necessary to prepare an effective insanity defense. A criminal trial is fundamentally unfair if the state proceeds against an indigent without making certain that he has an adequate opportunity to present his claims fairly within the adversarial system. There is a real risk of error if psychiatric assistance is not provided. *Ake v. Oklahoma* (1985).

(3) A state violates due process and equal protection when it dismisses an appeal from a trial court decree terminating a mother's parental rights for unfitness because of her inability to pay record preparation fees. While the Constitution does not guarantee a right to appellate review, once a state affords that right, *Griffin v. Illinois* (1956) establishes that there must be open and *equal* access to the courts. The present case falls within "a narrow category of civil cases in which the State must provide access to its judicial processes without regard to a party's ability to pay court fees." Since the present case involves the State's authority to permanently sever the parent-child bond based on parental unfitness, it requires the "close consideration" required for associational rights "of basic importance to our society." When measured against the magnitude and permanence of the loss the mother faces and the importance of the transcript to her interests, the State's interest in offsetting the costs to its court systems is inadequate. The State may not withhold from the parent a record of sufficient completeness to permit proper appellate consideration of her claim. *M.L.B. v. S.L.J.* (1996).

(4) Plaintiff brought an action alleging that the Government had violated her right of access to the courts by withholding information relating to her husband's capture and execution by Guatemalan army forces. She alleged that

had the Government not lied to her, she might have been able to take legal action to save her husband. The Court held that she failed to state an actionable constitutional claim. The plaintiff failed to identify the cause of action she might have had that was lost by the alleged deception and failed to identify a remedy not otherwise available under other claims of her complaint. *Christopher v. Harbury* (2002).

OTHER IMPORTANT INTERESTS. *The fact that the classification significantly burdens critically important interests such as decent housing, medical care, welfare, or education will not itself trigger a stricter standard of review than rationality. Equal protection is satisfied so long as the classification is not arbitrary.*

g. Education

1) *While education is an important social and individual interest, it has not yet been held to be a constitutional right. The rational basis test is, therefore, usually the appropriate standard of review.*

   Examples: (1) Use of local property taxes to finance local education does not violate equal protection even though there are wide differences in the value of property, and hence, educational resources, among school districts. There was no showing that the state was not providing at least the minimal skills necessary for the exercise of constitutional rights, such as speech and voting. The state financing scheme bears a rational relation to the state objective of promoting local control of education. *San Antonio Ind. School Dist. v. Rodriguez* (1973).

   (2) A state law authorizing non-reorganized school districts to charge a fee for school bus service does not violate equal protection. The law applies equally to all families who pay a user fee for the service. The statute is rationally related to the state's legitimate interest in fulfilling the expectations of residents of reorganized districts that they would enjoy free busing arrangements as a result of the reorganization plans. *Kadrmas v. Dickinson Public Schools* (1988).

2) *However, when education is totally denied to a discrete underclass of children while it is freely provided for other classes, the Court has applied*

a more searching standard of review—only a law furthering a "substantial" state goal will satisfy equal protection.

Examples: (1) A Texas statute that denies free public education to children of illegal aliens while providing it to children of citizens or legally-admitted aliens violates equal protection. While illegal alien children are not a suspect class, they do constitute an underclass ("a permanent caste") in our society. While education is not a constitutional right, it has "a fundamental role in maintaining the fabric of our society." The state failed to show that the discrimination was justified by a substantial state interest. *Plyler v. Doe* (1982). But note that the Court upheld a Texas law denying tuition-free education to a minor living apart from his or her parent or guardian whose presence in the school district is primarily for the purpose of securing a free public education. The law was held to be a bona fide residence requirement. *Martinez v. Bynum* (1983).

(2) In *Kadrmas, supra,* the Court distinguished *Plyler* since the child was not penalized because of any illegal conduct by her parents. She was denied bus service only because her parents would not pay the same user fee charged to all families using the service. *Plyler* involved "unique circumstances" that provoked a "unique confluence of theories and rationales."

h. Welfare

While welfare assistance involves basic human needs, welfare legislation is judged by the rational basis test unless a suspect classification or fundamental right is involved.

Example: A state law which imposes a dollar ceiling ($250 per month) on the amount of aid an AFDC family received was held constitutional. Each recipient child would receive benefits according to need until the ceiling was reached and after-born children would provide no additional benefits. Since this was deemed to be social and economic legislation, not involving any suspect classification or fundamental right, the rational basis test applied. The grant ceiling was rationally related to promoting employment among welfare recipients. *Dandridge v. Williams* (1970).

D. Review Questions

1. **T or F** When the rationality standard of review is used the classification is always upheld.

2. **T or F** When a government enactment has the effect of discriminating on the basis of race, strict scrutiny applies.

3. **T or F** If a decision is motivated in part by racial discrimination, equal protection is violated.

4. **T or F** If a school district is adjudged to be *de jure* segregated, it may not take action that has a segregative effect.

5. **T or F** If a school district subject to a desegregation order complies in good faith with the decree and eliminates past discrimination to the extent practicable, it can adopt policies even if they have the effect of resegregating the district school.

6. **T or F** While strict scrutiny is used for reviewing state and local affirmative action programs, federal affirmative action programs are constitutional if they satisfy intermediate review (i.e., they are substantially related to an important government interest).

7. **T or F** A university student admissions policy that seeks to promote diversity by considering the race and ethnicity of applicants as factors in an individualized determination is benign and is subject to intermediate review.

8. **T or F** Following *Grutter v. Bollinger* (2003), university admission programs that promote diversity in the student body by considering the race and ethnicity of the applicants are constitutional.

9. **T or F** The Court has held that using race in the placement of students in public elementary and secondary schools in order to achieve the educational and social benefits of racial diversity is unconstitutional.

10. **T or F** Alienage classifications, imposed by a state, are subject to an intermediate form of review, *i.e.*, the classification must be substantially related to an important government interest.

11. **T or F**   While peremptory jury strikes on the basis of race violate the Equal Protection Clause, the same strikes on the basis of gender will pass the intermediate standard review required of gender classifications.

12. **T or F**   State classifications which have the effect of burdening women more severely than men must be substantially related to an important government interest.

13. **T or F**   In *United States v. Virginia* (1996), the Court held that all publicly-funded single sex education violates equal protection.

14. **T or F**   Classifications which discriminate against men in order to remedy past discrimination against women are constitutional if they are narrowly drawn to achieve the benign purpose.

15. **T or F**   Illegitimacy is a suspect classification subject to strict scrutiny.

16. **T or F**   The Court has held that classifications based on sexual orientation are quasi-suspect and are to be reviewed using intermediate review.

17. **T or F**   When a classification significantly burdens the exercise of a fundamental constitutional right, the Court generally requires that government prove that the classification is necessary to a compelling government interest.

18. **T or F**   A classification which places an obstacle to free interstate movement will be judged by strict scrutiny standards.

19. **T or F**   While voting has not been held to be a fundamental constitutional right, the Court has applied strict scrutiny to restrictions on the franchise.

20. **T or F**   Residency requirements significantly burden the exercise of the franchise and the right of interstate travel and are generally held to violate equal protection.

21. **T or F**   One person-one vote applies to all local apportionment schemes as a command of the Equal Protection Clause.

22. **T or F**   The Court has held that an equal protection challenge to a political gerrymander represents a nonjusticiable political question.

23. **T or F**   Classifications which deny education to a discrete underclass of children are judged by a more demanding standard of review than rationality.

24. Which of the following are elements of strict scrutiny equal protection review?

  a. Burden of justification on the government.

  b. The government interest must be compelling.

  c. The classification must be necessary to achieve this objective.

  d. No less burdensome alternatives must be available.

  e. All of the above are elements of the strict scrutiny standard.

25. Which of the following classifying traits will *not* trigger a stricter standard of equal protection review?

  a. Race.

  b. National origin.

  c. Gender.

  d. Wealth.

  e. Illegitimacy.

26. Which of the following has *not* been held to be a fundamental right requiring a more stringent standard of equal protection review?

  a. Interstate travel.

  b. Privacy.

  c. Housing.

  d. Marriage.

  e. All of the above have been held to be fundamental rights.

27. Welfare recipients under the joint federal-state financed Aid to Families With Dependent Children program challenged a state of West Lincoln "maximum" grant regulation which set "an upper limit on the total amount of money any one family unit may receive" on the basis of a formula which did not take into account the fact that there was a disparity in family size among welfare recipients in the state. A three judge federal district court found the regulation violative of equal protection. The case was then appealed to the Supreme Court. Does the West Lincoln Welfare program described above violate the Equal Protection Clause of the Fourteenth Amendment? Why or why not?

28. The state of Neuter enacts a law requiring the sterilization of all welfare recipients having a third illegitimate child. Statistics indicate that the state's welfare rolls have a disproportionate proportion of blacks. A black welfare recipient who has been ordered to be sterilized following the birth of her third illegitimate child has brought suit alleging the law violates the Equal Protection Clause. Discuss the issues that would be raised in determining if the sterilization law violates equal protection.

VIII

Freedom of Expression

■ *ANALYSIS*

A. The Basic Doctrine of Freedom of Expression

The First Amendment to the U.S. Constitution states: "Congress shall make no law respecting an establishment of religion, or prohibiting the free exercise thereof; or abridging the freedom of speech, or of the press; or the right of the people peaceably to assemble, and to petition for a redress of grievances."

The First Amendment has a specific addressee, Congress, by which is meant the federal government generally. It was only in 1925 that the Supreme Court held that the states were bound by the "fundamental personal rights" of freedom of speech and press of the First Amendment through the Due Process Clause of the Fourteenth Amendment. *Gitlow v. New York* (1925).

The First Amendment guarantees, but does not define, freedom of speech and press. Although it has often been contended that these guarantees provide absolute protection, the course of constitutional interpretation does not support this contention. A variety of by no means consistent doctrines have emanated from the Supreme Court which seek to define the meaning and extent of the protection accorded to freedom of speech and press under the First Amendment. The Court has generally adhered to the principle that the vital functions served by the First Amendment requires close judicial scrutiny when First Amendment rights are burdened. The present chapter focuses on freedom of expression. Freedom of religion is discussed in Chapter IX.

1. First Amendment Rationale

a. Marketplace of Ideas

The marketplace of ideas theory is based on the principle that the First Amendment forbids government from taking sides in the natural struggle of ideas. If government does not limit or restrain the marketplace of ideas, full and free expression will push the best ideas toward acceptance and lead to the defeat of less worthy ones. "[T]he best test of truth is the power of the thought to get itself accepted in the competition of the market." *Abrams v. United States* (1919).

b. The Citizen Participant Model

In the famous libel case, *New York Times v. Sullivan* (1964), the Court declared that the central meaning of the First Amendment was to encourage the vigorous, robust discussion of public issues and public officials. Such discussion is central to democratic government in order that the people may actively participate in governing.

c. The Individual Liberty Model

Freedom of expression serves individual values as well as societal goals. Liberty is valued both "as an end and as a means." *Whitney v. California* (1927). Freedom of expression promotes individual autonomy and furthers self-determination.

2. First Amendment Methodology

The First Amendment could be read literally as an absolute prohibition on laws regulating speech. But as Justice Holmes stated: "The most stringent protection of free speech would not protect a man in falsely shouting fire in a theatre." *Schenck v. United States* (1919). The Court employs a variety of methodologies designed to reconcile freedom of expression with other legitimate public interests.

a. Categories of Speech

At times, the Court has held that certain categories of speech are not entitled to full First Amendment protection (*e.g.*, commercial speech) or to any First Amendment protection (*e.g.*, fighting words, obscenity, child pornography). "[S]uch utterances are of such slight social value as a step to truth that any benefit that may be derived from them is clearly out-weighed by the social interest in order and morality." *Chaplinsky v. New Hampshire* (1942). *These are "historic and traditional categories long familiar to the bar" and are "well-defined and narrowly limited classes of speech." United States v. Stevens* (2010). See Ch. VIII, I, 7.

But the Court has also held that such categories of speech are subject to First Amendment review under certain circumstances. What these categories mean "is that these areas of speech can, consistently with the First Amendment, be regulated because of their constitutionally prescribable content (obscenity, defamation, etc.)—not that they are categories of speech entirely invisible to the Constitution, so that they may be made the vehicles for content discrimination unrelated to their distinctively prescribable content." The "unprotected features of the words are, despite their verbal character, essentially a 'nonspeech' element of communication." Government regulates the "mode of speech" as a manner of communicating the idea. *R.A.V. v. City of St. Paul* (1992).

Example: The St. Paul hate speech law had been interpreted as limited to the "unprotected" category of fighting words. But the law applied only to fighting words that insult or provoke violence "on the bases of race, color, creed, religion or gender." Other fighting words were not proscribed. The discrimination between forms of fighting words was held to be an unconstitutional regulation based on speech content which failed to satisfy strict scrutiny review. Three justices who concurred in the judgment argued that "the content of the subject [of such speech] is by definition worthless and undeserving of constitutional protection." *R.A.V. v. City of St. Paul* (1992).

b. Strict Scrutiny

On other occasions, the Court has employed tests which impose a heavy burden of justification on government when it seeks to regulate speech content (*e.g.*, clear and present danger test, necessary to a compelling state interest). In such cases, the ordinary presumption of constitutionality is not applicable; the law is presumptively invalid.

c. Balancing

When a law only indirectly or incidentally burdens freedom of speech, the Court is more likely to engage in some form of overt balancing of the competing interests to determine if the law is *reasonable.* The interests of the government in regulating the activity are weighed against the burden on free speech interests. At times, the availability of less burdensome alternatives to achieve the government interests are considered. But it is not necessary that government adopt the least-restrictive means. *Ward v. Rock Against Racism* (1989). The degree of judicial scrutiny in interest balancing varies widely. In some cases, the courts engage in simple ad hoc balancing of the competing interests. In other cases, a more weighted balancing is used, *e.g.*, the law must be narrowly-tailored to achieve an important government interest. Some commentators view the clear and present danger doctrine and strict scrutiny as more stringent forms of interest balancing.

3. Content–Based v. Content–Neutral Regulation

a. Content–Based Regulation

1) *When government undertakes to regulate expression because of the content of the speech, i.e., because of what is being said, the law is presumptively invalid.* Simon & Schuster, Inc. v. Members of the New York State Crime Victims Board (1991). "[A]bove all else the First Amendment means that government has no power to restrict expression because

of its message, its ideas, its subject matter, or its content." *Police Department of the City of Chicago v. Mosley* (1972) (law prohibiting picketing around schools, but exempting labor picketing, held to be unconstitutional content-based regulation).

2) Laws are content-based if they discriminate on the basis of viewpoint or if they categorize speech based on its subject-matter. Subject-matter discrimination is presumptively invalid because there is concern that government will distort the public debate or favor particular messages. While a law may facially discriminate on the basis of content, "even a regulation neutral on its face may be content-based if its manifest purpose is to regulate speech because of the message it conveys." *Turner Broadcasting Systems, Inc. v. F.C.C.* (1994). The Court has also used the Equal Protection Clause to prevent government discrimination against particular speech, ideas, or speakers. *Police Department of the City of Chicago v. Mosley* (1972).

3) The courts "apply the most exacting scrutiny to regulations that suppress, disadvantage, or impose differential burdens upon speech because of its content." *Turner Broadcasting Systems, Inc. v. F.C.C.* (1994). *When regulating on the basis of content, government must prove that the law falls into a category of low-value or no-value speech or must justify the law by establishing that the differential treatment "is necessary to serve a compelling state interest and is narrowly drawn to achieve that end."* Simon & Schuster, Inc. v. Members of the New York State Crime Victims Board (1991).

Examples: (1) A provision of an ordinance prohibiting the display of signs within 500 feet of a foreign embassy if they tend to bring that government into public disrepute violates the First Amendment. The display clause, while not viewpoint-based, is a content-based regulation of core political speech—it focuses solely on the content of the speech and is sought to be justified as necessary to protect the dignity of embassy personnel by shielding them from critical speech. Even assuming this dignity interest is compelling, the regulation is not narrowly tailored since there are less restrictive alternatives available. *Boos v. Barry* (1988).

(2) The New York "Son of Sam" law required that an accused or convicted criminal's income from works

describing the crime be deposited by the publisher in an escrow account. The funds could then be used to compensate victims of the crime and satisfy the writer's creditors. The Court applied strict scrutiny because the law "imposes a financial burden on speakers because of the content of their speech." The state had a compelling interest in ensuring that victims of crime are compensated by their assailants and that the assailants do not benefit from their crime. But the statute was over-inclusive because it applied to "works on any subject, provided that they express the author's thoughts or recollections about his crime however tangentially or incidentally." The law was not narrowly-tailored since many valuable works would be unnecessarily covered. *Simon & Schuster, Inc. v. Members of the New York State Criminal Victims Board* (1991).

(3) Tennessee law prohibited the solicitation of votes and the display of campaign materials within 100 feet of the entrance to a polling place on election day. The law thus regulated core political speech; it was held to be a content-based regulation. Nevertheless, the law was upheld because Tennessee had a "compelling interest in preventing voter intimidation and election fraud." States generally seek to protect the fundamental electoral right through "a secret ballot secured in part by a restricted zone around voting compartments." *Burson v. Freeman* (1992).

(4) The Court 6–3 held that the Stolen Valor Act of 2005, criminalizing false representations that one has been awarded U.S. military decorations or medals and providing enhanced penalties for lying about being awarded the Congressional Medal of Honor, violates the First Amendment. A plurality, composed of Justice Kennedy, joined by Chief Justice Roberts and Justices Ginsburg and Sotomayor, concluded that the Government failed to show that the law satisfies the "exacting scrutiny" applicable to content-based restrictions. Except for a "few 'historic and traditional categories long familiar to the bar,' " content-based restrictions are

"presumed invalid" and the Government bears "the burden of showing their constitutionality." The Government argued that "false statements have no First Amendment value in themselves" and "are protected only to the extent needed to avoid chilling falsely protected speech." The plurality rejected recognizing a categorical rule denying First Amendment protection to false statements absent "some other legally cognizable harm associated with a false statement." While falsity of the speech may bear upon whether the speech is protected, false speech is not "in a general category that is presumptively unprotected." The claimed government censorial power would be unlimited.

The Plurality concluded that the Act did not satisfy the most exacting scrutiny. "The Government interest in protecting the integrity of the Medal of Honor is beyond question." But the restrictions must be "actually necessary" to achieve the interest. Justice Kennedy said: "There must be a direct causal link between the restriction imposed and the injury to be protected." The link between the interest in protecting the integrity of the military honors system and the Act's restriction on the false claims of liars "has not been shown." The Government did not provide evidence that the public's general perception of military awards is diluted by such false claims nor was the Government able to show "why counter speech would not suffice to achieve its interest." Finally, the restriction had not been shown to be the "least restrictive means among available effective alternatives." For example, a Government-created database could list winners of the Congressional Medal of Honor.

Justice Breyer, joined by Justice Kagan, concurred in the judgment, but rejected the "strict categorical" analysis in favor of an analysis showing "that the statute works First Amendment harm, while the Government can achieve its legitimate objectives in less restrictive ways." Strict scrutiny, Justice Breyer argued, is inappropriate when dealing as here, with regulations concerning "false statements about easily verifiable facts," that do not concern speech about "philosophy, religion, history, the social sciences, the arts," "where valuable contributions to the marketplace of ideas might be threatened." For the type of speech here, "intermediate scrutiny" should be used. Nevertheless, the statute failed such intermediate review. Justice Breyer accepted reading the law to criminalize only false factual statements, made with knowledge of their falsity and with intent that they be taken as true. But the statute contains no limiting features but applies broadly, risking significant First Amendment harms, including in the political arena. While the statute has "substantial justification," the Government's objective can be achieved "in less burdensome ways."

Justice Alito, joined by Justice Scalia and Thomas, dissenting, argued that the First Amendment does not protect "false factual statements that inflict real harm and serve no legitimate interest." Such statements "have no value in and of themselves, and prescribing them does not chill any valuable speech." The speech is verifiably false, lacks intrinsic value and "fails to serve any instrumental purpose that the First Amendment might protect." No one has suggested any truthful speech that the Act might chill. Justice Alito argued that the plurality and concurring opinion are actually based on a concern that the Act suffers from overbreadth but they fail to show any "substantial overbreadth relative to the Act's legitimate sweep." *United States v. Alvarez* (2012).

4) But if a law implicates national security and foreign affairs, the Court will give "deference" to Executive and Congressional findings of fact in determining whether a particular statute is necessary.

Example: The Court held 6–3 that a federal statute prohibiting provision of "material support or resources" to certain foreign groups designated as foreign terrorist groups, does not violate First Amendment freedom of speech as applied to support for training, expert advice or assistance, service and personnel even if limited to support only for lawful, nonviolent purposes of the groups. Since the law applies to conduct communicating a message, the Court applied "a more demanding standard." Applying the standard, Chief Justice Roberts stated: "Everyone agrees that the government's interest in combatting terrorism is an urgent objective of the highest order." In determining whether applying the statutory prohibition to "support" included promotion of peaceable, lawful conduct is a constitutional means, the Court stressed that support is fungible freeing up resources that may be used for violent ends. Further, plaintiff's support promotes the legitimacy of the foreign terrorist groups. The Chief Justice stressed that the statute reaches only support "coordinated with or under the direction of a designated foreign terrorist organization;" it does not prevent independent advocacy on behalf of foreign terrorist groups. Executive experience supports congressional factual findings that all contributions to designated foreign terrorist groups furthers terrorism. That government evaluation "is entitled to deference."

Justice Breyer, joined by Justice Ginsburg and Sotomayor, dissenting, argued that strict scrutiny should apply and that the Government did not meet its burden of showing that the means used are needed. The Government had not proven that plaintiff's political advocacy is fungible with support for terrorist activities. Even if support does provide "legitimacy," Justice Breyer said, this cannot justify suppression of advocacy for peaceable purposes. Such reasoning has no natural stopping place; it applies to all advocacy. And the dissent questioned the deference given the Government's factual findings. Under *Whitney v. California* (1927), it is for the Court to determine whether there is sufficient justification for criminalizing speech activity otherwise protected by the First Amendment. The dissent also questioned whether the Court's analysis was consistent with *Brandenburg v. Ohio. See Ch. VIII, E, 1, a. Holder v. Humanitarian Law Project* (2010).

b. Content–Neutral Regulation

1) *Government regulations that are unrelated to the content of speech are subject to a lesser degree of judicial scrutiny, even though speech may be incidentally burdened.* Such laws usually "pose a less substantial risk of excising certain ideas or viewpoints from the public dialogue." *Turner Broadcasting System, Inc. v. F.C.C.* (1994).

2) *If a law is justified without reference to the content of the regulated speech, it may be held to be content-neutral.* Thus, a law regulating the location of adult theaters was held to be content-neutral because it was directed at the "secondary effects" of adult theaters and not the adult content of the movie themes. Any burden on speech was deemed only incidental. *City of Renton v. Playtime Theatres* (1986).

3) *The courts generally apply a less demanding form of balancing analysis to content-neutral time, place and manner regulations.* For example, the Court will require that the law be "narrowly tailored to serve a significant government interest and leave open ample alternative channels of communication." *Perry Education Association v. Perry Local Educator's Association* (1983).

4) One of the most frequently used formulations is that of O'Brien v. United States (1968): *"A government regulation is sufficiently justified * * * if it furthers an important or substantial government interest; if the government interest is unrelated to the suppression of free expression; and if the incidental restriction of alleged First Amendment freedoms is no greater than is essential to the furtherance of that interest."* This does not require that government use the least burdensome means, if the means are direct and effective.

   Examples: (1) A regulation permitting police to disperse demonstrators within 500 feet of an embassy is constitutional. The congregation clause was narrowly interpreted by the lower court to permit dispersal of demonstrators only when police reasonably believe that a threat to the security or peace of the embassy is present. As interpreted, the law is not facially overbroad, but is a reasonable regulation of the place and manner of certain demonstrations. *Boos v. Barry* (1988).

(2) Provisions of the 1992 Cable Act requiring cable systems to carry local broadcast and public broadcast transmissions are content-neutral and are to be reviewed under the *O'Brien* "intermediate level of scrutiny" applicable to incidental burdens on speech. The Court stated: "Congress's overriding objective in enacting must-carry was not to favor programming of a particular subject matter, viewpoint, or format, but rather to preserve access to free television programming for the 40 percent of Americans without cable." The case was remanded to allow the parties to develop a more thorough factual record. *Turner Broadcasting Systems v. F.C.C.* (1994) (*Turner I*). On remand, the must-carry rules were upheld as "narrowly tailored to preserve a multiplicity of broadcast stations for the 40 percent of American households without cable." *Turner Broadcasting Systems, Inc. v. FCC* (1997) (*Turner II*).

4. The Doctrine of Prior Restraint: Forms of Control

Prior restraints involve government restraints on freedom of expression which operate prior to the time that the expression enters the marketplace of ideas, e.g., licensing, permit systems, censorship, injunctions. Such restraints on expression should be distinguished from restraints operating after speech, e.g., breach of the peace, disorderly conduct, defamation laws.

Prior restraints are highly suspect, both substantively and procedurally, and there is a substantial presumption against their constitutionality. The government bears a heavy burden of showing justification for the imposition of such a restraint.

a. Historically, the original understanding of the First Amendment may have been limited to a prohibition on prior restraints. Attack on administrative censorship and licensing provided the spawning ground for the development of theories of freedom of expression. Also, prior restraints tend to be more sweeping and inhibiting than post hoc restraints and cannot be collaterally attacked. Such restraints impose immediate and irreversible sanctions.

b. While not per se impermissible, prior restraints are subject to close judicial scrutiny. *Near v. Minnesota* (1931). Generally, the Court has employed the clear and present danger test, strict scrutiny, or a similar demanding standard in reviewing such prior restraints.

Examples: (1) In a per curiam opinion, the Court held that, absent a statute, a court could not constitutionally issue an injunction at the request of government restraining the publication by a newspaper of a classified study on the Vietnam War. The government failed to overcome the presumption of unconstitutionality to meet its heavy burden of justification. For example, the government failed to demonstrate that the publication would necessarily involve "direct, immediate, and irreparable damage to our Nation or its people." *New York Times Co. v. United States* (1971).

(2) Judicial orders restraining criminal pretrial news publications, while intended to preserve Sixth Amendment rights to a fair trial, involve prior restraints which are the most serious and least tolerable infringements on First Amendment rights. Only a showing by government that there is a clear and present danger to the administration of justice could justify such a prior restraint. In imposing such an order, a trial judge must determine (1) the nature and extent of pretrial news coverage; (2) whether other measures would be likely to mitigate the effects of unrestrained pretrial publicity; (3) the effectiveness of a restraining order in avoiding the danger. The failure to consider alternatives to a restraining order and the probable ineffectiveness of the order in promoting fair trial made such a "gag order" impermissible in the present case. *Nebraska Press Assn. v. Stuart* (1976).

(3) Seizure of the assets of the operator of numerous adult entertainment businesses under the forfeiture provisions of the Racketeer Influenced and Corrupt Organizations Act (RICO) is not a prior restraint. The government seized and destroyed millions of dollars worth of books and videos, most of which had not been held to be legally obscene. The RICO forfeiture order was imposed as a punishment following conviction after a full criminal trial for engaging in racketeering activities. The order "does not forbid [the defendant] from engaging in any expressive activities in the future, nor does it require him to obtain prior approval for any expressive activities." Any chill on protected expression is comparable to that from stiff criminal penalties

for obscenity offenses or other forfeiture of expressive materials as punishment for criminal conduct. *Alexander v. United States* (1993).

(4) A broad injunction prohibiting speech about a prominent lawyer, Johnnie Cochran, issued as a remedy following a finding of defamation and coercion "lost its underlying rationale" when Cochran died. The Court held that "the injunction, as written now amounts to an overly broad prior restraint upon speech, lacking plausible justification. As such, the Constitution forbids it." *Tory v. Cochran* (2005).

c. Not all injunctions are prior restraints subject to the heavy presumption of unconstitutionality.

1) If the injunction only *incidentally* affects expression, if it is content-neutral, the prior restraint doctrine does not apply. However, because of the differences between an injunction and a generally applicable law, *e.g.*, the greater danger of censorship and discriminatory application, the Court employs a somewhat more stringent standard than normally used for reviewing content-neutral regulations. *The Court asks "whether the challenged provisions of the injunction burden no more speech than necessary to serve a significant government interest."* Madsen v. Women's Health Center *(1994)*.

Examples: (1) An injunction restricting anti-abortion protesters from demonstrating in certain places and in certain ways outside of a health clinic that performs abortions is not content-or viewpoint-based and hence is not subject to strict scrutiny. The state court imposed the injunction "without reference to the content of the speech." Since speech is only incidentally affected by the content-neutral restriction, it is not a classic prior restraint which would be presumptively invalid.

An injunction prohibiting creating a 36 foot buffer zone in front of an abortion clinic does not violate the First Amendment because of the need to provide access to and from the clinic. However, the same buffer zone on the back and side of the clinic burdens more speech than necessary because no access to the clinic is being blocked. A noise restriction on the use of sound amplifiers to project messages into the clinic is valid under the First Amendment. Such a restriction is necessary to ensure that medical procedures inside the clinic can be performed efficiently and to protect the mental and emotional health of the clinic's patients. A similar ban on "images observable" from within the clinic violates the First Amendment because patients and employees can simply avert their eyes from the message. The First Amendment is also violated by a blanket ban that precludes approaching anyone seeking the services of the clinic without their consent within 300 feet of the clinic and a provision creating a 300–foot buffer zone around residences of clinic staff. *Madsen v. Women's Health Center* (1994).

(2) Applying *Madsen v. Women's Health Center* (1994), the Court upheld an injunction imposing a variety of restrictions on antiabortion protestors to prevent their blocking abortion clinics or engaging in other illegal activities. However, the Court struck down floating buffer zones (*i.e.* prohibiting demonstrations within fifteen feet of any person or vehicle entering or leaving the clinics), "because they burden more speech than is necessary to serve the relevant governmental interests." The lack of certainty in the restriction led to a substantial risk that speech protected by the First Amendment would be hindered. *Schenck v. Pro–Choice Network of Western New York* (1997).

2) While content-based permit systems are burdened substantively and procedurally, a content-neutral permit system not involving censorship concerns need only contain adequate standards to guide administrative discretion and render the official's actions subject to judicial review. *Thomas v. Chicago Park District* (2002).

Example: A municipal park ordinance requiring a permit before conducting large scale events or engaging in activities involving sound amplification is constitutional. The law provides 13 specified grounds for denial of the permit, none of which has anything to do with what a speaker might say. The law is not directed at communicative activity as such but to all park activity. Facially the law provides narrowly drawn, reasonable and definite standards guiding discretion. *Thomas v. Chicago Park District* (2002).

5. First Amendment Vagueness and Overbreadth

Throughout your review of First Amendment law, keep in mind that a law may be attacked as facially invalid or invalid as applied given the facts in the particular case. If the language of a law is unconstitutionally vague or overbroad on its face, the fact that it is applied in a narrow, constitutional manner will not save the law. And even a precise, narrowly drawn law can be applied in a sweeping unconstitutional way in a particular case.

a. Vagueness

A law is facially invalid if it is not drawn with sufficient clarity and definiteness to inform persons of ordinary intelligence what actions are proscribed. A vague statute regulating the First Amendment activity is fundamentally unfair, violating both due process and freedom of expression. The First Amendment demands special clarity in both criminal and civil laws burdening freedom of expression so that protected expression will not be chilled or suppressed, *e.g.*, standards in administrative licensing laws must be drawn with precision and clarity.

Example: A provision in the Antiterrorism and Effective Death Penalty Act (AEDPA) which prohibits providing "material support or resources" to designated terrorist organizations, is not unconstitutionally vague on its face. Statutory terms such as "training," "expert advice or assistance," "service," and "personnel" do not require "untethered, subjective judgments" to determine their meaning. And Congress has provided narrowing definitions over time. Further a requirement that the support be given "knowing" of the groups' connection to terrorism further reduces its vagueness. The "dispositive point here is that the statutory terms are clear in their application to plaintiff's proposed conduct. [T]he statutory terms are not vague as applied to plaintiffs." If the statute is clear in its application to plaintiffs, the statute is not unconstitutional *as applied* to the plaintiffs. *Holder v. Humanitarian Law Project* (2010).

b. Overbreadth

A law may also be void on its face if it is substantially overbroad in that the law indiscriminately reaches both constitutionally protected and unprotected activ-

ity. A statute regulating First Amendment activities must be precisely drawn so that protected behavior is not chilled or suppressed.

Examples: (1) A city ordinance making it a crime for "one or more persons to assemble * * * on any of the sidewalks * * * and there conduct themselves in a manner annoying to persons passing by * * * "is unconstitutional on its face. It is vague and an excessive intrusion on free assembly and association. *Coates v. Cincinnati* (1971).

(2) A resolution banning all "First Amendment activities" within the central terminal of a local airport is facially unconstitutional under the First Amendment overbreadth doctrine regardless of whether or not the terminal is a public forum. The ban is so sweeping that virtually any individual within the terminal is subject to legal action for protected expression, even individuals not posing a threat to the proffered governmental interest in preventing congestion and disruption. Such an absolute prohibition is a substantially overbroad invasion of protected speech that could not be justified by any conceivable governmental interest. Thus, it was not necessary for the Court to rule whether the affected forum was public or nonpublic; under any degree of scrutiny the law would have been unreasonable. Further the resolution was not amenable to a saving construction—it was too broad to construe it differently from its plain meaning without a series of adjudications. *Board of Airport Comm'rs of Los Angeles v. Jews for Jesus, Inc.* (1987).

1) **Third Party Standing**

A litigant has standing to challenge the constitutionality of an overbroad statute even though his activities could be reached under a properly drawn statute. Persons whose conduct could not be regulated under a properly drawn law may be chilled in the exercise of their First Amendment rights. Further, such laws invite selective enforcement.

2) **Substantial Overbreadth**

Increasingly, the Court is requiring real and substantial overbreadth for facial invalidity. The courts will consider the likelihood that a significant amount of protected speech will be burdened and the potential constitutional applications of the law. *Broadrick v. Oklahoma* (1973) (state law restricting political activities of state employees held constitutional); *New York v. Ferber* (1982) (child pornography law held constitutional); *Board of Airport Comm'rs of Los Angeles v. Jews for Jesus Inc.* (1987) (regulation prohibiting "First Amendment activities" in the airport terminal held unconstitutional).

Examples: (1) A city public housing authority trespass policy forbidding reentry to a fenced-off block of public housing to any nonresident who did not have a "legitimate business or social purpose for being on the premises," and who had been duly notified by police to leave and not return, is not unconstitutionally overbroad. Following notification, the defendant, who was arrested for trespass, claimed that the policy was being used to bar persons engaged in constitutionally protected speech. But the basis for the defendant's arrest was violation of the notice-barment rule, not speech. The defendant failed to show that "the trespass policy taken as a whole is substantially overbroad in relation to its plainly legitimate sweep." Applications of the policy that would violate the First Amendment could be remedied through as-applied litigation, rather than the "strong medicine" of overbreadth. *Virginia v. Hicks* (2003).

(2) A federal statute prohibiting the knowing sale, creation, or possession of depictions of animal cruelty with the intent of commercial gain, where illegal in the place where the video was created, sold, or possessed, was held unconstitutional 8–1 on grounds of overbreadth. The statute lacked a precise definition of "animal cruelty," and only required that the conduct depicted be "illegal." Chief Justice Roberts, for the Court, wrote that the state "created a criminal prohibition of alarming breadth." It would cover videos depicting animals "wounded or killed" even if no animal cruelty is involved. Anyone trying to comply with the statute would face "a bewildering maze of regulations from at least 56 separate jurisdictions;" jurisdictions where the

video was created, sold, or possessed may have differing laws on illegal conduct involving animals. While the statute makes exceptions for depictions with redeeming "instructional value," many hunting videos lack "instructional value" and could now be illegal to sell. The Government said it would enforce the statute only against "acts of extreme cruelty," but prosecutorial assurances cannot save a statute that prohibits speech "presumptively protected by the First Amendment." *United States v. Stevens* (2010).

B. Freedom of Association and Belief

While freedom of association and belief is not expressly enumerated in the Constitution, it has been held that such a right is implicit in the First Amendment speech, press, assembly, and the Fifth and Fourteenth Amendment due process "liberty," guarantees. *Increasingly, the Court has employed more stringent standards in reviewing government regulations significantly burdening the right to associate for politically expressive purposes. "Infringements * * * may be justified by regulations adopted to serve compelling state interests, unrelated to the suppression of ideas, that cannot be achieved through means significantly less restrictive of associational freedoms."* Roberts v. United States Jaycees *(1984).*

The First Amendment guarantee is limited to expressive association; it does not include a generalized right of social association. It is a right to associate for protected First Amendment purposes that is constitutionally protected. *City of Dallas v. Stanglin* (1989) (city ordinance limiting adult admission to teenage dance halls does not violate any First Amendment right of minors and adults to associate).

1. Restraints on Membership and Associational Action

a. *Membership in an organization that engages in illegal advocacy cannot be punished or penalized unless the law is limited to active membership which requires (1) knowing membership in the organization (scienter); (2) with specific intent to further the illegal objectives of the organization.*

   Example: A membership clause in a federal statute which makes it a felony for any person to be a member of an organization which advocates the forceful overthrow of the government knowing the purposes of the organization is valid. The Court validated the statute by declaring that the statute could only be enforced against a defendant if specific intent to engage in illegal advocacy could be shown. *Scales v. United States* (1961).

b. The right of association includes the right to engage in joint political action to further the organization's legitimate objectives. But it does not impose on government any affirmative obligation to promote those objectives or to support the activity.

> *Examples:* (1) Neither the NAACP nor its members could be held liable for damages resulting from a civil rights boycott of white merchants absent a showing of participation in illegal activity causing the harm. There was no showing that any member had actual or apparent authority from the NAACP to foster illegal conduct. The fact that some participants in the boycott may have acted illegally does not justify liability for those engaged only in peaceful political associational activity. *NAACP v. Claiborne Hardware Co.* (1982).
>
> (2) Use of a defendant's membership in the white racist group, Aryan Brotherhood, in a sentencing proceeding violates the First Amendment where the prosecutor made no showing of its relevance. The defendant, who was white, was accused of killing a white person and there was no evidence presented that the group had committed any unlawful or violent acts which might establish aggravating circumstances. Thus, the evidence "tended to prove nothing more than the abstract beliefs of the defendant [and] had no bearing on the issue being tried." *Dawson v. Delaware* (1992).

2. Group Registration and Disclosure Requirement

a. While a law prohibiting membership in an organization is a direct restraint on the right to associate, the restraint is generally more indirect, *e.g.*, requiring that an organization register and disclose its membership. In such cases, the Court balances the extent of the interference with the right to associate against the interests of government in the regulation.

b. In a series of cases involving subversive or extremist groups, the Court employed ad hoc balancing with deference to the legislative judgment.

In other cases, involving more "legitimate" groups, the Court employed strict scrutiny. Comparing these two lines of cases, some commentators suggest that the right of association is essentially the right to engage in activities otherwise independently protected by the First Amendment. Alternatively, the enhanced review used in more recent cases may simply reflect the different times.

Examples: (1) A federal statute requiring registration of the Communist Party and disclosure of its membership as a condition for organizing was held constitutional. The Court deferred to the congressional findings concerning the magnitude of the public interests in disclosure, the pertinence of the requirement to protecting those interests, and the minimal burden on associational rights. *Communist Party of America v. Subversive Activities Control Board* (1961).

(2) A state law requiring that the Ku Klux Klan disclose the names of its officers and members, pursuant to the state's efforts to control the KKK's illegal activities, is constitutional. The conviction of a member of the Klan for attending meetings knowing that the group had not satisfied the disclosure requirement was upheld. *New York ex rel. Bryant v. Zimmerman* (1928).

(3) A state attorney general may not require the NAACP to disclose to the state a list of its members in the state. Such compelled disclosure violates the First Amendment since the inviolability of privacy in group association and its indispensability to preservation of freedom of association, given the danger of reprisals, outweighs the governmental need for the information. *NAACP v. Alabama ex rel. Patterson* (1958).

(4) Application of a state law requiring political parties to report the names and addresses of campaign contributors and recipients of campaign disbursements to the Socialist Workers Party (SWP) (a minor political party which has historically been the object of governmental and private harassment) violates privacy of association and belief. The government interests in disclosure, *i.e.,* enhancement of voters' knowledge, deterrence of corruption and enforcement of contribution limitations, are weaker in the case of

minor parties while the threat to First Amendment values is greater when the disclosure involves contributors and recipients. Since the lower court concluded that the evidence established a reasonable probability that disclosure would subject contributors and recipients to threats, harassment and reprisals, the disclosure law cannot be applied to the SWP consistent with the First Amendment. *Brown v. Socialist Workers '74 Campaign Comm.* (1982).

3. Restraints on Government Employment and Benefits

a. General Principles

(1) Principles governing punishment of membership in an organization also apply to non-criminal penalties imposed on persons enjoying benefits and privileges provided by government, *e.g.*, bar membership, government employment. *No distinction can be made today regarding whether the person is exercising a right or a privilege. Civil penalties cannot be imposed for membership alone, absent scienter and specific intent.*

(2) Unconstitutional Conditions. Government may not condition the receipt of government benefits on the surrender of First Amendment rights.

> *Example:* A refusal by a state board of bar examiners to admit an applicant to its bar solely because of past association, *i.e.*, the use of aliases, former connection with subversive organizations, and a record of arrests is invalid. In the light of the ancient vintage of the objectionable past associations and the forceful showing of good moral character in intervening years, the action of the state board violated the Constitution. *Schware v. Board of Bar Examiners of State of New Mexico* (1957).

(3) Government has a substantial interest in the fitness, qualifications, and loyalty of its employees. In implementing this interest, it has employed a variety of means, *e.g.*, loyalty programs and loyalty oaths, disclosure requirements, legislative investigations. Reconciling these requirements with freedom of speech, association and belief has produced a mass of case law, varying over time, and often inconsistent in result. *Generally, however, the Court has employed a*

balancing approach, weighing the interest of government as employer in maintaining the particular regulation against the burden on First Amendment rights.

b. Loyalty Programs and Loyalty Oaths

1) Loyalty Programs

Loyalty programs designed to remove risks from government employment cannot employ means which excessively intrude on First Amendment rights. Government must use means which have a less drastic impact on First Amendment rights. This frequently is determined by balancing the respective interests involved.

Examples: (1) A federal statute which prohibited members of communist-action organizations under a final order to register from engaging "in any employment in any defense facility" was held invalid. The statute was too broadly drawn (overbreadth) and Congress could have used less drastic means in terms of the effect on First Amendment prohibitions in order to accomplish its legislative purpose. *United States v. Robel* (1967).

(2) A complicated and intricate scheme for determining teachers' loyalty was held unconstitutional. Mere knowing membership, without any requirement of specific intent, was proscribed. The Court held that the law was insufficiently precise and not drawn with narrow specificity. Further, less drastic means were available. *Keyishian v. Board of Regents* (1967).

2) Loyalty Oaths

a) Positive Oaths

Employment may not be conditioned on an oath that one has not or will not engage in protected speech activities, such as criticism of government, discussing political doctrine, or supporting certain candidates for office. Positive oaths as a condition of government employment which promise support of the Constitution in the future are constitutional as long as the oath has reasonable relation to the individual's present and future competency for the position.

Example: Since there is no constitutionally protected right to overthrow a government by force, violence, or illegal or unconstitutional means, no constitutional right is impaired by a state requirement that a state employee must take an oath to live by the constitutional system in the future as a precondition to employment. *Cole v. Richardson* (1972).

b) Overbreadth

A broader oath probing the individual's association with organizations having illegal purposes must be limited to membership in the organization knowing *its illegal goals with* specific intent *to promote those illegal objectives.*

Example: A state loyalty oath which conditioned employment on taking an oath that the employee had not knowingly and wilfully become or remained a member of an organization seeking the forcible overthrow of government was held unconstitutional since there was no requirement of specific intent. *Elfbrandt v. Russell* (1966).

c) Vagueness

An oath cannot be framed in terms so broad that persons of ordinary intelligence could not know what is being attested. Such an oath would violate due process requirements of fairness and might chill individuals from engaging in constitutionally protected activities.

Example: An oath requiring teachers to swear that they would "by precept and example promote respect for the flag and the institutions of the [United States] and that they were not members of a 'subversive organization'" was held unconstitutionally vague. *Baggett v. Bullitt* (1964).

c. Individual Membership Disclosure: Bar Admission Requirements

Government has an interest in limiting admission to the legal profession to those who establish their fitness and competency to practice law. Failure to cooperate with a bar committee's inquiry when the questions have a substantial relevance to such qualifications is a grounds for denying bar admission.

Example: A bar applicant is not constitutionally authorized to refuse to say whether he was a member of the Communist Party.

The Court declared that a state is not prohibited from denying admission to the bar to an applicant who refuses to provide unprivileged answers to questions having a substantial relevance to his qualifications. *Konigsberg v. State Bar of California* (1957).

1) But the questions must be relevant to the applicant's fitness and narrowly tailored to serve the government interest. Broad questions concerning associational memberships without reference to the character of the membership violate due process.

    Example: A state bar committee cannot deny admission to the bar to an applicant who refuses to answer questions concerning whether he had ever been a member of an organization advocating the forceful overthrow of the government. Since the questions did not probe knowledge or specific intent, the inquiry was an overbroad intrusion on First Amendment rights. *Baird v. State Bar* (1971).

2) But a more narrowly tailored inquiry into past associations, including inquiries into knowledge and specific intent, is permissible.

    Example: A state bar committee may validly ask a bar applicant whether he or she belongs to an organization advocating the violent overthrow of the government and whether during the period of membership(s) he had the specific intent to further the organization's illegal goals. Bar examiners may inquire about Communist affiliations as a prelude to further inquiry about the nature of the applicant's association and an applicant may be excluded from admission to the bar for refusal to answer. *Law Students Civil Rights Research Council, Inc. v. Wadmond* (1971).

d. Political Patronage

1) *Government may not discharge public employees for refusing to support a political party or its candidates, unless political affiliation is a reasonably appropriate requirement for the job in question. Government cannot condition public employment on an employee's exercise of his or her First Amendment rights.*

2) These principles also apply to promotion, transfer, recall and hiring decisions. "The First Amendment prevents the Government, except in the most compelling circumstances, from wielding its power to interfere with its employees' freedom to believe and associate, or not to believe and not to associate." *Rutan v. Republican Party* (1990).

3) These principles also apply to contractors, or other regular providers of services to protect "the exercise of rights of political association or the expression of political allegiance." *O'Hare Truck Service, Inc. v. City of Northlake* (1996).

> ***Examples:*** (1) The discharge of Republican non-civil service employees by a newly-elected county sheriff because of their party affiliation violated the First Amendment. A majority of justices agreed that subjecting a nonconfidential, non-policymaking employee to a penalty for the exercise of the rights of political association was equivalent to imposing an unconstitutional condition. The Court held that the discharge was not justified under a heightened standard of review by Government interests in assuring government efficiency, assuring the political loyalty of government employees or preserving the democratic process and the integrity of the political party system. *Elrod v. Burns* (1976).
>
> (2) The discharge of assistant public defenders who were performing their jobs because of their political affiliation was unconstitutional. The Court reasoned that "party affiliation is not necessarily relevant to every policymaking or confidential position." Rather, the Court held: "[T]he ultimate inquiry is not whether the label 'policymakers' or 'confidential' fits the particular position; rather, the question is whether the hiring authority can demonstrate that a party affiliation is an appropriate requirement for the effective performance of the public office involved." A public defender's effectiveness turned on how he responded to his client's need, not his political affiliation. *Branti v. Finkel* (1980).
>
> (3) The First Amendment safeguards for political association apply to a city's removal of a company from

a rotation list of available companies to perform towing services after its owner refused to contribute to the mayor's reelection campaign and instead supported his opponent. Distinguishing between Government employees and independent contractors in the context of political patronage would invite manipulation by Government, which could avoid liability by attaching particular labels to different jobs. The absolute right to enforce a patronage system as a means of retaining control over independent contractors has not been shown to be a necessary part of a legitimate political system in all instances. *O'Hare Truck Service, Inc. v. City of Northlake* (1996).

4. Legislative Investigations and Forced Disclosures

a. Investigatory Power

Pursuant to the necessary and proper clause, government can investigate in order to legislate. The grant of authority to an investigatory committee must be specific and explicit. Questions propounded to a witness must be "pertinent," *i.e.,* as precise and clear as due process requires in criminal cases.

b. First Amendment Limitations

In determining whether the investigation intrudes on First Amendment rights, the Court has at times balanced the government interests against the individual interests. Barenblatt v. United States *(1959). More recently, the Court has held that when an investigation intrudes on First Amendment rights of speech and association, government must show a substantial relation between that information sought and a subject of overriding and compelling government interest.* Gibson v. Florida Legislative Investigation Comm. *(1963);* DeGregory v. Attorney General *(1966).*

c. Disclosure Requirements and Self–Incrimination

1) Confessions given by government employees under threat of discharge cannot be used as a basis for a subsequent criminal prosecution since it violates the employee's privilege against self-incrimination. *Garrity v. New Jersey* (1967). The employee cannot be required to forego this privilege against self-incrimination as a condition of employment. *Gardner v. Broderick* (1968).

2) An employee who is granted immunity from criminal prosecution may not refuse to answer questions specifically, directly, and narrowly relating to the performance of his official duties. Failure to answer can be grounds for dismissal. If the employee answers, he may be discharged because of his answers.

3) If the inquiry is broad-ranging into associations and beliefs, it is arguably barred by the First Amendment. However, it may be possible for the employee to be removed for failure to cooperate with a relevant government inquiry.

5. Group Litigation

Litigation engaged in by groups to further organizational goals is viewed as expressive and associational conduct entitled to First Amendment protection. Government may regulate group litigation and legal services only for substantial reasons and with specificity.

Example: A state may not punish a lawyer affiliated with a non-profitmaking organization who, seeking to further ideological and political goals, informs a lay person of her legal rights and tells her free representation is available from the organization. The lawyer's activity is a form of political expression and is near the core of the First Amendment. Regulations in this area must be narrowly drawn, and a showing of merely potential danger cannot justify punishment. *In re Primus* (1978).

C. Freedom From Compelled Expression

The First Amendment includes both the right to speak freely and the right to refrain from speaking at all. Since there is a constitutional right of freedom of association and belief, there is a correlative right to be free of compelled association and beliefs. "If there is any fixed star in our constitutional constellation, it is that no official, high or petty, can prescribe what shall be orthodox in politics, nationalism, religion, or other matters of opinion." West Va. State Bd. of Educ. v. Barnette (1943) (compulsory flag salute held unconstitutional). Freedom from compelled orthodoxy is a vital component of self-determination protected by due process liberty.

1. In determining whether the right not to speak or associate is significantly burdened, the Courts will consider factors such as whether there is a particular message prescribed by government, the probability that the public will mistakenly associate the idea with the claimant of the right, the ability of the claimant to disavow the idea or message, and the impact of the compelled expression on a group's structure or message.

2. If freedom from compelled expression is significantly burdened by government, the more stringent standards of review apply. The regulation must be narrowly tailored to serve a compelling or overriding government interest. "[T]he fundamental rule under the First Amendment [is] that a speaker has the autonomy to choose the content of his own message." *Hurley v. Irish–American Gay Group of Boston* (1995).

1. Compelled Speech

The freedom from compelled expression includes the right to refuse to express support for ideas and activities which one opposes. *"Freedom of speech prohibits the government from telling people what they must say."* Rumsfeld v. FAIR *(2006). The freedom from compelled expression also includes freedom from being forced "to host or accommodate another speaker's message."* Id.

Examples: (1) A state may not constitutionally enforce criminal sanctions against persons who cover the motto "live free or die" on passenger vehicle license plates because that motto is repugnant to their moral and religious beliefs. The right of freedom of thought protected by the First Amendment includes the right to speak freely and the right to refrain from speaking at all. The latter limits the ability of the state to require an individual to participate in the dissemination of an ideological message by displaying it on his private property in a manner and for the express purpose that it be observed and read by the public. The state's interests in facilitating the identification of passenger vehicles and promoting the appreciation of history, individualism, and state pride are not sufficiently compelling to override the First Amendment interest at stake. *Wooley v. Maynard* (1977).

(2) A state law permitting the use of privately owned shopping centers for speech purposes does not violate the property owner's rights of belief and association. Since the shopping center is a public place, there is no likelihood that the property owners will be identified with the views being expressed and they can expressly disavow any such association. Finally, government is not prescribing the message being expressed. *Prune Yard Shopping Center v. Robins* (1980).

(3) A Massachusetts court, in seeking to enforce its public accommodations law, may not constitutionally require the private sponsor of the St. Patrick's Day parade to include

among the marchers a group of gay persons of Irish descent. The parade is a form of expressive conduct which need not be limited to any particularized message. The group of gay marchers is seeking to express a message that the sponsors do not wish to include. The state may not seek to promote the gay marchers message by forcing the parade organizers to alter their expression. Nor may it seek to discourage discrimination by forcing a speaker to alter his or her message. The state "is not free to interfere with speech for no better reason than promoting an approved message or discouraging a disfavored one, however enlightened either purpose may strike the government." *Hurley v. Irish–American Gay Group of Boston* (1995).

(4) The Solomon Amendment provides that educational institutions that fail to provide military recruiters access equal to that provided other recruiters will lose certain federal funds. A group of law schools opposed to the government's discriminatory policy towards homosexuals in the military (Forum for Academic and Institutional Rights (FAIR)) brought a suit claiming that the Amendment violated their First Amendment freedoms of speech and association. The Supreme Court unanimously rejected the claims.

Because the schools were not speaking when they allowed recruiters to access campus [See VIII, F on Expressive Conduct], the government was not compelling the schools to endorse any message nor was it interfering with any message by the schools. "The compelled speech to which the law schools point is plainly incidental to the Solomon Amendment's regulation of conduct, and 'it has never been deemed an abridgment of freedom of speech or press to make a course of conduct illegal merely because the conduct was in part initiated, evidenced, or carried out by means of language, either spoken, written, or printed.'" *Rumsfeld v. FAIR* (2006).

2. Compelled Association

If an organization engages in "expressive activity," being forced to accept certain persons as members may be inconsistent with that expression and can involve a significant burden on the right not to associate. However, forced interaction may not interfere with First Amendment-protected expressive association, which is focused largely on whether a group is forced to accept someone as a member.

Examples: (1) An interpretation of a state human rights law barring gender discrimination by public business facilities to the males-only membership rules of the United States Jaycees does not violate the right to be free of compelled association. The state has a compelling interest in eliminating gender discrimination in publicly available goods and services. There was no showing that inclusion of females would impede the organization's ability to engage in protected activities or to disseminate its views. The state had selected the "least restrictive means of achieving its ends." *Roberts v. United States Jaycees* (1984). These principles were reaffirmed and applied in *Board of Dirs. of Rotary Int'l v. Rotary Club of Duarte* (1987).

(2) A city law prohibiting discrimination in institutions with over four hundred members, defined to include certain private clubs, is not unconstitutionally overbroad. On its face, the statute does not significantly affect the ability of individuals to form associations to advocate public or private viewpoints. Clubs are not required to abandon or alter any activities protected by the First Amendment. There is ample opportunity under the law to assure that any overbreadth in its coverage will be curable through case-by-case analysis of specific facts. *New York State Club Ass'n v. City of New York* (1988).

(3) Application of a state public accommodations law to prevent the Boy Scouts of America from denying membership to an avowed homosexual assistant scoutmaster violates the Boy Scouts right of expressive association. The Court initially found that the organization engages in expressive activity by seeking to transmit a system of values. It then held that the forced inclusion of an avowed homosexual as an assistant scoutmaster would significantly burden the Scouts' message that "homosexual conduct is not morally straight" and its desire not "to promote homosexual conduct as a legitimate form of behavior." The Court relied on *Hurley v. Irish–American Gay Group of Boston* (1995) (Ch. VIII, C, 1) and deferred to the Scout's claim that Dale's membership would impair its expressive activity. Rejecting applicability of *O'Brien's* intermediate scrutiny standard and again relying on the analysis in *Hurley*, the Court held 5–4 that the States antidiscrimination interests did not justify the direct and immediate effect on the organization's First Amendment associational rights. *Boy Scouts of America v. Dale (2000).*

(4) The Solomon Amendment, which requires that law schools provide equal access to military recruiters or lose federal funds, does not interfere with their "right of expressive association." A group of law schools (FAIR) objected to providing access to military recruiters because the forced association significantly affected their ability to express their message that discrimination based on sexual orientation is wrong. The Court unanimously rejected the First Amendment claim concluding that recruiters were not made members of the law school community. The law school was not forced to accept members it didn't want. Unlike *Dale*, "[r]ecruiters are, by definition, outsiders who come onto campus for the limited purpose of trying to hire students—not to become members of the school's expressive association." *Rumsfeld v. FAIR* (2005).

(5) Hastings Law School has an all-comers policy for student groups—any group that wants recognition from the Law School has to allow all students membership in the group regardless of the student's status or beliefs. Christian Legal Society was denied recognition because it does not allow LGBT students or non-Christians to be members of the group. This denial was not a form of compelled association as in other cases where policies of forced inclusion in groups were overturned as violating rights of expressive association. Here CLS is not forced to accept any new members, but simply must forego official recognition and accompanying benefits if it chooses not to allow all students to participate. *Christian Legal Society (CLS) v. Martinez* (2010). See VIII, E, 2, a. on the use of limited public forum analysis in the *CLS* case.

3. Compulsory Fees and Dues

Compelling an individual to provide financial support for messages and programs that one opposes implicates the First Amendment right not to speak or associate. But reasonable fees and charges that reflect comparable benefits provided are generally constitutional.

Examples: (1) Insofar as service charges imposed by a union on non-members as part of an agency shop arrangement permitted by state law are used to finance expenditures by the union for the purposes of collective bargaining, contract administration, and grievance adjustment, there is no First Amendment violation even for public employees. However, a state cannot constitutionally compel public employees to contribute to union political activities or ideological causes not germane to the union's duties as collective bargaining representative consistent with the First Amendment guarantee of freedom of belief and association. Such expenditures must be financed by charges on employees who do not object to advancing those ideas and who are not coerced into doing so against their will by the threat of loss of government employment. *Abood v. Detroit Board of Education* (1977).

(2) The use of mandatory membership dues by the California State Bar to promote political and ideological causes with which some members disagree violates those members' First Amendment rights. *Abood* is controlling. In order to be permissible, the challenged expenditures must be "necessarily or reasonably incurred for the purpose of regulating the legal profession or 'improving the quality of legal service available to the people of the State.' " *Keller v. State Bar of California* (1990).

(3) *Abood* and *Keller* were distinguished in upholding compelled student fees in a state university setting. The University was not required to use the mandatory fees for funding only activities "germane" to the University mission. The Court stated: "If it is difficult to define germane speech with ease or precision where a union [*Abood*] or bar association [*Keller*] is the party, the standard becomes all the more unmanageable in the public University setting, particularly where the State undertakes to stimulate the whole universe of speech and ideas." *Board of Regents of University of Wisconsin v. Southworth* (2000).

(4) The state of Washington authorizes public-sector unions to negotiate agency-shop agreements. A public sector union challenged a state voter initiative (§ 760) requiring that unions obtain nonmembers' affirmative authorization before using collected fees for election-related activities. The Court, per Justice Scalia, unanimously held that § 760 does not violate the First Amendment as applied to public sector unions. Justice Scalia said that Washington could have gone much further; it could have restricted agency fees to the portion of union dues devoted to collective bargaining or could have eliminated

agency fees entirely. It follows that the less restrictive limitation imposed by Washington is constitutional. Justice Scalia said that prior agency fee cases did not balance constitutional rights; unions have no constitutional right to fees from nonmember-employees. Justice Scalia rejected the relevance of campaign finance cases, reasoning that "§ 760 is not fairly described as a restriction on how the union can spend 'its' money; it is a condition placed upon the union's extraordinary *state* entitlement to acquire and spend *other people's* money." *Davenport v. Washington Education Association* (2007).

(5) The First Amendment is not violated when a local public union charges non-member employees a service fee that includes litigation fees incurred by the national union on behalf of other locals so long as "(1) the subject matter of the (extra-local) litigation is of a kind that would be chargeable if the litigation were local, *e.g.*, litigation appropriately related to collective bargaining rather than political activities, and (2) the litigation charge is reciprocal in nature, *i.e.*, the contributing local reasonably expects other locals to contribute similarly to the national's resources used for costs of similar litigation on behalf of the contributing local if and when it takes place." The Court unanimously held that the "service fee" that the Maine State Employees Association charged nonmembers, which included an "affiliation fee" paid to the national union that did not directly benefit the local union, was constitutional. Justice Breyer, for the Court, explained that the nature and the level of reciprocity of the national litigation in this case were determinative of the fees' constitutionality. First, the national litigation concerned "activities that [were] of a chargeable kind," such as those relating to collective bargaining. Second, it was possible that a nonmember could "benefit from national litigation aimed at helping other units if the national or those other units will similarly contribute to the cost of litigation on the local union's behalf." *Locke v. Karass* (2009).

(6) Nonmembers of a public-sector union in an agency shop were given an annual opportunity to opt out of paying for the Union's political advocacy but were notified that the agency fee was subject to increase at any time without further notice. During the year, the Union imposed a "special assessment"

solely for political advocacy. Nonmembers were not given an opportunity to opt out although nonmembers who had previously opted out of the original charge were required to pay only a portion of the special assessment. Nonmembers sued.

The Court held 7–2 that the procedure used by the Union violated the First Amendment. Justice Alito, writing for the Court, said: "[P]rocedures for collecting fees from nonmembers must be carefully tailored to minimize infringement on First Amendment rights and the procedures used in this case cannot possibly be considered to have met that standard." But Justice Alito went on to state that the Union "should have sent out a new notice allowing members to opt in to the special fee rather than requiring them to opt out." So that a nonmember can make a choice, the Union must provide a fresh notice and "may not exact any funds from nonmembers without their aforementioned consent." The Court's opinion suggested strong support for further limitations on compulsory union fees which "constituted a form of compelled speech and association that imposes a 'significant impingement on First Amendment rights.'" Justice Alito suggested that the Court's precedent had been excessively tolerant and he criticized the use of opt out procedures generally. The Court did not reach the issue whether the use of opt out procedures is unconstitutional.

Justice Sotomayor, joined by Justice Ginsburg, concurred only in the judgment. The First Amendment was violated by not affording nonmembers "an opportunity to opt out of the contributions of funds." Justice Breyer, joined by Justice Kagan, dissented, arguing that the procedures used resulted in no significant harm to nonmembers. *Knox v. Service Employees International Union* (2012).

4. Compelled Market Assessments

When government regulation requires market producers to contribute funds to a mandatory advertising program, the First Amendment freedom from compelled expression is implicated. But the Court has failed to fashion any consistent principle.

(1) A federal regulation imposing assessments on growers, handlers, and processors of California fruit trees to pay the costs of generic advertising

of California nectarines, plums and peaches, does not violate the First Amendment. The compelled speech precedent is inapplicable since the law does not require the challenger to repeat an objectionable message, to use their property to convey an antagonistic ideological message or force them to speak when they would prefer to remain silent. There is no abridgement of the right to speak freely. Although some of the challengers might prefer to advertise personally, rather than generically, this restraint is common in regulatory programs benefitting an entire market. *Glickman v. Wileman Bros. & Elliot* (1997).

(2) The Court distinguished *Glickman* in upholding a First Amendment challenge to a federal assessment on mushroom producers to fund advertising of mushrooms generally. United Foods wanted to advertise the superiority of its mushrooms rather than engage in general mushroom advertising. *Glickman* was said to involve mandatory advertising assessments as part of a general regulatory scheme of an industry. In this case, "the advertising itself, far from being of the ancillary, is the principal object of the regulatory scheme." *United States v. United Foods, Inc.* (2001).

(3) *United Foods* was distinguished in upholding a federal assessment on beef producers to fund beef-related promotional campaigns designed and approved by the Secretary of Agriculture. The Court's decision in *United Foods* was based on the premise that the advertising in question was private, not government, speech. In this case, the "message set out in the beef promotions is from beginning to end the message established by the Federal Government." While the government solicits assistance from nongovernmental sources in developing specific messages, "the government sets the overall message to be communicated and approves every word that is disseminated." The Court upheld the assessment since the "compelled support of government—even those programs of government one does not approve—is of course perfectly constitutional" and "does not alone raise First Amendment concerns." *Johanns v. Livestock Marketing Assn.* (2005).

D. The Electoral Process

Speech involving the electoral process is at the "core" of the First Amendment. Similarly, First Amendment concerns are at their zenith when government seeks to regulate political association, including both the freedom of the individual to associate and the freedom of political parties to pursue common action. The rigor of judicial review of electoral regulation depends on the extent to which the challenged provision burdens freedom of speech, association and belief. A "severe" restriction must survive strict scrutiny. *Norman v. Reed* (1992). "But when a state election law provision imposes only 'reasonable, non-discriminatory restrictions' upon the First and Fourteenth Amendment rights of voters, 'the States's important regulatory interests are generally sufficient to justify' the restrictions." *Burdick v. Takushi* (1992).

1. Political Speech and Association

a. *Direct restrictions on what is said during an election campaign are tested under strict scrutiny. The restriction must be necessary to achieve a compelling government interest or be a form of unprotected expression.*

Examples: (1) A state may not, consistent with the First Amendment, declare an election void because the victorious candidate violated a state law in announcing to voters during the campaign that he intended to serve at a salary less than that fixed by law. Such a statement differs from the corrupting agreements and solicitations recognized as un-protected speech. Nor can the proscription be justified as facilitating the candidacy of persons lacking independent wealth. The means are unacceptable since government cannot restrict the free exchange of ideas because voters may make a bad choice. Finally, the state interest in preventing factual misstatements is inadequate since the law excessively chills political debate—there was no show-ing of knowledge of falsity or reckless disregard of truth or falsity. *Brown v. Hartlage* (1982).

(2) A statute prohibiting solicitation of votes and display of campaign materials within 100 feet of the polling place entrance is a constitutional content-based manner regula-tion. The wide-spread and time-tested use of such a restricted zone indicates that it is necessary to serve the compelling interest in preventing voter intimidation and election fraud. *Burson v. Freeman* (1992).

(3) The Court held, 5–4, that the First Amendment is violated by a State Supreme Court rule, known as the Announce Clause, prohibiting candidates for judicial elec-tion from announcing their views on disputed legal and

political issues. The mere statement of the candidate's position, even if she does not bind herself to maintain that position after the election, violates the Announce Clause, although candidates can criticize past decisions and discuss judicial philosophy generally. This content-based regulation of core First Amendment political speech was reviewed using "strict scrutiny." The rule does not serve the claimed interest in maintaining the impartiality, or appearance of impartiality, of state judges, understood as the lack of bias for or against either party to proceedings, since it restricts speech regarding certain issues, not parties. Impartiality, understood as lack of a preconception in favor or against a particular legal view, is not a compelling interest since eliminating such judicial preconceptions on legal issues is neither possible, nor desirable. Impartiality, understood as openmindedness, was inadequate since this was not the purpose of the Announce Clause. The rule would be "woefully underinclusive" since candidates regularly announce a position on legal issues before becoming a candidate and after being elected.

The dissent stressed the differences between election of judges and election of legislative and executive officials. They argued that the Announce Clause was a constitutional effort by the states to balance the interest in preserving the integrity of its judges, and the appearance of fairness, with its desire to have popular election of judges. *Republican Party of Minnesota v. White* (2002).

b. The First and Fourteenth Amendments provide constitutional protection for citizens to create and develop new political parties. The Court has recognized "the constitutional interest of like-minded voters to gather in pursuit of common political ends, thus enlarging the opportunities of all voters to express their own political preferences." *Norman v. Reed* (1992). State restrictions on access to the ballot of independents and minor political parties can significantly burden this right. *The courts generally require that such regulation of the mechanics of the electoral process be "reasonable, nondiscriminatory restrictions."*

Examples: (1) An Ohio law requiring independent candidates, such as presidential candidate John Anderson, to file nominating petitions in March in order to be placed on the November ballot violated the First Amendment rights of voters and candidates. Such an early filing date severely burdens the right of like-minded citizens to associate and limits the field from which voters might choose. The state interests in promoting political stability, voter awareness, and equal treatment of candidates were insufficient to justify such a significant burden on associational rights. *Anderson v. Celebrezze* (1983).

(2) A Hawaiian prohibition against write-in voting, where candidates had ample opportunity to secure access to the ballot before the primary, is constitutional. Since the burden "on voters' rights to make free choices and to associate politically through the vote" was limited, strict scrutiny was inappropriate. The prohibition was deemed presumptively valid and justified by the state's legitimate interest in preventing excessive factionalism in general elections. *Burdick v. Takushi* (1992).

(3) Minnesota's anti-fusion law prohibiting a candidate from appearing on the ballot as the candidate of more than one party does not violate associational rights protected by the First Amendment. The restriction does not severely burden the party's associational rights. It does not restrict the ability of a political party and its members "to endorse, support, or vote for anyone they like." The law does not directly limit a party's access to the ballot or its internal structure, governance or policy-making. The laws only slightly limit who may appear on the ballot as the party's candidate and its ability to express its message. Since the burden is not severe, strict scrutiny is not required; the state's asserted regulatory interest must be "sufficiently weighty to justify the limitation." "The restriction is justified as a means of protecting the integrity, fairness and efficiency of ballots and the processes for electing officials, assuring that minor and third parties actually have required electoral support, the State's strong interest in the stability of its political system by avoiding party-splintering and excessive factionalism, even if that in practice favors the traditional two party system." *Timmons v. Twin Cities Area New Party* (1997).

(4) The Court invalidated three state provisions limiting ballot initiatives. Beginning from the premise that petition circulation is core political speech involving interactive communication concerning political change, the Court held that the three restrictions significantly inhibited communication with voters and were not narrowly tailored to serve compelling state interests in administrative efficiency, fraud detection or informing voters. First, a requirement that initiative and petition circulators have to be registered voters drastically reduced the number of persons available to circulate petitions. The state interest in policing lawbreakers among circulators was already served by existing laws. Second, the requirement that circulators display their names on identification badges inhibited participation by depriving the circulator of anonymity at the precise moment when the circulator is most likely to be subject to harassment because of her political message. There are less burdensome affidavit requirements for dealing with misconduct. Finally, a final report requiring specific identifying information of the circulator and the amount paid to each circulator were unnecessary given other disclosure provisions indicating the influence of special interest groups on the initiative process. *Buckley v. American Constitutional Law Foundation* (1999).

c. "Under our Constitution, anonymous pamphleteering is not a pernicious fraudulent practice, but an honorable tradition of advocacy and of dissent." *Laws which prohibit the distribution of anonymous campaign literature regulate the content of speech at the core of the protection afforded by the First Amendment and are subject to "exacting scrutiny"—they must be "narrowly tailored to serve an overriding state interest."* McIntyre v. Ohio Elections Commission *(1995).*

   Example: An Ohio statute prohibiting the distribution of anonymous materials "designed to influence the voters in any election" is unconstitutional. In *Talley v. California* (1960), the Court invalidated a city ordinance prohibiting all anonymous leafleting and First Amendment protection was afforded to urging an economic boycott. While the Ohio law in this case applied only to the electoral context, "the Court's reasoning [in *Talley*] embraced a respected tradition of anonymity in the advocacy of political causes." Unlike cases regulating the mechanics of the electoral process, this law requiring disclosure regulates the content of core political speech. Applying exacting scrutiny, the Court held that "[t]he simple interest in providing voters with additional relevant information does not justify a state requirement that a writer make statements or disclosures she would otherwise omit." While the State has a more weighty interest in the electoral context in preventing fraud and libel, the Ohio law was not so limited and Ohio had other laws dealing with these concerns. The ancillary benefit did not justify this "extremely broad prohibition." *McIntyre v. Ohio Elections Commission* (1995).

2. Regulating Political Parties

a. State efforts to control national political parties are likely to be held unconstitutional. States cannot enforce their laws extraterritorially to regulate national parties.

Examples: (1) The First Amendment right of political association is violated when a state seeks to compel a national political party to seat a delegation at its convention chosen in a way that violates the party's rules. A state statute requiring that state delegates to the Democratic Party's national convention be seated even though those delegates were chosen through a process that included a binding state preference primary election in which voters do not declare their party affiliation was held unconstitutional. The National Democratic Party requires that only Democrats select delegates to the convention. Even though a state has a substantial interest in the manner in which its elections are conducted, it has no compelling justification for this substantial interference with the national party's right of political association. *Democratic Party of U.S. v. Wisconsin ex rel. La Follette* (1981).

(2) A state law banning the governing bodies of political parties from endorsing candidates in the party primaries and regulating the governance of such bodies violates freedom of speech and association. The restriction directly

affects speech at the core of the electoral process by hampering the ability of a party to spread its message and the ability of voters seeking information. It interferes with the freedom of association of political parties by limiting the ability to promote candidates through concerted action. The state lacks a compelling government interest in either promoting a stable political system or protecting primary voters from confusion or undue influence that would justify such burdens. Nor did the state establish that its regulation of internal party governance is necessary to the integrity of the electoral process. *Eu v. San Francisco Cty. Democratic Cent. Comm.* (1989).

b. State laws significantly burdening the ability of a political party to select their candidate are subject to strict scrutiny. Laws imposing a lesser burden on associational rights are constitutional if they are reasonable.

> *Examples:* (1) A state statute requiring voters in party primaries to be registered members of that party violates the First Amendment right to political association of the Republican Party, which allows independent voters to participate in primaries. The state power to regulate the time, place, and manner of elections does not justify restricting political association. State interests in easing its financial burden in administrating the political process, preventing raiding, avoiding voter confusion and in maintaining political integrity are either not sufficiently substantial or not adequately furthered by the state law to justify the burden on constitutional association. A political party may determine its own sphere of association free from excessive state interference. *Tashjian v. Republican Party of Connecticut* (1986).
>
> (2) A California law establishing a blanket primary allowing voters to vote for the candidate of their choice for an office regardless of party affiliation is invalid. The system violated the parties' right of expressive association by allowing the parties' nominee to be determined by nonadherents or adherents of an opposing party. Such forced association changes the parties' message. There was no compelling state interest narrowly served by the system. *California Democratic Party v. Jones* (2000).

(3) An Oklahoma statute which allows political parties to open their party primary only to voters who are registered with the party or who are registered as independents does not violate the right of political association. *Tashjian* is distinguished since it involved a statute which prevented a political party from opening its primary election to independent voters. The Oklahoma semi-closed primary system allows independent voters to vote in any primary open to them but prevents a party from opening its primary to voters registered in another party. The Libertarian Party of Oklahoma (LPO) is prevented from opening its primary to all registered Oklahoma voters. Voters affiliated with another political party must disaffiliate and register as independents or as Libertarians in order to vote in the LPO party primary. The imposition of this minimal burden was justified by the state's interests in preserving the identity and viability of political parties, enhancing party-building efforts, and protecting against party raiding. *Clingman v. Beaver* (2005).

(4) Washington voters passed Initiative 872 providing that candidates could designate their "party preference" regardless of whether they were affiliated with the party or the wishes of the party. The top two votegetters, regardless of party preference, would advance to the general election. The Court held 7–2 that I–872 was not violative of the First Amendment. Justice Thomas, writing for the Court, concluded that "I–872 does not on its face impose a severe burden on political parties' associational rights." Unlike *Jones*, the I–872 primary does not choose the parties' nominees; it simply limits the number of candidates from which the top two advance to the general election, regardless of their party preference.

The political parties claimed that their associational rights were still severely burdened by being compelled to associate with candidates they didn't endorse, by having their message altered and by being forced to engage in counterspeech to disassociate themselves from candidates. Justice Thomas replied that these claims were not based on facial requirements of I–872 but on the possibility that voters would misinterpret a candidate's party-preference designation as reflecting a party endorsement. The *possibility* of voter confusion would not justify striking down the law *on its face*. Since I–872 did not severely burden associational rights, the State need not assert a compelling interest. The State's asserted interest in providing voters with relevant information was a sufficiently important interest to sustain I–872.

Justice Scalia, joined by Justice Kennedy, dissenting, argued that I–872 severely burdened political parties' associational rights by "thrusting an unwelcome, self-proclaimed association upon the party" whenever a candidate indicated his preference for the party on the ballot. Applying strict scrutiny, Justice Scalia argued that the state had no compelling interest in telling voters that a candidate says he favors a particular political party. Nor did the law protect that interest with "minimal intrusion" on parties' rights. *Washington State Grange v. Washington State Republican Party* (2008).

(5) New York requires political parties to select their nominees for State Supreme Court Justices by a convention of delegates chosen by party members in a primary election. Convention nominees appear on the general election ballot along with independent candidates meeting statutory requirements. Candidates who failed to secure a party nomination brought suit claiming that the convention system burdened their First Amendment right to have "a fair chance of prevailing in their parties' candidate selection process." They claimed that the party leadership inevitably determines the party nominees. The Court unanimously rejected the First Amendment claim. Justice Scalia, for the Court, rejected any claim based on the *parties'* associational rights. As for the candidate's rights, the success of the party leadership's candidates says nothing more than that it has more widespread support than non-endorsed candidates. Precedent does not establish "an individual's constitutional right to have a 'fair shot' at winning the party's nomination." Justice Scalia concluded: "Selection by convention has been a traditional means of

choosing party nominees. While a State may determine it is not desirable and replace it, it is not unconstitutional." Nor did the existence of party entrenched one-party rule create any First Amendment basis for judicial intervention. *New York State Board of Election v. Lopez–Torres* (2008).

3. Limitations on Contributions and Expenditures

a. Campaign Spending

1) Noncorporate Spending—*Attempts to limit contributions and expenditures for political campaigns constitute a burden on the rights of association and expression. However, reasonable limitations on contributions by individuals and groups, designed to serve substantial governmental interests, are permissible, since such laws permit display of support and do not impair the ability to discuss issues. Restrictions on independent expenditures by individuals and groups, however, excessively reduce the quality and quantity of communication, and are unconstitutional.*

   Examples: (1) The provisions of the Federal Election Campaign Act of 1971 limiting political *contributions* to candidates for federal elective office are constitutional but the provisions of the statute limiting *independent expenditures* by contributors or groups relative to a clearly identified candidate are not valid. The statute's primary purpose, *i.e.*, limiting the actuality and appearance of corruption resulting from large individual financial contributions, is a sufficient justification for the marginal intrusion on freedom of political association which is a consequence of the limitation on political contributions. The speech is done by someone other than the contributors. However, the expenditure limitations are invalid since they place substantial and direct restrictions on the ability of individuals, candidates, and associations to engage in political expression. None of the asserted government interests was sufficient to justify the burden on First Amendment rights. *Buckley v. Valeo* (1976).

   (2) A section of the Presidential Election Campaign Fund Act making it a criminal offense for an independent political action committee (PAC) to expend more

than $1000 to further the election of a presidential candidate who accepts public financing violates the First Amendment. Restrictions on the amount of money which a group can spend on political communication during a campaign would reduce the quantity of expression because virtually every means of expressing ideas in mass society requires the expenditure of money. While the government has a compelling interest in preventing corruption of the political process or the appearance of corruption, there is not sufficient evidence that PACs cause political corruption to enable the spending limitation provision to survive a rigorous First Amendment standard of review. Even if sufficient evidence could be found, the section is fatally overbroad because it applies equally to multi-million dollar and small neighborhood PACs. *Federal Election Comm'n v. National Conservative Political Action Committee* (1985).

(3) Vermont campaign finance law limited the amount that candidates for state office could spend on campaigns, as well as the amount that individuals and organizations could contribute to campaigns. The Court held 6–3 that the limits on candidate expenditures violated the First Amendment under *Buckley v. Valeo*. While campaign contributions can be limited, Vermont's limits were set unconstitutionally low. In a plurality opinion, Justice Breyer, joined by Chief Justice Roberts and Justice Alito, relied on *Buckley* in concluding that restrictions on expenditures were much more restrictive on the quantity and quality of expression than limits on contributions.

Justice Breyer used a five factor test that led the Court to find Vermont's limits unconstitutionally low. First, the limits were lower than limits previously upheld and comparable limits in other States, creating the danger that challengers would be unable to run effective campaigns against incumbents; this would which reduce democratic accountability. Second, subjecting political parties to the same low limits as individuals "threatens harm to a particularly important political right, the right to associate in a political party." Third, since the statute treated the costs incurred by volunteers as contributions, it limited the ability to associate. Fourth, the limits were not adjusted for inflation over time. And fifth, Vermont claimed no interest, apart from those already considered in *Buckley*, that justified the exceptionally low limits. Taken together, these factors convinced the Court that the contribution limits "burden First Amendment interests in a manner that is disproportionate to the public purposes they were enacted to advance." Justices Thomas, joined by Justice Scalia, argued that *Buckley* provides insufficient protection to political speech and should be overruled. Justice Kennedy, concurred in the judgment, noting his skepticism regarding *Buckley* and its operation. Justices Stevens, Souter and Ginsburg, dissented. *Randall v. Sorrell* (2006).

(5) The Court 5–4 held that the "Millionaire's Amendment" (§ 319(a)) to BCRA, which allows a non self-financing candidate to receive contributions at three times the normal limit if his opponent contributes more than $350,000 in personal funds to his own campaign, is unconstitutional. Under *Buckley v. Valeo*, limits on candidate expenditures are usually unconstitutional. Justice Alito, writing for the Court, reasoned that, although the Amendment was not a direct cap on expenditures, "Section 319(a) requires a candidate to choose between the First Amendment right to engage in unfettered political speech and subjection to discriminatory fundraising limitations." Because a self-financing candidate cannot exercise his right to make unlimited personal expenditures without discriminatory contributions limits being imposed, the Amendment placed an unconstitutional burden on self-financing candidates.

The Court held that the government did not provide any compelling state interest to justify the burden. As it did in *Buckley*, the Court rejected the argument that the government interest in eliminating corruption or the threat of corruption was furthered by expenditure limits. In fact, self-financing reduces a candidate's reliance on outside contributions. The Court also rejected the desire to level electoral opportunities for candidates of different personal wealth as justification for the burden on speech. There are numerous factors which distinguish candidates, and " 'the concept that government may restrict the speech of some elements of our society in order to enhance the relative voice of others is wholly foreign to the First Amendment.' *Buckley v. Valeo.*"

Justice Stevens, joined in part by Justices Ginsburg, Souter and Breyer, defended the Millionaire's Amendment as "a modest, sensible, and plainly constitutional attempt by Congress to minimize the advantages enjoyed by wealthy candidates vis-a-vis those who must rely on the support of others to fund their pursuit of public office." Justice Stevens argued no burden was placed on a self-financing candidate, as the Amendment did not restrict his speech, but merely assisted the speech of his opponent. "[T]his amplification in no way mutes the voice of the millionaire, who remains able to speak as loud and as long as he likes in support of his campaign." But even assuming that a burden was placed on self-financing candidates, the dissent found that the government interest in "reducing both the influence of wealth on the outcomes of elections, and the appearance that wealth alone dictates those results" justified the burden. *Davis v. FEC* (2008).

2) Political Party Spending—Expenditures by political parties that are independent of the candidate's control may not be restricted. *Colorado Republican Federal Campaign Committee v. Federal Election Commission* (1996). But expenditures that are coordinated with a candidate are deemed contributions subject to limitation. Otherwise the regulation of contributions could be circumvented by channeling donor contributions through the political parties. *Federal Election Commission v. Colorado Republican Federal Campaign Committee* (2001).

Provisions of the Bipartisan Campaign Reform Act of 2002 (BCRA) prohibiting political parties from soliciting, receiving, or spending "soft money," and a host of ancillary provisions intended to prevent circumvention of the ban by funneling money through other sources, including state and local candidates, are constitutional. *McConnell v. Federal Election Commission* (2003).

Example: "Soft money" describes political donations which were not previously subject to the limitations on contributions to candidates contained in the Federal Election Campaign Act of 1971. Under the prior system of laws, individuals and corporations could make unlimited donations to the national political parties, which could then spend it however they wished, as long as the money was not used to specifically advocate the election of a particular candidate. This restriction was easily avoided, however, by running "issue ads" (ads aimed at attacking or supporting a candidate's position on a particular issue, rather than advocating the election or defeat of that candidate), and generic party ads encouraging voters to vote the Democratic or Republican ticket, or by conducting activities such as voter registration drives targeting voters likely to vote for the party's candidate.

The Court held that the limitation in BCRA on soft money is a limit on contributions, rather than expenditures. Therefore, regulations are subject to a lesser degree of scrutiny under *Buckley v. Valeo.* The contribution restriction must only be "closely drawn" to serve an important interest. Because most of the largest soft money contributors give to both parties, contributions appeared to be attempts to buy access or avoid retaliation, rather than expressions of support for a particular ideology. Thus, the First Amendment rights of donors are not as strongly implicated. Congress has a sufficiently important interest in combating corruption and the appearance of corruption created by the sheer size of soft money contributions. Banning soft money and creating anti-circumvention measures are measures reasonably tailored to serve the interest in anti-

corruption. The Court emphasized that limits on contributions are not limits on expenditures by the parties
themselves. *McConnell v. Federal Election Commission*
(2003).

3) Corporate Spending—*Overruling precedent, the Supreme Court held
that government prohibition of a corporation's independent expenditures
from its treasury for political speech is an unconstitutional restriction on
its First Amendment right of freedom of speech.* Corporations, and
probably unions, are free to spend unlimited amounts on political
communications. *Citizens United v. Federal Election Commission* (2010).
The Court, in *American Tradition Partnership, Inc. v. Bullock* (2012) [*per
curiam* decision holding that a Montana ban on corporate electoral
spending violates the First Amendment], declined to reconsider or
distinguish *Citizens United*.

Example: A provision of the Bipartisan Campaign Reform Act of
2002 (BCRA), prohibiting corporations and unions from
using their general treasury funds to make independent expenditures for speech that is an "electioneering
communication" or speech that expressly advocates the
election or defeat of a candidate within 30 days of a
primary election or 60 days of a general election was
held, 5–4, to be facially unconstitutional. Citizens United,
a nonprofit corporation, produced a documentary critical of candidate Hilary Clinton, which it planned to
make available through video on demand on cable TV
near election time. Concerned that this would violate
the BCRA prohibition on corporate electoral spending,
it sought declaratory and injunctive relief, arguing the
provision was unconstitutional as applied. The Court
overruled precedent which had upheld prohibition of
independent corporate political spending. See *Austin v.
Michigan Chamber of Commerce* (1990); *McConnell v.
Federal Election Commission* (2003).

Writing for the Court, Justice Kennedy stated: "The
Government may regulate corporate political speech
through disclaimer and disclosure requirements, but it
may not suppress that speech altogether." Justice Kennedy
characterized the law as a criminal ban carrying crim-

inal penalties; it was censorship akin to a prior restraint. While corporations could still speak through a
PAC under BCRA, Justice Kennedy argued that PACs
are an expensive alternative and are subject to extensive
regulations. The ban, he said, "necessarily reduces the
quantity of expression by reducing the number of
issues discussed, the depth of their exploration, and the
size of the audience reached." The purpose and effect of
the law was "to silence entities whose voices the
government deems to be suspect." Justice Kennedy
concluded that such laws are subject to strict scrutiny.
Prohibiting corporate spending distinguished between
speakers which was often simply a means to control
content. Precedent had established that the First Amendment protections extend to corporations; the fact that
they are not natural persons does not diminish the
protection accorded their political speech. [*First National Bank of Boston v. Bellotti* (1978); *Buckley v. Valeo*
(1976)].

The Court then considered justifications previously
relied on for upholding restrictions on corporate political speech. The government, Justice Kennedy said, did
not really rely on an antidistortion rationale which
would allow Government to ban political speech simply because the speech was that of an association using
the corporate form. Reliance on the great economic
resources a corporation acquires, he argued, is inconsistent with *Buckley's* rejection of a governmental interest in equalizing the relative ability of individuals or
groups to influence election outcomes. The fact that
state law provides advantages to corporations allowing
them to acquire such assets does not mean that corporations can be forced to surrender First Amendment
rights as a quid pro quo. Media corporations would be
endangered under this rationale. In particular, the
Court rejected the *Austin* rationale that there is a
compelling government interest in preventing the "corrosive and distorting effects of immense aggregations
of wealth that are accumulated with the help of the
corporate form and that have little or no correlation to

the public's support for the corporation's political ideas." *Austin v. Michigan* (1990).

Nor was there sufficient evidence that independent expenditures made by corporations, gives rise to corruption or the appearance of corruption. Justice Kennedy reasoned that *Buckley* had relied on quid pro quo corruption; greater influence and increased access, on the other hand, does not make officials corrupt. There was no evidence that independent spending—not coordinated with the candidate—fosters corruption.

Justice Stevens, joined by Justices Ginsburg, Breyer, and Sotomayor, dissenting, argued that the majority violated principles of *stare decisis* by abandoning the *Austin* and *McConnell* precedent. Congress and the courts had accepted legislative restrictions on corporate spending dating back to 1907 because of a "recurrent need to regulate corporate participation in elections to preserve the integrity of the electoral process, prevent corruption, and protect the expressive interests of the shareholders." Justice Stevens argued further that the majority misconstrued the statute as an absolute ban on corporate political speech when in reality it only banned certain forms of political speech and left open many other avenues for corporations to engage in political speech, e.g. Political Action Committees (PACs) and segregated funds established by a corporation for political purposes. The dissent characterized the majority's approach as a claim that the only sufficiently important government interest in preventing corruption is limited to *quid pro quo* corruption, e.g., bribing a government official to get preferential treatment. Justice Stevens argued that corruption operates on a spectrum. But even from the quid pro quo perspective, "many independent corporate expenditures had become essentially interchangeable with direct contributions in their capacity to generate *quid pro quo* arrangements." The dissent concluded that corporations are not natural persons and have characteristics that distinguish their participation in the democratic process which were developed in *Austin* and *McConnell. Citizens United v. Federal Election Commission* (2010).

b. Ballot Referenda

Limitations on contributions in ballot referenda disputes are generally invalid. State interests supporting such laws are inadequate to satisfy the exacting scrutiny applicable to such significant restrictions on freedom of association and freedom of expression.

Example: A city ordinance placing a limitation of $250 on contributions by persons to committees formed to support or oppose a ballot referendum on rent control violates freedom of expression and association. A restriction on contributions to groups burdens freedom of association and is subject to "exacting scrutiny." The restriction also operates to significantly affect expenditures and thus restrains freedom of expression. The exception recognized in *Buckley* based on the public interest in preventing corruption of officials does not apply to ballot referenda campaigns. *Citizens Against Rent Control/Coalition for Fair Housing v. City of Berkeley* (1981).

c. Disclaimer and Disclosure Requirements

Disclaimer and disclosure requirements are subject to "exacting scrutiny" which requires a substantial relation between the requirement and a "sufficiently important governmental interest." They are upheld if narrowly drawn to inform the public about sources of election-related spending or help to implement contribution limitations. *Buckley v. Valeo* (1976); *Citizens United v. FEC* (2010). They are invalid if there is a showing that disclosure will subject the party to threats, harassment, or reprisals from either government officials or private parties; or a showing of chill and harassment of associational rights. *Citizens United v. FEC* (2010); *NAACP v. Alabama ex rel. Patterson* (1958).

E. Speech in the Local Forum

Government has legitimate interests in protecting against harm from violence and disorder and generally in preventing illegal conduct. Abusive and offensive conduct directed at individuals and groups can produce emotional harm and impede our Nation's policy commitment to combating discrimination and to equality values. Nevertheless, the Court has recognized our "profound national commitment to the principle that debate on public issues shall be uninhibited, robust, and wide open * * *." *New York Times v. Sullivan (1964). When government regulates for the purpose of preventing harms associated with a speaker's message, i.e., content-based regulation, the law is presumptively invalid. Government must establish that the law satisfies a stringent standard of review, e.g., strict scrutiny, or that the regulated speech falls into a category of unprotected or low value speech.*

Government also regulates speech in the local forum for content-neutral reasons. There are legitimate governmental concerns over competing uses of public places, preventing littering, protecting privacy interests, and controlling against visual blight. Nevertheless, such government regulation can incidentally and significantly burden freedom of expression. *In reviewing such regulations, courts determine if the regulation is reasonable using a balancing test. The governmental interest is weighed against the First Amendment right. Balancing analysis is often criticized for ignoring the societal interest in preserving First Amendment values.*

1. Controlling Speech Content

a. The Clear and Present Danger Test

Advocacy of the idea of illegal conduct, without more, is constitutionally protected. Only "where such advocacy is directed to inciting or producing imminent lawless action and is likely to incite or produce such actions," may the speech be suppressed because of its content. Brandenburg v. Ohio (1969).

1) The Early Formulation

   a) In its most influential formulation, the clear and present danger doctrine was defined as follows: a restraint on the rights to free speech and assembly because of the threat of illegal conduct is permissible only if there actually exists an imminent and probable danger and an apprehended evil so substantial as to justify the governmental restraint. The focus was on the proximity and degree of the danger of illegal conduct under the circumstances existing at the time of the speech.

   b) The clear and present danger test provides that where the threatened danger is serious, likely, and imminent, the State, in such emergency circumstances, will be permitted to do what in normal circumstances it is not permitted to do, *i.e.,* restrain expression because of its content. The reason such restraint is permitted is because it is concluded there is insufficient time to permit full and free discussion to achieve its normally curative function. As Mr. Justice Brandeis expressed it: "Only an emergency can justify repression."

c) A *legislative* judgment that the danger is too immediate and too serious to permit the normal reliance on free discussion is not conclusive even if it is reasonable. The *court* must conclude that a particular restraint is justified because of the danger. *Whitney v. California* (1927) (concurring opinion of Mr. Justice Brandeis).

d) Judge Learned Hand in *Masses Publishing Co. v. Patten* (1917), offered an alternative to clear and present danger doctrine's focus on the factual circumstances. Hand argued that only urging others to act illegally, *i.e.*, incitement, could be punished consistent with the First Amendment. Such incitement was not within the guarantee of the freedom of speech. In modern terms, incitement of illegal conduct is categorically excluded from the First Amendment. The focus is on the nature of the speech, not the circumstances.

2) **The Doctrine Distorted**

In 1951, in a famous Smith Act case, the Supreme Court appeared to discount the importance of the criterion of time as an integral part of the clear and present danger doctrine and thereby removed an essential feature of the test designed to afford extensive protection to free expression. The clear and present danger doctrine, said the Court, does not mean that the governmental restraint on expression is prohibited "until the putsch is about to be executed." The contention was rejected that success or probability of success is the criterion. Instead, "[i]n each case, [courts] must ask whether the gravity of the 'evil,' discounted by its improbability, justified such invasion of speech as is necessary to avoid the danger." *Dennis v. United States* (1951).

3) **Advocacy v. Incitement**

Later the Court retreated from the *Dennis* holding and declared that *Dennis* was only intended to uphold restriction on advocacy of unlawful action, *i.e.*, incitement, and was not intended to restrict advocacy of abstract doctrine. *Yates v. United States* (1957). Although the *Yates* Court did not directly address the constitutional issue, *Yates* has been understood to impliedly repudiate the *Dennis* revision of clear and present danger.

4) **The Modern Test: Incitement and Danger**

a) *The modern formulation of the clear and present danger test focuses on both the nature of the speech and the danger it presents. First, only intentional incitement of unlawful conduct, not advocacy of abstract doctrine, can be punished. Second, only incitement to "imminent lawless action" which is "likely to incite or produce such actions," may be reached.* Brandenburg v. Ohio *(1969).*

Examples: (1) Julian Bond had been excluded from the Georgia legislature because he signed a statement of sympathy for draft resisters to the Vietnam War. The Court held that the exclusion violated the First Amendment because Bond had not urged draft resistance but had simply advocated opposition to the war. *Bond v. Floyd* (1966).

(2) Watts, a black activist who said in a speech to a small crowd—"If they ever make me carry a rifle, the first man I want to get in my sights is L.B.J. They are not going to make me kill my black brothers"—was convicted of intentionally threatening to kill the President. The Court reversed the conviction, reasoning that Watts had not made a true threat but had merely used political hyperbole. *Watts v. United States* (1969).

(3) Brandenburg, a KKK leader, said at a rally—"We're not a revengent organization, but if our President, our Congress, our Supreme Court, continues to suppress the white, Caucasian race, its possible that there might have to be some revengence taken." The Court overturned his conviction under the Ohio Syndicalism law, overruling *Whitney*. Only "where such advocacy is directed to inciting or producing imminent lawless action and is likely to incite or produce such action," can such speech be proscribed. The syndicalism law failed to draw this distinction and therefore, is unconstitutional. *Brandenburg v. Ohio* (1969).

b) Some commentators argue that the clear and present danger test is a form of weighted interest balancing using the rubrics of a formula. Others argue that it is a category of speech that is unprotected by the First Amendment. Incitement is often referred to separately by courts as a form of speech categorically excluded from First Amendment protection.

Examples: (1) The state may not punish an individual for wearing a leather jacket bearing the words "Fuck the Draft" in a courthouse for breach of the peace. Absent a showing of an intent to incite illegal conduct, *i.e.*, not mere advocacy, an individual cannot be punished for the content of his speech. Nor did any of the categorical exclusions permitting regulation based on speech content apply. *Cohen v. California* (1971).

(2) An antiwar demonstrator could not be convicted for using words such as "we'll take the fucking street later." At worst, this amounted to nothing more than advocacy of illegal action at some future time. There was no showing that the defendant's words "were intended to produce, and likely to produce, *imminent* disorder." *Hess v. Indiana* (1973).

(3) A speech by NAACP leader Charles Evers warning of "discipline" against blacks violating an economic boycott of white merchants was protected speech. While constituting "strong language," Evers' speech did not authorize, ratify, or directly threaten acts of violence. He did not engage in advocacy directed at inciting or producing imminent lawless action. No contemporaneous violence in fact ensued. Since Evers engaged only in protected expression, neither he nor the NAACP could be held liable for the lost earnings of white merchants in a state court action. *NAACP v. Claiborne Hardware Co.* (1982).

(4) A federal statute prohibiting giving "material support or resources" to foreign terrorist groups even where such advocacy is to promote only the lawful, nonviolent purposes of foreign terrorist groups was held constitutional where the advocacy was "coordinated or under the direction of

the foreign terrorist group" and where the support was determined to be fungible with other resources. *Holder v. Humanitarian Law Project* (2010). See Ch. VIII, A, 3, a.

b. The Fighting Words Doctrine

Government can impose content-based regulation when the speech constitutes fighting words—"[words] which by their very utterance inflict injury or tend to incite an immediate breach of the peace." Chaplinsky v. New Hampshire (1942). *The Court indicated: "The test is what men of common intelligence would understand would be words likely to cause an average addressee to fight."* Chaplinsky. *Fighting words includes personally abusive epithets, which are "inherently likely to provoke violent reaction."* Cohen v. California *(1971).* Government has the power to punish the use of fighting words under carefully drawn statutes not susceptible of application to protected expression.

1) Rationale

The fighting words doctrine is based on the theory that fighting words are of such slight value as a step to truth as not to merit First Amendment protection. The focus is on the nature of the speech rather than on the context. It has been said that such a form of speech is categorically excluded from First Amendment protection. While the doctrine originally was limited to face to face verbal encounters that are likely to produce a violent reaction from a reasonable person, it has increasingly been merged into the modern clear and present danger doctrine requiring incitement threatening imminent lawless action.

2) Overbreadth and Vagueness

The Court has provided little guidance on what words constitute fighting words. Instead, it has tended to hold that the statute in question is not limited to fighting words, and therefore is overbroad or is so unclear as to be vague. Such laws are facially unconstitutional regardless of their application in the particular case.

Examples: (1) A Jehovah's Witness who called the City Marshal a "Goddamned racketeer" and a "damned fascist" could be validly prosecuted under a state statute which had received a narrowing construction from the state supreme court limited to punishing only those words which had a "direct tendency to cause acts of violence by the persons to whom individually the remark is addressed." *Chaplinsky v. New Hampshire* (1942).

(2) Use of the words "Fuck the Draft" on the back of a jacket worn in the courthouse does not constitute fighting words. The words were not directed to a particular person and no one present could reasonably regard the words as a direct personal insult. Nor was there any showing that anyone was in fact violently aroused. *Cohen v. California* (1971).

(3) A state statute punishing the use of "opprobrious words or abusive language, tending to cause a breach of the peace" is unconstitutional. The law had not been construed by the state courts as limited to fighting words but had been read broadly to punish offensive language. *Gooding v. Wilson* (1972).

(4) An individual was prosecuted for saying to a police officer acting in the performance of his duties: "[Y]ou god damn m.f. police * * *." A narrowing construction by a state supreme court attempting to validate the statute under which the prosecution was brought making it unlawful "to curse or revile or to use obscene or opprobrious language" to a police officer fails where the state supreme court's construction is not limited to "fighting words" but extends to "words conveying or intending to convey disgrace." A statute so construed is constitutionally overbroad and facially invalid. *Lewis v. New Orleans* (1974).

(5) A municipal ordinance making it unlawful to intentionally "oppose, molest, abuse or interrupt any policeman in the execution of his duties" is unconstitutionally overbroad under the First Amendment. Although city officials argued that the law dealt only with "core criminal conduct" and was content-neutral, the Court found that the ordinance also outlawed a substantial amount of constitutionally protected speech. It was not narrowly tailored to reach only fighting words nor was it limited to situations presenting a

clear and present danger of disorderly conduct. The law accorded police unconstitutional discretion in enforcement. The Court suggested that the fighting words exception is narrower where police officers are involved, since they may be reasonably expected to exercise restraint in the face of such verbal challenges. *Houston v. Hill* (1987).

3) "Protected" Fighting Words

a) Even if a law regulates fighting words, if it discriminates on the basis of subject matter or viewpoint to create subcategories of fighting words, government must demonstrate that the discrimination is necessary to a compelling government interest. Fighting words may not "be made the vehicles for content discrimination unrelated to their distinctively proscribable character." *R.A.V. v. City of St. Paul* (1992).

b) However, when the content-discrimination in a proscribable category of speech does not create the possibility that government is seeking to drive certain ideas or viewpoints from the marketplace, strict scrutiny does not apply. First, "[W]hen the basis for the content discrimination consists entirely of the very reason the entire class of speech at issue is proscribable, no significant danger of idea or viewpoint discrimination exists." For example, proscribable threats of violence have special force when directed against the President. Second, if the subclass is associated with particular "secondary effects" so that the different treatment is justified without reference to speech content, strict scrutiny is not needed. For example, the Title VII prohibition against sexual discrimination in employment practices may be applied against sexually derogatory fighting words.

Example: A city ordinance, interpreted to prohibit fighting words that insult or provoke violence "on the basis of race, color, creed, religion or gender," is facially unconstitutional. Since other fighting words are not proscribed, the law imposes a content-based discrimination. The city failed to show that the proscribed fighting words communicate ideas in an especially threatening or offensive manner. The city's interest in protecting against victimization of especially vulnerable persons or groups is not a "secondary effect" since it is based on listeners' reactions to the speech.

The law does not survive strict scrutiny. The city has a compelling interest in ensuring the basic human rights of members of groups historically subject to discrimination. But the law is not "necessary" to achieve this interest since there are adequate content-neutral alternatives. All fighting words could be proscribed. Four concurring justices argued that requiring a wider category of speech be banned "appears to be a general renunciation of strict scrutiny review, a fundamental tool of First Amendment analysis." The concurring justices would have held the law overbroad since it criminalized conduct "that causes only hurt feelings, offense, or resentment." *R.A.V. v. City of St. Paul (1992).*

c. **Hostile Audiences**

1) *If the source of impending violence is a crowd of listeners hostile to the speaker's lawful message, the police usually must proceed against the crowd and protect the speaker.* Gregory v. Chicago *(1969).* The First Amendment protects speech even if it "induces a condition of unrest, creates dissatisfaction with conditions as they are, or even stirs people to anger." *Terminiello v. Chicago* (1949).

2) There is precedent, never overruled, that if the threatened disruption is due to the speaker's own intentional provocation, then the speaker can be punished under narrowly drawn laws proscribing incitement to likely, imminent lawless action. *Feiner v. New York* (1951). But the Court's response to civil rights demonstrations raises question on the scope of *Feiner.* Generalized fears of possible disorder do not justify police in stopping the demonstrators. *Edwards v. South Carolina* (1963); *Cox v. Louisiana* (1965).

d. **Offensive and Abusive Language**

1) In *Chaplinsky v. New Hampshire* (1942), the Court indicated that insulting or abusive language constituted fighting words—words

which by their very utterance inflict an injury (*i.e.,* verbal assault). This part of the original fighting words doctrine has been largely repudiated by the Court. As the concurring justices stated in *R.A.V. v. St. Paul* (1992): "The mere fact that expressive activity causes hurt feelings, offense, or resentment does not render the expression unprotected."

2) Government has no power to punish the use of words that are merely offensive, abusive, profane, or vulgar. Even abusive offensive dialogue can contribute to the marketplace of ideas. Government efforts to control such expression generally lack ascertainable standards. Further, often the emotive force of particular words is of equal or greater importance than their cognitive value. Finally, in suppressing offensive speech there is a substantial risk that ideas will also be suppressed.

Example: A defendant cannot be constitutionally convicted for wearing a jacket bearing the words "Fuck the Draft" in a county courthouse. Absent a particularized and compelling justification, the government cannot punish the use of offensive expletives. *Cohen v. California* (1971).

3) The First Amendment is violated if civil liability is imposed where the regulated speech is of "public concern, as determined by all the circumstances of the case." Such speech "is entitled to 'special protection' under the First Amendment" and cannot be prohibited simply because the idea is offensive or disagreeable. *Snyder v. Phelps* (2011).

Example: Members of the Westboro Baptist Church protested at the military funeral of Matthew Snyder, a Marine killed in Iraq. Reflecting the Church's view that the U.S. is overly tolerant of the sin of homosexuality and that God kills soldiers as punishment, they carried signs saying: "Thank God for Dead Soldiers," "God Hates You," "God Hates America," "Semper fi Fags," "Priests Rape Boys," and "You're Going to Hell." The Church notified authorities in advance and followed instructions in staging the protest 1000 feet from the funeral. The protest was peaceful and was on public land, out of sight of those at the funeral. Matthew Snyder's father sued on five tort claims, including intentional inflection of emotional distress. The jury awarded millions of dollars to Snyder.

The Supreme Court, per Chief Justice Roberts, 8–1, held that because Westboro's speech was on "matters of public concern," rather than on "matters of purely private concern," the First Amendment barred Snyder from recovery. Speech on matters of public concern includes speech "on subjects of 'general interest and of value and concern to the public.'" Whether speech is of public concern, is "determined by all the circumstances of the case;" the court examines the "content, form, and context of the speech . . . including what was said, where it was said, and how it is said."

Applying these standards to the Westboro speech, "the overall thrust and dominant theme" of the speech related "to broad issues of interest to society at large." The fact that the speech was connected to a funeral "cannot by itself transform the nature of Westboro's speech." The demonstration was on public land, next to a public street. This protest was one of many similar church protests held nationwide; there was nothing indicating that Westboro's speech on public matters was intended to mask an attack on Snyder on a private matter. "Given that Westboro's speech was at a public place on a matter of public concern, that speech is entitled to 'special protection' under the First Amendment." The fact that society finds that the speech is "upsetting or arouses contempt," that it is "offensive or disagreeable," or that the jury determines that the picketing is "outrageous" does not overcome this special First Amendment protection. Westboro's picketing is subject to reasonable content-neutral time, place or manner regulation; but in this case any distress turned on "the content and viewpoint of the message conveyed," rather than any interference with the funeral.

Justice Alito, writing as the sole dissenter, argued that the speech of the protestors went "far beyond commentary on matters of public concern," and became a personal attack on the family of the deceased. Such speech should not be protected solely because it touches on both private and public matters. *Snyder v. Phelps* (2011).

e. True Threats

1) The First Amendment permits a State to ban a "true threat" since it is a category of speech "subject to regulation consistent with the Constitution." *Virginia v. Black* (2003).

2) "True threats" include "those statements where the speaker means to communicate a serious expression of an intent to commit an act of unlawful violence to a particular individual or group of individuals. See *Watts v. United States* ('political hyperbole' is not a true threat). . . . Intimidation in the constitutionally proscribable sense of the word is a type of true threat." *Virginia v. Black* (2003).

3) True threats are constitutionally proscribable because their prohibition "protects individuals from the fear of violence" and from the "disruption that fear engenders" and protects people "from the possibility that the threatened violence will occur." *R.A.V. v. City of St. Paul* (1992).

   Example: The portion of a Virginia statute making it a felony to burn a cross on another person's property "with the intent of intimidating any person or group of persons" is constitutional because it proscribes symbolic speech that falls within the unprotected category of "true threats." Although the law did discriminate on the basis of content, it did not violate *R.A.V. v. City of St. Paul* (1992) because, in spite of the strong association of cross-burning with racist intimidation, the statute did not "single out for opprobrium only that speech directed toward [that] disfavored [topic]." The statute fell within one of the exceptions laid out in *R.A.V.* because "the basis for the content discrimination consist[ed] entirely of the very reason the entire class of speech at issue [was] proscribable." Cross burnings, when done with an intent to intimidate, are "a particularly virulent form of intimidation." They are a form of intimidation that is most likely to inspire the fear of impending violence. Virginia could "choose to regulate this subset of intimidating messages in light of cross burning's long and pernicious history as a signal of impending violence."

But because a provision of the Virginia statute made the burning of a cross prima facie evidence of an intent "to intimidate a person or group of persons," the statute was held to be unconstitutional on its face. As interpreted by the state courts, the provision made the burning of a cross, by itself, sufficient evidence from which a jury could infer the required intent. But this ignored all the contextual factors needed to decide whether a particular cross burning is intended to intimidate, or instead is a protected statement of ideology or group solidarity. As interpreted, the provision chilled constitutionally protected political speech by increasing the possibility of prosecution and conviction. *Virginia v. Black* (2003).

f. Equal Protection as a First Amendment Doctrine

Discrimination regarding the speech allowed in the public forum generally involves content-based distinctions. The Court subjects such content-based controls to strict scrutiny and demands substantial justification for discriminatory treatment which significantly burdens the fundamental rights of freedom of expression. Both the First Amendment and the Equal Protection Clause are used.

Example: A state statute barring all residential picketing except for labor disputes is unconstitutional. "When government regulation discriminates among speech-related activities in a public forum the Equal Protection Clause mandates that the legislation be finely tailored to serve substantial state interests, and the justifications offered for any distinctions it draws must be carefully scrutinized." The ban on non-labor picketing was not narrowly tailored to promote privacy in the home. *Carey v. Brown* (1980).

g. Hate Speech

1) Some states, localities, and public colleges have enacted laws or codes prohibiting expression that incites hatred of, or which is

insulting or derogatory towards, traditionally vulnerable groups—racial minorities, women, ethnic or religious groups, homosexuals. It is argued that such speech inflicts emotional harm, promotes discrimination and violence and has the effect of silencing the speech of its victims. While it does not meaningfully promote First Amendment values, it undermines the values of the Equal Protection Clause.

But apart from the context of threatened violence, *Cohen v. California*, *R.A.V.* and the First Amendment principles discussed above raise serious doubts about the constitutionality of such laws. Lower courts have found such laws and codes constitute content-based regulations violative of the First Amendment protection afforded offensive and abusive speech.

2) However, laws which punish racially motivated harmful conduct or which enhance the penalty for crimes when inspired by racial bias are consistent with the First Amendment. The racial bias motive must be established beyond a reasonable doubt. *Apprendi v. New Jersey* (2000).

Example: A state statute which enhanced the sentence of a black defendant who beat a white boy from two to seven years because the victim was selected on the basis of race is constitutional. Such enhancement does not violate the First Amendment protection afforded thought and beliefs. "[W]hereas the ordinance struck down in *R.A.V.* was explicitly directed at expression (i.e., 'speech' or 'message'), the statute in this case is aimed at conduct unprotected by the First Amendment." Bias-inspired crime may be singled out because it "is thought to inflict greater individual and societal harm." The claim that penalty enhancement might cause an individual to avoid bigoted, offensive speech is "too speculative to support an overbreadth claim." Finally there is no First Amendment barrier against the "evidentiary use of speech" in order to prove the elements of a crime. *Wisconsin v. Mitchell* (1993).

2. Regulating Public Property

In *Hague v. C.I.O.* (1939), the Court established that the use of streets and public places for expressive purposes has traditionally "been a part of the privileges, immunities, rights, and liberties of citizens." From this principle, there developed the concept of the "public forum" available to the citizen for expressive activity. As indicated above, this First Amendment *right of access* to public property has been complemented by the First Amendment equal protection concept of the *right of equal access*. But even the public forum is subject to a Robert's Rules of Order to reconcile competing uses of the forum. Further, not all government controlled property is part of the public forum available for First Amendment activity. The Court has rejected the claim that "people who want to propagandize protests or views have a constitutional right to do so whenever and however and wherever they please." *Adderley v. Florida* (1966).

If the government regulates speech in the "traditional" or "designated" public forum, regulation based on speech content must fall into a category of low-value speech or be justified using strict scrutiny. Burson v. Freeman (1992). *Content-neutral regulation of the traditional or designated public forum is constitutional if the law is narrowly-tailored to serve a "significant governmental interest," and leaves open ample alternative channels for communication of the information.* Heffron v. International Society for Krishna Consciousness (1981). *If public property is determined to be a limited or non-public forum, the government regulation may be based on speech content or the identity of the speaker but may not discriminate on the basis of viewpoint and must be reasonable.* Perry Educ. Assn. v. Perry Local Educators' Assn. (1983).

a.   The Nature of the Forum

The Court presently adopts a formalistic, categorical approach in designating the nature of a forum. A sharp distinction is drawn between the regulatory and proprietary roles of government. "Where the government is acting as a proprietor, managing its internal operations rather than acting as a lawmaker with the power to regulate or license, its action will not be subjected to the heightened review to which its actions as a lawmaker may be subject." *International Society for Krishna Consciousness, Inc. v. Lee* (1992).

A minority position rejects the categorical approach and its strict doctrinal line between government's proprietary and regulatory functions. Emphasis is placed on the need for citizens to be able to gather and speak in public places. The categorical approach is viewed as giving government almost unlimited authority to restrict speech on its property and as leaving inadequate opportunity for development of new public forums. The alternative view would adopt a different standard for identifying a public forum: "If the objective, physical characteristics of the property at issue and the actual public access and uses which have been permitted by the government indicate that expressive activity would be appropriate and compatible with those uses, the property is a public forum." *Lee* (Kennedy, J., concurring in the judgement).

1) Traditional Public Forum

   A traditional public forum is public property that has historically had as "a principal purpose the free exchange of ideas." Cornelius v. NAACP Legal Defense & Education Fund (1985). Government may not bar all communicative activity from the "quintessential" public forum, *e.g.*, streets and parks. Such places have historically been associated with expressive activity. *Hague v. CIO* (1939). They are a natural and proper place for disseminating information. *Schneider v. New Jersey* (1939).

   Examples: (1) Civil rights demonstrators who clapped, spoke, and sang but were otherwise peaceful may not be validly prosecuted for conducting a protest on traditionally public state capitol grounds. The state statute upon which the prosecution is based is so broad and all embracing as to jeopardize speech, press, assembly, and petition. *Edwards v. South Carolina* (1963).

   (2) A law barring all picketing and leafleting on the public sidewalks surrounding the Supreme Court is unconstitutional. Such a broad prohibition of "public forum property" does not narrowly serve the public interests in protecting persons and property or maintaining proper order and decorum. *United States v. Grace* (1983).

2) Designated Public Forum

   a) In a number of early cases, the public forum was held to include other public property where expressive activity was not incompatible with the normal use to which the property is put.

      Example: The First Amendment protects civil rights protesters engaged in a peaceful protest against segregation in a segregated public library from prosecution under a breach of peace statute. A reasonable, orderly, and limited exercise of First Amendment rights even in a public library is permissible. *Brown v. Louisiana* (1966).

b) Increasingly, whether a public forum exists is determined by government intent to open the property for expressive activity. When the government *designates* property as a public forum, it is subject to the same standard of review as applies to a traditional public forum. However, government may withdraw the place from public forum designation. Government does not create a public forum by inaction. It must be shown that the practice and policy of the government indicate an intent to open a nontraditional forum for general public discourse. *Cornelius v. NAACP Legal Defense & Education Fund* (1985). If the government excludes speakers who are within the class to which a designated public forum is made generally available, its action is subject to strict scrutiny.

Examples: (1) A state rule limiting the sale or distribution of goods and materials at a state fair to fixed locations, applied to prevent Krishnas from personal solicitation, is constitutional. State fairgrounds constitute a limited public forum. The fixed location rule is content-neutral and is narrowly-tailored to further the important state interest in traffic control on the crowded fairgrounds. Alternative forums such as speech at the fixed locations or personal contact off the fairgrounds, are available. *Heffron v. International Society for Krishna Consciousness* (1981).

(2) A university which has created a forum generally open for use by student groups violates the First Amendment freedom of speech and association when it discriminates in use of its facilities by denying access "for purposes of religious worship or religious teaching." In order to justify such discrimination in access to the public forum based on the religious content of the group's intended speech, the university must show "that its regulation is necessary to serve a compelling

state interest and that it is narrowly drawn to achieve that end." The university policy is not justified by the desire to maintain separation of church and state mandated by the state and federal constitutions. *Widmar v. Vincent* (1981). See Ch. IX, A, 1, d.

3) Limited or Nonpublic Forums

a) Public property which is not by tradition or designation a forum for public communication constitutes a limited or nonpublic forum. *Regulation of access to such property need only be viewpoint-neutral and reasonable.* Reasonableness has been marked by judicial deference to government, akin to a rationality test. But viewpoint neutrality is required: "the government must abstain from regulating speech when the specific motivating ideology or the opinion or perspective of the speaker is the rationale for the restriction." *Rosenberger v. University of Virginia* (1995). See Ch. VIII, J, 3.

b) The sole fact that particular property is owned by the government does not make it part of the public forum. Certain publicly-owned places are inappropriate for any assembly or protest. "The State, no less than a private owner of property, has power to preserve the property under its control for the use to which it is lawfully dedicated." *Adderley v. Florida* (1966). Military bases, jails or prisons, rapid-transit cars, and mail boxes have been placed in this category.

c) *General v. Selective Access.* A designated public forum is not created when the government grants only *selective* access for individual speakers rather than general access for a class of speakers. When the government grants eligibility for access to the forum to a particular class of speakers, whose members must then, as individuals, obtain permission to enter, only a *limited public forum* exists. *Cornelius v. NAACP Legal Defense & Educ. Fund, Inc.* (1985); *Arkansas Educational Television Commission v. Forbes* (1998).

Examples: (1) A number of students who were engaged in a demonstration at the county jail to protest the arrest on the day previous of other student civil rights demonstrators were validly convicted of trespass because not all public property is amenable to the exercise of First Amendment rights. While public property such as state capitol grounds may be open to the public, jails, built for security purposes, are not. *Adderley v. Florida* (1966).

(2) A school district's grant of exclusive access to the interschool mail system and teacher mailboxes to the bargaining representative for the district's school teachers does not violate the First Amendment rights of a rival teacher group. School mail facilities are not by tradition or designation a public forum. They are not open to the general public or to other groups similar to a teacher's union. There was no evidence that the school district sought to discourage one viewpoint and advance another. Since use of the mail facilities allows the exclusive bargaining representative to perform effectively its obligations to all school district teachers, the differential access is reasonable. Substantial alternative channels of union-teacher communication remain open to the rival union. Equal protection cases requiring equal access apply only if there is a public forum. *Perry Educ. Assn. v. Perry Local Educators' Assn.* (1983).

(3) A regulation prohibiting solicitation and receipt of funds in airport terminals managed by the Port Authority of New York and New Jersey is constitutional. Airports are not traditional public fora. "[T]he tradition of airport activity does not demonstrate that airports have historically been made available for speech activity." The principal purpose of airports is facilitating passenger air travel, not "promoting the exchange of ideas." Nor are the airport terminals designated public fora intentionally opened to speech activity—"the frequent and continuing litigation evidencing the operators' objections belies any such claim." The solicitation rule is a reasonable content-neutral

regulation given the disruptive effect of solicitation on the normal flow of traffic, and the potential for fraud and duress of harried travelers.

Justice Kennedy, joined by three other Justices, argued that airport terminals are public fora. Airports share physical similarities with other public fora. Based on experience, time, place and manner regulation can assure that "expressive activity is quite compatible with the uses of major airports." While Justice Kennedy concurred that the ban on solicitation and receipt of funds is a content-neutral regulation of the public forum, the other justices dissented, arguing that the solicitation ban is not narrowly-tailored. *International Society for Krishna Consciousness, Inc. v. Lee* (1992).

(4) A public television broadcaster's exclusion of an independent candidate from a debate does not violate the First Amendment. Public broadcasters have First Amendment obligations and candidate debates are an exception to the general rule that public television is not normally subject to analysis under the forum doctrine. The debate is a nonpublic forum, rather than a designated public forum. The government creates a designated public forum only by purposeful action opening property to general public access and not by simply granting access to selected speakers. The broadcaster created a limited public forum by restricting eligibility to candidates for a specific congressional seat and making candidate-by-candidate determinations based on viability and public support. This was selective, not general, access. Requiring that all qualified candidates be allowed to participate might well deter broadcasters from sponsoring debates given the limited time available. The candidate's exclusion was based on his lack of public support rather than his viewpoint and, given time constraints, was a reasonable

exercise of discretion consistent with the First Amendment. *Arkansas Educational Television Commission v. Forbes* (1998).

(5) The Court applied its limited public-forum precedent in holding that a public law school could condition official recognition of a student group (along with the school funds and other benefits that accompany such recognition) on the student group's agreement to open membership and leadership eligibility to all students. The University of California Hastings College of Law has an "all-comers" policy which requires all groups seeking to become a Registered Student Organization (RSO) to accept all students regardless of their status or beliefs. The Christian Legal Society (CLS), which was denied RSO status because it discriminated on the basis of religion and sexual orientation, challenged the constitutionality of denying it RSO status.

The Court, 5–4, per Justice Ginsburg, held that the Hasting's "all-comers" policy was reasonable and viewpoint-neutral. The policy did not violate freedom of speech, expressive association, or the Free Exercise Clause. In finding that the policy was reasonable, the Court accorded the College "due decent respect" given its expertise and experience. Justice Ginsburg reasoned that the "all-comers" policy "insures that the leadership, educational, and social opportunities afforded by [RSOs] are available to all students." Further, it supports the school's nondiscrimination policy. And, by bringing together individuals with diverse backgrounds and beliefs, it encourages learning among students. The Court also noted the availability of substantial alternative channels of communication available to CLS. The burden was only incidental; CLS could use the school's facilities and define its membership as it wished if it chose not to seek RSO status. The majority also held that the policy was viewpoint neutral: "It is, after all, hard to imagine a more viewpoint-neutral policy than one requiring *all* student groups to accept *all* comers. No group is singled out because of its point of view; no discrimination is based on speech content."

Justice Alito, joined by the Chief Justice and Justices Scalia and Thomas, dissenting, argued that, as applied, the Hastings policy permitted "expressive association" for student groups except "groups that formed to express a religious message." "Forced inclusion" in CLS of students whose status or beliefs violated the group's beliefs amounted to a violation of its right of "expressive association." Because it was applied only to religious groups, applications of the policy amounted to viewpoint discrimination. *Christian Legal Society v. Martinez* (2010).

4) Privately–Owned Property

   a) Only when privately-owned property has taken on all of the attributes of publicly-owned property can it be labeled part of the public forum.

   b) Generally, political protest on privately-owned property, such as shopping centers, is not privileged under the First Amendment. Trespass statutes may be constitutionally used to restrain even peaceful hand-billing or demonstrations.

   Examples: (1) Arrest of a Jehovah's Witness under a trespass law for distributing literature in a privately-owned company town violated freedom of speech. The property in this instance had acquired all of the attributes of a municipal area. *Marsh v. Alabama* (1946).

   (2) A privately-owned shopping center may prohibit, consistent with the First Amendment, picketing on its property, even though the picketing is related to a labor dispute between the picketers

and one of the lessees of the shopping center. The content of the picketing cannot render private property the functional equivalent of a municipality. Even a municipality could not discriminate in the regulation of expression on the basis of the content of that expression. If there is no First Amendment right to go on private property with respect to matters unrelated to the site of the protest, there is also no First Amendment right to go on private property with respect to a matter related to the site of the protest. *Hudgens v. NLRB* (1976).

b. The Demand for Reasonable Regulation

1) The *O'Brien* Standards

The Court sometimes employs the *O'Brien* standards in reviewing regulations of the local forum. This is essentially the same standard applied to content-neutral regulation in public forum cases.

> *Example:* A law prohibiting the posting of signs on public property (utility poles) does not unconstitutionally abridge freedom of speech. Citing *O'Brien*, the Court concluded that the law is a reasonable regulation of the manner of communication closely tailored to serve the government's interest in improving the appearance of the city. The law is content-neutral and there are alternative channels of effective communication available. The mere fact that the government property could be used as a vehicle for communication does not mean the Constitution requires such uses to be permitted. Appellee failed to demonstrate the existence of a traditional right of access to utility poles for communication purposes nor had they been designated for such use. *Members of City Council of City of Los Angeles v. Taxpayers for Vincent* (1984).

2) Determining Reasonableness

When government regulates speech in the public forum, any time, place and manner control must be clear and precise. *The regulation must be justified without reference to the content of the speech.* Content-neutrality is not lost simply because a regulation incidentally burdens some speakers more than others. *Renton v. Playtime Theatres, Inc.* (1986). *Regulation of the public forum must be narrowly drawn to further a substantial government interest but need not be the least-restrictive or least-intrusive means of achieving the interest. It is sufficient if the government interest would be achieved less effectively absent the regulation.* Ward v. Rock Against Racism *(1989).* As the public forum cases indicate, this is essentially a matter of interest balancing.

Examples: (1) Two hundred protesters who conducted a protest one hundred feet from a high school, complaining that the principal had failed to redress the grievances of black students were declared to have been validly convicted pursuant to an "antinoise" ordinance directed to protecting schools. The ordinance was upheld because it was not a vague breach of the peace ordinance but a specific statute limited to protest during school hours. The same expressive conduct which may be constitutionally protected at other places or other times, may, when conducted next to a school while classes are in session, be validly prohibited. *Grayned v. Rockford* (1972).

(2) A Port Authority regulation prohibiting the sale and distribution of written or printed materials in airport terminals preventing Krishnas from disseminating literature, is unconstitutional. Four justices, using public forum analysis, concluded that the almost total prohibition was not drawn in narrow terms and did not leave open ample alternative channels of communication. Problems of congestion could be addressed through narrow restrictions on the time and place of expressive activity. Justice O'Connor, applying nonpublic forum standards, concluded that the rule was unreasonable. Peaceful pamphleteering is not "incompatible with the multipurpose environment of the Port Authority airports." The record did not justify a total ban of the expressive activity. *Lee v. International Society for Krishna Consciousness, Inc.* (1992).

a) Speech Plus

The fact that assembly and protest involves picketing, handbilling, or solicitation of funds does not deprive the conduct of First Amendment protection. *However, the Court frequently has suggested that when expression takes the form of "speech plus conduct," it is not entitled to the same degree of protection as "pure speech."*

Examples: (1) A statute prohibiting willful obstruction of public passages, used to convict chanting, picketing, marching black protesters on the sidewalks across the street from the jailhouse, was held vague and overbroad. But the Court rejected the proposition "that the First and Fourteenth Amendments afford the same kind of freedom to those who would communicate ideas by conduct such as patrolling, marching, and picketing * * * as these amendments afford to those who communicate ideas by pure speech." *Cox v. Louisiana* (1965).

(2) *Compare:* The Court characterized clapping, speeches, singing, and marching by a crowd of demonstrators on statehouse grounds as "an exercise of (First Amendment) rights in their most pristine and classic form." *Edwards v. South Carolina* (1963).

b) Sound Amplification and Interest Balancing

Communication in the public forum can be subjected to content-neutral regulation in the interest of privacy and tranquility. Principles of freedom of speech used for the soap box orator do not necessarily apply to forms of communication technology such as sound trucks. While such broadcasting is protected under the First Amendment, it may be subject to content-neutral, reasonable regulation.

Example: A New York City ordinance designed to regulate the volume of amplified music at a bandshell in Central Park by requiring use of sound-amplification equipment and a sound technician provided by the

City is constitutional. While the content-neutral law employs flexible guidelines and vests considerable discretion in administrators, "perfect clarity and precise guidance have never been required even of regulators that restrict expressive activity." New York has substantial interests in protecting its citizens from unwelcome noise even in the streets and parks and in assuring its citizens of adequate sound amplification at the bandshell. The regulation is narrowly tailored since the government's substantial interest in limiting sound volume is served in a direct and effective way by requiring use of the city's sound technician but giving the sponsor autonomy regarding the sound mix. Since the city regulation is limited only to the extent of the amplification, the guidelines leave open ample alternative channels of communication. *Ward v. Rock Against Racism* (1989).

c) **Captive Audience**

Generally in public places, the burden of avoiding disagreeable speech is on the viewer or listener to avert his eyes or close his ears. *Erznoznik v. Jacksonville* (1975). "We are often captives outside the sanctuary of the home." *Rowan v. U.S. Post Office Dept.* (1970). Thus the government's ability "to shut off discourse solely to protect others from hearing it is . . . dependent upon a showing that substantial privacy interests are being invaded in an essentially intolerable manner." *Cohen v. California* (1971). The Court has "accepted the argument that a captive audience can be protected only sparingly and only as a factor in a balancing analysis." Homeowners can refuse to accept offensive mail (*Rowan*); targeted picketing intruding on the privacy of the home can be regulated (*Frisby v. Schultz* (1988)).

Example: It was argued that the father of a Marine killed in Iraq was part of a captive audience while attending the funeral and that the Westboro protesters therefore were not protected from liability. See Ch. VIII, A, 3, a. But the Court refused to extend the captive audience doctrine to these circumstances. The Westboro protestors stayed well away from the funeral service, Snyder could see only the tops of the signs when driving to the funeral and "there is no indication that the picketing in any way interfered with the funeral service itself." *Snyder v. Phelps* (2011).

3) Protecting the Homeowner

Canvassing, handbilling and solicitation of homeowners is constitutionally protected activity. *Martin v. Struthers* (1943) (ban on residential handbilling held unconstitutional). It is, however, subject to clear, narrowly-drawn regulation designed to protect the privacy of the homeowners or to prevent fraud or other criminal activity.

Examples: (1) An ordinance prohibiting door-to-door solicitations without the advance consent of the homeowner, used to bar magazine sales, is a reasonable means of protecting the privacy of the homeowner. *Breard v. City of Alexandria* (1951).

(2) An ordinance requiring advance written notice for purposes of identification by "any person desiring to canvass, solicit, or call from house to house [for] a recognized charitable [or] political campaign or cause" was held unconstitutionally vague. While solicitors may be required to identify themselves, the ordinance vested the undefined power in officials to determine what messages residents could hear. *Hynes v. Mayor of Oradell* (1976).

(3) A local ordinance prohibiting door-to-door solicitation of contributions by charitable organizations that do not use at least 75% of their receipts for charitable purposes violates the First Amendment. It is facially overbroad and unconstitutional regardless of whether or not a narrowly drawn statute could be applied against the challenging organization. While the village has a substantial interest in preventing fraud and crime and undue invasion of privacy, these interests could be sufficiently served by measures less destructive of First Amendment rights. *Village of Schaumburg v. Citizens for a Better Environment* (1980). Compare

Illinois ex rel. Madigan v. Telemarketing Associates (2003) where the Court upheld a fraud complaint filed by a state attorney general against a telemarketing firm that had contracted with a charity to conduct phone solicitations, where the telemarketing firm kept 85% of the funds it raised, while only 15% went to the charity. The government alleged that the telemarketing operators had exaggerated the percentage of the funds that would go towards charitable purposes to prospective donors and that the 85% fee was not justified by the firm's expenses. The Court held that the alleged false statements constituted "public deception," unprotected by the First Amendment. The Court distinguished the broad prior restraints at issue in cases like *Village of Schaumburg*, and per se percentage limitations on fundraising costs, from actions, such as this, targeting "misleading affirmative representations."

(4) A content-neutral city ordinance banning picketing "before or about" any residence, is constitutional. The law, as construed, prohibits only picketing focused on, and taking place in front of, a particular residence. The regulation of such focused picketing serves the significant governmental interest in protecting residential privacy and, as interpreted, leaves open ample alternative means of communicating a message. The ban is narrowly tailored since it eliminates no more than the exact evil it seeks to remedy; it forbids only targeted picketing directed at "captive" residents who are presumptively unwilling to receive the speech. *Frisby v. Schultz* (1988).

(5) A municipal ordinance that requires one to obtain a permit prior to engaging in the door-to-door advocacy of a political cause and to display upon demand the permit, which contains one's name, violates the First Amendment protection accorded anonymous pamphleteering or discourse, even though officials exercise no discretion in granting or denying the permit. While the Court found it unnecessary to choose a particular standard of review because of the breadth of the

speech affected by the ordinance and the nature of the regulation, the Court balanced the competing interests.

The Court accepted that the Government's interest in preventing fraud, preventing crime and protecting residents' privacy are important interests justifying some form of regulation of solicitation. But the ordinance is excessively broad covering anonymous speech supporting unpopular causes, speech of citizens holding religious or patriotic views, and spontaneous speech. Nor is the ordinance tailored to the claimed interests. The ability of unwilling listeners to deal with solicitors adequately protects privacy. Requiring a permit is unlikely to prevent crime. *Watchtower Bible and Tract Society of New York, Inc. v. Village of Stratton* (2002).

4) Licensing, Prior Restraint and the Duty to Obey

Prior restraints on access to the public forum, embodied in permit systems, licensing requirements and court injunctions, are constitutional if they are clear, narrowly-drawn, time, place, and manner regulations. In determining whether the regulation is reasonable, the courts balance the First Amendment interests against the government interests in preventing serious interference with the normal usage of the streets and in maintaining public peace and order.

Example: Conviction of protestors under a state statute prohibiting street parades without a permit and imposing a licensing fee was held constitutional. "If a municipality has authority to control the use of its public streets for parades or processions, as it undoubtedly has, it cannot be denied authority to give consideration, without unfair discrimination to time, place and manner in relation to the other proper uses of the streets." *Cox v. New Hampshire* (1941).

a) Facial Validity—Vagueness and Overbreadth

Prior restraints on the use of the public forum are valid only if the regulation is drawn with precision and specificity. Vague and imprecise regulations, vesting excessive discretion in public officials, are invalid on their face, regardless of the manner in which they are administered.

Examples: (1) Conviction of civil rights demonstrators who marched without a permit required by an ordinance directing issuance of such permits unless in the city commission's judgment "the public welfare, peace, safety, health, decency, good order, morals, or convenience require that it be refused" was overturned. As written, the ordinance was facially invalid since it vested "virtually unbridled and absolute power" in local officials. While the statute was given a narrowing interpretation by the lower court, the defendants could not have anticipated the saving construction. *Shuttlesworth v. Birmingham* (1969).

(2) A city ordinance giving the Mayor unfettered discretion to deny a permit for the placement of newsracks on public property as "not in the public interest" (he did have to give reasons) and unlimited authority to condition a permit on any terms he deems "necessary and reasonable" violates the First Amendment. The Constitution requires neutral licensing criteria to assure that official decisions are not based on the content or viewpoint of the speech being considered. *City of Lakewood v. Plain Dealer Publishing Co.* (1988).

(3) An ordinance requiring parade or assembly applicants to pay a permit fee of up to $1,000, the amount to be determined by the county administrator based on the costs of providing security for the event, is unconstitutional on its face. The ordinance gave overbroad discretion to a government official, creating the possibility of censorship. Moreover, the ordinance often requires that the fee be based on the content of speech since estimated costs may be higher for controversial parade applicants. The Court also rejected the

argument that $1,000 cap made the ordinance content-neutral. "A tax based on the content of speech does not become more constitutional because it is a small tax." *Forsyth County, Georgia v. The Nationalist Movement* (1992).

b) The Duty to Obey

1) *Laws*—A licensing statute or ordinance which, if valid on its face but unconstitutionally administered, must be obeyed, until the action of the administrator is overturned. *Poulos v. New Hampshire* (1953) (denial of a license to conduct religious services in a park). However, if the law is facially unconstitutional, it may be ignored and its invalidity established at the time of prosecution. The law is void *ab initio. Shuttlesworth v. Birmingham* (1969).

2) *Injunctions*—But if the prior restraint is in the form of an injunction, it must be obeyed even if it is facially invalid. Only if the injunction is frivolous or if the court lacks jurisdiction may it be ignored. Otherwise you must obey and establish its invalidity on appellate review before marching.

Example: An ex parte injunction issued pursuant to the ordinance later invalidated in *Shuttlesworth* could not be ignored. Conviction for contempt of court of marchers violating the injunction was upheld. The Court concluded that the protestors were not free "to ignore all the procedures of the law and carry their battle to the streets." *Walker v. Birmingham* (1967).

c) Procedural Standards
A content-neutral permit system must contain adequate standards to guide administrative discretion and render the official's actions subject to judicial review.

F. Symbolic Speech (Expressive Conduct)

While conduct may be used as a vehicle for communicating ideas, it may also embody the idea itself—the medium can be the message. Such expressive conduct is referred to as symbolic speech. You should employ a two-part analysis in symbolic speech cases. First, ask if the conduct is expressive. Second, ask if the expressive conduct is protected by the First Amendment guarantee.

1. Is the Conduct Communicative?

In determining whether conduct is speech, the Court often examines the nature of the conduct, factual context, and environment to determine if the actor has an intent to communicate a message and whether the audience viewing the conduct would understand the message. Spence v. Washington *(1974). However, conduct cannot "be labeled 'speech' whenever the person engaging in the conduct intends thereby to express an idea."* United States v. O'Brien (1968). *Rather, the Court has "extended First Amendment protection only to conduct that is inherently expressive."* Rumsfeld v. FAIR (2006). *Often the Court will assume* arguendo *that the conduct is expressive.*

Example: A First Amendment challenge to a Nevada statute providing that legislators may not vote upon or "advocate the passage or failure" of a matter if they have a conflict of interest was rejected by a unanimous Court. The Court, per Justice Scalia, began by stating that the prohibition of advocacy is not unconstitutional unless the prohibition on voting is unconstitutional. A legislative vote is not protected speech. "[T]he act of voting symbolizes nothing. It *discloses* . . . that the legislator wishes (for whatever reason) that the proposition on the floor be adopted, just as a physical assault discloses that the attacker dislikes the victim. But neither the one nor the other is an act of communication." Justice Scalia said that the Court had rejected the proposition "that the First Amendment confers a right to use government mechanics to convey a message." Justice Alito, concurring in part and concurring in the judgment, argued that legislators often use votes to express "deeply held and highly unpopular views often at great personal or political peril." Voting is an "inherently expressive act" meriting First Amendment protection. *Nevada Commission on Ethics v. Carrigan* (2011).

2. Is the Speech Protected?

When speech and nonspeech elements are combined in the same course of conduct, government regulation of symbolic speech is permissible if (1) it furthers an important or substantial governmental interest; (2) if the governmental interest is unrelated to the suppression of free expression; and (3) if the incidental restriction on alleged First Amendment freedom is no greater than is essential to the furtherance of that interest. O'Brien v. United States *(1968).* If the regulation is based on the content of the symbolic speech, "the most exacting scrutiny" applies. *Texas v. Johnson* (1989). The determination whether the government's interest is unrelated to the suppression of free speech is essentially the same as asking whether the regulation is content-based or content-neutral. The *O'Brien* test applies only if the regulation is content neutral. The *O'Brien* test is essentially the same standard used in reviewing content neutral regulation of the public forum. *Clark v. Community for Creative Non–Violence* (1984).

Examples: (1) The governmental interest in the effective functioning of the Selective Service System is sufficiently legitimate and substantial to justify a law prohibiting the conduct of burning draft cards in spite of the incidental restraint on First Amendment expression. Assuring the continued availability of the certificates is an appropriately narrow means of protecting this government interest which is unrelated to the idea expressed; no alternative means would more precisely and narrowly serve the governmental interest. *United States v. O'Brien* (1968).

(2) The wearing of a black armband in school to protest the Vietnam War was "akin to pure speech" and hence protected by the First Amendment. In the absence of evidence that the symbolic conduct would "materially and substantially interfere with the requirements of appropriate discipline in the operation of the school," prohibition by school officials of the wearing of the armbands is impermissible. *Tinker v. Des Moines Independent Community School Dist.* (1969).

(3) A flag misuse statute cannot be used to convict a person for displaying an American flag with a superimposed peace symbol on his own property. The nature of the activity, given the factual context and the environment, establishes this as a form of protected expression. Even assuming, arguendo, that the state has substantial interest in the physical integrity of the national flag as a symbol of our country, there was no impairment of this interest or any other governmental interest in this case. *Spence v. Washington* (1974).

(4) Application of a Park Service regulation to prohibit sleeping in Lafayette Park and the Mall in Washington, D.C., as part of a demonstration to protest homelessness, does not violate the First Amendment. Assuming that the demonstration is expres-

sive conduct protected to some extent by the First Amendment, application of the regulation satisfies the *O'Brien* standards for content-neutral time, place, and manner regulations. The regulation banning camping in these parks is narrowly focused to prevent wear and tear on the parks and preserve them in an attractive and intact condition. There were ample alternative channels for communication. *Clark v. Community for Creative Non–Violence* (1984).

(5) A Texas statute prohibiting desecration of a venerated object could not constitutionally be applied to convict a demonstrator for burning an American flag as part of a political protest at the Republican National Convention. The expressive and overtly political character of the flag burning as part of a protest when Ronald Reagan was renominated by the convention was intentional and apparent.

While the state sought to justify the application of the law by its interest in preventing breaches of the peace, no disturbance occurred or was threatened. The state may not presume provocative, offensive words will produce disorder and the expressive conduct involved did not constitute fighting words. The state's alternative interest in preserving the flag as a symbol of nationhood and national unity arises only from the content of the flag burner's message and is therefore content-based.

The state interest in deterring the flag burning does not justify the means selected by the State—criminal punishment of a person for burning a flag as a means of political protest. Whether dealing with verbal speech or expressive nonverbal conduct, the State cannot proscribe speech because it is critical of the flag. *"If there is a bedrock principle underlying the First Amendment, it is that the Government may not prohibit the expression of an idea simply because society finds this idea itself offensive or disagreeable."* Texas v. Johnson (1989).

(6) The federal Flag Protection Act of 1989, which criminalizes the act of one who "knowingly mutilates, defaces, physically defiles, burns, maintains on the floor or ground, or tramples upon" a United States flag, except for conduct related to disposal of a "worn or soiled" flag, is unconstitutional. Although there is no explicit content-based limit in the scope of

the ban, the government interest in protecting the "physical integrity" of a privately owned flag is based on a perceived need to preserve the symbolic value of the flag. That value is implicated only when the person's treatment of the flag communicates a message that is inconsistent with the ideas which the flag symbolizes. The language of the Act also focused on disrespectful treatment of the flag and on acts likely to damage the flag's symbolic value. Since the Act is concerned with communicative impact, it is subject to the most exacting scrutiny. While the government may create and promote national symbols, it cannot proscribe expressive conduct because of its likely communicative impact, citing *Texas v. Johnson. United States v. Eichman* (1990).

(7) A state public indecency law which prohibits knowingly or intentionally appearing in a state of nudity in a public place, can be constitutionally applied to non-obscene nude dancing. While non-obscene nude dancing is expressive conduct "within the outer perimeters of the First Amendment, though * * * only marginally so," it can be regulated under the *O'Brien* test. A plurality held that the state regulation furthers the substantial state interest in protecting societal order and morality. This state interest is unrelated to free expression since the perceived evil is public nudity not erotic dancing. The means is also not greater than necessary since the requirements of pasties and G-strings are "the bare minimum necessary to achieve the state's purpose." Justice Souter, concurring, reasoned that the regulation was a constitutional means of furthering "the State's substantial interest in combating the secondary effects of adult entertainment establishments." Justice Scalia, concurring, argued that the First Amendment is not implicated by "a general law regulating conduct and not specifically directed at expression." *Barnes v. Glen Theatre* (1991).

(8) The Solomon Amendment provides that educational institutions that deny military recruiters access equal to that provided other recruiters would lose certain federal funds. Forum for Academic and Institutional Rights (FAIR), a group of law schools opposed to the military's policy towards homosexuals (*i.e.*, "Don't Ask, Don't Tell") sued, alleging that the Amend-

ment denied them their First Amendment freedoms of speech and association. The Supreme Court unanimously rejected the First Amendment claims.

Chief Justice Roberts, writing for the Court, reasoned that "the Amendment regulates conduct, not speech: It affects what law schools must do—afford equal access to military recruiters—not what they may or may not say." Nor did the alleged expressive nature of the conduct regulated by the Amendment bring the conduct within the First Amendment's protection. The conduct of excluding military recruiters was not "inherently expressive." Any expressive component would come only from speech that accompanies the conduct. Conduct cannot become expressive merely by talking about it. Even if recruiting could be construed as expressive conduct, the Chief Justice reasoned, the government would satisfy its burden under *O'Brien*. "Military recruiting promotes the substantial Government interest in raising and supporting the Armed Forces—an objective that would be achieved less effectively if the military were forced to recruit on less favorable terms than other employers." The Court went on to hold that the Solomon Amendment did not compel expression violative of the First Amendment. (See Ch. VIII, C). *Rumsfeld v. FAIR* (2006).

G. Commercial Speech

1. Definition

The Court has characterized expression that does "no more than propose a commercial transaction" as "classic commercial speech." *Virginia State Bd. of Pharmacy v. Virginia Citizens Consumer Council, Inc.* (1976). The Court has defined commercial speech as "expression related solely to the economic interests of the speaker and its audience." *Central Hudson Gas & Electric Corp. v. Public Service Comm'n of New York* (1980). Nevertheless, there remains considerable uncertainty in determining what speech is commercial speech.

Example: Application of a federal law prohibiting the mailing of unsolicited advertisements for contraceptives to ban promotional and informational material which not only promotes a product but which discusses venereal disease and family planning was held unconstitutional. The Court initially determined that the material regulated did constitute commercial speech. Most of the mailings fell within the core notion of commercial speech in simply proposing a commercial transaction. The informational material did not become commercial speech simply by being included in an advertisement including references to products. Nor did the drug company's economic motivation turn the materials into commercial speech. But the combination of these considerations justified the lower court determination that the mailings constitute commercial speech. The Court then went on to hold that the application of the law to ban the mailings in question violated the *Central Hudson* test discussed below. *Bolger v. Youngs Drug Prods. Corp.* (1983).

2. **Applying the First Amendment**

    a. In early cases, the Court suggested that purely commercial speech was not First Amendment speech since it does not relate to self-government or promote individual self-dignity. See *Valentine v. Chrestensen* (1942). Further, there has been concern over the effect of extending First Amendment protection on government regulation of the economic marketplace.

    b. It is now established that even commercial advertising (assuming the activity advertised is legal) enjoys some First Amendment protection. The protection, however, is not as substantial as the constitutional protection afforded political, social, or religious speech. It is argued that commercial speech has greater objectivity and hardiness permitting greater state regulation. For example, the prior restraint doctrine does not apply. The overbreadth doctrine applies only to the extent that the regulation applies to *noncommercial* speech; restriction of commercial speech will not be facially invalidated because of overbreadth. Further, even when government regulation is based on the content of the speech, the courts consider the commercial character of the speech as one factor, among others, in balancing the First Amendment interests against the governmental interests furthered by the regulation.

        Example: A state statute declaring it unprofessional conduct for a licensed pharmacist to advertise the prices of prescription drugs was held invalid. Purely commercial speech is not removed from First Amendment protection. The fact that an advertiser's interest in a commercial advertisement is purely economic does not disqualify him from First Amendment protection. The consumer and society have a strong interest in the free flow of commercial information. *Virginia State Board of Pharmacy v. Virginia Citizens Consumer Council* (1976).

3. Unprotected Commercial Speech

Commercial speech providing information about activities which are illegal or contrary to public policy is not protected under the First Amendment. *Pittsburgh Press Co. v. Pittsburgh Com'n on Human Relations* (1973) (sex-designated help wanted ads, constituting illegal sex discrimination, not protected). Similarly, false and misleading advertising is not protected. *Friedman v. Rogers* (1979) (state statute prohibiting use of trade names by those practicing optometry held constitutional). Note that false defamatory publication, not involving commercial speech, does enjoy constitutional protection.

4. The Modern Test

a. *The Court now applies a four-part test to determine the constitutional protection provided commercial speech. First, the speech must not be misleading or related to unlawful activity—such speech is not protected by the First Amendment. Second, the asserted government interest must be substantial. Third, the government regulation must directly advance the governmental interest asserted. Fourth, the regulation must not be more extensive than is necessary to serve that interest. A prophylactic regulation designed to avert the potential for deception is seldom sufficient to meet this test.* Central Hudson Gas & Elec. Corp. v. Public Service Comm'n of New York (1980).

b. The government must show that the challenged regulation advances the governmental interest "in a direct and material way." It must show that the potential harms are real and that the regulation will alleviate them to a material degree. The relationship cannot be left to "speculation or conjecture." *Edenfield v. Fane* (1993).

c. The Court has held that a law can be "necessary" even if it is not the least restrictive means of achieving the substantial state interests; it is suffi-cient if there is a "reasonable fit." *Board of Trustees of State Univ. of New York v. Fox* (1989). But the Court has indicated that the availability of less burdensome alternatives remains relevant in determining if the fit is reasonable. *City of Cincinnati v. Discovery Network, Inc.* (1993).

Examples: (1) A state prohibition on utility advertising to promote the use of electricity violates the First and Fourteenth Amendments. First, the commercial speech does not concern illegal activity and is not misleading, and, therefore, the First Amendment applies. Second, the government interests in fair rates and energy conservation are clear and substantial. Third, the prohibition of advertising does directly advance the government interest in energy conservation since advertising is designed to increase the use of electricity. Fourth, while promotional advertising is directly related to the state's interest in energy conservation, a total prohibition is more extensive than is necessary to further the state's energy conservation interest. *Central Hudson Gas & Elec. Corp. v. Public Service Comm'n of New York* (1980).

(2) A state university has a substantial interest in regulating commercial speech in the form of Tupperware parties in college dorms, *e.g.*, promoting an educational rather than a commercial atmosphere, promoting safety and security, preventing commercial exploitation of students and preserving residential tranquility. A regulation is narrowly tailored to advance these interests if the State proves that the law does not burden substantially more speech than is necessary to further the interest; there must be a "reasonable" fit. The case was remanded for a determination whether the regulation is constitutional as applied to commercial speech and to determine if the regulation is facially overbroad in reaching certain noncommercial speech. *Board of Trustees of State Univ. of New York v. Fox* (1989).

(3) Although safety and esthetics are legitimate interests, banning newsracks which distribute commercial publications without banning newsracks for newspapers was not a reasonable fit between state interests and the means chosen to fulfill those interests. Banning the 62 commercial publications newsracks would still leave 1,500 to 2,000 newsracks on the street. Thus, any improvement in safety and esthetics would be marginal. *Cincinnati v. Discovery Network* (1993).

d. There is doubt about the future of the *Central Hudson* test and the commercial speech doctrine generally. While still adhering to *Central*

Hudson, the Court has been less deferential in its application and a number of justices have questioned its use for reviewing regulation of truthful, nonmisleading information.

Examples: (1) A federal law prohibiting beer labels from displaying alcohol content violates the First Amendment. Applying *Central Hudson*, the Court accepted that the government has a "substantial interest" in curbing strength wars by beer brewers who might seek to compete for customers based on alcoholic content given the social harm. But the law does not directly and materially advance this interest because other provisions of federal law allow beer advertising of alcohol content unless the state prohibits such advertising. Since advertising is a more influential weapon than labeling in any strength war, the regulatory scheme is irrational. Nor was the federal law sufficiently tailored to its goal since available alternatives to the labeling ban exist which would be less intrusive on First Amendment rights. The ban was more extensive than necessary. *Rubin v. Coors Brewing Co.* (1995).

(2) Rhode Island laws banning the advertisement of retail liquor prices except at the place of sale violate the First Amendment, and the Twenty-first Amendment does not qualify the First Amendment prohibition. While this holding was unanimous, a plurality would have held that "when a State entirely prohibits the dissemination of truthful, nonmisleading commercial messages for reasons unrelated to the preservation of a fair bargaining process, there is less reason to depart from the rigorous review that the First Amendment generally demands." Another plurality indicated that laws entirely banning such speech for reasons other than consumer protection must be reviewed with "special care." It was agreed that the Rhode Island ban could not survive even under *Central Hudson.* The state had not produced evidence that the ban would significantly reduce market-wide alcohol consumption. There are alternative forms of regulation that would not restrict speech and that would be more likely to achieve the state's goal of promoting temperance. Justices Scalia and Thomas

expressed a general discomfort with the limited review under *Central Hudson*. *44 Liquormart, Inc. v. Rhode Island* (1996).

(3) A federal law exempting compounded drugs from FDA drug approval requirements as long as the provider does not solicit the prescription and does not advertise or promote the compounded drug was held, 5–4, to be an unconstitutional restriction on commercial speech under *Central Hudson*. The Government has substantial interests in preserving the effectiveness and integrity of the new FDA drug approval process and of the public health and preserving the availability of compounded drugs by assuring its economic feasibility. Assuming that the prohibition on advertising "directly advances" these interests, the Government failed to demonstrate the restrictions are not more extensive than necessary. The Government did not show (or even consider) why various alternatives, alone or in combination, would be insufficient to prevent compounding from occurring on such a scale that it would undermine the new drug approval process. Further the law would prohibit a significant amount of beneficial speech. The dissent argued that the Court gave insufficient weight to the Government's regulatory rationale and too readily assumed the existence of practical alternatives. "It thereby applies the commercial speech doctrine too strictly." *Thompson v. Western States Medical Center* (2002).

(4) A Vermont statute prohibited pharmacies from selling or disclosing information that reveals the prescribing practices of doctors to pharmaceutical manufacturers for marketing purposes without the prescriber's consent and prohibited pharmaceutical manufacturers from using such prescriber-identifying information in marketing. The Supreme Court, 6–3, per Justice Kennedy, held the law unconstitutional. The Court said that a law imposing specific content-based and speaker-based restrictions on speech, including commercial speech, is subject to "heightened judicial scrutiny." The statute was more than an "incidental burden"—it disfavored speech based on marketing content and disfavored specific speakers—pharmaceutical

manufacturers. "As in previous cases, the outcome is the same whether a special speech inquiry or a stricter form of judicial scrutiny is applied." Citing *Central Hudson*, the Court said that "the State must show at least that the statute directly advances a substantial governmental interest and that the measure is drawn to achieve that interest." The Court held that Vermont failed to satisfy that standard. The State argued that the law was needed to protect medical privacy and to achieve improved public health and reduced healthcare costs. But the Court concluded that the law is not drawn to serve the physician interest in confidentiality. Prescription information can be freely shared except for use in marketing and everyone—except pharmaceutical companies—can use the information and doctors can avoid harassment by not meeting with marketing agents. The fear that marketing speech might be persuasive and thereby affect doctor-patient relationships is not a reason for silencing speech.

The Court also concluded that the law does not advance medical policy objectives in a permissible way. The fear that people might make bad decisions if given truthful information cannot justify content-based burdens. In fact, there is a difference of opinion on the value of prescriber-identified information in achieving treatment decisions. The state has imposed content and viewer-based burdens on speech it found too persuasive while leaving unburdened that speech which is in accord with its views.

Justice Breyer, joined by Justice Ginsburg and Kagan, dissenting, argued that the Vermont law was simply economic regulation which is not subject to heightened review. And, in any case, the law satisfies the review standards used when government regulates commercial speech. The Court defers to legislative judgment when reviewing economic regulation that has a less direct effect on speech. The Court has not used heightened scrutiny for content-based and speaker-based restrictions when commercial speech is involved. In this case, the record evidence is sufficient to permit a legislature to conclude that the statute "directly advances" the "substantial" state interests claimed. "The speech-related consequences here are indirect, incidental, and entirely commercial." Justice Breyer warned of reawakening *Lochner's* threat of "substituting judicial for democratic decision-making where ordinary economic regulation is at issue." *Sorrell v. IMS Health Inc.* (2011).

5. Lawyer and Other Professional Advertising

Lawyer advertising concerning routine legal services is constitutionally protected. But not all regulation of lawyer and professional advertising is unconstitutional under the modern commercial speech test. In-person solicitation by lawyers for pecuniary gain, for example, involves potential harm to the public that the state may seek to prevent. *Ohralik v. Ohio State Bar Association* (1978).

Examples: (1) A flat state ban on advertising by lawyers violates the First Amendment at least in the case of advertising routine legal services describing the price and the nature of the services offered. The First Amendment interest in informed and reliable consumer decision-making necessitates invalidating a flat ban on advertising by lawyers. However, the Court left open whether competing state interests would authorize some regulation where advertising claims of quality are concerned or where the advertising is false and deceptive. Similarly, the problem of lawyer advertising in the unique context of the broadcast media was left unresolved. *Bates v. State Bar of Arizona* (1977).

(2) A state bar association constitutionally may discipline a lawyer for soliciting clients in person for pecuniary gain. In-person solicitation is not unprotected by the First Amendment. However, because it is essentially a business transaction of which speech is merely a part, the level of scrutiny is lower. The states have a strong interest in preventing the harm solicitation can cause. Disciplinary action in circumstances posing only potential danger is permissible as a prophylactic measure. *Ohralik v. Ohio State Bar Assoc.* (1978). *Compare In re Primus* (1978) (state concern over the potential for deception does not justify sanctions against an ACLU lawyer informing potential clients of the possibility of litigation).

(3) Missouri rules regulating lawyer advertising: (1) specify ten categories of information which may be included in a published advertisement in newspapers, periodicals, or the yellow pages and exclude all other information such as the jurisdiction in which the lawyer is licensed to practice; (2) delineate the precise manner in which the area or areas of practice may be described in ads; and (3) limit the mailing of professional announcement cards solely to "lawyers, clients, former clients, personal friends and relatives." Application of these rules to discipline an attorney in the absence of any showing that the lawyer's speech was misleading or that restrictions short of an absolute prohibition would be insufficient to prevent deception violates the First and Fourteenth Amendments. *In re R.M.J.* (1982).

(4) A state supreme court reprimand of an attorney for newspaper advertising soliciting business from those injured by use of Dalkon Shields is unconstitutional. The ads were neither false nor deceptive and the government interest in the potential for deception is inadequate to justify a ban. Nor could the ban on the use of illustrations stand; the illustration involved was an accurate representation and the state's interest in preserving the dignity of the legal profession is not sufficient to justify a ban on all illustrations. However, the decision to discipline the attorney for failure to disclose in his ads that clients might be liable for litigation costs if the lawsuit is unsuccessful does not violate the First Amendment. Because extension of the First Amendment to commercial speech is justified by the value to the consumers of the information provided by the speech, the attorney's interest in not providing particular factual information is minimal. *Zauderer v. Office of Disciplinary Counsel of the Supreme Court of Ohio* (1985).

(5) A state may not prohibit lawyers from sending truthful, non-deceptive letters to potential clients known to face particular legal problems. There is much less risk of overreaching and undue influence from a mailed solicitation than from in-person solicitation. Nor does such mailed solicitation involve any special invasion of the recipient's privacy. A rule totally banning targeted, direct-mail solicitation by lawyers for pecuniary gain, without a particularized finding that the solicitation is false or misleading, violates the First Amendment. *Shapero v. Kentucky Bar Ass'n* (1988).

(6) The censure of an Illinois attorney by the Illinois Supreme Court for advertising himself as "Certified Civil Trial Specialist by the National Board of Trial Advocacy" on his letterhead is unconstitutional. The state cannot prohibit the advertising of facts that are true and verifiable simply because they are potentially deceptive. Only if the information is actually or inherently misleading does the state meet its heavy burden of justifying a categorical prohibition against disseminating accurate commercial information. The letterhead was neither actually nor inherently misleading and there is no dispute over the bona fides and relevance of NBTA certification. *Peel v. Attorney Registration and Disciplinary Comm'n of Illinois* (1990).

(7) Disciplining for "false, deceptive and misleading advertising" of an attorney, who is a certified public accountant (CPA) and a certified financial planner (CFP), for using the designations CPA and CFP after her name in advertising, violates the First Amendment. Since the lawyer did hold an active CPA license, the advertising was not misleading. Nor is the fact that the term CFP is a private, not a state recognized designation, "sufficient to overcome the constitutional presumption favoring disclosure over concealment." The Court warned against excessive state reliance on "potentially misleading" risks rather than real risk of harm. *Ibanez v. Florida Department of Business and Professional Regulation.* (1994).

(8) The Court held, 5–4, that rules of the Florida Bar prohibiting injury lawyers from sending targeted direct-mail solicitations to victims and their relatives for 30 days following an accident do not violate the First Amendment. The Court applied the intermediate scrutiny test of *Central Hudson*. The state has a substantial interest in protecting the privacy and personal tranquility of victims and their loved ones against intrusive, unsolicited contact by lawyers. An unrebutted Bar study provided statistical and anecdotal evidence establishing that the rules directly and materially advance that interest. The palliative rule is narrowly drawn in both duration and scope. There are many other ways citizens can learn about the availability of legal representation. *Florida Bar v. Went For It, Inc.* (1995).

6. Advertising Harmful Activity

The Supreme Court has indicated that truthful advertising on lawful but potentially harmful activity can be prohibited if the *Central Hudson* standards are met. In applying *Central Hudson*, the Court initially deferred to the legislative judgment on the appropriateness of the means the legislature can ban advertising if this is a reasonable means. If government has the greater power to completely ban the activity, it has "the lesser power to ban advertising." *Posadas de Puerto Rico Assoc. v. Tourism Co. of Puerto Rico* (1986). But in *Greater New Orleans Broadcast Association v. United States* (1999), the Court rejected the principle.

Examples: (1) Although Puerto Rico has legalized casino gambling, it may ban advertising for casino gambling to the Puerto Rican public, while permitting restricted advertising outside of Puerto Rico. The government has a substantial "health, safety and welfare" interest in reducing the demand for casino gambling by the residents of Puerto Rico (even though casino gambling by the residents is lawful). This interest is "directly advanced" by the ban since the legislature could reasonably conclude that ads would increase the demand. Puerto Rico's regulations are no more extensive than necessary since they apply only to ads aimed at residents, not tourists. It is for the legislature to decide whether to use a ban rather than a "counterspeech" policy of seeking to discourage gambling since the legislature could decide that residents, while aware of the risks of such gambling, would still be induced to engage in the harmful activity by the advertising. *Posadas de Puerto Rico Assoc. v. Tourism Co. of Puerto Rico* (1986).

(2) A federal prohibition on lottery advertisements for broadcast stations located in states which outlaw lotteries does not violate the First Amendment. Edge Broadcasting owned and operated a radio station in North Carolina, near the border of Virginia. Most of Edge's listeners and advertisers were from Virginia. Although North Carolina outlawed lotteries, Virginia permitted lotteries. The statutes at issue directly advanced the legitimate federalism interest of balancing the interests of lottery and non-lottery states by supporting North Carolina's laws against gambling. The federal law also was a reasonable fit to achieve that legitimate end even if it may not significantly further the government's purpose in an individual case. *United States v. Edge Broadcasting Co.* (1993).

(3) Rhode Island laws banning the advertisement of retail liquor prices except at the place of sale violate the First Amendment. A plurality of four justices concluded "that a state legislature does not have the broad discretion to suppress truthful, nonmisleading information for paternalistic purposes that the *Posadas* majority was willing to tolerate." The plurality rejected the claim of *Posadas* that the "greater" power to regulate commercial activity included the power to regulate speech. Any "vice" exception to First Amendment protection "would be difficult, if not impossible, to define." Other justices, concurring, felt it sufficient to hold that Rhode Island law failed to satisfy "[t]he closer look that we have required since *Posadas*" in applying *Central Hudson*. *44 Liquormart, Inc. v. Rhode Island* (1996).

(4) A federal law banning accurate and nonmisleading broadcast advertising of private casino gambling in states where it is legal violates the First Amendment. The Court applied *Central Hudson*, concluding that the law does not directly and materially advance the Government's interest in limiting casino gambling. The exemptions and inconsistencies in the federal law rendered it unreasonable. Without dissent, the Court states that "the power to prohibit or to regulate particular conduct does not necessarily include power to prohibit or regulate speech about that conduct." *Greater New Orleans Broadcast Association v. United States* (1999).

(5) Provisions of Massachusetts law regulating advertising of smokeless tobacco or cigars, which were designed to protect minors, were held unconstitutional. The law prohibited such outdoor advertising within 1000 feet of schools or playgrounds and prohibited such indoor advertising if placed lower than five feet from the floor. The prohibitions, while directly advancing the government interest, were not narrowly tailored given their broad geographic sweep and the range of communications restricted. The height restrictions did not directly advance the government interest given the varying height of children and their ability to look up. Nor were the restrictions narrowly tailored. Another provision banning self-service displays was held constitutional under *Central Hudson*. The Court did not reach the constitutional issues raised by state provisions regu-

lating cigarette advertising since such regulation was pre-empted by federal law. *Lorillard Tobacco Co. v. Reilly* (2001).

H. Freedom of the Press

While it has been suggested that the Press Clause of the First Amendment be read independently of the Speech Clause to afford the media special constitutional protection, the Court has not accepted this reading. The Press Clause is read together with the Speech Clause as a single guarantee. Further, the Court has held that the press enjoys no First Amendment privileges or immunities beyond those afforded the ordinary citizen.

The protection afforded the press from restraints on publication is dealt with in a number of other places in the outline, *e.g.*, prior restraint, obscenity. However, there are a number of issues of relevance to the media deserving special attention. Generally, the constitutional protection afforded the press in the pre-publication, newsgathering stage is less extensive than the constitutional protection accorded against restraints on publication.

The media is subject to generally applicable regulation and taxation laws. However, discriminatory taxation against the press, or between different forms of media, which "is directed at, or presents the danger of suppressing particular ideas," violates the First Amendment. *Leathers v. Medlock* (1991).

Examples: (1) A special state use tax imposed on the use of paper and ink in publishing violates freedom of the press regardless of the absence of any censorial motive. While the press was benefited by a specific exemption from the general sales tax, the Court held that differential taxation of the press is permitted only if the state demonstrates "a counterbalancing interest of compelling importance that it cannot achieve without differential taxation."

The state interest in raising revenues could be achieved by a generally applicable tax of businesses. Even though the state scheme imposed a lesser tax burden on the press than was applied to other businesses under the general tax laws, the Court concluded that the threat of different treatment of the press nevertheless has a censorial effect. Further, judicial assessment of the actual economic burdens of respective tax schemes was said to present too great a risk of error.

An exemption for the first $100,000 of ink and paper consumed, defended by the state as designed to create an equitable tax scheme, also was impermissible. The exemption presented a potential for abuse by singling out a few members of the press for special treatment while penalizing the remainder. The state failed to meet its heavy burden of justification. *Minneapolis Star & Tribune Co. v. Minnesota Com'r of Rev.* (1983).

(2) An Arkansas tax on general interest magazines which allows an exemption for newspapers and religious, professional, trade, and sports journals violates the freedom of the press. Selective taxation of a certain group of magazines poses a particular danger toward freedom of the press. Particularly disturbing is that such discrimination is content-based—magazines dealing with certain subjects are exempt from taxation. Applying strict scrutiny, the Court held that the tax was not necessary to the proffered state interests of raising revenue, encouraging low volume publications, or fostering communication on certain subjects. *Arkansas Writers' Project, Inc. v. Ragland* (1987).

(3) An Arkansas sales tax imposed on cable television services, but exempting newspapers, magazines and antenna satellite services, does not violate the First Amendment. Prior cases forbid discriminatory taxes only when "the tax is directed at, or presents the danger of suppressing, particular ideas." The Arkansas sales tax is a generally applicable tax which does not involve the kind of discrimination which threatens censoring of particular ideas or viewpoints. The tax structure does not resemble a penalty for a small number or speakers and is not based on media content. *Leathers v. Medlock* (1991).

1. Defamation

a. Public Officials and Public Figures

The First Amendment limits the ability of government to protect the reputation of citizens through defamation actions by erecting a qualified privilege to publish. A public official may recover damages for a defamatory falsehood relating to his official conduct only if he proves by clear and convincing evidence that the statement was made with "actual malice", i.e., with knowledge of its falsity or with reckless disregard of whether it was true or false. New York Times v. Sullivan *(1964). The* New York Times *privilege has been extended to public figures.* Curtis Publishing Co. v. Butts *(1967). Both the public official and the public figure plaintiff also bear the burden of establishing that a defamatory publication involving matters of public concern is false.* Philadelphia Newspapers, Inc. v. Hepps *(1986).*

1) Rationale

a) The First Amendment represents a profound national commit-ment to uninhibited, robust and wide-open debate on public issues free from government censorship or the need for self-censorship. Further, a qualified constitutional privilege for the citizen-critic of government is a necessary corollary of the privilege protecting public officials in performing their public duties.

b) But these interests do not require protection of calculated falsehood. Defamatory publication made with actual malice is not protected speech under the First Amendment.

2) Who Is a Public Official?

a) Public officials include all "those among the hierarchy of government employees who have, or appear to the public to have, substantial responsibility for or control over the conduct of governmental affairs." *Rosenblatt v. Baer* (1966) (nonelected supervisor of a publicly owned recreation area held to be a public official). Lower courts have tended to extend the term to almost any government employee. Candidates for public office are also included.

b) The privilege extends to "anything which might touch an official's fitness for office." *Garrison v. Louisiana* (1964) (charge that certain judges were inefficient, lazy and hampering an investigation held privileged). Today, almost all publications concerning public officials probably fall within the privilege, including charges of criminal conduct, *Monitor Patriot Co. v. Roy* (1971) (claim that a candidate was former bootlegger); *Ocala Star–Banner Co. v. Damron* (1971) (claim that mayor had been charged with perjury).

3) Who Is a Public Figure?

a) All–Purpose Public Figures
A person "may achieve such pervasive fame or notoriety that he becomes a public figure for all purposes and in all contexts." *Gertz v. Robert Welch, Inc.* (1974).

b) Limited Purpose "Vortex" Public Figures
A person may become a public figure for a particular range of issues if he is drawn into a public controversy and if he

voluntarily injects himself into that public controversy in order to influence the outcome. *Gertz v. Robert Welch, Inc.* (1974). The Court has required a *voluntary* involvement in a *public controversy* in order to qualify as a public figure.

Examples: (1) Where a magazine article libeled a reputable attorney, the fact that the lawyer was active in community and professional affairs does not render him a public figure for all purposes. Absent clear evidence of general fame or notoriety in the community, and pervasive involvement in the affairs of society, an individual should not be deemed a public personality for all aspects of his life. This is particularly true where the libel plaintiff did not discuss the matter in controversy with the press, and did not thrust himself into the vortex of the public issue, nor engage the public attention in an attempt to influence the outcome of the case. *Gertz v. Robert Welch, Inc.* (1974).

(2) When a magazine reported that a divorce had been granted on the basis of the wife's adultery but the divorce court had not made such a finding, and the wife brought a libel action against the magazine, the wife should not be deemed a public figure simply by virtue of her having been drawn into litigation. The wife, a prominent socialite, did not otherwise occupy a role of special prominence in the affairs of society and had not thrust herself to the forefront of particular public controversies in order to influence the issues involved. *Time, Inc. v. Firestone* (1976).

(3) A researcher who received Senator Proxmire's "Golden Fleece" award criticizing federal support of his research is not a public figure in a defamation action against the Senator. The researcher had not voluntarily sought the public spotlight, his professional writings reached a limited audience, and the only public controversy was that created by the Senator's award. *Hutchinson v. Proxmire* (1979).

(4) The fact that a person had refused to appear before a grand jury investigation of Soviet intelligence activities and was cited for contempt does not make him a public figure. He had not voluntarily sought public attention. Mere involvement in a matter attracting public attention does not make a person a public figure. *Wolston v. Readers' Digest Ass'n., Inc.* (1979).

4) Actual Malice

a) Do not confuse the "actual malice" required to overcome constitutional privilege with common law malice, *i.e.,* ill will or spite. Actual malice requires knowledge of falsity of the defamatory statement or recklessness. Recklessness is not satisfied by proving that the publisher acted unreasonably. Only sufficient evidence demonstrating that the publisher "entertained serious doubts as to the truth of his publication" will suffice. *St. Amant v. Thompson* (1968).

b) Because actual malice requires proof of the subjective bad faith of the publisher, the plaintiff may ask questions during discovery probing the state of mind of the publisher and inquiring into the editorial process. *Herbert v. Lando* (1979).

c) A journalist's alteration of quotations does not establish actual malice "unless the alteration results in a material change in the meaning conveyed by the statement." *Masson v. New Yorker Magazine, Inc.* (1991).

d) An appellate court reviewing a jury finding of actual malice must review the entire record and exercise its own independent judgment to determine if actual malice has been proven by clear and convincing evidence. *Bose Corp. v. Consumer Union* (1984). The appellate court must itself examine the statements at issue and the circumstances to determine whether the speech is constitutionally protected. However, a jury's credibility determinations are reviewed under a "clearly erroneous" standard and are not subject to de novo review. *Harte–Hanks Communications, Inc. v. Connaughton* (1989).

b. Private Figures

1) **Standards of Review**

   Even when the plaintiff is not a public official or public figure, the First Amendment imposes some limitations, at least where matters of public interest are involved. So long as a state does not impose liability without fault, it may define for itself the appropriate standard of liability for a publisher or broadcaster of defamatory falsehood injurious to a private individual. Gertz v. Robert Welch, Inc. *(1974).*

   a) A state may not employ liability without fault (*i.e.*, strict liability) at least where a public issue is involved. A standard of negligence is the minimum required by the First Amendment. Most states have adopted negligence as the standard of liability.

   b) The private individual lacks the access to the channels of communication available to public officials and public figures and hence has less effective means to counteract false statements. Further, he has not voluntarily exposed himself to public view.

   c) This principle represents a balance of the First Amendment interest in avoiding media self-censorship and the state interest in protecting private reputation.

   d) *Dun & Bradstreet, infra,* raises serious question whether the constitutional ban against strict liability in private plaintiff defamation actions applies if the subject matter is solely a matter of private concern.

2) **Presumed and Punitive Damages**

   a) If the subject matter of the defamation involves a matter of public interest, only actual damages, not presumed damages, are permitted. States may not permit recovery of punitive damages at least in the absence of a showing of actual malice. *Gertz v. Robert Welch, Inc.* (1974). However, actual damages includes not only out of pocket costs but also injury to reputation, humiliation, and mental suffering. *Time, Inc. v. Firestone* (1976).

   b) But in matters of purely private concern, the state may award presumed and punitive damages even absent a showing of actual malice.

Example: In a report circulated to five subscribers, Dun & Bradstreet, a credit reporting agency, falsely indicated that Greenmoss Builders, a construction contractor, had filed a voluntary petition for bankruptcy. A jury awarded $50,000 in compensatory or presumed damages and $300,000 in punitive damages. The Supreme Court held, 5–4, that such an award does not violate the First Amendment even if actual malice is not established. A plurality reasoned that the state interest in protecting reputation was sufficient to support such awards, even absent actual malice, "[i]n light of the reduced constitutional value of speech involving no matters of public concern." In determining that the speech involved "no public issue," the plurality stressed the limited, specific audience to whom the defamation was addressed and the commercial character of the information communicated. Two concurring Justices would overrule *Gertz. Dun & Bradstreet, Inc. v. Greenmoss Builders, Inc.* (1985).

c. Proof of Falsity

The private figure plaintiff, like the public official and public figure plaintiff, bears the burden in the defamation action of proving that the statements at issue are false, at least where the statements involve matters of public concern. The common law presumption that defamatory speech is false cannot stand when a plaintiff seeks damages against a media defendant for speech involving matters of public concern. *Philadelphia Newspapers, Inc. v. Hepps* (1986). *Dun & Bradstreet* raises a serious question whether this principle applies in private plaintiff defamation actions involving solely matters of private concern.

d. The Fact–Opinion Dichotomy

"Under the First Amendment there is no such thing as a false idea." *Gertz.* But this principle does not mean that there is a First Amendment privilege for matters of opinion. If a statement of opinion includes or implies false, defamatory statements of fact, a defamation action can be maintained. First Amendment concerns are adequately protected by the requirement that the plaintiff prove fault and falsity and the principle that a defamation action will not lie for publications that cannot reasonably be interpreted as stating actual facts about an individual. *Milkovich v. Lorain Journal Co.* (1990).

2. Privacy

a. Invasions of Privacy

Freedom of expression also limits the ability of government to award damages for invasions of privacy. But the scope of the constitutional protection available is uncertain.

b. False Light Privacy

A privacy action against the media cannot be maintained merely on grounds that the report was false if it was newsworthy. The Court has required that the plaintiff show that the publication was made with actual malice. Time, Inc. v. Hill *(1967).* Whether *Gertz v. Robert Welch, Inc. (1974),* alters this rule remains unclear.

> *Example:* Life magazine contained a picture story on a play providing a misleading portrayal of the hostage ordeal of the Hill family, who had been held captive in their home by escaped convicts. The Hills brought suit under a privacy statute providing a cause of action even as to newsworthy events if the publication was fictionalized. The Court held that freedom of speech and the press require a showing of actual malice in order to recover for false publications. *Time, Inc. v. Hill* (1967).

c. Disclosure of Private Facts

Most states provide a privacy action for publication of private facts, not of legitimate concern to the public, in a manner highly offensive to a reasonable person. A recurring question is whether the press can be held liable for such truthful publications consistent with the First Amendment.

1) The press has a right to truthfully report facts disclosed in public court proceedings and in court records open to the public. However, the Court has declared that no *New York Times v. Sullivan* privilege will extend to shield a libel defendant if the publication is based on an inaccurate report of judicial records. *Time, Inc. v. Firestone* (1976).

> *Example:* A cause of action for invasion of privacy pursuant to a state statute prohibiting publication of a rape victim's

name may not be maintained where the information is a matter of public record. *Cox Broadcasting Corp. v. Cohn* (1975).

2) The Court, thus far, has been unwilling to hold that truthful publication can never be punished consistent with the First Amendment. *But "[i]f a newspaper lawfully obtains truthful information about a matter of public significance then state officials may not constitutionally punish publication of the information absent a need to further a state interest of the highest order."* Smith v. Daily Mail Pub. Co. (1979).

Example: An award of civil damages against a newspaper for negligently publishing the name of a rape victim lawfully obtained from a police report, where a state statute prohibited such publication, was held unconstitutional. Imposition of damages was not a narrowly tailored means of furthering the state's interest in protecting privacy since government itself could take greater care in safeguarding private information. The law was deemed underinclusive since it punished disclosure by the media of the identity of the rape victims but not disclosure by other means. *Florida Star v. B.J.F.* (1989).

3) Closed Public Records. The Court has not yet decided the extent to which a state constitutionally may deny public access to its records. However, a state law punishing a newspaper for publishing confidential material in connection with state judicial disciplinary commission proceedings is invalid. Discussion of judicial affairs lies near the "core of the First Amendment" and the state interest in protecting the reputation of judges and the judiciary was insufficient to constitute a clear and present danger to the administration of justice. *Landmark Communications, Inc. v. Virginia* (1978). A state cannot prohibit a grand jury witness from disclosing his own testimony after the grand jury term has ended. *Butterworth v. Smith* (1990).

d. Disclosure of Illegally Obtained Information

Where the press plays no part in the illegal activity and the information is lawfully obtained, the disclosure of truthful information involving matters of public concern is constitutionally protected absent a need of the highest order. But the Court has refused to answer the question "whether truthful information may ever be punished consistent with the First Amendment." *Bartnicki v. Vopper* (2001).

Example: An anonymous eavesdropper recorded a telephone conversation between Bartnicki, a teacher's union negotiator, and Kane, the union president, discussing possible violent actions. The tape was sent to Yocum, a third party who gave it to others, including a radio station where Vopper, a broadcaster, played it. Bartnicki and Kane sued Yocum and the broadcaster under federal and state laws prohibiting the nonconsentual interception of the communication and its subsequent use and disclosure with knowledge or reason to know of its illegal origin. The Court, 6–3, held the disclosure provisions unconstitutional as applied to these facts. The Court held that the law was content-neutral since it was not concerned with the content of the recording, nor was it justified by reference to the content but by the source of the information. Nevertheless, it was "a regulation of pure speech," not conduct. Citing *Smith v. Daily Mail* and *Florida Star v. B.J.F.*, the Court stressed that the information was truthful, lawfully obtained, and of public significance. Citing *New York Times Co. v. United States* (1971) (*Pentagon Papers*), the fact that the information is known to be illegally obtained is not determinative.

The government interest in removing an incentive for illegal interception of communications is inadequate since "[i]t would be quite remarkable to hold that speech by a law-abiding possessor of information can be suppressed in order to deter conduct by a non-law-abiding third party." While the interest in minimizing the harm to the privacy interests of victims of the intercept is much stronger, on balance it was insufficient. Enforcement in this case "implicates the core purposes of the First Amendment because it imposes sanctions on the publication of truthful information of public concern."

Justices Breyer and O'Connor concurred to explain why "the Court's holding does not imply a significantly broader constitutional immunity for the media." They stressed the need to ask "whether the statutes strike a reasonable balance between their speech-restricting and speech-enhancing consequences." Here, the speakers' legitimate privacy expectations were drastically low and the public interest in defeating them was unusually high.

The dissent emphasized that the laws were content-neutral and justified by the government interests in "drying up the market" for illegally-seized information and protecting private communication. *Bartnicki v. Vopper* (2001).

e. Right of Publicity

Government protection of a person's "right of publicity," *i.e.*, the publicity value of his name and activities, while permissible, is subject to constitutional limitations. However, an action for damages against a television station for broadcasting a performer's entire act does not violate the First Amendment. *Zacchini v. Scripps–Howard Broadcasting Co.* (1977).

3. Intentional Infliction of Emotional Distress

a. Public Persons

Public officials and public figures may not recover for the tort of intentional infliction of emotional distress without showing that the publication contains a false statement of fact which was made with actual malice.

Example: Hustler Magazine published a parody portraying the Reverend Jerry Falwell as a drunken hypocrite whose first time sexual encounter was with his mother in an outhouse. A judgment for Falwell for intentional infliction of emotional distress was unanimously reversed by the Supreme Court. Bad motive may not be made controlling for tort purposes in the area of public debate about public figures. "Outrageousness," a critical element of the tort, has an inherent subjectiveness about it which permits juries to impose liability based on a dislike for the expression. The publication could not reasonably have been interpreted as stating actual facts about Falwell. "[P]ublic figures and public officials may not recover for defamation without showing that the publication contains a false statement of fact which was made with actual malice, *i.e.*, with knowledge that the statement was false or with reckless disregard as to whether or not it was true." This provides "breathing space" for First Amendment freedoms. *Hustler Magazine v. Falwell* (1988).

b.   Private Persons

The Supreme Court has not yet decided what limitations, if any, the First Amendment imposes in an action for infliction of emotional distress brought by a plaintiff who is not a public official or public figure. The Court avoided the issue in *Snyder v. Phelps*, Ch. VIII, E, 1, d, 3), holding that the First Amendment barred tort recovery because the speech was on "matters of public concern," rather than on "matters of private concern."

4.   Newsgathering

The First Amendment does extend some protection to the newsgathering process. However, the press generally has not been accorded a privilege to gather information beyond that of the ordinary citizen. The court will balance the effect of a regulation on the free flow of information to the public with the state interest in maintaining the regulation. In determining the responsibilities of journalists to comply with the ordinary and neutral requirements of civil and criminal procedure, the standard appears to be that the press should not be either specially burdened or specially advantaged.

a.   Newsman's Privilege

1)   The First Amendment affords journalists no privilege, qualified or absolute, to refuse to give evidence to a grand jury at least so long as it is conducted as a good faith law enforcement effort and not as a harassment device. The uncertain burden on newsgathering by requiring disclosure is outweighed by the public interest in fair and effective law enforcement. *Branzburg v. Hayes* (1972). The Court indicated its continued adherence to *Branzburg* in rejecting a First Amendment privilege for confidential peer review information. *University of Pennsylvania v. E.E.O.C.* (1990). However, a number of lower courts have recognized a First Amendment-based journalist's privilege from forced disclosure in a variety of criminal and civil proceedings.

2)   If a journalist has promised confidentiality to a source and then breaches that promise by publishing the source's name, the press

can be held liable for damages under the generally applicable law of promissory estoppel. Any burden on the journalist's First Amendment right to gather and disseminate the news is incidental. *Cohen v. Cowles Media Co.* (1991).

b. Access to Public Information and Institutions

1) Prisons

a) Censorship of Mail

Censorship of prisoners' outgoing mail violates the First Amendment right of the recipient unless (1) it furthers substantial government interests in security, order, or inmate rehabilitation; and (2) it is no greater than is necessary to further this substantial government interest. *Procunier v. Martinez* (1974). Internal correspondence may be limited if the regulation reasonably relates to legitimate penological objectives. *Turner v. Safley* (1987). This more lenient standard of judicial review has also been applied to censorship of incoming material which is perceived as presenting more of a risk than outgoing materials. *Thornburgh v. Abbott* (1989).

b) Interviewing Prisoners

Where there is a reasonable basis for a government regulation on journalist interviews with prison inmates, and alternative avenues of communication are available, it is established that the state may restrict particular modes of communication between inmates and the public. *Pell v. Procunier* (1974). It is also clear that the press has no special right of access to the prisons beyond that of the public. It is unclear whether there is any First Amendment public right of access to the prisons. However, if public access is granted, government may not discriminate against the press. *Houchins v. KQED, Inc.* (1978).

2) Judicial Proceedings

a) Criminal Trials

Since criminal trial proceedings have historically been open and public access makes the trial process function more effectively, there is a First Amendment right of access. A presumption of openness inheres in the very nature of a criminal trial under our system which can be overcome only by "findings that closure is essential to preserve higher values and is narrowly tailored to serve that interest." *Press–Enterprise Co. v. Superior Court* (1984) (*Press–Enterprise I*).

Examples: (1) Closure of the fourth trial of a murder charge, ordered on defendant's motion, without objection by the prosecution, was held to violate the First Amendment. Citing the tradition and value of open criminal trials, a Court plurality held that absent an overriding interest, articulated in trial court findings, the trial of a criminal case must be open to the public. There were no such findings. *Richmond Newspapers, Inc. v. Virginia* (1980).

(2) A state statute requiring closure of trials of designated sex offenses during the testimony of minor witnesses is unconstitutional. The government interest in encouraging young victims of sex offenses to come forward and to protect them from psychological harm is compelling. However, automatic closure, rather than case-by-case determination, is not narrowly tailored but is, rather, excessively broad. *Globe Newspaper Co. v. Superior Court* (1982).

(3) *Voir Dire.* The examination of prospective jurors in a criminal trial, like the trial itself, is presumptively open. This presumption can be overcome "only by an overriding interest based on findings that closure is essential to preserve higher values and is narrowly tailored to serve that interest." Closing all but 3 days of a 6 week voir dire is not narrowly tailored to protect jurors' privacy. *Press–Enterprise Co. v. Superior Court* (1984) (*Press–Enterprise I*).

b) Pretrial Proceedings

The Court has employed a two-part test in determining if pretrial proceedings should be open. First, is there a tradition of openness? Second, does public access aid the actual functioning of the proceeding? If there is First Amendment right of access, closure must be based on specific findings that it is essential to preserve higher values and that the closure order is narrowly tailored to serve that interest.

Examples: (1) The Sixth Amendment guarantee of an open trial is a personal right of the accused and does not create a right of public access to pretrial suppression hearings. However, a badly split Court avoided deciding the question whether the First Amendment guarantees a public right of access to suppression hearings. *Gannett Co. v. DePasquale* (1979).

(2) A qualified First Amendment right of access to preliminary hearings which have traditionally been open to the public and which play "a particularly significant and positive role in the actual functioning of the process" exists. Openness is critical where the preliminary hearing "is often the final and most important step in the criminal proceeding." Given the importance of public access to such proceedings, they "cannot be closed unless specific, on the record findings are made demonstrating that 'closure is essential to preserve higher values and is narrowly tailored to serve that interest.' " If the interest is that of an accused to a fair trial, closure is allowed only if "there is a substantial probability that the defendant's right to a fair trial will be prejudiced by publicity that closure would present and, second, reasonable alternative to closure cannot adequately protect the defendant's free trial rights." *Press–Enterprise Co. v. Superior Court* (1986) (*Press–Enterprise II*).

(3) The Supreme Court held 7–2, that the Sixth Amendment right to a public trial is violated when a court closes a *voir dire* proceeding without first considering reasonable alternatives to closure. As *voir dire* was about to begin in Presley's

trial for cocaine trafficking, the trial judge ordered the accused's uncle to leave the court and the floor where the proceeding was held because of concern that jurors might be prejudiced by "inadvertent comment or conversation" by the uncle. In a *per curiam* opinion, the Supreme Court relied on both First Amendment and Sixth Amendment precedent in holding that it was "well-settled" that the Sixth Amendment extends to jury *voir dire*. The Court added that the Sixth Amendment, like the First Amendment, requires trial courts "to consider alternatives to closure even when they are not offered by the parties." While potential prejudice to the jury might justify closure, the trial judge is required to make specific findings to that effect in the record. *Presley v. Georgia* (2010).

c. Newsroom Searches and Seizures

The First Amendment does not afford the press any special privilege from otherwise constitutional searches and seizures beyond that of the ordinary citizen. However, warrant requirements must be applied with particular searching exactitude when the search involves the newsroom. *Zurcher v. The Stanford Daily* (1978). *Compare New York v. P.J. Video, Inc.* (1986), holding, in an obscenity context, that an application for a warrant authorizing the seizure of materials presumptively protected by the First Amendment should be evaluated by the same standard of probable cause used to review warrant applications generally.

d. Cameras in the Courtroom

Permitting radio, television, and still photographic coverage of criminal trials for public broadcast, even over the objections of the defendant, does not violate due process, absent a showing of prejudice to the defendant depriving him of a fair trial. *Chandler v. Florida* (1981).

e. Copyright

The First Amendment does not protect the publishing of an as-yet unpublished copyrighted expression of a public figure. The substantial import of the subject matter and the fact that the words themselves which the author has used may be newsworthy does not excuse a use of material which would not ordinarily be permitted nor does it justify the unauthorized copying of the author's expression prior to publication.

Copyright law protects the First Amendment interest in free expression by distinguishing between copyrightable expression and uncopyrightable facts and ideas. To create a public figure exception to copyright would impede the copyright's functions of increasing knowledge. Moreover, First Amendment protection of freedom of thought and expression includes the right to refrain from speaking. *Harper & Row Publishers, Inc. v. Nation Enterprises* (1985).

f. Silencing Trial Participants

Gag orders directed against the media are content-based prior restraints which are presumptively unconstitutional. *Nebraska Press Association v. Stuart* (1976). As an alternative method of curbing prejudicial publicity and maintaining confidentiality, courts often issue orders designed to silence trial participants. The media argues that such gag orders violate First Amendment newsgathering rights. *A rule prohibiting lawyers from making extrajudicial statements "if the lawyer knows or reasonably should know that it will have a substantial likelihood of materially prejudicing an adjudicative proceeding" is constitutional.* Gentile v. State Bar of Nevada (1991).

Example: Nevada State Bar Rules used to discipline a defense attorney who held a press conference to argue that his client was being made a scapegoat for police corruption are void for vagueness. The "substantial likelihood of material prejudice" standard embodied in the Rules constitutes a constitutionally permissible balance between the First Amendment rights of lawyers and the state's interest in protecting fair trial rights. The lawyer is an officer of the court with special access to information increasing the danger from extrajudicial commentary. However, a "safe harbors" provision in the Nevada Rules, allowing the attorney to state without elaboration the general nature of the defense provided insufficient guidance to attorneys seeking to determine what is allowed and what is forbidden. *Gentile v. State Bar of Nevada* (1991).

g. Media Ride Alongs

Law enforcement officers violate the Fourth Amendment by allowing the media or other third persons accompany them into a private home in execution of an arrest warrant when the third party presence is not in aid of the execution of the warrant.

Example: Law enforcement officers invited a press reporter and photographer to accompany them on an arrest pursuant to a warrant. While the fugitive was not at home, his parents were in their bedrooms. They sued the officers for damages, claiming a violation of their Fourth Amendment rights. The Court held that core Fourth Amendment rights of residential privacy were violated by bringing the media into the home but that the officers enjoyed qualified immunity. While the press plays an important role in informing the public about the criminal justice system, this did not make the media's intrusion into a private home reasonable. *Wilson v. Layne* (1999).

5. Regulation of Electronic Media (See Ch. VIII, I, On Obscenity)

a. Regulating Broadcasting

1) Full First Amendment protection does not extend to broadcasting. Under the Communications Act, the Federal Communications Commission regulates broadcasting licensees "consistent with the public interest, convenience [and] necessity." Historically, this increased regulation has been justified under the scarcity theory—the broadcast spectrum is technologically limited and must be treated as a scarce public resource. See, e.g., *Red Lion Broadcasting Co. v. FCC* (1969) (holding constitutional FCC fairness doctrine requiring broadcast licensees to provide balanced treatment of controversial ideas). More recently, the Court has also emphasized the pervasiveness and influence of broadcasting and its impact on our society, as justification for the greater regulatory power of government. *FCC v. Pacifica Foundation* (1978) ("[O]f all forms of communication, it is broadcasting that has received the most limited First Amendment protection."). The Court has recently avoided First Amendment review of the FCC's regulation of broadcasting indecent speech. *FCC v. Fox TV Station, Inc.* (2012).

Examples: (1) George Carlin's 10–minute satiric monologue, "Filthy Words," was aired at two o'clock in the afternoon by a radio station owned by Pacifica. A man, who claimed that he had heard the broadcast while driving with his young son, complained to the FCC. The Court upheld the FCC's power to regulate indecent programming under a nuisance rationale stressing the factual context. Broadcasting's "uniquely pervasive presence in the lives of all Americans" and its unique accessibility to children justify special treatment of government regulation of broadcasting. The deliberate repeated use of vulgar, offensive and shocking language, describing sexual and excretory functions in a patently offensive manner, broadcast at a time when children were undoubtedly in the audience, justified civil regulation. *FCC v. Pacifica Foundation* (1978).

(2) The Supreme Court held that a finding by the FCC that Fox TV and ABC TV had violated its Order against the broadcast of fleeting expletives and even brief nudity violated the Fifth Amendment Due Process Clause. The broadcasts in question preceded the issuance of the FCC Order expressly banning fleeting expletives and nudity. The Court, per Justice Kennedy, held that the Commission failed to give Fox or ABC fair notice that the broadcasts could be found "actionably indecent" under then-existing indecency policies. Justice Kennedy observed that since the case was decided on fair notice grounds under the Due Process Clause, the Court need not address the First Amendment implications of the Commission's indecency policy. He did note that the FCC is free to modify its current broadcast indecency policy. Justice Ginsburg, concurring, said that *Pacifica* "was wrong when it was issued" and that "[t]ime, technological advances, and the Commission's untenable rulings in the cases now before the Court show why *Pacifica* bears reconsideration." *FCC v. Fox Television Stations, Inc.* (2012).

2) Nonprint means of communication are not necessarily subject to the diminished protection accorded broadcasting. Regulation of programming content on other media has been subjected to more exacting standards of review.

   Example: A total ban on sexually-oriented indecent, but nonobscene, telephone messages, is unconstitutional. Such speech can be regulated on the basis of its content only if the regulation is carefully tailored to achieve compelling government interest; government must use the least restrictive means available. *Pacifica* was based on the unique aspects of broadcasting. Telephone communications require the recipient to take affirmative steps to receive the communication. There is no "captive audience" and dial-a-porn service "is not so invasive or surprising that it prevents an unwilling listener from avoiding exposure to it." There were feasible and effective ways to protect children other than a total ban. The Court also upheld a statutory prohibition on obscene dial-a-porn telephone communication. *Sable Communications of California, Inc. v. FCC* (1989).

b. Regulating Cable Television

Cable operators "engage in and transmit speech." The reduced First Amendment protection applicable to broadcasting generally does not apply to cable which does not suffer from the "unique physical limitations of the broadcast media." While the unique physical characteristics of cable transmission may affect the constitutionality of particular cable regulation, "they do not require the alteration of settled principles of our First Amendment jurisprudence." *Turner Broadcasting System, Inc. v. FCC* (1994). But the Court has not yet clearly established that cable is subject to the same standards as the print media, *Denver Area Educational Telecommunications Consortium, Inc. v. FCC* (1996), although it appears that full First Amendment protection does apply. *United States v. Playboy Entertainment Group, Inc.* (2000).

Examples: (1) The district court erred in granting summary judgment to the government upholding federal must-carry provisions, which require cable operators to carry the signals of a specified number of local broadcast television stations. The must-carry rules are content-neutral regulations which are to reviewed using the *O'Brien* intermediate level of scrutiny. The regulation serves a variety of important interests, unrelated to the suppression of free expansion: (1) preserving the benefits of free broadcast televisions; (2) promoting widespread dissemination of diverse information; and (3) promoting competition for television broadcasting. But there are serious issues of material fact as to whether the must-carry rules suppress "substantially more speech than necessary." The case was remanded to develop a more thorough factual record. *Turner Broadcasting System, Inc. v. FCC* (1994).

(2) Following remand, the Supreme Court held, 5–4, that substantial evidence existed to support the congressional judgment that the must-carry rules were narrowly-tailored to the important interest in preserving the existence of local on-air broadcast stations. Absent the regulation, many broadcast stations would be denied carriage which would cause them serious financial difficulties, jeopardizing their survival. *Turner Broadcasting System, Inc. v. FCC* (1997).

(3) In reviewing the constitutionality of various indecency provisions in the Cable Act, the Court was sharply divided. Justice Kennedy urged that leased access channels be treated like a common carrier so that content-based regulation of cable is subject to strict scrutiny. Justice Thomas argued that the cable operator has the predominant First Amendment interest. Four justices, per Justice Breyer, declined to fix a particular standard by analogizing cable to other media.

Section 10(a) of the Cable Act permitting operators of leased channels to decide whether or not to broadcast "patently offensive" programs was held constitutional. The plurality engaged in "closely scrutinizing § 10(a) to assure that it properly addresses an extremely important problem, without imposing, in light of the relevant interests, an unnecessarily great restriction on speech." The need to protect children from accessible cable programming (as in *Pacifica*), consideration of the complex interests of the cable operators and those programmers granted access, and the likelihood that the permissive standard would not restrict excessive speech, led the plurality to hold that § 10(a) is sufficiently narrowly tailored. Three justices (Justices Thomas and Scalia and Chief Justice Rehnquist) concurred analogizing cable to the print media and recognizing "the general primacy of the cable operator's editorial rights over the rights of programmers and viewers."

Section 10(b) of the Cable Act requiring operators of leased channels to segregate and block potentially offensive programming if they decide to broadcast such programs is unconstitutional. While protection of children is a compelling interest, the Court concluded that requirement is not narrowly tailored, is more extensive than necessary and is not a "least restrictive alternative" (i.e., it does not satisfy "strict" or "less strict" standards).

Section 10(c) of the Cable Act permitting operators of public access channels required by local governments for public interest programming to allow or prohibit patently offensive programming is unconstitutional. Justice Breyer, joined by Justices Stevens and Souter, held that the provision was not necessary to protect children. It gives cable operators a censorship power over programming beyond that which they previously had and such programming is already subject to extensive supervision. Further, such content control is more likely to erroneously exclude borderline programs than to protect children. Finally there is no evidence that patently offensive programming on public access channels is a serious enough problem to justify the regulation. Justices Kennedy and Ginsburg concurred, arguing that such channels are "designated public forums." *Denver Area Educational Telecommunications Consortium, Inc. v. FCC* (1996).

(4) A "signal bleed" provision of the Telecommunications Act requiring cable operators either to scramble sexually explicit channels or to limit programming to certain hours is unconstitutional. The law is a "content-based restriction subject to strict scrutiny." The government failed to satisfy the less restrictive means test. Since existing technology could not prevent signal bleed in most cases, cable operators would broadcast sexually explicit programming only in the safe hours, thereby limiting programer's access during prime hours. The less restrictive alternative of promoting viewer blocking of such programs on an individual basis was available and would be effective in protecting children. *United States v. Playboy Entertainment Group, Inc.* (2000).

c. Regulating the Internet

The internet is a network of interconnected computers providing worldwide communications and information retrieval. The Court has stated that "our cases provide no basis for qualifying the level of First Amendment scrutiny that should be applied to this medium." The internet has not been subject "to the type of government regulation that has attended the broadcast industry. Moreover, the internet is not as 'invasive' as radio or television." Finally, "the internet can hardly be considered a 'scarce' expressive commodity," since it provides "relatively unlimited, low-cost capacity for communications of all kinds." *Reno v. American Civil Liberties Union* (1997).

Examples: (1) Provisions of the Communications Decency Act of 1996 prohibiting the knowing transmission over the internet of "indecent" or "patently offensive" material to a person under 18 years of age is unconstitutional. Since the law is a content based, criminal regulation of speech, strict scrutiny applies. The law must be narrowly-tailored to promote the Government's compelling interest in protecting children. But the Act uses different undefined terms—"indecent" and "patently offensive"—producing uncertainty in speakers and presenting a greater threat of censorship of protected speech than even obscenity laws. The CDA effectively suppresses a large amount of speech adults have a right to receive and communicate. The fact that there are ample alternative channels for communication, that the Act requires knowledge that the person is a minor, and the possibility that material with redeeming social value would not fall within the statutory bans, do not avoid the statute's overbreadth. Statutory defenses based on good faith, reasonable and effective action to prevent transmission to minors, do not constitute sufficient narrow tailoring to avoid the patently invalid, overbroad provisions. *Reno v. American Civil Liberties Union* (1997).

(2) The reliance on community standards in identifying "material that is harmful to minors" in the Child Online Protection Act *"does not by itself* render the statute substantially overbroad for purposes of the First Amendment." But the Court was in disagreement on other matters. It did not decide whether COPA otherwise was substantially

overbroad or vague or whether, as the district court had held, it would not survive strict scrutiny. *Ashcroft v. American Civil Liberties Union* (2002).

6. Public Access to the Media

a. Public Access to the Electronic Media

The public has a First Amendment right to receive suitable access to social, political, esthetic, moral, and other ideas and experiences. First Amendment protection extends not only to the interests of the speaker but also to those of the listener. This is necessary in order to preserve an uninhibited marketplace of ideas and to promote the role of the citizenry as citizen-critics of government action.

1) **Fairness Doctrine**

The government may constitutionally require broadcasters to discuss public issues and to provide coverage to each side of an issue. This doctrine—the fairness doctrine—promotes First Amendment values in avoiding monopolization of the limited airwaves and in producing a more informed public. *Red Lion Broadcasting Co. v. FCC* (1969). The FCC has rejected the fairness doctrine.

2) **A Right of Access**

There is no First Amendment right of public access to the broadcast media. Government is not constitutionally required to assure that broadcasters provide access to ideas and issues. However, a limited, reasonable congressionally-mandated statutory right of access to broadcast time is constitutional.

Examples: (1) The First Amendment does not mandate that the FCC require broadcast licensees to accept paid editorials on controversial topics. Such a doctrine would not promote the public interest in access since it would intrude on journalistic independence by involving the government excessively into decisions on what to broadcast and would tend to permit the affluent to determine the issues to be discussed. *CBS v. Democratic Nat'l Comm.* (1973).

(2) Refusal to sell air time to a legally qualified candidate for federal elective office violates the Fed-

eral Election Campaign Act of 1971, which creates an affirmative, enforceable right of reasonable access to the use of broadcast stations for individual candidates seeking elective office. This holding does not create a general right of access to the media, but rather recognizes a limited statutory right to reasonable access that pertains only to legally qualified federal candidates. *CBS v. FCC* (1981).

b. Public Access to the Print Media

Newspapers cannot be compelled to publish that which they do not choose to print. Unlike the situation in the electronic media, in the case of the print media, government may not perform the editorial function.

Example:　A state statute granting a political candidate a right to equal space to reply to personal attacks by a newspaper violates the First Amendment. Government regulation of what materials should go into a newspaper with respect to size and content of the paper, and the treatment of public issues and public officials constitutes an impermissible exercise of editorial control and judgment. *Miami Herald Publishing Co. v. Tornillo* (1974).

I. Obscenity

1. No First Amendment Protection

Lewdness, indecency, offensiveness, and profanity are not excluded from First Amendment protection. Cohen v. California *(1971). ("Fuck the Draft" emblazoned on a leather jacket is constitutionally protected speech). However, obscenity is not entitled to First Amendment protection since such expression lacks social importance.* Roth v. United States *(1957). The lack of protection afforded to obscene speech is limited in its application; the categorical exclusion of obscenity does not extend to animal cruelty and violence.* United v. Stevens *(2010) (animal cruelty);* Brown v. Entertainment Merchants Assn *(2011) (violence).*

a. Rationality Satisfied

The only substantive requirement, therefore, is that government obscenity regulations be rationally related to permissible state interests. The Court has stated that such regulations further the public interest "in the quality of life and the total community environment, the tone of commerce in the great city centers, and, possibly, the public safety itself * * *." *Paris Adult Theatre I v. Slaton* (1973).

b. A Matter of Definition

Since obscenity is not First Amendment speech or press, the essential focus is on the definition of "obscenity." Prior to 1973, no definition of obscenity was able to win support of a majority of justices.

2. The Modern Definition

Each element of a three-part test must be satisfied in order to define material as obscene: "(a) whether the average person, applying contemporary community standards would find that the work, taken as a whole, appeals to the prurient interest, (b) whether the work depicts or describes, in a patently offensive way, sexual conduct specifically defined by the applicable state law, and (c) whether the work, taken as a whole, lacks serious literary, artistic, political, or scientific value." Miller v. California *(1973).*

a. Contemporary Community Standards

1) No National Community Standard

In applying the standards relating to pruriency and patent offensiveness, the courts need not apply any national community standard. The jury may be instructed to apply "contemporary community standards" without further specification. Use of "community standards" to identify material harmful to minors in regulating obscenity on the internet does not itself render a law substantially overbroad. *Ashcroft v. American Civil Liberties Union* (2002).

2) Federal Jury Standard

In a federal proceeding, the prevailing community standard in the area from which the jurors are drawn may be used. *Hamling v. United States* (1974).

3) Identifying "Community" Members

In obscenity trials, children are not to be considered a part of the "community" for purposes of determining community standards. However, sensitive persons may be considered "community" members. *Pinkus v. United States* (1978).

4) Experts

Since the determination of pruriency and patent offensiveness are determined by community standards, no expert evidence is required to establish obscenity. *Paris Adult Theater I v. Slaton* (1973). Further, since community members can differ in their evaluation of materials, the fact that similar material to that in question is available in the community is not evidentiary. *Hamling v. United States* (1974).

5) Appellate Review

While *Miller* was meant to leave the determination of obscenity to local communities, this does not preclude independent judicial review *even* of the jury determination of obscenity. Constitutional standards must be satisfied.

Example: Conviction of a movie theater owner for showing the film "Carnal Knowledge" was reversed by the Supreme Court. While questions of pruriency and patent offensiveness are questions of fact for the jury, the Constitution does not permit condemnation of materials unless they "depict or describe patently offensive 'hard core' sexual conduct." The nude scenes in "Carnal Knowledge" did not satisfy this standard. *Jenkins v. Georgia* (1974).

b. Defining the Relevant Audience

1) The Average Person

Obscenity is to be judged in terms of the effect of the material on a person of average susceptibility. Neither the especially sensitive person nor the insensitive person is the measure, even though they are included in defining community standards.

2) Variable Obscenity: Minors and Deviants

Obscenity may be determined by considering the target audience to whom the work is addressed and their peculiar susceptibilities. Thus, a properly-drafted statute directed at distribution to minors would be constitutional. *Ginsberg v. New York* (1968). Similarly, jurors may be instructed to consider whether the material appeals to the prurient interest of members of sexually deviant groups, *e.g.,* sado-masochists. *Mishkin v. New York* (1966); *Pinkus v. United States* (1978).

c. The Demand for Specificity

1) Vagueness

The Court consistently has rejected the claim that all definitions of obscenity are necessarily unconstitutionally vague.

2) Overbreadth

    (a) Sex and obscenity are not synonymous, although only *sexual* material may be obscene. Examples of obscene material include "patently offensive representations or descriptions of ultimate sexual acts, normal or perverted, actual or simulated" and "patently offensive representations or descriptions of masturbation, excretory functions, and lewd exhibitions of the genitals." *Miller v. California* (1973).

    (b) In *Miller*, the Court stated: "Conduct must be specifically defined by the applicable state law, as written or authoritatively construed, to make obscenity regulation constitutional." In fact, the courts often construe the obscenity laws to embody the obscenity standards and specific types of acts set forth in *Miller* and uphold the statutes. *Ward v. Illinois* (1977) (state statute read to incorporate the patently offensive standard of *Miller* and its examples of patently offensive acts).

    (c) The fact that an obscenity statute is overbroad in part does not mean that the entire statute is invalid.

        Example: A statute defining "prurient" to include lust and not limited to shameful or morbid interest in sex is overbroad. However since the overbreadth is not incurable and need not taint all applications of the statute, it should be invalidated "only in so far as the word 'lust' is understood as reaching protected materials." *Brockett v. Spokane Arcades, Inc.* (1985).

3) Pandering

In determining whether the three-fold definition of obscenity is satisfied, the circumstances of the presentation and dissemination of the material are material. *Splawn v. California* (1977).

    Example: Where a publisher sought mailing privileges from the postmasters of Intercourse and Blue Ball, Pennsylvania, and where the leer of the sensualist permeated all the advertising for his publications, the purveyor's sole emphasis on the sexually provocative aspects of his publications can be decisive in the determination of obscenity. Inquiry can be validly directed to the context of such commercial exploitation in determining whether the material at issue can be treated as protected expression. *Ginzburg v. United States* (1966).

4) Racketeering Laws

There is no constitutional bar to the inclusion of substantive obscenity offenses under a state criminal RICO law. *Fort Wayne Books, Inc. v. Indiana* (1989).

d. Serious Value

Miller clearly rejects the requirement, fashioned in *Memoirs v. Massachusetts* (1966) that, to be labeled obscene, a work must be "utterly without redeeming social value." Today, the work, judged as a whole, must lack *serious* literary, artistic, political, or scientific value. Note that this element of the test is *not* judged by local community standards. The third prong is to be determined, not on a local community, but on an objective basis, *i.e.*, whether a reasonable person would find serious literary, artistic, political, or scientific value in the material, taken as a whole, not whether such value would be found under contemporary community standards. *Pope v. Illinois* (1987).

3. Privacy and Obscenity

a. *The mere possession of obscene matter cannot constitutionally be made a crime. Privacy, a fundamental right, protects what an individual reads or watches in his own home.*

> *Example:* In the course of a search of a home for evidence of bookmaking activities, the police found obscene films and the accused was arrested and charged with possession of obscene matter. The Court declared that punishment of mere private possession of obscene material violates the right or privacy even though the public distribution of the very same material could be constitutionally punished. Public distribution, unlike private possession, may be punished because of the possibility such material may fall into the hands of children or may intrude upon the sensibilities or privacy of the general public. *Stanley v. Georgia* (1969).

b. But the right of privacy does not protect obscene displays in places of public accommodation even when effective safeguards are employed against exposure to juveniles and passersby. *Paris Adult Theater v. Slaton* (1973).

c. Nor does *Stanley* extend to child pornography. The state's compelling interests in protecting the physical and psychological well-being of minors and in destroying the market for the exploitative use of children distinguish the child pornography context from *Stanley. Osborne v. Ohio* (1990).

4. Civil Control of Obscenity and Indecency

a. Prior Restraints

Control of obscenity may also take the form of civil statutes such as nuisance or zoning laws. Such controls usually constitute prior restraints involving licensing, injunction, and administrative censorship. However, the Court generally has taken a more favorable attitude to such prior restraints on the theory that they avoid many of the evils of obscenity control pursued through criminal laws. *Paris Adult Theater v. Slaton* (1973).

b. Content–Neutral Regulation

Frequently, zoning laws are treated as time, place, and manner regulations rather than content controls. In cases where the regulation significantly effects protected activity, the law must be designed to achieve a substantial government interest and must leave open reasonable alternative channels of communication.

Examples: (1) A zoning ordinance barring adult bookstores, theatres, etc., from being in a defined locational proximity is not an invalid prior restraint violative of the First Amendment or Fourteenth Amendment equal protection. While government must maintain neutrality regarding speech content, regulation of such establishments is unaffected by the content message in the films. Such a regulation is a place regulation, a reasonable means of implementing the city's interest in preserving the character of its neighborhoods. *Young v. American Mini Theatres, Inc.* (1976).

(2) A zoning ordinance which prohibits adult movie theatres from locating within 1000 feet of residential property, churches, parks, or schools does not violate the First Amendment. Such a regulation is a "content-neutral" time, place, and manner regulation aimed at the "secondary effects" of adult theaters. As such, it is acceptable under the

First Amendment so long as it is designed to serve a substantial government interest and there are reasonable alternative avenues of communication. A city's interest in attempting to preserve the quality of urban life is an interest which must be accorded high respect. The law left open reasonable alternative channels of communication since 5% of the city's land could be used by adult theaters. The city need not engage in fact-finding regarding the harm in Renton but can rely on findings and experience of other cities. *City of Renton v. Playtime Theatres, Inc.* (1986).

(3) The Court relied on *City of Renton's* "secondary effects" doctrine in upholding a city ordinance that not only dispersed adult businesses but prohibited more than one adult entertainment business in the same building. The city could reasonably rely on an earlier study relating crime patterns to a concentration of adult establishments in prohibiting multiple-use adult establishments. *City of Los Angeles v. Alameda Books, Inc.* (2002).

c. Vagueness and Overbreadth

1) "Indecent" publications and expressive activity which is not obscene remain constitutionally protected expression. Like criminal laws, civil regulations of obscene materials must be narrowly drawn to satisfy the three-fold test of obscenity. The sexual conduct proscribed must be specifically defined in the statute or be read in through authoritative judicial construction. Otherwise, when government seeks to shield the public from some kinds of speech or press on the ground of its special offensiveness by regulation, the First Amendment strictly limits its power.

Examples: (1) An ordinance that prohibits as a public nuisance drive-in theatres from showing films containing nudity ("bare buttocks * * * female bare breasts, or human bare pubic areas") when visible from a public street or public place sweeps too far beyond the permissible restraints on obscenity. Such an ordinance invalidly reaches films directed not only against sexually explicit nudity but reaches any nudity however innocent or educational. In such circumstances, the burden should be on the viewer to protect his sensibilities merely by averting his eyes. *Erznoznik v. Jacksonville* (1975).

(2) A zoning ordinance carrying penalties which excludes all commercial live entertainment, including nonobscene nude dancing, while permitting other commercial activity, violates the First and Fourteenth Amendment guarantee of freedom of expression. Nude dancing is not without its First Amendment protection from official regulation. But whatever protection nudity is afforded, this zoning ordinance was a substantial and overbroad intrusion on protected rights. It was not narrowly drawn to further a substantial governmental interest. State interests in traffic control and waste disposal, even if real, could be achieved by a more selective measure. It was not a reasonable time, place and manner control. *Schad v. Mount Ephraim* (1981).

(3) The New York Alcoholic Beverage Control Law which prohibits nude dancing in establishments licensed by the state to sell liquor for on-premises consumption, does not constitute a violation of the First Amendment. The State's power to ban the sale of alcoholic beverages includes the lesser power to ban the sale of liquor on premises where topless dancing occurs. The elected representatives of New York have chosen to avoid the disturbances associated with mixing alcohol and nude dancing by means of a reasonable restriction upon establishments that sell liquor for on-premises consumption. Whatever artistic or communicative value may attach to topless dancing is overcome by the state's exercise of its broad powers and "the added presumption in favor of the state regulation" conferred by the Twenty–First Amendment. *New York State Liquor Authority v. Bellanca* (1981).

2) *If the regulation does not significantly burden expression or the effects of speech, the First Amendment protection does not apply and the law need only be rational.*

Example: The First Amendment does not bar enforcement of a statute authorizing closure of premises found to be used as a place for prostitution and lewdness simply because the premises are also used as an adult bookstore. The appellate court erred in applying *O'Brien* since the sexual activity being regulated in the present case involves no element of protected expression. The legislature properly sought to protect the environment of the community by directing the sanction at places knowingly used for unlawful activity involving no protected expression. The Court characterized the incidental burden on First Amendment activity as minimal; the owners remained free to sell their materials at another location. *Arcara v. Cloud Books, Inc.* (1986).

5. Broadcasting and Indecent Speech

a.   Full First Amendment protection does not extend to broadcasting. The pervasiveness of broadcasting and concern over the presence of children in the audience allows reasonable FCC regulation of indecent programming. See *FCC v. Pacifica Foundation* (1978) (See Ch. VIII, H, 5).

b.   But nonprint means of communication are not necessarily subject to the diminished protection accorded broadcasting. Regulation of indecency on other forms of media have been subject to the more exacting standards of review normally used for content control. See Ch. VIII, H, 5.

6. Child Pornography

Child pornography is a "category of material outside the protection of the First Amendment." Government can punish pornographic depictions of children even if the *Miller* standards are not satisfied. However, virtual child pornography, where no actual child is used, is protected speech. *Ashcroft v. Free Speech Coalition* (2002). The possession or pandering of child pornography—even virtual child pornography—can be criminalized. But the government regulation must be limited to child pornography and fall within its rationale for speech restriction. *United States v. Williams* (2008).

Examples: (1) A New York criminal statute prohibiting persons from knowingly promoting sexual performances by children under the age of 16 by distributing such material is constitutional. The state has a compelling interest in protecting minors; distribution of such visual material is intrinsically related to production involving sexual abuse of children; the economic benefits from distribution stimulate production of the materials; such productions have minimal constitutional value. The Court did limit its decision to live performances or visual reproduction of live performances, *i.e.*, production involving child actors. Since the New York law was not "substantially overbroad," it was not facially unconstitutional. The Court did not decide if "socially valuable" works are constitutionally protected. *New York v. Ferber* (1982).

(2) An Ohio statute which criminalized possession of any material depicting a nude minor, except under a number of limited circumstances and for proper purposes was found constitutional. The statute itself was not unconstitutionally overbroad, because the construction of the statute by the Ohio Supreme Court narrowly limited application of the law to lewd displays of nudity where such nudity involves a lewd exhibition or involves a graphic focus on genitals, and not merely nudity. The law was also read to include a requirement of scienter. However, since it was unclear that the jury had been properly instructed on the elements of the offense as due process requires, the conviction was reversed and the case remanded. *Osborne v. Ohio* (1990).

(3) A federal law which extends the ban against child pornography to "virtual child pornography," *i.e.*, visual depiction that "appears to be" of minors engaging in sexually explicit conduct, is overbroad and unconstitutional. Similarly, a provision extending the law to any sexually explicit image that is "advertised, promoted, presented, described, or distributed in such a manner that conveys the impression it depicts a minor engaging in sexually explicit conduct" is overbroad and unconstitutional.

The law goes beyond the categories of proscribable speech recognized in *Miller* and *Ferber*. The law goes beyond *Ferber* since it focuses not on the harm to child participants involved in the production of the work but "prohibits speech that records no crime and creates no victims by its production." Virtual child pornography is not intrinsically related to the sexual abuse of children. Nor does the Government otherwise justify the prohibition. The tendency of virtual pornography to encourage unlawful acts cannot justify suppressing it absent a showing of a more direct connection between the speech and resulting child abuse.

The prohibition of the manner of distribution is also unconstitutionally overbroad. The law prohibits a substantial amount of speech that falls outside of *Ginzburg's* pandering rationale. It prohibits possession of the tainted material, even though the person in possession bears no responsibility for how it was marketed, sold, or described in promotion. *Ashcroft v. Free Speech Coalition* (2002).

(4) Following *Free Speech Coalition*, Congress enacted a new law criminalizing, under certain circumstances, the pandering or solicitation of child pornography. The Court held 7–2 that the Act was not unconstitutionally overbroad or vague. Justice Scalia, writing for the Court, noted that the Act prohibits offers to provide and requests to obtain child pornography. The statute "precisely tracks the material held constitutionally proscribeable in *Ferber* and *Miller*." Justice Scalia identified important features of the law. It includes a scienter requirement—all of the elements must be done "knowingly." The string of operative verbs—advertise, promotes, distributes, solicits—penalize speech that accompanies transactions involving the transfer of child pornography. The defendant must have held the subjective belief that the material was child pornography and must objectively manifest that belief. The defendant must subjectively intend that the listener believe that the material is child pornography and use speech that he thinks will engender that belief. The definition of "sexually explicit conduct" is very similar to that used in the statute upheld in *Ferber*.

Justice Scalia then asked the critical overbreadth question: as construed, does the statute criminalize a substantial amount of protected expression? The statute "criminalizes only offers to provide or requests to obtain contraband—child obscenity and child pornography involving actual children, both of which are proscribed and the proscription of which is constitutional." Justice Scalia concluded: "we hold that offers to provide or requests to obtain child pornography are categorically excluded from the First Amendment."

Nor was the statute void for vagueness. Justice Scalia argued that what renders a statute unconstitutionally vague is indeterminacy as to precisely what the incriminating fact is. Here the statute requires that the defendant believes, and makes a statement that reflects the belief, that the material is child pornography or that he communicate with the intent to cause another to believe the material is child pornography. These are factual questions involving true-or-false determinations. That it may be difficult in some cases to make the determinations doesn't make the statute impermissibly vague. *United States v. Williams* (2008).

7.   Beyond Obscenity—Animal Cruelty? Violence?

Recent efforts to expand the categories of "unprotected speech" have been unsuccessful. While the Court left open the possibility of such categories, the Court has stressed that categorical exclusion does not rest on a "balancing of the interests," but on the historic, long-established treatment of such speech. *United States v. Stevens* (2010). For example, laws restricting the depiction of violence are not categorically unprotected because "violence is not obscene" and there is no long standing history of restricting children's access to depictions of violence. *Brown v. Entertainment Merchant's Association* (2010).

Examples: (1) A federal statute prohibiting the knowing sale, creation, or possession of depictions of animal cruelty with the intent of commercial gain and where it was in violation of local law where created, sold, or possessed, was held unconstitutional by the Supreme Court on the grounds of substantial overbreadth. See VIII, B, 2. The Court rejected efforts to treat animal cruelty like obscenity or child pornography. There exists no "similar tradition excluding depictions of animal cruelty from 'the freedom of speech' codified in the First Amendment." Whether a category of speech qualifies for First Amendment protection does not depend on balancing the value of the speech against its costs to society, because the First Amendment "reflects a judgment that the benefits of its restrictions on the Government outweigh the costs." Here, the Court found no evidence of a long standing historical view that "depictions of animal cruelty" is a category of unprotected speech.

Justice Alito, the sole dissent, argued that the reasoning in *Ferber* focusing on the underlying harm to society and the need to support local criminal laws applied equally to depictions of animal cruelty. Though he noted animal cruelty did not rise to the gravity of harm caused by child pornography, "there is still a compelling interest" on the part of the Government to prevent commercial gain from the sale of media featuring animal cruelty. *United States v. Stevens* (2010).

(2) A California statue which restricts the sale or rental of violent video games to minors without the consent of a parent if they "include killing, maiming, dismembering, or sexually assaulting an image of a human being" is unconstitutional. The statute mimicked the language for regulating obscenity for minors upheld in *Ginsberg v. New York* (See Ch. VIII, I, 2, b, 2), but focused on violence that a "reasonable person" using "community standards" would find unsuitable for minors which has no "value to minors." Unlike obscenity, there is no "longstanding tradition" restricting the access children have to depictions of violence. "New categories of unprotected speech may not be added to the list by a legislature that concludes certain speech is too harmful to be tolerated." The statute was subject to traditional strict scrutiny review because "violence is not obscene." Video games are a medium of speech entitled to the same amount of protection from government regulations as other media such as literature and radio, as they all enter "the marketplace of ideas." The statute was not proven to be narrowly tailored. The Government failed to prove that exposure to violence in video games caused violent behavior; depictions of violence in other media is not restricted. *Brown v. Entertainment Merchants Association* (2011).

8. Procedural Fairness

a. Administrative Regulation

1) Prior restraints are burdened procedurally as well as substantively. At least if the restraint involves content-based administrative censorship, the following procedural requirements must be satisfied:

   (a) The censor has the burden of demonstrating that the material is unprotected.

   (b) There must be a prompt judicial proceeding in order to impose a valid final restraint on publication.

(c) The censor must either issue a license for publication or go to court to justify the restraint. *Freedman v. Maryland* (1965).

Example: A Dallas ordinance embodying zoning, licensing, and inspections of sexually oriented businesses was invalidated as an impermissible prior restraint which failed to provide the procedural protections required by *Freedman v. Maryland* (1965). The ordinance failed to place limits on the time within which the decision maker must issue the license and failed to provide for prompt judicial review. These faults made the law unconstitutional under *Freedman.* Three members of the Court would also have held, however, that since no censorship was involved in the licensing scheme, the city need not bear the burden of going to court and justifying the restraint as required by *Freedman.* Three justices would still apply all the *Freedman* standards to such licensing and three justices would not have applied any of the *Freedman* standards in the absence of content censorship. *FW/PBS, Inc. v. City of Dallas* (1990).

2) A content-neutral permit system regulating speech in a public forum, not involving censorship concerns, does not have to satisfy the procedural requirements of *Freedman.* It must contain adequate standards to guide the official's decision and render it subject to judicial review. *Thomas v. Chicago Park Dist.* (2002).

b. Judicial Censorship

Procedural due process also limits the judicial determination of obscenity both at the hearing stage and in framing a remedy.

Example: A state nuisance statute authorizing a prior restraint of indefinite duration on the future exhibition of motion pictures that have not been judicially determined to be obscene was held unconstitutional. The restraint against future filming was based on a determination that obscene films had been shown in the past. The Court held that such an injunction must adhere to more narrowly drawn procedures than normally used in nuisance cases and that the burden of justifying such a prior restraint is greater than for justifying a criminal sanction for past activities. *Vance v. Universal Amusement Co., Inc.* (1980).

c. Search and Seizure

1) Large-scale civil seizure of indecent materials for the purpose of their suppression or destruction must be preceded by an adversarial determination of obscenity. *Quantity of Books v. Kansas* (1964). This principle remains applicable if the seizure is taken pursuant to state civil racketeering (RICO) laws. *Fort Wayne Books v. Indiana* (1989).

2) Search and seizure of a single copy of a work or film for use as evidence in a criminal proceeding pursuant to a warrant, describing the material to be seized, issued on a finding of probable obscenity, is permissible even if the warrant is issued *ex parte*. There is no requirement in this context for a prior adversary determination of obscenity. *Heller v. New York* (1973).

J. Special Contexts

In certain special contexts or "restricted environments," the ordinary speech-protective doctrines and rules are either not applied or applied in a markedly altered form. The laws regulating speech are not generally applicable laws but regulate only the speech of persons who have a special relationship to the government. *In cases involving the military, government employees, prisons, and children in school, the special government interests involved result in a more deferential form of judicial review.*

1. Political Activity by Government Employees

a. *In determining what limitations may be placed on political action by government employees, the Court employs a two-part test. First, the Court must determine if the speech involves a matter of public concern or only a matter involving the personal interests of the employee.* Connick v. Myers (1983). *If the latter, the First Amendment is inapplicable. Second, if public interest speech is involved, the Court employs a balancing test. The interest of the employee as a citizen in participating in the political process is weighed against the interest of the government as employer in assuring the efficiency of its operations.* Pickering v. Board of Education *(1968). However, when public employees make statements pursuant to their official duties, the employees are not speaking as citizens for First Amendment purposes, and the Constitution does not insulate their communications from employer discipline.* Garcetti v. Ceballos (2006).

Examples: (1) Federal employees may be validly prohibited by the Hatch Act from undertaking an active and visible role in political management and political campaigning. The Court upheld the balance struck by Congress subordinating the interest of the employee as citizen to the interest of government in assuring efficiency and preserving public confidence by means of the prohibition. *United States Civil Service Commission v. National Association of Letter Carriers* (1973).

(2) Although the state has interests as an employer in regulating the speech of its employees that differ significantly from those it possesses with respect to regulating the speech of the citizenry in general, a teacher may not, consistent with the First Amendment, be dismissed for making comments on matters of educational policy that are substantially correct. In such situations, a balancing test should be used to weigh the need for confidentiality as it relates to the function the state is performing against the interest of a teacher in commenting upon matters of public concern. The teacher did not have a close working relationship with the Board requiring loyalty and confidence. There was no showing that the statements, even if false, threatened the professional reputation of administrators and there was no showing of actual malice. *Pickering v. Board of Education* (1968).

(3) A county law enforcement employee was overheard to say on hearing of an attempt on President Reagan's life, "If they go for him again, I hope they get him." She was fired because of her statement. The government's interest in discharging the employee under such circumstances did not outweigh her rights under the First Amendment. The employee was fired because of the content of her speech. Since the employee served no confidential, policy-making or public contact role, the danger to governmental interests was minimal. Although a statement which constituted a threat to kill the President would not be protected by the First Amendment, this statement made in the context of a conversation which addressed the policies of the President's administration could not be so characterized. The

employee's statement constituted protected speech on a matter of public concern. *Rankin v. McPherson* (1987).

(4) A provision of the Ethics in Government Act prohibiting federal Government employees from accepting an honorarium for speeches and articles is unconstitutional as applied to employees below the policymaking level. The speech falls within the protected category of citizen comment on matters of public concern. While applying *Pickering*, the Court noted the Government has a greater burden when it uses a wholesale deterrent to a broad category of speech by a large number of potential speakers. The ban applied to speech addressed to a public audience, made outside the workplace and often involved content largely unrelated to their Government work. While the Government's interest that federal officers not misuse or appear to misuse power by accepting rewards is "undeniably powerful," the Government cited no evidence of misconduct by low level federal employees. Although the Government also argued that efficiency concerns justified the law, the Act's numerous exceptions made any benefits speculative. The sweeping ban was a "crudely crafted" device for achieving the Act's objectives. The Court declined to fashion a broad remedy, holding the Act unconstitutional as applied to the plaintiffs. *United States v. National Treasury Employees Union* (1995).

(5) The Court unanimously held that a statewide voluntary association of public and private schools did not violate the First Amendment free speech rights of member schools when it prohibited coaches from using "undue influence" in recruiting activities because the "athletic league's interest in enforcing its rules sometimes warrant[s] curtailing the speech of its voluntary participants." While the First Amendment protected the schools' right to publish truthful information about its programs, where speech impaired the proper administration of education or athletics, the association could restrict the speech of its members. Similar to the balancing test used in government employee speech cases, the Court stated that, in this case, the association had an adequate interest in preventing an

exploitation of student athletes. *Tennessee Secondary School Athletic Association v. Brentwood Academy* (2007).

b.   When the speech involves only matters of personal interest, rather than public concern, the courts exercise deference. "[W]hen a public employee speaks as an employee upon matters of personal interest, absent the most unusual circumstances, a federal court is not the appropriate forum in which to review the wisdom of a personnel decision taken by a public agency allegedly in reaction to the employee's behavior." *Connick v. Myers* (1983).

> *Example:*   Discharge of an assistant district attorney for protesting her transfer and for circulating a questionnaire to other assistant district attorneys requesting their views on transfer policies, office morale, confidence in supervisors, etc., does not violate the First Amendment. The government need not prove that the speech "substantially interfered" with official responsibility. The employer could reasonably believe the employee's behavior would disrupt the office, undermine his authority and destroy close working relationships. *Connick v. Myers* (1983).

c.   Not all employee speech involving matters of public concern is citizen speech subject to *Pickering* and *Connick v. Myers*. Government as an employer and manager needs to have a significant degree of control over employee speech made in performing official duties. "*[W]hen public employees make statements pursuant to their official duties, the employees are not speaking as citizens for First Amendment purposes, and the Constitution does not insulate their communications from employer discipline.*" Garcetti v. Ceballos (2006). But the Court did not decide whether its new *per se* rule would apply in the same manner to employee speech involved in scholarship or teaching.

> *Example:*   Richard Ceballos, a deputy district attorney, pursuant to his supervisory responsibilities, wrote a memorandum to his supervisors detailing inaccuracies in an affidavit used to obtain a search warrant. While he recommended dismissing the prosecution, his supervisors rejected his recommendation. He informed the defense counsel of his views and testified pursuant to a subpoena. Ceballos claims that subsequently he was subjected to retaliation because he had exercised his free speech rights. The Court held, 5–4, that

Ceballos spoke as an employee, not as a citizen for First Amendment purposes; his claim of unconstitutional retaliation failed. Justice Kennedy, writing for the Court, said that the significant point was that the memo was written pursuant to the attorney's official duties advising his supervisors on how to handle a case. Conducting a balancing test for all employee communications "would commit state and federal courts to a new, permanent, and intrusive role, mandating judicial oversight of communications between and among government employees and their supervisors in the course of official business. The displacement of managerial discretion by judicial supervision finds no support in our precedents." Since there was no dispute that Ceballos' memo was written pursuant to his official responsibilities the Court did not find it necessary to fashion a "comprehensive framework" for defining an employee's duties. But an employer cannot restrict employees' rights by broad job descriptions. Justice Kennedy also noted the myriad of legal protections available to whistleblowers.

Justice Stevens, dissenting, argued that the First Amendment " 'Sometimes,' not 'Never,' " protects government employee speech relating to official duties. He rejected the Court's categorical distinction between speaking as a citizen and speaking in the course of one's official responsibilities. Justice Souter, joined by Justices Stevens and Ginsburg, dissenting, argued that First Amendment balancing should be applied because "private and public interests in addressing official wrongdoing and threats to health and safety can outweigh the government's stake in the efficient implementation of policy." But an employee should not prevail unless he speaks on a matter of unusual importance and satisfies a high standard of responsibility. Justice Breyer, dissenting, would require balancing only where the employee was speaking on a matter of public concern and where there was "augmented need for constitutional protection and diminished risk of undue judicial interference with governmental management of the public's affairs." *Garcetti v. Ceballos* (2006).

d. In order to establish a prima facie case, the government employee must prove that the protected activity was a substantial factor, *i.e.*, a cause, of the adverse government action against her.

Example: An untenured teacher who claims that his dismissal violates his First and Fourteenth Amendment rights has the burden of showing that his conduct was constitutionally protected and that this conduct was a substantial factor, a motivating factor, in the school board's decision not to rehire him. The burden is then on the school board to show by a preponderance of the evidence "that it would have reached the same decision as to respondent's reemployment even in the absence of the protected conduct." The Court concluded that "[t]he constitutional principle at stake is sufficiently vindicated if such an employee is placed in no worse a position than if he had not engaged in the conduct." *Mt. Healthy City School Dist. Bd. of Educ. v. Doyle* (1977).

e. The public concern test also applies to retaliation claims made by government employees under the Petition Clause. While the clauses are not identical, the right to speak and the right to petition are "cognate rights," integral to the democratic process. But the substantial government interest in protecting the efficient and effective operation of government requires "a cautious and restrained approach" under both clauses. *Borough of Duryea v. Guarnieri* (2011).

Example: Following his termination, the chief of police of the Borough of Duryea filed a union grievance. An arbitrator reinstated the chief following a suspension. The Borough issued directives limiting his powers and the chief filed a second union grievance claiming retaliation for filing a grievance protected by the Petition Clause. Justice Kennedy, writing for the Court, held that a public employee must satisfy the public concern test. The Petition Clause does not "justify the imposition of broader liability when an employee invokes its protection instead of the protection afforded by the Speech Clause." The government interests that restrain speech by public employees also apply to petition claims. The government must have the power to restrict employees who "use petitions to frustrate progress" towards its goals. Allowing plaintiffs to circumvent the public concern test by using the Petition Clause would burden the government unduly and create an increase in frivolous lawsuits. The Supreme Court vacated and remanded. *Borough of Duryea v. Guarnieri* (2011).

f. The First Amendment principles applicable to government employees also protect independent contractors from termination of even contracts at will in retaliation for their exercise of freedom of speech.

> *Example:* After an independent contractor criticized the county and its board of commissioners, his contract with the county was not renewed. The contractor sued the county, claiming that the non-renewal of his contract was a violation of his First Amendment rights. The Court held that there is no difference of constitutional magnitude between government employees and independent contractors. Application of a nuanced *Pickering* approach, recognizing the different interests involved between government employees and contractors is superior to a bright line rule giving government *carte blanche* to terminate contracts in retaliation for exercise of First Amendment rights. On remand, the court should balance the government and private interests. The plaintiff has the burden of showing that the termination was motivated by his speech on a matter of public concern. If the plaintiff meets that burden, the Government may show that, given the knowledge, perceptions and policies at the time, it would have terminated the contract regardless of the speech or "that the county's legitimate interests as contractor, deferentially viewed outweighed the free speech interests at stake." *Board of Commissioners, Wabaunsee County v. Umbehr* (1996).

2. The Academic Forum

Public education may properly seek to "inculcate fundamental values necessary to the maintenance of a democratic political system." *Ambach v. Norwick* (1979). Further, school officials have a special responsibility acting *in loco parentis* for the protection of students. On the other hand, public school officials may not impose political orthodoxy or exclude expression simply because of disagreement with the ideas expressed. Students retain First Amendment rights even in the schoolhouse, but "the special characteristics of the school environment" must be considered. *Tinker v. Des Moines Independent Community School Dist.* (1969).

a. Library Censorship

The Court has held that the First Amendment does impose some limits on the power of a local school board to remove books from the school library. A plurality of the Court concluded that books could not be removed from public high school for the purpose of restricting access to ideas with which the board disagreed. The justices generally agreed that books could be removed because they were pervasively vulgar or educationally inappropriate. *Board of Education v. Pico* (1982).

b. Student Speech

1) Student rights of free expression in the schoolhouse are not coextensive with the rights of adults in other settings. Schools can bar speech or expressive action that intrudes upon the work of the schools or the rights of other students.

   Examples: (1) The wearing of a black armband in school to protest the Vietnam War was "akin to pure speech" and hence protected by the First Amendment. In the absence of evidence that the symbolic conduct would "materially and substantially interfere with the requirements of appropriate discipline in the operation of the school," prohibition by school officials of the wearing of the armbands is impermissible. *Tinker v. Des Moines Independent Community School Dist.* (1969).

   (2) A school district does not violate the Constitution by suspending a high school student for two days for delivering a speech at a student political assembly heavily laden with sexual innuendo which the Court characterized as vulgar and offensively lewd. Society has an overriding interest in teaching students "the boundaries of socially appropriate behavior." School officials could determine that such offensive speech would undermine the school's basic educational mission. The school disciplinary rule proscribing "obscene" language was held to have provided adequate warning to the student of the potential for the sanctions. *Bethel School Dist. No. 403 v. Fraser* (1986).

   (3) A school may "restrict student speech at a school event, when that speech is reasonably viewed as

promoting illegal drug use." At a school sanctioned and supervised viewing of the passing of the Olympic Torch, Frederick, a student, unfurled a banner, which read "BONG HiTS 4 JESUS." Morse, the school principal, confiscated the banner and later suspended Frederick. The Court held 6–3 that Frederick's First Amendment rights were not violated. Chief Justice Roberts, writing for the Court, joined by Justices Scalia, Kennedy, Thomas and Alito, first determined that, under the circumstances, this was a student speech case, even through the events occurred off school property. It occurred during school hours, was a school sanctioned event, teachers and administrators participated and the banner's message was plainly visible to students. While the banner's message was cryptic, Morse reasonably regarded it as advocating or promoting illegal drug use in violation of school policy. Various interpretations of what the words might mean support Morse's interpretation and there is a paucity of alternative interpretations. Given Morse's reasonable understanding of the message, she could restrict Frederick's speech. *Tinker* does not state the only basis for restricting student speech. "The 'special characteristics of the school environment,' *Tinker*, and the governmental interest in stopping student drug abuse—reflected in the policies of Congress and myriad school boards . . . —allow schools to restrict student expression that they reasonably regard as promoting illegal drug use." However, the Chief Justice rejected the argument that Frederick's speech was proscribable because it was "offensive"—"much political and religious speech might be perceived as offensive to some."

Justice Thomas, concurring, to urged that *Tinker* be overruled. Justice Alito, joined by Justice Kennedy, concurring, stressed that the Court's holding was limited to circumstances where a reasonable observer would interpret the student speech as advocating illegal drug use. It did not approve "restriction of speech that can plausibly be interpreted as commenting on any political or social issue," including the debate over drug policy. Justice Alito rejected a broad reading of the holding which would support restrictions on student speech threatening the school's "educational mission;" the Court's holding "does not endorse any further extension." Justice Breyer, concurring in part and dissenting in part, would have avoided the constitutional question and would have dismissed the student's claim for damages on grounds of the qualified immunity of the school officials. He reasoned that it will be difficult to limit the Court's approval of this "viewpoint restriction" to the facts of this case. Justice Stevens, joined by Justices Souter and Ginsburg, dissenting, argued that "the First Amendment protects student speech if the message itself neither violates a permissible rule nor expressly advocates conduct that is illegal and harmful to students." Here, Morse disciplined Frederick for a nonsense message—not advocacy—without showing any likely connection between the supposed advocacy and feared consequences. *Morse v. Frederick* (2007).

2) *School facilities are public forums only if school officials have by policy or practice opened those facilities for general public use or for use by some segment of the public, e.g., student organizations. Schools can regulate "school sponsored" student speech that occurs in "curricular" activities so long as there is some reasonable basis, some legitimate pedagogical concern, for the regulation.*

Example: Spectrum, a school newspaper written and edited by a school journalism class, carried two articles on teenage pregnancy and divorce which the school principal believed were "inappropriate, personal, sensitive and unsuitable." He deleted two full pages of the paper without any notice to the student editors. The censorship was held constitutional.

There was insufficient evidence that school officials intended to make the school newspaper a public forum. It was a supervised learning experience for journalism students. Hence, the *Tinker* standard was not applicable—

only reasonableness was required. Further, *Tinker* had not considered whether a school must affirmatively promote particular student speech. A school, acting in its capacity as sponsor of student speech, may disassociate itself from particular expression. In the school-sponsored expressive activity of publishing a newspaper the principal made a reasonable pedagogical decision that the articles in question were not suitable for publication. *Hazelwood School Dist. v. Kuhlmeier* (1988).

c. Academic Freedom

As the cases involving freedom of association and belief indicate, the First Amendment does extend protection to teachers from excessive governmental interference, including who may teach and what is taught. See, *e.g., Keyishian v. Board of Regents* (1967) (loyalty program held unconstitutional); *Sweezy v. New Hampshire* (1957) (conviction of teacher for contempt for refusing to answer questions about the contents of a lecture held unconstitutional). While the First Amendment embraces a concept of academic freedom, the First Amendment does not protect against every incidental burden on academic freedom. *University of Pennsylvania v. E.E.O.C.* (1990) (the First Amendment right of academic freedom did not protect peer review materials involved in tenure decisions at universities from disclosure).

3. Subsidized Speech

a. *"[G]overnment speech is not restricted by the Free Speech Clause."* Pleasant Grove City v. Summum (2009). *When Government acts as a speaker or funds a selected private group to express its message, it need not fund alternative viewpoints. In a democratic society, Government can endorse some positions and not others.*

b. *The Free Speech Clause does apply when Government subsidizes private speech. When Government provides grants to private speakers, it cannot discriminate on the basis of viewpoint. But if the subsidy program demands government discretion, it is less likely that it will be held to be unconstitutional viewpoint-discrimination.*

c. ***Unconstitutional Conditions Doctrine.*** *Government cannot condition the receipt of public benefits on the surrender of constitutional rights. Further, the government cannot deny benefits to a person on a basis that denies First Amendment rights even if a person has no right to the benefits.*

d.   *Application of these broad principles often produces seemingly inconsistent results.*

Examples: (1) Federal regulations which prohibit federally funded family planning projects from abortion counseling, from referring clients to abortion clinics, and from engaging in activities that encourage, promote or advocate abortion and requiring that any such abortion activities be separated physically and financially from the federally funded project do not violate the First Amendment. Government does not deny anyone the right to engage in abortion related activities or engage in pro-abortion speech. The government only refuses to fund such activities with federal monies. The condition is placed on the program receiving the grant; it is not an unconstitutional condition on those willing to engage in constitutionally protected activity. *Rust v. Sullivan* (1991).

(2) The University of Virginia's denial of student activity funds provided to help cover the printing costs of publications produced by student groups to a Christian student newspaper because of its Christian editorial viewpoint is unconstitutional. The University subsidy program was held to constitute a limited public forum. The University expended funds not to express a particular message, as in *Rust v. Sullivan*, but to "encourage a diversity of viewpoints from private speakers." The university policy did not simply prevent discussion of the subject of religion in student publications, but rather denied funding to any group with a religious editorial position. This constituted unconstitutional viewpoint discrimination. The Establishment Clause does not justify viewpoint discrimination against religious speakers since such financial support for religious groups does not violate neutrality. *Rosenberger v. Rector and Visitors of the University of Virginia* (1995).

(3) A statutory provision requiring that the National Endowment for the Arts (NEA) consider "general standards of decency and respect for the diverse beliefs and values of the American public" in awarding grants does not facially violate the First Amendment. Facial challenges are disfa-

vored; *substantial* overbreadth is required. While government grant programs will violate the First Amendment if they discriminate on the basis of viewpoint, the NEA provision is not viewpoint based. Unlike the statutory provision that prohibits grants for obscene works, the provision in question only requires that the NEA *consider* indecency and disrespect in making its decisions; indecent or disrespectful projects can still be funded. Ideological bias is unlikely given the lack of consensus on what is indecent. Unlike *Rosenberger*, in funding the arts Government does not indiscriminately "encourage a diversity of viewpoints" but makes selective choices based on aesthetic judgments and excellence. While the law is facially constitutional, claims that the grant program is administered in a viewpoint discriminatory manner (*i.e.*, as applied challenges) can still be made. The First Amendment is not as demanding in terms of clarity and specificity when Government is not regulating, so a vagueness challenge is rejected. *National Endowment for the Arts v. Finley* (1998).

(4) Congress engaged in impermissible viewpoint restriction when it prohibited lawyers for legal services organizations receiving federal funds from assisting clients in challenging the validity of existing state and federal welfare laws. The restriction prevented LSC attorneys from arguing that any state or federal welfare law was invalid or should be amended and required attorneys to withdraw from representation when the validity of a constitutional or statutory challenge became apparent. The Court distinguished the case from government speech cases like *Rust v. Sullivan* (1991), because here, the government was not using private speakers to transmit its own message, but was facilitating private speech. This case was more analogous to limited public forum cases such as *FCC v. League of Women Voters* (1984) and *Rosenberger v. Rector and Visitors of the University of Virginia* (1995): "Just as government in those cases could not elect to use a broadcasting network or a college publication structure in a regime which prohibits speech necessary to the proper functioning of those systems, it may not design a subsidy to effect this serious and fundamental restriction on advocacy of attorneys and

the functioning of the judiciary." The restriction distorted the role of the attorney, whose professional mission was to present all the reasonable and well-grounded arguments necessary for proper resolution of the case, and threatened severe impairment of the judicial function by insulating certain laws from judicial inquiry. *Legal Services Corp. v. Velazquez* (2001).

(5) The Children's Internet Protection Act ("CIPA") does not facially violate the First Amendment by conditioning federal assistance to public libraries for providing Internet access on installation of blocking software to filter images constituting obscenity or child pornography. A plurality opinion by Chief Justice Rehnquist reasoned that public libraries do not create a public forum by providing Internet terminals to the public because Internet access is not provided in order to encourage a diversity of viewpoints, but to facilitate research and learning. Therefore, heightened judicial scrutiny is not appropriate. The fact that the software can result in erroneous blocking is not of constitutional significance, because patrons can simply request to have a site unblocked or to have the filter temporarily disabled. Although the restriction is content-oriented, "[p]ublic library staffs necessarily consider content in making collection decisions and [have] broad discretion in making them." Nor is the government imposing an unconstitutional condition on funding because it does not force libraries to violate their patrons' First Amendment rights. Citing *Rust v. Sullivan* (1991), the plurality reasoned that the government is entitled to insist that "public funds be spent for the purposes for which they were authorized."

Justice Kennedy, concurring, agreed that CIPA is facially constitutional since a librarian can unblock a site or disable the filtering device. If an adult viewer's election to view constitutionally protected Internet material is substantially burdened, an as-applied challenge could be brought. Justice Breyer, concurring, would apply a form of heightened scrutiny, examining the requirements with special care, since CIPA restricts public receipt of information through critically important sources—libraries and the Internet. He concluded that the comparatively small burden imposed on a library patron seeking legitimate Internet materials was not disproportionate given CIPA's legitimate objectives.

Justice Stevens, dissenting, argued that CIPA was an excessive restraint on adult access to constitutionally protected speech and constituted an unconstitutional condition on receipt of federal funds. Justice Souter, joined by Justice Ginsburg, dissenting, added that CIPA mandates actions by recipient libraries that would be unconstitutional if the libraries took the actions on their own. *United States v. American Library Association* (2003).

(6) Summum, a religious organization, requested permission from Pleasant Grove City to erect a monument containing the Seven Aphorisms of Summum in Pioneer Park, a public park which already had at least 11 privately donated monuments, including a Ten Commandments monument. When the city denied the request, Summum sued claiming that the city violated the Free Speech Clause by accepting the Ten Commandments monument but rejecting its monument. The Supreme Court unanimously rejected the claim.

Justice Alito, for the Court, reasoned that in permitting privately donated monuments to be erected in the Park, Pleasant Grove was engaging in its own expressive conduct, *i.e.*, government speech. Therefore, the Free Speech Clause, has no application; while the Clause limits government regulation of private speech, "it does not regulate government speech." Government is free to decide what views it wishes to express whether it speaks itself or uses private sources to deliver its message. It is still subject to other constitutional limitations such as the Establishment Clause and other legal and political limitations. The permanent Park monuments are government speech and the city "effectively controlled" the message by selecting which monuments were to be included. The city does not necessarily endorse the message of the donor and the monument's message or messages may change over time.

While a public park may be a public forum, the Court rejected application of public forum precedent to the city's program of accepting permanent monuments. Forum doctrine is used where government-owned property or a government program is capable of accommodating a large number of speakers without defeating the essential public function. "By contrast, public parks can accommodate only a limited number of permanent monuments." The monuments monopolize the use of the public space permanently interfering with other uses. Further, if government were required to observe viewpoint-neutrality in accepting donated monuments, it would bring the program to an end. Every use would require accommodation of competing causes. *Pleasant Grove City v. Summum* (2009).

K. Review Questions

1. **T or F** Whether the burden on freedom of speech imposed by a government regulation is directly based on content or merely incidental, the courts will require that the law be necessary to a compelling governmental interest.

2. **T or F** Fighting words are of such minimal social value that the First Amendment does not apply to the speech.

3. **T or F** A law which discriminates against particular speech based on viewpoint or subject-matter is presumptively invalid.

4. **T or F** Advocacy of illegal conduct is constitutionally protected speech.

5. **T or F** Prior restraints on expression are prohibited by the First Amendment, *i.e.*, they are *per se* impermissible.

6. **T or F** A law that is vague and overbroad is unconstitutional even if it is applied narrowly in a way that conforms to First Amendment standards.

7. **T or F** The validity of a law that burdens freedom of association and belief is generally determined by a rationality test.

8. **T or F** Government may not condition the receipt even of public benefits and privileges on the surrender of First Amendment rights.

9. **T or F** The political activities of government employees, like citizens generally, are not subject to government restriction unless such activity is illegal.

10. **T or F** Government employees can be punished for speech that is made pursuant to their official duties without First Amendment limitations.

11. **T or F** The First Amendment does not limit Government when it terminates public contracts with independent contractors because of their political affiliation (*i.e.*, political patronage).

12. **T or F** Reasonable limitations on campaign expenditures by a candidate or a group are constitutional.

13. **T or F** The freedom of association and belief implies a right not to associate and a freedom from compelled beliefs.

14. **T or F** In implementing its civil rights policies, a city cannot force private parade organizers to include marchers (*e.g.*, gays and lesbians) imparting a message the organizers do not wish to convey.

15. **T or F** Government can punish fighting or offensive speech.

16. **T or F** When a speaker's message arouses a hostile crowd to take action against him or her, the police may arrest the speaker in order to preserve public peace and order.

17. **T or F** All content-based discrimination between classes of fighting words is subject to strict scrutiny.

18. **T or F** Speech in all publicly owned places is subject to regulation only if such a law serves a significant government interest and leaves open alternative channels of communication.

19. **T or F** While pure speech is constitutionally protected, when speech is joined with conduct, First Amendment standards no longer apply.

20. **T or F** Government is as free to regulate speech and speakers in a nonpublic forum as a private property owner is free to control speech on her property.

21. **T or F** In expressive conduct cases, if the First Amendment is implicated, the regulation need only further an important government interest and not burden speech any more than is essential to the furtherance of the government interest.

22. **T or F** Content-neutral licensing of First Amendment expression is constitutional if reasonable.

23. **T or F** Court injunctions usually must be obeyed even if they are facially invalid.

24. **T or F** In modern times, commercial speech receives the same constitutional protection afforded political speech.

25. **T or F** The press enjoys special privileges and immunities under the Press Clause of the First Amendment.

26. **T or F** There is a First Amendment-based right of access to criminal trials.

27. **T or F** The Supreme Court has applied less demanding First Amendment standards to content-based regulations of telephones and the Internet by analogizing those communications media to broadcasting.

28. **T or F** There is a First Amendment right of access to the media.

29. **T or F** Government restraints on indecent, but not obscene, language in broadcasting are unconstitutional.

30. **T or F** Government regulation of cable television is reviewed under the same First Amendment standards that apply to government regulation of broadcasting.

31. **T or F** Criminal proscription of the distribution of books and magazines which describe minor children in indecent, but not obscene, activity is constitutional.

32. **T or F** Public figure plaintiffs who are not public officials, suing in defamation, can recover if they can prove that the defendant media published with gross negligence concerning the truth or falsity of the defamatory statement.

33. **T or F** Private figure plaintiffs can never recover presumed or punitive damages absent proof of actual malice.

34. **T or F** There is a constitutional right of equality of access to public property when the expressive activity is not incompatible with the normal use to which the property is put.

35. **T or F** When a government employee is disciplined for the content of his speech, strict scrutiny applies.

36. **T or F** Government speech which discriminates based on viewpoint violates the First Amendment absent compelling justification.

37. **T or F** While the Solomon Amendment, (which requires law schools to provide equal access to military recruiters or suffer loss of federal

funds) significantly burdens the freedom of speech rights of law schools by compelling speech, the Government provided compelling justification for the Amendment.

38. Which of the following is a *per se* restraint on freedom of association and belief that is unconstitutional regardless of the government interests:

    a. Prohibition on membership in an association advocating illegal conduct.

    b. Forced disclosure of the membership lists of such an association.

    c. Loyalty oaths.

    d. All of the above (a, b, c) are *per se* invalid.

    e. None of the above (a, b, c) are *per se* invalid.

39. Which of the following standards is *not* used in assessing the constitutionality of time, place and manner controls of speech in the public forum?

    a. The law must be clear and precise.

    b. The law must be content neutral or satisfy strict scrutiny.

    c. The law must be narrowly drawn to reflect a significant government interest.

    d. The availability of alternative forums will be considered.

    e. All of the above standards are used in determining the validity of time, place and manner controls.

40. Which of the following is *not* true?

    a. A public airport is a nonpublic forum.

    b. A prohibition on solicitation in public airports is constitutional.

    c. A prohibition on distributing leaflets in public airports is constitutional.

41. Which of the following most accurately describes the legal status of "symbolic speech" or "expressive conduct"?

    a. It is conduct which does not involve First Amendment law.

b. If the nature, factual content, and environment indicate that the conduct is intended and understood as communication, any restraint violates the First Amendment.

c. Conduct which qualifies as "symbolic speech" is judged by First Amendment standards.

d. Conduct labeled "symbolic speech" receives the same constitutional protection as obscenity.

42. Which of the following is most accurate under the present public law of defamation?

a. Defamation of public officials is fully protected under the First Amendment.

b. The law of defamation of public figures and private persons is left to the states.

c. In defining the defamation standards relating to private figures, states may choose actual malice, negligence, or strict liability.

d. Defamation actions by public officials and public figures are permitted only if actual malice is shown.

e. Punitive and presumed damages can be recovered.

43. Which of the following is *not* part of the present test of obscenity?

a. The material must appeal to the prurient interests of the average person applying contemporary community standards.

b. The work must be patently offensive.

c. The work must lack redeeming social value.

d. Pruriency and patent offensiveness need not be judged by a national community standard.

44. Which of the following procedures are constitutionally required for valid civil censorship of obscene materials?

a. The publisher has the burden of demonstrating that the material is protected.

b. Administrative censorship must not be used.

c. Only a judicial determination of obscenity will suffice to permanently restrain publication.

d. The publisher must appeal the censor's determination to a court to eliminate the restraint.

45. Which of the following is most accurate regarding the First Amendment status of student speech?

a. There is no difference between the First Amendment rights of students in school or out of school.

b. A school may restrict student speech, but only when it is unrelated to the content of speech.

c. A school may restrict student speech that promotes any illegal activity.

d. A school may restrict student speech that substantially disrupts its educational mission.

e. C and D.

46. An ordinance has recently been enacted by the City Council of Lincoln City, West Lincoln, prohibiting the posting of real estate "For Sale" and "Sold" signs. During the 1970s, the non-white population of Lincoln City rose from 60 to over 5000, or from .005% of the population to 18.2%. The City Council enacted the new ordinance because, in the words of a city councilman, "a major cause in the decline in the white population was 'panic selling' exploited by unscrupulous real estate brokers and salesmen who have been encouraging whites to sell their houses at low prices in order that they might sell them at much higher prices to incoming black residents." A real estate company, Beautiful Homes, Inc., has filed suit in the appropriate federal district court asking for a declaratory judgment that the ordinance is unconstitutional and requesting injunctive relief to prevent its enforcement. At the trial, expert real estate witnesses testified that only 2% of the homes that had been sold in Lincoln City during the past decade were chiefly sold because of the panic selling techniques of a few real estate agents. Is the ordinance constitutional? Why or why not?

47. The state of Eureka has enacted a law requiring all groups advocating racial hatred to register with the state Attorney General and to disclose the organization's membership lists. Pursuant to the law, the state has ordered the Ku Klux Klan to register and file a disclosure statement. Discuss the First Amendment claims that might be raised by the KKK in challenging the Eureka law.

IX

Freedom of Religion

■ *ANALYSIS*

The First Amendment guarantees both the "free exercise" of religion and freedom from any "law respecting an establishment of religion." Both guarantees have been incorporated into the Due Process Clause and are therefore applicable to the states. However, these guarantees are often in conflict. For example, providing fire and police services constitute government support for religious institutions. But denial of such services, critical to their survival, might be said to impair the free exercise of religion. Remember, both guarantees may be involved in a freedom of religion case and the tensions will have to be reconciled. While the basic command is government neutrality, courts have wavered as to how strict the neutrality must be and how much government accommodation of religion is permissible.

A. The Meaning of the "Establishment" Clause

In most cases, the courts have employed a three-fold test to determine if the command of neutrality imposed by the Establishment Clause is violated. Each of the three requirements must be satisfied: (1) the government action must have a secular legislative purpose; (2) the primary effect of the government action must be one that neither advances nor inhibits religion; (3) the government action must not foster an excessive government entanglement with religion. Lemon v. Kurtzman *(1971). But the* Lemon *test is under attack. The Court has increasingly asked whether a law constitutes a message of endorsement or disapproval of religion or a particular religious belief. In other cases, the Court has used a coercion test, asking whether the government has coerced anyone to support or participate in religion or its exercise. The alternatives to the* Lemon *test are considered more tolerant of government accommodations of religion. The endorsement and coercion tests are sometimes used as criteria for determining whether a law has an impermissible effect. Whether a law involves an excessive governmental entanglement is, at times, also treated as part of the effects test. See* Agostini v. Felton *(1997).*

The Establishment Clause is not merely a prohibition of a government-sponsored religion or simply a command of equal treatment among religions. Government cannot "pass laws which aid one religion, or prefer one religion over another." Everson v. Board of Educ. *(1947).*

Examples: (1) A state statute vesting in the governing bodies of churches and schools the power effectively to veto applications for liquor licenses within a five hundred foot radius of the church or school violates the Establishment Clause. While the state can regulate the environment around schools, churches, hospitals, etc., when the state delegates its zoning power to a private religious entity, the deference due to legislative zoning (including the deference accorded under the 21st

Amendment) is inappropriate. While the law has a valid secular purpose (in protecting the centers from the hurly-burly associated with liquor outlets), it has a primary effect of advancing religion. Since the law is standardless, it "does not by its terms require that churches' power be used in a religiously neutral way." Further, the law provides "significant symbolic benefit to religion" by creating a joint exercise of legislative authority. Finally, the third test is violated since the law "enmeshes churches in the exercise of substantial governmental powers." *Larkin v. Grendel's Den, Inc.* (1982).

(2) A special state statute creating a separate school district along the lines of a village which is a religious enclave of Satmar Hasidim, practitioners of a strict form of Judaism, violates the principle of neutrality mandated by the Establishment Clause. The fact that the delegation of civic power was to the qualified voters of the village, rather than to a religious institution as in *Larkin*, was not of constitutional significance. The state purposefully delegated its "discretionary authority over public schools to a group defined by its character as a religious community in a legal and historical context that gives no assurance that governmental power has been or will be exercised neutrally." The statute is "tantamount to an allocation of political power on a religious criterion." Since a particular religious sect is given special treatment, the statute is not a permissible legislative accommodation of religion. *Board of Education of Kiryas Joel School District v. Grumet* (1994).

1. Religion in the Schools

a. Released Time

Released time for religious education conducted off-school premises is a permissible accommodation of religion. *Zorach v. Clauson* (1952). However, it violates the First Amendment to conduct the classes within the schools. An on-premises religious program involves the expenditure of public resources for promoting religious goals, places public support behind the programs, and involves a close working relationship between public and religious authorities. Therefore, it has a primary effect which is sectarian, which violates the Establishment Clause. *McCollum v. Board of Education* (1948).

b. Prayers, Bible Reading, Moments of Silence and Devotional Exercises

1) While an objective study of the Bible or religion may be included as part of a secular program of study, government may not require religious exercises in the schools. *Required prayers, even when non-denominational, or other religious exercises have the purpose and primary effect of aiding religion.* Engel v. Vitale (1962) *(required recitation of prayer, composed by Board of Regents, held unconstitutional).*

2) *Excusal or exemption to avoid coercion of students having religious objections to the exercises is irrelevant.* When the state aids or encourages religion in violation of the Establishment Clause, accommodation for free exercise claims is not determinative.

   Example: The First Amendment forbids state-required recitation of a prayer and daily Bible reading even though the state provides for excusal of the nonconforming child upon the written request of a parent and even though the prayer is not state—composed. Even if it argued that the purpose of the mandatory Bible reading is non-religious in character and designed to serve secular values, such as promotion of moral values and the teaching of literature, the religious character of the exercise is manifest from, among other things, the provision for nonattendance at the exercises by nonconforming children. In such circumstances, the primary effect of the enactment is the impermissible advancement of religion. *School District of Abington Township v. Schempp* (1963).

3) A moment of silent prayer is a religious exercise designed to promote prayer and endorse religion and therefore violates the Establishment Clause. Whether a moment of silence with no reference to prayer or religion would survive Establishment Clause review remains undecided.

   Example: A state statute which authorizes a period of silence for "meditation or voluntary prayer," which is proven to be motivated by a legislative purpose to endorse religion and by no secular purpose, violates the Establishment Clause. Enacted to convey a message of state endorsement and promotion of prayer, the statute is not consistent with the established principle that the government must pursue a course of neutrality toward religion. *Wallace v. Jaffree* (1985).

4) School-sponsored prayers offered by clerics at a baccalaureate exercise of a public high school violate the Establishment Clause.

Example: Pervasive government involvement with religion by sponsoring and directing a religious exercise—a nonsectarian invocation and benediction offered by clergy selected by the principal—at an official graduation ceremony violates the Establishment Clause. The school district's supervision and control of the ceremony places public and peer pressure on attending students to participate or maintain respectful silence; there is "subtle coercive pressure" on the student. That the student need not attend the ceremony is not determinative. "It is a tenet of the First Amendment that the State cannot require one of its citizens to forfeit his or her rights and benefits [to attend this important event] as the price of resisting conformance to state-sponsored religious practice."

Four concurring justices would have found the religious exercise an endorsement of religion. They argued that, while there was coercion, proof of coercion is not essential for an Establishment Clause violation. Four dissenting justices argued that the traditional recognition of invocations and benedictions at graduation ceremonies indicated there was no Establishment Clause violation. Only coercion backed "by force of law and threat of penalty" matters under the Establishment Clause. *Lee v. Weisman* (1992).

5) A school policy allowing student-led, student-initiated prayers at public high school football games violates the Establishment Clause.

Example: Prior to 1995, a school district provided a student chaplain to deliver a prayer over the public address system prior to each varsity football game. After being sued, the district adopted a new policy. Students would vote on whether there should be invocations, and then select the student to deliver it. The district court modified the policy to require only nonsectarian, nonproselytizing prayer. The Court 6–3 held that, even as modified, the policy violated the Establishment Clause. The Court rejected the argument that the Clause was inapplicable because the messages constituted "private speech." These invocations were authorized by government policy, took place on government property, and at government-sponsored school-related events. This was not a forum open to indiscriminate use by the student body generally but was open to only one student, selected by the majority, whose message was subject to regulation. It placed the minority at the mercy of the majority. The school had not maintained a neutral, hands-off policy. The degree of its involvement constituted an endorsement of religion, *e.g.*, the speaker delivered an "invocation" consistent with the purpose of solemnizing the events thereby inviting and encouraging religious messages. Courts must distinguish sham secular purposes from sincere ones. As in *Lee v. Weisman*, the program was coercive. It is the school district that decided to have elections, which encourages divisiveness along religious lines. Nor is attendance at the games really voluntary for many and, in any case, the school uses social pressure to enforce orthodoxy. *Santa Fe Independent School District v. Doe* (2000).

c. Teaching Religious Values

1) Curriculum Control

While the state has broad leeway in prescribing the school curriculum, it may not use the power to advance particular religious tenets or beliefs.

Examples: (1) A state statute prohibiting the teaching of evolution in public schools is unconstitutional. A particular segment of a body of knowledge cannot be proscribed "for the sole reason that it is deemed to conflict with a particular religious doctrine." The anti-evolution or "monkey law" was clearly enacted for a religious purpose. *Epperson v. Arkansas* (1968).

(2) A state statute which forbids the teaching of the theory of evolution in public schools unless accompanied by instruction in the theory of "creation science" is facially invalid as violative of the Establishment Clause because it lacks a clear secular purpose. While the Court is "normally deferential to a State's articulation of a secular purpose," the statement of a secular purpose must be "sincere and not a sham." The state "creationism" law sought to discredit evolution by counterbalancing the teaching of evolution "at every turn with the teaching of creation science." The state statute impermissibly attempted to endorse religion by advancing "the religious viewpoint that a supernatural being created humankind." *Edwards v. Aguillard* (1987).

2) Covert Religious Purpose

Even when the state seeks to justify a law by claiming that it serves secular objectives of teaching fundamental values and traditions, the law will not be upheld if the Court determines that the program or practice is primarily religious in character or has the purpose of advancing religion.

Example: A state statute requiring the posting of the Ten Commandments in public schools furthers only sectarian purposes and hence violates the Establishment Clause of the First Amendment. The fact that the public school displays carry a statement on the importance of the Ten Commandments in our laws and our legal system and that the display was paid for with private funds is insufficient to negate the religious purpose. *Stone v. Graham* (1980).

d. **Equal Access**

1) As the released time cases indicate, not all government accommodation of religious programs in public forums violates the Establishment Clause. *Discrimination against groups in the use of the public forum based on the religious content of their message burdens freedom of speech and association which can be justified only by showing a compelling government interest. See Ch. VIII, E, 2, a, 2), on equal access to the public forum.*

Examples: (1) A university which has created a forum generally open for use by student groups violates the First Amendment freedom of speech and association when it discriminates in use of its facilities by denying access "for purposes of religious worship or religious teaching." The university policy is not justified by the desire to maintain separation of church and state, mandated by the state and federal Constitutions.

While compliance with the federal non-establishment principle is a compelling interest, an equal access policy is not incompatible with the non-establishment requirement. An open forum policy would serve a secular purpose of promoting exchange of student ideas and would not foster excessive entanglement of government with religion since enforcement of the exclusion policy risks greater entanglement, *i.e.*, determining which groups are to be excluded and monitoring meetings to assure compliance. Nor does equal access have a primary effect of advancing religion since the policy does not confer any imprimatur of state approval on the religion and the benefit is available to a broad spectrum of groups, secular and sectarian. *Widmar v. Vincent* (1981).

(2) A State University's denial of a subsidy authorized for printing student publications to a Christian student newspaper because it "primarily promotes or manifests a particular belief in or about a deity or an ultimate reality" violates freedom of speech. The University's subsidy program was a limited public forum. While content discrimination may be permissible if it preserves the purposes of the limited forum, viewpoint discrimination within the designated class of speakers is presumptively unconstitutional. The University does not simply discriminate on the basis of religious subject matter. The State discriminates in access to the subsidy on the basis of viewpoint. It is subject to strict scrutiny. Scarcity of resources does not justify viewpoint discrimination among speakers. Nor is the viewpoint bias justified by the necessity of

complying with the Establishment Clause. "We have held that the guarantee of neutrality is respected, not offended, when the government, following neutral criteria and evenhanded policies, extends benefits to recipients whose ideologies and viewpoints, including religious ones, are broad and diverse." By engaging in viewpoint discrimination requiring public officials to review and interpret publications, the State program compromises the very neutrality the Establishment Clause requires. *Rosenberger v. Rector & Visitors of University of Virginia* (1995).

(3) State refusal to allow the Ku Klux Klan to erect a ten foot cross on a public square adjoining the Capitol building violates freedom of speech. The cross display is private religious speech which "is a fully protected under the Free Speech Clause as secular private expression." Since the square is a traditional public forum, content based regulation is subject to strict scrutiny review. While compliance with the Establishment Clause can be a compelling government interest, it was insufficient in this case since there was no government endorsement: "The State did not sponsor [the Klan's] expression, the expression was made on government property that had been opened to the public for speech, and permission was requested through the same application process and on the same terms required of the private groups." *Capitol Square Review Board v. Pinette* (1995).

(4) An elementary school which has authorized after hours community use of its facilities engages in unconstitutional viewpoint discrimination when it excludes a Christian Club for children because it would engage in religious worship. The Club addressed a subject otherwise permitted under the school's use rules, the teaching of morals and character development, from a religious standpoint. The fact that the Club would use live storytelling and prayer, rather than films, is inconsequential. While avoiding Establishment Clause violations may be characterized as a

compelling interest justifying content-based discrimination, here the school had no valid Establishment Clause interest. The meetings would be after hours, not sponsored by the school, open to non-club members and the forum was open to nonreligious groups. Neutrality would be furthered. Even though it is elementary age children, there is no coercion of children involved. There was little danger of any perceived endorsement of religion. The free speech rights of the Club and its members cannot be overcome simply because of some risk that small children might perceive the meeting as an endorsement of religion. *Good News Club v. Milford Central School* (2001).

2) Laws designed to promote equal access to school facilities by prohibiting discrimination against religious speech do not violate the Establishment Clause.

   Example: The 1984 federal Equal Access Act, extending *Widmar* to public secondary schools, does not violate the Establishment Clause. Since Westwood High School allows one or more "noncurriculum related groups" to meet on school premises, it creates a "limited open forum" under the Act, and is therefore prevented from discriminating based on speech content. Denial of a request to form a religious group and meet on school premises during noninstructional time is a denial of "equal access" which violates the Act.

   The logic of *Widmar* applies with equal force to the Equal Access Act. A plurality applied the *Lemon* test. Congress' avowed purpose of preventing discrimination against religious and other types of speech is "undeniably secular." The Act grants equal access to both secular and religious speech; its purpose is not to endorse or disapprove of religion. Nor does the Act have the primary effect of advancing religion. Secondary school students are sufficiently mature to appreciate that a school does not endorse student speech merely because it is permitted on a nondiscriminatory basis. Participation of school officials is expressly limited under the Act, minimizing the possibility of official endorsement or coercion. The wide spectrum of clubs at the school also limits any possible message of official endorsement or preference. The limited oversight role of school officials does not impermissibly entangle government in religious activities. *Board of Educ. of the Westside Community Schools v. Mergens* (1990).

2. Financial Assistance to Religious Institutions

a. Public Benefits

The fact that government action provides some aid to religion does not necessarily mean it is an impermissible establishment of religion. *If the state only acts for the secular purpose of serving the public welfare and well-being, the fact that religion is incidentally benefitted does not condemn the program.*

Examples: (1) A state law authorizing reimbursement to parents for the expense of bus transportation for their children on buses operated by the public transportation system does not violate the Establishment Clause of the First Amendment. The law was designed to provide safe transportation to school age children, not to aid private schools. State power is no more to be used as to handicap religions than it is to favor them. *Everson v. Board of Education* (1947).

(2) A state law permitting the loan of state-approved secular textbooks to children in secondary schools does not violate the Establishment Clause. The purpose of the law is to advance the education of the young. Parents and children, rather than the religious school, receive the primary financial benefits of the law. *Board of Educ. of Central School Dist. No. 1 v. Allen* (1968).

(3) A state law of general applicability requiring the state to provide a sign language interpreter for a deaf student attending a Catholic high school does not violate the Establishment Clause. "[G]overnment programs that neutrally provide benefits to a broad class of citizens defined without reference to religion are not readily subject to an Establishment Clause challenge just because sectarian in-

stitutions may also receive an attenuated financial benefit." The key is that the assignment of the state interpreter in the sectarian school results from the parents' decision to move their deaf son to the private school, not because of any decision made by the state. *Zobrest v. Catalina Foothills School District* (1993).

b. Financial Aid to Schools

The Court is sharply divided on the application of the Establishment Clause to various forms of aid to religious schools. While the three-part test is applied, each case is decided on an ad hoc basis reflecting shifting coalitions of the justices. While aid is usually found to be in furtherance of a permissible secular purpose, it may be held to have a primary sectarian effect or involve excessive government entanglement with religion.

Among the factors you should consider in evaluating aid programs are: (1) whether the aid is to elementary and secondary education or to higher education; (2) the type of assistance provided (especially whether the aid is directed to citizens generally or is given directly to the religious institution, whether the aid is available generally or is limited to benefitting religious institutions, and whether it involves a continuing church-state relationship or affords an opportunity for inculcating religious values); (3) the location of the assistance, i.e., on public or private school grounds.

1) Elementary–Secondary v. Higher Education

Aid to elementary and secondary education is more likely to be held unconstitutional since the pupils are more impressionable and subject to ideological persuasion. Political divisiveness is more common at this level of education. Higher education has its own internal discipline and stresses academic freedom.

Examples: (1) State salary supplements for the teachers of secular subjects in non-public elementary schools involves excessive government entanglement with religion since parochial schools have substantial religious activity, the teacher is amenable to religious discipline, such aid involves a continuing government relationship with the schools, the children are of impressionable age and there is danger of political divisiveness. *Lemon v. Kurtzman* (1971).

(2) Federal construction grants for buildings and facilities to be used strictly for secular activities at private colleges are constitutional, although only a 20–year limit on the use to which such facilities could be put violates the First Amendment. Such construction aid is dispensed on a one-time basis, is religiously neutral involving limited government surveillance, and does not involve institutions permeated with religious education involved in educating impressionable young people. *Tilton v. Richardson* (1971).

(3) State annual non-categorical grants to private colleges, including sectarian institutions requiring theology courses, is not unconstitutional. First, the purpose is secular, *i.e.,* supporting higher education generally. Second, the state aid did not go to institutions so "pervasively sectarian" that secular and sectarian activities could not be separated—the aid was directed exclusively to the secular activities. No entangling relationship was created given the character of the institutions aided, review of the class content was not required in the approval process, and there was minimal danger of political divisiveness. *Roemer v. Board of Public Works of Maryland* (1976).

2) Testing, Recordkeeping, and Other Services and Equipment

The validity of state support for such services in elementary and secondary schools is likely to turn on the opportunity the particular program affords for indoctrination, *e.g.,* whether state officials or private school administrators prepare the test, and whether the program is neutral or has the primary effect of furthering the school's religious mission. Also, if the program takes place on public school grounds and under the supervision of public school officials, it is more likely to be upheld. But the Court has held "that a federally funded program providing supplemental, remedial instruction to disadvantaged children on a neutral basis is not invalid under the Establishment Clause when such instruction is given on the premises of sectarian schools by government employees pursuant to a program containing safeguards such as those present here." *Agostini v. Felton* (1997).

Examples: (1) The Court upheld a statute authorizing the state to furnish pupils in non-public schools with standardized tests and scoring services. Similarly, the Court upheld the furnishing by public employees of speech, hearing, and psychological diagnostic services, stressing the non-ideological character of the aid. However, the Court did rule unconstitutional those portions of the statute providing for the loan of instructional materials and equipment to non-public school parents or their children and providing for field trip services to non-public schools since such services could be used to disseminate religious teachings. *Wolman v. Walter* (1977).

(2) State cash reimbursement of non-public schools for state required testing and reporting services does not violate the Establishment Clause. The state retained total control over the content of the tests and the grading and recordkeeping could not be used as a part of religious teaching. The non-ideological services are discrete and readily identifiable and the pervasive religious atmosphere of the schools is not determinative. *Committee for Public Educ. & Rel. Lib. v. Regan* (1980).

(3) In *School District of Grand Rapids v. Ball* (1985), the Court had invalidated a Shared Time program in which remedial and enrichment classes were offered during regular school hours to children attending non-public schools. The classes were taught by public employees on the premises of the non-public school. Using the *Lemon* test, the Court had concluded that the program had the impermissible effect of advancing religion by risking state-sponsored indoctrination, creating a symbolic public endorsement of religion and impermissibly subsidizing the religious mission of the schools.

In *Aguilar v. Felton* (1985), the Court had invalidated the use of federal funds to pay the salaries of teachers providing remedial education to disadvantaged children in parochial schools. The use of extensive ongoing monitoring to prevent the religious effects of public aid in the pervasive sectarian environment of parochial schools created a danger of excessive governmental entanglement which violated the *Lemon* test.

But in *Agostini v. Felton* (1997) the Court overruled *Aguilar* and the holding of *Ball* on the Shared Time Program. While still purporting to apply the *Lemon* test, the Court uses different criteria in holding that the same federal program used in *Aguilar* does not violate the Establishment Clause. First, *Zobrest* establishes that the placement of public employees on parochial school grounds does not invariably result in state-sponsored indoctrination or constitute a symbolic union of government and religion. Second, *Witters* rejects the principle that all government aid that directly aids the educational function of religious schools is invalid. When aid is allocated on the basis of neutral, secular criteria that neither favors nor disfavors religion, and is made available to both religious and secular beneficiaries on a nondiscriminatory basis, the aid is not likely to have the effect of advancing religion. Further, entanglement must be excessive to violate the Establishment Clause and the entanglement inquiry is properly treated as an aspect of the inquiry into the statute's effects. The considerations above indicate that the law's provisions for public monitoring, the need for administrative cooperation, and the danger of political divisiveness do not establish *excessive* entanglement. In sum, the federal program is administered on a neutral basis and does not have an impermissible effect of endorsing religion. *Agostini v. Felton* (1997).

(4) A federal program channeling financial aid to state educational agencies which then lend educational materials and equipment to public and private schools to implement "secular, neutral and nonideological" programs is constitutional. A majority of the Court

continues to accept that proof of actual diversion of aid to religious uses would violate the Establishment Clause. Justice O'Connor, joined by Justice Breyer, concurring, agreed with the plurality that *Wolman v. Walter, supra*, which suggested that any aid that is reasonably divertible to religious uses is prohibited, should be overruled. But she argued that actual diversion would violate the Establishment Clause. A government aid program does not pass constitutional muster solely because it employs neutral criteria. But in this case the *Agostini* criteria was satisfied. The program neither endorsed religion nor had the effect of advancing religion. *Mitchell v. Helms* (2000).

3) **Tax Relief and Tuition Benefits**

When the aid is given to citizens rather than provided directly to the religious institutions, it is more likely to be upheld. But if the aid is limited only to citizens involved with religious institutions rather than to citizens generally, it may still be held unconstitutional. However, not all aid that directly benefits the educational functions of parochial schools is unconstitutional. *Agostini v. Felton* (1997). *"[W]here a government aid program is neutral with respect to religion, and provides assistance directly to a broad class of citizens who, in turn, direct government aid to religious schools wholly as a result of their own genuine and independent private choice, the program is not readily subject to challenge under the Establishment Clause."* Zelman v. Simmons–Harris (2002). *Neutrality* and *free private choice* are the key requirements.

Examples: (1) A state law providing direct unrestricted reimbursement grants to parents with children in non-public elementary and secondary schools was held to have the direct and immediate effect of aiding religion. Similarly, state tax relief to the parents was held unconstitutional. Finally, grants for the maintenance and repair of facilities and equipment was struck down. There was no assurance that any of these grants would be used to support solely the secular activities of the schools. *Committee for Public Educ. & Religious Liberty v. Nyquist* (1973).

(2) A state law permitting taxpayers to deduct certain educational expenses is constitutional. Assuring a

well-educated citizenry is the secular purpose of the law and the legislature could conclude that assuring the financial health of private schools serves that end to the benefit of taxpayers generally. Nor does the aid have a primary effect of advancing the sectarian aims of the private schools. Education is only one of the many deductions allowed, encouraging desirable expenditures. "Most importantly, the deduction is available for educational expenses incurred by *all* parents, including those whose children attend public schools and those whose children attend non-sectarian private schools or sectarian private schools." This neutrality of the program distinguishes *Nyquist*. Further, "by channeling whatever assistance it may provide to parochial schools through individual parents, [the state] has reduced the Establishment Clause objectives. * * * " The Court rejected the usefulness of statistical evidence indicating that the law primarily benefits religious institutions. *Mueller v. Allen* (1983).

(3) State vocational rehabilitation aid to a blind student which is used by him for education at a Christian college is not precluded by the Establishment Clause. The second prong of the *Lemon* test is not violated. First, the state aid goes directly to the student and flows to the religious institution only as a result of the independent and private choice of the recipient, *i.e.*, it is not a "direct subsidy" to the religious school. Further, it is not likely that any significant part of the aid expended under the program would support religious education. Finally, the aid is in no way skewed towards religion and creates no financial incentive for students to attend sectarian institutions. Nor is there any state endorsement of religion. *Witters v. Washington Dept. of Services for the Blind* (1986). The Court applied *Mueller v. Allen* and *Witters* in holding that the Establishment Clause is not violated when a public school district provides a sign-language interpreter for a deaf ninth-grader in a Catholic high school. *Zobrest v. Catalina Foothills School District* (1993).

(4) An Ohio program of tuition aid based on financial need for students in the Cleveland school district to attend participating public or private schools of their parent's choosing and tutorial aid for students choosing to remain enrolled in public school does not violate the Establishment Clause. The voucher program was upheld 5–4 even though 86% of the participating private schools had a religious affiliation and 96% of the students in the program enrolled in religiously affiliated schools. The program had a valid secular purpose of providing educational assistance to poor children in a demonstrably failing public school system.

The Court held that the program did not have the forbidden effect of advancing or inhibiting religion. Citing *Mueller*, *Witters* and *Zobrest*, the Court stated: "Where a government aid program is neutral with respect to religion, and provides assistance directly to a broad class of citizens who, in turn, direct government aid to religious schools wholly as a result of their own genuine and independent private choice, the program is not readily subject to challenge under the Establishment Clause." Any "incidental" advancement of a religious mission or "perceived endorsement of a religious message" is "reasonably attributable" to the choice of the choice of the individual recipient, not the government.

The Ohio program is one of true private choice, neutral in all respects towards religion. It provides educational benefits to any parent with of school age children in Cleveland and participation is open to all schools in the district, religious or nonreligious. There are no special incentives for religious schools. Parents have a genuine choice among religious and nonreligious organizations in deciding where to direct their aid. While more religious schools may participate and more children enroll in religious schools, this does not prevent a program from being neutral, where there is true private choice.

The dissent stressed that, in Cleveland, the overwhelming proportion of voucher money must be spent on religious schools and will be spent in amounts that cover almost all of tuition. Thus, it will pay substantial public money for instruction in not only secular, but also religious, subjects. The invocation of neutrality and private choice are only examples of verbal formalism. While all schools participate in the program, voucher tuition payments will predominantly benefit religious schools—the program is not truly "neutral." *Zelman v. Simmons–Harris* (2002).

3. Other Establishment Contexts

a. Blue Laws

1) The Court has thus far upheld Sunday closing laws against challenges based on the Establishment and Free Exercise Clauses.

2) Whatever the historical purpose of the Blue Laws, the Court considered that their present purpose and effect is secular. They are designed to promote a common day of rest. *McGowan v. Maryland* (1961).

3) However, if it were established that a particular law was enacted for the purpose of advancing religion, it would be unconstitutional, even if it also had the secular effect of providing a day of rest. See *Epperson v. Arkansas* (1968). Further, a law affording an employee with an absolute unqualified right not to work on the Sabbath of his choice was held to have the primary effect of advancing a religious practice in violation of the Establishment Clause. *Estate of Thornton v. Caldor, Inc.* (1985).

4) Note that, unlike the religious exemptions granted in many free exercise cases, the law in *Estate of Thornton* did not exempt the employee from any government-imposed obligation in order to further free exercise concerns. The Court has stated: "[I]t is a permissible legislative purpose to alleviate significant governmental interference with the ability of religious organizations to define and carry out their religious missions." *Corporation of Presiding Bishop of the Church of Jesus Christ of Latter–Day Saints v. Amos* (1987) (religious exemption from Title VII prohibition against discrimination in

employment is a permissible accommodation consistent with the Establishment Clause). Granting a religious exemption from generally applicable laws does not necessarily violate the Establishment Clause. Indeed, the Court has suggested, (1) that such legislation is valid; and (2) that it is more appropriate that such exemptions be created by the legislatures than by the courts.

b. Tax Exemptions

Property tax exemptions for places of religious worship as part of a general scheme relieving nonprofit organizations from tax obligations are constitutional in spite of the indirect support provided religion. A history of exemption has demonstrated that such benefits do not involve sponsorship, *i.e.*, money is not given to support religion. Tax exemptions, in fact, result in less government administrative entanglement with religion than would tax assessments, liens, foreclosures, etc. This is "benevolent neutrality." *Walz v. Tax Comm'n* (1970). However, a state may not grant exemptions from sales and use taxes exclusively to religious periodicals. Such exemptions violate the Establishment Clause in that they constitute a state endorsement of religious beliefs. Such a subsidy to religion does not have the secular purpose and primary effect mandated by the Establishment Clause. *Texas Monthly, Inc. v. Bullock* (1989).

c. Social Welfare Programs

The fact that religious institutions are incidentally benefitted as participants in a generally applicable, secular governmental social welfare program, does not violate the Establishment Clause. If a significant portion of the funds go to pervasively sectarian institutions, a law could have the primary effect of advancing religion in violation of the anti-establishment principle.

Example: The Adolescent Family Life Act, authorizing federal grants to public and private groups, including religious organizations, for research, services and counseling in adolescent sexuality and pregnancy, is not facially unconstitutional under the Establishment Clause. Using the *Lemon* test, the Act has the secular purpose of dealing with problems relating to teenage sexuality. While religious institutions are specifically included as grantees, any effect of advancing religion is "incidental and remote." Religious institutions are not disabled by the First Amendment from participating in social welfare programs. On its face, the Act does not indicate "that a significant proportion of the federal funds will be disbursed to 'pervasively sectarian' institutions." There is no indication that the monitoring under the Act will result in government involvement in the day to day activities of religious grantees producing "excessive entanglement." *Bowen v. Kendrick* (1988).

d. Legislative Prayer

While prayer in the schools has been invalidated by the Court, legislative-opening prayer led by a state-paid chaplain has been upheld. Instead of employing the *Lemon* three-part test, the Court relied on history in holding that those who drafted the First Amendment had not perceived legislative prayer as a threat to the Establishment Clause. The First Congress voted to pay a chaplain to open sessions with a prayer. *Marsh v. Chambers* (1983).

e. Religious Displays

The Court has employed history and tradition in upholding governmental recognition of holidays and displays with some religious significance. However, government may not display religious symbols in a way that has an ostensible and predominantly religious purpose. *McCreary County v. ACLU* (2005), or which endorses religion.

Examples: (1) Inclusion of a nativity scene as part of a municipal Christmas display does not violate the Establishment Clause. The Court emphasized "the government's acknowledgment of our religious heritage and governmental sponsorship of graphic manifestation of that heritage." While minimizing the value of the *Lemon* test, the Court characterized the display as having the secular purpose of celebrating the holiday. Any benefit to religion from use of the nativity scene to depict the origins of the holiday was "indirect, remote and incidental." There was no entanglement since minimal funds were involved and there were no contacts between church and city authorities. *Lynch v. Donnelly* (1984).

(2) The placement of a Christmas creche on the Grand Staircase, the main part of the Allegheny County Courthouse, given the setting, violates the Establishment Clause.

The creche stood alone with no other secular symbols of the holiday season. In this context, the display endorsed a patently Christian message glorifying God for the birth of Jesus Christ. On the other hand, the placement of an 18–foot Chanukah menorah in front of a government building, next to a Christmas tree and a sign saluting liberty, does not violate the Establishment Clause. In this context, the menorah is part of an overall holiday setting; a secular celebration of the cultural event of Christmas coupled with an acknowledgment of Chanukah as "a contemporaneous alternative tradition." It is not "sufficiently likely" that citizens will interpret the display as an endorsement or disapproval of religious choices. *Allegheny County v. ACLU* (1989). See *Capitol Square Review Board v. Pinette* (1995), Ch. IX, A, 1, d.

(3) The display of the Ten Commandments on county courthouse walls where the context establishes that the predominant purpose of the display is religious violates the Establishment Clause. In 1999, two Kentucky counties placed a framed copy of the King James version of the Ten Commandments on display. The Court would characterize this display as "an unmistakably religious statement dealing with religious obligations and with morality subject to religious sanction." When the ACLU filed an action, the counties adopted resolutions authorizing an expanded but altered display since the Ten Commandments are Kentucky's "precedent legal code." The second display included eight smaller documents, all having a religious theme or religious element. The Court would state: "Together the display and resolution presented an indisputable and undisputed showing of an impermissible purpose." After the district court issued a preliminary injunction and the counties got new lawyers, a third display appeared, "The Foundation of American Law and Government Display," consisting of an educational display of nine historical documents, including the Ten Commandments, all of the same size.

The Court 5–4 held the display violates the Establishment Clause. Justice Souter, for the Court, rejected the counties' effort to have the Court abandon the *Lemon* test, since the purpose was "unknowable." Instead, Justice Souter stated: "When the government acts with the ostensible and predominant purpose of advancing religion, it violates the central Establishment Clause value of official neutrality, there being no neutrality when the government's ostensible object is to take sides." See *Stone v. Graham* (1980) (Ch. IX, A, I, c, 2) (holding display of Ten Commandments in public school had predominantly religious purpose and violated the Establishment Clause). Under the *Lemon* test, while the government's statement of purpose receives deference, "the secular purpose has to be genuine not a sham and not merely secondary to a religious objective." Nor was the Court willing to focus only on the third display, ignoring its evolutionary context. Justice O'Connor, concurring, reasoned: "The purpose behind the counties' display is relevant because it conveys an unmistakable message of endorsement to the reasonable observer."

Justice Scalia, for the dissent, challenged the claim that government cannot favor religious over irreligion or that religion in the public forum has to be completely nondenominational. In addition, he argued that the Court had changed the *Lemon* test. "First, the Court justifies inquiry into legislative purpose, not as an end in itself, but as a means to ascertain the appearance of the government action to an objective observer." Second, he argued that the Court replaced the requirement that government have a secular purpose with a heightened requirement that the secular purpose "predominate" over any purpose to advance religion. Even applying the *Lemon* test, the dissent argued that neither the first nor second display necessarily evidenced an intent to further religious practice. There was "no evidence of a purpose to advance religion in a way that is inconsistent with our cases." *McCreary County v. ACLU* (2005).

(4) Display of a 6–foot monument inscribed with the Ten Commandments on the grounds of the Texas state capitol together with 16 other monuments and 21 historical markers said by the state "to compose Texas identity," does not

violate the Establishment Clause. Chief Justice Rehnquist, writing for a plurality, argued that the *Lemon* test was not useful in dealing with the sort of "passive monument" in this case. The Ten Commandments are religious and the monument has religious significance. But, "[s]imply having religious content or promoting a message consistent with a religious doctrine does not run afoul of the Establishment Clause." The Ten Commandments, he said, plays an important role in our heritage which is acknowledged by displays throughout America.

Justice Breyer, indicating that he viewed this as "a borderline case," concurred in the judgment, but not in the plurality opinion. While indicating his belief that the display would satisfy the *Lemon* test, he stressed that review should be based on the basic purposes of the Religion Clauses, e.g., the fullest possible scope of religious liberty and tolerance for all and avoiding divisiveness. "Here the tablets have been used as part of a display that communicates not simply a religious message, but a secular message as well. The circumstances surrounding the display's placement on the Capitol grounds and its physical setting suggest that the State intended the latter nonreligious aspects of the tablets' message to predominate." Justice Breyer emphasized that the monuments had a 40–year history on the Texas State grounds without significant controversy.

Justice Stevens, joined by Justice Ginsburg, dissenting, argued from the neutrality principle. The Decalogue prefers the Judeo–Christian message over other religions and over the irreligious. Justice Souter, joined by Justices Stevens and Ginsburg, argued that *Graham v. Stone* was controlling. The government put the Commandments on display to be seen and Texas had done nothing to blunt its religious message. Justice O'Connor also dissented for the reasons given by Justice Souter and in her concurrence in *McCreary County*. *Van Orden v. Perry* (2005).

(5) In 1934, the Veterans of Foreign Wars (VFW) placed a cross on federal land to honor American soldiers killed in

World War I. About seventy years later, Frank Buono brought an action claiming that the Government's permitting the cross was a violation of the Establishment Clause. The federal district court agreed and issued an injunction, reasoning that a "reasonable observer" would view the cross as an endorsement of religion. While an appeal was pending, Congress enacted a statute providing for a transfer of the cross and one acre of land on which it was erected to the VFW in exchange for other land. The Ninth Circuit affirmed the district court's decision in the original action but did not deal with the effect of the transfer. Buono secured another order from the district court permanently enjoining the land transfer, reasoning that the transfer statute had been enacted to protect the cross display which had previously been enjoined. The Ninth Circuit affirmed. The Supreme Court reversed and remanded.

In a plurality opinion, Justice Kennedy, joined by the Chief Justice, and, in part, by Justice Alito, reasoned that the district court had not correctly assessed the transfer statute's significance. By dismissing Congress' motives as illicit, the district court ignored the fact that private citizens had erected the cross to honor war heroes and not to promote a religious message. Further, the cross had stood and been privately maintained for almost seventy years before the statute was enacted. After the first injunction was issued, Congress was prevented from allowing the cross, but did not wish to convey disrespect for those whom the cross was honoring. The statute reflected Congress' effort to resolve the dilemma; the effort at accommodation deserved judicial respect. Finally, while the first injunction had been issued based solely on the district court's conclusions regarding reasonable perceptions, the later injunction was issued on a different basis—the Court's suspicion of an illicit government purpose. Enjoining the transfer in these circumstances was improper. The case was remanded for a proper consideration of the effect of the statute in the context. Justice Alito, concurring, would not have remanded since the factual record established that the transfer statute was constitutional. Justice Scalia, joined by

Justice Thomas, concurred in the judgment because they believed that Buono lacked Article III standing.

Justice Stevens, joined by Justices Ginsburg and Sotomayor, dissenting, argued that the injunction preventing the land-transfer should be affirmed. The land transfer would continue the Government's endorsement of the religious message of the cross. Justice Breyer, dissenting, decided that there was no federal question of significance presented; certiorari should not have been granted. *Salazar v. Buono* (2010).

f. Denominational Preferences

The Court has suggested that when a law aids or advances only selected religions, rather than religions generally, i.e., it grants denominational preferences, the law is suspect and a strict scrutiny standard applies. Government must demonstrate that the law is closely tailored to furthering a compelling public interest. The Lemon three-part test must be satisfied.

Examples: (1) A Minnesota law imposing registration and reporting requirements only on religious organizations that solicit more than 50 percent of their funds from nonmembers violates the Establishment Clause. The clear command of the clause is that one religious denomination cannot be officially preferred over another. Such a law must be closely fitted to furthering a compelling interest. While the state has a compelling interest in protecting its citizens from abusive practices in solicitations, the law is not closely fitted to further that interest. The record does not support the assumption that membership control over solicitation will occur when the 50 percent figure is reached, that this will protect the public and that the need for public disclosure rises in proportion with the percentage of non-member contributions. While the *Lemon v. Kurtzman* Establishment Clause test is intended to apply to laws affording a uniform benefit to all religions rather than a discriminatory law, the "excessive entanglement" test of *Kurtzman* is implicated since the law creates a risk of politicizing religion. *Larson v. Valente* (1982).

(2) The refusal of the IRS to recognize payments made by members of the Church of Scientology to that church for

training and auditing sessions as charitable contributions does not violate the Establishment Clause. The applicable section of the IRS code was neutral in design and purpose, even though it might impose a disparate burden on certain groups that rely on sales for fundraising. There is no unconstitutional denominational preference since the rule applies to all religious entities. There is no significant danger of an excessive entanglement between church and state through enforcement of the rule since it involves routine regulatory action rather than any inquiry into religious doctrine. *Hernandez v. CIR* (1989).

(3) Imposition of a state sales and use tax on religious materials sold by a religious organization does not violate the Establishment Clause. Applying the *Lemon* test, the Court first concluded that the tax was "neutral and non-discriminatory on questions of religious beliefs." Nor was there a danger of excessive entanglement. Even assuming that there were significant administrative burdens imposed by the tax, this would not violate the Establishment Clause. Since the materials are subject to the tax regardless of content or motive, government would not be required to inquire into the religious basis for selling the materials. *Jimmy Swaggart Ministries v. Board of Equalization* (1990).

g. Internal Church Disputes

Courts are not to decide purely internal church disputes. However, courts may decide legal questions, which can be settled by the application of "neutral principles of law", i.e., questions which will not require an inquiry into religious doctrine. Jones v. Wolf *(1979)* (state court could decide which group would control church property following a separation within the church).

Example: Cheryl Perich, a commissioned minister of the Hosanna–Tabor Evangelical Lutheran Church and School, was fired as a teacher at the school after a disability leave. She claimed she was fired in retaliation for threatening to file an ADA lawsuit. The Court unanimously held that a "ministerial exception" barred her claim. Chief Justice Roberts, writing for the Court, while not adopting any rigid formula, concluded that Perich was a minister "given all the circumstances of her employment." The Chief Justice considered her formal title as a "commissioned minister," the substance reflected in the title given the training she received and the process of commissioning, and the significant religious functions she performed for the church, even though she had secular duties and other lay teachers in the school also performed the same religious activities. Because she was a minister, the First Amendment required the dismissal of her employment discrimination claim. "Both Religion Clauses bar the government from interfering with the decision of a religious group to fire one of its ministers." The Establishment Clause is violated when the government involves itself in ecclesiastical decisions of appointing ministers. The Free Exercise Clause is violated by the government imposing unwanted ministers on the religious group. The Court held that a "ministerial exception" grounded in the Religion Clauses applies to application of legislation such as the Americans with Disabilities Act. *Hosanna–Tabor Evangelical Lutheran Church and School v. EEOC (2012).*

h. Institutionalized Persons

A federal law intended to protect religious exercise by institutionalized persons was held to qualify, on its face, as a permissible legislative accommodation of religion.

Example: A section of the Religious Land Use and Institutionalized Persons Act of 2000 (RLUIPA) providing that "[n]o government shall impose a substantial burden on the religious exercise of a person residing in or confined to an institution" unless the burden furthers "a compelling governmental interest," and does so by "the least restrictive means," does not, on its face, violate the Establishment Clause. The law "alleviates exceptional government-created burdens on private religious exercise" by protecting institutionalized persons who are dependent on government's permission and accommodation to practice their religion. In doing so, the statute requires courts to "take adequate account of the burdens a requested accommodation may impose on nonbeneficiaries" and requires courts to be satisfied "that the Act's prescriptions are and will be administered neutrally among different faiths." The Act does not elevate religious accommodation over an institution's needs to maintain order and safety. *Cutter v. Wilkinson* (2005).

B. The Meaning of the "Free Exercise" Clause

If government undertakes to burden persons because of their religious beliefs, there is a violation of the Free Exercise Clause. Most laws, however, only incidentally burden or coerce religious beliefs while pursuing a secular public welfare objective. Coercion of religious belief is the essence of a free exercise claim.

Free exercise cases generally involve a claimed exemption from an otherwise generally applicable law. In reconciling the secular public welfare interests of government with the free exercise interests of the individual, the courts engage in balancing. For example, it is doubtful whether the members of a religious group which did not believe in paying taxes to the state would be permitted to withhold their taxes.

Since the 1960's, the courts have employed a two-step test. Initially, the court examines the severity of the burden on the individual's religion. If the burden is significant, government must demonstrate that the law is narrowly tailored to achieve a compelling state interest. The availability of less burdensome alternatives is considered. Doctrines employed in freedom of expression cases, *e.g.*, the prior restraint doctrine, prohibition against vagueness and overbreadth, are often applied in free exercise cases. In many cases, this strict scrutiny standard has resulted in an exemption from religion-neutral laws that have the effect of significantly burdening a religion.

However, in Employment Div., Dept. of Human Resources of Oregon v. Smith *(1990), and* Lyng v. Northwest Indian Cemetery Protective Ass'n *(1988), discussed below, the Court held that this strict scrutiny standard did not apply to a generally applicable and otherwise constitutional law, even though application of the law incidentally imposed a significant burden on a religion. These holdings may portend a general doctrinal revision rejecting strict scrutiny review of laws having only an incidental effect of significantly burdening religious freedom. If this approach triumphs, a key question will become whether the challenged government action directly, rather than incidentally, burdens free exercise. Incidental burdens on religion would be insufficient to generate strict scrutiny review.*

1. Belief–Conduct

While religious belief and opinion is absolutely protected, the practice of religious activities must be accommodated to valid government interests. The interest of the government in regulating conduct injurious to the public well-being is balanced against the burden on the individual's exercise of his religion if the conduct is prohibited.

Examples: (1) Application of a federal law prohibiting polygamy to a Mormon who claims that polygamy is a fundamental tenet of his faith does not violate the Free Exercise Clause. The law is a permissible regulation of conduct which is subversive of good order and violative of social duties. *Reynolds v. United States* (1878).

(2) A state law compelling a flag salute by public school children in violation of their religious beliefs offends the guarantee of freedom of speech and religion. The state cannot prescribe what is orthodox in politics, nationalism, and matters of opinion. Religious freedom is susceptible of restriction only to prevent grave and immediate dangers to interests which the state may lawfully protect. *West Virginia Bd. of Educ. v. Barnette* (1943).

(3) A state law prohibiting clergymen from being delegates to the state constitutional convention violates the free exercise guarantee. Treating the law as directed at conduct rather than beliefs, the Court still found no state interest of sufficient magnitude to justify the significant burden on religion. *McDaniel v. Paty* (1978).

2. Centrality and Sincerity

In resolving free exercise claims, the courts are prohibited from assessing the truth or falsity of the claimant's religious beliefs. United States v. Ballard *(1944)* (lower court erred in allowing jury to consider truth or falsity of religious claims of a member of the "I Am" movement who was being prosecuted for using the mail for false pretense). *However, the courts can inquire into whether the religious belief is sincerely held. The courts have also probed the centrality of a belief or practice to a religion in assessing the significance of the burden on free exercise.* Wisconsin v. Yoder *(1972).* However, in *Employment Div., Dept. of Human Resources of Oregon v. Smith* (1990), discussed below, the Court states: "It is no more appropriate for judges to determine the 'centrality' of religious belief before applying a 'compelling interest' test in the free exercise field, than it would be for them to determine the 'importance' of an idea before applying the 'compelling' interest test in the free speech field." This may be the prelude to eliminating the centrality inquiry in free exercise cases.

3. General Indirect Burdens

The fact that a religion-neutral, generally applicable law imposes a burden on a religious group does not, without more, require an exemption under the Free Exercise Clause. Absent a significant burden on the claimant's free exercise of her religious beliefs, *i.e.,* a uniquely religious impact, strict scrutiny is not appropriate.

Examples: (1) Application of the Fair Labor Standards Act (FLSA) to workers (identified as "employees" under the Act because they are not truly "volunteers" but receive "wages" in the form of benefits) engaged in the commercial activities of a religious foundation (identified as a business "enterprise" under the Act) does not violate the Free Exercise or Establishment Clauses. The Free Exercise Clause requires an exemption from a governmental program only if the law actually burdens the claimant's freedom to exercise religious rights. Application of the FLSA does not force the workers to accept wages nor does it prevent their returning the wages to the Foundation. Nor does the recordkeeping required by the FLSA foster an excessive government entanglement with religion violative of the Establishment Clause. The Act is limited to commercial activities and the inquiries made relate only to routine factual information and are not equal to significantly intrusive "government surveillance" into religious affairs. *Tony & Susan Alamo Foundation v. Secretary of Labor* (1985).

(2) California's imposition of sales and use tax liability on religious materials does not violate the Free Exercise Clause. The incrementally larger tax burden experienced by the religious group does not significantly burden their free exercise of their religious beliefs. Claimant's religious beliefs do not forbid payment of the tax. California's generally applicable tax is not a flat license fee imposed as a precondition for evangelical activity; it is not a prior restraint to engaging in religious activity. Compare *Murdock v. Pennsylvania* (1943) (convictions of Jehovah's Witnesses for soliciting without a license requiring payment of a license fee held unconstitutional). The Free Exercise Clause does not require the state to grant an exemption from its generally applicable tax absent proof of a more significant burden on religious freedom. *Jimmy Swaggart Ministries v. Board of Equalization* (1990).

(3) Hastings College of Law's all-comers policy for student groups, requires that, for official recognition of a student group, the group must allow anyone to join. The Court held that the policy does not deny free exercise of religion to a Christian group that discriminates on the basis of religion and sexual orientation in membership. The policy was viewpoint-neutral and was reasonable. It only denied the group official recognition, still allowing them to use the school's facilities. It was only an incidental burden on the group's free exercise of religion. *Christian Legal Society v. Martinez* (2010).

4. Blue Laws

The Court has rejected a challenge to Sunday closing laws based on the Free Exercise Clause by characterizing the laws as imposing only an indirect economic burden on the Sabbatarian. Balanced against the state interest in having a uniform day of rest, the free exercise claim failed.

Example: An orthodox Jewish merchant who celebrates the Sabbath on Saturday and closes his shop that day but who keeps his shop open on Sunday may be validly prosecuted under a state Sunday closing law. When the state regulates conduct by enacting a general law within its power, the purpose and primary effect of which is to advance the state's secular goals, the statute is valid despite its indirect burden, (*i.e.*, an economic hardship on religious observance), unless the state may accomplish its purpose by means which do not impose such a burden. *Braunfeld v. Brown* (1961).

5. Conditioning Public Welfare Benefits

a.   *The government cannot condition the receipt of governmental benefits on the surrender of constitutional rights, including the free exercise of one's religion. Conditioning the receipt of public benefits, such as unemployment compensation, on the willingness to violate one's religious principles, imposes a significant burden on free exercise. Only a compelling government interest, which cannot be realized by means less burdensome on constitutional values, justifies such coercion.*

Examples: (1) A Seventh Day Adventist was disqualified for benefits under a state unemployment compensation law because she would not work on Saturday, the Sabbath day of her faith, thus running afoul of a provision in the state law disqualifying those who refuse to accept "suitable work when offered * * *." The state may not force an individual to choose between following the precepts of her religion and forfeiting governmental benefits. The application of the provision violated free exercise because it involved a significant burden and no compelling state interest was advanced to justify such a burden. *Sherbert v. Verner* (1963).

(2) A state denial of unemployment benefits to a claimant who terminates his job because his religious beliefs forbade participation in production of armaments violates the free exercise guarantee. As long as the person terminates his work because of an honest conviction that such work was forbidden by his religion, he can make a free exercise claim. The state interests in avoiding widespread unemployment and avoiding detailed probing by employers of a job applicant's religious beliefs were not sufficiently compelling to justify the substantial burden placed on the employee's religious liberty. *Thomas v. Indiana Employment Security Div.* (1981).

(3) A state denial of unemployment benefits because of the "misconduct" of a Seventh Day Adventist who, because of religious objections, refused to work her assigned hours, violates the Free Exercise Clause. Even though her religious objections developed after she commenced employment, *Sherbert* and *Thomas* controlled. *Hobbie v. Unemployment Appeals Comm'n* (1987).

(4) The federal statutory requirement that a state agency "shall utilize" social security numbers in administering federal assistance programs does not violate the Free Exercise Clause even where the claim is made that state compliance with the requirement would burden the litigant's religious beliefs. The Free Exercise Clause does not afford an individual a right to dictate the conduct of the government's internal procedures on religious grounds. The law, requiring use of Social Security numbers already in the government's possession, imposes no significant burden on the claimant's ability to exercise his religion.

A further requirement was that the number be provided by the individual as a condition for welfare eligibility. Three justices stressed that eligibility for welfare benefits rather than government compulsion of conduct was involved and would not apply strict scrutiny. Since the requirement is facially neutral in religious terms applying to all applicants for the benefits involved, and clearly promotes a legitimate and important governmental interest, they would uphold the requirement. Preventing fraud in these programs is an important goal, and the social security number requirement is a reasonable means of promoting that goal. Four justices would have decided the case using strict scrutiny on the basis of *Thomas* and *Sherbert.* Two justices did not reach the issue. *Bowen v. Roy* (1986).

(5) State denial of unemployment benefits to a worker who refused a job because of his belief that as a Christian he could not work on Sunday as the job required, violates the free exercise guarantee. A person cannot be made to choose between fidelity to religious belief and employment absent compelling justification. *Frazee v. Illinois Dept. of Emp. Sec.* (1989).

Exception: Employment Div., Dept. of Human Resources of Oregon v. Smith (1990), discussed below, indicates that benefits can be denied if the denial is only the incidental effect of applying a generally applicable and otherwise valid criminal law. *In such a case, strict scrutiny is not applicable.* Since prohibition of the religious practice is constitutional, imposition of the lesser burden of denying unemployment benefits to persons engaging in the proscribed conduct is constitutional. *Employment Div., Dept. of Human Resources of Oregon v. Smith* (1988) (*Smith* I).

6. Compelled Expression

a. When government requires an individual to engage in practices contrary to central tenets of his or her religion, it imposes a direct burden on the free exercise of religion. Only a compelling or overriding government interest justifies such a significant burden on free exercise.

Examples: (1) State prosecutions of members of the Amish church who refuse to send their children to public school after the eighth grade thus violating a state law compelling public school attendance to age 16 violates the free exercise guarantee. Utilizing a balancing test, the Court ruled the prosecutions invalid on the ground that the Amish had sustained the heavy and difficult burden of showing that their alternative mode of continuing informal vocational education served to meet exactly those interests advanced by the state in support of its requirement of compulsory high school attendance. In such circumstances, the legitimate claims to free exercise of religion overbalance the interests of the state. *Wisconsin v. Yoder* (1972).

(2) Imposition of social security taxes on a member of the Amish faith who objected on religious grounds to receipt of public insurance benefits and to payment of taxes to support public insurance funds does not violate the free exercise guarantee. While payment of such taxes does violate Amish religious beliefs, the government limitation on religious liberty is justified by its showing that "it is essential to accomplish an overriding governmental interest." Government has a vital interest in maintaining a mandatory and continuous participation in and contribution to the social security system since widespread individual voluntary coverage would undermine the system. *United States v. Lee* (1982).

b. But the courts exercise extreme deference to government authority in reviewing free exercise claims by military personnel.

Example: The First Amendment does not preclude an Air Force regulation, prohibiting members of the Air Force from wearing headgear while indoors, from being applied to an Orthodox Jew's wearing of a yarmulke even though the effect is to restrict the wearing of the headgear required by his religious beliefs. Review of military regulations challenged on First Amendment grounds is far more deferential than constitutional review of similar laws or regulations designed for civilian society. When evaluating whether military needs justify a particular restriction on religiously motivated conduct, courts must give great deference to the professional judgment of military authorities concerning the relative importance of a particular military interest. The regulation reasonably and evenhandedly served the military's perceived need for uniformity in visible apparel. *Goldman v. Weinberger* (1986).

7. Noncoercive Laws

If the government regulation has the incidental effect of making it significantly more difficult to practice a religion, but does not compel or coerce action contrary to a religious belief, strict scrutiny does not apply. Note that the government is not required by the Free Exercise Clause to accommodate its own internal processes and operations to the religious needs and desires of particular claimants, even if the government action imposes a significant burden on religious belief. See also *Bowen v. Roy* (1986), where the Court characterized the burdensome effect of such government action as insignificant.

Examples: (1) The Free Exercise Clause does not bar the federal government from permitting timber harvesting and road construction in a national forest traditionally used for religious purposes by three Indian tribes. Such an incidental effect on religion does not constitute a "prohibition" of free exercise. Even if the government action "would virtually destroy" the religious practice, government could not operate if it were required to satisfy every citizen's religious needs and desires. *Lyng v. Northwest Indian Cemetery Protective Ass'n* (1988).

(2) Washington state could, pursuant to the stronger anti-establishment guarantee in its own constitution, deny funding from its "Promise Scholarship Program" to students pursuing degrees that were religiously "devotional in nature or designed to induce religious faith." Although the state "could, consistent with the Federal Constitution, permit Promise Scholars to pursue a degree in devotional theology," the Free Exercise Clause did not compel them to do so over the restrictions of their own state constitution. There was no "presumptive unconstitutionality" based on the fact that the law is not facially neutral with respect to religion since the state has imposed no burdens but has merely chosen not to fund a particular category of instruction. The state's interest in upholding the anti-establishment values expressed in its constitution was substantial, and the exclusion placed only a minor burden on recipients of the scholarships. There is tension between the

Establishment and the Free Exercise Clauses. But "there is room for play in the joints." The Court concluded: "if any room exists between the two Religion Clauses, it must be here." *Locke v. Davey* (2004).

8. Proscribed Religious Practices

a. *The free exercise guarantee is not violated by a generally applicable and otherwise constitutional criminal law which has the incidental effect of prohibiting a religious practice. Such religion-neutral laws are presumptively valid; strict scrutiny does not apply. This principle applies even if the proscribed practice is central to a religion. However, if a law which imposes a substantial burden on religion is not generally applicable and neutral, strict scrutiny does apply.*

Examples: (1) Denial of unemployment compensation to workers who were fired from their jobs with a private drug rehabilitation organization for work-related misconduct resulting from the use of the drug peyote during sacramental worship of the Native American Church did not deny free exercise of religion. The use of peyote violates state criminal drug laws which make no exception for religiously inspired uses. Such a prohibition is permissible under the Free Exercise Clause.

Strict scrutiny is inapplicable to challenges to "an across-the-board criminal prohibition on a particular form of conduct." The *Sherbert* strict scrutiny test has never been used to invalidate government action outside the context of unemployment compensation, a context where individualized assessment of the reasons for the government action is appropriate. A rule of presumptive invalidity "would open the prospect of constitutionally required religious exemptions from civic obligations of almost every conceivable kind." Such religious accommodation should be left to the legislature. *Employment Div., Dept. of Human Resources of Oregon v. Smith* (1990).

(2) City ordinances prohibiting religious animal sacrifice, but exempting nonreligious animal slaughtering, violate the Free Exercise Clause. The laws were not neutral since their object was to suppress the Santeria religion and its

ritual. Nor were the ordinances of general applicability since the city's secular interests in promoting public health and preventing cruelty to animals, were pursued "only against conduct motivated by religious belief." Since the laws directly burdened religion, they "must undergo the most rigorous of scrutiny." The laws were not narrowly tailored since they were underinclusive, exempting all non-religious animal slaughtering. Nor were the city's secular interests compelling since the city failed to prohibit conduct producing the same or greater harm. *Church of the Lukumi Babalu Aye, Inc. v. Hialeah (1993).*

(3) Even though the Americans with Disabilities Act is a valid and neutral law of general applicability, it cannot be applied when the case "concerns an internal church decision that affects the faith and mission of the church itself," such as the firing of a commissioned member of a religious organization. *Hosanna–Tabor Evangelical Lutheran Church and School v. EEOC (2012).* See Ch. IX, A, 3, g.

b. In the Religious Freedom Restoration Act of 1993 (RFRA), Congress rejected *Smith* and sought "to restore the compelling interest test as set forth in *Sherbert v. Verner* and *Wisconsin v. Yoder* and to guarantee its application in all cases where free exercise of religion is substantially burdened." The Act provides: "Government shall not substantially burden a person's exercise of religion even if that burden results from a rule of general applicability" unless the burden, "(1) is in furtherance of a compelling governmental interest; and (2) is the least restrictive means of furthering that compelling governmental interest." RFRA specifically provides that it is not intended to affect Establishment Clause cases.

But in *City of Boerne v. Flores* (1997), the Court held RFRA unconstitutional insofar as it applies to state action. Because the Act exceeded Congress' remedial powers under the Fourteenth Amendment, § 5. (See Ch. XI, B, 1). However, in *Gonzales v. O Centro Espirita Beneficente Unias do Vegetal* (2006), the Court applied RFRA to invalidate federal action preventing use of a banned drug in a sacramental tea.

Examples: (1) RFRA is unconstitutional as applied state action (here, the denial of a building permit to enlarge a church) because it exceeds Congress' power under § 5 of the Fourteenth Amendment. Congress' enforcement power is corrective; it is a power to provide remedies or enact preventive measures. It does not include the power to define the substantive rights guaranteed in the Fourteenth Amendment, § 1. It is the judicial role to say what the law is under *Marbury v. Madison.*

In using its Fourteenth Amendment, § 5 enforcement powers, Congress can reach conduct which is not itself unconstitutional as a means of preventing unconstitutional state action. But there must be a congruence and proportionality between the wrong to be prevented or remedied and the means Congress uses. RFRA failed this test since it would invalidate an excessive number of state laws as a means of preventing states from directly, intentionally burdening the free exercise of religion. There was no evidence that generally applicable laws are regularly used to covertly burden religious freedom. *City of Boerne v. Flores* (1997).

(2) The federal government sought to prohibit O Centro Espirita Beneficente Unias do Vegetal (UDV), a religious group, from using *hoasca*, a hallucinogen banned under the federal Controlled Substances Act (CSA). *Hoasca* was used in a sacramental tea taken as a central part of UDV's communion ceremony. UDV successfully moved for a preliminary injunction. The Supreme Court unanimously affirmed, holding that the Government had not carried the burden placed on it by RFRA. Chief Justice Roberts, for the Court, first held that RFRA placed the burden of proving a compelling interest on the Government and "burdens at the preliminary injunction stage track the burdens at trial." Turning to the merits, the Court rejected the Government's claim that it had a compelling interest in the *uniform* application of the CSA, which admitted of no exceptions.

The Court, rejecting this categorical approach, said that RFRA requires that the Government show that "the compelling interest test is satisfied through the application of the challenged law 'to the person'—the particular claimant whose sincere belief is being substantially burdened." "[T]here is no indication that Congress, in classifying [the substance], considered the harms posed by the particular use at issue here—the circumscribed, sacramental use of *hoasca* by the UDV." Provision in the CSA for waivers and exemption—especially the exemption for Native American religious use of peyote—undermines the Government's claim that CSA establish "a closed regulatory" system, admitting of no exemptions.

The Government failed to provide evidence that granting UDV an exemption would cause administrative harms recognized as a compelling interest *e.g.*, that it would undermine the CSA. Finally, the Court said that the Government did not even submit evidence of any international consequences of granting an exemption for the UDV that might create a compelling interest in complying with the U.N. Convention on Psychotropic Substances. *Gonzales v. O Centro Espirita Beneficente Uniao do Vegetal* (2006).

c.   Further, the Court has upheld a federal law modeled on RFRA applicable to institutionalized persons.

Example: The Religious Land Use and Institutionalized Persons Act of 2000 (RLUIPA) providing that "no government shall impose a substantial burden on the religious exercise of a person residing in or confined to an institution," unless the burden furthers a "compelling governmental interest" and does so by "the least restrictive means" does not violate the Establishment Clause. A unanimous Court noted that the law alleviates exceptional government-created burdens on private religious exercise by protecting institutionalized persons who depend on the government's permission and accommodation for exercise of their religion. *Cutter v. Wilkenson* (2005) (See Ch. IX, A, 3, h).

C.   The Meaning of Religion

The Court has not directly addressed itself to the question of what qualifies as a religion or a religious belief under the Establishment and the Free Exercise Clauses. Indeed, it is not even clear that it is appropriate for a court to probe the meaning of "religion." But the Court has stated: "Although a determination of what is a 'religious' belief or practice entitled to constitutional protection may present a most delicate question, the very concept of ordered liberty precludes allowing every person to make his own standards on matters of conduct in which society as a whole has important interests." *Wisconsin v. Yoder* (1972).

The Court has clearly rejected any limitation of "religion" to theistic religions. *Torcaso v. Watkins* (1961). While there must be a sincerely held "religious belief" to qualify for free exercise protection, it is not required that the claimant be a member of organized religion or a particular sect. *Frazee v. Illinois Dept. of Emp. Sec.* (1989) (denial of religious exemption to a claimant for unemployment compensation who belonged to no sect, but sincerely believed that as a Christian he could not work on Sunday as the job required, violates free exercise).

1. Conscientious Objection

    a.   In cases involving the conscientious objector provisions of the draft laws, the Court has indicated that the test of whether a belief is religious "is whether a given belief that is sincere and meaningful occupies a place in the life of its possessor parallel to that filled by the orthodox belief in God * * *."

    b.   A plurality of the Court has gone even further, extending conscientious objector status even to those whose objections primarily reflect public policy considerations. *Welsh v. United States* (1970). However, the Court has refused an exemption to those opposed to a particular "unjust" war and has upheld the exclusion of such persons as based on neutral and secular reasons. *Gillette v. United States* (1971).

D. Review Questions

1. **T or F** State authorization of a religious community's control over a school district so that special education can be provided to children within the community is a constitutional accommodation of religion.

2. **T or F** Released time for religious instruction, on or off school grounds, violates the Establishment Clause.

3. **T or F** Requiring non-denominational prayers violates the First Amendment even if objecting students are excused.

4. **T or F** Prayers offered at graduation ceremonies do not violate the Establishment Clause, provided that students are excused from participating, since such ceremonies are traditional and any benefits to religion are only incidental.

5. **T or F** Religious groups can be excluded from using public school property generally open to outside groups in order to avoid an Establishment Clause violation.

6. **T or F** Use of state funds for busing or the loan of state approved textbooks for students attending religious-affiliated schools does not violate the Establishment Clause.

7. **T or F**   Assignment of a public employee to serve as an interpreter for a deaf student in a parochial school violates the Establishment Clause.

8. **T or F**   State tax relief provided only for parents with children in religiously-affiliated elementary and secondary schools violates the Establishment Clause.

9. **T or F**   Public assistance for tuition expenses, available to all citizens, is constitutional even if, statistically, sectarian schools receive the primary economic benefit.

10. **T or F**   A program of remedial education for disadvantaged children attending parochial schools is unconstitutional if the teachers are public employees and the classes are taught in the parochial school.

11. **T or F**   A law providing more favorable treatment for traditional religions with a large, established membership is probably constitutional.

12. **T or F**   A state law granting a religious exemption from a generally applicable law has the purpose of aiding religion and therefore violates the Establishment Clause.

13. **T or F**   Courts may not decide legal questions involving ownership of religious property.

14. **T or F**   While religious belief is absolutely protected, religious practices are subject to public regulation.

15. **T or F**   If a government regulation of conduct significantly burdens a sincerely held religious belief, it necessarily violates the Free Exercise Clause.

16. **T or F**   An exemption from generally-applicable laws for persons having a sincere religious objection to conforming is always required by the Free Exercise Clause.

17. **T or F**   Courts cannot constitutionally inquire into the meaning of "religion" or "religious belief."

18. **T or F**   If a law significantly burdens a religious belief, strict scrutiny is always required by the Free Exercise Clause.

19. Which of the following programs would be most likely to violate the Establishment Clause?

a. Tax exemption for churches and other property owned by religions.

b. A requirement that the Ten Commandments be posted in public school classrooms.

c. Sunday Closing Laws.

d. State building grants to colleges.

e. State reimbursement of non-public elementary schools for state required testing and reporting.

20. Which of the following is the *least accurate* statement of the law relating to the Establishment of Religion Clause?

a. The government action must have a secular legislative purpose to be valid.

b. The Establishment Clause is directed principally against laws discriminating among religions.

c. If the primary effect of a law is to advance or inhibit religion, the Establishment Clause is violated.

d. Laws fostering an excessive entanglement with religion, or promoting political divisiveness, violate the non-establishment guarantee.

21. A city ordinance prohibits religious animal sacrifice, but exempts nonreligious animal slaughtering. A religious group, which use animal sacrifice as a central part of its religious worship challenges the constitutionality of the city ordinance. Discuss the merits of the Free Exercise Clause challenge.

X

State Action

■ ANALYSIS

The mechanism that makes most constitutional guarantees operative is state action. In the Civil Rights Cases of 1883, the Court delimited the significance of state action under the Fourteenth Amendment: "Individual invasion of individual rights is not the subject matter of the Amendment." In other words, private discrimination against other individuals with respect to jobs, housing, and services are not a constitutional (as distinguished from a statutory) matter reached by the Fourteenth Amendment. This is equally true of most rights and liberties protected by the Constitution—it is government wrongdoing that provides the subject matter for constitutional judicial review. In applying the state action requirement, the Court has described it as preservative of personal liberty, federalism and separation of powers.

In the fairly recent past, efforts were made, with some success, to have the Court view private action as quasi-public and therefore subject to constitutional standards. Thus, where a private activity fulfills a public function or where the state involvement and the private involvement were intertwined, the Court has been willing to categorize an entire activity as the equivalent of state action.

In the 1970's, the movement to judicially expand the state action concept to reach more private conduct came to a halt. The Court has significantly increased the level of government involvement in private conduct that is needed to establish state action and has required litigants to demonstrate a close nexus between government and the particular private action being challenged. In other words, the Court is limiting the occasions when private conduct will be subject to constitutional limitations.

A. The State Action Requirement

1. Thirteenth Amendment

The Thirteenth Amendment provides that "neither slavery nor involuntary servitude * * * shall exist within the United States * * *." It is not limited to state or public action denying the guarantee but applies directly against private action as well.

2. Fourteenth Amendment

The Fourteenth Amendment, § 1, provides that "no *State* shall make or enforce any law which shall abridge the privileges or immunities of citizens of the United States; nor shall any *State* deprive any person of life, liberty, or property, without due process of law; nor [may the State] deny to any person within its jurisdiction the equal protection of the laws." [Emphasis added.] It has been held that state action is required if the courts are to find these guarantees violated. *Civil Rights Cases* (1883).

3. Fifteenth Amendment

Similarly, the Fifteenth Amendment, § 1 requires governmental action in order to prove a violation. It provides that "the right of citizens of the United States to vote shall not be denied or abridged *by the United States or by any State* on account of race, color, or previous condition of servitude." [Emphasis added.]

4. The Present Standard—State Responsibility

The mere fact that the government is somehow involved in challenged private action is not sufficient to establish "state action." It is only when the government is so significantly involved in the action that it can be said that the government is "engaged in the challenged conduct or is responsible for it" that the requisite threshold is satisfied. There must be a close nexus between government and the particular private conduct being challenged.

B. Official Misconduct and Joint Action

1. Action Contrary to Law

Challenges to laws and to official action pursuant to a law clearly involve state action. But even if an official acts contrary to law, the state action requirement is satisfied. The government has put the official in a position of authority where he can misuse his power.

Example: Three state law enforcement officials beat and killed a young black man. Suit was brought against the officers under a federal civil rights statute alleging that the officers, acting under color of law, had violated the victim's due process rights to life, trial, and punishment according to law. The acts of the officers were considered by the Court to be under "color of law" because that term embraces acts of officers who undertake to perform official duty whether they act properly or improperly. *Screws v. United States* (1945).

2. Public Administration

Official supervision, control, or management of a facility, even when the government is only indirectly entwined in the management, constitutes state action.

Examples: (1) A testator left a park as a gift to a city on condition that it be used only by whites. The park was maintained by the city as a public facility and was also granted a tax exemption. The appointment of "private" trustees did not take the park out of the public sector and did not dissipate the momentum the park acquired as a public facility. If the city remains entwined in the management or control of the park, it is subject to Fourteenth Amendment standards. In such circumstances, even if the formal title to the park is in private hands, the public character of the park requires that it be subject to the commands of the Fourteenth Amendment. *Evans v. Newton* (1966).

(2) Action by Amtrak in rejecting displays for its billboards is subject to First Amendment review. Amtrak is an agency or instrumentality of the United States for constitutional purposes. "[W]here, as here, government creates a corporation by special law, for the furtherance of governmental objectives, and retains for itself permanent authority to appoint a majority of the directors of that corporation, the corporation is part of the Government for purposes of the First Amendment." *Lebron v. National Railroad Passenger Corp.* (1995).

3. Joint Action

If a private individual engages in joint activity with government officials, state action is established.

> *Example:* Eighteen defendants, three of them state law officers, were responsible for the deaths of three civil rights workers. The lower court upheld counts charging a violation of a federal civil rights statute against the three law officers but dismissed as to the fifteen private individuals on the ground that they had not acted under color of law. The Supreme Court reversed, holding that one acts under color of law if he is a willful participant in a joint activity with the state or its agents. *United States v. Price* (1966).

C. Public Functions

Some activities are so public in character that the government will not be allowed to disclaim responsibility. Government inaction in the face of private actions in such areas will be deemed to establish state action. Only if a function is traditionally and exclusively a function of government will it constitute state action.

1. White Primaries

Primary elections are "an important function relating to the exercise of sovereignty by the people." Even when the primary is administered by normally private persons or groups, the action remains that of the government. *Terry v. Adams* (1953). (primary held by a private group prior to regular Democratic primary which was tantamount to election, held to constitute state action).

2. Company Towns

If a privately-owned place becomes the functional equivalent of a public forum, such as a municipality, it may become part of the public forum.

Examples: (1) When a company-owned town refused to permit a Jehovah's Witness to distribute religious pamphlets on the town's main street, the Court declared that such a company-owned town, where no alternative forum was present, should be deemed sufficiently public as to prevent a restraint on First Amendment rights. The touchstone of this decision was that the streets of the company town, albeit privately owned, served a public or governmental function sufficient to cause them to be viewed as quasi-public for purposes of application of the state action concept. *Marsh v. Alabama* (1946).

(2) The Court has suggested that operation of a park could constitute a public function. "The service rendered even by a private park of this character is municipal in nature," citing *Marsh*. *Evans v. Newton* (1966). But, this approach has not prevailed. *Evans v. Abney* (1970).

3. Traditionally and Exclusively Sovereign

At the present time, the Court requires that the private entity must be exercising powers traditionally and exclusively reserved to government, *i.e.*, powers "traditionally associated with sovereignty, such as eminent domain," in order to find state action using the public function theory. *Jackson v. Metropolitan Edison Co.* (1974) (privately-owned utility is not engaged in state action).

Examples: (1) A warehouseman's enforcement of a lien by the sale of the stored goods, as authorized by New York's Uniform Commercial Code, was held not to constitute state action. In authorizing self-help as a means of resolving private disputes, the statute does not delegate a function "traditionally and exclusively reserved to the state," because there remains a wide range of debtor's remedies available and the state has not delegated to the creditor "an exclusive prerogative of the sovereign." The statute is merely a legislative determination that courts should not prevent self-help in this situation. State acquiescence in private action does not constitute state action. *Flagg Bros. Inc. v. Brooks* (1978).

(2) Operation of a nominally private school for maladjusted high school students, located on private grounds and managed by a private Board of Directors, is not state action, for purposes of a lawsuit alleging denial of free speech and due process rights of an employee. Until recently, the state had not undertaken responsibility for students who could not be served by traditional public schools. Nor is education of maladjusted students the *exclusive* province of the state merely because it extensively funds the private education. *Rendell–Baker v. Kohn* (1982).

(3) Operation of a nursing home which houses Medicare patients, who are challenging their transfer or discharge without notice or hearing, does not constitute state action. The fact that the state has legally assumed financial responsibility for the nursing care of such patients does make the activity state action. The decisions made in the day-to-day administration of a nursing home are not the kind of decisions "traditionally and exclusively made by the sovereign for and on behalf of the public." *Blum v. Yaretsky* (1982).

D. Significant State Involvement

1. Symbiotic Relationships

a. *The Court will sometimes inquire into the facts and circumstances to determine whether the aggregate of all the contacts between the government and the private actor constitute such a significant involvement as to make the government responsible for the private action. Critical in such a weighing is the existence of a "symbiotic relationship" between the government and the private actor.*

Example: A privately-owned restaurant, located within a municipal parking authority, which refused to serve a Black man food or drink solely because of his race was held bound by the proscriptions of the Fourteenth Amendment. The land and building were publicly owned, acquired, constructed, and maintained. Guests of the restaurant were thereby afforded a convenient place to park their autos, and the restaurant's convenience for diners may well have provided more business for the Parking Authority. In short, the state had so far insinuated itself into a position of interdependence with the restaurant that the state had to be recognized as a joint participant in the challenged activity. Therefore, the restaurant could not be viewed as so "purely private" as to fall outside the scope of the Fourteenth Amendment. *Burton v. Wilmington Parking Authority* (1961).

b. The fact that the government and private party are in a close working relationship or even in a contractual relationship does not necessarily establish a symbiotic relationship or joint action.

   Example: Disciplinary actions taken by the University of Nevada Las Vegas (UNLV) against its basketball coach, Jerry Tarkanian, under threat of sanction for violation of NCAA rules, does not mean that the NCAA engaged in state action. This case is the "mirror image" of the usual state action case since it was the state that performed the final act complained of in response to the influence of the private party. Since UNLV actively resisted the imposition of sanctions, the parties were more in an adversarial posture than partners. The NCAA was not an agent of the state but acted in response to its other members to enforce its rules. UNLV was free to leave the NCAA and establish its own standards. No power was delegated by the state to the NCAA to discipline a state employee; the rules were enforceable only by sanctions against the University itself. The NCAA imposition of sanctions was not taken pursuant to Nevada law and the organization remained a private entity acting at odds with the state. *National Collegiate Athletic Ass'n v. Tarkanian* (1988).

c. *If there is a sufficiently close relationship between the government and the private party that the acts of the latter may reasonably be treated as the acts of the state itself, i.e., they are entwined, state action may be found.*

   Example: The Tennessee Secondary School Athletic Association, a non-profit statewide athletic association which regulates interscholastic sports at public and private high schools, was held 5–4 to be engaged in state action in enforcing one of its rules against a member school. *Tarkanian* was distinguished because the NCAA did not act as a surrogate for a single state. In this case, the Court found two types of "entwinement." There is entwinement from the bottom up since 84% of the Association's membership were public schools "represented by their officials acting in their official capacity to provide an integral element of secondary public schooling." The officials overwhelmingly perform the acts by which the Association runs high school sports. The Court concluded: "Entwinement will support a conclusion that an ostensibly private organization ought to be charged with a public character and judged by constitutional standards; entwinement to the degree shown here requires it." The dissent warned that "if the majority's new entwinement test develops in future years, it could affect many organizations that foster activities, enforce rules, and sponsor extracurricular competitions among high schools—not just in athletics. . . ." *Brentwood Academy v. Tennessee Secondary School Athletic Association* (2001).

2.　Government Regulation and Licensing

Even extensive government regulation of a private activity or the provision of public benefits on a neutral basis is not, without more, sufficient to constitute state action. Further, the fact that the state licenses the actor does not make the state a partner to the actions of the licensee.

Example:　A Black American who was refused service by a national fraternal organization, contended that because the state liquor board had issued the organization a private club liquor license, the refusal of service to him was state action for purposes of the Equal Protection Clause. The Court rejected this contention, reasoning that discrimination by an otherwise private entity does not violate the Equal Protection Clause merely because the private entity receives some state benefit or is subject to extensive state regulation. The Court emphasized that unlike *Burton v. Wilmington Parking Authority* (1961), there was nothing in the record to suggest the presence of a symbiotic relationship between the private entity and the state. *Moose Lodge No. 107 v. Irvis* (1972).

3. Government Financial Support

The fact that government provides financial support for a private actor does not necessarily make the conduct of the private action into state action. Numerous privately-owned businesses and institutions rely on government contracts. Further, government grants and subsidies flow to numerous persons and institutions. Only if the assistance somehow makes the government a partner to the challenged conduct by encouraging, authorizing, or approving it (see below) is it likely to constitute state action.

Examples: (1) The fact that a state directly reimburses 90 percent of the medical expenses of the patients in privately-owned nursing facilities and subsidizes the operating and capital costs of the home does not make the state constitutionally responsible for the home's decisions. *Blum v. Yaretsky* (1982).

(2) The fact that a privately-owned and operated school depends on public funds for 90 to 99 percent of its operating budget does not make the acts of the administrators the acts of the state. *Rendell–Baker v. Kohn* (1982).

(3) State purchase of textbooks, like state tuition grants, directed to students attending public and private schools, regardless of whether the participating school practiced racial discrimination violates the Fourteenth Amendment. Such support is a form of financial assistance money to the benefit of the private school itself. *Norwood v. Harrison* (1973).

(4) A city under a desegregation order violates equal protection when it permits exclusive use of its recreational facilities, even on a temporary basis, by segregated private schools since it makes attendance at such schools more attractive. The Court remanded the question of whether non-exclusive use would constitute state action to the lower court. *Gilmore v. Montgomery* (1974).

E. Encouragement, Authorization and Approval

1. Neutral Law Enforcement

Generally, the neutral enforcement of its laws by state officials will not, without more, constitute state action. In the absence of any encouragement, authorization, or approval of the challenged act, the state is not responsible for the conduct.

Example: A public park could not constitutionally be operated on a racially discriminatory basis as directed by the testator who had asked that his property be held in trust by the city as a park "for whites only." The state court's refusal to apply the *cy pres* doctrine to the will in order to keep the park open to all races and its decision permitting the trust property to revert to the heirs of the testator did not violate the Fourteenth Amendment. The Court emphasized that there was not the slightest indication that the state judges were motivated by any discriminatory intent in construing the will. Similarly, there was no indication that the testator had been persuaded to draw his will as he did by the fact that state statutes permitted racial restrictions at the time of the writing of the will. *Evans v. Abney* (1970).

2. Involuntary Discrimination

However, even a neutral enforcement of state law by a state official cannot be used to force racial discrimination on unwilling parties.

Example: A willing seller may not be barred from transacting a sale of real estate with a willing buyer because of state judicial enforcement of restrictive covenants, designed to exclude persons from the ownership of real property on the basis of race. Such judicial action bears the clear and unmistakable imprimatur of the state. Judicial action is no less state action under the Fourteenth Amendment because taken under a state's common law policy or because the particular private discrimination, enforced by the state, has its original impetus in a private agreement. This conclusion is fortified by the public policy against housing discrimination and in favor of free alienation of property. *Shelley v. Kraemer* (1948).

3. Significant Encouragement

When the challenged private actions are overtly or covertly encouraged by public officials or government measures, state action is present.

Examples: (1) Convictions against civil rights demonstrators participating in a "sit-in" protesting segregation in a privately-owned restaurant were reversed by the Court because the facts disclosed that the separation of the races which was being protested had been precipitated by the oral command of the police superintendent and the mayor. *Lombard v. Louisiana* (1963).

(2) A new provision of a state constitution was submitted to the electorate by referendum which was designed to prevent the enactment by the state of legislation designed to secure fair housing, *i.e.,* to prevent racial discrimination in the rental and sale of real estate. The Court held that the embodiment of a right of discrimination on racial grounds in the state's charter would encourage private racial discrimination to a degree which would offend the Fourteenth Amendment. *Reitman v. Mulkey* (1967).

4. Authorization and Approval

a.   *The fact that the government acquiesces in the wrongful acts of a private party does not make the government responsible for the conduct. Only if the government authorizes or compels the particular conduct being challenged, thus making itself responsible for the action, is there a sufficient nexus to satisfy the state action requirement.*

Examples: (1) The termination of a customer's electric service by a privately-owned utility company for non-payment, in the absence of notice, hearing and an opportunity to pay any amounts found due, is not attributable to the state. This is so even though the state public utilities commission approved a tariff which authorized termination of service in such circumstances. State action was still not present because the state public utility commission had not directly approved or authorized the termination provision. The fact that public utility regulation by the state is extremely comprehensive does not in itself establish state action. *Jackson v. Metropolitan Edison Co.* (1974).

(2) A warehouseman's enforcement of a lien by the sale of stored goods, as authorized by the state Commercial Code, did not constitute state action. Action by a private party, without any action by public officials, did not make the person a public actor. In the absence of "something more," there was no state action. *Flagg Brothers, Inc. v. Brooks* (1978).

(3) Dismissal of employees by a privately-owned school because of their speech activity does not constitute state action. Even though the school was heavily regulated,

there was no showing that the personnel decisions were "compelled or even influenced" by the state regulation. *Rendell–Baker v. Kohn* (1982).

(4) A private nursing home's decision to discharge or transfer a Medicaid patient is not state action sufficient to support a § 1983 claim. The fact that the state required the facility's staff to evaluate a patient's condition on a particular form, to make "all possible efforts" to place the patient in a facility providing the "appropriate level of care," and the fact that the state could impose penalties on nursing homes, was not deemed to be regulation that would "dictate the decision to discharge or transfer in a particular case." Here, the ultimate decision turned on medical judgments made by private parties according to professional standards not established by the state. *Blum v. Yaretsky* (1982).

b. *In order to find state authorization and approval of private conduct, two conditions must be satisfied. "First, the deprivation [of the right] must be caused by the exercise of some right or privilege created by the state or by a rule of conduct imposed by the state or by a person for whom the state is responsible. Second, the party charged with the deprivation must be a person who may fairly be said to be a state actor."*

Examples: (1) Invocation of state prejudgment attachment proceedings by a private party, whereby the county sheriff executes a writ of attachment issued by the clerk of the state court, constitutes state action. The constitutional challenge was to the state law creating the attachment proceeding thus satisfying the first test. The private party's joint participation with state officials in the seizure of the disputed property was sufficient to make the private party a "state action" under the second test. *Lugar v. Edmondson Oil Co., Inc.* (1982).

(2) The use of race-based peremptory challenges to potential jurors by private litigants in civil proceedings constitutes state action. *Lugar v. Edmondson*'s two-part test is satisfied. First, peremptory challenges are authorized by state law. Second, government officials engage in "overt, significant participation" in the system of peremptory

challenges and in civil litigation generally. It is the government that summons the jury and regulates the process. The judge participates in the *voir dire* and administers the use of peremptory challenges. When private parties are given power to select the members of a governmental body, "the private body will be bound by the constitutional mandate of race-neutrality." Finally, the government makes the injury move severe by permitting it to occur in the courthouse. *Edmonson v. Leesville Concrete Co.* (1991).

(3) A private insurer's decision to withhold, as authorized by state law, workmen's compensation payments for disputed medical treatment pending a "utilization review," to determine if the expenses are "reasonable and necessary," is not state action. Applying *Lugar*, the Court accepted that the private insurer acted with knowledge of and pursuant to the state statute. But the act of withholding payments was not "fairly attributable to the State." The fact that the State extensively regulated the insurers was not sufficient to establish state action. Rather, it was necessary to determine if a "closeness" between the State and the disputed private conduct exists. The mere fact that the State authorized suspension of payments during the review was not sufficient authorization or encouragement. "We have never held that the mere availability of a remedy for wrongful conduct, even when the private use of that remedy serves important public interests, so significantly encourages the private activity as to make the State responsible for it." Nor was the "public function" precedent applicable. The legal obligation to provide benefits was imposed on employers, not the State. Before the laws regulating workmens' compensation were enacted, the insurer was free to withhold payment of medical expenses without any State involvement. There was no "joint participation" since the private insurers were providing services that the State would not necessarily provide. *American Manufacturers Mutual Insurance Co. v. Sullivan* (1999).

F. Review Questions

1. **T or F**   The Thirteenth Amendment applies to private conduct.

2. **T or F**   Any government involvement with private discrimination will establish the requisite state action under the Fourteenth Amendment.

3. **T or F**   When a public official acts contrary to state law, this is not state action under the Fourteenth or Fifteenth Amendments.

4. **T or F**   If the government financially contributes a substantial portion of the funds of a private concern, the action of that concern constitutes state action.

5. **T or F**   If an activity is traditionally and exclusively a function of the sovereign, government will not be allowed to disclaim responsibility for it.

6. **T or F**   Neutral law enforcement which forces unwilling private parties to racially discriminate constitutes state action violative of the Equal Protection guarantee.

7. **T or F**   Even state authorization and approval of the challenged private action does not constitute state action if the government is not in a joint venture with the private actor.

8. Which of the following is the *least likely* basis for a funding of state action?

   a. State management of a facility.

   b. Joint action by public officials and private persons.

   c. Government regulation and licensing.

   d. Public encouragement of the challenged act.

   e. The existence of a symbiotic relationship between government and the private actor.

9. Which of the following is most likely to constitute state action?

   a. Warehouseman's enforcement of a lien by selling the stored goods, as authorized by the State Commercial Code.

   b. Termination of a customer's electric service by a privately-owned utility service subject to extensive state regulation.

   c. Dismissal of employees by a privately-owned school receiving 90% of its funds from the government.

d. Invocation of a state prejudgment attachment law by a private party, whereby the sheriff executes a writ of attachment issued by the clerk of the state court.

10. Western Broadcasting Company, which operates a radio station in Lincoln City, West Lincoln, had a policy of requiring political candidates to submit the script of their campaign messages prior to broadcast to the station news director in order to insure the material was in good taste. On several occasions, one of the candidates for mayor of Lincoln City, Joe Luzer, was ordered by the station news director, Carr E. Full, to excise from his campaign messages material the news director considered to be in bad taste. Station news director Full never found it necessary to review the scripts of Abel Goode, the winning candidate for mayor. Luzer has filed suit for damages in the federal district court on the grounds that the censorship of his campaign messages by the station violated his First Amendment rights. The defendant station has moved to dismiss. What is the principal constitutional law ground for the motion to dismiss? Explain.

XI

Congressional Legislation in Aid of Civil Rights and Liberties

■ *ANALYSIS*

A. In General: Federal Legislative Jurisdiction

1. Commerce Clause

As indicated in Ch. II of the Outline, Congress has plenary power to regulate interstate commerce even for social welfare purposes. It has used this constitutional power in the 1964 Civil Rights Act to provide remedies for private and state discrimination in places of public accommodation. *Heart of Atlanta Motel v. United States* (1964); *Katzenbach v. McClung* (1964).

2. Spending Power

As indicated in Ch. II of this Outline, Congress has power to condition federal grants in the exercise of its spending powers so long as the conditions are not so coercive as to constitute compulsion. Congress used this constitutional power in Title VI of the 1964 Civil Rights Act providing for the termination of federal funds to grantees who discriminate.

3. Federal Rights

Congress also has power to reach state or private action which interferes with the exercise of "federal rights" arising from the relationship of the citizen to the national government.

Examples: (1) In an action based on a federal civil rights statute brought by blacks for damages against white persons who mistook them for civil rights workers, stopped them on the highway and beat them, the Court found (1) that the statute could constitutionally be applied to protect the right of interstate movement; (2) that the right did not necessarily rest on the Fourteenth Amendment; and (3) that right was assertible against private as well as governmental interference. *Griffin v. Breckenridge* (1971).

(2) A provision of the 1970 federal Voting Rights Act eliminating the use of state residency requirements in presidential and vice-presidential elections is constitutional since the imposition of durational residency requirements unreasonably burdens the privilege of taking up residence in another state. The constitutional authorization for the legislation in this regard was based on the power of Congress to protect the privileges of federal citizenship without reference to § 5 of the Fourteenth Amendment despite the availability of that source of legislative power. *Oregon v. Mitchell* (1970).

4. Authority to Enforce Amendments

The Thirteenth, Fourteenth, Fifteenth, Nineteenth (women's rights to vote), Twenty-third (vote for the District of Columbia in presidential elections), Twenty-fourth (abolishes poll tax), and Twenty-sixth (18 year old vote) Amendments all have provisions giving Congress power to enforce the amendment by appropriate legislation.

B. Enforcing the Thirteenth Amendment

1. Private Action Covered

The guarantee of the Thirteenth Amendment, § 1, against the imposition of slavery or involuntary servitude, runs against private as well as governmental action.

2. Badges of Slavery

Section 2 of the Thirteenth Amendment gives Congress authority "to enforce this article by appropriate legislation." Congress has power under this provision to enact direct and primary legislation which is necessary and proper for abolishing all badges and incidents of slavery in the United States. As long as the legislation is a rational means of achieving that end, Congress has power to act under the Thirteenth Amendment, subject only to rights and liberties guaranteed by the Constitution.

Examples: (1) White sellers who refused to sell a home to blacks were sued pursuant to 42 U.S.C. § 1982 which provides: "All citizens of the United States shall have the same right, in every State and Territory, as is enjoyed by white citizens thereof to inherit, purchase, lease, sell, hold, and convey real and personal property." The Court held that § 1982 bars *all* racial discrimination, private as well as public, in the sale or rental of property, and that the statute thus construed is a valid exercise of the power of Congress to enforce the Thirteenth Amendment. Under the Thirteenth Amendment, Congress has the power to legislate against the badges and incidents of slavery such as those imposed by racial barriers to the acquisition of real and personal property. *Jones v. Alfred H. Mayer Co.* (1968).

(2) A federal statute interpreted to prohibit discrimination against blacks by private commercially operated nonsectarian schools constitutes a valid exercise of federal legislative power under § 2 of the Thirteenth Amendment. Such an interpretation does not offend freedom of association. Although parents have

a First Amendment right to send their children to schools teaching segregation, the First Amendment does not protect the practice of excluding racial minorities from such institutions. Parents still have a due process right to send their children to private schools. *Runyon v. McCrary* (1976).

C. Enforcing the Fourteenth Amendment

Section 5 of the Fourteenth Amendment provides that "Congress shall have power to enforce, by appropriate legislation, the provisions of this article." This provision gives Congress the power to enforce the privileges and immunities, due process and equal protection guarantees of the Fourteenth Amendment, § 1. As long as Congress could reasonably conclude that legislation is appropriate to securing the guarantees of the Fourteenth Amendment, the legislation is constitutional.

1. Scope of the Enforcement Power

a. Congress has broad power to enact legislation which is reasonably designed to secure Fourteenth Amendment rights. Congress in the exercise of this enforcement power may prohibit conduct which is not itself unconstitutional and even regulate conduct in areas previously reserved to the states.

b. But the power to enforce Fourteenth Amendment guarantees is a remedial or corrective power, not a power to define the substantive rights. "The design of the Amendment and the text of § 5 are inconsistent with the suggestion that Congress has the power to decree the substance of the Fourteenth Amendment's restrictions on the States." *City of Boerne v. Flores* (1997). Congress can neither increase nor dilute Fourteenth Amendment rights.

c. *In determining if enforcement legislation is designed to deter or remedy unconstitutional action, "there must be a congruence and proportionality between the injury to be prevented or remedied and the means adopted to that end. Lacking such a connection, legislation may become substantive in operation and effect."* City of Boerne v. Flores (1997).

Examples: (1) Section 4(e) of the federal Voting Rights Act of 1965 provides that no person who had successfully completed the sixth grade in school in Puerto Rico in which the language of instruction was other than English shall be denied the right to vote because of inability to read or write

English. The federal statute served to prohibit the enforcement of New York laws making literacy in English a condition to voting, even though the Court had previously held that literacy tests do not necessarily violate equal protection. The Court held that Congress could have reasonably concluded that elimination of literacy requirements was a means of eliminating discriminatory treatment by government in providing and administering public services.

The Court also held that Congress could reasonably conclude that barring the literacy tests was an appropriate means of eliminating discrimination in voting qualifications. There was a basis on which Congress could determine that requiring literacy in the circumstances was not an appropriate means of assuring intelligent voting. Justice Harlan, dissenting, argued that the Court was in fact defining the substantive scope of the Fourteenth Amendment right in violation of the separation of powers principle established in *Marbury v. Madison*. However, an alternative interpretation of the Court's opinion is that Congress was merely defining a remedy for unconstitutional voting discrimination by New York. *Katzenbach v. Morgan* (1966).

(2) The Religious Freedom Restoration Act (RFRA) was enacted by Congress in response to the Supreme Court's refusal to apply heightened scrutiny to incidental burdens imposed by generally applicable laws on the free exercise of religion. Congress prohibited " '[g]overnment' from 'substantially burden[ing]' a person's exercise of religion even if the burden results from a rule of general applicability unless the government can demonstrate the burden '(1) is in furtherance of a compelling governmental interest; and (2) is the least restrictive means of furthering that * * * interest'." Insofar as RFRA applies to action by states, Congress relied on its enforcement powers under the Fourteenth Amendment, § 5. RFRA was invoked in an effort to prevent a local zoning board from denying a building permit to a church.

But the Court held RFRA unconstitutional insofar as it applied to action by the states, declaring: "Although Congress certainly can enact legislation enforcing the constitutional right to the free exercise of religion * * * Congress does not enforce a constitutional right by changing what the right is." Even the dissenting justices did not reject the principle that Congress' enforcement power under the Fourteenth Amendment is remedial, not substantive. The Court did not reach the constitutionality of RFRA as it applies to federal action.

RFRA is not a proper enforcement measure under the Fourteenth Amendment, § 5 since it is out of proportion to any supposed remedial or preventive objective. It attempts a substantive change in constitutional rights. While preventive rules designed to deter unconstitutional state action can be appropriate remedial measures, RFRA goes too far since it is not limited to state laws likely to be held unconstitutional when challenged because of their treatment of religion. The broad coverage of RFRA ensures its intrusion on a host of official actions at every level of state and local government. There would be extensive litigation and many general regulatory laws would fail under the strict scrutiny review mandated by RFRA, including the least restrictive means requirement. "Remedial legislation under § 5 'should be adapted to the mischief and wrong which the [Fourteenth] [A]mendment was intended to provide against'."

In addition, separation of powers concerns indicated the unconstitutionality of RFRA as applied to the states. "[T]he Court retains the power, as they have since *Marbury v. Madison*, to determine if Congress has exceeded its authority under the Constitution * * * RFRA contradicts vital principles necessary to maintain separation of powers and the federal balance." *City of Boerne v. Flores* (1997).

But the Court did uphold a narrower federal law protecting religious exercise by institutionalized persons, absent a "compelling government interest" and use of "the least restrictive means." *Cutter v. Wilkinson* (2005) (See Ch. IX, B, 8, c, holding that the Act, on its face, does not violate the Establishment Clause).

2. Constitutional Limits on Enforcement Powers

a. Tenth Amendment

Congress cannot violate other provisions of the Constitution in the exercise of its Fourteenth Amendment, § 5, powers. But the fact that enforcement legislation intrudes into "legislative spheres of autonomy previously reserved to the States does not make the law violative of the Tenth Amendment. *Fitzpatrick v. Bitzer* (1976)." *City of Boerne v. Flores* (1997).

Example: The provision of the federal Voting Rights Act of 1970 lowering the voting age to 18 in state elections is invalid. Art. I, § 2, makes clear that the states are to determine the qualifications of their own voters for state officers. Congress has power, however, to set aside state voter qualifications when those qualifications reflect racial discrimination. In the latter circumstance, the explicit ban on racial discrimination reflected in the Civil War Amendments to the Constitution necessarily qualifies the division of powers between the state and national governments. *Oregon v. Mitchell* (1970).

b. Sovereign Immunity

1)   *Fitzpatrick v. Bitzer* held that Congress could authorize suits against state governments using its enforcement power under the Fourteenth Amendment, § 5. The Fourteenth Amendment embodies limitations on state authority. In enacting "appropriate legislation," Congress might provide for private suits against States or state officials that would otherwise be barred by the Eleventh Amendment. See Ch. I, C, 1, a, on the Eleventh Amendment.

2)   But under *City of Boerne*, the constitutionality of any such legislation depends on whether there is a "congruence and proportionality between the constitutional injury to be prevented or remedied and the means adopted to that end." In a number of recent cases, the Court has imposed stringent requirements in holding various congressional statutes authorizing suits against state governments (*i.e.,* abrogating state sovereign immunity) did not satisfy this standard and were unconstitutional.

Examples: (1) The Patent Remedy Act made States subject to suit in federal court for patent infringements. The legislative record failed to provide evidence of any pattern of patent infringements by states that would violate due process. Therefore the abrogation of state sovereign immunity was not proportionate or congruent with any constitutional violation to be remedied. *Florida Prepaid Postsecondary Education Expense Board v. College Savings Bank* (1999).

(2) The federal Trademark Remedy Clarification Act abrogated state immunity from suit in federal court for false and deceptive advertizing in violation of the Trademark Act. But the Court held that the right to be free of false advertising about your product and to be secure in your business interests are not "property" rights protected by the Due Process Clause. Hence, suits could not be justified under the enforcement clause of the Fourteenth Amendment. *College Savings Bank v. Florida Prepaid Postseconday Expense Education Board* (1999).

(3) The Age Discrimination in Employment Act makes it unlawful for employers, including States, to engage in various forms of age discrimination. Although ADEA has a clear statement abrogating State immunity, the abrogation exceeded Congress' authority under the Fourteenth Amendment, § 5. Precedent established that age discrimination is subject only to rationality review under the Equal Protection Clause. States may engage in age discrimination where it is rational without violating equal protection. But the ADEA makes the State liable for all age discrimination thereby prohibiting substantially more state employment decisions than would likely be held unconstitutional. The ADEA legislative record reveals no pattern of age discrimination by States that is unconstitutional. The ADEA remedy therefore is out of proportion to any constitutional violation to be remedied or prevented. *Kimel v. Florida Board of Regents* (2000).

(4) Title I of the Americans with Disabilities Act prohibits, employers, including States, from discrimi-

nating against qualified individuals because of their disabilities in various employment contexts and authorizes suits. The Court held 5–4 that Title I of the ADA exceeds Congress' power under the Fourteenth Amendment, § 5. In enacting the ADA, Congress had extensively documented that states as employers often engage in disability discrimination. But, as in *Kimel*, state discrimination against the disabled is unconstitutional only if it is irrational. And the Court concluded, after closely examining the legislative record, that Congress had not identified "a pattern of irrational state discrimination in employment against the disabled." Further, the ADA's requirement of reasonable accommodation of disabilities involved significant costs which was not a congruent and proportional response to any state action that was unconstitutional. *Board of Trustees of the University of Alabama v. Garrett* (2001).

3) But the Court has upheld federal legislation abrogating state sovereign immunity based on Congress' power under the Fourteenth Amendment, § 5, in situations where the state would be subject to more demanding standards of judicial review than rationality.

> *Examples:* (1) State employees may recover money damages based on a state's failure to comply with the Family and Medical Leave Act. The Act allows eligible employees, both men and women, to take up to twelve weeks of unpaid leave for certain reasons, including care of the employee's spouse. Congress was within its § 5 authority to abrogate state immunity under the Act as a means of remedying and deterring gender-based discrimination, even though it includes in the proscription conduct which is facially constitutional. Intentional gender-based discrimination is subject to heightened review under equal protection and it is therefore easier for Congress to show a pattern of state constitutional violations. Congress had significant evidence of extensive state gender-based discrimination in leave benefits. The Act was congruent and propor-

tional to the prevention of gender discrimination because it was targeted at "the formerly state-sanctioned stereotype that only women are responsible for family caregiving, thereby reducing employers' incentives to engage in discrimination by basing hiring and promotion decisions on stereotypes." Also, Congress had previously attempted unsuccessfully to alleviate this type of discrimination through another statute (Title VII) and the present Act was a narrower intrusion on state sovereignty than previous laws held unconstitutional by the Court. *Nevada Dep't of Human Res. v. Hibbs* (2003).

(2) Title II of the Americans with Disabilities Act, which prohibits discrimination against individuals with disabilities in public services, programs, or activities, is a constitutional exercise of Congress § 5 enforcement power "as it applies to the class of cases implicating the accessibility of judicial services." Two paraplegic individuals brought suit against the state claiming they were denied access to courthouses in violation of the Act. Congress had made findings after compiling an extensive record of disability discrimination in judicial services that had not been remedied by other means. Unlike statutes invalidated in *Garrett* and *Kimel* that were designed to enforce rights subject only to rationality review, the discrimination in access to state courthouse and court proceedings involves rights under the Due Process Clause, First Amendment, and Sixth Amendment that are subject to heightened scrutiny. The Act is appropriate prophylactic legislation as applied: "Title II's requirement of program accessibility is congruent and proportional to its object of enforcing the right of access to the courts." *Tennessee v. Lane* (2004).

(3) But the Court held 5–4 that the self-care provision of the 1993 Family and Medical Leave Act (FMLA), requiring employers to grant unpaid leave for self-care for a serious medical condition, is not a valid exercise of Congress' power under section 5 to abrogate state

sovereign immunity from lawsuits. In a plurality opinion, Justice Kennedy reasoned that, unlike *Hibbs*, Congress had not provided evidence of a pattern of sex-based discrimination and a remedy narrowly-drawn to address or prevent such violation. The record did not establish that states maintained discriminatory policies, or administered neutral policies in a discriminatory way or used sex-based stereotypes in administering self-care provisions. Finally, even if the self-care provision does address neutral leave policies having a disparate *impact* on women, the remedy would not be congruent and proportional to any *constitutional* violation. Justice Ginsburg, writing for the dissent, stressed the overriding purpose of the FMLA was to make it feasible for women to work while sustaining family life. This required leave policies that would not encourage employers to prefer men over women. The self-care provision, she argued, was seen by Congress as an integral part of that objective. *Coleman v. Court of Appeals of Maryland* (2012).

4) Further, the Court has reaffirmed that, while there is disagreement as to the scope of Congress "prophylactic" powers, it is accepted that *Congress has power under § 5 to create a private cause of action for "actual" violations by the State of the Fourteenth Amendment, including the power to abrogate state sovereign immunity.*

Example: Tony Goodman, a paraplegic inmate at a Georgia state prison, alleged that he was confined for 23–24 hours per day in a 12–by–3 foot cell in which he could not turn his wheelchair around, that he was denied use of toilet and shower facilities because of inaccessibility and a lack of assistance, forcing him to sit in his own bodily waste, and that he was denied access to medical treatment and prison programs because of his disability. Goodman sued state defendants under Title II of the ADA (Americans with Disabilities Act), seeking injunctive relief and money damages.

The Supreme Court held that Goodman's allegation of the denial of the benefits of the prison's services, programs and activities could be conduct that "independently violated" the provisions of the Due Process Clause which incorporate the Eighth Amendment's guarantee against cruel and unusual punishment. Because of a lack of clarity in Goodman's complaint, the case was remanded "to determine in the first instance, on a claim-by-claim basis, (1) which aspects of the State's alleged conduct violated Title II; (2) to what extent such conduct also violated the Fourteenth Amendment; and (3) insofar as such misconduct violated Title II but did not violate the Fourteenth Amendment, whether Congress's purported abrogation of sovereign immunity as to that class of conduct is nevertheless valid." *United States v. Georgia* (2006).

5) On the basis of the above cases, in determining if Congress has constitutionally abrogated state sovereign immunity, consider the following three questions: (1) Does the plaintiff complain of an actual independent violation by the State of a Fourteenth Amendment right for which Congress had created a private cause of action against the State? (2) Does the plaintiff, in a private suit against the state based on congressional statute authorizing the action, allege that there is a "congruence and proportionality between the constitutional injury to be prevented or remedied and the means adopted to that end"? (3) Does the plaintiff allege a kind of discrimination which would involve a more demanding standard of review than rationality, or a fundamental right, for which Congress has provided a private cause of action?

3. Private Action

Since the Fourteenth Amendment, § 1 requires state action when judicially enforced, it is questionable whether Congress, using its Fourteenth Amendment, § 5 powers could legislate against private action.

a. Historic Barrier

In the *Civil Rights Cases* (1883), the Court held that Congress had power only to provide remedies for state action violating the Fourteenth Amendment, § 1. Section 5 did not give Congress power to enact the equivalent of a municipal code for private rights.

b. Basis for Expansion

However, six justices in concurring opinions in *United States v. Guest* (1966), would have held that where the right secured by the Fourteenth

Amendment runs against private interference (in that case, the right to use state-owned facilities free from racial discrimination), Congress may use its § 5 powers to legislate against such interference, governmental or private. It could be argued that such legislation against private conduct could be an appropriate means of preventing or deterring unconstitutional state action.

c.   The Expansionist Approach Rejected

But in *United States v. Morrison* (2000) (See Ch. II, B, 5), the Court reaffirmed the historic limitation in the *Civil Rights Cases* on Congress' enforcement powers, *limiting it to remedying or preventing unconstitutional governmental action, not private conduct*. The "naked dicta" of *Guest* did not cast doubt on the "enduring vitality" of the *Civil Rights Cases* limiting the corrective power in § 5 to its object—"to counteract and redress the operation of such prohibited state laws or proceedings of [s]tate officers."

Example: Congress did not have constitutional authority to enact the Violence Against Women Act under the Fourteenth Amendment, § 5. In enacting the VAW Act, Congress found pervasive bias in various state justice systems against victims of gender-motivated violence. Petitioners argued that this bias denied such victims equal protection and that Congress acted appropriately in enacting a private civil remedy against the perpetrators of such violence. But the Fourteenth Amendment prohibits only state action, not private conduct, however discriminatory or wrongful. Petitioners alternatively argued that there has been gender-based disparate treatment by state authorities. But the Act is not aimed at proscribing discrimination by officials which the Fourteenth Amendment might not itself proscribe. It is not directed at any state or state actor but at individuals who commit criminal acts. No consequence is visited on any state official by the Act. The VAW Act a provides nationwide remedy but there is pervasive bias in only some states. It did not have the requisite congruence and proportionality required by *City of Boerne v. Flores. United States v. Morrison* (2000).

d.   But Congress can legislate against private action using its commerce and spending powers and its enforcement powers under the Thirteenth Amendment, § 2.

D. Enforcing the Fifteenth Amendment

1. Constitutional Text

The Fifteenth Amendment, § 1 provides that "the right of citizens of the United States to vote shall not be denied or abridged by the United States or by any State on account of race, color, or previous condition of servitude."

2. Enforcement Clause

a. *Section 2 of the Fifteenth Amendment gives Congress the power to enforce this article by appropriate legislation. Any legislation which Congress could rationally conclude is appropriate to effectuate the constitutional prohibition against racial discrimination in voting is a constitutional exercise of Congress' power under the Fifteenth Amendment, § 2.*

b. The Court's holding in City of *Boerne v. Flores* (1997) that Congress' enforcement power under the Fourteenth Amendment, § 5, does not include power to define the substantive right almost certainly applies to Congress' power under the Fifteenth Amendment, § 2. Also recall the Court's statement in *City of Boerne*: "Legislation which deters or remedies constitutional violations can fall within the sweep of Congress' enforcement power even if in the process it prohibits conduct which is not itself unconstitutional and intrudes into 'legislative spheres of autonomy previously reserved to the States.' *Fitzpatrick v. Bitzer*."

Examples: (1) The federal Voting Rights Act of 1965 prohibiting voter registration requirements denying the right to vote on the basis of race was upheld. Congress had legislative jurisdiction to enact the statute under § 2 of the Fifteenth Amendment. As against the reserved powers of the states, Congress may use any rational means to effectuate the constitutional prohibition of racial discrimination in voting. The Court declared that the powers of Congress, under § 2 of the Fifteenth Amendment, is complete in itself, may be exercised to its utmost extent, and acknowledges no limitations, other than are prescribed in the Constitution. *South Carolina v. Katzenbach* (1966).

(2) The provisions of the federal Voters Right Act prohibiting literacy tests were upheld as a proper exercise of congressional legislative jurisdiction under § 2 of the Fifteenth Amendment in view of the long history of discrim-

inatory use of literacy tests to disenfranchise voters on account of their race. *Oregon v. Mitchell* (1970).

(3) Even if only purposeful racial discrimination in voting violates the Fifteenth Amendment, Congress under § 2 of that Amendment may outlaw voting practices that are discriminatory in effect. While such practices do not themselves violate § 1 of the Amendment, prohibitions against practices having a discriminatory racial effect on voting are "appropriate" and "reasonable" means of enforcing the voting guarantees of the Fifteenth Amendment. The extension of the Voting Rights Act of 1965 for an additional seven years was held to be a reasonable means of promoting the purposes of the Fifteenth Amendment. *City of Rome v. United States* (1980).

(4) A multimember electoral scheme which resulted in black voters having less opportunity to elect representatives of their choice was challenged as violative of Sec. 2 of the Voting Rights Act. In 1982, Congress had amended Sec. 2 to provide that the Act is violated if the "totality of the circumstances" established that a voting standard or practice "results in a denial or abridgement of the right" to vote on a racial basis. According to the Court, the Amendment was to make clear that "a violation could be proven by showing discriminatory effect alone and to establish as the relevant legal standard the results test * * *." A district court finding that Sec. 2, as interpreted, was violated was not clearly erroneous. *City of Rome* had established that Congress has power to legislate against discriminatory effects under the Fifteenth Amendment, even if Sec. 1 of the Fifteenth Amendment requires a showing of racially discriminatory purpose. *Thornburg v. Gingles* (1986).

(5) The Court has suggested that Sec. 5 of the Voting Rights Act of 1965 may no longer be a constitutional remedy. Sec. 5 prevents all changes in election procedures by covered jurisdictions having a history of racial discrimination in voting until they are submitted to, and approved by a D.C. federal district court or the Attorney General. The Court avoided the constitutional question by interpreting

the Act to allow the complaining jurisdiction to avoid coverage. Chief Justice Roberts, writing for the Court, noted the "substantial federalism costs" of Sec. 5 and said that the Act's current burdens "must be justified by current needs." The past successes achieved using Sec. 5 do not justify its present use. But "[t]he Fifteenth Amendment empowers 'Congress', not the Court, to determine in the first instance what legislation is needed to enforce it." *Northwest Austin Municipal Utility District Number One v. Holder* (2009).

E. Review Questions

1. **T or F**   Congress can legislate against private action under its commerce and spending powers.

2. **T or F**   Congress can legislate against private action imposing "badges of slavery."

3. **T or F**   Congress can provide remedies to enforce the guarantees of the Fourteenth and Fifteenth Amendments as long as the laws are reasonable.

4. **T or F**   In the exercise of its plenary enforcement powers under the Fourteenth and Fifteenth Amendments, Congress can increase or diminish the rights as defined by the courts.

5. **T or F**   In order to be an appropriate preventive or remedial measure under the Fourteenth Amendment, § 5, the means adopted must be proportional to the injury Congress seeks to prevent or remedy.

6. **T or F**   It is established that Congress cannot use its enforcement powers under the Fourteenth and Fifteenth Amendments against private action.

7. **T or F**   In enforcing the Fifteenth Amendment, Congress can legislate against state action that has the *effect* of racially discriminating in the exercise of the franchise.

8. **T or F**   Congress can abrogate State sovereign immunity under the Fourteenth Amendment, § 5, if such legislation rationally furthers the guarantees of the Fourteenth Amendment, § 1.

9. Which of the following congressional enactments is the *least likely* to be upheld pursuant to Congress' enforcement powers under the Thirteenth, Fourteenth, and Fifteenth Amendments?

   a. A law prohibiting the use of literacy tests.

   b. A law lowering the voting age to age 18 in federal elections.

   c. A law prohibiting gender discrimination in private schools.

   d. A law prohibiting private racial discrimination in the sale or rental of housing.

10. A federal statute, 42 U.S.C. § 1981, has been read to prohibit private schools from excluding qualified children solely because they are black. A private commercially operated non-sectarian school contends that this statute so interpreted constitutes an invalid exercise of federal legislative power under Section 2 of the Thirteenth Amendment. Does it?

APPENDIX A

Answers to Review Questions

PART ONE: THE ALLOCATION OF GOVERNMENTAL POWER: NATIONAL AND STATE

Chapter I: Judicial Review

1. *False.* Although it is possible to argue on the basis of the grant of judicial power in Art. III and constitutional supremacy in Art. VI that there is a textual basis for judicial review, most authorities agree that Justice Marshall in *Marbury v. Madison* (1803) created the doctrine. It is, at best, an implied power.

2. *False.* The doctrine of judicial review applies to the actions of all government officials, state or federal, as was held by the Supreme Court in *Cooper v. Aaron* (1958) and *United States v. Nixon* (1974).

3. *True.* Art. VI of the Constitution has been read to give state courts concurrent jurisdiction in federal constitutional matters.

4. *False*. The Supreme Court of the United States has constitutional power to review cases coming from the state as well as the federal courts because Art.

III makes the touchstone for review the case and not the tribunal. This helps to further the policy of assuring uniformity of constitutional interpretation.

5. *False.* The policy of judicial self-restraint counsels that the courts not anticipate constitutional questions. Instead, the courts should decide the constitutional question only when there is no alternative basis for deciding the case.

6. *True.* While it might be held today that separation of powers principles would be violated by such a massive assault on the federal courts, a critical reading of Art. III which refers to lower federal courts which Congress "may create," supports this conclusion.

7. *True.* While the Eleventh Amendment bans suits against a sovereign state in federal courts (absent the state's consent), *Ex parte Young* (1908) has created an enduring exception permitting suit for injunctive relief against a state official who acts unconstitutionally.

8. *False.* The Supreme Court in *Seminole Tribe of Florida v. Florida* (1996) overruled an earlier plurality decision and held that the Eleventh Amendment prevents congressional authorization of suits against unconsenting states, even when the Constitution vests plenary regulatory power over a particular area in Congress. Congress can authorize suits against the states using its remedial powers under the Fourteenth Amendment, § 5.

9. *True.* The Art. III requirement of "case and controversy" requires that a litigant demonstrate a factual injury caused by the government action being challenged. The injury must be "fairly traceable" to the action and must be "redressable" if the court grants the requested relief.

10. *False.* At least in the absence of congressional legislation authorizing suit, a citizen lacks Art. III standing.

11. *False.* The *jus tertii*-third-party standing rule is not a requirement of Art. III. It proceeds from the belief that the best plaintiff is the one most directly involved in the controversy. But the facts of the particular case may move a federal court to decide that the interests favoring decision on the merits outweigh the reasons underlying the rule.

12. *False.* Congress can, by statute, create legal interests which are sufficient to satisfy Art. III "even where the plaintiff would have suffered no judicially cognizable injury in the absence of statute." *Warth v. Seldin* (1975). However,

the Art. III minimum requirements of an injury in fact, which is fairly traceable to the government action being challenged and which is redressable by the sought-after remedy, must be satisfied. Congress can remove prudential obstacles to standing.

13. *False.* It is true that generally a case is moot when factual circumstances change so that a judicial decision could not remedy any existing injury. However, a claim is not moot if there has been a voluntary cessation of the illegal conduct, if the government's action has important collateral consequences or if the claim is one "capable of repetition, yet evading review." Pregnancy is "capable of repetition" and will generally end prior to appeal. *Roe v. Wade* (1973).

14. *True.* Under *Younger v. Harris* (1971), a federal court should exercise its discretion and abstain, absent a showing of bad faith harassment, when a state criminal prosecution is pending. If no good faith prosecution is pending, a federal court may issue injunctive and declaratory relief against a vague and overbroad intrusion on First Amendment rights.

15. *True.* The courts decide many cases involving political matters, *e.g., United States v. Nixon* (1974). The political question doctrine is based on separation of powers concerns or the constitutional commitment of the issue to another branch of government which indicate that the case is not appropriate for judicial resolution.

16. *False.* In *Nixon v. United States* (1993), the Court held only that Judge Nixon's challenge to Senate rules, providing for a Senate committee to hear and report on the evidence, involved a non-justiciable political question. The Court reasoned that Art. I, § 3, cl. 6, provides that the "sole" power to try impeachments is vested in the Senate. However, if an "identifiable textual limitation" is violated by Congress, the matter could be justiciable. In *Nixon*, the Court held that the word "try" was not such a constitutional limit but the Court did not necessarily hold that impeachment challenges always involve a political question.

17. **c.** Art. III federal courts cannot give advisory opinions because of the Art. III requirement of a case and controversy. All of the other limitations on judicial review indicated are prudential rules born of judicial self-restraint, *e.g.,* avoidance of judicial review until necessary, the desire to secure the best plaintiff.

18. **b.** While state officials can be sued for injunctive relief when they act illegally (hence, c is a wrong answer), suit is barred if the award would be a

retroactive charge on the state treasury. A is wrong since a state may waive its sovereign immunity. D is wrong since ancillary monetary relief, such as attorney's fees, is permitted in spite of the Eleventh Amendment. Similarly, e is wrong since prospective relief, such as a desegregation order involving busing (which involves added costs), has been approved by the Court.

19. **b.** A builder seeking to build housing in the area who is prevented from doing so by the zoning ordinance has injury in fact caused by the challenged enactment. A is wrong since any injury suffered by Metro taxpayers would be speculative and the causation would be questionable. C is not the best answer since simply being a member of a racial minority has not been held sufficient to establish standing—the black plaintiff would have to prove he or she was prevented from living in Suburbia because of the ordinance. D is not the best answer. While an association may have standing to represent its members, it must demonstrate that the members have Art. III standing. There are no facts indicated that establish this prerequisite.

20. **d.** (D) is correct because a State has standing to assert its own rights and protect its own territorial interests when Congress has authorized a procedural right to enforce the Clean Air Act. The state has suffered a personal injury due to the rise in sea levels that was damaging its territory. *Massachusetts v. EPA* (2007). (A) is incorrect because citizens cannot use lawsuits as a means of airing general grievances to ensure that the law is followed. *Lance v. Coffman* (2007). (B) is incorrect because, even though Congress has authorized a procedural right to comment on US Forest Service procedures, that commenting process must be necessary to protect a personal interest of the plaintiff in order for that plaintiff to have standing. Since members of the environmental group did not have plans to study or visit other forests where the US Forest Service has similar projects, there is no imminent injury. *Summers v. Earth Island Institute* (2009). (C) is incorrect because, like federal taxpayers, state taxpayers do not have a significant stake in state funds because the injury felt by each taxpayer is so small. *DaimlerChrysler v. Cuno* (2006).

21. **e. None of the above.** This is a state tax break, therefore a group of federal taxpayers would not be injured because the funds affected are state funds, not federal funds. State taxpayers also would not have standing because the harm suffered by any individual state taxpayer due to a loss in state funds is not direct enough to satisfy the Art. III requirements. Municipal taxpayers also do no have standing because, while they could challenge a decision of the municipal government to grant tax breaks, in this case they are still

challenging a state decision and there was no guarantee that repealing the tax break would have any effect on that particular municipality. *DaimlerChrysler v. Cuno* (2006).

22. The awarded back pay does not offend the Eleventh Amendment. In *Edelman v. Jordan* (1974), the Supreme Court held that even in a suit directed against a public official, if relief involves a charge on the general revenue of the state, cannot be distinguished from an award of damages against the state. Therefore, the Eleventh Amendment would bar such an award. However, the award in this case is different. In this case, unlike *Edelman*, Congress has specifically provided for suits against the state pursuant to the authority it possesses under § 5 of the Fourteenth Amendment. The Eleventh Amendment bar to a back pay award against the state without its consent is limited by the Fourteenth Amendment duty imposed on states and the accompanying power of Congress to provide remedies for violation of the state's duties pursuant to § 5. In short, the threshold fact of congressional authorization distinguishes this case from *Edelman*. Or, to put it another way, the Eleventh Amendment is *pro tanto* qualified by § 5 of the Fourteenth Amendment in these circumstances. *Fitzpatrick v. Bitzer* (1976).

23. Since Doctor Kildare would benefit financially from the grant of the injunction against the Sterilization Law, he has standing under Art. III to challenge its constitutionality. He alleges financial injury resulting from the operation of the Purity law that would be abated by the grant of the injunction. This satisfies the standing requirement derived from the Art. III case and controversy mandate. While the Third Party Standing Doctrine would normally prevent a doctor from raising the rights of a person not before the court, this is a rule of judicial self-restraint. In the present case, the doctor can claim the rights of his female patients given the closeness of the doctor-patient relationship, the difficulty of the woman's raising her own privacy claims and the intimate involvement of the doctor in the woman's sterilization decision. See *Singleton v. Wulff* (1976).

Chapter II: National Legislative Powers

1. *False.* This is a government of enumerated powers. Congress has no inherent domestic legislative powers. There must be a constitutional grant of power, express or implied, in order for Congress to legislate.

2. *True.* While Justice Marshall in *McCulloch* indicated that a granted power cannot be used as a pretext for legislating in regard to matters outside congressional power, this pretext principle has not endured. The courts will

not probe the motive or purpose behind otherwise valid exercises of congressional powers. Congress, therefore, can achieve social welfare objectives by using broad powers, such as the commerce power.

3. *True.* Congress can regulate local activity if it can rationally conclude that such activity has a substantial adverse effect on interstate commerce. Since federal law overrides contrary state law under the Art. VI Supremacy Clause, the displacement of state police powers does not make the federal law unconstitutional. Insofar as federal regulation of *private* activity is concerned, the Tenth Amendment is a truism. *United States v. Darby* (1941). But the fact that the federal law regulates activity historically subject to state sovereignty may bear on the reasonableness of the federal law. *Lopez v. United States* (1995); *United States v. Morrison* (2000).

4. *False.* Under the Affectation Doctrine, Congress can regulate local activities if it has a rational basis for concluding that the activity substantially affects interstate commerce. In *United States v. Lopez* (1995), the Court invalidated a federal law making it an offense for individuals to posses firearms in a school zone. The Act had no jurisdictional nexus, there was no congressional fact finding, the activity regulated was not commercial, and it involved matters historically subject to state sovereignty. Also, in *National Federation of Independent Business v. Sebelius* (2012), five justices concluded that Congress' power under the Commerce Clause was insufficient to justify a mandate in the Affordable Care Act of 2010 requiring individuals to purchase health insurance or pay a penalty. Although, individuals not possessing health insurance can have substantial financial effects on the interstate healthcare industry, the regulation would require individuals not engaged in an activity to engage in commercial activity, i.e., buying health insurance. This exceeds Congress' Commerce Clause power.

5. *True.* While the taxing power is a fiscal power rather than a regulatory power, the courts today do not probe the congressional motive or purpose. If the law is facially a revenue-producing tax measure, it will not be held to be invalid under the penalty doctrine.

6. *False.* Congress has power to tax and to spend for the general welfare. But these are fiscal, not regulatory, powers.

7. *True.* Congress may define the conditions under which federal monies are spent. While states may thereby be induced to submit to federal regulation in order to obtain needed funds, they remain free to refuse the monies and the accompanying conditions. In modern times, the Tenth Amendment has not

proven an impediment to such indirect federal regulation. As *National Federation of Independent Business v. Sebelius* (2012) held, the conditions placed upon the States cannot be so coercive as to make it fiscally impossible for the states to refuse the monies with the conditions.

8. *False.* While this statement might have had some validity under *National League of Cities*, it is clearly false under *Garcia*. The *Garcia* Court rejected judicial efforts to identify provinces of state autonomy. It is the national political process, with exceptions, that protects federalism. The judicial role generally is limited to assuring that this political process is working.

9. *True.* In *McCulloch v. Maryland*, the Necessary and Proper Clause was broadly interpreted to cover all reasonable means for achieving the delegated powers. Under Art. VI Supremacy Clause doctrine, Congress can preempt state law.

10. *False.* Congress can preempt state legislation and can offer states the alternative of legislating consistent with federal standards or face federal preemption. However, in *New York v. United States* (1992), the Court indicated that Congress cannot, consistent with state sovereignty, directly order a state to legislate. When Congress compels state regulation rather than simply encouraging it, Congress undermines political accountability.

11. *False.* "Since Congress cannot force states to regulate, 'State officials cannot consent to the enlargement of powers of Congress beyond those enumerated in the Constitution.' " *New York v. United States* (1992). The constitutional authority of Congress cannot be expanded by the consent of a governmental institution—whether the States or the Executive—whose power is narrowed.

12. *False.* The federal government cannot compel State officials to administer a federal regulatory program. *Printz v. United States* (1997). Balancing is inappropriate when a law compromises the structural framework of dual sovereignty. Such a federal law offends the principle of separate state sovereignty, "and no comparative assessment of the various interests can overcome that fundamental defect."

13. **c.** Congress can tax and spend money derived therefrom for the general welfare. Congress can impose taxes even if the law has an incidental regulatory effect. The courts will not probe Congress' purpose. Further, A is wrong since a law will not be invalidated as a penalty if it is facially revenue-producing. B is wrong since Congress can only spend, not regulate, for the general welfare. D is wrong since Congress can impose reasonable conditions as a prerequisite to receiving federal monies. The state is free to reject the grant.

14. No, the town does not have a constitutional defense. The *Garcia* case establishes that the judiciary cannot interpose itself between what would otherwise be the appropriate exercise of federal legislation, such as the FLSA, validly authorized by the federal Commerce Clause and the states. The Tenth Amendment and state sovereignty are generally not limitations on federal commerce power jurisdiction. There is an exception for federal regulation which is applicable only to states and which compels states to regulate (*New York v. United States* (1992)) but it is unlikely that the courts would find that these facts fall within this exception. The Tenth Amendment today serves only as a minimal limitation on the congressional commerce power to assure that the political processes are working. Even if the Supreme Court were inclined to resurrect some portion of *National League of Cities*, it is questionable that the provision of lifeguard service at municipal beaches would be considered such an essential element of state or local sovereignty as to override the fact that the federal interests served by that legislation have been considered appropriated for Commerce Clause regulation.

Chapter III: State Power in American Federalism

1. *True.* In *U.S. Term Limits, Inc. v. Thornton* (1995), the Court held unconstitutional a State law setting term limits for members of Congress. Even if the Constitution did not divest the states of such power (which it did), the Tenth Amendment did not reserve such a power to states since it was not within the "original powers" of the states. Electing representatives to the national legislature was a new right established by the Constitution itself. It created a direct link between the national government and the people of the United States.

2. *False.* The commerce power is, at least partially, a shared power. While Congress has plenary power over interstate commerce, this is not necessarily inconsistent with state regulation of the same subject.

3. *False.* The Dormant Commerce Clause, as interpreted by the courts, has "negative implications" which limit the states' ability to regulate when interstate commerce is burdened.

4. *False.* The central purpose of the Commerce Clause, *i.e.*, to assure a national Common Market, is violated by protectionist laws. Such barriers are "virtually per se" impermissible.

5. *True.* State laws which discriminate in the means used or in their impact are, at least in theory, capable of justification. The state must show a legitimate

local purpose which could not be adequately served by nondiscriminatory alternatives.

6. *False.* If a law imposes a heavier burden on out-of-state interests than on in-state interests, it is discriminatory even if local citizens are also burdened. *West Lynn Creamery v. Healy* (1994). The fact that a local law which discriminates against out-of-state commerce also burdens other political subdivisions of a state will not negate the discrimination. *Fort Gratiot Sanitary Landfill, Inc. v. Michigan Department of Natural Resources* (1992). It will still be subject to stricter scrutiny under the Dormant Commerce Clause.

7. *False.* A subsidy program funded from general revenues may be constitutional. However, funding the subsidy through a tax applicable to goods produced outside the state, even though facially nondiscriminatory, has a discriminatory effect violative of the Dormant Commerce Clause. The subsidy offsets the burden imposed by the tax. The program operates to protect local farmers against competition from out-of-state goods. *West Lynn Creamery v. Healy* (1994).

8. *False.* Even if the state law is nondiscriminatory, it will be held unconstitutional if it imposes an undue burden on interstate commerce. Determination of whether a burden is excessive is determined by ad hoc balancing. There is some sentiment on the Court for limiting the Dormant Commerce Clause to discriminatory state laws. The Court, however, has not thus far abandoned undue burdens analysis involving a balancing of the national and state interests.

9. *False.* A state may be able to prefer an in-state entity, so long as that entity is publicly operated, serving a traditional public function, if it continues to treat all private entities (both in state and out of state) the same. This is true even where the State is acting as a regulator, rather than as a market participant. However, State preference for any private in-state entity would constitute discrimination against interstate commerce in violation of the Dormant Commerce Clause. *United Haulers Association v. Oneida–Herkimer Solid Waste Management Authority (2007).*

10. *True.* Given the historic local control of highway management, state highway laws enjoy a heavier presumption of validity. But states cannot excessively burden interstate commerce even when regulating highways.

11. *True.* When a state is not regulating commerce, but instead is participating in the marketplace, the negative implications of the Dormant Commerce Clause will not prohibit a state from favoring its own citizens.

12. *True.* While Art. IV, § 2, prohibits unreasonable discrimination against out-of-state citizens, the Court has held that the Clause is implicated only if fundamental interests, which bear on the vitality of the Nation as an entity, are burdened.

13. *True.* When the state runs a business in the marketplace, it acts as a market participant, not as a regulator. In such a capacity, it is not subject to the Dormant Commerce Clause.

14. *False.* Interstate commerce can be made to pay its way but the burden imposed by the taxing state must reasonably reflect the benefits the taxpayer receives in doing business in the state.

15. *False.* It is the economic incidence of the tax, not its name, that determines its validity. The modern test requires that: (1) the activity taxed must be sufficiently connected to the taxing state; (2) the tax must be fairly related to the benefits provided the taxpayer; (3) the tax must not discriminate against interstate commerce; (4) the tax must be fairly apportioned in light of the local contacts and the benefits received by the taxpayer.

16. **d.** The Court in *Commonwealth Edison v. Montana* (1981) upheld the state tax under the *Complete Auto Transit* test which is indicated in answer d. State taxes regularly burden out-of-state consumers (answer a) and out-of-state businesses (answer c) but are nevertheless upheld. Answer b is wrong since the tax applies regardless of the destination of the coal.

17. *False.* State legislation is preempted only if it conflicts with federal law, Congress has expressly precluded state regulation on the area, or an analysis of the congressional action indicates an intent to occupy exclusively the field.

18. *False.* Congress has plenary regulatory power over interstate commerce and may legitimate state laws which would otherwise violate the Dormant Commerce Clause. But Congress must manifest an "unambiguous intent" before a statute will be read to permit state discrimination against interstate commerce.

19. **e.** When the courts determine if federal law is intended to preempt state law, the courts will consider each of the factors as well as legislative history and

the historic federal and state roles in regulating the subject. Preemption turns on the particular facts of each case.

20. The law is constitutional. It creates no barriers whatsoever against interstate independent dealers. It does not prevent the flow of interstate goods, nor does it place added costs upon them. Furthermore, the statute does not distinguish between in-state and out-of-state companies in the retail market. While some out-of-state integrated petroleum companies will not enjoy the same privileged status in the West Lincoln market that they have in the past, the statute does not give a competitive advantage to in-state independent dealers against out-of-state dealers. The presence of discriminatory impact here—the fact that the burden of a state regulation falls on interstate companies—does not by itself establish a claim of discrimination against interstate commerce. The negative implications which flow from the Commerce Clause are not offended by this kind of state regulation. *Exxon Corp. v. Governor of Maryland* (1978).

Chapter IV: The Executive Power

1. *False.* At least in the absence of an extreme emergency, the President has no inherent domestic law-making power. However, his power to see that the laws are faithfully executed does appear to create some power to act subject to congressional authority.

2. *False.* When Congress performs legislative acts, it must act pursuant to Art. I, §§ 1 and 7, requiring Bicameralism and Presentment. The legislative power must be exercised "in accord with a single, finely wrought and exhaustively considered procedure." *INS v. Chadha* (1983).

3. *True.* While not expressly provided for in the Constitution, the Court in *United States v. Nixon* (1974) recognized such a constitutionally based privilege for confidential matters based on the separation of powers principle and the powers set forth in Art. II.

4. *False.* The President's power of removal of officials exercising quasi-judicial or quasi-legislative functions is subject to congressional control. While Congress' power to restrict the President's removal of purely executive officials is more circumscribed, limited restrictions which do not impede the President's ability to perform his constitutional duty are constitutional.

5. *False.* The determination of whether such a delegation violates separation of powers will depend on whether it constitutes a legislative usurpation of

Executive Branch functions or prevents the Executive from performing its constitutionally assigned functions. The Court held that provisions in the Ethics in Government Act authorizing appointment of an independent counsel to perform prosecutorial functions and limiting the President's power to control such functions does not violate separation of powers. *Morrison v. Olson* (1988).

6. *True.* While the President has acquired a dominant role in foreign affairs, both Congress and the Executive have constitutional powers in foreign affairs.

7. *True.* While there is no express constitutional authority for executive agreements, their legality is now established. As federal law, they prevail over state law in cases of conflict.

8. *True.* Art. I, § 8, vests the power to *declare* war in Congress. However, as Commander-in-Chief (Art. II, § 2), the President has power to make war and some ill-defined power to commit the nation to hostilities. The war power, therefore, is a shared power.

9. *False.* The President's unique role in our constitutional scheme has been held to afford him absolute immunity against civil suits even when he acts in the "outside perimeter of his official responsibility." But he does not enjoy even temporary constitutional immunity from civil litigation arising from unofficial acts that allegedly took place prior to his taking office. *Clinton v. Jones* (1997).

10. *False.* Although the Supreme Court in *Hamdi v. Rumsfeld* (2004) declined to decide whether the President has inherent Art. II power to detain U.S. citizens as enemy combatants, the Court held that the President could not detain such persons pursuant to a congressional statute without providing due process. Thus, even where the President's authority is at its highest [*Youngstown Sheet & Tube Co. v. Sawyer* (1952) (Jackson, J., concurring)], detainees must be provided some due process rights.

11. *False.* In *Hamdi v. Rumsfeld* (2004) the Court held that executive detentions of U.S. citizens, as enemy combatants, when authorized by Congress, was constitutional if due process were afforded. The Court never reached the questions of whether the President possessed Art. II power to order detention of American citizens absent Congressional authorization.

12. *True.* In *Boumediene v. Bush* (2008), the Court held that the habeas corpus privilege applies to aliens detained at Guantanamo Bay, even though the

United States does not have sovereignty over the area. Procedures provided by Congress for review of detainee status were held to be an inadequate and ineffective substitute for habeas corpus.

13. *False.* In *Hamdan v. Rumsfeld* (2006), the Court held that the military commission convened to try Hamdan lacked power because its structure and procedure violated the Uniform Code of Military Justice and the Geneva Convention.

14. **b.** *Hamdi v. Rumsfeld* (2004) upheld military detention of an American citizen captured in Afghanistan and detained as an enemy combatant under a congressional resolution authorizing the President to "use all necessary and appropriate force" against individuals associated with the 9/11 terrorist attack. A is inaccurate since the Court did not decide whether the President's Article II powers would support such detention absent the congressional resolution. Justice Thomas would accept this position. C represents the view of Justice Scalia and Stevens dissenting in *Hamdi.*

15. **c.** When the President invokes privilege, it is presumptively valid and the burden is on the party seeking disclosure to make a strong showing of the need for rejecting the privilege. "A" may be true in foreign affairs and national security matters since this has not yet been decided, but it has been rejected in domestic matters. Since a presumption of validity attaches to the claim of privilege, b is not the best answer. *United States v. Nixon* (1974) establishes that the courts are the final arbiters of a claim of privilege. Therefore, d is not correct.

16. **c.** Members of Congress and their aides enjoy constitutional immunity for "legislative acts." They are subject to prosecution but the prosecutors cannot rely on legislative acts in securing a conviction.

17. Yes, the legislation was unconstitutional. Article 2, § 2, cl. 2, establishes the power to appoint officers of the United States and provides that the Congress may vest the appointment of inferior officers in either the President alone, in the courts of law, or in the heads of departments. Congress violated Article 2 by providing that a majority of the voting members of the Federal Election Commission should be appointed by the President pro tem of the Senate and the Speaker of the House. Neither of these legislative officials come within the terms "courts of law" or "heads of departments" as required by the Appointments Clause. *Buckley v. Valeo* (1976).

PART TWO: INDIVIDUAL RIGHTS AND LIBERTIES: CONSTITUTIONAL LIMITATIONS ON GOVERNMENTAL POWER

Chapter V: Historical Perspectives

1. *True.* In *Barron v. Baltimore* (1833), the Court held that the Bill of Rights was intended only as a limit on the national government. Fundamental rights in the Bill of Rights have since been applied through selective incorporation to limit state governments using the Fourteenth Amendment due process protection of "liberty."

2. *False.* The sole function of the Privileges or Immunities Clause of the Fourteenth Amendment is to protect rights secured to individuals in their capacity as federal citizens. The Clause has not been interpreted, as has the Due Process Clause, to incorporate Bill of Rights guarantees.

3. *False.* In *District of Columbia v. Heller* (2008), the Supreme Court ruled that the Second Amendment guarantees an "individual right to possess and carry weapons in cases of confrontation."

4. *False.* In *McDonald v. City of Chicago* (2010), the Court held that the Second Amendment right limits the states through the Fourteenth Amendment. However, the plurality rejected reliance on the Privilege or Immunities Clause using instead the Due Process Clause of the Fourteenth Amendment. Only Justice Thomas accepted the argument that the right to possess and bear arms is a privilege or immunity of United State's citizenship.

5. No, he is wrong. The Supreme Court has definitely held that the Privileges or Immunities Clause of the Fourteenth Amendment was not designed to protect individual economic liberties against state legislation. The sole function, it has been held, of the Privileges or Immunities Clause of the Fourteenth Amendment is to protect the rights secured to individuals in their relationship to the federal government, *i.e.*, in their capacity as federal citizens. *Slaughterhouse Cases* (1873).

Chapter VI: Due Process of Law

1. *True.* A law violates the Contracts Clause (Art. I, § 10 for state laws) or the Fifth Amendment Due Process Clause (federal laws), only if it unreasonably and severely impairs contract relationships on which the parties have relied.

2. *False.* A state may contract away its fiscal powers but it may thereafter impair the contract if it is necessary to do so to serve important state interests.

3. *False.* While "taking" is not limited to condemnation of land, the mere fact that property values are diminished will not require just compensation under the Fifth Amendment (federal laws) or Fourteenth Amendment Due Process Clause (state law). If a regulation is a reasonable use of governmental power, *e.g.*, the state police power, it is probably not a taking even if property values decline.

4. *True.* Such a "confiscatory taking" requires compensation as does a physical occupation of property. Only if preexisting state nuisance or property law limits the ownership to the property can just compensation be avoided. *Lucas v. South Carolina Coastal Council* (1992).

5. *False.* In determining if a condition is a reasonable regulation or a compensable taking, a two-part test is applied. First, there must be an "essential nexus" between the condition and a legitimate state interest. Second, an individualized finding must establish facts showing that the condition has a "rough proportionality" to the impact of the development. This is a more demanding standard than rational basis review. *Dolan v. City of Tigard* (1994).

6. *True.* Social and economic regulatory and tax legislation which does not significantly interfere with fundamental constitutional rights is reviewed under the traditional rational basis test. The law is presumed constitutional and the burden is on the challenging party to establish that it is arbitrary and irrational. This burden is essentially insurmountable.

7. *False.* The Court adheres to a selective incorporation approach, applying only those guarantees determined to be essential to "the concept of ordered liberty" or "fundamental to the American scheme of justice" to the state. Thus far, the Third Amendment, the Seventh Amendment right to trial by jury in civil cases, the right to grant jury indictment, freedom from excessive bail and the requirements of a 12–person jury and of a unanimous verdict for conviction, have not been incorporated.

8. *True.* Once a Bill of Rights provision is held applicable to the states under the Fourteenth Amendment, it has the same substantive meaning as it has for the national government. But note that the Court has, at times, read the Bill of Rights guarantees narrowly, thus leaving the states free to pursue their own policies.

9. *True.* When a fundamental right is significantly burdened, the Court employs a stricter standard of review. Usually the government bears the burden of demonstrating that the law is necessary to further a compelling government

interest. In other cases, a less demanding standard is used, *e.g.*, a law must be narrowly tailored to achieve an overriding government objective.

10. **True.** This part of the holding of *Roe v. Wade* (1973) was reaffirmed in *Planned Parenthood of Southeastern Pennsylvania v. Casey* (1992). The law would impose an undue burden on the woman's protected liberty right. The state may proscribe abortion only after viability and only if an exception is made when the abortion is necessary for the mother's life or health.

11. **False.** In *Casey*, the Court abandoned strict scrutiny and the trimester test. The constitutionality of the regulation would probably depend on whether the regulation imposed an "undue burden" on the woman's right to terminate her pregnancy, *i.e., does the regulation have the purpose or effect of placing a substantial obstacle in the path of the woman seeking an abortion of a nonviable fetus.*

12. **False.** In *Gonzales v. Carhart* (2007) the Supreme Court upheld a ban on partial-birth abortions against a facial attack, despite the absence of any provisions exempting mothers whose health was at risk. The Court reasoned that this did not create an undue burden on women because there was medical uncertainty as to whether a partial-birth abortion would ever be necessary to preserve a mother's health and safe alternatives were available.

13. **True.** The right of privacy is not unduly burdened if government fails to make the right of privacy effective by funding abortions for those dependent on government-supplied medical care. There is no right to abortion funding. Nor is equal protection violated.

14. **False.** In *Washington v. Glucksberg* (1997), the Court held there is no fundamental right to suicide or to assisted suicide. Such an interest is not "deeply rooted in our Nation's history and tradition" and is not "implicit in the concept to ordered liberty." *Cruzan v. Director, Missouri Dept. of Health* (1990) did recognize that a competent person may have a liberty right to refuse unwanted medical treatment. But the Court held only that a state may require clear and convincing evidence of the patient's choice even if there is such a right.

15. **False.** While the right to travel interstate is a fundamental right, the Court has never clearly identified the source of the right. It has been variously ascribed to the Privileges or Immunities Clauses of the Fourteenth Amendment or Art. IV, § 2, or to be an inherent federal right arising from the character of our National Union.

16. *False.* Procedural due process must be accorded only if the government deprives a person of significant life, liberty, or property interests which are presently enjoyed. Once this threshold is met, the Courts balance the following interests: (1) the severity of the harm if procedures are not given; (2) the risk of error if the procedures are not afforded; and (3) the administrative difficulty and cost of providing the added procedures.

17. *True.* The Court has held that imposition of a stigma by government officials does not, without more, qualify as a liberty interest. But when the official action affects a legal interest or status created by law, or, perhaps, when a tangible interest is lost, liberty interests are implicated.

18. *True.* There is no requirement that a public employee "take the bitter with the sweet." While a state may so condition the property interest that it does not constitute property, the courts, not the state, are the final arbiter as to what process is required once a property interest has been found. One must separate the finding of a life, liberty, or property interest from the inquiry into whether the employee was granted the process that was due.

19. *False.* Denial of an opportunity to challenge critical facts which are presumed true, which results in the loss of fundamental liberty or property interests, generally does violate due process. However, when no significant liberty or property interest is impaired by the presumption, *e.g.*, non-contractual claims to public benefits, the presumption is constitutional if it is rationally based.

20. *False.* The right-privilege distinction has been abandoned. Whether the person's interest is characterized as a constitutional right or is only a life, liberty or property interest, due process must be accorded.

21. *False.* The Constitution "require[s] recusal when 'the probability of actual bias on the part of the judge or decisionmaker is too high to be constitutionally tolerable.'" If the circumstances objectively lead one to think that a particular judge is biased in a certain case, Due Process requires that he recuse himself in the interest of a "fair trial in a fair tribunal." *Caperton v. A.T. Massey Coal Company* (2008).

22. *True.* The minimum procedures demanded by due process are notice and hearing. What procedures are required to assure fundamental fairness in the context requires balancing the interests favoring summary determination against the protected harm to the individual. *Matthews v. Eldridge* (1976).

23. **a.** The courts generally do not probe to discover the true legislative purpose in reviewing laws under the rationality standard. It is sufficient if there is a

permissible government objective. That a law may incidentally serve other objectives that would be impermissible, will not render a law unconstitutional.

24. **d.** *Bowers v. Hardwick* (1986) held that there was no fundamental right to engage in homosexual sodomy. But *Lawrence v. Texas* overruled *Bowers v. Hardwick*, holding that a state law criminalizing private adult homosexual sodomy violates due process liberty and privacy. Liberty protects the right of the individual, regardless of sexual orientation, to make the choice to engage in intimate sexual conduct in the privacy of the home. The state interest in furthering the moral choices of its citizen is not a legitimate state interest sufficient to justify intrusion into the personal and private life of the individual. The Court expressly indicated it was deciding the case under the Due Process Clause rather than the Equal Protection Clause to prevent persons from arguing that a sodomy law drawn to cover different-sex participants might be constitutional. A, B, and C are wrong under *Lawrence v. Texas* (2003).

25. **d.** Such a law was held unconstitutional in *Casey*. Parental consent laws, with provision for judicial bypass, are constitutional (A would be wrong). A law requiring a second physician (selection b) was upheld even during the more demanding regimen of *Roe*. It would almost certainly survive under the more lenient standards of *Casey*. While a law requiring that abortions be performed in a hospital (selection c) was held unconstitutional in *City of Akron*, under the standards of *Roe*, the validity of such a law would be uncertain under *Casey*. The best answer is therefore d.

26. **c.** B and d are both incorrect because professional disqualification and deportation have both been declared civil penalties by the Court. The Ex Post Facto Clause only forbids retroactive application of criminal laws. A is incorrect because such a law has been determined by the Court to apply prospectively. The penalty is only being applied to the third, as yet uncommitted, crime rather than the first two crimes. C is correct because the Ex Post Facto Clause applies to laws making conduct criminal which was not a crime when performed.

27. **b.** A mere subjective expectancy of continued employment is not enough to qualify as a property interest. Similarly, if the government specifically conditions the character of the entitlement afforded, making it only a limited employment interest, it will not suffice as a property interest. However, if government creates an entitlement, either expressly or impliedly, it will

constitute a property interest. A, c, and d have all been held sufficient to require due process to be afforded.

28. Yes, it is. The Supreme Court no longer follows the line of decisions which used to exalt substantive due process by striking down state legislation which a majority of the Court deemed unwise. State legislatures are not to be put in a straitjacket when they attempt to deal with economic situations which they regard as offensive to the public welfare. The courts may not use the Due Process Clause of the Fourteenth Amendment to sit as a super-legislature to weigh the wisdom of legislation. The West Lincoln statute may be wise or unwise but relief, if it is needed, should be addressed to the legislature of West Lincoln and not to the courts. Since the law is rationally related to promoting the public health and safety, it is constitutional. *North Dakota State Board of Pharmacy v. Snyder's Drugstores* (1973).

Chapter VII: Equal Protection

1. *False.* Like due process law, equal protection generally affords a wide measure of discretion to government in fashioning classifications. The burden is on the challenger to prove that the classification is not rationally related to any permissible government interest. If any state of facts reasonably can be conceived that would sustain a law, the existence of that state of facts at the time of enactment will be presumed. But in some cases, the Court has employed rationality with bite and has held laws unconstitutional using the Equal Protection Clause. See, e.g., *City of Cleburne v. Cleburne Living Center* (1985). Also in *Romer v. Evans* (1996), the Court invalidated a broad discriminatory law against gays purportedly using rational basis review. In both cases, the Court seemed to be concerned with possible prejudice or animus against the disadvantaged group.

2. *False.* Before strict scrutiny is used, the challenger must prove that the discrimination was purposeful, either overtly or covertly. Discriminatory impact may be evidentiary of this impermissible purpose but it is seldom sufficient alone to prove discriminatory purpose.

3. *False.* If a decision is motivated even in part by racial hostility, government may save the law by proving that it *would* have reached the same decision regardless of the discriminatory purpose.

4. *True.* A *de jure* segregated school district is under an affirmative duty to desegregate. Action that has the effect of impeding fulfillment of that duty is prohibited.

5. *True.* Once a school district, acting in good faith, takes all practicable steps to desegregate, it has remedied its constitutional wrong. It has no constitutional duty to avoid the unintended segregative effects of its policies. *Board of Education of Oklahoma City v. Dowell* (1991).

6. *False*. *Adarand Constructors, Inc. v. Pena* (1995) held that "all racial classifications, imposed by whatever federal, state, or local governmental actor, must be analyzed by a reviewing court under strict scrutiny." This reflects the principle of congruence—equal protection analysis is the same under the Fifth and Fourteenth Amendments. However, this does not necessarily mean that strict scrutiny will be applied in the same way to federal and state programs. It is possible that the courts will afford greater deference to federal programs.

7. *False*. Strict scrutiny is used for reviewing all racial classifications. *Adarand Constructors, Inc. v. Pena* (1995). A university admissions program which is narrowly drawn to further a compelling interest in promoting the diversity of the student body is constitutional. *Grutter v. Bollinger* (2003).

8. *False*. While *Grutter v. Bollinger* (2003) holds that diversity in the student body can be a compelling interest for a race-based admissions program, the program must also be narrowly tailored. The program cannot involve the mechanistic and inflexible use of race. It must involve individualized determinations in which race or ethnicity may be factors to be considered but they cannot virtually determine of the outcome. *Gratz v. Bollinger* (2003).

9. *False.* The Supreme Court in *Parents Involved in Community Schools v. Seattle School District No. 1* (2007) held that Seattle's use of race in its tiebreaker system was not narrowly tailored because the system was not individualized, race was decisive by itself when it was used, and only a limited notion of diversity was used. The Court did not decide whether the educational and social benefits from racial diversity in public elementary and secondary schools could be a compelling interest. *Grutter* was limited to the university context. A plurality of justices did appear to endorse a Colorblind Constitution prohibiting the use of race in school admission.

10. *False.* State classifications based on alienage are judged by strict scrutiny, unless the political community exception applies. When states set qualifications for voting or for appointment of officials to important government positions, only a rational basis for the classification is required.

11. *False.* Peremptory jury strikes purposefully made on the basis or race or gender violate the Equal Protection Clause. In either case, if a prima facie

showing of intentional discrimination is made, the burden is on the opposing party to explain the reason for the strike. If it can be shown that the strike was based on a juror characteristic other than race or gender, the Equal Protection Clause has not been violated. *J.E.B. v. Alabama* (1994).

12. *False.* It is only *purposeful* gender classifications which must meet the higher standard of review. Since gender is not a suspect classification, but shares some common characteristics with race, an intermediate standard is used— but only when the discrimination is intentional.

13. *False.* The Court held that the single sex program at VMI failed to satisfy intermediate review because it did not truly promote diversity and the adversative program was not inherently unsuitable for women. The Court did not consider programs of single sex education for men and women that were truly comparable and not created solely to remedy an equal protection violation.

14. *True.* Benign gender classifications are generally upheld when narrowly drawn. But the Court will probe the legislative purpose in order to determine if the classification is truly benign.

15. *False.* Illegitimacy, while sharing some characteristics with race as a classifying trait, is not suspect. Like gender, it generally receives intermediate scrutiny, *i.e.*, the classification must be substantially related to an important government interest.

16. *False.* In *Romer v. Evans* (1996) the Court held that a state constitutional amendment discriminating against homosexuals was irrational and violative of equal protection. But the Court did not decide that classifications based on sexual orientation are suspect, requiring heightened judicial scrutiny.

17. *True.* Strict scrutiny may be used because of the nature of the personal interest which is burdened. If government significantly burdens the exercise of a constitutional right, rational basis review would be inappropriate. Generally, the Court will employ strict scrutiny—the classification must be necessary to a compelling government interest.

18. *False.* Only a significant burden on the right of interstate travel will trigger strict scrutiny review. The Court has required a showing of deterrence or a penalty on the right. On occasion the Court, purporting to use a rational basis test, has invalidated laws burdening interstate travel.

19. *True.* There is no express right to vote in the Constitution, nor has such a right been implied. But equality of access to the franchise is a fundamental right

protected by the Equal Protection Clause itself. The franchise is an interest of such vital importance that classifications significantly burdening the exercise of the franchise in both general and special purpose elections have been judged under a strict scrutiny standard of review, *i.e.*, the classification must be necessary to a compelling interest.

20. *False.* Residency requirements are generally held not to violate equal protection. It is durational residency requirements that are judged by the more stringent standard of review. Nevertheless, even durational residency requirements may be upheld when of short duration and narrowly tailored to prevent electoral fraud.

21. *False.* It is only when a local government uses popular elections relating to the performance of governmental functions and employs single member districting that one person-one vote applies.

22. *False.* The Court in *Davis v. Bandemer* (1986) held that equal protection challenges to political gerrymanders are justiciable. A plurality in *Vieth v. Jubelirer* (2004) argued that the courts lacked judicially manageable standards for resolving such questions. While Justice Kennedy, concurring, agreed that there were as yet no workable standards, he concluded that the Court should allow more time for developing such a standard. The Court did not overrule *Bandemer.*

23. *True.* While education is not a constitutional right, when this fundamental interest is denied to a discrete underclass of children, *e.g.*, illegal aliens, while it is available to other children, more than rationality is required. Only a law furthering a "substantial" state goal will satisfy equal protection.

24. **e.** When the strict scrutiny standard is used, the ordinary presumption of validity no longer applies. The government bears the extremely difficult burden of proving that the classification is necessary to a compelling government interest and that no less burdensome alternative is available.

25. **d.** Wealth classifications, without more, are judged under the traditional rationality standard. Race and national origin classifications (a & b) are subject to strict scrutiny. Gender and illegitimacy classifications (c & e) are judged by an intermediate form of review, *i.e.*, the classification must be substantially related to an important government interest.

26. **c.** While decent housing is an important social interest, it has not been held to be a fundamental right. Classifications significantly burdening access to

housing, like access to welfare benefits, are subject only to traditional rational basis review.

27. No, the West Lincoln Welfare program does not violate the Equal Protection Clause. In the area of social and economic legislation, a state does not violate the Equal Protection Clause merely because the classifications made by its laws are imperfect. There is no suspect classification or fundamental right involved. As long as the classification has a reasonable basis, it is constitutionally permissible even though the classification may in practice result in some inequality. A basis for this legislation can be found in the legitimate state interest in encouraging employment and avoiding discrimination between welfare families and the families of the working poor. The Equal Protection Clause does not require a state to choose between attacking every aspect of a problem or not attacking the problem at all. The state's action need only be reasonably based and free from invidious discrimination, a test which the statute meets. The courts may not second-guess state officials in their task of the allocation of limited public welfare funds among competing categories of potential recipients. *Dandridge v. Williams* (1970).

28. A law is generally constitutional under the Equal Protection Clause if the classification is rationally related to a permissible government interest. In the present case, however, the recipient would claim that the burden of the law impacts more severely on blacks and that such a racial classification must be shown to be necessary to a compelling government interest. However, a disproportionate racial impact is insufficient to trigger this strict scrutiny standard. Only if it is shown that the law was born of a purpose to racially discriminate will the Court depart from rationality review. The recipient would also claim that the law's classification significantly burdens the fundamental right of privacy. If this allegation is established, the state would be required to prove that the classification is necessary to a compelling governmental objective. It is doubtful that the state interest in curtailing welfare costs or discouraging illegitimacy would support the law. If the rationality standard is used, the law would probably be held constitutional under the Equal Protection Clause.

Chapter VIII: Freedom of Expression

1. *False.* When government regulates freedom of speech directly because of the content of the speech, the courts demand either that the speech be in a category of reduced First Amendment protection (*e.g.,* fighting words, obscenity) or that Government establish that the regulation is necessary to a

compelling Government interest (*i.e.*, strict scrutiny). But when the law only incidentally burdens free expression, *e.g.*, content-neutral time, place or manner regulation, a lesser degree of judicial scrutiny is used, *e.g.*, interest balancing, to determine the reasonableness of the law.

2. *False.* Fighting words are an area of speech that can be regulated consistent with the First Amendment "because of their constitutionally proscribeable content." The categories of proscribeable speech, however, are not "entirely invisible to the Constitution"; they cannot "be made vehicles for content discrimination unrelated to their distinctively proscribeable content." *R.A.V. v. City of St. Paul* (1992).

3. *True.* When government undertakes to regulate speech because of its content, it is presumptively invalid. Unless it falls into a category of proscribeable speech, it is subject to strict scrutiny. Laws are content-based if they discriminate on the basis of subject matter or viewpoint. *Simon & Schuster, Inc. v. Members of the New York State Board* (1972). Government may discriminate on the basis of content in regulating speech in a non-public forum.

4. *True.* Advocacy of illegal conduct, without more, is protected. It is only when the advocacy takes the form of incitement that will probably produce imminent lawless action that the expression may be controlled because of the content of the speech. However, the Court did uphold a law prohibiting advocacy of illegal conduct taking the form of "material support" to designated foreign terrorist organizations. *Holder v. Humanitarian Law Project* (2010).

5. *False.* Prior restraints are highly suspect, both substantively and procedurally, and there is a heavy presumption against their constitutionality. The government bears a heavy burden of justification when it seeks to use such a restraint. Content-neutral injunctions, however, must only "burden no more speech than necessary to serve a significant government interest." *Madsen v. Women's Health Center* (1994). Nor must content-neutral permit systems meet the demanding procedural rules applicable to content-based prior restraints.

6. *True.* A law that fails to inform persons of ordinary intelligence what actions are proscribed and thereby burdens First Amendment speech is facially unconstitutional. Similarly, if a law indiscriminately reaches both protected and unprotected activity, it is facially invalid. Substantial overbreadth is required. Such facial unconstitutionality cannot be redeemed by a narrow application of the law.

7. *False.* Freedom of association and belief are implicit in the First Amendment guarantees. The extent of the burden imposed by a law on the individual rights to associate and hold particular political, economic, or social beliefs is weighed against the interests of the government in maintaining the regulation. The courts often employ more stringent forms of review, including strict scrutiny.

8. *True.* This is the Unconstitutional Conditions Doctrine. Such a forced surrender of constitutional rights is itself unconstitutional.

9. *False.* The government employee's political activities are subject to greater restraint than those of the ordinary citizen. The Court employs a balancing test, weighing the interests of the employee as a citizen against the interests of the government as employer. If private speech is involved, only rationality is required.

10. *True.* When public employees make statements pursuant to their official duties, the employees are not speaking as citizens for First Amendment purposes. The Constitution does not insulate their communications from employer discipline because the government has a strong interest in controlling speech that can affect its operations. However, government employees are protected by the First Amendment when they speak as private citizens, rather than as government employees. *Garcetti v. Ceballos* (2006).

11. *False. Elrod v. Burns* (1976) and *Branti v. Finkel* (1980) hold that Government may not discharge public employees for refusing to support a political party or its candidate, unless political affiliation is a reasonably appropriate requirement for the job in question. This principle has been applied when government retaliates against a contractor for the exercise of rights of political association or the expression of political allegiance. *O'Hare Truck Service, Inc. v. City of Northlake* (1996). Similarly, the First Amendment protects independent contractors from the termination of their contracts in retaliation for the exercise of freedom of speech. *Bd. of County Commissioners v. Umbehr* (1996).

12. *False.* Restrictions on expenditures excessively reduce the quality and quantity of communications about political matters, and, therefore, violate the First Amendment. Reasonable regulation of campaign contributions are constitutional.

13. *True.* Government may not define what is orthodox in politics or other matters of opinion. An individual possesses a First Amendment right to be

free of government-compelled association and belief. Only a compelling government interest will justify such a restraint.

14. *True.* In *Hurley v. Irish–American Gay Group of Boston* (1995) the Court struck down such a requirement. A fundamental rule of the First Amendment is that government cannot interfere with the autonomy of speakers to determine the content of their message. "[W]hen dissemination of a view contrary to one's own is forced upon a speaker intimately connected with the communication advanced, the speaker's autonomy is compromised."

15. *False.* Government can punish fighting words under carefully drawn laws which are not susceptible of application to protected expression, *i.e.*, not vague or overbroad. However, government has no power to punish the use of words that are merely offensive, abusive, vulgar, or profane.

16. *False.* If impending violence is due to a speaker's incitement of a crowd to imminent and probable illegal conduct, then the speaker can be punished under properly drawn laws. But if the source of the disruption is a hostile audience and the speaker is not seeking to incite illegal conduct, the police must generally proceed against the crowd and protect the speaker. "Heckler's veto" is inconsistent with the First Amendment.

17. *False.* The Court in *R.A.V. v. City of St. Paul* (1992) indicates that content-based discrimination in a category of proscribable speech is not prohibited when the discrimination does not raise "the specter that the Government may effectively drive certain ideas or viewpoints from the marketplace." For example, if the basis for the content discrimination reflects the very reason the category of speech is proscribable, there is no danger of viewpoint discrimination.

18. *False.* The more demanding standard of review is limited to speech in places that are parts of the "public forum." Speech in publicly-owned places that are not parts of the "public forum," *e.g.*, military bases, jails or prisons, rapid transit cars, mailboxes, can be regulated by laws that are viewpoint-neutral and reasonable.

19. *False.* The Court has at times suggested that when expression takes the form of "speech plus conduct," it is not entitled to the same degree of First Amendment protection accorded "pure speech." Nevertheless, conduct which provides the means for communication, *e.g.*, handbilling, picketing, or solicitation of funds, is protected under the First Amendment. "Expressive conduct" is subject to the *O'Brien* test.

20. *False.* Even when regulating speech in a nonpublic forum, government is subject to the First Amendment. Regulation of speech in a nonpublic forum must be viewpoint neutral and reasonable. Private property owners are not similarly limited.

21. *False.* The less demanding *O'Brien* standard applies only if the government interest is unrelated to the suppression of free expression. If the regulation of expressive conduct is content-based as in *Texas v. Johnson* (1989), strict scrutiny applies.

22. *True.* Prior restraints on access to the public forum are constitutional if they are clear, narrowly drawn, *i.e.,* not vague or overbroad time, place and manner controls. When the regulation is content-neutral, reasonableness is determined by balancing the severity of the burden on First Amendment expression against the government interests in preventing excessive interference with the normal usage of the streets and in maintaining public peace and order. The Court has held that content-neutral injunctions are constitutional if they "burden no more speech than necessary to serve a significant government interest." *Madsen v. Women's Health Center* (1994).

23. *True.* While statutes that are facially invalid may be disobeyed and tested at the time of prosecution, court injunctions must generally be obeyed even if they are patently invalid. Only if the order is frivolous or if the issuing court lacks jurisdiction may it be ignored.

24. *False.* While commercial speech is protected under the First Amendment, its hardiness and the ability of the speaker to determine its accuracy causes it to be subject to a lesser standard of First Amendment protection. A four-part standard is used for commercial speech: (1) the speech must not be false or misleading since such speech is unprotected under the First Amendment; (2) the government interest in regulating must be substantial; (3) the regulation must directly advance the substantial government interest; and (4) the regulation must be no broader than is necessary to achieve that interest. *Central Hudson Gas & Elec. Corp. v. Public Service Comm'n of New York* (1980). A law is "necessary" if there is a "reasonable fit."

25. *False.* The Press Clause and the Speech Clause are read as a single guarantee. The press enjoys no special privileges or immunities under the First Amendment beyond those afforded the ordinary citizen.

26. *True.* Criminal trials are presumptively open under the First Amendment. This First Amendment right of access is based on a history of openness and

on the value of openness to the functioning of criminal trials. "The presumption of openness may be overcome only by an overriding interest based on findings that closure is essential to preserve higher values and is narrowly tailored to serve that interest." *Press–Enterprise v. Riverside County Superior Court* (1984) (*Press–Enterprise I*). The right of access to criminal trials has been extended to pre-trial proceedings unless the judge makes specific findings that prejudice would occur if the public witnessed the proceedings. *Presley v. Georgia* (2010).

27. *False.* In *Sable Communications of California, Inc. v. FCC* (1989), the Court distinguished *Pacifica* and the broadcasting context in applying strict scrutiny to invalidate a total ban on sexually indecent (but nonobscene) telephone messages. In *Reno v. ACLU* (1997), the Court again distinguished *Pacifica* and the broadcasting context in striking down regulations on indecent speech on the internet as an overbroad intrusion on the First Amendment.

28. *False.* The First Amendment does not impose any duty on the government to intrude on journalistic discretion by forcing either the electronic or print media to make access available. Further, the First Amendment prohibits laws that require the print media to publish particular material. However, the First Amendment is not violated by a limited, reasonable, congressionally-mandated statutory right of access to broadcast time.

29. *False.* While indecent or offensive speech and print publication is constitutionally protected, the unique context of broadcasting, *e.g.,* the limitations on its availability, its pervasiveness and the need to protect children, have been held to permit broader government control, including regulation of indecent programming.

30. *False.* *Turner Broadcasting System, Inc. v. F.C.C.* (1994), applies traditional First Amendment principles to cable television: "The broadcast cases are inapposite because cable television does not suffer from the inherent limitations that characterize the broadcast medium." *Denver Area Educ. Telecom. Consortium v. FCC* (1996), while leaving the standards for cable unsettled, does not apply the reduced broadcast standards.

31. *False.* The exclusion of the distribution of materials involving child pornography was limited to live productions and reproductions of live productions. If no live actors are involved, distribution does not promote production involving child abuse.

32. *False.* Public figure plaintiffs, like public officials, must prove actual malice by clear and convincing evidence (*i.e.,* knowledge of the falsity of the

defamatory publication or reckless disregard of its truth or falsity).

33. *False.* While *Gertz* does suggest such a broad principle, *Dun & Bradstreet* limits the constitutional bar on presumed and punitive damages to matters of public concern. If the defamation in a private figure plaintiff case involves only a matter of purely private concern, the state may award such damages.

34. *False.* Characterization of public property as part of the limited public forum increasingly turns on government intent to designate it as open to expressive activity. While the compatibility of the speech with the normal functions of a place is evidentiary of government intent, it is not determinative. Outside of the traditional public forum, government can close public property to particular speech or speakers so long as it acts in a viewpoint-neutral, reasonable manner.

35. *False.* In reviewing government regulation of the speech of government employees, the Court employs a two-part test. First, the Court asks whether the speech involves a matter of public interest. If speech involves only matters of personal interest, the Court defers to the government employer. Second, if the speech does involve the public interest, the Court balances the interests of the employee as citizen against the interests of the government in assuring efficiency.

36. *False.* While the Free Speech Clause would subject government regulation of private speech in a public forum to strict scrutiny, the Government possesses the right to choose its own expression when it is speaking for itself, "[G]overnment speech is not restricted by the Free Speech Clause." *Pleasant Grove City v. Summum* (2008).

37. *False.* In *Rumsfeld v. FAIR* (2006), the Court held that the Solomon Amendment did not burden freedom of speech. The Amendment regulated conduct, not speech, by telling law schools what they must do. Excluding recruiters is not expressive speech protected by the First Amendment. The Amendment does not compel speech or dictate the content of law school speech. Nothing in the recruiting suggests that law schools agree with the military's policy and nothing in the Amendment restricts what law schools say about the military's policies.

38. **e.** Laws burdening the rights of association and belief are constitutional, if reasonable, which is determined by a balancing test. Restraints on group membership (answer a) are valid if limited to active membership which requires knowledge of the organization's illegal objectives (scienter) and

specific intent to further those illegal objectives. Forced disclosure of a group's membership lists may be constitutional if the government's interests in a narrowly tailored law are sufficiently compelling. Even loyalty oaths probing an individual's associations may be constitutional if vagueness and overbreadth are avoided.

39. **e.** While government regulation of speech outside of the public forum need only be content-neutral and reasonable, a more demanding standard of review is used for time, place and manner control of speech in the public forum. In defining this more stringent standard, the Court uses all of the elements indicated in a, b, c, and d.

40. **c.** A public airport was held to be a nonpublic forum in *Int'l. Society for Krishna Consciousness v. Lee* (1992) (a is true). A ban on solicitation was held to be a reasonable means of preventing fraud and delay and inconvenience to airport users (b is true). But a ban on handbilling, which does not involve the same degree of such dangers, was held to be unreasonable (c is not true).

41. **c.** When conduct embodies the idea itself, such symbolic speech—or "expressive conduct"—is judged under the First Amendment (answers a and d are wrong). Conduct qualifies as symbolic speech if all the circumstances indicate that the speaker intends to communicate and the audience understands the speech. But even symbolic speech is subject to regulation if the law meets First Amendment requirements (b is wrong).

42. **d.** Public officials and public figures may recover in defamation only if they prove that the publication was made with knowledge of its falsity or reckless disregard of its truth or falsity, *i.e.,* actual malice (a is wrong and d is correct). While states may define the applicable standards for private figures, public figures enjoy the same measure of First Amendment privilege as public officials (b is wrong). In defining the applicable standard for private figures, states may not impose strict liability (c is wrong). Note that *Dun & Bradstreet, Inc.,* may portend a change in this principle if the defamatory material involves solely a matter of private concern. Absent proof of actual malice, presumed and punitive damages cannot be recovered if the defamation involves a matter of public concern (e is not completely accurate). Even in private figure defamation cases, presumed and punitive damages can be recovered only if actual malice is shown, unless private speech is involved (e is not accurate).

43. **c.** The modern obscenity definition set forth in *Miller* requires only that the work, taken as a whole, lacks serious literary, artistic, political, or scientific

value. The requirements of prurient interest (answer a) and patent offensiveness (answer b) are subject to "contemporary community standards" which need not be a national community (answer d). Thus, a, b, and d are all accurate statements of the modern obscenity definition.

44. **c.** Temporary administrative censorship, under narrowly drawn procedures, does not violate the First Amendment (b is wrong). But, the censor has the burden of demonstrating that the material is unprotected (a is wrong) and it is the censor who must remove the restraint or go to court to justify it (d is wrong). Only a prompt judicial determination that the material is obscene justifies a permanent suppression of the materials.

45. **d.** Schools are allowed to restrict student speech when it creates a substantial disruption and undermines its educational mission. *Tinker v. Des Moines Independent Community School District* (1969). C is not correct. Schools may limit speech when it promotes illegal activity, but thus far, the Court limited its holding to the context of illegal drug use. *Morse v. Frederick* (2007). B is incorrect. *Tinker* and subsequent student speech cases involved content-based regulation. A is incorrect. The Court has applied different First Amendment standards only to student speech in the academic forum. Even in *Morse v. Frederick* (2007) which occurred off school property, the Court tied the context to the school's educational program.

46. The Government has a substantial interest in promoting a stable, racially integrated community and stemming "white flight." But this end cannot be achieved by keeping its citizens from obtaining information. The fact that the ordinance here restricts only one method of communication has some significance to First Amendment analysis. A law which regulates the time, place, or manner of expression has a different status than a law prohibiting a category of expression altogether. Nevertheless, the ordinance is still unconstitutional since reasonable alternative means of communication do not exist here. Leaflets, sound trucks, demonstrations—all of them alternative forms of expression—would be no substitute in this context for "For Sale" signs.

Furthermore, this ordinance is not a time, place, or manner regulation since the basis for the ordinance must be ascribed to the town's interest in regulating the content of the communication rather than on the interest in regulating the form of expression, *i.e.*, the place. Thus, the town has not prohibited all signs but only "For Sale" signs indicating that content rather than the form of expression is the purpose behind the ordinance. See *Linmark Associates, Inc. v. Township of Willingboro* (1977) and *City of Ladue v. Gilleo* (1994).

47. The Klan would allege that the law violates the rights of association and belief of Klan members. While no right of association and belief is expressly guaranteed by the First Amendment, the right, including a right of privacy in associational memberships, has been implied from the express rights and has been applied to the states as a guarantee of the Fourteenth Amendment Due Process Liberty Clause. Whether the Eureka law violates this right would be determined by a balancing test. The burden on the protected rights would be weighed against the state interest in maintaining public order and discouraging racial conflict and dissension. The Klan would argue that the Court should employ strict scrutiny since the registration and disclosure law significantly burdens protected First Amendment activity. *DeGregory v. Attorney General of New Hampshire* (1966). In the past, however, the Court has tended to employ strict scrutiny for "legitimate" groups engaged in First Amendment activity, using ad hoc balancing for groups such as the Communist Party and the KKK. *New York ex rel. Bryant v. Zimmerman* (1928). This differs from constitutional viewpoint-neutral laws that may incidentally place a greater burden on groups with discriminatory policies while still promoting legitimate government interests. *Christian Legal Society v. Martinez* (2010). In any case, it would be argued that the law is a vague and overbroad intrusion on the rights of association and belief. It would be argued that persons of common intelligence could not determine which groups are covered by the "advocating racial hatred" provision. Since advocacy, even of illegal conduct, is constitutionally protected, it would be argued that the law is unconstitutionally overbroad. It should be noted that the recent decision in *Holder v. Humanitarian Law Project* (2010), indicates that if hate organizations such as the KKK are designated as terrorist organizations, advocacy in the form of "material support" of these groups could constitutionally be made illegal.

Chapter IX: Freedom of Religion

1. *False.* Such authorization constitutes the allocation of political power on a religious criterion in violation of the Establishment Clause. Neutrality is violated since there is no assurance that government will treat other similarly situated groups in the same fashion. Accommodation of religion cannot be pursued by affording a religious sect special treatment. *Board of Education of Kiryas Joel School District v. Grumet* (1994).

2. *False.* Released time, off school grounds, is a permissible accommodation of religion. On-campus released time programs have a primary effect which is sectarian by placing public support behind religious programs.

3. *True.* The First Amendment forbids required recitation of prayers or Bible reading. Even if the prayer is non-denominational and students are excused, the Establishment Clause is violated. A moment of silent *prayer,* for the purpose of endorsing religion, has also been held unconstitutional.

4. *False.* When government is involved with religion by sponsoring a religious exercise, the Establishment Clause is violated. The school's involvement in the ceremony imposes a "subtle coercive pressure" on students to participate. A student cannot constitutionally be forced to forgo attendance at the ceremony as the price of avoiding a state-sponsored religious practice. *Lee v. Weisman* (1992).

5. *False.* Discrimination on the basis of religious viewpoint violates freedom of speech. The Establishment Clause is not violated by a non-discriminatory open access policy since any benefit to religion is only incidental. There is no realistic danger that the government would be perceived as endorsing religion. *Widmar v. Vincent* (1981); *Lamb's Chapel v. Center Moriches School District* (1983). The principle that the Establishment Clause is not violated by a neutral, non-discriminatory access policy which includes religious speakers was extended to subsidy programs in *Rosenberger v. Rector & Visitors of University of Virginia* (1995). These principles apply even in an elementary school context and even if the group plans to conduct prayer services. *Good New Club v. Milford Central School* (2001).

6. *True.* If a state acts for the secular purpose of serving the public welfare, the fact that the program incidentally benefits religion does not condemn the program. Such non-ideological aid as busing and books does not have a *primary* effect of fostering religion and does not involve excessive government entanglement with religion. This aid can even go so far as to include tax credits for taxpayers who contribute to organizations providing scholarships for private, including sectarian, schools. *Arizona Christian School Tuition Organization v. Winn* (2011).

7. *False.* "Government programs that neutrally provide benefits to a broad class of citizens defined without reference to religion are not readily subject to an Establishment Clause challenge just because sectarian institutions may also receive an attenuated financial benefit." The placement of the interpreter in the parochial school results from the decision of the parents, not the government. *Zobrest v. Catalina Foothills School District* (1993).

8. *True.* Such assistance, directed at religious schools and parents with children in religious schools, has been held to have the direct and immediate effect of aiding religion.

9. *True.* Aid for meeting tuition expenses available only to parents having children in sectarian schools is unconstitutional. *Committee for Public Educ. and Religious Liberty v. Nyquist* (1973). But a neutral tuition aid program, available to citizens generally, where the parents freely choose how the tuition assistance is directed, is constitutional, even if substantial public funds are provided to religious schools. *Zelman v. Simmons–Harris* (2002).

10. *False.* In *Agostini v. Felton* (1997), the Court held that the Establishment Clause is not violated when federal funds are used to send public school teachers into parochial schools to provide remedial education. The aid was provided on a neutral basis and there were safeguards provided. The fact that the aid is given in the sectarian schools by public employees is not determinative. The carefully constrained program did not have the effect of advocating or endorsing religion. *Aguilar v. Felton* (1985) and portions of *School District of Grand Rapids v. Ball* (1985) to the contrary were overruled.

11. *False.* When a law aids or advances only selected religions, rather than religions generally, *i.e.,* it grants denominational preferences, the law is suspect and must meet the rigorous strict scrutiny standard. Only if the law is necessary to a compelling government interest is it constitutional.

12. *False.* Accommodation of religion by granting exemptions from significant burdens on a religious belief or practice which would result from application of general laws is a legitimate public purpose. The Court has indicated that it is more appropriate for the legislature than the courts to fashion such exemptions. Any such preference must be nondenominational, *i.e.,* it must not prefer particular religions over others.

13. *False.* Courts may not decide purely internal church disputes. However, they may apply neutral principles of law, not requiring an inquiry into religious doctrines, to settle questions of ownership of religious property.

14. *True.* Religious belief and opinion are not subject to government control. However, conduct, even when it is an expression of religious beliefs, must be accommodated to overriding government interests.

15. *False.* The Court applies a two-part test in free exercise cases. If a burden on religion is determined to be significant, the government must demonstrate a compelling or overriding interest for the law. There must be no less burdensome alternative available. But even a significant burden on religion can be justified.

16. *False.* Government cannot condition the receipt of public benefits on the surrender of free exercise rights. Further, a direct burden on a religious

adherent by requiring conduct contrary to one's faith demands substantial justification. But even though neutral laws of general applicability may impose a significant burden on a religious adherent, the government may require uniform application if this is essential to achieve an overriding government interest, if the law does not coerce the surrender of religious beliefs, or if the law is a general criminal prohibition which only incidentally burdens religion.

17. *False.* While the Court has not yet directly addressed the meaning of "religion" in the First Amendment, the Court has recognized that ordered liberty precludes allowing every person to provide their own constitutional standard of religion. The closest the Court has come to addressing this issue is the parallel beliefs doctrine which asks whether a particular belief occupies a place in the life of its possessor parallel to that filled by the orthodox belief in God.

18. *False.* Even if a generally applicable law incidentally imposes a significant burden on religion, strict scrutiny is not required if the law does not coerce surrender of religious freedom. Further, strict scrutiny is not applied to a generally applicable criminal law that has only the incidental effect of significantly burdening a particular religion or religious practice.

19. **b.** Such a law has been held unconstitutional even where private funds were used. While the state argued that the law served secular purposes, the Court held that it was religious in purpose and primary effect. Tax exemptions, Sunday Closing Laws, government funds for college buildings, and non-ideological aid for state-required activities all have been upheld as secular in purpose and primary effect and as not involving excessive government entanglement with religion.

20. **b.** The Establishment Clause is not merely a command of equal treatment among religions, but instead is a command of government neutrality as to religion generally. Answers a, c, and d embody the three-part test used in Establishment Clause cases. If a law is secular in purpose or primary effect or fosters excessive government entanglement with religion, the Clause is violated.

21. The city ordinance is unconstitutional. A law which is a generally applicable and neutral, having only an incidental effect on religion, is presumptively valid. *Employment Div. Dept. of Human Resources v. Smith* (1990). However, the city ordinance on its face is directed only against the religious ritual, exempting other nonreligious animal slaughtering. The direct, primary

purpose of the law is to curb the religious activity. Strict scrutiny applies to laws that directly impose a significant burden on religion. Ritual animal slaughtering is a central part of plaintiff's religion so the burden is significant. The city's interest in promoting public health and preventing cruelty to animals is not compelling since the law does not prohibit conduct involving the same or greater evil. Nor is the ordinance narrowly-tailored since it is under-inclusive, exempting nonreligious animal slaughtering. *Church of the Lacombe Babalu Aye, Inc. v Hialeah* (1993).

Chapter X: State Action

1. *True.* Unlike the Fourteenth and Fifteenth Amendments, the Thirteenth Amendment is not limited to state action but applies directly against private action. Slavery or involuntary servitude is prohibited, regardless of its source.

2. *False.* The modern Court is increasingly narrowing the concept of state action. It is only significant involvement in the particular conduct being challenged, making the government responsible for the challenged activity, that will satisfy the state action requirement.

3. *False.* While illegal action by a public official may not be the action of the state for Eleventh Amendment purposes, it is state action under the Fourteenth and Fifteenth Amendments. The official has been clothed with state authority, thus putting him in a position where he or she can misuse public power.

4. *False.* The fact that the government financially supports a private actor does not necessarily make the state a partner to the activities of that actor. Only if the government funds are shown to constitute encouragement, authorization, or approval of the activity being challenged is a finding of state action likely.

5. *True.* Some activities, such as elections or maintaining public order on municipal streets are so public in character that even state failure to control private actions, constitute state actions. However, the Court today requires that the activity be *traditionally and exclusively* a function of sovereign government in order to apply the Public Function Doctrine.

6. *True.* Generally, neutral enforcement of valid state laws does not constitute state action violative of the Fourteenth Amendment. However, the Court has held that the neutral judicial enforcement of a racially restrictive covenant against a willing white seller does constitute impermissible state action. *Shelley v. Kraemer* (1948).

7. *False.* While government acquiescence in the wrongful action does not make the state responsible for the conduct, if the state authorizes or compels the particular conduct being challenged, it is a responsible party. Joint action is a means of establishing state action but it is not the only test of state action.

8. c. Neutral enforcement of government regulations will not constitute state action. Even pervasive regulation and licensing of a private actor engaged in discrimination does not make the state responsible for the discrimination. However, if government actually manages or supervises the challenged activity (answer a) or public officials become vicariously responsible by acting in concert with the discriminating party (answer b) or the government encourages, authorizes, or approves the challenged action (answer d), there is state action. Similarly, if government and the private actor are so interdependent that a symbiotic relationship exists, state action is present.

9. **d.** The action was taken pursuant to a state law authorizing the private action and the private party's joint participation with the public officials fairly makes him a state actor. *Lugar v. Edmondson Oil Co., Inc.* (1982). "A" was held not to constitute state action in the absence of some public enforcement—it was held to be only a policy of noninvolvement. *Flagg Bros., Inc. v. Brooks* (1978). "B" was held not to constitute state action in absence of a showing of government authorization or approval of the policy under which service was terminated. Pervasive government regulation of private action is inadequate. *Jackson v. Metropolitan Edison Co.* (1974). Financial support of a private actor (answer c), without a closer government involvement in the challenged act, does not constitute state action. *Rendell–Baker v. Kohn* (1982).

10. The state action principle is the principal constitutional law ground for the motion to dismiss. The mere fact that broadcasting is a licensed industry is not sufficient to establish "state action." First Amendment obligations run only to the government and not to private broadcasters. The mere fact that the broadcasting industry is extensively regulated by government does not serve to transform the actions of this private industry into state action. Furthermore, the fact that government licenses the actor does not make the state a partner to the action.

Chapter XI: Congressional Legislation in Aid of Civil Rights and Liberties

1. *True.* Congress may use its plenary commerce and spending powers against private action detrimental to civil rights and liberties. Similarly, Congress can legislate against private or state action which interferes with the exercise of

"federal rights" protected by the Constitution.

2. *True.* Section 2 of the Thirteenth Amendment gives Congress authority to enforce the prohibition against slavery and involuntary servitude. Legislation designed to eradicate the badges of slavery is a reasonable means of enforcing the Thirteenth Amendment guarantee which reaches even private action.

3. *True.* Section 5 of the Fourteenth Amendment and § 2 of the Fifteenth Amendment grant power to Congress to enforce the substantive guarantees in those amendments. Congress can enact reasonable laws to protect against conduct which the courts hold violates these amendments.

4. *False.* While there is language in *Katzenbach v. Morgan* that could be read to indicate that Congress has power to define the substantive content of the Fourteenth and Fifteenth Amendment rights, this principle was rejected in *City of Boerne v. Flores* (1997). Congress' power under the enforcement clauses is to prevent or remedy unconstitutional action, not to determine what is a constitutional violation.

5. *True.* *City of Boerne v. Flores* (1997) held that there must be congruence and proportionality between the injury to be prevented or remedied and the means adopted to that end. The Religious Freedom Restoration Act was held to be out of proportion to preventing or remedying state laws likely to be held unconstitutional because of their treatment of religion. The Act's adoption of strict scrutiny with its "least restrictive means" requirement was held to be broader than appropriate.

6. *True.* In the *Civil Rights Cases* (1883), the Court held that Congress in exercising its enforcement powers could provide remedies only against "state action." But there was judicial support for the proposition that Congress can legislate against private conduct which interferes with Fourteenth Amendment rights. *United States v. Guest* (1966) (concurring opinions). But in *United States v. Morrison* (2000), the Court rejected the dicta in *Guest* and reaffirmed the principle that the enforcement power is limited to its object, remedying or preventing unconstitutional state action, not private conduct.

7. *True.* Even if a showing of discriminatory state purpose is required to establish a Fourteenth or Fifteenth Amendment violation, Congress, in the exercise of its enforcement powers, can legislate against discriminatory impact. As long as the law is a reasonable means of implementing the constitutional guarantee in the Amendment, it is constitutional.

8. *False*. While Congress can enact appropriate corrective legislation under its enforcement powers, such remedies or preventive laws must be congruent and proportional to the unconstitutional action. In a number of recent cases, the Court has imposed demanding standards in invaliding congressional legislation abrogating State sovereign immunity.

9. **c.** While it is possible that this law might be upheld, it is the *least likely* to be held valid. The Thirteenth Amendment, which provides possible support for the law, is generally held to be limited to racial (not gender) discrimination. The Fourteenth Amendment, which would reach gender discrimination, at least thus far, usually requires state action. "A" was upheld in *Oregon v. Mitchell* (1970) as a reasonable means of enforcing the Fifteenth Amendment. "B" was also upheld in *Oregon v. Mitchell*, although a provision lowering the voting age in state elections was held unconstitutional. "D" was upheld in *Jones v. Mayer* (1968), under Congress' Thirteenth Amendment, § 2, powers, as a reasonable means of eradicating "badges of slavery."

10. No, it does not. Congress has power to legislate under Section 2 of the Thirteenth Amendment to enact direct and primary legislation which is necessary and proper for abolition of badges and incidents of slavery, subject only to the rights and liberties guaranteed by the Constitution. The interpretation of 42 U.S.C. § 1981 prohibiting discrimination against Blacks by private schools does not offend freedom of association. Although parents have a First Amendment right to send their children to schools which teach segregation as a value, the First Amendment does not protect the practice of excluding racial minorities from such institutions. *Runyon v. McCrary* (1976). The statutory interpretation of § 1981 as reaching private conduct was reaffirmed in *Patterson v. McLean Credit Union* (1989).

APPENDIX B

Practice Examination

Read each question carefully and organize your answer. Do not make unnecessary assumptions. If you feel that any assumptions are necessary to enable you to develop an issue, state these assumptions in your answer and indicate why they are necessary. If you believe additional information is necessary to properly resolve an issue, state the nature of the required information and why it is needed. Even if you decide that a particular theory decides the issue, you are required to discuss alternative theories. Formulate your answers, whenever possible, to reflect the competing policy considerations or values that are involved. A mere statement of issues without analysis or of rules with no analysis of their rationale is to be avoided. Once you discuss a subject do not repeat the discussion—merely cross-reference to your original discussion.

Question I

(1 1/2 Hours)

The community of Purewhite is a high-income residential community. Less than 1% of the community is non-white. While there are three luxury apartment units in the town, it is primarily composed of single-family dwellings built on large lots. The average price of these homes is approximately $500,000 and land values have risen rapidly. Schools in the community are among the finest in the country and the municipal services provided are correspondingly excellent. While various land-use controls of Purewhite have been struck down by the courts as racially discriminatory, Purewhite remains heavily segregated. Purewhite has never applied for federal funds available to assist in developing lower-income racially integrated housing.

Purewhite is across the river from the city of Urbana. A typical urban area, Urbana has become increasingly populated by non-whites as whites have fled to Purewhite and other adjoining white communities. Metropolitan Urbana is over 60% non-white. The declining tax base of Urbana has aggravated the municipality's problems. Little new housing is being built and older housing is falling into a severe state of disrepair. Urbana has made a number of efforts to secure assistance from surrounding white communities, including Purewhite, in meeting its problems but has been consistently rebuffed.

In 1990, Bild–A–Lot, Inc., a privately-owned, open housing developer, announced plans to build a large-scale, racially-integrated, low-income, multi-unit apartment housing project in Purewhite on land on which it holds an option. Architects were hired and plans were drafted for the project. A furor of adverse reaction broke out in Purewhite. Under public pressure, the Purewhite Community Council took the unusual step of scheduling a public meeting on the subject of the future development of Purewhite. At the meeting, there were statements made about "undesirable elements" entering the community and even blatantly racist appeals. But there were also statements reflecting economic and aesthetic concerns.

Shortly thereafter, the Purewhite Council enacted an "Anti–Apartment Ordinance," zoning the entire town to exclude any further apartment dwellings. Provision was made for individual exceptions or variances granted by the zoning board and for the apartment units already built. The ordinance recited the high costs to the community of multi-unit developments created by the need to provide schools, fire and police protection, sewage and sanitation, adequate access roads, etc. Bild–A–Lot applied to the zoning board for an exception or variance. A hearing was held but the application was denied, citing the problems indicated in the Anti–Apartment Ordinance.

A. A black resident of Urbana who desires housing in Purewhite, a small number of white residents of Purewhite who desire to enjoy the social and economic benefits of living in an integrated community, and Bild–A–Lot Inc., want to bring suit to challenge the Anti–Apartment Ordinance as violative of the Equal Protection Clause of the Fourteenth Amendment. However, the plaintiffs are concerned over standing problems if the suit is brought in federal district court. Discuss the nature of the standing problems. In your answer, assume there is no applicable federal fair housing law.

B. Assuming that standing problems are overcome, discuss the merits of a federal court challenge to the Purewhite ordinance based on the Equal Protection Clause. Do not discuss equal protection law involving fundamental rights and interests.

Question II

(45 Minutes)

The trucking freight business in the state of Utopia has hit hard times. Almost all local Utopia trucking firms do business primarily within the state using conventional single unit trucks. However, many interstate trucking companies using large double and triple unit trucks are seriously cutting into local truckers' business. Because of the large capacity of the double and triple unit trucks, interstate companies are able to carry a number of loads at one time. They are generally able to deliver freight between points within a state (as part of a larger shipment) at cheaper rates than can be charged by domestic companies using single unit trucks. Trucking companies in Utopia have been lobbying the state legislature for relief.

Utopia's Department of Transportation has been concerned with the road safety hazards posed by large doubles and triples. Studies indicate that they are involved in a disproportionate number of road accidents. When accidents do occur, they tend to be more severe and produce far greater road congestion than other highway accidents. The studies show that the large trucks, when temporarily parked on road shoulders, often hang out into the roadway producing increased highway danger. All this information, derived from the Department's studies, has been forwarded to appropriate committees of the Utopia state legislature.

In 1990, the Utopia legislature enacted the "Highway Safety Act" (HSA), which provides: "All companies doing business with the state of Utopia are required to use only single unit trucks, (i.e., no double or triple unit trucks may be used) for all their business involving hauling." The HSA applies to companies doing business with the state which use their own trucks for hauling as well as those companies doing business with the state which hire trucking freight companies to haul their products.

Suit has been brought challenging the HSA as violative of the Commerce Clause. Discuss the issues that will be raised in the litigation. Limit your discussion solely to Commerce Clause issues.

Question III

(30 Minutes)

Studies indicate that a highly disproportionate number of drunk driving accidents involve drivers under 21. Drivers under 21 are responsible for 20% of all traffic related accidents although they comprise only 8% of all licensed drivers. It is estimated that alcohol related accidents involving drivers under 21 cost the nation $2 billion a year in lost wages, productivity, medical and legal costs and purchasing power. In states where the drinking age has been raised to 21, alcohol-related fatalities in the 16–20 years old age group have dropped an average of 28%. The Chairman of the National Transportation Safety Board has stated that if the drinking age is raised to 21 across the nation, over 1,250 lives can be saved per year.

Congress is presently considering two bills designed to combat drunken driving. The first, "Drunk Driving Regulation Act" (DDRA), would make drunken driving "in or affecting interstate commerce," a federal criminal offense. Stringent criminal penalties, enforced by federal authorities, would be prescribed. The second, the "Drunken Driving Spending Act" (DDSA) would require states to adopt stringent criminal sanctions for drunken driving as a condition for receiving federal highway funds. Cut-off of federal highway funds would follow a determination by the U.S. Department of Transportation that the state laws fail to meet federal standards.

Critics of the proposed legislation claim that Congress lacks constitutional power to enact either law and that either measure would violate the powers reserved to the states under the Tenth Amendment. Discuss the merits of these claims.

Question IV

(45 Minutes)

Malcom Y, accompanied by 50 followers, marched to a local neighborhood park on Martin Luther King's birthday. At the park, Malcom made a fiery speech, stressing that King had made one serious mistake—he had ruled out violence. Malcom stated:

> Violence is all that whites understand. You've got to burn, destroy and kill to make it. And you have to start now. Knock the whites down and don't let them up.

Pointing to some white construction workers standing near by, he said, "Look at those fucking sons of bitches. Those are the ones who have the jobs you need." As he continued, his followers became increasingly agitated and so did the whites in the area. One of the construction workers said, "We should shut that son of a bitch up." At this point, police moved in, arrested Malcom Y and dispersed the crowd.

Malcom Y was convicted of violating the Penal Code, § 111 which provides:

> Sec. 111 *Disorderly Conduct.* It shall be unlawful and constitute disorderly conduct for any person to intentionally use language that is racially offensive or abusive, or indecent, or to use language that threatens to produce immediate violence and disorder.

Malcom has appealed his conviction. Discuss the constitutional issues that might be raised on the appeal.

Question V

(One Hour)

St. Mark's Church is located in the central business district of the town of Hustler. Erotica Bookstore wishes to move into a location only 500 feet from St. Mark's. In doing so, Erotica would violate a Hustler township ordinance (Adult Business Activity Ordinance, ABAO) providing that an "adult entertainment business" may not locate within 1000 feet of any lot upon which there is located a school, a public park, another adult entertainment business, or a church. The ordinance does not apply to preexisting uses; it was applicable only to future locational decisions. An adult business activity includes adult bookstores, defined as:

> An establishment having as a principal activity the sale of material which emphasizes portrayals of human genitals and pubic regions or act of human masturbation, sexual intercourse or sodomy.

No other definitions are provided.

The Adult Business Activity Ordinance (ABAO) was enacted in 1990 after a number of protests at Hustler town hall by religious organizations and civic groups. Many of the protestors expressed moral outrage at the influx of "indecency and filth" into the town and expressed concern "for the well-being of children." These sentiments as well as expressions of concern over the effect of the intrusion of adult business activity in the town on the civility of community life, the threat of urban deterioration, and effect on the township's image were repeated in the debate of the Hustler town council leading to the enactment of ABAO. There were no specific findings by the council or any government agencies on the effects of the location of adult establishments, although some council members noted the increasing use of such zoning ordinances in other communities and the Supreme Court decisions that have upheld similar ordinances. It was noted in the debate that the area of land in Hustler township where adult businesses could locate under the ordinance is approximately 3% of the total urban area; most of the land where adult businesses could locate would be outside of the central business area.

Erotica Bookstore filed suit in federal district court seeking a declaration that the Hustler ABAO is unconstitutional and an injunction against the ordinance's enforcement. Discuss the issues raised by the suit.

Question VI

(30 Minutes)

Prior to 1983, Ohio law required that all abortions after the first trimester (90 days) be performed in a hospital. Outpatient facilities would not qualify as "hospitals" under the law. In 1983, the Ohio hospitalization law was declared unconstitutional on the authority of *Roe v. Wade*.

Assume that in 1993, after the Supreme Court's decision in *Planned Parenthood of Southeastern Pa. v. Casey*, Ohio reenacted its hospitalization law. An action has been brought challenging the constitutionality of the Ohio hospitalization law, claiming that it violates the Due Process Clause.

Discuss the issues raised by the constitutional challenge to Ohio's hospitalization law.

ANSWERS

Question I

A.   Standing raises the question whether the litigant is entitled to have the court decide the case on the merits. This involves both constitutional limitations on federal court jurisdiction and prudential rules governing the proper exercise of the judicial review powers.

Art. III of the Constitution requires that litigation be presented in an adversary form and context capable of judicial resolution and that its resolution not violate separation of powers principles, *i.e.*, that there be a "case or controversy." Art. III standing requires that the plaintiff demonstrate a "personal stake" in the outcome of the controversy. In order to establish this personal stake, the plaintiff must establish actual or threatened "injury in fact," which is "fairly traceable" to the government action being challenged, and which is "redressable" through judicial relief.

Even assuming *arguendo* that the Purewhite Anti–Apartment Ordinance is purposefully racially discriminatory, the black resident of Urbana would not, simply by reason of his race, satisfy Art. III standing requirements. Stigmatic injury is sufficient only if the litigant is personally denied equal treatment by the discriminatory treatment. The minority litigant must prove that his inability to find suitable housing in Purewhite is fairly traceable to the restrictive ordinance and that absent the ordinance there is a substantial probability that he could live in the community. *Warth v. Seldin* (1975). However, if the black plaintiff could establish that he is seeking apartment housing such as that planned in the Bild–A–Lot project (or similar project) which is actually being stopped because of the challenged law, and that he would qualify for such housing, the indirect injury can satisfy Art. III. *Village of Arlington Heights v. Metropolitan Housing Dev. Corp.* (1977).

The white residents of Purewhite claim injury in fact to their interest in the social and economic benefits from living in an integrated community. Such an intangible injury can satisfy Art. III standing requirements. However, a generalized grievance common to citizens generally is not sufficiently personal to the plaintiff to satisfy Art. III requirements; ideological injury common to all citizens is insufficient. In *Gladstone Realtors v. Village of Bellwood* (1979), the white plaintiffs claimed under federal fair housing laws recognizing their intangible interest. The denial of their statutory interest then provided the requisite injury in fact. Further they were residents of a 12–13 block racially integrated neighborhood being transformed by the challenged practices. While injury to this interest was held sufficient to satisfy Art. III standing requirements, it is less likely that the more attenuated interests of Purewhite residents in the racial integration of the community generally would suffice.

The developer Bild–A–Lot would have the clearest claim to Art. III standing. Bild–A–Lot has been denied a variance under the challenged ordinance and seeks to remove the obstacle which would allow it to build. It thus satisfies the causation requirement that the injury be fairly traceable and redressable.

If the Art. III standing requirements are satisfied, both the white resident plaintiffs and Bild–A–Lot would still have to overcome prudential obstacles, insofar as they rely on the equal protection claim of racial discrimination suffered by racial minorities. Generally, litigants are not allowed to raise the legal claims of third parties not before the court, *i.e.,* the third party standing rule. Courts will decide a constitutional question only when necessary and usually only when litigated by plaintiffs who can fully represent the legal interests at stake.

But the *jus tertii* rule is a prudential doctrine, a non-jurisdictional rule of judicial self-restraint, which can be overcome when there are overriding considerations. The close relationship of the racial discrimination claim to the interests of the white resident plaintiffs and the developer might suffice. On the other hand, there is no apparent reason why the disappointed members of the racial low-income minority cannot litigate their own legal claim. If the black resident of Urbana is found to have standing, the third party standing rule would pose no obstacle to litigating the equal protection claim.

B.   The plaintiffs challenge the Purewhite ordinance as violative of the Fourteenth Amendment Equal Protection Clause. In most equal protection cases, the plaintiff has the burden of proving that the classification is not "rationally related to furthering a legitimate government interest." He must prove that the law is arbitrary and irrational. The courts will assume that the legislature found any state of facts that would sustain the law. In short, the courts traditionally defer to the legislature or agency when reviewing socioeconomic legislation under the Equal Protection Clause and the law is generally sustained. Given the economic and aesthetic interest recited in the Anti–Apartment ordinance, a general ban on future building with provision for variances when appropriate would probably be upheld.

While the Supreme Court in some socio-economic cases has invoked a more demanding mode of equal protection review, the facially neutral, generally applicable, *i.e.,* nondiscriminatory, character of the Purewhite apartment ban makes the present case an unlikely candidate for more intensive judicial review.

The plaintiffs will endeavor to have the court invoke a more demanding review than that used in traditional socio-economic cases. However, the fact that the ordinance discriminates against the poor, will not, without more, produce a stricter standard of review.

The plaintiffs' best argument will be that the Purewhite ordinance is a racially discriminatory law. When the state intentionally discriminates on the basis of race, it has the burden of establishing that the classification is necessary to a compelling interest. There must be no less burdensome alternative available. However, to trigger this strict scrutiny standard of review, the plaintiffs must prove that the Anti–Apartment law, while facially neutral, was covertly enacted for the purpose of racial classification and causes the discriminatory effect.

The requirement of discriminatory purpose cannot be satisfied by proving that the government knew or could have foreseen the discriminatory consequences of the law. The government must act "because of" and not merely "in spite of" its impact on the racial minority. But the purpose to racially classify need not be the sole or even the dominant purpose for using the electoral system; race must be shown to have been a motivating factor in the decision.

In determining whether there is discriminatory purpose, the courts are to consider the totality of the relevant facts, including circumstantial and direct evidence of intent.

In proving the intentional use of race in enacting the Purewhite ordinance, plaintiffs will use statistical evidence indicating a disproportionate burden on racial minorities and the foreseeability of increased racial segregation resulting from the exclusion of apartment dwellings such as the Bild–A–Lot project (*e.g.*, while metropolitan Urbana is 60% non-white, Purewhite is only 1% non-white). The plaintiffs can also employ other contextual evidence such as the community reaction to the Bild–A–Lot project, the departure from normal procedures in calling the public meeting, and racist remarks made at the meeting. This can be added to evidence indicating past racial housing discrimination in Purewhite, the socio-economic conditions in the metropolitan area, Purewhite's refusal to aid Urbana, and its failure to participate in federal fair housing programs (although it has no legal obligation to participate).

If the plaintiffs succeed in establishing a prima facie case of purposeful race discrimination, the burden would shift to the government. Purewhite could seek to rebut the prima facie case by arguing that the racial segregation is a product of wealth disparities (*e.g.*, cost of housing) and not race, that the public meeting was meant to provide a forum for differing views on the future development of the community faced with a major new housing development, that the testimony at the meeting was mixed and that there were pressing public welfare (i.e., aesthetic and economic) concerns reflected in the ordinance.

The community can also argue that even if the enactment of the Anti–Apartment ordinance was partially motivated by racial considerations, the law would have been enacted in any case given the economic and aesthetic concerns of the community. Finally, the community could argue that the apartment ban is necessary to compelling public interest in avoiding the adverse social consequences of high density dwellings. However it is unlikely that the community could meet the strict scrutiny standard of review which generally is "strict in theory, fatal in fact."

Question II

Utopia's "Highway Safety Act" (HSA) can be challenged as violative of the negative implications of the Dormant Commerce Clause. Although the commerce power is a concurrent power, a state cannot adopt policies which discriminate against interstate commerce or which unduly burden the free flow of interstate commerce. But laws which benefit publicly owned or operated activities, while treating all private businesses the same, do not discriminate against interstate commerce. *United Haulers Ass'n Inc. v. Oneida–Herkimer Solid Waste Management Auth.* (2007).

If the Court finds that the purpose of HSA is to favor local trucking firms against competition from out-of-state truckers, then it is virtually *per se* impermissible. Such a discriminatory purpose would violate the intent of the Commerce Clause to establish a National Common Market. Moreover, out-of-state citizens lack recourse to the state's political process for redress of such discrimination. Since the burden of the law would not fall on local residents, there is no internal political check. While HSA is facially neutral in that it applies to all truckers, it could be argued that there is evidence of discriminatory purpose in that Utopia's trucking business has hit hard times, almost all local firms use single unit trucks, and local truckers have been lobbying for relief. The Court, however, has been increasingly reluctant to probe behind an asserted state interest to find a covert discriminatory purpose.

The Court could also find that HSA, while intended to serve the state's interest in highway safety, is discriminatory in impact. Arguably, HSA is discriminatory in that the restriction on trucking impacts more heavily on out-of-state truckers who use doubles and triples and eliminates a competitive advantage they previously held over local trucking firms which use singles. If the Court accepts this argument, the state would have to prove that HSA promotes a legitimate state interest and that no less discriminatory alternative legislation is available.

In defense of HSA, Utopia could argue that the law is not discriminatory since it applies to all trucking companies using doubles and triples, whether in-state or out-of-state. Further, out-of-state trucking firms are not restricted from doing business in Utopia as long as they use singles. The fact that the structure of the trucking industry is such that most local firms use single unit trucks, while out-of-state trucking firms use double and triples, does not make the law discriminatory.

If the Court finds that HSA is not discriminatory, the law might still violate the Dormant Commerce Clause if it unduly burdens the free flow of interstate commerce. The burden on interstate commerce must be balanced against Utopia's interest in highway safety. Utopia can argue that the highway safety interests of the state have traditionally been given great weight by the Court. In fact, if the safety interests are not illusory, the Court has indicated that it would not second-guess the legislative judgment by balancing the competing interests. Further, under the HSA, out-of-state firms remain free to do business in the state using doubles and triples, only companies doing business *with* the state are affected. The out-of-state firms, on the other hand, will stress the loss of business and the resulting pressure to convert to singles for business in Utopia which would impair their competitive advantage. They may also challenge the state's safety evidence and note the alternatives available to the state to promote highway safety.

Utopia would argue that the law is justified as a safety measure, citing the disproportionate number of road accidents from doubles and triples and that the law is limited only to companies doing business with the State. The plaintiffs would cite the cost and delays produced by Utopia's law, the protectionist effects of the law, the disparity (if any) with other state laws, and any evidence challenging the safety claims of Utopia.

The analysis above proceeds on the assumption that the state is *regulating* the marketplace. While the law is directed at companies doing business with the state, the Government is regulating the market, not benefitting public businesses. However, the state might assert that it is acting as a market participant rather than a market regulator. When a state participates in the marketplace, the normal negative implications of the Dormant Commerce Clause do not apply. The Commerce Clause is directed solely at state regulation and not at state action taken to provide benefits to its citizens. Further, when the state enters the market, fairness dictates that it be treated similarly to private participants who are not subject to the Dormant Commerce Clause. Utopia would argue that it is directly acting in the marketplace by choosing those companies with whom it will deal and defining the conditions of the contract.

The interstate truckers, on the other hand, would argue that the effects of the HSA are not limited only to firms entering contracts with the state but others as well. Businesses dealing with the state must limit their trucking contracts to firms using singles. Further, this requirement appears to apply to all of the hauling business of the company, even if Utopia is not a party. When a state imposes conditions that effect parties who are not in privity to the contract and with which it has no business relationship, *i.e.*, a "ripple" effect, it acts as a regulator rather than as a participant. If Utopia is held to be a market regulator rather than a market participant, the negative implications of the Dormant Commerce Clause, discussed above, would apply.

Question III

The claim that Congress lacks constitutional power to enact DDRA should be rejected. The Commerce Clause provides a plenary source of constitutional power to regulate driving in interstate commerce, including the power to limit or exclude such commerce. This regulatory power to define the substantive conditions under which interstate commerce shall occur is complete in itself, subject only to the limitations of the Constitution.

Congress also has implied power to enact reasonable regulations to effectuate the Commerce Clause. Pursuant to this implied grant, Congress may regulate local intrastate activity if Congress could rationally conclude that such activity has a substantial effect on interstate driving activity, even if the effect is only indirect. This includes the power to impose criminal sanctions even absent proof that the particular defendant is engaged in activity affecting interstate activity—"[w]here the *class of activities* is regulated and that *class* is within the reach of federal power, the courts have no power 'to excise, as trivial, individual instances' of the class." *Perez v. United States* (1971). While the means selected must be reasonable, Congress is the judge in the first instance of what means are to be employed in the exercise of its granted powers.

But there are limits. In *United States v. Lopez* (1995), holding unconstitutional a law criminalizing gun possession near a school, and *United States v. Morrison* (2000), holding unconstitutional a federal law proving a civil remedy for victims of gender-motivated violence, the Court stressed that there must be a rational basis for Congress' concluding that the regulated act *substantially* affects interstate commerce. Among the factors discussed by the Court, the following appear especially relevant. First, the absence of any jurisdictional nexus between the regulated act and interstate commerce makes it more difficult to identify the requisite effect. Second, the regulated activity must be commercial in character, unless it is an important part of a regulatory scheme for regulating an interstate economic market. *Gonzalez v. Raich* (2005). Third, the absence of congressional findings of fact indicating a substantial effect makes it more difficult to evaluate Congress' judgment, although such findings are not required. Fourth, the fact that the federal law regulates local activity having only a remote, attenuated causal effect on interstate commerce. If Congress regulates in such areas such as criminal law, education or family law where States have historically been sovereign, this may bear on the reasonableness of a federal law.

Nevertheless, the proposed DDRA should be held constitutional. The Act is expressly drawn in terms of drunk driving "in or affecting interstate commerce." The Act regulates activity, not inactivity. *National Federation of Independent Business v. Sebelius* (2012). In light of the statistical evidence concerning the relationship of drunken driving and automobile accidents, Congress could rationally conclude that stringent federal criminal sanctions applied to the whole class of drunk drivers is an appropriate means of regulating the movement of interstate commerce. Drunken driving causing traffic accidents is closely related to commercial activity. The fact that the law furthers police power objectives or that its primary effect is local is immaterial since the regulated activity substantially affects interstate commerce. The courts will not inquire into the purpose and motive of Congress. While highway safety is a traditional local concern it is also of national importance and a regular subject of federal regulation. Finally, it would be difficult to distinguish intra- and interstate driving. Congress has power to assure the effectiveness of its regulations of interstate commerce even if that involves the regulation of intrastate commerce.

Until recently, the constitutional objections to the "Drunken Driving Spending Act" (DDSA) would be rejected outright because Congress is granted power to spend for the general welfare. *U.S. Const. Art I § 8.* In *National Federation of Independent Business v. Sebelius* (2012) Congress attempted to withhold all existing Medicaid funding from a State if it did not comply with an expansion to Medicaid. However, the Supreme Court limited the spending power by not allowing withholding of previously committed monetary grants for an entire federal program if a State refused to comply with a newly enacted modification or expansion of that program.

The DDSA attempts to withhold all federal highway funding, including existing funding, from the states if they do not adopt stringent criminal sanctions for drunk driving. This seems similar to *Sebeilus* because it is an enactment that expands federal power over federal highway funding and conditions all federal highway funding on this new expansion. The constitutionality of this will hinge on whether the *Sebelius* rationale extends to a new program that takes away funding from a previously exiting program, because the DDSA is a completely new program and not technically an expansion, unlike the legislation in *Sebelius*. It may still be unconstitutional because it "is economic dragooning" that "leaves the States with no real option" but to comply with the new regulation.

As indicated above, there is ample basis for congressional regulation of drunk driving. It is a matter of national concern subject to the congressional spending power. The condition imposed by DDSA is reasonably related to the subject of the grant, *i.e.*, highway safety.

While the Court has held that the Tenth Amendment limits the commerce power when Congress regulates the sovereign States (*New York v. United States* (1992); *Printz v. United States* (1997)) that principle applies only when the congressional law compels the States to enact or enforce federal regulatory programs. It does not apply to generally applicable laws regulating private and public activity. It is the political process that protects federalism. (*Garcia v. San Antonio Metropolitan Transit Auth.* (1985), overruling *National League of Cities v. Usery* (1976)). Insofar as the proposed laws would displace state police power to regulate private activity, *i.e.,* highway safety, the Tenth Amendment is not a limitation. In the context of regulation of private activity, the Tenth Amendment is only a truism—that Congress may not regulate if it lacks power. But Congress can act when it has power to regulate the private conduct even if the federal law displaces state power in a traditional area of local concern. As indicated above, Congress' commerce power extends to private driving activity and the Tenth Amendment, therefore, provides no barrier to this exercise of the commerce power.

It could be argued that the Tenth Amendment limits Congress' ability to use its spending power to require that the state use its sovereign legislative powers against drunken driving. Indeed, in overruling *National League of Cities,* the Court in *Garcia* indicated that there may be some remaining "affirmative limits" that the "constitutional structure might impose on federal action affecting the states under the Commerce Clause." In *New York v. United States* (1992) and *Printz v. United States* (1997), the Court did hold that a law requiring states to regulate or enforce a federal regulatory program violates the Tenth Amendment. It could be argued that the condition imposed by the DDSA causes the states to adopt criminal sanctions in violation of *New York* or enforce the federal standards in violation of *Printz.* But in *South Dakota v. Dole* (1987), the Court rejected such a Tenth Amendment argument under the spending power since the state remained free to reject the federal grant and the attached condition. When a state voluntarily participates in a federal spending program, it accepts reasonable conditions attached to the grant. Sovereignty is preserved by the state's ability to refuse to participate in the federal program.

South Dakota v. Dole (1987) did indicate that in some circumstances the financial inducement offered by Congress might be so coercive as to pass the point at which pressure turns into compulsion. The threatened cutoff of all federal highway funds might satisfy this limitation. However, the Court has consistently rejected all such Tenth Amendment limitations on the Spending Power and might well do so in the present case.

Question IV

Malcom Y will challenge his conviction as a violation of his First Amendment right of freedom of speech made applicable to the states as part of Fourteenth Amendment liberty. Malcom would argue that his remarks, while abusive and offensive are constitutionally protected. The state will argue that Malcom's speech constitutes "fighting words," *i.e.,* words which have a direct tendency to cause acts of violence by the person to whom, individually, the remarks are addressed. Fighting words are so devoid of social worth as to enjoy little, if any, First Amendment protection. If Malcom's abusive remarks to the construction workers are held to constitute fighting words, the Disorderly Conduct statute could be constitutionally applied to punish Malcom because of the content of his speech. The conviction, therefore, would be affirmed.

Alternatively, the state could contend that Malcom's speech presented a clear and present danger of violence which government could prevent by suppressing his speech. The government would have to establish that Malcom's speech was intended to incite or produce imminent unlawful action and that such imminent lawless action was likely to result. *Brandenburg v. Ohio* (1969). The mere abstract advocacy of unlawful conduct would be insufficient to justify Malcom's conviction. Malcom's language must be held to have constituted advocacy of action, *i.e.,* incitement. Further, there must have existed a real probable and imminent threat that violence would result from the indictment if the conviction is to be upheld.

This incident would also not fall under the protections outlined by Chief Justice Roberts in *Snyder v. Phelps* (2010) for protestors and demonstrators speaking hateful and inflammatory messages. Unlike the protestors in *Snyder* who were located away from the affected audience and complied with all regulations, Malcom Y pointed directly at onlookers and personally insulted them, as well as advocated for violence. The direct contact and pointed remarks at least implied advocacy of violence, unlike the speech in *Snyder* which "was on a matter of public concern" without directly attacking nearby individuals.

If the danger of violence arose only because of a hostile audience reaction to Malcom's otherwise protected speech, the conviction should be reversed. Speech that is offensive, vehement and caustic is constitutionally protected even if it produces an angry hostile crowd reaction. Normally the police must protect the speaker from the hostile crowd; there is no "heckler's veto."

Assuming that the Court held that Malcom's speech was not constitutionally protected, Malcom could still seek to overturn his conviction by arguing that the Disorderly Conduct Statute is facially unconstitutional since it is vague and overbroad. Even though Malcom could be convicted under a properly drawn law, under the First Amendment overbreadth doctrine, he has standing to challenge the facial constitutionality of the statute. This is an exception to the third party standing rule that a litigant normally cannot raise the legal claims of parties not before the Court who might be chilled from asserting their own rights.

Malcom's challenge to the facial validity of § 111 might well succeed. First, the statute does not satisfy the special demand for precision and clarity when First Amendment rights are at stake. Since it does not clearly define the types of proscribed speech, persons of ordinary intelligence would be forced to guess at its meaning and could differ as to its application. This, in turn, chills free speech and leads to indiscriminate and improper law enforcement. Second, the statute arguably is overbroad, *i.e.,* it proscribes both protected and unprotected speech. Abusive, offensive and indecent speech, which the statute proscribes, is protected by the First Amendment unless perhaps the speech is imposed upon a "captive" audience. The statute is not limited to fighting words or speech which is intended to, and is likely to, incite imminent unlawful acts or true threats. It seems unlikely that the Court would provide a savings construction which would limit the statute to unprotected speech and the law would probably be held facially unconstitutional.

Further, even if the statute were narrowly interpreted to limit it to fighting words, it might still be presumptively unconstitutional under *R.A.V. v. City of St. Paul* (1992). When the state discriminates among fighting words on the basis of content unrelated to their distinctly proscribable character, the discriminatory regulation must be shown to be necessary to a compelling state interest. Section 111 of the Penal Code singles out racially abusive or offensive language for punishment— this constitutes subject matter discrimination. The state has a compelling interest in preventing verbal assaults against racial minorities, given our history of racial discrimination. However, the law is not narrowly-tailored, since all fighting words could be proscribed.

The government could argue that the law falls within an exception recognized in *R.A.V.,* *i.e.,* where the discrimination does not create a danger of viewpoint discrimination. See, e.g., *Virginia v. Black* (2003) (cross burning with an intent to intimidate is an especially virulent form of true threat). It could be argued that racial fighting words are an especially intolerable and socially unnecessary mode of expressing the speaker's message. But in *R.A.V.,* the Court rejected a similar argument since government had not selected only speech most likely to produce violence but rather those fighting words that were especially intolerable or odious. This form of selectivity threatens viewpoint bias.

Question V

Erotica will argue that the Hustler ordinance violates freedom of speech protected by the First and Fourteenth Amendments. While obscene publications are not part of the "freedom of speech" protected by the Constitution, the First Amendment does protect sexually offensive and indecent adult materials and businesses that deal in such materials. This constitutional protection applies to both criminal and civil regulation, *e.g.*, the zoning law involved in the present case. While a plurality of the Court has asserted that indecent and offensive speech enjoys a lesser degree of constitutional protection than other fully-protected speech, *e.g.*, political speech, this has not been accepted by a majority of the Court.

However, the Court has upheld two adult zoning ordinances similar to that employed by Hustler township on the basis that they were reasonable, content-neutral time, place and manner regulations. *City of Renton v. Playtime Theatres* (1986) and *Young v. American Mini Theatres, Inc.* (1976).

The initial issue is whether the Hustler ordinance is content-based or content-neutral. If the law was enacted for the purpose of burdening the content of the speech it would presumptively violate the First Amendment. Such a content-based law is valid only when the speech is categorically excluded from "the freedom of speech," (*e.g.*, obscenity), or if the law is narrowly-tailored to serve compelling government interests.

While the Hustler ordinance does distinguish between bookstores whose principal activity is the sale of designated adult materials and other materials—facially a discrimination reflecting the content of the materials sold—this does not necessarily mean that the law is content-based. If the law is enacted for a predominant, primary purpose which is not based on the content of the regulated speech, it may still be deemed content-neutral. The fact that *one* of the motivating factors for a law is speech content will not necessarily trigger strict scrutiny review.

In this case, Hustler township will argue that the law was enacted because of the expressed concerns over the tone and civility of communal life, the image of the community and urban deterioration. Erotica will argue that the context in which the law was enacted (*i.e.*, the protests and lobbying focused on concerns of offensiveness and indecency), the legislative debate reflecting these concerns and the lack of governmental findings on urban blight prove that the primary concern of the Hustler town council was combatting sexually offensive, indecent expression. Given the Court's reluctance to probe behind a facially valid purpose, it seems unlikely that the Court would accept the argument that the law is content-based.

If the ordinance is held to be a content-neutral time, place and manner regulation, the Court will apply the *United States v. O'Brien* test, asking whether the law furthers an important or substantial governmental interest unrelated to the restriction of free expression and if the incidental restriction on alleged First Amendment freedoms is no greater than is essential to the furtherance of that interest. This does not require the state to adopt the least burdensome alternative. If the law directly and effectively furthers its legitimate objective, it is constitutional. Further, courts have traditionally extended presumptive validity to a city's use of its zoning powers.

However, Erotica will argue that Hustler has failed to prove that the claimed state interests are really threatened by adult business activities in the town. In *American Mini Theatres,* Detroit had made extensive factual findings on the effect of adult businesses on urban life. In *City of Renton,* the city had relied heavily on studies produced by other cities. While the *City of Renton* Court did not require the city to produce its own studies, it did note the city's reliance on some particularized studies. Erotica will argue that the court should invalidate adult zoning based solely on unsupported declarations and not based on factual findings.

Hustler township can argue that precedent does not require conclusions and explicit findings of fact in the legislative record. The city can rely on the findings of other cities and the Supreme Court decisions accepting the legislative recognition of the documented relation of adult business activities and urban deterioration. They will contend that as long as there is expressed justification for the city ordinance, the city need not make explicit findings.

Erotica will also argue that the ordinance does not leave "reasonable alternative avenues of communication." The effect of the ordinance is to ban adult businesses from most of the central business areas. Only 3% of total city area is available to such establishments whereas 5% of the land area was available in Renton. The Hustler ordinance suppresses or greatly restricts access to lawful speech.

Hustler township will argue that the zoning ordinance affects only future locational decisions. It permits location of adult businesses in approximately 3% of the land area, including portions of the central business area. The community has not used its zoning power to exclude adult businesses; adult businesses remain free to operate in Hustler. Hustler has not denied adult bookstores a reasonable opportunity to operate.

Erotica may also argue that the Hustler ordinance is unconstitutionally vague. The ordinance applies to business establishments having as a "principal activity" the sale of the designated materials. But the ordinance nowhere defines "principal activity." In the First Amendment area, laws must be narrow and specific. Persons of common intelligence must be able to ascertain its meaning. Precision and clarity in drafting are essential to assure that protected speech will not be chilled and that the law will be properly enforced.

Hustler township will argue that, to the extent that any ambiguity exists in the ordinance, it can be given a narrowing construction by the state courts. Further, there is nothing in the record indicating that Erotica is not clearly subject to the ordinance; any lack of warning does not harm this plaintiff.

Question VI

The Ohio hospitalization law will be challenged as violating liberty guaranteed by the Fourteenth Amendment Due Process Clause. *Planned Parenthood v. Casey (1992)* reaffirmed the "essential" holding of *Roe v. Wade*: 1) the right of a woman to have an abortion of a nonviable fetus without undue state interference; 2) a recognition of the state's ability to regulate post-viability abortions, as long as an exception is provided in cases where the mother's health is endangered; and 3) a recognition of a state interest in the potential life and health of the fetus from the point of conception.

Liberty extends to the woman's decision to terminate a pregnancy because it involves a choice central to personal dignity and autonomy of the person. While the *Casey* Court did not adopt the language of fundamental rights, a majority of the justices accepted the importance and significance of the liberty right to an abortion prior to viability and the need for heightened scrutiny when the state burdens the right.

The state may argue, as did the dissent in *Casey*, that while abortion implicates liberty, the woman's interest is not fundamental and not subject to heightened judicial scrutiny. Abortion has been traditionally proscribed and stringently regulated. It is not implicit in the concept of ordered liberty since our system of justice would survive even if abortion is regulated. Finally, the state's interest in protection of the fetus makes abortion sui generis. The state would argue that the hospitalization law is rationally related to the state interest in protecting the health of the mother. Given the judicial deference accorded state regulation under this standard, the law would be constitutional.

The challenger would argue for heightened judicial review because of the significance of the liberty right. They might argue for strict scrutiny, *i.e.*, the law must be necessary to a compelling interest. If the Court adopted this standard, this law would fail. Under *Roe*, the state would have a "compelling" interest after the first trimester (90 days). However, the requirement of hospitalization is not narrowly tailored to this interest given the safety of many second-trimester abortions and the costs to the woman. However, the Court in *Casey* rejected *Roe's* trimester framework and did not adopt strict scrutiny. Indeed, only Justice Blackmun—no longer on the Court—used the strict scrutiny standard. The trimester approach was deemed inadequately sensitive to the substantial state interests involved and unnecessary to protect the woman's rights.

Most likely, the Court would adopt the "undue burdens" test. *Gonzales v. Carhart* (2007). Under the undue burdens test, a law must not have the purpose or effect of placing a substantial obstacle in the path of a woman seeking the abortion of a nonviable fetus. The test focuses on the burden on a woman's right to choose whether or not to have an abortion and does not directly address the state interests in maintaining the regulation.

The state will argue that the hospital law does not impose an undue burden since the woman remains free to choose whether or not to have an abortion. The fact that any abortion occurring 90 days or more after the onset of pregnancy must be performed in a hospital and not in an outpatient facility, involving added costs and inconvenience is an incidental, indirect burden. The state might also argue that its health interest outweighs any incidental burden on the woman given the superior health care available at such a facility. This would be relevant if the Court adopts an interest-balancing approach.

The challenging party will argue that the woman's informed decisionmaking is not furthered by the law. Further, the costs and difficulties of securing hospital abortions, *e.g.*, travel, the fact that many hospitals don't perform abortions, and that outpatient facilities do not qualify as hospitals, constitute a substantial obstacle for many women. This is especially true for the poor and in cases where the spouse opposes abortion. However, similar arguments failed in a facial challenge to a 24–hour waiting period requirement in *Casey*. Even if the facial challenge to this hospital law fails, the application of the law might be challenged as imposing an undue burden in the particular case.

Glossary

A

Abortion The Fourteenth Amendment guarantee of liberty protects the decision of a woman to terminate a pregnancy. While the state has legitimate interests from the outset of pregnancy in protecting the woman's health and life of the fetus, it may not proscribe abortion prior to fetal viability. After viability, a state may even proscribe abortion, so long as an exception is made for the mother's life or health. In regulating abortion, a state may not impose "undue burdens," *i.e.*, laws having the purpose or effect of placing a substantial obstacle in the path of a woman seeking an abortion.

While the minor female has a right to privacy, extending to abortion, the state has a greater interest in regulating the abortion of minors. Parental notification and consent laws are constitutional if narrowly drawn and if they include a judicial bypass provision. *Hodgson v. Minnesota* (1990).

Abortion Funding Government has no affirmative constitutional duty to provide funds for abortions for those who could not otherwise, because of financial reasons, obtain them. This is so even though government may choose to provide financial assistance to those who need it to encourage childbirth.

Abstention Federal courts use the discretionary "abstention" doctrine to avoid the unnecessary adjudication of a constitutional issue, especially where such issue rests on an unsettled interpretation of state law. Thus, a federal court may give a state court the chance to interpret a challenged state statute or to complete a pending state trial, even if the federal court has jurisdiction. Also, a federal court will not enjoin a pending state criminal proceeding (and some civil proceedings) nor grant declaratory relief, absent bad faith harassment.

Adequate State Grounds The Supreme Court will not review state court judgments that clearly and expressly rest on "adequate and independent state grounds," even if the state court erroneously decided an alternate federal ground. This is based on the principle that courts should not reach federal constitutional questions unnecessarily.

Advisory Opinions Art. III, § 2, of the Constitution confines federal court jurisdiction to "cases and controversies." The Court has interpreted this as a bar to any Art. III court rendering an "advisory opinion." *Muskrat v. United States* (1911). Federal courts have jurisdiction under Article III to decide real controversies between parties but no jurisdiction to provide legal counsel to the other branches of government.

Affirmative Action Race-based affirmative action is constitutional only if the law satisfies strict scrutiny, *i.e.,* necessary to a compelling government interest. The plan must be narrowly drawn and race-neutral means must be considered. Remedial programs, narrowly tailored to remedy specific identified illegal discrimination, can satisfy the strict scrutiny standard.

Affectation Doctrine Congress can regulate local activities which it could reasonably conclude have a substantial effect on interstate commerce. Such regulation is necessary and proper to effectuating Congress' power to regulate "Commerce among the states." There are limits. Factors which the Court considered in holding a law unconstitutional for exceeding Congress' Commerce Power include: the fact that the regulated activity was not commercial or economic activity, the absence of a jurisdictional nexus with interstate commerce, the lack of congressional fact-finding or an adequate record, and intrusion on traditional areas of state control. *United States v. Lopez* (1995).

Alienage Classifications (Standard of Review) When a state classifies on the basis of alienage, strict scrutiny normally applies. The reason for this is said to be that such classifications involve a discrete and insular minority requiring special judicial protection. However, where a state regulates on the basis of an alienage classification in matters concerning qualifications for voting or for appointment of officials to important government positions that involve the definition of self-government (*i.e.,* political function exception), the traditional equal protection-rational basis test applies.

Appellate Jurisdiction Art. III vests the appellate jurisdiction in the Supreme Court, subject to congressional exceptions. The failure of Congress to grant jurisdiction is treated as an implied exception. While the power of Congress to withdraw appellate jurisdiction may be plenary, it may be subject to limitations arising from separation of powers principles and constitutional rights and liberties.

Appointment Power Art. II, § 2, cl. 2, vests the power to appoint principal federal officials, subject to the Senate's advice and consent, in the President. Congress may vest the power to appoint inferior officers in the President, courts of law, or heads of departments. Congress may not vest appointment powers in itself. *Buckley v. Valeo* (1976). Whether an officer is a principal or inferior officer depends on a functional analysis of the official's subordination or independence, the scope of her jurisdiction, and the extent of the functions performed. *Morrison v. Olson* (1988).

Association and Belief While the First Amendment does not expressly mention a right of association and belief, it has been interpreted to protect a right of expressive association to achieve First Amendment objectives and a freedom of belief. Burdens on these implied rights are usually reviewed by a balancing test, often strict scrutiny.

Authorization and Approval (State Action) The fact that the state acquiesces in the wrongful acts of a private party does not make the state responsible for the conduct. The termination of a customer's electric service by a privately-owned public utility company for non-payment, in the absence of notice, hearing, and an opportunity to pay any amounts found due, is not attributable to the state. Only if the state authorizes or compels the particular conduct being challenged, thus making itself responsible for the action, is there state action. *Jackson v. Metropolitan Edison Co.* (1974).

B

Badges of Slavery (Thirteenth Amendment, Enforcement of) Congress has power under § 2 of the Thirteenth Amendment to enact direct and primary legislation which is necessary and proper for abolishing all badges and incidents of slavery in the United States. Thus, it has been held that 42 U.S.C. § 1982, which has been construed to bar *all* racial discrimination, private as well as public, in the sale or rental of property, is a valid exercise of the power of Congress to enforce the Thirteenth Amendment. *Jones v. Mayer* (1968).

Balance of Interests Test (Interstate Commerce) Even non-discriminatory state regulation of interstate commerce may violate the Commerce Clause if it excessively burdens interstate commerce (Negative Implications or Dormant

Commerce Clause Doctrine). The courts weigh the burden on the free flow of interstate commerce against the state interests furthered by the regulation. The balancing includes consideration of factors such as (1) the nature and function of the state regulation; (2) the character of business involved; and, (3) the actual effect on the flow of commerce. Some justices argue that such balancing is properly a legislative, not a judicial function; the Dormant Commerce Clause is satisfied if the regulation is not discriminatory.

Balancing Test (First Amendment) When government regulation only indirectly burdens First Amendment rights, the courts apply a balancing test. For example, in reviewing content-neutral regulations the courts use the test set forth in *O'Brien v. United States* (1968): "A government regulation is sufficiently justified * * * if it furthers an important or substantial government interest; if the government interest is unrelated to the suppression of free expression; and if the incidental restriction of alleged First Amendment freedoms is no greater than is essential to the furtherance of that interest." Under this test, it is not necessary that government adopt the least-restrictive means. Balancing takes a variety of forms including simple ad hoc balancing of interests to more stringent forms of review requiring a more narrow tailoring of means to overriding government objectives, including use of the least restrictive means.

Belief–Conduct Distinction, Freedom of Religion While religious belief and opinion is absolutely protected, the practice of religious activities must be accommodated to valid government interests. Thus, a federal law prohibiting polygamy was enforceable against a nineteenth century Mormon who claimed that polygamy was a practice fundamental to his faith. The federal law did not violate the Free Exercise Clause but was a permissible regulation of conduct which was subversive of good order and violative of social duties. *Reynolds v. United States* (1878).

Bicameralism The constitutional requirement contained in Art. I, §§ 1, 7, that no federal law can take effect without the concurrence of the prescribed majority of members of both Houses of Congress. *Immigration & Naturalization Services v. Chadha* (1983). See *Presentment*.

Blue Laws (Freedom of Religion) Thus far, challenges to Sunday closing laws based on the Free Exercise Clause have been rejected. The Supreme Court has balanced the state interest in a common day of rest against the free exercise claims of Sabbatarians and concluded that Blue Laws impose only an indirect economic burden on the Sabbatarian. *Braunfeld v. Brown* (1961).

C

Campaign Finance (Contributions v. Expenditures) The rights of association and expression are burdened by attempts to limit contributions and expenditures for political campaigns. However, reasonable limits on contributions by individuals and groups are permissible since the government has a substantial interest in preventing corruption or the appearance of corruption resulting from large contributions. Expenditure restrictions, though, are unconstitutional because they excessively reduce the quality and quantity of communication. *Buckley v. Valeo* (1976). However, restrictions on expenditures by corporations are constitutional if they are narrowly drawn to serve the state's compelling interest in preventing the distorting and corrosive effect of corporate wealth on the political process. *Austin v. Michigan Chamber of Commerce* (1990).

Case and Controversy The Art. III limitation of federal judicial power to various enumerated "cases" and "controversies" requires that a case be in an adversary form and context which is capable of judicial resolution and that its resolution not violate separation of powers principles.

Child Pornography Sexually indecent live productions involving minors or visual reproductions of such performances are not protected by the First Amendment. The state may criminally punish those who knowingly promote such activity by distributing child pornographic material. *New York v. Ferber* (1982). "Virtual Child Pornography, not involving minors in the production of the visual depiction is constitutionally prohibited speech." *Ashcroft v. The Free Speech Coalition* (2002).

Clear and Present Danger "The most stringent protection of free speech would not protect a man in falsely shouting fire in a theatre and causing a panic. * * * The question in every case is whether the words used are used in such circumstances and are of such a nature as to create a clear and present danger that they will bring about the substantive evils that Congress has a right to prevent." *Schenck v. United States* (1919). "[F]ree speech and free press do not permit a state to forbid or proscribe advocacy of the use of force or of law violation except where such advocacy is directed to inciting or producing imminent lawless action and is likely to incite or produce such actions." *Brandenburg v. Ohio* (1969).

Commerce Power Congress has the power to regulate "commerce among the states" which has come to mean interstate commerce. There are three broad categories of activity that Congress may regulate under its Commerce Power. "First, Congress may regulate the use of the channels of interstate commerce. Second, Congress may regulate and protect the instrumentalities of interstate commerce, or persons or things in interstate commerce, even though the threat may come only from intrastate activities. Finally, Congress' commerce authority includes the power to regulate those activities having a substantial relation to interstate commerce, *i.e.,* those activities that substantially affect interstate commerce." *United States v. Lopez* (1995). In reviewing laws enacted pursuant to the Commerce Power, courts will not probe the congressional purpose or the local effects of the law in determining whether Congress has power to act. Thus, Congress may achieve social welfare objectives through the use of the Commerce Power.

Commercial Speech Precisely what speech will be labeled commercial speech remains uncertain. The Court has noted that "expression related solely to the economic interests of the speaker and its audience," constitutes commercial speech. *Central Hudson Gas & Electric Corp. v. Public Service Corp.* (1980).

Commercial speech, such as commercial advertising, does enjoy First Amendment protection but not as extensive as that enjoyed by political, social, or religious speech. *Virginia State Board of Pharmacy v. Virginia Citizens Consumer Council* (1976). *Central Hudson* sets forth a four-part test for determining the constitutionality of commercial speech regulations: (1) The speech must not be false or misleading or related to unlawful activity; (2) the asserted government interest must be substantial; (3) the regulation must directly advance the government interest; (4) the regulation must be no more extensive than necessary. Regulation of truthful, nonmisleading commercial speech, reflecting simple paternalism, is likely to be held unconstitutional. The Court recently has been exercising a "closer look" in reviewing commercial speech regulation.

Compact Clause Article I, § 10, cl. 3, requires that Congress consent to any agreement or compact by a state with another state or with a foreign country. This consent requirement has been limited by judicial interpretation to apply to agreements which increase the powers of the states in such a way as to potentially interfere with federal supremacy.

Company Towns (State Action) If a privately-owned town operates as the functional equivalent of a municipality, it may be deemed a public forum. Thus, where the streets of a company owned town are denied to Jehovah's Witnesses for purposes of distributing religious pamphlets, and no alternative forum is present, they will be deemed quasi-public for purposes of the state action concept. The action of the company town denying access to its streets to the Jehovah's Witnesses will be deemed sufficiently public to render the town's action a violation of the constitutional rights of the Jehovah's Witnesses. *Marsh v. Alabama* (1946).

Compelled Speech Since the First Amendment protects the right to speak and the right of freedom of association and belief, it has been held that there also must be a correlative right to be free from compelled association and compelled speech. *Wooley v. Maynard* (1977). When government burdens expresses advocacy or association by forcing a person or group to speak, or to provide support for ideas that they oppose, it may be held to violate the First Amendment.

Conclusive Presumption A conclusive presumption is created when a law irrebuttably presumes that certain facts exist which result in categorizing individuals into a class. The class is subjected to burdens not visited on others, even though in fact the presumption may be incorrect as applied to a particular individual whom the presumption places in the class. The denial of the opportunity to challenge the presumption in regard to fundamental liberty or property interests has generally been held to violate due process. *Cleveland Board of Education v. LaFleur* (1974).

Congressional Immunity Art. I, § 6, the Speech and Debate Clause, provides absolute immunity for "legislative acts," *i.e.*, matters which are an integral part of the communicative and deliberative process. Congressional aides can share in this constitutional immunity.

Contemporary Community Standards, Obscenity, Definition of In applying the standards relating to pruriency and patent offensiveness as aspects of the definition of what is obscene, *i.e.*, unprotected expression under the First Amendment, the courts need not seek to apply a "national community standard" but may instruct the jury without further specification.

Content Control Government regulation based on the viewpoint or subject matter of speech. Content-based control is considered a form of regulation which requires substantial justification under the First Amendment. When a regulation is based on the content of the speech, *e.g.*, a harm associated with the message, government must establish that the regulation is necessary to a compelling government interest.

Content–Neutral Regulation If a law is justified without reference to the content of speech, the courts apply a less-demanding form of balancing (intermediate scrutiny), e.g., the law must be "narrowly tailored to serve a significant government interest and leave open ample alternative channels of communication" or the *O'Brien* test. Government need not use the least burdensome means, if the means are direct and effective.

Cooley Doctrine In determining whether a state regulation is valid under the dormant Commerce Clause, the Cooley Doctrine focuses on the subject of the regulation. When the subject is national, requiring uniformity of regulation, the states may not regulate. Today, the doctrine is generally used as part of the balancing of national and local interests to determine if the state regulation is an undue burden on interstate commerce.

Cumulative Effects Doctrine Even though the impact of a particular transaction on interstate commerce may be trivial in itself, it still may be sufficient to be covered under federal regulation pursuant to the Commerce Clause, when it is considered that the impact of the transaction, taken together with many others similarly situated, is far from trivial. Hence, taken overall, the transaction can be seen to substantially affect interstate commerce. *Wickard v. Filburn* (1942).

D

Defamation (Private Persons) The private figure plaintiff has not voluntarily sought the public spotlight on matters of public concern and generally lacks access to the media for self-defense. "[S]o long as they do not impose liability without fault, the states may define for themselves the appropriate standard of liability for a publisher or broadcaster of defamatory falsehood injurious to a private individual." *Gertz v. Robert Welch, Inc.* (1974). In addition to fault, the private figure plaintiff must prove actual damages and falsity. If the defamation involves a matter of purely private concern, the private figure plaintiff can recover presumed and punitive damages, even absent actual malice. *Dun & Bradstreet, Inc. v. Greenmoss Builders, Inc.* (1985).

Defamation (Public Officials and Public Figures) "The constitutional guarantees (of freedom of speech and press) require, we think, a federal rule that prohibits a public official from recovering damages for a defamatory falsehood relating to his official conduct unless he proves that the statement was made with 'actual malice'—that is, with knowledge that it was false or not." Actual malice, which must be established by clear and convincing evidence, also includes reckless disregard of truth or falsity. *New York Times Co. v. Sullivan* (1964). The actual malice requirement also applies to public figures. Whether he is a public official, public figure, or private person, the plaintiff also has the burden of proving falsity, at least for defamation involving matters of public concern. (See *Public Figure*)

De Jure and De Facto Segregation De Jure segregation is racial separation created by purposeful, government action. De Jure segregation in the public school is inherently unequal and violative of equal protection. *Brown v. Board of Educ.* (1954). This principle has been extended to public facilities such as beaches and parks. A de jure segregated school system is under an affirmative duty to desegregate.

De Facto segregation is not intentionally created by government action. It is the product of factors such as housing patterns and migration. The Court has held that de facto segregation does not violate equal protection.

Delegation of Legislative Powers Congress can delegate legislative powers to the Executive or to independent agencies if it formulates reasonable standards to guide the exercise of the delegated powers. The courts today defer to the congressional judgment of reasonableness.

Deprivation (Procedural Due Process) When an individual is injured by a negligent rather than a deliberate act, no "deprivation" requiring procedural due process protection arises. The lack of due care by government officials does not constitute the type of abusive treatment that the Due Process Clause was designed to protect against. *Davidson v. Cannon* (1986); *Daniels v. Williams* (1986).

Diluting the Franchise Government regulations limiting the effectiveness of the vote of particular classes may significantly burden equality of access to the franchise in violation of the Equal Protection Clause. The franchise is diluted by unreasonable state limits on access to the ballot of minority parties and independents or by legislative reapportionment which denies the equal protection right to vote on a one person-one vote basis, *Reynolds v. Sims* (1967), or by a political gerrymander *Davis v. Bandemer* (1986).

Direct v. Indirect Burden (Free Exercise) A direct burden on the free exercise of religion results when government requires an individual to engage in practices contrary to central tenets of his or her religion. Only a compelling government interest justifies such a significant burden on free exercise. The free exercise of religion is severely burdened where a state prosecutes Amish church members for refusing to send their children to school as required by law. *Wisconsin v. Yoder* (1972).

An indirect burden on the free exercise of religion results when government places an incidental burden on religious observance. The Court has held that when a state regulates conduct by enacting Blue Laws, the purpose of which is to advance the secular goal of a uniform day of rest, the statute is valid despite its indirect burden on religious observance unless the state may accomplish its purpose by less restrictive means. *Braunfeld v. Brown* (1961). In an apparent repudiation of the direct-indirect burden test, the Court has usually reviewed indirect burdens under the same strict scrutiny standards used for direct burdens. *Sherbert v. Verner* (1963); *Frazee v. Illinois Dep't. of Emp. Sec.* (1989). However, the Court has held that a law that is generally applicable and religion-neutral, which imposes only incidental burdens on a particular religion, will not be reviewed by strict scrutiny. *Employment Div., Dept. of Human Resources of Oregon v. Smith* (1990).

Discrimination (Interstate Commerce) State laws which discriminate against out-of-state interests in favor of local interests are likely to be held violative of the negative implications of the Dormant Commerce Clause. "The statute must serve a legitimate local purpose and the purpose must be one that cannot be served as well by available nondiscriminatory means." *Maine v. Taylor* (1986). Discriminatory laws violate the historic purpose of the Commerce Clause and its common market philosophy. Out-of-state interests lack political power to protect themselves in the legislature of the regulating state.

Division of Powers Federalism reflects the values of diversity while preserving unity. Governmental powers in the United States are allocated between the national government and the states. Governmental powers not delegated to the national government are, under the Tenth Amendment, reserved to the States, or to the people. Today, the Tenth Amendment is not a meaningful limit on the national power to regulate private action and provides only a limited check on Congress' power to regulate the states through generally applicable laws. See *Garcia v. SAMTA* (1985). But the Tenth Amendment is used to invalidate federal laws applicable to the states (not private parties), requiring them to regulate or to enforce federal programs. See *New York v. United States* (1992); *Printz v. United States* (1997).

Dormant Commerce Clause Even if Congress has not legislated, the Dormant Commerce Clause limits the ability of states to regulate interstate commerce. States may not discriminate against interstate commerce unless the law is narrowly tailored to legitimate state interests and nondiscriminatory alternatives are not available. Even a nondiscriminatory law may violate the Dormant Commerce Clause if it unreasonably burdens interstate commerce. Whether the burden is excessive is determined by balancing the competing interests. *Pike v. Bruce Church, Inc.* (1970) See *Balance of Interests Test, Interstate Commerce; Discrimination (Interstate Commerce)*.

Due Process (Procedural) The guarantee of procedural fairness which flows from both the Fifth and Fourteenth Amendment Due Process Clauses. For the guarantees of procedural due process to apply, it must first be shown that a deprivation of a significant life, liberty, or property interest has occurred. This is necessary to bring the Due Process Clause into play. Minimal procedural due process requires notice and hearing. Procedures which due process requires beyond that minimum must be determined by a balancing analysis based on the specific factual context.

Due Process (Economic Substantive) The idea that certain notions of substantive social policy, such as freedom of contract or the right to enjoy property without any interference by government regulation, should be read into the Due Process Clause of the Fourteenth Amendment, particularly the words "liberty" and "property" in that clause. Thus, freedom of contract was declared to be part of the liberty of the individual protected by the Due Process Clause of the Fourteenth Amendment. Today, social and economic regulation which does not interfere with specific fundamental rights is not accorded close scrutiny by the courts. State and federal regulation in the economic area is, therefore, routinely upheld as long as there is any rational basis for the legislation in question. (See *Fundamental Rights*).

Durational Residency Requirements While residency requirements for voting do not violate equal protection, durational residency requirements do significantly burden the exercise of the franchise and impair the fundamental personal right to travel. A one year state residency requirement as a precondition for voting has been held to be an unconstitutional denial of equal protection. *Dunn v. Blumstein* (1972).

E

Editorial Autonomy (First Amendment) The exercise of editorial judgment in the print media, unlike the situation in broadcasting media, may not be scrutinized by government. Editorial autonomy in the print media is protected by the First Amendment. *Miami Herald Publishing Co. v. Tornillo* (1974). The courts are presently working out the extent to which editorial autonomy applies to other media.

Eleventh Amendment The Amendment, as interpreted, provides that the judicial power does not extend to suits against a state or its agencies by citizens of another state or a foreign country or by its own citizens. However, the Amendment does not bar suit in federal court against local governments, where the state has waived immunity, where a state official is sued in his or her individual capacity or where Congress has authorized suit pursuant to a proper use of its enforcement powers under the Fourteenth Amendment, § 5. But the courts have been increasingly restrictive on defining the scope of Congress' enforcement powers in abrogating state sovereign immunity.

Entwinement An ostensibly private organization may be charged with a public character and be judged by constitutional standards when it is significantly entwined with government, *e.g.*, public officials actively involved in the private organization or the organization is actively involved in enforcing rules or implementing activities of public entities. *Brentwood Academy v. Tennessee Secondary School Athletic Association* (2001).

Equal Protection (Administrative or Enforcement Discrimination) Although a law is nondiscriminatory on its face, if it is applied and administered by public authority unfairly so as to illegally discriminate between persons in similar circumstances, equal protection is nonetheless still violated. *Yick Wo v. Hopkins* (1886).

Equal Protection (Discriminatory Purpose and Effect) While discriminatory effect may be evidence of discriminatory purpose, it does not in itself trigger review beyond the rational basis test. In order to authorize the judicial departure from the traditional equal protection standard of review, a governmental purpose to discriminate must be shown.

Equal Protection (Federal) There is no specific textual guarantee of equal protection vis-a-vis the federal government in the Constitution. However, the federal government has been held to be bound by "equal protection" through an interpretation of the Due Process Clause of the Fifth Amendment. *Bolling v. Sharpe* (1954).

Equal Protection (Traditional) Classifications which do not intentionally discriminate on the basis of a suspect or quasi-suspect trait or significantly burden fundamental rights are reviewed under traditional equal protection standards. Usually the classification will be upheld if it is rationally related to a legitimate government interest. The burden is on the challenging party. Over- and under-inclusion is not fatal. The Court has occasionally employed a more searching review demanding a greater showing of justification for the classification.

Establishment Clause, Test for Violation of The Establishment Clause has been interpreted to mean that the government may not aid one religion, may not prefer one religion over another, and may not aid religion in general. For government action to survive a constitutional attack under the Establishment Clause, three criteria must be met: (1) The government action must have a secular legislative purpose; (2) the primary effect of the government action must be one that neither advances nor inhibits religion; and (3) the government action must not foster an excessive government entanglement with religion. *Lemon v. Kurtzman* (1971). Increasingly, the entanglement element of *Lemon* has been treated as part of the inquiry into effects. In interpreting the effects element, the Court has asked whether the law or activity involves a message of endorsing religion. See *Agostini v. Felton* (1997).

Executive Agreements Executive Agreements are agreements entered into by the Executive with foreign powers. They do not require Senate concurrence. Executive Agreements prevail over contrary state law. Even though there is no express constitutional authority for such agreements, their constitutional validity has been long established. *United States v. Belmont* (1937).

Executive Immunity The President of the United States enjoys absolute immunity from civil damages for actions while in office within the "outside perimeters" of his official responsibilities. He does not enjoy immunity from civil actions for conduct prior to assuming office. *Clinton v. Jones* (1997). Lower executive officials enjoy only a qualified immunity. They are liable for violations of clearly established rights knowable to a reasonable person.

Executive Impoundment The President impounds funds when he withholds or delays the expenditure of congressionally appropriated funds. Whether this is a constitutional exercise of the executive power to execute the laws (*e.g.* budget limits) or in an intrusion on the legislative power to make the laws, has not been finally decided.

Executive Privilege The Court has recognized executive privilege regarding confidential domestic matters. A claim of privilege is presumptively valid, imposing a heavy burden of justification on the party seeking disclosure. Courts are the final arbiter of this domestic privilege which takes its life from the separation of powers doctrine. Executive privilege is designed to protect the expectations of a President in the confidentiality of his conversations and correspondence. The President and those who work with him in the executive branch must be able freely to explore policy alternatives. The Court reasoned that this would be impossible unless the privacy of executive deliberations were at least presumptively protected. *United States v. Nixon* (1974).

Executive Removal Power Quasi-legislative and quasi-judicial officers can be removed only for cause and only by the processes indicated in the legislation creating the office. The President has greater freedom to remove purely executive officials. But congressional restrictions on such removal may be constitutional if they do not impede the President's constitutional duties. *Morrison v. Olson* (1988). Congress violates separation of powers by vesting executive functions in officials subject to its power of removal. *Bowsher v. Synar* (1986).

Ex Post Facto Law This is a specific limitation on federal and state government, found in Art. I, § 9, cl. 3, and Art. I, § 10, cl. 1, which prohibits the enactment of retroactive criminal legislation that significantly disadvantages the offender. It should be remembered that the *ex post facto* law prohibition does not apply to civil legislation.

F

False Light Privacy Where a privacy action is brought against the media because a report has been published that is false, the privacy plaintiff will be required to show, if the report was newsworthy, that the publication was made with actual malice. *Time, Inc. v. Hill* (1967).

Fighting Words "There are certain well-defined and narrowly limited classes of speech, the prevention and punishment of which have never been thought to raise any (First Amendment) problem. These include 'fighting' words—those which by their very utterance inflict injury or tend to incite an immediate breach of the peace." *Chaplinsky v. New Hampshire* (1942). Words which have a direct tendency to cause acts of violence by the person to whom, individually, the remarks are addressed may be punished by government under carefully drawn statutes not susceptible of application to protected expression. It had been held that such verbal assaults are not part of "the freedom of speech." But content-based discrimination among fighting words is subject to strict scrutiny.

Fourteenth Amendment, § 5, Enforcement Powers In *Katzenbach v. Morgan* (1966), the Court held that the language of § 5 of the Fourteenth Amendment ("The Congress shall have power to enforce, by appropriate legislation, the provisions of this article") gives to Congress "the same broad powers expressed in the Necessary and Proper Clause, Art. I, § 8, cl. 18." Laws which deter or remedy constitutional violations are constitutional even if they prohibit conduct which is itself constitutional or intrude into areas traditionally reserved to the states. There must be a congruence and a proportionality between the injury to be prevented or remedied and the means adopted. The enforcement power does not include the power to define the substantive right. *City of Boerne v. Flores* (1997).

Free Exercise, Test for Violation of If government undertakes to burden persons because of their religious beliefs, there is a violation of the Free Exercise Clause. Coercion of religious belief is the heart of the free exercise claim. Today, courts examine the severity of the alleged governmental burden on the individual religious beliefs. If the burden is significant and direct, government usually will be required to demonstrate a compelling or overriding public interest. Here, as elsewhere in First Amendment law, the availability of less burdensome alternatives to realize the governmental interest will be considered. However, if the law is a generally applicable, religion-neutral law, which only incidentally burdens religious freedom, strict scrutiny is not used even if the burden is significant. *Employment Div., Dept. of Human Resources of Oregon v. Smith* (1990). Legislation to overturn *Smith* in reviewing state action was held unconstitutional in *City of Boerne v. Flores* (1997).

Fundamental Rights Challenged legislation that significantly burdens a "fundamental right" (examples include First Amendment rights, privacy, and the right to travel interstate) will be reviewed under a stricter standard of review. A law will be held violative of the Due Process Clause if it is not closely tailored to promote a compelling or overriding interest of government. A similar principle applies under Equal Protection law.

G

Gender Classifications (Standard of Review) The Court applies an intermediate standard of review for gender classifications. This standard of review is arguably not as severe as the strict scrutiny standard of review, which is used in racial discrimination cases. However, it is more difficult for the state to meet than the traditional equal protection-rational basis standard of review. Under the intermediate standard of review, purposeful gender classifications "must serve important governmental objectives and must be substantially related to achievement of those objectives." *Craig v. Boren* (1976). Although such laws are subject to "particularly careful scrutiny," this standard of review is not as exacting as strict scrutiny.

Group Litigation (First Amendment) Litigation engaged in by groups to further organizational goals is viewed as expressive and associational conduct entitled to First Amendment protection. Government may regulate group litigation and legal services only for substantial reasons and with specificity. *In re Primus* (1978).

I

Illegitimacy Classifications (Standard of Review) The Court appears to use an intermediate standard of review for illegitimacy classifications. For classifications directed against illegitimates to be upheld, the state must usually show that the classification is substantially related to an important government interest. Although illegitimacy classifications have many of the characteristics of suspectness, *i.e.,* it is a status beyond the control of the child, there is a history of pervasive discrimination, and illegitimates are a politically insular minority, the Court has as yet declined to treat illegitimacy classifications as suspect classifications warranting the application of the strict scrutiny standard of review.

Incorporation The Court has held that some, but not all, of the provisions of the Bill of Rights are incorporated by the guarantee of liberty in the Due Process Clause of the Fourteenth Amendment and thus are applicable against the states. But this is not the limit of the rights guaranteed by Due Process liberty. In accepting this process of "Selective Incorporation," the Court has rejected the argument that the Due Process Clause incorporates all of the Bill of Rights, *i.e.,* "Total Incorporation."

Intergovernmental Immunities (In General) Under the Supremacy Clause (Art. VI), the states may not tax or regulate the national government or its instrumentalities. "[T]he power to tax involves the power to destroy * * * "*McCulloch v. Maryland* (1819). Nor may the state discriminate against the federal government and those dealing with the federal government. Nondiscriminatory federal taxes on the states, which are reasonable in light of the benefits conferred on the state, are constitutional.

Intergovernmental Immunities (Federal Regulation of States) In *National League of Cities v. Usery* (1976) the doctrine of state sovereignty, reflected in the Tenth Amendment, was interpreted to hold that federal regulations should not displace state choices involving the integral operations of state governments thereby interfering with their traditional governmental functions. *National League* was overruled in *Garcia v. San Antonio Metropolitan Transit Auth.* (1985). The test for identifying traditional functions was said to be unworkable. It was deemed inappropriate for unelected federal judges to determine what functions are traditional or integral to state sovereignty. Federalist values are best protected by the political process. But Congress cannot order a state to regulate (*New York v. United States* (1992)) or to enforce federal standards. *Printz v. United States* (1997).

Intermediate Review A middle tier form of review between deferential rationality review and demanding strict scrutiny. The law must be substantially related to an important or significant government interest but the government need not use the least restrictive means.

Interpretivism/Non–Interpretivism These two approaches reflect different views on how Courts should make constitutional decisions. Interpretivism emphasizes reliance on the Constitution itself as the basic norm for decision. Non–Interpretivism looks both at the Constitution and outside the document itself for values to guide the determination of constitutional questions.

J

Joint Action (State Action) If a private individual is engaged in joint activity with state officials, state action is established. A private individual acts under color of law if he is a willful participant in a joint activity with the state or its agents. *United States v. Price* (1966).

Journalist Privilege The idea that journalists should have a privilege, either qualified or absolute, to refuse to give evidence is based on the theory that such disclosures would dry up their news sources and thus work to the detriment of First Amendment interests. The First Amendment does not afford journalists the privilege, qualified or absolute, to refuse to give evidence to a grand jury, at least where the grand jury is undertaking a good-faith law enforcement effort.

Branzburg v. Hayes (1972). However, lower courts have increasingly recognized a qualified privilege, especially in civil cases where the journalist is not a litigant.

Judicial Review "[T]he particular phraseology of the Constitution of the United States confirms and strengthens the principle, supposed to be essential to all written constitutions, that a law repugnant to the Constitution is void." *Marbury v. Madison* (1803). The power of constitutional review by the courts is also extended to executive and judicial acts, national and state. "The judicial power shall extend to all Cases, in Law and Equity, arising under this Constitution, the Laws of the United States, and Treaties made, or which shall be made, under their Authority; * * * "U.S. Constitution, Art. III, § 2.

Just Compensation The Fifth Amendment requires the payment of just compensation when private property is taken by government for public use. A similar limitation is applicable to the states as part of Fourteenth Amendment Due Process. Just compensation is measured by fair market value.

Justiciability The Court has used justiciability to refer both to case and controversy jurisdictional limitations on judicial power and prudential limitations on judicial power. It is used to refer to considerations of judicial self-restraint relating to the proper role of the federal courts in our constitutional system, *i.e.,* the ability of the federal courts to define duties and rights and fashion remedies.

L

Legislative Investigations (First Amendment Limitations) When an investigation intrudes on First Amendment rights of speech and association, government must show a substantial relation between the information sought and a subject of overriding and compelling government interest. *Gibson v. Florida Legislative Investigation Comm.* (1963).

Legislative Veto Congress delegates authority to the Executive but retains power to review and veto the exercise of such authority. In *Immigration & Naturalization Service v. Chadha* (1983), the Court held a one-house veto of executive orders involving deportation violative of the Bicameralism and Presentment Clauses since legislative action was involved.

Legitimization Since Congress has plenary power over interstate commerce, it can legitimize state action which would be unconstitutional under the Dormant Commerce Clause. Where Congress allows a state to regulate an area of interstate commerce, "any action taken by a State within the scope of the congressional authorization is rendered invulnerable to Commerce Clause challenge." *Western*

& Southern Life Ins. Co. v. State Bd. of Equalization (1981). Thus, Congress can legitimize a discriminatory state tax on out-of-state companies in interstate commerce. *Prudential Ins. Co. v. Benjamin* (1946).

Liberty Interest (Procedural Due Process) The broad concept of liberty is not limited to conditions of confinement such as imprisonment. Liberty also includes fundamental constitutional rights such as the freedom of choice to marry and raise a family. Liberty interests also include values which have special importance in American society. Reputation may be a liberty interest but the Court has held that injury to reputation alone, without any more tangible interest, does not constitute liberty. *Paul v. Davis* (1976). The Due Process Clause mandates that no person's liberty interest may be deprived without fair processes.

Line Item Veto. The Line Item Veto Act authorized the President to cancel certain spending provisions after he signed an act into law. The cancelled provisions would then be submitted to Congress for reconsideration. The Act was held violative of the Presentment Clause of Art. I, § 7, which provides that a measure becomes law only after passage by both houses, followed by presidential approval or disapproval of the measure. The presidential cancellation had the effect of changing the law by a partial repeal which is inconsistent with the veto power. *Clinton v. City of New York* (1998).

M

Marketplace of Ideas Theory The principle that it is the responsibility of government not to limit or restrain dialogue in the marketplace of ideas. The theory, Darwinian in essence, is that if government does not intrude, free play will be given to the struggle of ideas and those with the greatest social value will triumph. "[T]he best test of truth is the power of the thought to get itself accepted in the competition of the market." *Abrams v. United States* (1919).

Market Participant (Interstate Commerce) When the state acts as a participant in the marketplace rather than as a regulator of the market, the Dormant Commerce Clause Doctrine does not apply. Like any private actor, the Dormant Commerce Clause imposes no limitation. The state may choose those with whom it will deal.

The more that state action affects parties who are not in any contractual relation with the state, *i.e.*, the "ripple effect" of state contractual activity, the more likely it is that the state will be treated as a regulator.

Mootness Judicial review will be denied under the "mootness" doctrine if a judicial determination is no longer necessary to compel the result originally sought. Exceptions to this doctrine include: (1) cases which are capable of repetition, yet evading review; (2) the continued existence of collateral consequences; (3) voluntary cessation of illegal actions where there is a reasonable likelihood they will reoccur.

N

Necessary and Proper Clause Art. I, § 8, states: "The Congress shall have Power * * * To make all Laws which shall be necessary and proper for carrying into Execution the foregoing [enumerated] powers, and all other Powers vested by this Constitution in the Government of the United States." In its historic discussion of implied powers in *McCulloch v. Maryland* (1819), the Court gave the Clause a broad interpretation: "Let the end be legitimate, let it be within the scope of the constitution, and all means which are appropriate, which are plainly adapted to that end, which are not prohibited, but consistent with the letter and spirit of the constitution, are constitutional." If the law is reasonably designed to effectuate an express constitutional power, it is constitutional in the absence of some other constitutional violation.

Negative Commerce Clause See *Dormant Commerce Clause.*

Neutrality The Establishment Clause is not merely a prohibition of a government sponsored religion or simply a command of equal treatment of religion. The basic command for government is neutrality. Challenged government action must have a secular purpose, not have a primary effect that advances or inhibits religion and it must not foster excessive government entanglement with religion. Government must not endorse religion or coerce its exercise.

Newsgathering (Access to Judicial Proceedings) The First Amendment extends some protection to the newsgathering process. Criminal trials may not be closed unless such closure is mandated by a compelling government interest and the closure is narrowly drawn to serve that interest. Absent an overriding interest articulated in trial court findings, the trial of a criminal case must be open to the public. *Richmond Newspapers, Inc. v. Virginia* (1980). The access right also extends to criminal preliminary hearings.

Nonpublic Forum Public property not designated or traditionally considered a public forum for communication constitutes the nonpublic forum. Government regulation of the nonpublic forum need only be viewpoint-neutral and reasonable to be constitutional. Regulation may be based on subject matter and be selective as to speakers given access as long as the government doesn't take sides. *Perry Education Assn. v. Perry Local Educators' Assn.* (1983). (See *Public Forum*).

O

Obscenity "Obscenity is not within the area of constitutionally protected speech or press." *Roth v. United States* (1957). In *Miller v. California* (1973), the Court set forth the modern test: "(a) whether 'the average person, applying contemporary community standards' would find that the work, taken as a whole, appeals to the prurient interest. * * * (b) whether the work depicts or describes, in a patently offensive way, sexual conduct specifically defined by the applicable state law, and (c) whether the work, taken as a whole, lacks serious literary, artistic, political, or scientific value."

Overbreadth A law may be void on its face if it is substantially overbroad in that the law indiscriminately reaches both constitutionally protected and unprotected activity. A statute regulating activity protected under the First Amendment must be precisely drawn so that protected expression is not chilled or suppressed. *Coates v. Cincinnati* (1971).

P

Pardon Power Under Art. II, § 2, the President has the power to grant pardons for offenses against the United States except for impeachment. The power of the President to pardon is plenary, but it is subject, possibly, to constitutional prohibitions.

Penalty (Equal Protection) When a classification significantly burdens the exercise of a fundamental right, the classification ordinarily must withstand strict scrutiny. If the law does not deter, penalize or otherwise significantly burden the exercise of the protected right, the classification must only satisfy the traditional rational basis test. For example, a one year state residency requirement for divorce did not violate the Equal Protection Clause since the state had an important interest in divorce and because of the insignificant burden of the alleged deprivation, *i.e.*, the petitioner was merely delayed. *Sosna v. Iowa* (1975).

Penalty Doctrine (Federal Taxing Power) A tax law which has the facial characteristics of regulation and punishment may be judged as a penalty rather than a tax. As such, it must be justified as an exercise of Congress' regulatory power rather than its fiscal powers. Today the courts will not probe the congressional purpose. If the law is facially revenue-producing, it is likely to be treated as a tax rather than a penalty. A federal tax has not been held to be a penalty for many years.

Pocket Veto The President can pocket veto a bill by not signing it or vetoing it prior to adjournment, or possibly a significant recess.

Police Power States have the power to act reasonably to further the public health, safety, morals and well being. Congress exercises the equivalent of a police power in protecting the channels of interstate commerce or persons or things in interstate commerce.

Political Gerrymanders The deliberate and arbitrary drawing of political district lines for partisan advantage is political gerrymandering. An equal protection challenge to such districting is justiciable. The challenger must prove both intent to discriminate against an identifiable group and an actual discriminatory effect on this group.

Political Question Under the "political question" doctrine, federal courts will not decide certain cases. While holding that reapportionment was not a political question, *Baker v. Carr* (1962) set forth several formulations of what a political question is, including classic, functional and political considerations such as: (1) "a textually demonstrable constitutional commitment of the issue to a coordinate political department"; (2) "the impossibility of deciding [the question] without an initial policy determination of a kind clearly for nonjudicial discretion;" and (3) "the impossibility of a court's undertaking independent resolution without expressing lack of the respect due coordinate branches of government". The political question doctrine reflects the concerns of justiciability and separation of powers. It focuses on the capabilities of the federal courts and their proper role *vis a vis* the Congress and the Executive.

Preemption Under the Supremacy Clause, a federal law or regulation preempts any conflicting state law or regulation. Further, a state law is preempted if it frustrates the full purposes and objectives of Congress. Finally, Congress may occupy a field of regulation. In determining congressional intent, courts look at factors which include: (1) the pervasiveness of the federal regulatory scheme; (2) whether national uniformity necessitates federal occupation of the field; (3) the danger of conflict between the state law and the administration of the federal program.

Prematurity and Abstractness Even if a case is sufficiently ripe to satisfy the Art. III requirement of a case and controversy, the Court may still decline to decide the case on the merits because the issue is premature or the record is too abstract. Such considerations, born of judicial self-restraint, are often included under the term "justiciability."

Presentment Pursuant to, Art. I, §§ 1, 7, legislative action must be presented to the President for approval or veto. Such legislative action must also be enacted by both Houses of Congress for it to become law. *Immigration and Naturalization Service v. Chadha* (1983). See *Bicameralism*.

Prior Restraint Prior restraints are especially burdened under the First Amendment. Government bears a heavy burden of justification when it undertakes to regulate speech or press prior to publication. *Nebraska Press Association v. Stuart* (1976). But a content-neutral prior restraint must only "burden no more speech than necessary to serve a significant government interest." *Madsen v. Women's Health Center* (1994).

Prior Restraint (Civil Obscenity Procedures) "[A] noncriminal process which requires the prior submission of a film to a censor avoids constitutional infirmity only if it takes place under procedural safeguards designed to obviate the dangers of a censorship system. * * * [T]he exhibitor must be assured, by statute or authoritative judicial construction, that the censor will, within a specified brief period, either issue a license or go to court to restrain showing the film." The court must promptly determine whether the material may be suppressed. The censor bears the burden of proof. *Freedman v. Maryland* (1965).

Privacy (Obscenity) "Whatever may be the justifications for other statutes regulating obscenity, we do not think they reach into the privacy of one's own home. If the First Amendment means anything, it means that a State has no business telling a man, sitting alone in his own house, what books he may read or what films he may watch." *Stanley v. Georgia* (1969).

Privacy (Sexual) In reviewing a state criminal statute which proscribed assisting in or counseling in the use of contraceptive devices, the Court recognized a constitutional "right of privacy" by reasoning that "specific guarantees in the Bill of Rights have penumbras." *Griswold v. Connecticut* (1965). This privacy right was extended to protect a woman's right to choose whether to terminate a pregnancy. *Roe v. Wade* (1973). But it does not include homosexual relations even in private. *Bowers v. Hardwick* (1986). The Court in *Planned Parenthood of Southeastern Pennsylvania v. Casey* (1992), did not expressly refer to a right of privacy but did interpret liberty to provide heightened judicial protection for abortion, "involving the most intimate and personal choices a person may make in a lifetime, choices central to personal dignity and autonomy."

Private Action (Thirteenth Amendment) The Thirteenth Amendment's prohibition against slavery or involuntary servitude encompasses private as well as governmental action.

Privileges and Immunities (Article IV) Absent substantial justification, the state is required to treat alike all citizens, resident and non-resident, with respect to those privileges and immunities which are fundamental to the nation as a single entity. Nonresidents must be shown to be a particular source of a problem and the law must bear a substantial relation to eradication of the problem.

Privileges and Immunities Clause (Fourteenth Amendment) This clause does not incorporate any of the Bill of Rights nor does it protect all civil rights of individual citizens against state action. Instead, it only protects those rights peculiar to federal citizenship. *Slaughterhouse Cases* (1873).

Property Interest (Procedural Due Process) A property interest requires a legal entitlement created by the state. Property is not limited to interests in realty or personalty, but the interest must be recognized by the state, *e.g.*, wages, welfare benefits, a driver's license. If the state seeks to deprive a person of a property interest, procedural due process must be accorded.

Public Benefit (Establishment Clause) Government action in the form of busing and books which provides some incidental aid to religion constitutes public benefits. If the state acts only for the secular purpose of serving the public welfare and well-being, the fact that religion is incidentally benefitted does not constitute an impermissible establishment of religion. *Everson v. Board of Educ.* (1947).

Public Figure, definition of Public figures, for purposes of the application of the *New York Times v. Sullivan—Gertz v. Welch* doctrines, have been defined into two categories as follows:

All-purpose public figure—a person who has achieved such pervasive fame or notoriety that he is deemed to be a public figure for all purposes and in all contexts. By universal acclamation, Johnny Carson falls in this category.

Limited-purpose (vortex) public figure—a person who would not otherwise be a public figure but who has become so for a particular range of issues because he has voluntarily injected himself into the vortex of a public controversy in order to influence its outcome. *Gertz v. Robert Welch, Inc.* (1974).

Public Forum Places like streets and parks, which have historically been associated with expressive activity, constitute the traditional public forum. *Hague v. CIO* (1939). The First Amendment bars government from restricting all communicative activity in natural and proper places for disseminating information. *Schneider v. New Jersey* (1939). The public forum has been expanded to include such property as the government may designate as a public forum (the limited or designated public forum). Government may impose content based regulation in the public forum only if it satisfies strict scrutiny or the regulation involves low value speech. Subject matter regulation of speech in a designated public forum must be consistent with the purposes for which the limited forum was created. Government may regulate the time, place and manner of speech in the public forum if the regulation is content-neutral, is narrowly tailored to serve a significant government interest and leaves open alternative channels of communication. *Perry Education Assn. v. Perry Local Educators Assn.* (1983). (See *Nonpublic Forum*).

Public Function (State Action) Some activities are so public in character that the government will not be allowed to disclaim responsibility even though the activity is entirely private in terms of ownership. To qualify as a public function, the activity must be traditionally and exclusively associated with sovereignty.

Public Records, First Amendment Protection For The press has a right to publish an accurate report of facts obtained from public court proceedings or from public court records. However, the actual malice test of *New York Times v. Sullivan* will not shield a defendant if the defamation was based on judicial records, even though public, if they were inaccurate. *Time, Inc. v. Firestone* (1976).

R

Rational Basis Review. A minimal level of judicial review in which the burden is on the challenging party to establish that the law is not rationally related to a permissible government interest. Any state of facts that would further a conceivable government interest will suffice. The court defers to the legislative judgment.

Released Time (Freedom of Religion) While released time for religious education is permissible, it violates the First Amendment to conduct the classes within the schools. Released time for religious instruction within the public schools provides religion so invaluable an aid that it constitutes a violation of the Establishment Clause. *McCollum v. Board of Education* (1948).

Religion, Meaning of The Court has not, thus far, provided any consistent definition of the meaning of "religion" in the First Amendment. The concept is not limited to theistic beliefs and practices. It protects sincere and meaningful beliefs which occupy a place in the life of the person claiming it parallel to that filled by more traditional notions of religious belief and practice.

Right to Assemble and Petition The First Amendment guarantees the right of the people to assemble peaceably and to petition the government for redress on grievances. This guarantee is applicable to the states through the Due Process Clause of the Fourteenth Amendment.

Right to Refuse Treatment The Court has recognized a significant liberty interest in avoiding the unwanted administration of medical treatment. This liberty interest includes the refusal of life supporting treatment. But, through a balancing test, the Court held that a state may require that the individual's intent to terminate such treatment be established by clear and convincing evidence. *Cruzan v. Director, Mo. Dept. of Health* (1990). The Court unanimously held that liberty does not include a right to assisted suicide. *Washington v. Glucksberg* (1997).

Ripeness Art. III "case and controversy" requires that there be an immediate injury or a threat of imminent injury for a case to be timely. The Court will consider (1) the hardship to the plaintiffs of delay; (2) the potential for inappropriate judicial interference with administrative action; and (3) whether courts would benefit from further factual development of the issues.

S

Selective Incorporation The theory that some, but not all, of the provisions of the Bill of Rights are incorporated by the Due Process Clause of the Fourteenth Amendment and are thus made applicable to the states.

Separate but Equal Doctrine In *Brown v. Board of Education* (Brown I) (1954), the Court stated that "segregation of children in public schools solely on the basis of race, even though the physical facilities and other 'tangible' factors may be equal, deprive(s) the children of the minority group of equal educational opportunities" in violation of the equal protection guarantee of the Fourteenth Amendment.

Separation of Powers Principles governing the allocation of powers among the three coordinate branches of the national government. When powers come into conflict, the courts consider whether one Branch is invading the constitutional prerogatives of another Branch or is usurping powers which are properly shared. Formalists tend to focus on the text of the Constitution and stress the formal separation of governmental functions. Functionalists stress the principle of checks and balances and the interaction of institutions sharing government powers.

Sexual Persuasion. Thus far, classification on the basis of sexual orientation has not been treated as a suspect or quasi-suspect classification requiring heightened equal protection review. However, a law making it more difficult for gays and lesbians as a class to seek aid from the government and which is so broad and discontinuous with the claimed government interests as to suggest animus towards the class has been held to be irrational and violative of equal protection. *Romer v. Evans* (1996).

Spending Power Congress has power to spend, but not directly regulate, for the general welfare. General welfare objectives are not limited to the specifics of Art.

I, § 8, but include all matters of national concern. Congress can attach reasonable conditions to its grants of money but it must be clear that they are conditions and not simply policy statements.

Standing Art. III standing has two requirements, both of which must be met if standing is to be present in litigation before an Art. III court. First, the litigant must show injury in fact; second, he must show that he will personally benefit from the required judicial relief and that but for the action of the defendant, the injury in fact of which he complains would not occur (*i.e.*, causation). This includes both a requirement that the injury is "fairly traceable" to the government act being challenged and that the injury is "redressable" if the court grants relief.

Standing (Federal Taxpayers) The barrier to taxpayer suits was lowered in a challenge by taxpayers to aid to religious schools under a federal statute. In *Flast v. Cohen* (1968), the Court stated, "A taxpayer may or may not have the requisite personal stake in the outcome, depending upon the circumstances of the particular case. * * * First, the taxpayer must establish a logical link between (taxpayer) status and the type of legislative enactment attacked. * * * Secondly, the taxpayer must establish a nexus between the status and the precise nature of the constitutional infringement alleged." A federal taxpayer must be challenging on the basis of a specific limitation on Congress' Taxing and Spending Power. Only the Establishment Clause has been held to be a specific limitation on the Taxing and Spending Power.

Standing (Third Party Rights) While a party generally does not have "standing" to assert the rights of a third party, a court may make an exception after weighing: (1) the importance of the relationship between the complainant and the third party; (2) the third party's ability to vindicate its own rights; and (3) the risk that third party rights will be diluted if standing to the complainant is not allowed. Associations have standing to litigate rights of members if "(a) members would otherwise have standing to sue in their own right; (b) the interests it seeks to protect are germane to the organization's purpose; (c) neither the claim-asserted nor the relief requested requires the participation of individual members in the law suit." *Hunt v. Washington State Apple Advertising Comm'n* (1977).

State Action Most constitutional guarantees are not violated by private action. Only significant government involvement, making the government responsible for the challenged acts, will constitute state action. The Court requires a close nexus between the government and the private actions being challenged.

State Taxation of Interstate Commerce States may tax interstate commerce if the tax reasonably reflects the benefits derived from the taxing state, the tax is not discriminatory, the taxpayer has minimal local contacts with the taxing state and the tax is fairly apportioned to avoid multiple burdens. *Complete Auto Transit, Inc. v. Brady* (1977).

Stream of Commerce In Commerce Clause analysis, local activities which are part of the current or stream of interstate commerce are considered part of the interstate movement. Congress can regulate such local incidents directly under its commerce power.

Strict Scrutiny. A demanding form of judicial review in which the burden is on the government to prove that the law is necessary to a compelling public interest. Government must use less restrictive means. The law is presumptively invalid. Such review is sometimes said to be "strict in theory, fatal in fact."

Supremacy Clause Article VI provides that "[t]his Constitution, and the Laws of the United States which shall be made in Pursuance thereof * * * shall be the Supreme Law of the Land * * *." State laws which conflict with federal law, impede federal objectives, or which are preempted, yield to the federal law.

Suspect Classifications The Court will employ the "strict scrutiny" standard under the Equal Protection Clause in determining the legitimacy of classifications that are based upon a trait which itself seems to contravene established constitutional principles so that any purposeful use of the classification may be deemed "suspect." Examples include race, national origin and alienage (with exceptions). While gender and illegitimacy are not suspect classifications, they are reviewed under an intermediate standard—the classification must be substantially related to an important government interest. Other classifying traits are reviewed under the rationality standard.

Symbiotic Relationship When the action of government and private actors is so intertwined as to constitute a "symbiotic relationship," their combined activities will be viewed by the courts as constituting state involvement sufficient to invoke the "state action" doctrine and thereby subject the private actor, in such circumstances, to constitutional obligation. *Burton v. Wilmington Parking Authority* (1961).

Symbolic Speech (Expressive Conduct) The Court has rejected both the view that there is no First Amendment protection if expression involves conduct and the idea that a "limitless variety of conduct can be labeled 'speech' whenever the person engaging in the conduct intends thereby to express an idea." Conduct is deemed symbolic speech when all the factual circumstances indicate that the actor intends to communicate and the audience can understand the communication. It is then necessary to determine if the law regulating the symbolic speech is constitutional under the First Amendment. "When 'speech' and 'nonspeech' elements are combined in the same course of conduct, a sufficiently important government interest in regulating the nonspeech element can justify incidental limitations on First Amendment freedoms." *United States v. O'Brien* (1968).

T

Takings Clause When government "takes" property for public use, the Fifth and Fourteenth Amendment require that just compensation be given. Courts distinguish condemnation and physical takings as well as categorical (per se) takings where the government deprives an owner of all economically valuable use of his property from regulatory takings. In determining whether a law constitutes a taking requiring just compensation or a regulation which does not, the courts consider the law's economic impact, investment expectations, and the character of the government action. A temporary moratorium on use of one's land, even of long duration, is not a categorical taking and is subject to the ad hoc balancing inquiry. *Tahoe Sierra Preservation Council Inc. v. Tahoe Regional Planning Agency* (2002).

Tax Exemptions Tax exemptions for places of religious worship are constitutional even though, indirectly, they provide support for religion. Tax exemption for religious institutions constitutes a historically-acceptable "benevolent neutrality" on the part of government because they involve, in fact, less government entanglement with religion than would tax assessments, liens, and foreclosures. *Walz v. Tax Commission* (1970).

Taxing Power Congress has the fiscal power to raise monies through taxes. But a regulatory "penalty" may not be imposed under the guise of raising revenue. If a law is revenue producing on its face, it is likely to be treated as a tax, not a penalty. *United States v. Kahriger* (1953).

Total Incorporation The idea that the Due Process Clause incorporates each of the Bill of Rights and makes them applicable against the states. The Court has never accepted the total incorporation theory. *Adamson v. California* (1947).

Travel (Interstate Migration) The right to interstate travel or interstate migration is protected under the Constitution. However, it does not have a specific constitutional locus. At various times, it has been said to be protected by the Commerce Clause, the Privileges and Immunities Clause of the Fourteenth Amendment, and the Interstate Privileges and Immunities Clause of Art. IV, § 2. At other times, it is referred to as a national right implicit in the federal Union established by the Constitution.

Tuition Aid (Establishment Clause) Tuition aid given to citizens generally is more likely to be upheld than aid given only to citizens involved with religious institutions. A state law allowing taxpayers to deduct tuition expenses is not violative of the Establishment Clause where its purpose is to promote a well-educated citizenry and where the deduction is available on a neutral basis to parents of all students. *Mueller v. Allen* (1983).

U

Unconstitutional Conditions, Doctrine of Government may not unconstitutionally condition the receipt of government benefits on the surrender of constitutional rights such as First Amendment rights.

Undue Burden A term used in Dormant Commerce Clause analysis to refer to the determination that, after a balancing of the interests, the state interests are insufficient to justify the burden on interstate commerce. See *Dormant Commerce Clause*.

V

Vagueness Doctrine A statute is void for vagueness if it is not drawn with sufficient clarity and definiteness to inform persons of the course of conduct they must follow to avoid the ban of the statute. The First Amendment requires special clarity so that protected expression will not be chilled or suppressed. Statutes which are void for vagueness are fundamentally unfair thus violating the due process guarantee as well.

Vestiture Clause Art. II, § 1, vests the Executive Power in the President. It may be a separate source of power, a reference to other Art. II powers, or a reference to the Framer's choice of a single Executive.

Viewpoint Control Government regulation which endorses a particular belief or opinion over competing positions is viewpoint-based. It is considered a form of censorship which is heavily burdened under the First Amendment. The courts will sustain such regulation "only if the government can show that the regulation is a precisely drawn means of serving a compelling state interest." *Consolidated Edison Co. of New York v. Public Service Comm'n. of New York* (1980).

Voting Practices, Racially Discriminatory in Effect (Congressional Power to Legislate Against Pursuant to § 2 of the Fifteenth Amendment) Under § 2, any legislation which Congress could rationally conclude is appropriate to effectuate the constitutional prohibition against racial discrimination in voting is constitutional. Even though only purposeful racial discrimination in voting violates the Fifteenth Amendment, Congress, under § 2 of that Amendment, may outlaw voting practices that are discriminatory in effect. While such practices do not violate § 1 of the Amendment, prohibitions against practices having a discriminatory racial effect on voting are "appropriate" and "reasonable" means of enforcing the voting guarantees of the Fifteenth Amendment. *City of Rome v. United States* (1980); *Thornburg v. Gingles* (1986).

W

Wealth Classifications In the absence of some fundamental right or interest, a classification which operates to disadvantage the poor is not suspect. The Court employs a rational basis standard of review.

Welfare Legislation (Standard of Equal Protection Review) While welfare assistance involves basic human needs, welfare legislation will be measured by the rational basis test unless a suspect classification is involved. *Dandridge v. Williams* (1970).

APPENDIX D

Table of Cases

APPENDIX E

Index

†